D0559492

SEXUAL STRANDS

Understanding and Treating Sexual Anomalies in Men

SEXUAL STRANDS

Understanding and Treating Sexual Anomalies in Men

Ron Langevin
Clarke Institute of Psychiatry
Toronto, Canada

LEA LAWRENCE ERLBAUM ASSOCIATES, PUBLISHERS
1983   Hillsdale, New Jersey   London

Lawrence Erlbaum Associates, Inc. Publishers
365 Broadway
Hillsdale, New Jersey 07642

Library of Congress Cataloging in Publication Data

Langevin, Ron.
   Sexual strands.

   Bibliography: p.
   Includes indexes.
   1. Sexual disorders.   2. Men—Sexual behavior.
I. Title.
RC556.L285   616.85'83'0088041   81-22056
ISBN 0-89859-205-4   AACR2

Printed in the United States of America
10 9 8 7 6 5 4 3 2 1

. . . . Birth, and copulation, and death.
That's all the facts when you come to brass tacks:
Birth and copulation and death.

From: Sweeney Agonistes Fragments of an Aristophanic Melodrama

by: T.S. Eliot
London: Faber & Faber Ltd., 1932

Contents

Preface

Sexual release is a basic drive we share with the lower animals. It is important for survival of the human race. Sex is central to the mainstream of scientific thinking about theories of human development and evolution. Few other behaviors studied by psychiatrists and psychologists qualify for such a claim. Moreover, sexual behavior is amenable to scientific study in a way few other behaviors are. Orgasm in the male is a clearly recognizable event to the individual experiencing it and to the scientist studying it. In contrast, research investigators who must communicate about mental health problems like schizophrenia are not sure they are even talking about the same thing. The behavior involved is very complex and not always readily elicited even from cooperative patients.

Orgasm is a phenomenon around which to organize and explain behavior. We can classify anomalies and derive definitions which are clear and which provide an easy measure of success for therapy studies. The criterion of orgasm can bring order into a seeming chaos and offers one of the surest pathways to the understanding of human sexual behavior.

It is therefore surprising that the study of sexual behavior is so heavily represented by theories and so short on facts. This book is an attempt to present the theories and facts so serious readers can appreciate the present state of knowledge. In so doing, it is hoped they will find avenues for research and will be able judiciously to select treatment goals.

The topic of sexual anomalies is interesting in itself but offers us some understanding of sexual behavior in general as well. Just as a congenital heart defect may tell a physician more about how the heart works, so sexual anomalies may tell us about sexual functioning in the average male. Some of the anomalies are important social problems such as rape and child molestation. Others are only considered to be a nuisance, like exhibiting, but they all offer some clues to understanding sexual behavior.

This work was written as a handbook for a variety of people; researchers, clinicians, social scientists, and patients with the afflicting problems. Forensic workers will find the information pertinent to the many issues they face in making decisions for the courts. Clinicians treating such individuals will find a detailed evaluation of therapy methods. Researchers will find that central issues have been raised and directions for studying them have been suggested. The patient will have a more thorough understanding of his sexual behavior and of treatments he may choose.

The book is only about men because they produce almost all of the problematic sexual behavior in the world. Professional literature on female homosexuality and prostitution is scant but growing. For these two reasons, female sexual anomalies are not discussed.

Theories related to each of the major sexual anomalies in men will be considered. Hard empirical evidence will be reviewed and will be given priority in formulations about each of the problems covered. The clinical and research literature on sexual anomalies is overrepresented by uncontrolled and unsystematic case studies which may offer clues to etiology and treatment but at best are suspect in the final formulation of any theory. The major therapeutic approaches to sexual anomalies will be considered and evaluated although behavior therapy has been most frequently used in the last 30 years. None of the treatments can be considered final answers to the problems but it is hoped that the review herein will provide clinicians with an informed frame of reference for selecting a treatment approach for clinical use or research investigation.

The book has been written in laymen's language and contains few tables of technical data or statistical analysis. Figures and case information used in the book are illustrative rather than strictly factual. However, a critical evaluation of the professional literature has been undertaken.

One concept recurs throughout: the stimulus response matrix. It is a very simple model of behavior but I have found it surprisingly useful as a frame of reference for organizing research data, evaluating treatment, and communicating information. Thus, it should be useful to teacher, student, clinician and researcher alike. An attempt has been made to be as thorough as possible and to summarize available knowledge to this point. Reference materials have been presented so the interested reader can examine the original articles in journals for more technical details.

Finally, the formulations used rely predominantly on objective sex data rather than psychodiagnostic interpretations. Studies using some form of penile measurement and orgasmic sexual history from standardized instruments have been given precedence. However, personality data and demographic information are also included to help understand fully the sexual behavior.

ACKNOWLEDGMENTS

The following is a summary of 10 years of work in research and treatment of sexual anomalies. During that time, I have accumulated much experience which would not have been possible without my colleagues on the Forensic Service of the Clarke Institute of Psychiatry. Kurt Freund, Department of Behavioral Sexology, Clarke Institute of Psychiatry, has shared his experience from a lifetime study in the area of sexual behavior. Many people have helped to produce this book by offering constructive comments and criticisms: Betty Steiner, Steve Hucker, Will Cupchik, Dan Paitich, Georges Ramsay, Suzanne Curnoe-Langevin, Ken Zucker and Kingsley Ferguson. The help of Bill & Queenie Curnoe & Max were indispensable for writing. The careful typing, editing and referencing for the book was done by Mitas Ongtengco and Merle Jaggernauth. The figures and illustrations were drawn by Andre Langevin and Pierre Fazzini. I wish to thank everyone for their assistance. Finally, the students and patients who have cooperated and who participated in data collection have made my involvement rewarding and interesting.

Ron Langevin
Clarke Institute of Psychiatry,
University of Toronto,
Toronto, Canada.

SEXUAL STRANDS

Understanding and Treating Sexual Anomalies in Men

INTRODUCTION TO THE ASSESSMENT AND TREATMENT OF SEXUAL ANOMALIES

1 A Model for Studying Sexual Anomalies

DEFINITION OF SEXUAL ANOMALY

A scientific definition of a concept should attempt to be as objective and value free as possible. This is not easy in the study of sexual behavior which is often laden with emotional and moral values. Older terms like "pervert" evoke a reaction even today. With current political movements to liberalizing attitudes toward sex, one is now faced with a battle of rhetoric. Ten years ago, "sexual deviation" seemed like a nonperjorative statistical concept but some individuals have deemed it unacceptable too. Terms such as "sexual variant" and "sexual anomaly" are currently popular although it may be just a matter of time before they also assume prejudicial connotation.

In practice, I have found the term "sexual anomaly" first suggested by Hirschfeld[6] and defined as "unusual sexual behavior" is nonthreatening to patients seeking help. The therapist's attitude to the sexual behavior, of course, is more important than the words he may use and it often is conveyed implicitly in his therapeutic approach. The term "sexual anomaly" has been selected for use in this book because it covers a wide range of behavior and it is familiar to therapists and theorists working in the area. It implies that the sexual behavior in question is not typical of the general population.

The Stimulus Response Matrix

One is faced with a dilemma in studying sexual anomalies. Although theories abound about their origin and nature, systematic controlled empirical studies are very few in number. Some theories appear to be based on a few case studies or on speculation alone. Often theories apply only to a single anomaly rather than to a range of them. Much basic research is still needed that focuses on the question of what stimulus the sexually anomalous male is responding to, and how he prefers to react. Since so little is available in the way of factual information, a simple organizing model—the stimulus response matrix—will be used. It attempts to bring together what is known and integrate it. Understanding exhibitionism, rape, and so forth offers a means for evaluating treatment as well. More complex theories such as psychoanalytic interpretations of sexual anomalies can be scrutinized in terms of the matrix. In this way, the book can be more empirical and factual and not be locked into preconceived notions.

Two questions recur throughout the book: *what* is the sexually anomalous male erotically reacting to and *how* is he reacting? The stimulus part of the matrix is what is being reacted to sexually. Table 1.1 shows the range of stimuli that have been studied and which are considered important in a wide range of sexual behaviors. The list will be elaborated as our knowledge grows with research studies.

TABLE 1.1
The Stimulus Response Matrix of Sexual Behavior

The Stimuli	The Responses

1. Body Characteristics
  A. Mature
  B. Immature
  C. Male shape
  D. Female shape
	1. Intercourse
	  A. Vaginal
	  B. Anal

	2. Oral-Genital

2. Gender Behavior
  A. Masculine
  B. Feminine
	3. Masturbation

	4. Exhibiting

3. Other Behaviors
  A. Pleasure-Pain
  B. Dominance-Submission
  C. Courtship
	5. Peeping

	6. Rape
	7. Touching

4. Miscellany
  A. Fetish - garments, hair
    fire, etc.
  B. Animals
	8. Frottage

	9. Obscene Calls

	10. Cross Gender Dressing
	  A. Transvestism
	  B. Transsexualism

The first set of stimuli is body characteristics. Normal men respond most erotically to the mature female body shape but also to some extent to the pubescent girl and the female child[4]. The great similarity between these body shapes may explain the reactions of normal healthy men. However, some men who are pedophiles (literally, lovers of children) react most to the female child. Analogous reactions apply to homosexual men. Most prefer the mature male body but some, the homosexual pedophiles, react most to male children. Differences in reactions to parts of the body are less variable than one may expect. The relative size of a mature woman's breasts may seem important to an individual but examined over a large number of men, it is not[7]. In fact, normal men react most erotically to the pubic area and less so to the breasts[4].

Males of most species are larger than females and size can influence sexual interaction. The dramatic influence of size on sexual behavior is illustrated by the laughing dove birds[2]. The male and female do not have clear color differences as many birds do. When a small male is caged near a larger one, he ceases to display in a male way and begins to show characteristically female behavior. Relative size may relate to dominance and submission in humans and may be important in homosexual behavior where both partners are same sexed and in pedophilia and incest when a great difference in size may be evident.

Men are usually taller and heavier than females but when a man is shorter and/or lighter than a woman, he may not be as sexually appealing in spite of 'good looks'. Body type may also play a role in erotic arousal. Traditional females tend to prefer the tapering "V" physique while less traditional females are more variable[9][14]. Negative feelings about one's body can relate to heterosexual difficulties[11]. Little research on sexual anomalies has been carried out on this seemingly important variable.

A second set of stimuli is the gender behavior of the potential sex partner. Tomboyish behavior in a mature female may turn off many men whereas ultra feminine behaviors may be a stimulus to excitement. For example, a woman in a pair of muddy jeans who is swearing and smoking a cigarillo would generally be less stimulating to the average North American male than a woman in a pretty dress who is clean and wearing a touch of perfume. However, tastes vary and different cultural subgroups may dictate what is important. Some men transgress cultural standards and dress like women (transvestites) or want to be converted into women by surgery (transsexuals). These anomalies are usually referred to as gender dysphoria and the concept of "gender identity" has received considerable attention in the professional literature.

When researchers have attempted to determine what is the "essence" of gender behavior, they usually come up against a blank wall. Questionnaires developed in the 1920's and 1930's are interesting to peruse because they reveal cultural stereotypes of what was characteristically male and what was female at the time[10] [13]. Taking a bath was considered more feminine and taking a shower more masculine. Occupational choices also reflect gender identification. The female would more appropriately desire clerical/secretarial work and the male manual labor. Considering that women did not work in business at all in the 1800's and now, in light of the women's rights movement, that they are working in many more fields, one can appreciate that such indices of gender identification or masculinity-femininity are time bound and suspect. Gender behavior has been considered important in sexual anomalies and it will be noted throughout the book.

Other stimulus behaviors in Table 1.1 include pleasure, pain, dominance, submission and courtship. These are rather ill defined for scientific purposes and have only begun to be studied in systematic research. Considering them intuitively for the time being, most men are excited when a female shows some sign of sexual response. Pleasure on her part in terms of gestures or verbal statements that she is enjoying the sexual interaction are arousing to them. However, some men may be more excited by a woman's pain, fear or displeasure in unwanted sexual events such as rape. Some males may find being dominant in a relationship facilitates intercourse and they may be rather rigid about it (See [15] for theoretical issues in animal related studies). *Mr. A,* a pedophilic patient, said the thing he liked most about children was their utter dependence on him, particularly his own children with whom he has sexual contact on a number of occasions. He was not generally sexually aroused by his wife until "she was in tears and on her knees at his mercy." Dominance will be discussed again under sadism and pedophilia.

Courtship behavior refers to the culturally determined sequence of events and exchanges between men and women, which are accepted in establishing a sexual relationship. This may be divided into four phases: searching, pretactile interaction, tactile interaction and genital union[3]. In the first stage, partners seek each other out or let each other know they are available. In our culture, going to socials, dances, and so forth is common. Once two individuals agree to "try each other out", there is a more or less prolonged exchange (dating, talking on the phone, etc.) prior to some preliminary sexual interaction (petting and kissing) until finally, intercourse completes the sequence. Men vary in their style of accomplishing this sequence and the rapidity of so doing. Women are similar and in fact may attract more men by their particular courtship behavior. Some men may show a pathological distortion of the usual sequence and this will be noted when exhibiting, peeping and rape are discussed later.

The final stimulus category is a miscellany of items, and there are others, but they are not encountered too often. One will find occasionally in a clinical setting some patients who exhibit fetishes, usually for female undergarments, hair or at times for fire. Rare also are cases of bestiality[8] or zoophilia (literally lover of animals) in which there is some sexual contact with an animal and cases of necrophilia which involves contact with a dead body. However the dynamics of zoophilia have been described[12].

The response side of the matrix describes how the sexually anomalous male reacts to the series of stimuli just listed. This can be in a variety of ways such as vaginal, oral or anal contact. Anal intercourse is rare but can be enjoyed by both heterosexuals and homosexuals. In some cases, it can be a means of degrading the victim or of causing pain.

Oral genital exchanges are common among both homosexuals and heterosexuals today in North America[8]. About 3/5 of males have oral-genital experiences and for this reason, it is difficult to label it "unusual" and to evaluate pathological implications.

Masturbation is commonly practiced by the sexually deprived and by younger men who do not have sex partners available to them or who are in-experienced in obtaining sexual gratification with a partner. However, it is also a major outlet for several sexual anomalies: exhibiting, peeping, touching, frottage, transvestism and various fetishes.

Exhibiting is the display of the genitals to a female stranger often apparently with no other interaction desired. Watching sexual intercourse or women undressing at the movies and burlesque theater is a pasttime for some young men but it only becomes an anomaly when it is a preference at maturity and is associated with orgasm. Rape is a familiar term and involves sexual intercourse with a nonconsenting female but there is more. Force may be involved and may be essential to the act. In addition, other forms of contact are often demanded; oral, genital and anal intercourse.

Touching, and frottage or rubbing involve a female stranger usually in a novel setting, and the act is carried out against her will. Such acts are sometimes but not always forerunners to rape.

Obscene phone calls can be a satisfying outlet in themselves. Usually, the caller masturbates while talking to an unknown female. He talks about sex and may use vulgar language. Sometimes, such patients can be quite in-genious. Mr. B. used to pose as a psychiatrist who would call housewives during the day and tell them that their husbands had seen him recently about sex problems they were having. The surprised wife would naturally offer intimate information about her marital sex relations in the interests of helping, only to find out she had been tricked when her husband returned home that evening.

Finally, some men dress in women's clothes, especially undergarments as an essential part of their sexual response. The transvestite will masturbate and be totally satisfied while touching or viewing himself in a mirror. The transsexual, on the other hand, does not seem to derive erotic gratification from the clothes themselves but wants to relate sexually to other men as a woman. He is willing to go to great extremes to do so, even to have an operation to have his penis and testicles removed. The relationship of transvestism and transsexualism is not clearly understood at present and it will be discussed in detail later.

Using the stimulus and the response elements of the matrix, one can describe most sexual anomalies. Each can be considered as a preference for certain stimuli and a preference to respond orgasmically in certain ways. Each is an interaction of stimulus and response and may produce a seemingly new entity. The absence of stimulus response connections in the matrix may also be revealing. The salient stimuli and responses for each anomaly will be noted in later chapters. Theories will be discussed and then the supporting empirical evidence with conclusions.

To any researcher or therapist, it is important to know how the elements of the stimulus response matrix are measured. A range of measurement possibilities present themselves but some are clearly better than others and are preferable in clinical assessments. Selections of clinical assessment procedures for sexually anomalous men are discussed in Chapter 2.

BIBLIOGRAPHY

1. Abernathy, V. Dominance and sexual behavior: A hypothesis. *American Journal of Psychiatry,* 1974, *131,* 813–817.
2. Craig, W. The voices of pigeons regarded as a means of social control. *American Journal of Sociology,* 1909, *14,* 86.
3. Freund, K. *Analysis of disorders of courtship phases.* Unpublished manuscript, Clarke Institute of Psychiatry, Toronto, 1978.
4. Freund, K., McKnight, C. K., Langevin, R., & Cibiri, S. The female child as a surrogate object. *Archives of Sexual Behavior,* 1972, *2,* 119–133.
5. Friedman, R. C. Critique of a hypothesis of dominance and sexual behavior. *American Journal of Psychiatry,* 1975, *132*(9), 967–969.
6. Hirshfeld, M. *Sexual Anomalies: The Origins, Nature and Treatment of Sexual Disorders.* New York: Emerson Books Inc., 1956.
7. Horvath, T. Physical attractiveness: the influence of selected torso parameters. *Archives of Sexual Behavior,* 1981, *10*(1), 21–24.
8. Kinsey, A. C., Pomeroy, W. B., & Martin, C. E. *Sexual behavior in the human male.* Philadelphia: W. B. Saunders, Co., 1948.
9. Lavrakas, P. J. Female preferences for male physiques. *Journal of Research in Personality,* 1975, *9*(4), 324–334.
10. Lunneborg, P. W. Dimensionality of MF. *Journal of Clinical Psychology,* 1972, *28*(3), 313–317.
11. Mitchell, K. R., & Orr, F. E. Heterosexual social competence, anxiety, avoidance and self-judged physical attractiveness. *Perceptual and Motor Skills,* 1976, *43,* 553–554.
12. Rappaport, E. A. Zoophily and zoerasty. *Psychoanalytic Quarterly,* 1968, *37,* 565–587.
13. Terman, L., & Miles, C. *Sex and personality.* New York: McGraw Hill, 1936.
14. Wiggins, N., & Wiggins, J. S. A typological analysis of male preferences for female body types. *Multivariate Behavior Research,* 1979, 89–102.

2 Assessment of Erotic Preferences

Assessment of sexual anomalies is often difficult because there are so many theoretical preconceptions and so few facts. Moreover, about half of clinical cases present more than one anomalous behavior[71] and the clinician is faced with making sense of the seemingly infinite combinations of behaviors. Some theorists have prematurely linked anomalies that may have occurred in a patient by chance. The large number of physiological measures used as indices of erotic arousal has also served to confuse the assessment process[110].

Order can be imposed and solutions to these problems derived by examining orgasmic preferences. That is, how does the individual *prefer* to have his sexual climax. Usually the most frequent behavior leading to orgasm reflects this preference but not always. A married man can have intercourse thousands of times with his wife and yet prefer young boys with whom he may only have risked contact a dozen times.

Two assessment tools are most valuable in working out erotic preference patterns; phallometry or measurement of penile reactions, and a standardized sex history questionnaire. These measures may seem personal, intrusive and embarrassing to some clinicians but there is good scientific reason for resorting to them. To date, penile reactions are the most valid index of erotic behavior in a cooperating individual. Researchers have attempted to use many other psychological measures of sexual arousal, which are less obtrusive than phallometry, but none have its validity nor its accuracy. Zuckerman[110] has reviewed the varied indices used to measure erotic arousal.

Sexual arousal has been measured via brain activity, sweating, heart rate and even pupillary dilation. Clever instrumentation has been devised to measure changes in pupil size[38] but the pupil dilates first and foremost to subtle changes in light intensity. The variability in size due to light and dark parts of a stimulus picture is so great, it obscures any erotic component to the reaction. It would be very expensive and complex to control the light patterns in stimulus pictures for experimental work. Having done this, the reliability and validity of eye changes in relation to erotic arousal remain to be established.

Another clever attempt to measure erotic arousal unobtrusively has been via brain activity in CNV or contingent negative variation[19]. One can examine brain waves before and after presenting stimulus pictures of men, women and neutral scenes. The change in brain activity pattern, presumably due to the stimulus, is the CNV. In the single study examining this factor, Costell and Wittner[19] found differences in CNV to pictures of men and women but the research participants of both sexes did not react differently. The apparently heterosexual men and women should have reacted differently to stimulus males and females if the CNV tapped erotic interest. Many other measures are similarly suspect as indices of erotic arousal. There is some relationship between some of these measures of general arousal such as galvanic skin response, or heart rate and erotic arousal but it is usually a weak and uncertain one[7][47][110].

Self report of sexual arousal is also important but may not reflect penile reactions. Freund, Barlow and I[29] compared penile reactions of normal men and their verbal report of "physical sexual arousal" to pictures of nude men and women. There was a positive relation between the two but one could only predict penile reactions with about 50% accuracy from verbal report. At best a 65% to 70% relationship has been found[57][79]. In addition, we found that when penile responses were examined for those pictures on which subjects said they did not respond, the penile measures still discriminated reactions to pictures of males and females in the expected direction for normal subjects. So one may use small reactions of which the subject may not be aware to examine sexual preference. However, the individual's report of his sex history is most important and cannot be ignored in the assessment. In fact laboratory studies of relative degree of arousal may not reflect the typical and extreme sexual arousal which culminates in orgasm. The latter can only be assessed from the individual's history, to which we will return later. Nevertheless, penile measurement of erotic preferences is to date, the only satisfactory physiological measure. This does not mean it is problem free.

Men and animals have erections associated with nonsexual fear, during sleep, and, when they have full bladders[7]. Research studies have to be carefully designed to control these extraneous factors. Usually well rested men, who are told to urinate prior to testing, serve as research participants.

They are shown the laboratory before consenting to participate in a study. The fact that they are volunteers is important since they are able to withdraw from the study at any time. In some of our studies we also relaxed the participant prior to testing by playing audiorecordings of relaxation exercises[46]. Thus many of the confounding factors in the study can be controlled.

Nevertheless the individual research participant, especially incarcerated patients, can and may attempt to control and fake penile reactions[27 28 52 78 79 87 88 89]. They may wish to show they do not react erotically to children but only to adult women. They may wish to show, perhaps to themselves, that after treatment, they are normal in erotic reactions and they may work at distorting responses. Thus we are forced to deal only with voluntary and honest research participants and patients at present. This is perhaps the most serious limitation of penile measurement but in spite of that, it is still the best measure available of erotic preference. It helps the clinician to clarify erotic preferences. For example, the psychologist often has no clue about what the cooperating patient is responding to. Nor can the patient tell his doctor because he often does not know. When a stimulus is complex, some aspect of it may be more arousing than another but the patient may not know this. Using penile measurement helps to find out[1 2].

PHALLOMETRY

Of all the possible approaches to studying sexual behavior, phallometry is one of the most concrete. First developed extensively by Kurt Freund and his colleagues[33], it attempts to examine the reactions of the human male's penis to erotica. Freund's original device measured penile volume changes and it has been imitated by others[45 57]. Some researchers have developed strain gauges which measure changes in penile circumference[6 10 50 51 53 72].

Two commonly used devices for measuring penile reactions are illustrated in Figure 2.1. The volume phallometer consists of a glass cylinder and an inflatable cuff made from a condom and a plastic ring. The cuff is placed at the base of the penis and the glass cylinder is locked on it to encase the penis. A brace with velcro fits over the cylinder and is secured by a waist belt also with velcro. The cuff is then inflated and forms a seal around the base of the penis. Any expansion or contraction of the penis forces the air up and out of the glass cylinder. The glass cylinder in turn is connected to a plastic tube and it, to some recording and measuring device. A graduated column of liquid may be used[33] or more conveniently a strain gauge attached to a polygraph which measures and records penile volume change[45]. The volume changes may be converted to a linear scale. The device is extremely accurate and measures as little as 0.02 milliliters change in volume, far less than any individual is usually aware of. The range of possible measurement extends up to 100 milliliters, again well beyond the usual size of reactions. Most recordings are in the 0 to 10 ml. range. The author recommends this device for research because it is far more accurate than the circumference gauge, the second device in Fig. 2.1, which is, however, more widely used because of its simplicity[29].

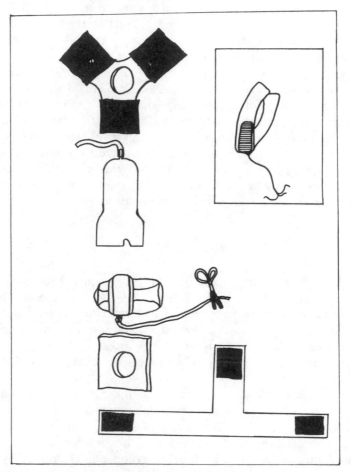

FIG. 2.1   VOLUME PHALLOMETER; Insert Circumference Strain Gauge.

The strain gauge consists of a small ring that fits over the shaft of the penis[6] [10]. There is disagreement in practice on the exact placement of the ring but the glans appears to be a favored location. The strain gauge is attached to the ring. It connects via electrical wires to a polygraph for measurement and recording. It also forms a linear relationship of circumference change to the paper printout of the polygraph. The ring is certainly more convenient than the volume phallometer but one must use longer stimulus presentation times with the former to obtain any response. The circumference is at best about 50% predictable from volume changes in the penis. Since the volumetric device measures all changes in the penis, including circumference, we must assume that some important reactions may be missed[29] [57] [92]. This is an important consideration when evaluating any research study. It will not be discussed further in the book but is worth remembering.

Once the patient or research subject is connected to the volume or circumference phallometer, a series of stimuli can be presented. The usual format has been to present movies or slides although movies tend to elicit larger reactions[30] [57] . Now one can conduct his research or assessment. If one wished to measure penile reactions of sexually anomalous men to pictures of nude males and females for example, he can do so with great accuracy in cooperative men.

Freund and his colleagues have developed a paradigm experiment[31]. Comparable groups of patients and nonpatients can serve as research participants, e.g., pedophiles and community volunteers matched on age and education. They are shown pictures of males and females from 6 years of age to maturity, in this case up to 25 years old. The age groups of stimuli can be divided into four for convenience; 6–8, 9–12, 13–15 or pubertal years, and 18–25 or physically mature individuals. Neutral or nonsexual pictures of landscapes or objects are included as a point of reference. There are six pictures in each sex-age category to measure reactions more reliably since a research participant may not like the face or body of a particular stimulus person. If only that picture were used, misleading results might be obtained.

Each picture is presented for 10 seconds and the participants' reactions are recorded before the stimulus is presented (baseline) at 10 seconds and at 20 seconds. Practice slides are used first to insure that the apparatus is working and the participant understands instructions. Then all 54 pictures are presented, allowing time in betweeen them for the penis to detumesce to baseline again. When all the participants have completed the study, statistical analysis will be computed to determine significant differences between the two groups across the stimulus categories.

Besides stimulus pictures, audio presentations have also been used. These often have a distinct advantage over visually presented stimuli, because it is difficult if not impossible to present visually, in a realistic form, the stimulus situation that arouses the patient, for example, a rape or exposing. When one stipulates that the female who was raped had a look of "fear" or "shock" on her face, it is almost impossible to produce a picture that most research participants will agree is "a look of shock", and so forth.

However, if one tells the patient to *fantasize* a look of fear or shock, he is more likely to do so. Fantasy is considered by sex researchers to be a major avenue into the sexual psyche of patients and is an invaluable tool with phallometry[1][2][101].

The phallometer has clear application in sex research and it can be a valuable tool in assessment and treatment[5]. It can serve to establish an index of the sexually anomalous patient's erotic preferences and provide him and his therapist with new information. Knowing this, a treatment program can be established which monitors changes in erotic reactivity via the phallo-meter. Thus a pedophilic patient undergoing assessment initially may show his greatest penile reactions to 9–11 year old girls and his smallest to adult females. After effective treatment, this should be reversed and one can watch the change develop during treatment by monitoring penile reactions. Although this procedure is not used as often as it should be, it provides for scientific scrutiny of the therapy process itself.

SEX HISTORY EXAMINATION

In spite of the utility of the phallometer, one still must find out how the patient usually attains his orgasms and what is his preferred mode of doing so. These are the most important data the clinician collects and for this purpose he uses a sex history examination. A detailed investigation by a trained clinician of the various possible sexually anomalous behaviors, of problems of impotence, premature ejaculation, etc. is of utmost importance.

A face to face interview is advisable in general but a number of investigators have attempted to develop self administered questionnaires[3][4][13][18][20][21][22][35][37][39][58][71][76][103][104][105][106][111]. Unfortunately, most have been developed to establish heterosexual experience with mature females and do not sample anomalous behavior at all. A thorough test, the Thorne Sex Inventory[105] is filled with psychodynamic interpretations which this author believes should be avoided at the present state of our knowledge. Derogatis[22] has developed a more basic measure which needs some work and my colleagues and I have developed our own measure[71], the Clarke Sex History Questionnaire for Males (SHQ) which has satisfactory reliability and validity. It examines frequency of erotic behaviors as well as desire and disgust for them. In this way, erotic preference patterns can be constructed for most sexual anomalies and it provides a good start to assessment. Since it will be used in many studies throughout the book, the questionnaire has been included as Appendix One.

A typical assessment would include a variety of psychological tests in addition to the Sex History Questionnaire, in order to examine other pertinent factors that will be discussed in the next session. The SHQ items may be computer scored or visually scanned for a profile of the patient. A sample profile appears in Appendix Two. The possible scales that may be scored represent the elements of the stimulus response matrix referred to earlier. The printout will tell you what behaviors have been engaged in by the patient including any sexually anomalous ones. In addition, the profile will compare him to other patients with the same sexual anomaly to indicate how strong the behavior is. Thus two reports may read:

| Exhibiting behavior | 15th percentile | Patient A |
| Exhibiting behavior | 90th percentile | Patient B |

This means in the first case that only 15% of exhibitionists have less experience than the patient in question. In the second case, however, 90% have had less experience, which confirms the habit strength of his exposing. This is an important clue to the sexual preferences of the patient.

The assessment may seem difficult at first glance because patients presenting at a clinic offer a disconcerting array of sexual behaviors. The label, "polymorphous perverse", is not uncommon and more than one sexual anomaly is typically listed in medical records. For example, an individual, *Mr. C,* charged with rape had homosexual experience with men and boys, intercourse with minors, peeped in windows, grabbed strange females on a crowded bus and dressed in female clothes. How does one make sense of all these? Some clinicians prefer to indicate the seemingly dominant sexual anomaly or even the one that is presented at that particular admission to hospital. However, there are two related ways of bringing order in the seeming chaos. First, one can determine what behavior is erotically preferred and/or, second, one can determine how the patient usually has his orgasm. Interviewing Mr. C, charged with rape, a clinician found that only rape and intercourse with a minor were associated with orgasm. When he did experience orgasm on one occasion while being fellated by a homosexual, he did not like the experience and would not repeat it. His other "sexually deviant experiences" simply reflected curiosity. The Sex History Questionnaire ascertains desire and disgust for the sexual behaviors under investigation. Disgust for homosexual behavior, for example, with a few orgasmic experiences often indicates a lack of true erotic interest. The "true" homosexual has orgasms and desires sex with a man and has no disgust for it.

Many seemingly normal individuals are also erotically aroused by children[31], exposing, peeping[48], and so forth, but never act on these impulses. The arousal is also much less than one would find from their preferred sexual outlet, that is, intercourse with an individual of the opposite sex. Peeping in windows is not uncommon and normal volunteers in research projects will indicate they have watched women undressing in windows at night or in alleyways. One may think, therefore, that all men are voyeurs. Careful inquiry with research participants and patients alike will uncover the fact that many of the incidences occurred by chance or for a lark with a group of young men. Moreover, orgasm occurred only rarely if at all in these cases even though the event may have been sexually exciting. This is typical for normal young men. However, when the true voyeur is questioned, one finds that he actively sought out the places where he could watch couples having intercourse or watch women undressing. In addition, he would masturbate to orgasm while watching such events or do so afterwards while fantasizing. To illustrate, compare the following segments from two interviews, the first with a normal research volunteer and the second, with a patient who preferred voyeurism.

Doctor: I see on your sex history questionnaire that you have peeped into a window to watch a woman undress on one occasion. Could you tell me more about it?

Volunteer: Well it was really an accident. It was the woman next door I happened to see from my bathroom one night. I had just turned out the light and was about to leave when I noticed her undressing. Naturally, I stayed to watch. (laughs)

Doctor: What did you do after that?

Volunteer: I watched until she left and then I left too.

Doctor: That was it?

Volunteer: That was it.

In contrast, a voyeur in treatment, said the following.

Patient: I must be stupid to do what I do. I swear I'm going to give it up. Last Saturday, I spent 45 minutes in a tree waiting for this chic to go to bed. Do you remember how cold it was last Saturday?

Doctor: Yes I do.

Patient: Well, I waited 45 minutes and then I thought at last she's going to get undressed. She started to take off her sweater and then she goes over and closed the f...... blind. Boy, was I hopping.

LATER.......

Doctor: Did you do any other peeping in the past week?

Patient: Yes. I watched a couple screwing in the park on Tuesday. I was so close to their car, I could touch them but they didn't see me (chuckles). I even came all over the guy's tire (chuckles again).

The latter had not had intercourse with a woman and was not sure he wanted it. He admitted to enjoying the peeping and also exposing himself.

He did not really want to change and a clear preference for the voyeurism and exhibiting was evident. The behavior of the research volunteer, on the other hand, was accidental and even when it is not, the behavior is rarely orgasmic or of long term interest.

The use of erotic preference is of great value in understanding sexual anomalies. It is rarely used by clinicians and researchers alike. Many theoretical formulations do not even recognize its value. Its power to increase our understanding of sexual anomalies cannot be overestimated at present. The wide range of behavior normal individuals will engage in when deprived or when curious can be misleading. The male in prison may seem to be homosexual but once released in the community, he suddenly loses his homosexual interest and again has intercourse with adult females. This man is clearly heterosexual and the homosexual acts in prison are surrogate in nature. He does it only because he was deprived of what he really wanted.

The idea of orgasmic preference and behavior preference will be used throughout the book and in the stimulus response matrix. Without it, sexual anomalies would seem a bewildering array of behaviors. Using both the phallometric testing and a sex history questionnaire, we can derive clear assessments and treatment evaluations.

IMPORTANT VARIABLES ASSOCIATED WITH SEXUAL ANOMALIES

An examination of sexual behavior, while most important, would not be complete in itself to the clinician who wants to do the best job possible for his patient. Other factors are important in understanding the total picture presented by the sexual anomalies. Only the five most important items usually considered in an assessment are discussed here and are used throughout the book: alcohol and drugs, criminal history, personality, parent child relations and sex hormones.

Alcohol and Drugs

Many sexual anomalies are also crimes in North America and alcohol is associated with some of them[107]. As an example, about half the charged rapists are drinking at the time of their offence, and a third of them are chronic alcoholics[81] [82]. Even a quarter of the victims are drinking[94].

While alcohol can be a complicating factor in many clinical and forensic problems, there are two problems peculiar to sexual anomalies. The first is how alcohol affects sex drive. Does alcohol disinhibit the imbiber in a way that augments his sex drive? Popular lore would suggest that alcohol increases the desire to perform sexual acts but it removes the ability to do so by rendering the drinker impotent. One might wonder then how it is possible for the intoxicated individual to have and maintain an erection to carry out the sexually anomalous act.

Unfortunately, there are only a few studies relating penile sexual arousal and alcohol consumption in men, none of whom had sexual anomalies[9] [16] [26] [55] [90] [108] [109]. The studies indicated that with increasing amounts of alcohol, penile circumference to the same stimulus decreases and ejaculation is retarded. Farkas and Rosen[26] found that small amounts of alcohol might increase arousal. However, it was not a statistically significant finding. Results of several studies were suspect since they repeated the same stimuli to the same people while giving them different amounts of alcohol. We know from other research[84] that men rapidly habituate to repeated sexual stimuli. There are other problems with the alcohol studies but they suggest that the folk lore about alcohol reducing potency are accurate.

Another issue which has not been studied well is how sexual arousal in chronic drinkers is affected by excessive amounts of alcohol. While some alcoholics suffer more or less permanent impotence because of their life style and may even suffer problems of feminization e.g., breast growth, loss of hair, etc., most do not[63]. In fact, the chronic drinker is usually more tolerant of large amounts of alcohol and will show fewer behavioral deficits than an inexperienced drinker[61]. *Mr. D.* was charged with raping a 32 year old divorcee who lived alone. Labeled a weekend alcoholic, he held down a regular job as a laborer. His typical weekend involved the consumption of 72 pints of beer and 120 ounces of rye whiskey. One Saturday evening in the middle of his drinking bout, he drove his car on city streets, picked up a hitchhiker and took her to a lonely road where he raped her. The average social drinker would be incapable of such behavior even if he were not very sick after drinking so much alcohol. Although there is no experimental evidence available, this case suggests that penile erections of this man would also be less affected than those of the average person who was drinking. The old adage about drink increasing the desire may still apply to the chronic drinker who can carry out his desires and does not suffer the impotence a social drinker would. This may well be what happens in some sexual offenses. However, the issue of tolerance to alcohol is complex and not well understood.

Tolerance is easily lost making clinical investigation difficult[60] [61]. The effect of alcohol on sexual arousal clearly requires more research. We need to study chronic abusers who are involved in sex offenses. In any assessment of a sexual anomaly, the usage of alcohol by the patient is important to know but he may not be seen for 3 weeks after arrest by which time his tolerance to such large amounts of alcohol may be lost.

In addition to directly influencing his sexual behavior, the sexually anomalous male may attribute his acting out sexually, especially if it is an offense, to the consumption of alcohol[56]. The forensic psychiatrist often hears, "I was drunk at the time, I don't remember" or "Yes, I did it but I was drunk." This may simply be lying to avoid incrimination or to reduce the anger of the courts to him.

This brings us to the second problem: can alcohol change erotic preferences? There is no evidence to suggest that this is the case, although some accused persons may make this claim. An intoxicated individual may do something for a dare (not too often in sexual offenses) or will genuinely not know what he is doing. Some sexually anomalous men cannot admit their desires to themselves, but will act out when drinking and attribute the behavior to the alcohol. *Mr. E* faced a charge of indecent assault on a 9 year old girl when first interviewed. He had a previous conviction for the same charge with an 8 year old girl. He vehemently denied both charges and said he was "framed" on the first charge. He was drinking on both occasions. When examined by phallometric testing on penile reactions to pictures of children and adults, he showed the largest reactions to 6-9-year-old girls, second largest to adult females and no reaction at all to males:

Doctor: We are only trying to help you Mr. E. You said you were not even on the scene for the charge you face. But you were seen touching Jane (9 year old girl) by 2 witnesses. How can I help you when you deny everything?

Mr. E: Well, I guess I was there but I was so drunk I didn't know what I was doing. Only a pervert would touch a kid!

Alcohol and drug usage can be considered from another perspective by the clinician. Even if alcohol were totally unrelated to sexual anomalies, which it is not, it may still be an important barometer in making decisions about treatment and disposition of a given client. Excessive consumption of alcohol may reflect a self centered life style, which indicates that this person is willing to indulge himself in other ways than sexual misbehavior and, at its extreme, reflects a psychopathic personality. Alcohol addiction in itself is difficult to treat and any therapy goals for sexual anomalies must first deal with the alcohol problem before any progress in sexual areas can be hoped for. An admission on the part of a patient that alcohol is a significant factor in his sexual acting out, but, at the same time, indicating that he is unwilling to give it up, may reflect poor prognosis in treatment of the sexual anomaly.

A particularly worrisome problem involves the release of hostile impulses with alcohol or drug use[63] [74]. The consumption of excessive amounts of alcohol and a history of violence in any form is an important but not well researched index of recidivism of violent sexual acting out.

Drug usage must also be assessed in any sexual anomaly. Use of aphrodisiacs[12] or medication with aphrodisiac effects like L-Dopa[15] is uncommon in clinical cases but antipsychotic medication and other tranquilizers used more often, can reduce sexual arousal to a point where it interferes with normal marital satisfaction. Choice and amount of medication must be carefully considered for use with any sexually anomalous patient. Generally, medication is not necessary except for the occasional complicating and/or accompanying psychiatric states, e.g., psychoses. Antiandrogens have been used to reduce sex drive and this treatment has its own problems, which will be discussed later under treatment.

A major concern for the clinician is the use of self administered non medical drugs, mainly narcotics and psychedelic drugs. Usage may vary in individual cases but marijuana is frequently encountered. Experimental research on the effects of marijuana on sexual arousal is very limited. Subjective reports suggest that it can enhance the sexual experience and generally, the intoxicated person is not especially aggressive[40 62 107].

One family of drugs that are of great concern is the amphetamines. Characteristically, "speed" as it is popularly called, produces a paranoid state. The seasoned user apparently learns to recognize this and ignore it. However, such a state is not always so easily controlled, and violent behavior may ensue[40]. Ms. F lived with her boyfriend and an elderly roomer in an apartment. All were unemployed and on welfare. When alone one day with the boarder, they drank a bottle of vodka together. It is uncertain whether sexual intercourse had occurred. She also had "a nickel" of speed toward early evening. About thirty minutes later, she had an irresistible impulse to hurt someone. The boarder who was now sick from the alcohol asked her for help. She strangled him to death and stabbed him 9 times in the chest. She attributed her act to the drug and noted that a few weeks earlier she had similar impulses and had tortured a cat while under the influence of speed as well.

In conjunction with sexual behavior, amphetamines may be extremely dangerous. In some cases sex drive may be reduced resulting in dissatisfaction[93]. Others may have increased libido, which can enhance sexually anomalous behavior[11]. The hyperexcitability resulting may be similar to states of cocaine intoxication. LSD has also been linked to violence[97] but the relation of drug use or alcohol and aggressive and/or sexual interaction is complex and not well understood at present[63 95]. The problem needs careful attention by research investigators. What has been said about alcohol and prognosis of course applies to drugs as well. Abuse may reflect poor social controls and poor prognosis in treatment.

Criminal History

Since so many sexual anomalies are also sexual offenses, clinic patients will often have criminal records. The forensic worker will want to know the number of charges, whether they are all sexual in nature or if other nonsexual offenses have occurred. It is important to ascertain whether the patient has a history of charges or only one. It may be the first charge for a patient, which reflects the fact that he is only 18 and this is the first time he was caught; or it may be a first charge for a 34-year-old male who has a history of blocking his anomalous sexual impulses. The latter case usually has a more certain prognosis than the former. Of course, he may be clever and/or lucky and never have been caught. Alternatively, the patient may have a long history of acting out in spite of many and varied treatment programs that have been offered. Prognosis is usually poor in cases of repeated acting out but eventually, many of these offenders "burn out" and lose interest in their anomalous outlet. In any event, the persistent offender indicates that he will carry out his socially deviant behavior in spite of any sanctions levied against him. This often means poor treatment prospects.

The second important fact about the criminal record of a sexually anomalous patient is the nature of the charges. If they relate only to his sexual behavior, treatment goals may be feasible, but if the charges are wide and varied, they may reflect a general antisocial person in which prognosis is very poor and incarceration would be the best course to recommend. Rapists, for example, often have extensive criminal records involving charges of theft, of common assault, and indecent assault as well as rape[82]. Although some experimental programs are currently being examined, the prognosis is poor in such cases. Perhaps, the duration of the problem which often extends into early childhood is the main contributing factor. Perhaps, it is the type of person they are, that is, sociopathic or psychopathic personalities. These questions remain to be researched adequately.

Clinicians must make a judgment about such patients. Their decision may become very different when the courts or defence request information on the accused patient's "dangerousness". What a vague concept! Danger may be social, political, moral or physical[102]. Even a mixture of these four may be implied and decision making can be complex and uncertain. Fortunately in the area of sexual anomalies, two factors are usually implied in the concept: will the accused act out again and will he physically harm someone? The use of orgasmic preferences provides a criterion for the clinician that is not available in nonsexual problems[77]. One can assess the preferred orgasmic outlet of the accused and determine the amount of force used in his past sexual acts. The fusion of sexual and aggressive urges can then be studied phallometrically and may offer invaluable information[2] [8] [80]. This is discussed later under specific sexual anomalies, especially rape.

The patient who has no criminal record often attends out of a true desire to change his anomalous behavior. In some cases, there is family pressure or social pressure to change, but usually prognosis is more favorable if the patient is attending voluntarily. Information obtained may be more reliable and the patient may work more readily at his therapy goals. In contrast, the incarcerated individual may not even admit his charges. Information may be biased or outright lies can invalidate any assessment that may be made. The clinician must be aware of these problems and make the appropriate judgments.

Personality

The personalities of males with sexual anomalies are as varied as those in the general population. Nevertheless, several traits recur in research and clinical reports. Most prominent is masculinity–femininity and/or gender identity. The gender behavior of the stimulus person to whom an individual is attracted and erotically aroused is important but the desired stimulus person is also selected in accordance with his own gender identity and behavior. Men usually select women as sex partners. The transsexual male, on the other hand, feels like a woman and may act like a woman, wanting normal male sex partners. The homosexual male is often identified as being effeminate but this is not invariably the case. However, many are more feminine in varying degrees than the typical heterosexual man. At the other extreme, the very masculine male may be a rapist or an exhibitionist, at least as theorized and reported in case studies. It has often been assumed that feminine gender identity or persistent effeminate behavior is a precursor of sexual anomalies like transsexualism and homosexuality, but this theory has only had limited testing. We will discuss this again in connection with transsexualism.

The terminology used to discuss gender behavior is rather technical and complex[83] [86] [96] [99] [100]. Shively and De Cecco[96] indicate four components that are important: (1) biological or anatomical sex, (2) gender identity or the conviction of being male or female, (3) social sex role or characteristics culturally associated with men or women and more commonly labeled masculinity/femininity and (4) sexual orientation or a preference for male or female sex partners, which is also commonly called sex object preference. Often all four components go together and appear inseparable but research evidence suggests there is some distinction. A physically normal male with male gender identity may engage in characteristic feminine behaviors like going to the ballet or knitting or he may show masculine sex role behavior and prefer male sex partners. Unfortunately, measurement instruments in this area are generally poor and few measure gender identity[32] [54].

A second dimension of personality that is theoretically important is introversion–extraversion[49] [59] [65]. This is basically a tendency to be outgoing with people (extraversion) or predominantly to keep to oneself (introversion). At its extremes, introversion may encompass shyness and feelings of inferiority and may even be associated with a psychotic illness. Introversion, including shyness, passivity and submissiveness, has long been considered to be part of sexual anomalies. However, the very few studies that have been carried out indicate that the association of the two is a rather weak one. Moreover, if an exhibitionist, for example, were to feel introverted and inferior, does this cause the sexual anomaly or is it the other way around? Does he have these bad feelings about himself because he has the problem? This is unknown but in practice it is difficult to assign introversion–extraversion an etiological status because of its inconsistent occurrence in sexually anomalous men.

Finally in examining personality the clinician will want to know if the patient is "psychotic" and/or "legally insane." The presence of a psychosis will make any treatment directed to the sexual anomaly difficult, if not impossible, before the psychosis itself is dealt with. In assessments, the forensic psychiatrist must determine if the patient is insane. This is rarely a problem in sexual anomalies since the majority are sane by any definition. Often, violent sexual anomalies are associated with personality pathology but seldom are such individuals labeled psychotic. Chronic drug and alcohol abuse may contribute to a seemingly bizarre history. Sometimes a change in the level of sexual functioning or bizarre sexual behavior may signal a psychotic state[17] [75] [98]. Generally, life long or persistent sexual anomalies have not been associated with psychiatric disorders. However, the more sexual outlets an individual engages in, the more emotionally disturbed he seems[49]. This may be the product of stimulus confusion, unreliable reporting or other factors. Such factors complicate both assessments and treatment. A careful examination of sexual outlets may reveal an underlying preference, or which factor is most important for the respondant.

Parent Child Relations

Most theories of human development stress the family as the socializing unit. The behavior and attitudes of each parent to the child are of great etiological significance in determining the type of person each child will be. Psychoanalytic theory even specifies an oedipal period of development that has a lasting influence on the sexual behavior of a child. During this period, the child desires the mother for himself and wishes to be rid of the father.

His fear of being castrated by the father leads to the development of the incest taboo and identification with the father. Unresolved problems lead to later sexual difficulties. An active mother and a passive or absent father may lead to strengthened mother identification and gender identity confusion[14]. One end product is assumed to be homosexuality and transsexualism although other sexual anomalies may develop as well. Since the oedipal conflict the child experiences may lead to a host of varied disorders, sexual and otherwise, its empirical value is thereby greatly diminished. Nevertheless, the establishment of gender identity has been considered to be largely determined by parenting. Research has been sparse and generally retrospective reports have been used. Fathers especially have been neglected as contributors to child development[24][44] and there are very few reliable and valid measures of parent child relations for adults[70].

Parents also influence a child's general attitude to himself. If he is constantly considered inferior or inadequate, he will carry these feelings with him as an adult and this may influence his sexual behavior and produce sexual problems. The feelings of inferiority experienced by a sexually anomalous patient may reflect such an upbringing.

Some theorists maintain that gender behavior and sexual preference is laid down very early in life and may even have a strong genetic component. A phenomenon common to some lower animals, called *imprinting* may be occurring in human beings as well[67]. Imprinting in birds involves the newborn following the mother, usually within 24 to 72 hours after birth. This ''following'' response is characterized by great distress on the part of the newborn when the mother draws away from it. The chick will squawk and run over to mother at which point it calms down. If this process is disrupted by removal of the mother, the chick develops in abnormal ways. One of the abnormalities that has been noted is unusual sexual behavior, or even its complete absence. If a bird is imprinted on another species rather than its own, it will display sexual behavior to them rather than its own kind at sexual maturity. Although there is no direct evidence yet, imprinting in humans may be important too.

The Harlows[36] have demonstrated the importance of early tactile experiences in the sexual development in monkeys. Monkeys were given mother surrogates that were wire mesh models with terry cloth bellies. Others had only the wire mesh and no soft material to cling to. The terry cloth babies behaved more normal than the wire mesh ones who displayed sexual abnormalities especially in their later mothering behavior. Does such a phenomenon occur in humans? No one knows for sure yet. Perhaps early experiences of deprivation either to children awaiting adoption in institutions or to children in abusive homes are critical determinants in this period of development and later sexual behavior.

Sex Hormones

Sex hormones play an important if uncertain role in sexual behavior. It is well known that removal of the testes from the male (castration) produces a dramatic reduction in sexual desire. However, it is still not clearly known how sex hormones influence sexual behavior, and in particular, if they are related to sexual anomalies in the adult male. The hormone that has received the most attention is testosterone. A number of studies[23] [25] [63] [68] [85] [91] have shown that higher levels of serum testosterone are positively related to aggressive behavior and in some cases sexually aggressive behavior. The direct relationship of sexual arousal and serum testosterone and other hormones is a positive but weak one[41] [43] [48]. Its relationship to aggressiveness is clearer. Whereas some authors claim confusion on this point, aggressiveness is positively related to testosterone in criminals and other groups where a history of violence is evident[85]. It is unrelated in studies of normal populations, which are often examined on questionnaire measures of aggressiveness. Use of restricted sampling of nonaggressive people and of unreliable or invalid questionnaires may explain these discrepancies.

Hormones may relate to feminization of the homosexual as well. Meyer-Bahlberg[64] has reviewed research studies with some skepticism. Study designs and controls are wanting and assaying procedures of hormones still need considerable development. Sampling of blood hormones is often inadequate as well[73] and at least three samples of blood should be drawn[34]. When some of these problems have been worked out, clearer answers on the relationship of sexual anomalies and hormones may be forthcoming. In the meantime, we have to keep in mind that they are important and speculate on their significance. Testosterone, aggression and alcohol consumption also interact in important ways that are not well understood but have significant implications for violent sexual anomalies[61] [63] [74].

Another component of early sexual development, which may be important, is the hormonal environment of the mother's uterus for the fetus. One theory claims that excessive female hormones in the mother at certain critical periods of fetal development may relate to homosexual orientation. Experiments with animals have demonstrated that some animals may appear to be anatomically male but behave as females when their mothers were injected with excessive amounts of female sex hormones (oestrogens) during their pregnancy[66]. Such abnormalities may be important in hermaphroditism. In such cases, the sex of the children are uncertain because they may possess sexual organs of both male and female. It may also be important in the more subtle cases of homosexuality in which the genitals are normal but the sexual orientation of the individual is inverted. Although there is no satisfactory evidence to support any of the above theories, hormones are certainly important in sexual development and research efforts are needed to understand their role. Genetic factors may also be important in sexual anomalies and some progress has been made in sex typing mammalian cells as male or female depending on the presence or absence of the Barr body[69] and in karyotyping or determining genetic sex. This will be discussed again later.

With each of the foregoing background factors, we can now consider general treatment approaches that have been employed.

BIBLIOGRAPHY

1. Abel, G. G., Barlow, D. H., Blanchard, E. B., & Mavissakalian, M. Measurement of sexual arousal in male homosexuals: Effects of instructions and stimulus modality. *Archives of Sexual Behavior*, 1975, *4*(6), 623–629.
2. Abel, G. G., & Blanchard, E. B. The measurement and generation of sexual arousal in male sexual deviates. In M. Hersen, R. M. Eisler, & P. M. Miller (Eds.), *Progress in Behavior Modification*, 1976, *2*, 99–136.
3. Abramson, P. R., & Mosher, D. L. Development of a measure of negative attitudes toward masturbation. *Journal of Consulting and Clinical Psychology*, 1975, *43*(4), 485–490.
4. Allen, R. M., & Haupt, T. D. The sex inventory: Test-retest reliabilities of scale scores and items. *Journal of Clinical Psychology*, 1966, *22*, 375–378.
5. Bancroft, J. The application of psychophysiological measures to the assessment and modification of sexual behavior. *Behavior Research & Therapy*, 1971, *9*, 119–130.
6. Bancroft, J., Jones, H., & Pullan, B. A simple transducer for measuring penile erection, with comments on its use in the treatment of sexual disorders. *Behavior Research & Therapy*, 1966, *4*, 239–241.
7. Bancroft, J., & Mathews, A. Autonomic correlates of penile erection. *Journal of Psychosomatic Research*, 1971, *15*, 159–167.
8. Barbaree, H. E., Marshall, W. L., & Lanther, R. D. Deviant sexual arousal in rapists. *Behavior Research & Therapy*, 1979, *17*(3), 215–222.
9. Barbaree, H. E., Marshall, W. L., Lightfoot-Barbaree, L. O., & Yates, E. *Alcohol Intoxication and Antisocial Behavior: Two Laboratory Studies*. Paper presented at the Annual Meeting of the Ontario Psychological Association, 1979.
10. Barlow, D. H., Becker, R., Leitenberg, H., & Agras, W. S. A mechanical strain gauge for recoding penile circumference change. *Journal of Applied Behavior Analysis*, 1970, *3*, 73–76.
11. Bell, D. S., & Trethowan, W. H. Amphetamine addiction and disturbed sexuality. *Archives of General Psychiatry*, 1961, *4*, 74–78.
12. Benedek, T. G. Aphrodisiacs: Fact and fable. *Medical Aspects of Human Sexuality*, 1975, *5*(12), 42–63.
13. Bentler, P. M. Heterosexual behavior assessment – I. Males. *Behavior Research & Therapy*, 1968, *6*, 21–25.
14. Bieber, I., Dain, H., Dince, P., Drellich, M., Grandh, H., Gundlach, R., Kremer, M., Rifkin A., Wilbur, C., & Bieber, T. *Homosexuality: A psychoanalytic study of male homosexuals*. New York: Basic Books, Inc., 1962.
15. Bowers, M. B., Van Woert, M., & Davis, L. Sexual behavior during L-dopa treatment for Parkinsonism. *American Journal of Psychiatry*, 1971, *127*(12), 127–129.

16. Briddell, D. W., & Wilson, G. T. Effects of alcohol and expectancy set on male sexual arousal. *Journal of Abnormal Psychology,* 1976, *85*(2), 225–234.

17. Chrzanowski, G. Sex behavior as clue to mental disease. *Medical Aspects of Human Sexuality,* 1971, *1*(1), 12–19.

18. Corriveau, D. P., Brown, W. A., & Monti, P. M. Orthogonal components of reported male sexual behavior. *Psychological Reports,* 1977, *41*, 57–58.

19. Costell, R. M., & Wittner, W. K. Contingent negative variation as an indicator of sexual object preference. *Science,* 1972, *177*, 718–720.

20. Cowden, J. E., & Pacht, A. R. The sex inventory as a classification instrument for sex offenders. *Journal of Clinical Psychology,* 1969, *25*, 57–60.

21. Croft, H. A. The sexual information examination. *Journal of Sex & Marital Therapy,* 1975, *1*(4), 319–325.

22. Derogatis, L. R., Meyer, J. K., & Vasquez, N. A psychological profile of the transsexual. *Journal of Nervous & Mental Disease,* 1978, *166*(4), 234–254.

23. Doering, C. H., Brodie, H. K., Kraemer, H., Moos, R., Becker, H., & Hamburg, D. Negative affect and plasma testosterone: A longitudinal human study. *Psychosomatic Medicine,* 1975, *37*(6), 484–491.

24. Earls, F. The fathers (not the mothers): Their importance and influence with infants and young children. *Psychiatry,* 1976, *39,* 209–226.

25. Ehrenkranz, J., Bliss, E., & Sheard, M. H. Plasma testosterone: Correlation with aggressive behavior and social dominance in man. *Psychosomatic Medicine,* 1974, *36*(6), 469–475.

26. Farkas, G. M., & Rosen, R. C. *The effects of ethanol on male sexual arousal.* Paper presented at the annual meeting of the Eastern Psychological Association, New York, 1975.

27. Freund, K. A laboratory differential diagnosis of homo- and heterosexuality—an experiment with faking. *Review of Czechoslovak Medicine,* 1961, *7,* 20–31.

28. Freund, K. A note on the use of the phallometric method of measuring mild sexual arousal in the male. *Behavior Therapy,* 1971, *2,* 223–238.

29. Freund, K., Langevin, R., & Barlow, D. Comparison of two penile measures of erotic arousal. *Behavior Research & Therapy,* 1974, *12,* 355–359.

30. Freund, K., Langevin, R., & Zajac, Y. A note on erotic arousal value of moving and stationary human forms. *Behavior Research & Therapy,* 1974, *12,* 117–119.

31. Freund, K., McKnight, C., Langevin, R., & Cibiri, S. The female child as a surrogate object. *Archives of Sexual Behavior,* 1972, *2,* 119–133.

32. Freund, K., Nagler, E., Langevin, R., Zajac, Z., & Steiner, B. Measuring feminine gender identity in homosexual males. *Archives of Sexual Behavior,* 1974, *3*(3), 249–260.

33. Freund, K., Sedlacek, F., & Knob, K. A simple transducer for mechanical plethysmography of the male genital. *Journal of Experimental Analysis of Behavior,* 1965, *8,* 169–170.

34. Goldzieher, J. W., Dozier, T. S., Smith, K. D., & Steinberger, E. Improving the diagnostic reliability of rapidly fluctuating plasma hormone levels by optimized multiple-sampling techniques. *Journal of Clinical Endocrinology and Metabolism,* 1976, *43*(4), 824–830.

35. Harbison, J., Graham, P., Quinn, J., McAllister, H., & Woodward, R. A questionnaire measure of sexual interest. *Archives of Sexual Behavior,* 1974, *3*(4), 357–366.

36. Harlow, H., & Harlow, M. The effect of rearing conditions on behavior. In J. Money (Ed.), *Sex research: New development.* New York: Holt Rinehart, 1965.

37. Haupt, T. D., & Allen, M. A multivariate analysis of variance of scale scores on the sex inventory, male form. *Journal of Clinical Psychology,* 1966, *22,* 387–395.

38. Hess, E. H., & Polt, J. M. Pupil size as related to interest value of visual stimuli. *Science,* 1960, *132,* 349–350.

39. Joe, V., & Brown, C. A test of the Zuckerman heterosexual scales. *Journal of Personality Assessment,* 1975, *39*(3), 271–272.

40. Kalant, O. J. *The Amphetamines: Toxicity and Addiction.* Toronto; University of Toronto Press, 1973.

41. Kling, A., Borowitz, G., & Cartwright, D. Plasma levels of 17-hydroxycorticosteroids during sexual arousal in man. *Journal of Psychosomatic Research,* 1972, *16,* 215–221.

42. Koff, W. C. Marijuana and sexual activity. *Journal of Sex Research,* 1974, *10*(3), 194–204.

43. Kraemer, H., Becker, B., Brodie, H., Doering, C., Moos, R., & Hamburg, D. Orgasmic frequency and plasma testosterone levels in normal human males. *Archives of Sexual Behavior,* 1976, *5*(2), 125–132.

44. Lamb, M. E. Fathers: Forgotten contributors to child development. *Human Development,* 1975, *18,* 245–266.

45. Langevin, R., & Martin, M. Can erotic responses be classically conditioned? *Behavior Therapy,* 1975, *6,* 350–355.

46. Langevin, R., Stanford, A., & Block, R. The effect of relaxation instructions on erotic arousal in homosexual and heterosexual males. *Behavior Therapy,* 1975, *6,* 453–458.

47. Langevin, R., Martin, M., & Handy, L. *Physiological correlates of erotic arousal.* Paper presented at the Annual Meeting of the Society for the Scientific Study of Sex, Inc., Beverly Hills, California, 1975.

48. Langevin, R., Paitich, D., Ramsay, G., Anderson, C., Kamrad, J., Pope, S., Geller, G., Pearl, L., & Newman, S. Experimental studies in the etiology of genital exhibitionism. *Archives of Sexual Behavior,* 1979, *8*(4), 307–331.

49. Langevin, R., Paitich, D., Freeman, R., Mann, K., & Handy, L. Personality characteristics and sexual anomalies in males. *Canadian Journal of Behavioral Science,* 1978, *10*(3), 222–238.

50. Laws, D. R., & Bow, R. A. An improved mechanical strain gauge for recording penile circumference. *Psychophysiology,* 1976, *13*(6), 596–599.

51. Laws, D. R. A comparison of the measurement characteristics of two circumferential penile transducers. *Archives of Sexual Behavior,* 1977, *6*(1), 45–52.

52. Laws, D. R., & Holmen, M. L. Sexual response faking by pedophiles. *Criminal Justice and Behavior,* 1978, *5*(4), 343–356.

53. Laws, D. R., & Pawlowski, A. V. A multi-purpose biofeedback device for penile plethysmography. *Behavior Therapy & Experimental Psychiatry,* 1973, *4,* 339–341.

54. Lunneborg, P. W. Dimensionality of MF. *Journal of Clinical Psychology,* 1972, *28,* 313–317.

55. Malatesta, V. J., Pollack, R. H., Wilbanks, W. A., & Adams, H. E. Alcohol effects on the orgasmic-ejaculatory response in human males. *Journal of Sex Research,* 1979, *15*(2), 101–107.

56. McCaghy, C. H. Drinking and deviance disavowal: the case of child molesters. *Sexual Problems,* 1968, *16*(1), 43–49.

57. McConaghy, N. Measurement of change in penile dimension. *Archives of Sexual Behavior,* 1974, *3*(4), 381–387.

58. McCoy, N. N., & D'Agostino, P. A. Factor analysis of the sexual interaction inventory. *Archives of Sexual Behavior,* 1977, *6*(1), 25–36.

59. McCreary, C. P. Personality profiles of persons convicted of indecent exposure. *Journal of Clinical Psychology,* 1975, *31,* 260–262.

60. Mello, N. K., & Mendelson, J. H. Alcohol and human behavior. In L. L. Iverson, S. D.

Iverson, & S. H. Snyder. *Handbook of psychopharmacology* (Vol. 12). New York: Plenum Press, 1978, 235-317.

61. Mendelson, J. H. Endocrines and aggression. *Psychopharmacology Bulletin,* 1977, *13*(1), 22-23.

62. Mendelson, J. H. Marijuana and sex. *Medical aspects of Human Sexuality,* 1976, *10,* 23-24.

63. Mendelson, J., & Mello, N. Alcohol, aggression and androgens. In S. H. Frazier (Ed.), *Aggression.* Baltimore: Williams & Wilkins, Co., 1974.

64. Meyer-Bahlburg, H. F. Sex hormones and male homosexuality in comparative perspective. *Archives of Sexual Behavior,* 1979, *8*(2), 101-120.

65. Mohr, J., Turner, R., & Ball, R. Exhibitionism and pedophilia. *Corrective Psychiatry and Journal of Social Therapy,* 1962, *8,* 172-186.

66. Money, J. Sexual dimorplism and homosexual gender identity. *Psychological Bulletin,* 1970, *74*(3), 425-440.

67. Money, J., Hampson, J. G., & Hampson, J. L. Imprinting and the establishment of gender role. *A.M.A. Archives of Neurology & Psychiatry,* 1957, *77,* 333-336.

68. Monti, P. M., Brown, W. A., & Corriveau, D. P. Testosterone and components of aggressive and sexual behavior in man. *American Journal of Psychiatry,* 1977, *134*(6), 692-694.

69. Moore, K. L., & Barr, M. L. Morphology of the nerve cell nucleus in mammals with special reference to the sex chromatin. *Journal of Comparative Neurology,* 1953, *98,* 213-231

70. Paitich, D., & Langevin, R. The Clarke parent-child relations questionnaire: A clinically useful test for adults. *Journal of Consulting & Clinical Psychology,* 1976, *44*(3), 428-436.

71. Paitich, D., Langevin, R., Freeman, R., Mann, K., & Handy, L. The Clarke SHQ: A clinical sex history questionnaire for males. *Archives of Sexual Behavior,* 1977, *6*(5), 421-435.

72. Pawlowski, A. V., & Laws, D. R. A multipurpose voltage controlled oscillator. *Behavior Research Methods and Instrumentation,* 1974, *6*(1), 27-28.

73. Perloff, W. H. Hormones and homosexuality. In J. Marmor (Ed.), *Sexual inversion.* New York: Basic Books, Inc., 1965, 44-69.

74. Persky, H., O'Brien, C., Fine, E., Howard, W., Khan, M., & Beck, R. The effect of alcohol and smoking on testosterone function and aggression in chronic alcoholics. *American Journal of Psychiatry,* 1977, *134*(6), 621-625.

75. Pinderhughes, C., Grace, E., & Reyna, L. Psychiatric disorders and sexual functioning. *American Journal of Psychiatry,* 1972, *128*(10), 96-103.

76. Posavac, E. J., Walker, R. E., Foley, J. M., & Sannito, T. Further factor-analytic investigation of the Thorne femininity study. *Journal of Clinical Psychology,* 1977, *33*(1), 24-31.

77. Quinsey, V. L. Assessments of the dangerousness of mental patients held in maximum security. *International Journal of Law and Psychiatry,* 1979, *2,* 389-406.

78. Quinsey, V. L., & Bergersen, S. G. Instructional control of penile circumference in assessments of sexual preference. *Behavior Therapy,* 1976, *7,* 489-493.

79. Quinsey, V. L., & Carrigan, W. F. Penile responses to visual stimuli. *Criminal Justice and Behavior,* 1978, *5*(4), 333-342.

80. Quinsey, V. L., Chaplin, T. C., & Varney, G. A comparison of rapists' and non-sex offenders' sexual preferences for mutually consenting sex, rape and sadistic acts. *Behavioral Assessment,* 1981, *3,* 127-135.

81. Rada, R. T. Alcoholism and forcible rape. *American Journal of Psychiatry,* 1975, *132*(4), 444-446.

82. Rada, R. T. *Clinical aspects of the rapist.* New York: Grune & Stratton, 1978.

83. Rekers, G. A., Willis, T. J., Yates, C. E., Rosen, A. C., & Low, B. P. Assessment of childhood gender behavior change. *Journal of Child Psychology & Psychiatry,* 1977, *18,* 53–65.

84. *Report of the Commission on Pornography and Obscenity.* Washington, D.C.: U.S. Gov't. Printing Office, 1970.

85. Rose, R. M. Testosterone, aggression and homosexuality: A review of the literature and implications for future research. In *Topics in Psychoendocrinology,* E. J. Sachar (Ed.), New York: Grune & Stratton, 1975.

86. Rosen, A. C., & Rekers, G. A. Toward a taxonomic framework for variables of sex and gender. *Genetic Psychology Monographs,* 1980, *102*(2), 191–218.

87. Rosen, R. C. Suppression of penile tumescence by instrumental conditioning. *Psychosomatic Medicine,* 1973, *35*(6), 509–514.

88. Rosen, R. C. *The control of penile tumescence in the human male.* Paper presented at the annual convention of the American Psychological Association, New Orleans, 1974.

89. Rosen, R. C., Shapiro, D., & Schwartz, G. Voluntary control of penile tumescence. *Psychosomatic Medicine,* 1975, *37*(6), 479–483.

90. Rubin, H. B., & Henson, D. E. Effects of alcohol on male sexual responding. *Psychopharmacology,* 1976, *47,* 123–134.

91. Scaramella, T. J., & Brown, W. A. Serum testosterone and aggressiveness in hockey players. *Psychosomatic Medicine,* 1978, *40*(3), 262–265.

92. Schaeffer, H., Tregerthan, G., & Colgan, A. Measured and self-estimated penile erection. *Behavior Therapy,* 1976, *7,* 1–7.

93. Segraves, R. T. Pharmacological agents causing sexual dysfunction. *Journal of Sex & Marital Therapy,* 1977, *3*(3), 157–176.

94. Selkin, J. Rape. *Psychology Today,* 1975, *8*(8), 71–76.

95. Sheard, M. H. The role of drugs in precipitating or inhibiting human aggression. *Psychopharmacology Bulletin,* 1977, *13*(1), 23–25.

96. Shively, M., & De Cecco, J. Components of sexual identity. *Journal of Homosexuality,* 1977, *3*(1), 41–48.

97. Smart, R. G., & Bateman, K. Unfavourable reactions to LSD: A review and analysis of the available case reports. *Canadian Medical Association Journal,* 1967, *97,* 1214–1221.

98. Spalt, L. Sexual behavior and affective disorders. *Diseases of the Nervous System,* 1975, *36*(12), 644–647.

99. Stoller, R. J. The term "transvestism". *Archives of General Psychiatry,* 1971, *24,* 230–237.

100. Stoller, R. J. *The transsexual experiment.* London: Hogarth Press, 1975.

101. Stoller, R. J. Sexual excitement. *Archives of General Psychiatry,* 1976, *33,* 899–909.

102. Tennent, T. G. The dangerous offender. *British Journal of Hospital Medicine,* 1971, *6,* 269–274.

103. Thorne, F. C. A factorial study of sexuality in adult males. *Journal of Clinical Psychology,* 1966, *22,* 378–386.

104. Thorne, F. C. Scales for rating sexual experience. *Journal of Clinical Psychology,* 1966, *22,* 404–407.

105. Thorne, F. C. The sex inventory. *Journal of Clinical Psychology,* 1966, *22,* 367–374.

106. Thorne, F. C., & Haupt, T. D. The objective measurement of sex attitudes and behavior in adult males. *Journal of Clinical Psychology,* 1966, *22,* 395–403.

107. Tinklenberg, J. R., & Woodrow, K. M. Drug use among youthful assaultive and sexual offenders. In S. H. Frazier (Ed.), *Aggression.* Baltimore: Williams & Wilkins Co., 1974.

108. Wilson, G. T. Alcohol and human sexual behavior. *Behavior Research & Therapy,* 1977, *15,* 239–252.
109. Wilson, G. T., & Lawson, D. M. Effects of alcohol and sexual arousal in women. *Journal of Abnormal Psychology,* 1976, *85*(5), 489–491.
110. Zuckerman, M. Physiological measures of sexual arousal in the human. *Psychological Bulletin,* 1971, *75*(5), 297–329.
111. Zuckerman, M. Scales for sex experience for males and females. *Journal of Consulting and Clinical Psychology,* 1973, *41*(1), 27–29.

3 Treatment Methods

INTRODUCTION

A limited number of treatment procedures have been applied to sexual anomalies. Rather than describe them repeatedly in detail, an overview of each major method is described in this chapter. Of all the treatments for sexual anomalies that have been developed by mental health professionals, behavior therapy has been reported most. Psychoanalysis and other psychotherapies, including group therapies have been employed as well but have not been reported as frequently in professional journals. In the past few years, chemical intervention in sexual behavior has gained increased popularity. In particular, antiandrogen drugs, which reduce sex drive have been employed. These methods will be reviewed along with an age old solution to sexual problems, castration. The reader who is familiar with the methods and the problems they entail may wish to skip this chapter.

BEHAVIOR THERAPY

Behavior therapy is also called behavior *modification* which describes the goal of treatment, to change or modify overt and/or quantifiable behavior. Incidental feelings of well being and attitudes may also be modified in the process but the behavior therapist restricts himself to overt behavior, knowing that if this is changed, as a matter of course, the patient's problems and bad feelings will disappear as well. Some concrete observable behavior is the usual target of treatment. In the case of sexual anomalies, the therapist tries either to reduce the frequency of erotic reactions to anomalous behavior or increase those to normal behavior, for example, reduce the frequency of exposing and increase the frequency of sexual intercourse.

Measuring the frequency of behavior.   In order to do this, the therapist counts the frequency of the sexual behaviors before any treatment is started. This is known as establishing the baseline rate of behavior. It is particularly important because some behavior is very sporadic and may create difficulties in evaluating treatment effectiveness. For example, if an exhibitionist exposes once or twice a year and only during the summer, in order to know if therapy has actually changed his life, one would have to wait at least a year to see if the behavior has recurred. On the other hand, if it occurs daily, the therapist can know within a week or so if his treatment method is effective in changing that patient. Thus it is crucial to establish the baseline rate of a behavior being modified.

In order to measure the changes occurring during treatment, the reported frequencies of the sexual behavior outside the treatment center are noted and penile reactions to stimuli used in treatment are monitored. Since single criterion are often unsatisfactory, several should be used. This may entail other measures of sexual behaviors including desires, disgust and/or pleasure in the so called *multiple baseline design*[53] [54]. Treatment and measures should be as simple as possible.

Measurement offers a great advantage. If the therapist is trying to reduce penile reactions to exposing stimuli and the patient continues to show unchanging large reactions to such stimuli, the method can be altered so that a change will be observed. The penile strain gauge or phallometer serve this purpose well and provide the behavior therapist with a distinct advantage over other treatment methods. He can know continually that the patient is progressing and the goals of treatment are being obtained. In contrast, the criteria of outcome in other approaches are much more complex and uncertain, such as in time consuming psychotherapy. This may be one more reason why behavior therapy has become so popular. With the phallometer, the therapist can continually monitor the process of therapy and know when to stop treatment. He can also follow up the patient using the same procedure, at 6 month intervals over a 3-or-4 year period to determine if the effectiveness of treatment is lasting.

Shaping procedures.   A commonly used procedure in many behavior therapy methods is shaping. Rather than try to change behavior all at once, a gradual alteration is attempted. Usually, a hierarchy of stimuli is constructed which depicts the patient's sexual activity in segments. The stimuli in the hierarchy are ranked from weakest to strongest either in terms of erotic arousal or anxiety arousing potential. Thus an exhibitionist would report the act of exposing in detail and indicate which locale, which reaction of the female, and so forth, are most and least sexually arousing. If he found intercourse with a girlfriend or wife aversive, that would be cataloged in the same way. For example:

Least arousing sexually	street setting, woman did not notice or ignored him, cold outside
More arousing sexually	street setting, woman notices but does not react
More arousing again	park, no one around, woman unreactive
More arousing again	park, woman smiles but hurries on
More arousing	street setting, woman notices and smiles at him, sees him masturbate
More arousing	street setting, woman smiles at him, seems interested, maybe turned on by exposing and masturbation
Most arousing	park, no one around, woman stops and watches him masturbate to climax

A hierarchy of aversion to intercourse can similarly be constructed. For example:

Least aversive	sitting with wife who says let's go to bed
More aversive	wife kisses him and looks like she wants sex and says let's go to bed
More aversive again	getting ready for bed, wife wants sex
More aversive	walking toward the bed, wife looks turned on sexually
More aversive	wife rolls over and kisses him in bed
More aversive	wife pushes her body against his
More aversive	wife touches his penis
Most aversive	wife guides his penis toward her vagina

The hierarchies are very useful because it is easier to change a weak behavior than a strong one. Moreover, since the weaker behaviors are more readily changed, the patient will be aware of some improvement in his condition and it will incite him to continue treatment and motivate him to change even more.

Starting treatment by changing the weak responses also weakens the related stronger behaviors. So in the example above, if one changes the "exposing in the steet to a woman who ignored him" so that the patient no longer found it arousing, the more powerful stimuli like exposing in the park to a smiling woman will also be less exciting for the patient. Gradually the strongest behavior will become weak and be extinguished. It is like pulling the bottom from a pyramid of tins in a grocery store. The whole structure does not fall but it is weakened considerably and removing other tins is easier and weakens the structure even more. This method is useful, in both enhancing and removing behaviors from a person's repertoire.

Another reason shaping is so useful is that the real behavior may be so complex that it cannot be readily changed. For example, if one wished to train a dog to climb up a ladder, then jump through a ring of fire, stand on its hind legs and dance around in circles, it is much easier to break the sequence down into 3 or more pieces and then add them together, that is, climb the ladder, then train to jump through the ring of fire, then dance on hind legs. Similarly, a sexually anomalous man may be reacting with fear to a complex of stimuli. An impotent man who is in a bedroom with his wife may feel an aversion to the room itself, to his wife's body and to the cues she offers that she wants intercourse. The behavior therapist may start breaking down the fear the patient experiences to the room alone, then to his wife's body and then to intercourse.

At other times, a single stimulus is so powerful and the patient reacts so strongly that it is difficult to progress beyond that point. In the example above, the exhibitionist who has an aversion to having intercourse with his wife may find the step "wife rolls over and kisses him in bed" so anxiety provoking that he blocks on changing it. The therapist can at that point break it down into sub-steps. For example:

1. wife looks at him in bed
2. wife smiles at him in bed
3. wife starts to turn toward him in bed
4. wife moves a few inches toward him
5. wife moves a few inches more
6. wife is a few inches from his face
7. wife's lips are about to touch his lips
8. wife's lips touch his lips
9. wife's lips press against his
10. wife's body is starting to roll closer
11. wife's body is a few inches closer again
12. wife's body is about to touch his

13. wife's body is in contact with his
14. wife's body is pressed against his.

So one step becomes 14 and the patient continues to progress through the sequence. A similar procedure could be used for the anomalous stimuli that are to be decreased in frequency.

Sometimes a lack of progress is evident because the frequency of behavior may not be changing but the intensity is. A patient may report that he continues to peep in windows 4 times a week at his pretreatment level but he may also claim that he did not enjoy it as much or that he only masturbated twice in the four times, while before treatment he always masturbated while peeping. Thus some progress may still be evident. Often the simple count of frequencies is sufficient but the therapist can avoid the difficulty just noted, by recording and following multiple baselines of sexual behavior such as urges, fantasies and orgasms related to the desired outlets, to masturbation and to intercourse.

Classical and Operant Conditioning

Two methods pervade just about every behavior therapy procedure: classical and operant conditioning. Classical conditioning was attributed first to Ivan Pavlov, a Russian physiologist who worked with dogs. He found that dogs would salivate to the sight of food. This could be described as an anticipatory response since the dogs would not actually have the food in their mouths but the sight and perhaps the smell would trigger a salivation reaction. When Pavlov rang a bell just before the presentation of food, the dogs would also salivate. After only a few repeated pairings of bell with food, they would salivate to the sound of the bell alone. This is termed a conditioned reaction or response. The dogs did not salivate to the bell alone as much as they would to the food but the reaction was large enough to be measured. Pavlov investigated the numerous factors that could affect the size of the conditioned reaction. For example, if the bell was a 2000 cycle per second sound, would the dogs salivate as much for a 3000 cps or 10000 cps tone? Pavlov set the study of conditioned behaviors into a scientific frame of reference and research continues today on the factors important in conditioned responses.

The second major method is operant conditioning and it has been known to animal trainers for hundreds of years. It was first systematically studied by B.F. Skinner in the 1920's. The method is simple: behavior followed by reward tends to recur more frequently, behavior followed by no reward or by punishment tends to disappear.

The paradigm experiment illustrating this method and known to many undergraduate psychology students is to train a hungry rat to press a bar for food. Usually this is carried out in an enclosure called a Skinner box that has a food receptacle and a bar in the wall. The student gives the rat a few bits of food to let it know the food is there, but does not give it enough to satisfy its hunger. It will explore the cage box naturally and will press the bar by chance which automatically produces a small pellet of food. If left alone, it may discover the connection between the bar and the food on its own. The bar pressing behavior, which is rewarded will increase in frequency until the rat is satiated. These are the basics of operant conditioning.

The shaping procedure is used to speed up the conditioning process. The student is provided with a remote control switch that activates the food dispenser. The student observes the rat and whenever it comes in the vicinity of the bar to be pressed, he gives it food. Gradually the behavior is more specified and the rat will sniff and/or touch the bar and the student gives it food. Soon the rat is spending much of its time around the bar and will touch it by accident perhaps, but soon it is pressing the bar at great frequency to get the food. When satiated, it will rest and perhaps preen itself. The next time it is placed in the box and is deprived of food, it will go right to the bar and press. If the experimenter disconnects the bar and pressing it is not followed by food, the frequency of bar pressing drops and the behavior is said to be *extinguished*. Alternatively, the experimenter may decide to *suppress* the behavior by giving the rat an electric shock every time he touches the bar. After one, perhaps two or three shocks, the rat will not touch the bar. Suppression is different from extinction because with time, the rat will come back to press the bar again especially if it is hungry. Researchers continue to argue today if this sort of punishment is effective in changing behavior.

Both classical and operant conditioning have been used repeatedly as the rationale for specific methods of treating sexual anomalies but the fit is not always satisfactory.

SPECIFIC BEHAVIOR THERAPY METHODS

Aversion therapy. Historically, classical conditioning was first used in the aversion treatment of sexual anomalies in 1935 by Max[77]. Using the Pavlovian model, he presented pictures of males to a homosexual patient as the conditioning stimulus parallel to the bell in Pavlov's study. The projected picture (conditioning stimulus) was followed by a strong electric shock (unconditioned stimulus). The shock would create an unconditioned aversive or fear reaction. Just as the dog salivated for the bell, so the homosexual patient would develop a conditioned aversive reaction to the pictures of males when repeatedly paired with the shock. Max noted that the patient lost his "homosexual fixation". The laboratory setting has changed since that time to become more sophisticated but the method underlying it is similar.

Max's work seemed to go unnoticed until Freund employed a chemical aversion procedure. When a person is administered apomorphine and emetine, shortly afterwards he has an irrestible urge to vomit. Thus it serves as an unconditioned reaction that is very unpleasant. The procedure was similar to Max's—the patients were presented with pictures of males (conditioning stimulus) and administered emetine hydrochloride and apomorphine. Soon the pictures elicited an unconditioned nausea reaction rather than the positive reaction they did formerly.

Researchers adopted the method and applied it to other sexual anomalies. Technically anything could be used as a conditioning stimulus and paired with nausea producing drugs or electric shock and result in a conditioned aversive reaction. Another chemical that was used as an aversive agent was scoline, a curarizing drug which left the individual paralyzed for a minute or two. Without the life support system of the attending physician, literally pumping oxygen into him, he would die, since the lungs were paralyzed. The logic of the method was still the same; present the conditioning stimuli, for example, clothes used by a transvestite in orgasmic crossdressing, and then introduce the aversive chemical until he is paralyzed. The clothes in this case would become aversive and future crossdressing should be less in frequency.

Therapists soon became disenchanted with the chemical method of aversion, perhaps because of outcries against such inhumane methods[113] but especially because they were imprecise and uncontrollable. One never knew exactly when the patient would vomit after receiving apomorphine and emetine hydrochloride[90] so there was little control over the timing of conditioning and unconditioned stimuli. Earlier work and theorizing suggested that the timing was crucial. In particular, about half a second between stimuli was optimal. Shorter than that or longer did not produce as effective conditioning. Chemical aversion therapy was expensive. Medical support staff had to attend the patient who would be admitted to the hospital for a few days at least so that repeated pairing of conditioning stimulus and chemical could take place. Support staff was especially necessary because of the danger to the patient. There was always the possibility of gastric rupture from continual vomiting, especially with nothing in the stomach. Body fluids might be lost and there could be salt depletion and possible cardiovascular sequelae. Some patients acquired a fever and became delerious and in one case died.

Scoline had more practical limitations in that very few people were willing to come back for a second session. Since a satisfactory conditioned response demands repeated pairings of the conditioning and aversive stimuli, this method is not very practical. Serious physical consequences also had to be taken into consideration in treating patients with this method. One had to ensure that the patient was healthy. Heart trouble would be a particular concern since one would not want to risk a heart attack. In light of the deficiencies of these procedures, practitioners turned to the less dangerous and more efficient electric shock once again.

Electrical aversion therapy has several advantages: the timing of the shock in relation to the conditioning stimulus could be very exact and controlled; the amount of shock delivered to the patient could be varied in a precise manner; the stimulus could be repeatedly presented at the same sitting unlike the chemical aversive agents that needed hours and sometimes days between presentations. One could be assured that the conditioning stimulus preceded the aversive one. This was not always possible with chemical agents and at times the conditioning stimulus came second. This so called "backward conditioning" had never been satisfactorily demonstrated to work.

The use of classical faradic conditioning as it was called, was reported in a few scattered studies but it was only in 1966 when the procedures were modified by Feldman and MacCulloch[28] and their colleagues to an operant conditioning model that research and interest in this method escalated. The operant approach they used has been labeled avoidance conditioning. Some theorists believe that such conditioning underlies all significant human behavior.

In this method, a warning stimulus is presented to the patient, for example, a tone which may last 8 to 10 seconds. When the tone ends he receives an electric shock. So far, this looks like an inefficient form of classical conditioning. However, the patient has an opportunity to respond during that 8 to 10 seconds by pressing a button to terminate the tone and prevent the shock from coming. Animal studies have illustrated the strength of such avoidance reactions since rats once trained will terminate the tone hundreds of times without further shocks.

The avoidance reaction was recognized as much more lasting in its impact on behavior and it was employed in treating sexual anomalies. Instead of the tone, attractive pictures of sex stimuli would be presented, for example, children to pedophilic men, and the task of the patient was to remove the picture before the shock came. Why should the patient not press the button all the time and receive no shock? Then he could go out in the real world and carry on as he chose. This in fact can happen with this method so it had to be modified somewhat.

It was changed in two ways to make it effective. First, on a third of the paired presentation trials the patient could not avoid shock, but he did not know which trials they were. This added an element of uncertainty which would keep up the anxiety level of the patient. Second, a third of the trials were unpunished anyway because it had been found in animal work that within limits, doing so created a stronger learning bond and the behavior was less likely to extinguish as quickly. This latter procedure is called *partial* *reinforcement,*as opposed to continuous reinforcement on which every pairing involves shock.

Unfortunately, the patient may still minimize the number of shocks he receives to 1/3 of the total. In theory, he should be shocked 2/3 of the time (unavoidable plus avoidable shock) which is a relatively effective procedure. In fact, it is more effective than shock delivered 100% of the time. However, if the patient always pushes the button from the start he will only be shocked 1/3 of the time and this results in poor learning. It seems that in spite of findings with animals over which the researcher has complete control; when working with humans who may wish to fool the therapist, there can be serious practical limitations to the method.

Covert sensitization.   There have been some ingenious variants of the classical and operant conditioning methods. One method is covert sensitization[18] in which both the conditioning and the aversive stimuli are *imagined.* These may be prerecorded on tape to provide a polished presentation. A typical description might be:

> Close your eyes and imagine the following. You are walking down the street alone at night and no one is around. As you walk along you notice an attractive young woman coming your way. You are really turned on and you think you would like to expose. As she comes closer, you unzip your fly and take out your privates. You are really excited now.

The foregoing would be akin to the conditioning stimulus. Then the aversive one is presented:

> As she comes closer, you feel a knot in your stomach. You feel like vomiting. You can feel it gushing up into your mouth. She is walking closer, she is really close now and you are about to expose. The vomit is in your mouth. You try to swallow it but it is too much. You start to throw up all over. It gushes out and lands all over your erection. The puke keeps coming, you have never been so sick in your life.

Then there is a relief sequence which takes the patient away from the exposing situation:

> You start to run away. You clean off yourself and get away. Your stomach feels better the farther away you get. You cannot see the woman anymore and your desire to expose is gone. You feel better now. You take in deep breaths of the cool clean evening air. You feel good the farther you walk away from there.

Of course all of the learning principles noted with the previous aversive methods apply here. One might wish to have no aversive sequence on 1/4 or 1/3 of the trials (partial reinforcement), time between conditioning stimulus and aversive stimulus is important, etc. However, when all the stimuli are imagined and unobservable, the therapist relinquishes considerable control over the treatment. This may be especially problematic when the unwilling patient is ordered by the court to be treated instead of going to jail.

Monitoring phallometric reactions can be an invaluable aid in this method since it provides some index that the subject is aroused (tumescence) and experiencing aversion (detumescence).

Shame aversion therapy. Another aversion method that involves no shock but appears to be a powerful operant method nonetheless, is shame aversion therapy. Several variants of this method have been independently reported in the last 10 years[102] [117] [119]. Basically the patient engages in his sexually anomalous behavior but it goes unrewarded and in fact he is humiliated or shamed after it. It additionally may be aversive because the patient is forced to maintain contact with the victim after his act. The therapy setting might be a room with 10 or 12 seated observers who just look at the patient engaging in his acts but they do not react in any way. For example, the patient may be a toucheur and grab ladies' breasts on the subway. In this instance, the patient would touch the breast of a passive disinterested female while a group of unreactive observers simply watch him. Only 2 or 3 sessions are used. Either this number of session is sufficient or the patient begins to like it and does not improve at all. The therapist has to be careful to ensure the patient is not depressed. The humiliation and "shame" may add to his existing feelings and backfire. Only a few cases are reported in the literature and one transvestite who seemed depressed, attempted suicide after the treatment session.

Anxiety relief conditioning. Punishing undesired behavior has long been considered insufficient as a treatment in itself to change sexually anomalous behavior[9]. If one simply suppresses or extinguishes exposing for example, what is the patient to do when he is sexually aroused? Therapists seem agreed that some form of appropriate heterosexual behavior should be encouraged and a number of treatments did develop just with that end in mind. When Freund first introduced chemical aversion conditioning for homosexual males, he concurrently used a procedure that might be called "exposure". He injected testosterone, a sexual stimulant, into the patients and when the stimulant took effect, he introduced them to pictures of women. Some claimed that they were sexually excited by women for the first time in their lives. The continuity of such feelings, of course, would be beneficial to the lasting satisfaction of the patient and to an established "cure".

Most therapists using aversive methods did not employ testosterone, however. They used anxiety relief conditioning. The logic of this method is to associate the termination of an aversive event like shock with a neutral stimulus, which then takes on positive qualities. The relief from tension could be associated with pictures of adult women for pedophilic patients. Hopefully, viewing the pictures would become relaxing and eventually have a positive erotic valence. To this day, such a method is used in conjunction with aversion trials. Thus the sequence of presentation for a homosexual is: picture of male, electric shock, picture of female.

In theory, the male becomes aversive and the female becomes relaxing. The jump from nonaversive to erotically arousing, however, is a big one. Moreover, the sequence "shock—female stimulus" looks like backward conditioning that does not appear to result in learning. In fact the sequence "male stimulus–shock–female stimulus" may produce two undesired results. First, analogous animal studies suggest that having the equivalent of a female stimulus after the shock reduces the amount of aversion to the male stimulus[106]. Second, if the female stimulus is aversive to begin with, as some theories claim, one is shunting the patient from one aversive state (shock) to another (female stimulus). This is not likely to relax the patient and produce a positive valence to the female. Rather, he may show an avoidance reaction to both shock and females, perhaps to the whole therapy situation if his anxiety level is sufficiently high. Other methods of enhancing heterosexual behaviors are more theoretically sound and practical.

Systematic desensitization. One such method is reciprocal inhibition therapy or systematic desensitization developed by Wolpe[120]. It has been used for cases in which the patient is anxious about sex relationships with mature females. The theory of the method is that one cannot be muscularly tense and relaxed at the same time since the muscles are either relaxed or contracted. The patient is first trained in deep muscle relaxation after Jacobson[51]. When he is well versed in this method and knows when his body tenses, he can learn to relax it under quiet and undemanding circumstances, that is, in the treatment room with his therapist. Then a hierarchy of anxiety producing stimuli is introduced, namely sexual interaction with a female. An attempt is made to extinguish the anxiety to the stimuli. The hierarchy describes parts of the interaction from a weak anxiety producing stimulus to a very strong one as noted earlier. Ordinarily, one might expect that talking to a woman versus actually engaging in vaginal penetration would be a linear sequence from least anxiety producing to most anxiety producing but this is not always the case. Each person has his idiosyncracies and the therapist has to construct a hierarchy for each patient. The case of Mr. A is an example of how the treatment is applied.

> *Doctor:*   Mr. A, you seem to be getting along well with the relaxation exercises. Do you feel you can recognize the differences between tension and relaxation now?
>
> *Mr. A:*   Yes, I think I can do it pretty well here. When I try it at home, I'm not always as successful. Sometimes I forget completely and then I realize how tense I am and try to relax but it is too late. I'm getting better doing it at home, it just takes practice.

Doctor: I think we are ready to move on to the next phase of treatment. You have indicated that you feel sexually excited when you expose but you feel tense when it is time to have intercourse with your wife and you have been avoiding it. What I would like to do for the rest of this session today is to look in detail at what makes you feel tense. What is the typical sequence of events before you have intercourse with your wife?

Mr. A: Usually it is at bed time or in the evening when we are alone. She might say, "Are you coming to bed now?" Just the way she says it, I know she is in the mood for sex. Often I'll make some excuse . . . I want to see the news on TV or read some more of my book. When I do go along with her, I get more and more tense as we brush our teeth and get ready for bed. Usually she is in bed before me and has that eager look on her face. That bothers me. Then I turn out the lights and get in beside her. She rolls over toward me and kisses me and I know she wants more. We can pet like that for a long time before I get an erection. Sometimes I imagine I'm exposing to a strange woman and I get aroused that way. Sometimes she will stroke and suck my penis and that gets me going, but it is hard work. I'm glad when it's over.

Doctor: Let's write down some of the things that are happening here:
wife asks if you're coming to bed . . . .
you get up and go to the washroom and brush your teeth . . .
you put on your pajamas . . .
she is putting on her pajamas . . .
you are finishing up in the washroom and walking toward the bed . . .
you see your wife lying in bed with eager look . . .
you turn out the light and lie beside her . . .
she leans over to kiss you . . .
she rolls her body against yours . . .
you start to pet . . .
you have intercourse . . .
Let's start with that list. Rate each item on a scale of how much tension it produces from 1 to 10. If there is no tension at all, give it a score of 1. If it is extremely tension generating, rate it 10. Of course the numbers in between are degrees of tension, a 5 would be a fair amount of tension somewhere in between the extremes of no tension and extreme tension. Think about each item in terms of the relaxation exercises we have been doing. How much does each situation produce muscular tension as we have discussed here? Any questions? Ok. Rate the items.

In the next session, the items would be presented from the least tension producing to the most tension producing. Perhaps only a few could be given because of the difficulty the patient experiences. The therapist may find he has to divide up a segment into finer pieces. An example from a therapy session illustrates this problem and how it is handled.

The preliminary relaxation exercises have been given, usually for 15 to 30 minutes, to have the patient in a state of deep relaxation. Doctor says in a quiet and relaxing voice:

If you are completely relaxed now, raise a finger to let me know. (Patient raises a finger). I'm going to ask you to imagine some scenes now. If you feel any tension let me know by raising a finger. I want you to imagine you are in your bathroom at home and brushing your teeth at bedtime. Your wife is lying in bed waiting to have sex with you...(pause). If you can imagine that raise a finger. (Patient raises a finger. Pause of about 10 seconds). Now clear that thought from your mind and relax. Concentrate on your body and relax any muscle that may have become tense. Breathe deeply and regularly and relax... If you felt tension during that scene raise a finger. (Patient does not). If you felt relaxed raise a finger. (Patient does).

After a few moments the therapist says again:

Now I want you to imagine you are in your washroom at home getting ready for bed. You leave the washroom and walk toward your wife lying in bed with an eager look in her eyes. (Patient raises a finger to indicate he experiences tension). Clear that thought from your mind and relax.

The therapist has two options at this point. First, he may try to repeat the stimulus hoping that the patient will not indicate tension. However, if the patient becomes tense, this time he says:

You turn out the light in the bathroom and take one step into the bedroom. You see your wife lying there.

This time the subject experiences no tension so the following step is:

You take two and three steps into the bedroom. Let me know when you start to feel the tension.

After 6 steps, the patient raises a finger and the therapist terminates the sequence. It is repeated and a seventh step is taken. This time there is no tension. Finally in this manner, the patient imagines getting into bed with no tension experienced.

A certain amount of training and skill are necessary to perform this sort of treatment but compared to other methods like psychoanalysis, it is inexpensive and quick. That is one reason behavior therapy methods have become so popular. This method has been found to be useful for phobias and anxiety generating situations. When there is anxiety associated with conventional heterosexual relations, such a method seems most appropriate. Some sexual anomalies are also considered to be anxiety motivated, that is, the behavior is caused as much by fear as by sexual arousal. In such cases, the method would seem to be applicable directly to changing the anomaly. The method offers the patient a sense of self control[37] over his behavior and cooperation is generally readily obtained.

Positive classical conditioning.   Another approach used to enhance heterosexual behavior has been simple classical conditioning but not the aversive variety described earlier. Conditioned reactions are built on the individual's existing erotic reactions to unconditioned stimuli, such as, reactions of homosexual men to males. The pictures of men elicit erotic arousal and by pairing them with pictures of females as conditioning stimuli, the latter take on erotic valence. Soon the patient is reacting to the pictures of females alone. This method has demonstrated effectiveness with just about any stimulus. In therapy analogue studies, gloves, random polygons and colored geometric figures have been used to demonstrate that a mild "fetish" can be created in normal men with such procedures[58] [78] [91]. The problem of course with this method is that the conditioned reaction is always smaller than the reaction to the unconditioned stimulus. In the example of homosexuality, the patient would always react less to females than to males. Moreover, the reactions created to the pictures of females may be subliminal or so weak that they are ineffective in producing positive changes in actual erotic interactions with women[58]. At the very least some other procedure must be implemented.

Fading.   A clever procedure developed by Barlow and Agras[10] which overcomes the problem of weak conditioned reactions is called *fading*. Two projectors are required with a rheostat so that the intensity of the projected slides can be varied. Two perfectly overlapping pictures are shown simultaneously but in different intensities, one of a male and one of a female. The male is shown first at 100% intensity and the patient is allowed to react erotically. His penile circumference change is monitored while the picture of the female is phased in. That is, the intensity of her image is increased from 0% to 20% and the image of the male is faded out to 80% intensity. The relative strength of the two images is varied so that the patient maintains at least 75% full erection. Eventually, the female image is gradually increased to 100% intensity and the male image is phased out to zero intensity while the patient maintains criterion erection. Thus the goal is having the patient eventually highly sexually aroused before a heterosexual stimulus. This method has an advantage over simple positive classical conditioning since the reaction to the female is at least as great as that to the male.

It is not clear if classical or operant conditioning is the main paradigm used here. If it were classical conditioning, the conditioning stimulus (female) is presented after the unconditioned stimulus (the male) and backward conditioning would be employed. This is not an effective method. On the other hand, the subject of the procedure is responding with penile erection and the reaction is reinforced with an aversive or neutral stimulus. Thus his reactivity to the female should not be enhanced but rather his reactivity to the male should decrease since it is being nonreinforced or even punished. Perhaps something is going on that is neither simple classical nor operant conditioning.

Some writers have stated that it does not matter if we are following learning principles, the important thing is that the method works. An analogy would be the Salk vaccine for polio. It is not yet clear how it works but it does work so use it. An unfortunate addendum to this is that we are not so sure the behavior therapy methods work. The parallel to the Salk vaccine is a poor one since there is a clear outcome, the number of polio cases has declined dramatically since its introduction. In contrast, we are unsure of the effect of the treatments described here on sexual anomalies. The reasons will become evident when we discuss treatment outcome later.

There are two other practical limitations to this method. First, we do not know what is going on in the patient's head. If he is using fantasies of the male or of homosexual interaction, he may continue to use them while the picture of the female is on, in fact ignoring the visual stimulus and attending to the imagined stimulus in his head. The therapist has little control over this. Moreover, the patient may now respond to females but continues to respond to males as well. Combined with this problem is the difficulty of obtaining full erections or even 75% erection in patients with slide materials and without the patient masturbating or manipulating himself. For some therapists, masturbation in therapy is ethically unacceptable and this may be a serious limitation to fading. Finally, the method seems applicable when there is a stimulus anomaly, as in pedophilia or homosexuality but would not be used for the majority of response anomalies such as exhibitionism in which there is already considerable penile reactivity to the mature female.

Orgasmic reconditioning.   Some other operant methods have developed that find a wider range of application. Orgasmic reconditioning is one technique[71] in which the sexually anomalous fantasies of the patient are used to advantage. In effect, the patient is allowed to fantasize whatever he wishes in order to obtain an erection and in approaching a climax via masturbation. However, at the last moment when ejaculation is inevitable, he must switch his fantasy to one of heterosexual intercourse or of a female under normal sexual circumstances. This heterosexual fantasy is shaped gradually so that it occupies increasing amounts of fantasy time and so displaces the anomalous fantasy until finally, he has only a normal heterosexual fantasy. Each session involves orgasm so that therapists may prefer to have the patient do the therapy exercise in the privacy of his home at a time when he ordinarily would masturbate. This creates a more ethically sound procedure than having him do it on instruction in the treatment unit. In orgasmic reconditioning, shaping is important and so is the speed with which one proceeds through the fantasies. In the treatment unit, the therapist can monitor from session to session how much the patient is reacting to his anomalous fantasies.

This method has been reported for a few cases but has drawbacks. In theory it is described as classical conditioning. The fantasy of the female precedes orgasm, but follows the fantasy of the anomalous behavior whatever it may be, of homosexual outlet, crossdressing, and so forth. If one considered the pairing of disordered and heterosexual normal stimuli, this could be described as aversive conditioning if the normal one is anxiety provoking. If the heterosexual stimulus is neutral and the anomalous one is positively reinforcing, it could be considered backward conditioning, again a procedure that should not work to change behavior. Thus there are theoretical problems that make the outcome of this procedure questionable in terms of learning theory. If the female or intercourse with her is simply uninteresting rather than aversive or erotic as many patients describe, pairing her with the anomalous fantasy should tend to make it neutral as well, according to the Premack principle[55]. In fact, my patients have reacted that way. The heterosexual stimulus does not become positive, everything tends to become uninteresting.

Penile operant conditioning.   Another operant method closer to the animal experiments involves depriving the patient of liquids and then reinforcing penile reactions to normal heteroerotic stimuli with liquid. As with so many of these methods, only a couple of cases are reported in professional literature. In one case reported by Quinn et al[89] a homosexual patient was required to abstain from liquids for 18 hours prior to treatment. He was also administered chemicals to increase his thirst. Penile circumference changes were monitored while he viewed slides of females. Whenever he showed any reaction to the pictures, however small, he was reinforced with a small amount of lime juice. Gradually the penile reaction was shaped to larger and larger circumference changes. The desired results were created in a very short time. A similar procedure was used in one of my cases but no chemical was used to increase thirst. In a matter of 5 thirty minute sessions, penile circumference was changed 25 fold over baseline and the homosexual patient had erotic reactions to females, in fact for the first time in his life. However, after seven sessions, a strange phenomenon occurred. While the patient continued to show increased in penile circumference, he indicated that "there was nothing going on in his head". It would appear that a penile reflex had been conditioned but more was necessary. This method could offer interesting avenues into understanding erotic behavior and more research appears warranted.

Assertion therapy.   Another operant procedure, which has wide application including treatment of sexual anomalies is assertion therapy. If patients show a deficiency in heterosexual behaviors, especially in approaching and interacting with females, assertion therapy can be useful. They may be trained to express feelings and thoughts in a straightforward and honest way while respecting the rights of others. It involves shaping the components of an assertive reaction, modelling the appropriate behavior for the patient, and coaching him on his own behavior, which may be deficient, and practicing appropriate behaviors in the therapeutic setting. Unassertive behavior may be conveyed in many ways by weak or uncertain voice, hesitation, stammering, glancing away instead of maintaining direct eye contact with the other person, slumped posture, soft voice, as well as by the content of the conversation. A sample session of a shy male coached on asking a girl for a date is:

Doctor: Ok. Let's try to ask Gloria for a date. You really think she is attractive and you would like to know her better. You would like to take her out this weekend.

Patient: Ok . . . . . . uh . . . Hi Gloria, nice day isn't it?

Doctor (Gloria):   Yes it is.

Patient: I . . uh . . I was wondering uh . . if you were . . uh busy this weekend?

Doctor (Gloria):   That depends.

Patient: Uh . . . uh (shrug his shoulders).

Doctor: Ok. Let's analyze what has happened. I said ask her for a date this weekend but that can be any of three days. It really leaves Gloria uncertain about what you want. It would be better to let her know first that you would like to spend time with her and then try to fix a date. Now you also did not look me directly in the eyes when you spoke. I'll think you really mean what you are saying if you do. Know what you want to say. Express what feelings are in your head and heart. That way you won't hesitate so much either. Let's try it again, ok?

Patient: Ok. Hi Gloria. It's nice to see you.

Doctor (Gloria):   Nice to see you too.

Patient: I've been wanting to spend some time with you. I was wondering if you were, uh . . . free some time this weekend?

Doctor (Gloria):   That would be nice. I'm free Saturday night.

Patient: Great.

Doctor: That was good. You said what you felt and Gloria returned her feelings. You looked her right in the eyes. I felt you meant what you said. That is the goal of assertive training. Now let's try it one more time. This time raise your voice just a little so it is loud and clear. That tells the other person too that you mean what you say.

In this way, the components of an assertive response are shaped. The patient is also given homework so that he can do in vivo exercises to change his life. A hierarchy of easy to difficult situations is developed for shaping and rewarding the patient's behavior.

In the treatment of sexual anomalies, heterosexual difficulties may be evident. Simply knowing about treating people in a civil and honest way, especially women, is not part of some men's repertoire, either through ignorance or bad example in their upbringing. The use of assertiveness training can be useful.

The literature on assertion training, including social skills training is an expanding one[2] [20] [21] [24] [25] [26] [35] [62] [63] [92] [104]. A variety of options can be used: rehearsal with the patient, coaching, modeling live or on videotape with feedback. The patient's own behavior can be played back so he can see his mistakes. One of course can purchase expensive equipment for the purpose of assertion therapy but there is no strong evidence that it improves results. Those on a limited budget can use assertion therapy effectively without any equipment. I have found it helpful for patients to read a book on assertiveness, either *I can if I want to*[63] or *Your perfect right*[2].

A major problem in the area of assertion therapy is the poor distinction between assertion and aggression[5] [76]. One must teach the expression of anger in an assertive way[49]. Anger can be expressed without name calling by a statement of feelings, "I am angry with you" but conceptually, there is much overlap of the two terms. This may be the case because of inadequate validation of popular measures. The physical signs, "eye contact, voice loudness", and so forth, do not form a unitary expression of assertiveness and their face validity must be questioned[47] [93]. It is also a concern whether treatment extends to the patient's everyday life.

Satiation therapy. A final method has recently been described and labeled satiation therapy[72]. Like orgasmic reconditioning, masturbation and fantasizing are a critical part of the treatment. The patient is required to masturbate to his favorite anomalous fantasy. However, he continues to do so past the point of satiation and climax. He may do so for an hour or more, even though he climaxed in a few minutes. A few cases have been reported successfully treated with this method but it does not follow any learning principle. The intensity of the erotic experience may diminish with repetition the sequence is still erotic fantasy followed by reinforcement either as climax or lesser erotic stimulation. In theory it should increase or stamp in the anomalous behavior.

The Behavior Therapy Treatment Unit

In the history of developing therapy methods, it became evident that the behavior therapist was gadget oriented. Audiovisual and physiological devices abound and there is a well developed business that caters to the needs of the behavior therapist. One has to be judicious in what he purchases and the treatment unit depicted in Fig. 3.1 offers a minimum required for most laboratories. The equipment depicted can also serve for research and is standard to many behavior therapy settings. The goals of treatment are to record the frequencies of anomalous behavior and note changes with therapy. Paper and pencil are all that is necessary in most instances.

The penile phallometer is also indispensable (See page 9). Penile reaction is one of the best indices of erotic arousal and should be monitored to determine the effectiveness of treatment. The price of systems to monitor such reactions can vary from a few hundred dollars to thousands of dollars. If one happens to have a multipurpose polygraph for recording reactions, that is fine but one can purchase systems for a few hundred dollars that are just as good. The recording system should have a paper printout so a permanent record is available for later examination. The therapist is busy during the treatment session and it is one less thing to do if a machine automatically records reactions of the patient. The penile circumference strain gauge developed by Barlow[11] and Laws[61], and their associates, are the best available, the latter being an improvement of the former in terms of its durability. These cost relatively little and can be connected to inexpensive monitoring systems. The mercury strain gauge is unreliable due to breaks in the mercury, and should be avoided.

A recording system may also contain polygraph channels for heart rate, galvanic skin response, and such, and their use will add substantially to the cost of the treatment unit. It is well to remember that such measures are unrelated to sexual arousal as determined by self report and penile reactivity. They also are tedious to score and expensive since a research assistant or time on a computer system is required. They have yet to prove their value in treatment of sexual anomalies. I think that at present they are unnecessary for sex research.

The phallometer which measures volume is more complete than the circumference strain gauge but it is more cumbersome to use repeatedly in therapy conducted weekly. Nevertheless, the individual may wish to use it and the complete mechanical system developed by Freund can be made of glass locally or ordered for a few hundred dollars. If one has access to a polygraph, the system can be connected via two standard laboratory beakers that serve as amplifiers[58].

The therapist constructing his treatment unit will have to choose among the alternatives within the limits of his budget. Usually the treatment unit requires a screen and projector for slides and if the therapist wishes, movies. Although the latter are more arousing sexually, movies are also more expensive. Sometimes the treatment may require statements rather than pictures, and slides are the most economical. The use of fantasy has also become prominent in treating sexual anomalies and audio descriptions are very effec-

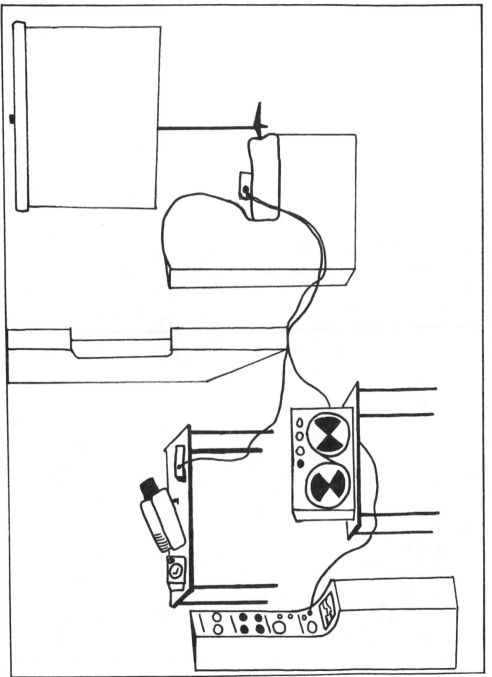

FIG. 3.1   The behavior therapy laboratory.

tive for this purpose[1]. So the unit should have a tape recorder preferably with earphones to block outside distractions. The recorder serves many purposes, recording sessions or playing tapes such as one uses in relaxation training described earlier. Deep muscle relaxation demands a comfortable chair such as a "lazy boy" to be used in the unit. Not only is it useful for relaxation but it makes the long session that may take an hour or more, less tedious.

In order to synchronize operations, one or more timers may be used. Simple timers are available, which serve as event recorders and can note important details such as onset of picture and end of picture. One has a much better idea of exactly what the patient is responding to.

If one wishes to use electrical aversion therapy, a shock box is required and the timer becomes essential in order to regulate the occurrence of the shock in reference to other stimuli and to control the duration of the shock. The massive change in electrical current usually interferes with polygraph measures including the penile circumference phallometer, but not necessarily the volume phallometer. One should consult an expert to ensure crosscurrents, the intensity of the shock and the placement of electrodes are not dangerous to the patient.

Finally a feedback switch for the patient may be useful to indicate to the therapist if he is reacting or not, or for terminating a shock, and so forth. The latter items are all inexpensive and if one has an in-house electrical or biomedical engineer, such gadgets can be made quickly and cheaply for the treatment unit. With the above items, most behavior therapy treatments can be efficiently carried out.

Critique of Behavior Therapy Methods

Criticisms have been leveled at behavior therapy from within the fold of practitioners as well as outside. A major item of controversy from outside the fold of practitioners has been the problem of symptom substitution. It is maintained by psychotherapists that treating only the symptom as behavior therapy does, will not remove the underlying problem and some other symptom will appear in place of the one removed. In this sense, the treatment is simplistic and ineffective. Behavior therapists have responded with data, noting that symptom substitution did not occur as predicted and the patients were well[40 86 122]. In fact, it is one of the few schools of treatment that is able to respond with systematic data.

A more serious criticism is that behavior therapy is most successful with disorders involving specific maladaptive behavior such as phobic and anxiety reactions, enuresis, stuttering and tics but has been disappointing with alcoholism and sexual anomalies[40]. However, the success is relative and behavior therapy is about as effective as the more expensive and time consuming psychotherapies in treating sexual anomalies.

Within the school of behavior therapy, both theory and practice have been criticized. Although the treatments are supposed to be based on learning theory and behaviorism, often only a flimsy justification is used. Some procedures described previously appear to violate the principles outright. Locke[67] for example, notes that systematic desensitization contradicts every major premise of behaviorism. In the procedure, the patient must introspect and reveal the content and intensity of his fears, imagine the scenes to be deconditioned and control the scenes in his "mind".

It has been argued that theory of treatment methods can presumably be investigated by returning to the laboratory and doing therapy analogue studies. Since the behavior therapy can be broken down into universal learning principles, one can also turn to animal studies or examine the procedures on normal individuals in the laboratory. Phobias of snakes, rats and spiders commonly have been used. The limited number of existing studies often have research errors and better studies are clearly needed to support the continued use of the procedures in therapy[16].

The learning principles on which the behavior therapy methods are supposed to be based are not as well established as one is led to believe. For example, the timing between conditioning stimulus and unconditioned stimulus is supposed to be critical and 0.5 seconds is presumed to be best. Yet the research evidence for that assertion is very limited[55]. One study showed that the more precisely timed electric shock aversion method did not differ in outcome from the imprecise chemical aversion method[79][80]. One has to wonder at the principles as well as what is producing the outcome in these studies.

Another disregard for the learning principles is illustrated by the assertion that during avoidance or other aversive conditioning, changes in physiological reactions is a good indicator of successful therapy[28]. A successfully treated patient will show increases in heart rate, perspiration, etc., during the presence of the conditioning stimuli. However, there is no satisfactory evidence that this is the case[41]. One experimental study shows that initially in classical conditioning, physiological activation increases but as conditioning occurs, there is a decrement in physiological activation. The best point to stop for optimal or sufficient learning is unknown at present.

It has been presumed that people who condition more readily will benefit more from aversion treatment. However, in examining the hypothesis, the only published study showed there was no relationship between conditionability and treatment outcome[69].

It has been suggested we ignore these problems and direct our energies to determining which treatments work better[68] and to develop empirical methods that work. Such arguments attempt to remove the very advantages of behavior therapy that make it an ideal treatment method. Although it is a worthwhile goal to develop new methods that work, it is also unethical and unscientific to use methods that have no logical basis and violate known principles of treatment. Therapy must be developed using reasons that are logically consistent.

Behavior modifiers have also been criticized for ignoring validity and reliability in their behavioral assessments[19]. This is especially easy to do in the area of sex research. Because sex is often embarrassing and because we have a clear cut idea of what sexual arousal is all about, it is common to ignore the cardinal features of our measurement techniques. It is therefore important to use questionnaires that are established and to show that phallometric measures consistently elicit the anomalous behavior in question. Behavioral studies have the advantage of research knowledge and design but they have been infrequently used. Less than 5% of studies use a control group, base line, and adequate follow up[81].

There are other assumptions made about behavior therapy methods that are not warranted. In most treatments, conditioning stimuli have been treated as if they were neutral. In the original classical and operant experiments, neutral stimuli were employed. Pavlov's dogs were exposed to a bell, which had no necessary positive or negative valence. Erotic stimuli are not neutral by their very nature. To pair a neutral bell tone with shock is very different from pairing a male nude with shock since the latter has a history of strong positive erotic valence.

Animal research suggests that when reward and punishment are associated with the same goal response, there is a paradoxical increase in the persistence of the behavior over using reward alone[73]. So by punishing sexually anomalous behavior, which is associated with rewarding orgasms, we may in fact be increasing its persistence[52]. This problem needs research in humans.

Some theorists think the learning is an inverted U-shaped function of general arousal. Learning improves with increases in the shock level up to some point and then it diminishes again until it is very inefficient. If a behavior is motivated by anxiety, the electric shock adds to the anxiety level and the reinforcement of the anomalous behavior is increased so the undesired behavior should occur more frequently.

It is argued that the stronger the negative reinforcer, the better the learning[113]. Thus make the punishment severe. A strong electric shock is better than a weaker one. Others say only a minimally aversive stimulus is necessary[69]. It may be the incompatibility of the response elicited by the aversive stimulus with the disordered behavior that is important rather than the intensity of the aversive stimulus[70]. Patients will habituate to a weak electric shock faster than to a stronger one but learning may not be different.

Suppression and extinction are not distinguished. It is different if a person loses a behavior pattern altogether versus suppresses it for a while. Some behavior therapy methods have resulted only in suppression and the behavior recurs soon after treatment. Therapists have suggested that *booster sessions* be used to reinforce the treatment sessions. Little evidence exists for the effectiveness of the booster session and in fact it may make no difference[113].

How many sessions are enough to prevent the anomalous behavior from coming back? Is it twenty? thirty? No one knows for sure. If treatment fails one can say there were not enough sessions but it is not clear what determines how much is enough.

Generalization is a problem for all therapy methods but it is evident in behavior therapy because it is so readily examined[66] [101]. Gains in therapy may only be evident in highly similar situations outside the treatment setting[56]. In some cases, only the stimuli used in the unit will become neutral or aversive. Imagining erotic exchanges with women in the treatment unit may be arousing, but not in the world outside. This is known to the therapist in some cases because only the pictures used in the treatment itself became aversive. When other pictures were substituted, the patient responded in his previously strong and anomalous fashion. Alternatively, too much generalization may occur. If a heterosexual pedophile is attracted to 14-year-old girls and is treated with aversive conditioning and develops an aversion to those girls, this reaction can generalize to older females as well. Initially, he might react much less to mature females and react considerably to girls. With repeated treatment, he reacts to none of the females but much less so to the mature females. This leaves him with no stimulus for sexual outlet.

Punishment and aversive methods in general have been criticized for being inhumane. Holden[50] noted that we have been sold modified behavior and not the relief of suffering. It may be our abhorrence of sexual anomalies that makes us want to use punishment procedures on them. Aversion methods were developed first and have been used most in the treatment of sexual anomalies. They outnumber other methods in treatment of sexual anomalies 2-to-1. Some writers indicate that punishment alone does not have a lasting effect on behavior[52]. Punishment of aggressive and anxiety motivated behavior may increase their likelihood of recurrence. Most existing theories of homosexuality for instance assume it is anxiety motivated and yet punishment has been used. One has to ask why.

I do not think we should throw out the baby with the bath water. Behavior therapy has provided us with many sound principles and I think they should be followed. Recording the occurrence of baseline behaviors, and assessing treatment as we go along are invaluable to research and treatment. Other treatment approaches would do well to copy behavior therapy in this respect. However, I do not believe we should persist in using inhumane methods like aversive procedures nor in using procedures that have no logical basis or demonstrated effectiveness. Moreover, the method should be applied to the anomaly with an understanding of the behavior involved[121]. This usually has not been done and the reader may become disillusioned with the existing methods. However, treatment of sexual anomalies is relatively new and not well understood. A research orientation to treatment is the healthiest at present. The assessment methods developed by behavior therapists are the best at present and I recommend their use. Both the understanding of sexual anomalies and their treatment offer a challenge to the researcher and therapist. The presentations in this book suggest directions for research into both treatment and etiology.

HYPNOTISM

Hypnotism or Mesmerism has long been fascinating and mysterious for laymen and professionals alike. It is often considered trickery or is relegated to the theater but Freud and his teacher, Charcot, took it seriously since they could remove physical symptoms of psychological origin temporarily with hypnosis[57]. Today, the tradition of hypnosis as a curative art continues and attempts have been made to scientifically explain it.

Hypnosis has been considered a form of conditioning[57][107]. When the hypnotherapist suggests a patient will engage in his sexually anomalous behavior and experience aversion, this sounds like covert sensitization. Then he suggests the patient imagine he is engaging in normal sexual behavior and will feel good doing it. This can be construed as positive classical conditioning.

It is noteworthy that fantasy and imagery exercises are prominent in the behavior therapies and in psychotherapies[1]. Barber[7][8] who has conducted extensive experimental work on hypnosis considers the hypnotic subject to be a willing partner who engages in vivid imagery at the suggestion of the therapist. Hypnosis works because the individual wants it to work. Barber considers this to be analogous to attending the theater during which considerable emotion is felt. He notes that we do not say, "he is only acting" because we want to experience the feelings the actors try to elicit. Similarly, we want to be hypnotized by the therapist to experience what he suggests because we are interested and find it worthwhile.

Barber and his colleagues have experimentally studied the many conditions important in hypnosis. Most important for our purposes in this book is that they found hypnosis will be more effective if the situation is defined as hypnosis and the therapist removes fears and misconceptions the subject may have. Then cooperation must be secured so the subject has expectancies of success in the end and the positive attitudes and motivation necessary to produce a willingness to think with and vividly imagine those things that are suggested. So far it sounds no different from any other therapy procedure. However, there is also the *trance* state which has been thought to be similar to sleep. The deeper the trance, it is maintained, the better the therapy[95]. Barber et al's research casts doubt on this theory and on the analogy to sleep. A study of brain wave patterns has shown that hypnotic subjects are awake and that the so called *trance-like* state may be primarily due to subjects having their eyes closed and relaxing.

Barber's work has normalized hypnosis and taken the mystery away. It appears to be an alternative imagery procedure that adds to the repertoire of methods useful in treating the sexual anomalies described in this book.

PSYCHOTHERAPY AND GROUP THERAPY

A large number of treatments fall under the label *psychotherapy* and it is not possible to review them all here. When particular procedures are used in conjunction with specific sexual anomalies, some detail will be provided along with source references for the interested reader.

Strupp[109] has suggested that there are three features common in psychotherapies, which are essential conditions of effective change in the patient. First, the therapist creates and maintains a helping role modelled on the parent child relationship. The therapist should have a characteristic respect, interest, understanding, tact, maturity and a firm belief in his ability to help. The parenting role provides the second condition, a power base to influence the patient to change by suggestion or persuasion, encouraging openness in communication, self scrutiny and honesty. The power allows the therapist to interpret the patient's self defeating behavior and distorted beliefs about reality. He also sets an example of maturity and he manipulates rewards that make him a behavior modifier in effect. Finally, it is necessary to have a patient who has the capacity and willingness to profit from the therapy experience. The cooperation of the patient is essential in all therapies including the seemingly mechanical behavior therapies[96]. Even conditioning is not brainwashing and a patient can beat it if he tries. The problem of uncooperativeness is especially important in evaluating sexual offenses, which can result in a court order for the treatment of an unwilling offender. Mohr[84] has indicated that treated sex offenders do not differ from untreated ones in later recidivism. Treatment would therefore seem pointless in such cases.

Frank[31] has described six somewhat different features from Strupp's that are common to all psychotherapies. There should be an intense emotionally charged confiding relationship with a helping person or group. Second, a rationale should be provided to explain the cause of the patient's distress and a method for relieving it. The rationale serves as a vehicle for transmitting the therapist's influence and transmitting to the patient the therapist's prestige thus strengthening confidence in him. Third, new information on the problem and alternative ways of dealing with it are provided. Fourth, the patient's expectations of help are strengthened by personal qualities of the therapist, his status in society and his work setting. Fifth, the patient is provided some successes, which heightens his hopes and enhances his sense of mastery and competence. Finally, therapy facilitates emotional arousal that is important to attitudinal and behavioral change. Behavior therapists prefer to work from behavior change to incidental emotional and attitudinal change. However, a positive attitude to treatment may be critical to successes in all therapies[14].

Other writers have also listed the important variables in psychotherapy but there is little research to support the claims[36][105]. Mintz[83] in an empirical study found that the recent onset of difficulties, relative mildness of dysfunction and good social assets like income and education are signs of positive therapy outcome. Whereas psychotherapists have traditionally been poor in specifying detailed criterion of therapy success, Mintz found global outcome ratings were to some degree self fulfilling prophesies. Their widespread use should therefore be discouraged.

Psychotherapy of sexual anomalies has typically been poorly reported and analyzed[103]. Since there are so many ways of interpreting and achieving the common objectives noted by Strupp and others, we often do not know what exactly has been done. There has been a recent trend to changing the situation but it has not yet affected reports of psychotherapy of sexual anomalies[15][30][39][64][118].

MISCELLANEOUS PROCEDURES

Two sensational methods have been publicized as treatments of sexual anomalies and dysfunctions: sexual interaction with therapist and the use of female surrogate sex partners. An ethical issue, which is particularly pertinent in sex therapy is the possibility of sexual contact between patient and therapist. In the few documented cases in which this has happened[22], the aging male therapists were in a depressed state and behaved indiscretely. They were certainly in no position to help the patients. The Psychologists' Code of Ethics quite clearly indicate that the practitioner must recognize the bounds of his competence while operating within accepted moral and legal standards. Sexual contact violates the code[42].

One may also question the use of *female surrogates*, either volunteers or prostitutes who introduce inadequate males to sexual intercourse. Masters and Johnson[74] consider the involvement of two partners in sex therapy an essential element in success. However, they generally use *committed* partners rather than strangers. This serves to place sexual intercourse within a broader social and interpersonal context that the use of a surrogate fails to provide.

It has been my general impression of sexually anomalous males that intercourse is not all that difficult a task. However, their lack of interest in relating to females in a broader and meaningful social sense may be more important and more difficult to do. I do not believe that female surrogates can provide that social element.

CHEMICAL INTERVENTION

Since psychiatry is a branch of medicine, some therapists find it appropriate to apply a disease model to sexual and other behaviors. It may also seem natural that various drugs would be used in attempts to alter sexual behavior. In recent years, chemical intervention has become popular as a means of changing the intensity if not the direction of sexually anomalous behavior.

Several chemicals have been used in order to reduce sex drive in patients. Cyproterone acetate is among the most effective[60]. It has been shown in animals to be 45 times more effective than its nearest competitor, medroxyprogesterone acetate, commercially called provera[13]. A number of studies have been conducted on humans but not comparative studies of the drugs. The basic mechanism of the drugs is that they compete at protein binding sites in the body with the male sex hormones, the androgens. Freund (1980) notes that provera and cyproterone appear to affect the level of circulating testosterone (See Freund[32] for a review of mechanisms of action). Usually within a few days of administration, one will notice a sharp drop in androgens in the male. The therapist can monitor this by taking blood samples and assaying serum testosterone. The patient should report a reduction in sexual drive with their use. It is important to note that he will not change his erotic preference. If one is treating a pedophile, he will continue to prefer children. He simply has a reduced sexual drive while on the drugs.

If the patient is married, difficulties could arise if he cannot have intercourse with his wife. Strong doses of the drugs will produce erectile difficulties as well as disinterest. Freund suggested a way around this problem. The dose of antiandrogen is titrated so that the "edge is taken off" the sex drive but the patient does not experience erectile difficulties. Thus the patient may be started at 100 mg. of provera. At his next visit, he may claim he cannot have an erection. He could be told to take the pills only every second day or the dosage could be reduced to 50 mg. On the other hand, if he reports too much erotic arousal, especially to anomalous stimuli, the dosage could be increased to 150 mg. or higher until it is not. The ideal balance occurs when the patient is not preoccupied with sex but can respond to body contact with his wife. In this way, marital relations are maintained and preoccupation with sexually anomalous stimuli is reduced.

The drugs are useful in relieving the pressure on a patient who is bothered by urges to act out sexually anomalous behavior but their long term use is suspect and dangerous. Unless a patient is willing to forego any erotic outlet, the drug in itself is ineffective as a long term treatment. At some point the patient's anomalous erotic preferences must be dealt with in therapy. Ideally one can treat his problem behavior while on the drug and then take him off it. However, most behavior therapy methods are not possible because one cannot attempt to modify erections while the patient is prevented from doing so by chemical means.

The effectiveness of the drugs is also suspect since the few systematic studies in the literature[6] [59] suggest that research participants report less arousal on provera and cyproterone but penile reactions do not change. How does this affect behavior in the real world? Would a powerful erotic stimulus elicit the anomalous behavior regardless of the amount of antiandrogen? The answer to the question is unknown at present but the two systematic controlled analog studies suggest that he would. Some patients state that provera only has a short term effect and then does not influence their sex drive. Other patients refuse the drugs because they feel demasculated and are not in control of their own behavior. This is another obstacle to treatment.

The drugs present dangers. Cyproterone acetate has been linked with testicular atrophy[13]. How much can one give a patient before that happens? In fact, does one wish to give it at all knowing this to be the case? What liver damage is caused by the drugs[87]? Provera has been linked with possible diabetic sequelae[116]. Moreover, the antiandrogen drugs are basically female hormones and the male may be feminized especially with cyproterone[108]. The following are possible side effects,[32] [108] which are reversible: weight gain, fatigability, increased sleep requirements and mood disturbance. Less often, there is loss of body hair, hot and cold flashes. Provera and other female hormones cause reduced ejaculation volume and decreased sperm production[48] and in conjunction with testosterone used to prevent atrophy of the genitalia and reduced sex drive, it may be an effective birth control agent for men[3] [17] [33] [34] [82] [115]. It has an interesting application in treatment of prostatic and renal cancers[88] [97] [98] [99]. It may be a useful treatment for sex offenders who do not respond to other methods of treatment[29].

All side effects are reversible when the drug is removed but would long term use make the side effects irreversible? This is unknown. Both of these drugs can only be used for a short term and used with discretion. They are not a treatment for sexual anomalies per se but only an adjunct while something else is done.

The major tranquilizers, thioridazine, fluphenazine, enanthate and benperidol also reduce sex drive but have not been used as extensively as the antiandrogens for that purpose[114]. Recent research has also indicated undesirable side effects from these drugs. The neuroleptic drugs reduce libido but can also cause stiffness, tremor, restlessness, blurred vision, upset stomach, constipation, photosensitivity, dry mouth, hypotension, fluid retention, amenorrhea and perhaps most disconcerting, tardive dyskinesia[100]. The latter includes purposeless movements, mainly blinking, licking, chewing and grinding, which may go unnoticed by the patient and not appear until years after use of the drugs. Removal of the drug makes the symptoms worse. This produces a dilemma for therapists. Their use for sexual anomalies is not recommended. In fact the therapist can avoid the use of all drugs by telling the cooperative patient to masturbate before the urge to act out gets too strong. This does not change the behavior either but can reduce the chance of involvement with the law and of possible danger to his victims. *Mr. C* is an example. He was a pedophile and liked 12-to-15-year-old girls. He noted:

> I try to masturbate in the morning before I shave. I get it over then for the day and I usually don't feel any urges throughout the day. I can go about my job without thinking about girls all the time. Sometimes I think about it anyway. If I pass a school I may be so turned on I can't help myself. In that case, I try to get to a washroom and masturbate. Usually that is effective. Occasionally, the urges can still be there but most often it works.

Since the patient will do this anyway without physical harm to himself, this method appears to be the safest at present for preventing acting out. It also leaves the patient in control of his own behavior, a feature some patients complain provera does not allow.

One must cope of course with the uncooperative and dangerous patient. When one is confronted with a rapist or sadistic murderer, release into the community is a perennial problem. In some such cases, castration has been suggested.

CASTRATION

Castration is an irreversible solution to the problem of sexual anomalies and is very controversial. Basically, the sexual drive of the patient is dramatically reduced by removing the testicles, which produce most but not all of the male sex hormone, testosterone[32 45]. This is distinct from sterilization in which the connections of testes to surrounding tissue (vasectomy) are severed. Sterilization does not influence the production of hormones and thus does not alter sexual activity in itself[111].

The operation for castration involves two incisions in the scrotum which holds the testes. When the testes are removed from the scrotal sac and severed, they are replaced for cosmetic reasons by glass, or more commonly, plastic; although marble, injections of petroleum jelly, ivory, celluloid, aluminum and silver have also been used.

Castration has been described historically among other things as a way of protecting harems. Sultans would train eunuchs to protect their harems but they would protect the harems from the eunuch by castration. This method could be used for the "treatment" of the persistent sexual offender but cases have been reported in which rapes occurred subsequent to the castration.

In general, however, recidivism for sexual offenses has been dramatically reduced by castration to under 10% and in some samples as low as 2%. The presurgery recidivism rates vary from first offenders at 7% to repeated offenders at 23%[111]. However, estimates are highly variable and in one study reviewed by Heim and Hursch[46], there was an 84% recidivism rate before castration and 2% after. Unfortunately in the reports, the focus has been on castration rather than on the type of sexual offender suitable for castration. Whereas terms like "repeated offender" or "dangerous" are used, the samples appear to include at least some exhibitionists, homosexuals and pedophiles. Heim and Hursch further point out that individuals who agree to castration surgery, or, who are forced to have it, may be a different group from those who are not castrated, such that recidivism rates are not comparable.

Large samples of patients have been followed up over long periods but only the ex-prisoners' self reports have been used in assessing the effectiveness of castration. The general statement of reduced sex drive has not been supported by animal studies that have shown that rats and dogs castrated after puberty continue to copulate for years after. In the one existing study of penile reactions of 38 castrated humans, it was found that 50% had full erections to a sex movie[46]. Thus the reactions of castrates are much more variable than earlier reports would indicate when controlled measures are used. The utility of castration has yet to be demonstrated.

In addition, one has to worry about side effects from surgery. There may be periods of sweating and blushing after surgery that eventually appear to stop. Body and facial hair is usually more sparse but head hair may become thicker. These are not so problematic but 50% of some samples of men become obese, which entails its own general health problems. Particular growth of fat about the breasts in about 10% of cases results in an undesirable female appearance. Some men lose weight and some are unchanged. However, obesity and gynecomasty (female breasts) are problematic. The skin generally becomes softer, thinner and more slack and flabby. About a quarter develop the "castrate-face" which is strangely puckered with many small wrinkles and a sallow complexion[46].

It is difficult to link disease clearly to the castration but some castrates reported heart disorders, respiratory difficulties, dorsalgia, night sweating or chronic body pain several years after surgery. Rachiopathy and osteoporosis have also been reported, the latter verified by x-ray in over 80% of one sample of 68 castrates. Osteoporosis is a porousness and fragility of the bones due to calcium imbalance. This appears to be mediated by sex hormones and treatment usually involves administration of oestrogen. The link to castration appears more than coincidental.

While earlier reports with poor methodology suggest no psychological sequelae to castration, worrisome numbers are depressed, or angry and may feel inadequate, isolated and too passive after surgery. A systematic study of psychic factors remains to be done. Freund[32] has argued that physical side effects are not serious if attended to and that mental health and social benefits to the patient should be compared to the medical problems.

MISCELLANEOUS PHYSICAL INTERVENTIONS

Three other physical procedures have been used in treating sexual anomalies; electroconvulsive therapy (ECT), psychosurgery and sex reassignment surgery. The latter has been widely used in the treatment of transsexuals and is discussed in Chapter 6.

ECT has been fallaciously associated with correcting sexual anomalies. The treatment has a history of overuse and abuse but today, it is accepted as a powerful and painless method of treating certain depressions. Thus ECT may be useful in some sexually anomalous men who are depressed but it will not change the sexual anomaly itself.

One may wish to draw similar conclusions about brain surgery and especially about lobotomies and leucotomies which serve to render some brain tissue nonfunctional. It has been found that some individuals who have abnormal brain conditions such as a temporal lobe tumor may display bizarre sexual behavior. When brain surgery is completed and the patient recovers, the unusual sex behavior also vanishes. The converse is not true. That is, individuals with sexual anomalies do not usually show obvious brain pathology so that brain surgery is not likely to alter their behavior unless they become vegetables.

Stereotaxic hypothalatomy has been used in West Germany since 1962[94] and, like castration, it is related to a low recidivism rate for sex delinquents. In this method, a probe electrode is inserted deep into the brain and areas of sexual functions in the hypothalamus are burned out by electric current. Placement of electrodes is very precise and surrounding tissue is unharmed. This method may be labeled "neural castration". Since only 75 cases have been so treated, its outcome is not yet clear. Permanent brain implants have also been used by Heath[44] in Louisiana for a couple of cases of homosexuality. Methodologically, the report is so poor that it is uncertain what the outcome was. In addition, dangers of infections to brain sites have not been adequately documented. My best guess is that this method would not find general applicability even if it were effective. Individuals who do not like chemical control of their bodies by antiandrogen drugs would likely object to being neural puppets.

The ethics of using brain surgery, implants and castration for sexual anomalies have not been clearly worked out but their inhumaneness and physical dangers indicate that if they are used at all, they need to be carefully controlled and individuals selected for such treatment well defined. At the very least, it is unethical to conduct anything but systematic, thorough and well designed controlled studies of these methods (cf. Freund,[32]).

EXAMINING OUTCOME OF THERAPY

The reader can see that a variety of approaches are available for treating the sexual anomalies and some choice must be made. It would be desirable in theory to understand what we are treating and then apply the most efficient and humane treatment. Unfortunately, there are an abundance of theories about sexual anomalies and a severe shortage of facts. Thus one must be practical and select the treatment that works best. Many approaches to treatment are atheoretical and simply try to alter the behavior. As desirable as it may seem, the goal of understanding what we are treating and then applying treatment is not available at present. It is hoped that this book will offer the reader some paths for obtaining that goal.

Society, the therapist and the patient.   Assuming we are simply going to change the sexual anomaly, what criteria of success should be used? We can look at the question from the perspective of the patient or of society and the practitioner who is often a mediator between the two[97]. Since many sexual anomalies are also offences, society may be quite satisfied if the therapist can prevent the patient from engaging in future sexual offences. Even the therapist may be satisfied with this criterion. It is in fact relatively easy to satisfy. No treatment is necessary, since the recidivism rate for sexual offences is rather low. Most crimes show a 40% chance of the individual engaging in further criminal acts but this percentage drops to less than 20% for sexual offenses[84]. So simply leaving the patient alone and placing him on probation for a year may be sufficient for most cases.

Unfortunately, when cases are reported in the literature, we often do not know if a chronic offender or a first time offender was treated. If it was a first offence the chance of acting out again on the average is slim. If it is a chronic offender who was successfully treated, it is a different story. It would help in most treatment evaluations if the author of the report indicated how often the patient was currently acting out or has acted out over the three months prior to the offense. It has been found that individuals who have a high frequency of acting out prior to the offense and at the start of treatment are likely to drop out of treatment or not to show signs of improvement[27][59]. This can serve as a warning to the therapist and as signs to the readers how effective treatment is.

Contrast *Mr. E* and *Mr. F* who are both exhibitionists. Both are facing charges of exposing and it is their second offense. Both were caught approximately two years prior to the present charge. *Mr. E* is a sporadic exposer and works hard at containing his urges.

Doctor:　How do you feel about the charge and being here?

Mr. E:　I wish I could die. I didn't ask to be an exhibitionist. I wish I could find the courage to kill myself but I know I don't have what it takes to commit suicide. Maybe I should run away from it all. Start over in South America, a new life where no one knows me or my past.

Doctor:　How often are you bothered by the urge to expose?

Mr. E:　It comes and goes every few weeks or so but I keep busy and don't think about it so nothing happens. Once in a while it is too much for me and the dam bursts.

Doctor:　How often does the dam burst and what do you do?

Mr. E:　Last summer (about 6 months ago), I was feeling so horny that I could hardly contain myself. I masturbated with pictures but it did not help and I exposed to a woman in the park. Sometimes masturbation relieves the tension and I don't expose. I didn't expose before last summer for a year and a half . . . my other charges as you know.

Mr. F on the other hand is angry and does not particularly care what happens. He knows the court will be lenient, and he replies to the same questions as follows:

Doctor:　How do you feel about the charge and being here?

Mr. F:　It's a pain in the ass but I'll likely get off with a fine, my lawyer said. He may even get the charges dropped. It costs a pile for the lawyer and it is inconvenient going to court and everything but that's about it. (Looks smugly at the therapist).

Doctor:　How often are you having the urge to expose?

Mr. F:　Oh, 3 or 4 times a week. I exposed on the way here to this cute chick at the bus terminal.

Doctor:　Do you expose every time you get the urge?

Mr. F:　Not everytime. Sometimes there is no one around so I can't do it. (Smiles). Other than that, ya, pretty well every time, a few times a week.

Mr. E needs no treatment for his sexual anomaly but counselling in his feelings about himself. One would have to wait two years to see if he exposes a couple of times. He is administering the best treatment to himself, but that is in terms of society's goals and not his. He would be very happy if some therapy method could remove his desires to expose altogether. If a treatment only suppresses the urge to act out in sexually anomalous ways, we leave the patient with the pain and suffering that accompanies controlling his socially unacceptable urges. If, on the other hand, we can *alter his erotic preferences*, he will be relieved of any pressure to act out in this way.

In the case of Mr. F, it would be difficult to devise any treatment that would work. He is hostile and unaccepting of treatment. He has totally given into his urges to expose and it is only lack of opportunity that restraints him. Even if he were cooperative, his high frequency of urges would give him a sense of failure, making progress in therapy difficult. An effective program for this man would be a significant addition to our therapeutic repertoire. Mr. F is the sort of individual who either does not respond to therapy or tends to discontinue treatment.

Dropping out of treatment is a complex phenomenon related to a variety of factors[4] including patient's social isolation, therapist's attitude and behavior, differences in patient's and therapist's expectations, passive aggressive behavior, family attitude and behavior, motivation, dependence, psychological mindedness, symptom intensity, socioeconomic status, sociopathy, alcohol/drug dependence, age, sex and social stability. The reader may wish to see review articles for details of these factors[4] but only one fact need concern us here. The dropouts from treatment may be peculiar in some way and research studies of therapy should take them into consideration in evaluating outcome. Often we do not know about dropouts from a study, and if we unknowingly try a treatment, we may discover by trial and error that many patients refuse that therapy.

Baekeland and his associates[4] suggest several ways of reducing the number of dropouts: (a) eliminate waiting lists; (b) refer alcohol/drug addicts to specialized treatment programs; (c) offer a wide range of ancillary services and (d) treatment modalities. Use the ones suited to the patient rather than the simple ones or the available one. (e) Explain clearly to the patient the aims, scope, probable results, side effects, duration and kind of treatment. (f) Minimize therapist absences. (g) Find out if he is a previous dropout and explore the reasons for it. (h) Maintain contact with other significant people in the patient's life. (i) In more symptomatic lower class patients, emphasize rapid symptom relief.

Sometimes the patient sincerely wants to change because he has been caught and genuinely feels guilty and is repentant. However, confession may be good for the soul so that the guilt is short lived and urges to act out are strong and satisfying enough that he wants to keep them more than he wants to stay out of trouble with the law or his family. Often the imposition of external force to be treated is unsatisfactory and a poorer treatment outcome can be anticipated but not always. Court orders for treatment as opposed to jail or in addition to jail make it hard to enact any worthwhile treatment program because treatment becomes a sentence rather than a therapy. Ultimately the willingness of the individual is most important and progress, if possible, will be best noted in such cooperative cases. Mr. H is such a case who changed.

Mr. H: When I was here 2 years ago, I really didn't give a damn. I came because I was caught. I really didn't want to help myself and I just didn't know it at that time. Now I feel different. There are no charges; I'm here because I want to be here and I want to change my life. I'm tired of having urges to expose and I want to understand why I have the urges and hopefully with your help (doctor) change so I don't have them. Is that possible?

The motivational state of the patient is paramount in treatment. There is no known treatment which will change the patient who does not want to change. One of the author's patients was proceeding in a course of treatment and reported that he was "getting better", since the urges were lesser to act out. A late night call from the police department suggested otherwise, since he was caught again while on probation. Another incident was described to the author in which several army alcoholics were treated with scoline aversion therapy described earlier. On this day, the alcoholics were treated one after the other. One patient noted: "It was payday and to celebrate both the treatment and payday, we all went over to the canteen for a drink."

Overall it seems that society's goals, and the therapist's goals are best met by a consideration of the patient's motivation and preferences. If the patient is willing to change, he will be best able to cope if his erotic preferences are changed so he is no longer aroused by sexually anomalous behavior.

Assessing Erotic Preferences

The single most important aspect of treating sexual anomalies is to determine erotic preferences by complete sex history and/or phallometric testing. Disposition is clearer in most cases. In some sexual offenses, the accused have normal erotic preferences. They need not concern the mental health system because they will not recidivate. Their offenses were situational in nature and perhaps due to some life stress. When the stress is removed or the patient learns to cope with the stress, the danger of acting out is almost zero. Mr. G is an example. A grandfather and a minister of the church, he had led a productive life and was an esteemed member of his community. He had fathered several children who were grown up and many had embarked on careers in various cities around the country. He had one daughter in the city who had two children, a boy and a girl. It was the girl that he engaged in sexual fondling. No charges were laid, but assessment and treatment were requested by the family. The event had occurred 3 months after the death of his wife to whom he was very close.

> *Mr. G:* I didn't mean to hurt my granddaughter. I love her very much. I love all my grandchildren. My wife, Betsie, and I both loved them dearly and wouldn't hurt them for the world. I do not know what made me do what I did. I guess I was just lonely.
>
> Since my wife passed away, I have been so lonely I don't know how to cope. I've prayed to God for help to cope and maybe even to take me away too, so I can be with my wife. But it is not his will and I am so alone.

Mr. G was considered to be suffering from a serious depression. A course of three sessions of electroconvulsive therapy relieved his depression at which point counselling in coping with his wife's death resulted in a dramatic improvement. Since he showed no previous pedophilic desires and was now no longer depressed, the odds were high he would not act again as he had.

When anomalous erotic preferences are evident, some therapy goals may seem more appropriate than others. For example, it may be easier to adapt a homosexual pedophile to adult males because he responds more to them than to any female. In any case, preferences can be examined before and after treatment to show that, in fact, they did change.

Assuming one has a motivated patient who shows a sexually anomalous erotic preference and it is deemed worthwhile to change such urges, how can one know if the therapy is successful?

One can examine the therapy sessions themselves, either by monitoring continuously operant conditioning of the penis or by having test probe sessions intermittently, to see if there is a change. If one notices a steady decline in the sexually anomalous reactions to stimuli, then therapy is affecting at least the right target. Follow up on rates of sexually anomalous behavior outside the treatment unit and enjoyment of normal sexual outlets would be other measures that would indicate successful treatment. To show that normal sexual intercourse is the new preferred mode of erotic outlet over the old preferred sexually anomalous behavior would be the ultimate criterion of success in treatment.

Using Controlled Studies

Unfortunately, most of the reports of treatment for sexual anomalies in the professional literature fail seriously in many aspects of the criteria discussed here. Many case reports of therapy are used with no control groups or condition. Even if a single case design control study were used, it would be a significant improvement in the existing state of affairs. The case studies are unsystematic, uncontrolled and generally so confounded that it is difficult to know what factors are operative in treatment outcome. *Mr. I*, an exhibitionist, who was seen over a period of six years whenever trouble arose, illustrates how inaccurate a case report may be.

Mr. I was seen at 21 years of age for the first time. He was recently married and charged with indecent exposure. He appeared to be a very guilty but very angry person. The therapist tried without success to have him express his anger directly but he continued to deny any anger for anyone. He indicated he worked very successfully at suppressing his urges to expose and only acted out every year or two. The last time he had acted out at 17 years of age, his father sent him to a psychiatrist to "get his head fixed". While treatment was deemed likely to fail, a short course in assertive training was undertaken at the time in the hopes it would improve his disposition and with the hope he would finally express that anger. After 6 months, he reported no urges to expose and indicated that treatment was great; he felt better and was ready for a new start. At this point many therapists are tempted to write up their case report and submit it for publication. In fact, the majority of case reports follow up the patient for only 3-to-6-months. A year is unusual for a follow up period, but even this can be inadequate. No report was published in this case and he only returned 2 years later, again charged with exposing. His marriage was on the rocks. Marital counselling appeared to be a stopgap for a while but the therapist was not satisfied that the anomaly had been treated or that the patient had changed. Finally 3 years later; five years after initial contact, the patient and his wife came in to discuss divorce since he was having an affair with another woman. His anger finally emerged:

> *Mr. I:*   I'm tired of being everyone's lacky. I'm saying now 'what about me.'
> I'm pissed off with everyone. With my wife, my family and I'm tired of
> being quiet about it. I'm speaking out and letting everyone know about it.
> My girlfriend is great because she encourages me to say what I feel. My
> wife doesn't. If our marriage can be saved, it has to change.
>
> LATER . . . .
>
> You know when I first came in here I was mad. You didn't know it but I
> was mad. My old man unloaded me and our problems one more time on
> someone else. I was angry at you for being there. I used to sit back and
> laugh to myself. He thinks I'm changing and I'm making a fool out of
> him. I'm going out every day and exposing and he thinks I'm cured. Well
> let him think that. I'll just sit back here and laugh at him without him
> suspecting a thing.

It is just as important for evaluating treatment to know if patients would "get better" spontaneously without treatment. An untreated control group may be used for this purpose. Spontaneous remission of symptoms has been a topic of controversy[110] [112] and it is especially important in sexual anomalies. First, there are fewer sexual offenders over 35 than under[85]. Either they "burn out" or are better at avoiding detection. In any case, one has to be wary of overly long treatments or of progams involving older offenders since in both cases, spontaneous remission is more likely. Second, for patients from puberty–to–20, anomalous behavior may disappear spontaneously for other reasons. Young men are extremely excitable and may engage in unusual behavior from high sex drive levels or simply from curiosity since they are novices. With maturity and passing exploratory behavior, they settle into socially acceptable sex behavior. In addition, shyness or lack of know how can result in anomalous behavior such as peeping, frottage or in homosexual outlet. These again tend to remit spontaneously with age. A comparable control group can be highly effective in sorting out these extraneous factors.

Many settings are opposed to untreated control groups for ethical reasons. However, a treatment cannot be properly evaluated without some form of control group. Many drugs used in psychiatric settings may have side effects that will only be evident when an untreated control group is used. Moreover, known side effects may be a danger to the individual. If for example it were shown that a depression can be treated with one course of ECT and 3 weeks of counselling, would this not be a better alternative than the use of drugs, which may take three weeks to show their effectiveness and which the patient may have to continue for months or even years? Some side effects are frightening. Amphetamines are prescribed for hyperactive children who appear to be turning into antisocial adults. These same chemicals have been linked in some cases to violent and unprovoked murder. Tardive dyskenesia is a long term side effect of neuroleptic drugs. Cyproterone acetate causes testicular atrophy. Provera may have side effects including diabetic symptoms. Do we have to risk this? Considering the low recidivism rate of sexual anomalies, would not a better starting point be a thorough evaluation of a treatment as opposed to the ethical objections of no treatment? An alternative is available that is acceptable to the opponents of control groups in psychiatric treatments: comparison of two therapies. Two alternative methods of treatment that are deemed suitable for a given sexual anomaly can be compared in terms of their effectiveness and efficiency. Thus one might compare aversive conditioning and reciprocal inhibition therapy in the treatment of pedophilia. In this way, all patients would receive some form of treatment and the researcher could see if one is more effective than the other. Even if both methods were successful, one might be faster than the other or have more lasting effects, have lower dropout rate, have better overall psychological effects on the patient, and so forth, which would offer the therapist a selection in the course of action he chose. One might discover that one treatment is better for some kinds of patients over others and this would be useful information for future treatment.

The use of uncontrolled studies at this juncture in our therapeutic history is unjustified and unnecessary. A hundred cases treated "successfully" is uninformative if there are no controls. The extraneous factors can be subtle and powerful as in the case of Mr. J, a homosexual pedophile, who came only for five therapy sessions before he "confessed his true feelings". He had shown dramatic and remarkable change in only three treatment sessions using an operant conditioning paradigm. This was the only clue the therapist had that anything was amiss; improvement was too good and too fast. However, *Mr. J*'s face was an unexpressive one and it was very difficult to know what he was feeling from his appearance. He deliberated over everything and gave carefully thought out answers to questions. He was motivated to change and had tried a number of treatments over a period of 8 years without success. On the fifth session, he said:

> *Mr. J:* It's no good going on with this treatment; it isn't working and I am only fooling myself thinking it is. The only reason there is a change is you. The first moment I walked into your office, I was electrified. I very quickly had a crush on you and I realized it is crazy. You are so obviously heterosexual that even if there was a hope of a romance, that would make it impossible. I realize that now. But these last few weeks I have been living with this infatuation and I think I'm over it now.

Some extraneous factors can be almost ludicruous. *Mr. K*, an exhibitionist, reported during the course of an experimental investigation of two treatments that he thought he would stop exposing either this week or next. With such a conscious effort evident in his statement, a surprised therapist asked "How come?"

> *Mr. K:* Oh, it's getting too cold. It snowed last weekend a bit and they say we are due for a heavy snow tomorrow. (He looked at the therapist who had an evident suprised look on his face). You don't think I'm going to freeze my nuts off do you?

We examined season of discharge as a variable in follow up of treated exhibitionists[59]. Statistically, significantly more patients recidivated when discharged in summer than in winter, the warm months as opposed to the cold months of the year. Using a single case study, one could say nothing about season of discharge from the hospital.

Behavior modifiers have attempted to improve the unsystematic case study so frequent in clinical journals by introducing the single case experimental design[12][23][38][65]. A therapy procedure is introduced after baseline measurement of the rate of the anomalous behavior. The frequency should decline with treatment. Once the behavior starts to change, the treatment or reinforcer is either withdrawn or reversed so the anomalous behavior should increase in frequency again. This serves to demonstrate that the treatment is in fact the significant influence on behavior. Since the anomalous behavior can vary in its intensity and frequency, and since nonspecific treatment factors can change behavior, this part of the procedure is an essential demonstration that therapy is working. The therapist then reintroduces treatment until the frequency of the target behavior is nil.

A multiple baseline procedure has also been effectively employed. That is, one examines not only the frequency of the anomalous behavior but also of normal or socially acceptable outlets such as heterosexual intercourse. One can simultaneously decrease anomalous behavior and increase the frequency of coitus. Theorists have debated the utility of this design and it has been suggested it is even superior to group studies[12]. Others are less enthusiastic[43].

It is valuable to sort out two factors in research studies: control and number of cases. Experimental control with demonstrated effectiveness of treatment is generally superior to an uncontrolled study. In this respect, the single case experimental design is superior to the uncontrolled study. However, the single case still involves only one individual who might be peculiar in some way and might be nonrepresentative of cases generally seen in a clinic. For this reason, a large number of cases is desirable. When the dimensions of control versus no control and number of patients versus single patient are compared, the combination of control and large number of individuals is the most conservative and the present writer recommends its acceptance since it more likely represents clinical reality.

Adequate Follow-up

The follow-up of patients is crucial to understanding treatment and evaluating its effectiveness. Periodic assessment will tell the therapist how lasting the treatment is or in effect if he had changed the patient's behavior at all. There is some question about how long follow up should be[75] but in the case of sexual anomalies at least a year or more is often necessary. Summertime is particularly problematic because of added stimulation from the environment in the form of bathing suits, scant clothing, and so forth, and follow up over two summers will usually indicate the strength of changed behavior. If the behavior occurs sporadically, for example, 3 or 4 times a year, additional time may be necessary to evaluate treatment effectiveness. A cursory review of the therapy literature will show that follow up is generally inadequate. Results of such studies should be considered with extreme caution.

Investigating the Effectiveness of Treatment

The sexual anomalies offer the investigating therapist an advantage over studying other mental health problems. There is a clearly defined criterion for examining the effectiveness of treatment—preferred and actual orgasmic outlet. The sex history can be examined for past behavior and a daily diary can be used to determine baseline frequency of the sexual anomaly in the past week or so. One may wish to have the patient keep a diary of acting out, urges, and thoughts. Some therapists prefer to score acting out, urges, and urges with masturbation, surrounding the anomalous behavior. This is a matter of preference. The rating of intensity of urges, and so forth, versus frequency may be of value. However, it is difficult to have patients keep diaries and the more you ask them to do, the less likely it will be done correctly if at all.

It is important to stress the need to record this behavior before treatment begins. I have found it helpful to make a plan with the patient when he will fill in the diary. My own preference is to record only orgasmic outlet and note if it was normal sexual outlet or the anomalous one. Often details are not remembered and asking for fantasies, and so forth, is not likely to be recorded even if the patient is serious. A diary that is not filled in during the evening can be done in the morning, if it only involves recording that he had intercourse the preceding evening. It is a lot simpler than remembering if he had a fantasy or two of exposing that evening. The diary can be kept throughout the course of therapy and provides an index of the effectiveness of treatment. With most behavior therapy techniques, progress should be evident in a few weeks. If there is none, therapy goals should be reconsidered or perhaps the treatment method should be changed. Of course the more traditional psychotherapies may take longer for change to be evident. In this case, behavior therapy methods may be used as an adjunct to treatment.

If the therapy chosen directly alters sexual behavior, phallometric measurement is an integral part of ongoing assessment. In the treatment unit, the therapist can assess at the start, the strength of reactivity to the preferred and anomalous stimuli. If during the course of treatment he does not change, it indicates something is amiss. If, however, he shows a steady decline in reactivity, treatment is likely having the desired effect. Follow-up at monthly intervals after treatment and then at 6 months can also involve assessment of the same parameters as measured during treatment. This provides an ongoing record of effectiveness. The younger the patient, the more important it is to determine what is happening. An inadequate follow up can be misleading.

In conclusion, I think the reader should be skeptical of treatment approaches that do not meet these criteria. They misled us all. We embark on ventures that are doomed to failure because they are improperly investigated. They offer a taste of plausibility and of cure, too often leaving the patient angry and disillusioned. If a treatment is to be used experimentally, the patient should know this and know that we do not have the answers. The therapeutic enterprise becomes a joint venture that involves cooperation and a surprising openness on the part of the patients. I feel this is the road to progress.

BIBLIOGRAPHY

1. Abel, G. G., & Blanchard, E. B. The role of fantasy in the treatment of sexual deviation. *Archives of General Psychiatry,* 1974, *30,* 467–475.
2. Alberti, R., & Emmons, M. L. *Your perfect right: A guide to assertion behavior.* San Luis Obispo, Ca.: Impact Press, 1970.
3. Alvarez-Sanchez, F., Faundes, A., Brache, V., & Leon, P. Attainment and maintenance of azoospermia with combined monthly injections of depot medroxyprogesterone acetate and testosterone enanthate. *Contraception,* 1977, *15*(6), 635–648.
4. Baekeland, F., & Lundwall, L. Dropping out of treatment: A critical review. *Psychological Bulletin,* 1975, *82*(5), 738–783.
5. Bakker, C. B., Bakker-Rabdau, M. K., & Breit, S. The measurement of assertiveness and aggressiveness. *Journal of Personality Assessment,* 1978, *42*(3), 277–284.
6. Bancroft, J., Tennent, G., Kypros, L. The control of deviant sexual behavior by drugs. *British Journal of Psychiatry,* 1974, *125,* 310–315.
7. Barber, T. X. Responding to 'hypnotic' suggestions: An introspective report. *American Journal of Clinical Hypnosis,* 1975, *18*(1), 6–22.
8. Barber, T. X., & De Moor, W. A theory of hypnotic induction procedures. *American Journal of Clinical Hypnosis,* 1972, *15*(2), 112–135.
9. Barlow, D. Aversive procedures. In W. S. Agras (Ed.), *Behavior modification: Principles and clinical application.* Boston: Little, Brown & Co., 1972, 87–125.
10. Barlow, D., Agras, S., & Leitenberg, H. *An Experimental Analysis of "Fading" to Increase Heterosexual Responsiveness in Homosexuality.* Paper presented at the 17th Annual Meeting of the Southern Psychological Association, Miami Beach, Florida, 1971.
11. Barlow, D., Becker, R., Leitenberg, H., & Agras, W. A mechanical strain gauge for recording penile circumference change. *Journal of Applied Behavior Analysis,* 1970, *3,* 73–76.
12. Barlow, D. H., & Hersen, M. Single case experimental designs: Uses in applied clinical research. *Archives of General Psychiatry,* 1973, *29,* 319–325.
13. Bastani, J. B. Treatment of male genital exhibitionism. *Comprehensive Psychiatry,* 1976, *17*(6), 769–774.
14. Bent, R. J., Putnam, D. G., Kiesler, D. J., & Nowicki, S. *Correlates of successful and unsuccessful psychotherapy.* Paper presented at the 84th APA Annual Convention, Washington, 1976.
15. Bergin, A. E., & Strupp, H. H. New directions in psychotherapy research. *Journal of Abnormal Psychology,* 1970, *76*(1), 13–26.
16. Bernstein, D. A., & Paul, G. L. Some comments on therapy analogue research with small animal "phobias". *Journal of Behavior Therapy & Experimental Psychiatry,* 1971, *2,* 225–237.

17. Brenner, P. F., Mishell, D. R., Bernstein, G. S., & Ortiz, A. Study of medroxyprogesterone acetate and testosterone enanthate as a male contraceptive. *Contraception,* 1977, *15*(6), 679–691.

18. Cautela, J. Covert reinforcement. *Behavior Therapy,* 1970, *1,* 33–50.

19. Cone, J. D. *What's relevant about reliability and validity for behavioral assessment?* Paper presented at the annual meeting of the American Psychological Association, Chicago, 1975.

20. Curran, J. P. Skills training as an approach to the treatment of heterosexual-social anxiety: A review. *Psychological Bulletin,* 1977, *84*(1), 140–157.

21. Curran, J. P., Gilbert, F. S., & Little, L. M. A comparison between behavioral replication training and sensitivity training approaches to heterosexual dating anxiety. *Journal of Counseling Psychology,* 1976, *23*(3), 190–196.

22. Dahlberg, C. C. Sexual contact between patient and therapist. *Medical Aspects of Human Sexuality,* 1971, *5,* 34–56.

23. Edgar, E., & Billingsley, F. Believability when N = 1. *Psychological Record,* 1974, *24,* 147–160.

24. Eisler, R. M. The behavioral assessment of social skills. In M. Hersen, & A. S. Bellack (Eds.), *Behavioral assessment: A practical handbook.* New York: Pergamon Press, 1976.

25. Eisler, R. M., Miller, P. M., & Hersen, M. Components of assertive behavior. *Journal of Clinical Psychology,* 1973, *24*(3), 295–299.

26. Eisler, R. M., Hersen, M., & Miller, P. M. Shaping components of assertive behavior with instructions and feedback. *American Journal of Psychiatry,* 1974, *131*(12), 1344–1347.

27. Evans, D. R. Subjective variables and treatment effects in aversion therapy. *Behavior Research & Therapy,* 1970, *8,* 147–152.

28. Feldman, M. P., & MacCulloch, M. J. *Homosexual behavior: Therapy and assessment.* Oxford: Pergamon Press, 1971.

29. Field, L. H., & Williams, M. The hormonal treatment of sexual offenders. *Medicine, Science and the Law,* 1970, *10,* 27–34.

30. Fiske, D. W., Hunt, H. F., Luborsky, L., Orne, M. T., Parloff, M. B., Reiser, M. F., & Tuma, A. H. Planning of research on effectiveness of psychotherapy. *American Psychologist,* 1971, *26,* 727–737.

31. Frank, J. D. Therapeutic factors in psychotherapy. *American Journal of Psychotherapy,* 1971, *25*(3), 350–361.

32. Freund, K. Therapeutic sex drive reduction. *Acta Psychiatrica Scandinavica,* 1980, *62,* 5–38.

33. Frick, J., Bartsch, G., & Weiske, W. H. The effect of monthly depot medroxyprogesterone acetate and testosterone on human spermatogenesis. I. Uniform dosage levels. *Contraception,* 1977, *15*(6), 619–668.

34. Frick, J., Bartsch, G., & Weiske, W. H. The effect of monthly depot medroxyprogesterone acetate and testosterone on human spermatogenesis. II. High initial dosage. *Contraception,* 1977, *15*(6), 669–677.

35. Galassi, J. P., Galassi, M. D., & Litz, M. C. Assertive training in groups using video feedback. *Journal of Consulting Psychology,* 1974, *21*(5), 390–394.

36. Garfield, S. L. What are the therapeutic variables in psychotherapy? *Psychotherapy and Psychosomatics,* 1974, *24,* 372–378.

37. Goldfried, M. R. Systematic desensitization as training in self-control. *Journal of Consulting and Clinical Psychology,* 1971, *37*(2), 228–234.

38. Gottman, J. M. N-of one and N-of two research in psychotherapy. *Psychological Bulletin,* 1973, *80*(2), 93–105.

39. Gross, S. J., & Miller, J. O. A research strategy for evaluating the effectiveness of psychotherapy. *Psychological Reports,* 1975, *37,* 1011–1021.

40. Grossberg, J. M. Behavior therapy: A review. *Psychological Bulletin,* 1964, *62*(2), 73–88.

41. Hallam, R., & Rachman, S. Theoretical problems of aversion therapy. *Behavior Research & Therapy,* 1972, *10,* 341–353.

42. Hare-Mustin, R. T. Ethical considerations in the use of sexual contact in psychotherapy. *Psychotherapy: Theory, Research and Practice,* 1974, *11*(4), 308–310.

43. Hartmann, D. P., & Atkinson, C. Having your cake and eating it too: A note on some apparent contradictions between therapeutic achievements and design requirements in N = 1 studies. *Behavior Therapy,* 1973, *4,* 589–591.

44. Heath, R. G. Pleasure and brain activity in man. *Journal of Nervous and Mental Disease,* 1972, *154,*(1), 3–18.

45. Heim, N. Sexual behavior of castrated sex offenders. *Archives of Sexual Behavior,* 1981, *10*(1), 11–19.

46. Heim, N., & Hursch, C. J. Castration for sex offenders: Treatment or punishment? A review and critique of recent European literature. *Archives of Sexual Behavior,* 1979, *8*(3), 281–304.

47. Heimberg, R. G., Montgomery, D., Madsen, C. H., & Heimberg, J. S. Assertion training: A review of the literature. *Behavior Therapy,* 1977, *8,* 953–971.

48. Heller, C. G., Laidlaw, W. M., Harvey, H. T., & Nelson, W. O. Effects of progestational compounds on the reproductive processes of the human male. *Annals of the New York Academy of Science,* 1958, *71,* 649–665.

49. Hewes, D. D. On effective assertive behavior: A brief note. *Behavior Therapy,* 1975, *6,* 269–271.

50. Holden, H. M. Behavior and aversion therapy in the treatment of delinquency. Should aversion and behavior therapy be used in the treatment of delinquency? *British Journal of Criminology,* 1965, *5,* 377–387.

51. Jacobson, E. *Progressive relaxation.* Chicago: University of Chicago Press, 1938.

52. Jones, H. G. Behavior and aversion therapy in the treatment of delinquency I. The techniques of behavior therapy and delinquent behavior. *British Journal of Criminology,* 1965, *5,* 355–365.

53. Kazdin, E., & Kople, S. A. On resolving ambiguities of the multiple-baseline design: Problems and recommendations. *Behavior Therapy,* 1975, *6,* 601–608.

54. Keniston, K., Boltax, S., & Almonds, R. Multiple criteria of treatment outcome. *Journal of Psychiatric Research,* 1971, *8,* 107–118.

55. Kimble, G. A. *Conditioning and learning.* New York: Apple Century Crofts, Inc., 1961.

56. Kirschner, N. M. Generalization of behaviorally oriented assertive training. *Psychological Record,* 1976, *26,* 117–125.

57. Kroger, W., & Fezler, W. *Hypnosis and Behavior Modification.* Philadelphia: Lippincott Co., 1976.

58. Langevin, R., & Martin, M. Can erotic responses be classically conditioned? *Behavior Therapy,* 1975, *6,* 350–355.

59. Langevin, R., Paitich, D., Hucker, S., Newman, S., Ramsay, G., Pope, S., Geller, G., & Anderson, C. The effect of assertiveness training, provera and sex of therapist in the treatment of genital exhibitionism. *Journal of Behavior Therapy & Experimental Psychiatry,* 1979, *10,* 275–282.

60. Laschet, U. Antiandrogen in the treatment of sex offenders: Mode of action and therapeutic outcome. In J. Zubin, & J. Money (Eds.), *Contemporary Sexual Behavior: Critical Issues in the 1970s.* Baltimore: Johns Hopkins University Press, 1973.

61. Laws, D. R., & Bow, R. A. An improved mechanical strain gauge for recording penile circumference. *Psychophysiology,* 1976, *13*(6), 596–599.
62. Lazarus, A. A. On assertive behavior: A brief note. *Behavior Therapy,* 1973, *4,* 697–699.
63. Lazarus, A. A., & Fay, A. *I Can If I Want To.* New York: William Morrow & Co., 1975.
64. Leeman, C. P. Outcome criteria in psychotherapy research. *Psychotherapy and Psychosomatics,* 1975, *25,* 229–235.
65. Leitenberg, H. The use of single-case methodology in psychotherapy research. *Journal of Abnormal Psychology,* 1973, *82*(1), 87–101.
66. Lick, J. R., & Unger, T. E. The external validity of behavioral fear assessment: the problem of generalizing from the laboratory to the natural environment. *Behavior Modification,* 1977, *1*(3), 283–306.
67. Locke, E. A. Is "behavior therapy" behavioristic? (An analysis of Wolpe's psychotherapeutic methods). *Psychological Bulletin,* 1971, *76*(5), 318–327.
68. London, P. The end of ideology in behavior modification. *American Psychologist,* 1972, *27,* 913–920.
69. MacCullough, M. J., Birtles, C. J., & Feldman, M. P. Anticipatory avoidance learning for the treatment of homosexuality: Recent developments and an automated aversion therapy system. *Behavior Therapy,* 1971, *2,* 151–169.
70. Mandel, K. H. Preliminary report on a new aversion therapy for male homosexuals. *Behavior Research & Therapy,* 1970, *8,* 93–95.
71. Marquis, J. N. Orgasmic reconditioning: Changing sexual object choice through controlling masturbation fantasies. *Journal of Behavior Therapy & Experimental Psychiatry,* 1970, *1,* 263–271.
72. Marshall, W. L., & Lippens, K. The clinical value of boredom: A procedure for reducing inappropriate sexual interests. *Journal of Nervous and Mental Disease,* 1977, *165*(4), 283–287.
73. Martin, B. Reward and punishment associated with the same goal response. *Psychological Bulletin,* 1963, *60*(5), 441–451.
74. Masters, W. H., & Johnson, V. E. *Homosexuality in perspective.* Boston: Little, Brown & Co., 1979.
75. Mash, E. J., Terdal, L. G. After the dance is over: Some issues and suggestions for follow-up assessment in behavior therapy. *Psychological Reports,* 1977, *41,* 1287–1308.
76. Mauger, P. A., Adkinson, D. R., Hernandez, S. K., Firestone, G., & Hook, J. D. *Can assertiveness be distinguished from aggressiveness using self report data?* Unpublished manuscript, Department of Psychology, Georgia State University, Atlanta, Georgia.
77. Max, L. Breaking up a homosexual fixation by the conditional reaction technique: A case study. *Psychological Bulletin,* 1935, *32,* 734.
78. McConaghy, N. Penile volume change to moving pictures of male and female in heterosexual and homosexual males. *Behavior Research & Therapy,* 1967, *5,* 43–48.
79. McConaghy, N. Subjective and penile plethysmograph responses following aversion-relief and apormorphine aversion therapy for homosexual impulses. *British Journal of Psychiatry,* 1969, 115, 723–730.
80. McConaghy, N. Penile response conditioning and its relationship to aversion therapy in homosexuals. *Behavior Therapy,* 1970, *1,* 213–221.
81. McNamara, J. R., & Macdonough, T. S. Some methodological considerations in the

design and implementation of behavior therapy research. *Behavior Therapy,* 1972, *3,* 361–378.

82. Melo, J. F., & Coutinho, E. M. Inhibition of spermatogenesis in men with monthly injections of medroxyprogesterone acetate and testosterone enanthate. *Contraception,* 1977, *15*(6), 627–634.

83. Mintz, J. What is "success" in psychotherapy? *Journal of Abnormal Psychology,* 1972, *80*(1), 11–19.

84. Mohr, J. W. Evaluation of treatment. *International Psychiatry Clinics,* 1972, *8*(4), 227–242.

85. Mohr, J. W., Turner, R., & Jerry, M. *Pedophilia and Exhibitionism.* Toronto: University of Toronto Press, 1964.

86. Nolan, J. D., Mattis, P. R., & Holliday, W. C. Long-term effects of behavior therapy: A 12-month follow-up. *Journal of Abnormal Psychology,* 1970, *76*(1), 88–92.

87. Novak, E., Hendrix, J.W., & Seckman, C. E. Effects of medroxyprogesterone acetate on some endocrine functions of healthy male volunteers. *Current Therapeutic Research,* 1977, *21*(3), 320–326.

88. Paine, C. H., Wright, F. W., & Ellis, F. The use of progestogen in the treatment of metastatic carcinoma of the kidney and uterine body. *British Journal of Cancer,* 1970, *24,* 277–282

89. Quinn, J. T., Harbison, J. J., & McAllister, H. An attempt to shape human penile responses. *Behavior Research & Therapy,* 1970, *8,* 213–216.

90. Rachman, S. Aversion therapy: Chemical or electrical? *Behavior Research Therapy,* 1965, *2,* 289–299.

91. Rachman, S. Sexual fetishism: an experimental analog. *Psychological Record,* 1966, *16,* 293–296.

92. Rachman, S. Clinical applications of observational learning, limitation and modeling. *Behavior Therapy,* 1972, *3,* 379–397.

93. Rich, A. R., & Schroeder, H. E. Research issues in assertiveness training. *Psychological Bulletin,* 1976, *83*(6), 1081–1096.

94. Rieber, I., & Sigusch, V. *Psychosurgery on sex offenders and sexual deviants. A critical review of the current practice in West Germany.* Paper presented at the annual meeting of the International Academy of Sex Research, Hamburg, 1976.

95. Roper, P. The use of hypnosis in the treatment of exhibitionism. *Canadian Medical Association Journal,* 1966, *94,* 72–77.

96. Ryan, V. L., & Gizynski, M. N. Behavior therapy in retrospect: Patients' feelings about their behavior therapies. *Journal of Consulting and Clinical Psychology,* 1971, *37,* 1–9.

97. Samuels, M. L., Sullivan, P., & Howe, C. D. Medroxyprogesterone acetate in the treatment of renal cell carcinoma (hypernephroma). *Cancer,* 1968, *22*(3), 525–532.

98. Scott, W. W., & Schirmer, H. K. A new oral progestational steroid effective in treating prostatic cancer. *Transactions of American Association of Genito-Urinary Surgeons,* 1966, *58,* 54–62.

99. Seal, U. S., Doe, R. P., Byar, D. P., & Corle, D. K. Response of plasma fibrinogen and plasminogen to hormone treatment and the relation of pretreatment values to mortality in patients with prostatic cancer. *Cancer,* 1976, *38,* 1108–1117.

100. Seeman, M. Tardive dyskinesia. *Montage,* 1979, *5*(2), 4.

101. Seligman, M. E. On the generality of the laws of learning. *Psychological Review,* 1970, *77,* 406–418.

102. Serber, M. Shame aversion therapy. *Journal of Behavior Therapy & Experimental Psychiatry,* 1970, *1,* 213–215.

103. Sethna, E. R., & Harrington, J. A. Evaluation of group psychotherapy. *British Journal of Psychiatry,* 1971, *118,* 641–658.

104. Shephard, G. Social skills training: The generalization problem. *Behavior Therapy,* 1977, *8,* 1008-1009.

105. Shostrom, E. L. The measurement of growth in psychotherapy. *Psychotherapy,* 1972, *9*(3), 194-198.

106. Siegel, P. S., & Milby, J. B. Secondary reinforcement in relation to shock termination: Second chapter. *Psychological Bulletin,* 1969, *72*(2), 146-156.

107. Spanos, N. P., & Barber, T. X. Toward a convergence in hypnosis research. *American Psychologist,* 1974, *29*(7), 500-511.

108. Spodak, M. K., Falck, A., & Rappeport, J. R. The hormonal treatment of sexual aggressives with depo-provera. *TSA News,* 1977, *1*(1), 2.

109. Strupp, H. H. On the basic ingredients of psychotherapy. *Journal of Consulting & Clinical Psychology,* 1973, *41*(1), 1-8.

110. Strupp, H. H. 'Spontaneous remission' and the nature of the therapeutic influence. *Psychotherapy and Psychosomatics,* 1974, *24,* 389-393.

111. Sturup, G. K. Castration: The total treatment. In H. L. Resnik, & M. E. Wolfgang (Eds.), *Sexual behaviors: Social, clinical and legal aspects.* Boston: Little, Brown & Co., 1972, 360-382.

112. Subotnik, L. Spontaneous remission: Fact or artefact? *Psychological Bulletin,* 1972, *77*(1), 32-48.

113. Tanner, B. A. Shock intensity and fear of shock in the modification of homosexual behavior in males by avoidance learning. *Behavior Research & Therapy,* 1973, *11,* 213-218.

114. Tennent, G., Bancroft, J., & Cass, J. The control of deviant sexual behavior by drugs: A double-blind controlled study of benperidol, chlorpromazine, and placebo. *Archives of Sexual Behavior,* 1974, *3*(3), 261-271.

115. Terner, C., & MacLaughlin, J. Effects of sex hormones on germinal cells of the rat testis: A rationale for the use of progestin and androgen combinations in the control of male fertility. *Journal of Reproduction and Fertility,* 1973, *32,* 453-464.

116. Walker, P., & Meyer, W. J. *Antiandrogen treatment for the paraphiliac sex offender.* Paper presented at the conference on Violence and the Violent Individual, Houston, Texas, 1978.

117. Wardlaw, G. R., & Miller, P. J. A controlled exposure technique in the elimination of exhibitionism. *Journal of Behavior Therapy & Experimental Psychiatry,* 1978, *9,* 27-32.

118. Westheimer, R. Evaluation criteria and psychotherapy research. *Psychotherapy and Psychosomatics,* 1975, *25,* 236-238.

119. Wickramsakera, I. Aversive behavior rehearsal for sexual exhibitionism. *Behavior Therapy,* 1976, *7,* 167-176.

120. Wolpe, J. *Psychotherapy by reciprocal inhibition.* Stanford, Ca.: Stanford University Press, 1958.

121. Wolpe, J. Inadequate behavior analysis: The Achilles heel of outcome research in behavior therapy. *Journal of Behavior Therapy & Experimental Psychiatry,* 1977, *8,* 1-3.

122. Yates, A. J. Misconceptions about behavior therapy: A point of view. *Behavior Therapy,* 1970, *1,* 92-107.

II STIMULUS PREFERENCE ANOMALIES

4 Homosexuality

In contemporary Western society, the topic of human rights for homosexuals polarizes opinion in public and professional circles. While gay men and women continue to suffer persecution, the swing of opinion has been to liberalizing attitudes toward homosexuality. Some countries have changed their laws so that homosexual acts in private between consenting adults are no longer criminal offenses. The American Psychiatric Association in 1973 changed its official classification of homosexuality to "sexual orientation disturbance". The trend has been to deemphasize the disease status of homosexuality[118] [169] [175]. Why then bother to include it in a book about sexual anomalies?

Although agreeing with the liberalizing of attitudes, I have included this chapter for two reasons. One aim of this book is to understand sexual anomalies. Homosexuality will remain an unusual sexual behavior in spite of any social changes and it therefore merits study in its own right. It offers one more avenue to understanding sexual behavior in general. Second, the majority of available treatments have been applied to homosexuality and not to other sexual anomalies. To discard it would ignore a great deal of our knowledge on treatment methods. We can learn from that history and perhaps we can apply much of what we have learned to other sexually anomalous behavior that has not and will likely not be socially acceptable in the near future. Knowing what treatments are available for homosexuality and knowing their outcome offers the maximum freedom to the individual. Some homosexuals may wish to change their sexual orientation in spite of social reform. They, as well as therapists, should know the extent to which this is possible. Clinicians who are concerned with relieving the suffering of patients including homosexuals, will be interested in the contents of this chapter.

Homosexuality has usually been defined as erotic interaction between persons of the same anatomical sex. Some clinicians are more specific and require that the interactions occur over a prolonged period of time and so represent a more or less stable behavior pattern. In the Kinsey scale of homosexuality–heterosexuality, the extreme poles indicate "exclusive" homosexual or heterosexual. According to Kinsey and his associates[90], 37% of the total male population in the United States has had at least some homosexual experience to the point of orgasm between adolescence and old age. However, only 4% were exclusive homosexuals throughout their lives. Other studies reviewed by West[189] have supported their findings.

Considered in terms of orgasmic preferences, such results may be confusing. How many of the 37% preferred male partners over female ones? Many may be acting out of curiosity or deprivation. Young and inexperienced boys may engage in mutual sexual stimulation because they are curious or too shy to approach a girl. Men on long sea duty or in prisons also engage in homosexual outlets, often out of mere deprivation[51]. How many do so is not easily ascertainable. However, the 4% who were exclusive homosexuals very likely represent men who have an established erotic preference. Although this incidence is low, it represents one of the most commonly reported sexual anomalies. It has accordingly received the most attention in the professional literature[25] and many treatment methods have been directed to it.

The percentage of men who are exclusive homosexuals remains an educated guess nonetheless. Many individuals would not admit to a stranger, even a researcher, that they are homosexual. The Kinsey studies were conducted during the war years and since admitting homosexuals are often rejected for military service, they may have a biased sample of individuals that overrepresents their numbers. This and other research studies often do not specify a criterion to gauge how exclusive the homosexual preference is. Self admission and use of friends of a gay student are uncertain criteria. This should be considered in evaluating results. Measurement of penile reactions and a sex history of exclusive homosexuality should be trusted first, but they are not used as often as they could be.

THE THEORIES

Psychoanalysis

There is a large and growing literature on homosexuality and it is not possible to include it all here. In fact, in this section, theories have been grouped into types: psychoanalytic, social learning, and organic. The interested reader may wish to see source materials or consult the Kinsey Institute that keeps a bibliography of publications on the topic[25].

Aversion to females. The most prominent theories come from the psychoanalysts who commonly associate homosexuality with anxiety. It is postulated that the homosexual male is afraid of the female in general and/or of heterosexual intercourse in particular[70]. This fear may be so general that any suggestion of sexual interaction on the part of a female may produce great distress[159]. *Mr. A*, who came for treatment of depression and concern over homosexuality, stated it this way:

> *Mr. A:*   The women at the office all want to go out with me. I don't know why. I'm not good looking and I don't encourage them at all. Maybe it's because I'm one of the few men there. They make me want to look for another job, preferably one with no women around at all.
>
> *Doctor:*   How do you know they all want to go out with you?
>
> *Mr. A:*   Oh, they have various ways of letting you know. Janet is always offering to get me a coffee and drops subtle hints that she would like to go here or there and letting me know she is free. It makes me feel sick. I don't want to hurt their feelings but I don't know what to do.

On the other hand, nonsexual relationships with women may not be threatening. On the contrary, there may even be a comraderie with females, a sharing of common interests in clothes, fashions, plants, etc.[131] but a specific revulsion for intercourse or contact with the female genitals. *Mr. B*, who had a problem with drugs but was unconcerned about being a homosexual, lived in a boarding house with several women and described them as "great friends" who were really understanding about his homosexuality. There was no fear of females until it came to sexual interaction:

> *Mr. B:*   Liz and I get along well. She is a great friend. We have so much in common. And we share our interest in fashion in a way nongay men can't. She said just the other day that it was great talking about clothes with me. She said I knew so much and could talk like a woman about it. (LATER . . . .)
>
> Women are ok, it's just the thought of touching their genitals I find disgusting. They are so wet and icky, there is no way I could put my penis in it.
>
> *Doctor:*   What do you think would happen if you did?
>
> *Mr. B:*   I couldn't, it would make me sick. It is so dirty.

Doctor: You mentioned previously that you enjoyed anal intercourse with your boyfriend. Do you consider that dirty too?

Mr. B: No, it's different. I make sure I have a bowel movement before, so the (rectal) chamber is empty. There is no problem. He is close to me and we love each other. It's great.

Whereas the fear may manifest itself in specific or general terms, psychoanalysts often see the anxiety as developing in the early family life of the child. In particular, during the phallic stage of development (3-to-5 years of age) when the male child's erotic energy is focused on his penis and when he considers it important and powerful, there can be trouble. Depending on parental attitudes and behavior, the child may experience an extreme fear that his important organ will be cut off (castration anxiety). The female to him is evidence that the organ has been removed in some people and he is afraid his powerful father will castrate him too. *Mr. C*, who had been in psychoanalytic treatment for 14 years was interested in behavior therapy to change his sexual orientation. He noted in his social history:

Mr. C: I used to sleep with my mother when my father was away on business trips. I liked that. I remembered one time rubbing my penis against her leg when I was 4 or 5 years old. She was asleep and didn't know about it, I think. At least she didn't say anything. I didn't like it when my dad came home again because I had to go back to my own bed and sleep alone.

In conjunction with a desire to possess mother and remove father, this fear can assume neurotic proportions and leave varying symptoms, among them, homosexuality.

Narcissism. A major division in homosexual etiology occurs in the assumption that the oral stage rather than the phallic stage is important in the development of homosexuality. The oral stage of development is the first in life and it is basically self centered or narcissistic. All activities center around the mouth and self gratification. Homosexuality is viewed as narcissistic because the male seeks out a love object that is like himself; analysts would say, represents himself[159]. His concern is self gratification, that is, autoeroticism as opposed to mutual gratification. Some patients report a phase of their development, in fact, in which they are autoerotic and perhaps, narcissistic. *Mr. F*, a married man for 20 years, decided to give the "gay life a try" and sought consultation on whether he was doing the "right thing". In describing his developmental history, he noted:

Mr. F: When we were growing up, the guys used to joke about homosexuals and might grab each other in the locker room showers as a joke. I used to go along with this but I was dead serious. They did not know that. I was scared to death that anyone would find out about it and I became really suspicious. Before I started my clandestine affairs with other gay men, I went through a period in which I didn't need anyone else. It wasn't just the worry. I was really turned on by my own body. I would look at myself in the mirror by the hour and masturbate again and again. If I could, I would have sucked my own penis. But that didn't matter; it was nice to touch myself and look at myself. I would soak in the bathtub by the hour too, watching my penis swaying in the water. I thought that happy period would never end. Then one day, I just lost interest. I started going to the gay bars for pick ups soon after.

A psychoanalyst might claim that he was only seeking substitutes for himself in looking for these other males. Some recent psychoanalytic writing has stressed narcissism over phallic concerns in sexually anomalous behavior. Cavenar, Spaulding and Butts[29] discussed autofellatio as a desire for self sufficiency. This behavior is as rare as it is difficult to do but in three cases described, the elements of self sufficiency and homosexual narcissism were noted. Goldberg[66] discussed "perverse activities" in general and considers them to be attempts to supply substitutes for the absent narcissistically invested self object. As noted in other chapters, narcissism seems to be a logical characteristic to investigate in sexual anomalies and it will be referred to again.

The male as female surrogate. An alternative explanation is that the sexual interaction with a male is only a substitute for an interaction with a female. This assumes the homosexual male has an erotic preference for females. Whereas the anxious and incapacitated male cannot interact sexually with a female, he selects a male as a surrogate but fantasizes sex with a woman or symbolically transforms the interaction into a sexual one with a woman. Such an interpretation would seem to apply to many cases of deprivation in which a female partner is not available, either physically such as in a prison, or psychologically as in cases of shy and inexperienced pubescent boys. *Mr. G*, a heterosexual by preference charged with repeated theft, was serving time in a maximum security prison. He described it this way:

Mr. G: You get hungry in there, really hungry. So some of the sweet things (younger and effeminate boys) look pretty good. When the guards are changing or when no one is around, you arrange to get one of these sweet things and have a go at it. You're so hungry and it feels good. At first, I felt like throwing up just thinking about it, then it didn't look so bad. I just imagined I was screwing a young chick and it was ok.

Many homosexual men would say that they do not have any fantasies of females at all during sex. However, some psychoanalysts would note that

sucking the penis symbolizes sucking the female breast and when anal intercourse is carried out, the anus is the symbolic equivalent of the vagina.
Specifically, the mother's vagina is represented and the homosexual act can
then be conceptualized as an incestuous desire, symbolically acted out.
Some clinicians make much of anal intercourse as a homosexual outlet, as
perhaps *the* homosexual outlet (See [189]). The lower incidence of such acts
makes this interpretation suspect[98].

Kinsey[90], on the other hand, maintained that neurotic symptoms are coincidental and occur because of the social unacceptability of homosexuality.
An example is *Mr. D*, who had a 6-year relationship with another man. He
came to our clinic in anger at a government employment service because in
his words, "seeing a shrink" was the only way he could get training for a
new career as a chef. He was rude to everyone concerned in our clinic:

Mr. D: This world drives me nuts. If I didn't have to work I'd have no contact with it. Government bureaucracy, employers who don't like the fact
I'm gay; rotten landlords who say they don't want queers around, it's bad
for the neighborhood, and the final degradation and insult—coming to
shrinks so I can get the training everyone else can who isn't gay, without
the hassle.

Doctor: Why do you put up with it all?

Mr. D: Because when Friday night comes, my lover and I are alone together.
We have a beautiful dinner. He cooks and sets the table. I bring home the
wine and some flowers for the table. We are alone, we make love and the
world doesn't matter any more.

Another homosexual in his twenties who was studying to be an engineer
was a research participant who looked normal in most respects but a clinician might wonder about these "neurotic" fears that developed while he
was growing up in a rural setting:

Mr. E: Do you know what it means to be the small town queer? Everyone
and I mean *everyone* knows. And do they let *you* know! Everyday, morning to night, they abuse you with, "Hey queer, wanna suck me?" or
"Hey fag, your slip is showing." Then there are the fights—what could
be more fun than beating up a queer after a good drunk? Try to get a
job—even as a grocery clerk or baby sitter—they don't want you around.
I finally had to get out, come to the anonymity of the big city. But the
persecution is still here although it's less. Looking back, I wonder what
they all had against me.

Feminine gender identity.   Another important theoretical facet of
homosexuality is masculinity–femininity and/or feminine gender identity.
The general trend in the homosexual male population is to greater feminiza-

tion and to feminine gender identity; the outcome of identification with mother as opposed to father. Bieber et al[22] maintain that the mother is the dominant member in the families of homosexuals and the father is either passive or frequently absent. Thus, many homosexual men describe themselves as "mother's favorite".

Psychoanalysts often presume that those men who are more feminine assume a passive sex role whereas those who are more father identified play a male role and are the more active sexually. An example is *Mr. B* noted earlier. He liked his partner to take care of him to the point of a neurotic dependency, which destroyed numerous relationships. He was a hairdresser who thought of being a fashion designer since he liked women's clothes so much. His effeminate mannerisms and occupation presented a stereotype layman often have of the homosexual[131]. Coupled with a desire for anal intercourse and to fellate his partner, he fits the theory. However, some men do not fit it too well. Mr. H, who was a media personality and actor, was asked whether he preferred to seduce or be seduced.

> *Mr. H:* It depends. As far as sex goes, I like everything it is possible to do. I like all kinds of men. If some handsome brute sweeps me off my feet, that's fine. If I have to initiate and be the aggressor, that's fine too. I'll take it every way I can get it.

It has also been assumed that a strong genital attachment to the father can produce homosexuality. There may be excessive fondling or overt seduction by the father[159]. Moreover, dependence on father for learning the "secrets of masculinity", of "acquiring the know how of dealing with women" can, through progressive dependence, create the conditions in which the child seeks fullfillment via a homosexual relationship. A number of personality traits are ascribed to homosexual men which follow from psychoanalytic theory. Among them, sadism resulting from an excessive interest in the anus; passivity, from a greater feminization; and dependency, which relates to substituting the penis for a breast. They show insecurity from an excessive fear of castration; hostility and lack of assertiveness since they cannot relate to women. There are many opinions about homosexuality in the psychoanalytic school and the interested reader should turn to the source literature[16 22 25 66 159 172 189].

Social Learning Theories

Homosexuality as learned.   A second broad set of attempts to explain homosexuality may be labeled social learning theories[189]. They are based on learning phenomenon, often occurring in childhood. Some interpretations are similar to those of the psychoanalysts. However, they assume that the homosexual behavior is the end product of a series of rewards and punishments, or reinforcers, which serve to shape the end product that the clinician sees. Such a formulation first came from animal research[89].

Using food, among other things, as rewards and electric shocks as punishments, it has been repeatedly demonstrated that simpler animals can learn an amazing variety of tasks. Recently, psychologists have claimed even to have taught chimpanzees the American Sign Language for the deaf using such methods[63]. Applying this method to humans, we may conclude that the feminine behaviors that often accompany homosexuality can be selectively encouraged by parents and other family members. Masculine behavior may be too rough for boys who are often labeled "sissies". *Mr. I* illustrates both this facet of theorized homosexual behavior and a poor father relationship:

> *Mr. I:*   I tried so hard to please him when I was a kid. I had to show him my report card before Mom saw it. But it was never good enough for him. When he was drunk, which was often, he said he wanted his son to be an athlete and he let me know in no uncertain terms that I didn't fill the bill. But I was terrified of being injured. I just couldn't play football or hockey. The kids at school thought I was a sissy because I would always back down from a fight.
>
> I remember the last effort I ever made to please my father. I was a runner in high school on the track and field. I gave it everything I had and I was good. I won a second place ribbon in interschool competition that year. All the parents came. I told my dad about it weeks in advance. When the day of the competition came, he was away on a week long drunk. I stopped trying to please him that day. We've hardly spoken since.

Inducement into homoerotic acts by older men would find a ready place in this set of theories. The rewarding nature of orgasm would stamp in the homosexual pattern. Marquis[113] has postulated that much of sexual behavior is learned by the association of stimuli with release of sexual tension. He argues that sexual fantasies followed by masturbation can alter overt sexual behavior. If homosexual outlet is all the boy knows then it may simply be conditioned in this fashion. If this outlet is the first or exclusive and repeated outlet for the novice, it may affect his life long pattern. Sagarin[155] notes that an estimated 40-to-50% of men entering prison will have homosexual experience. If this happens to be the first experience, it could be establishing a life long pattern. One cannot know if this theory is supported because usually we do not know if the person was homosexual or heterosexual before entering prison.

Some social learning theorists maintain that homosexuality is also a fusion of sex and anxiety drives (See [24] [146] and [149] for example). The actual sexual acts may be substitutes for female sex partners or be anxiety laden behavior in themselves. The "compulsive quality" of the act is considered to be a sign that anxiety and sexual drives are fused. Thus the gay male really desires a female but his anxiety is so great he turns to a male, which also generates anxiety but to a lesser extent. One might expect that the actual orgasmic act would not be very pleasurable. The powerful force of anxiety would cancel out the pleasure he could experience by the sexual arousal. This sort of experience is not uncommon in approach avoidance conflicts.

Many times, it is difficult to tell if the anxiety is connected to homosexuality itself, or, when homosexual acts are against the law, if the anxiety is simply fear of detection by the police. *Mr. J*, a 45-year-old business executive and self acknowledged homosexual, was shy and retiring and had as his only sexual outlet, the clandestine washroom exchange in which two men in adjacent cubicles would engage in mutual masturbation or fellatio. *Mr. J* described his usual experience as follows:

> *Mr. J:*   When I start feeling horny, I want to have contact with someone but at the same time I feel very tense. I'll go into a washroom in the subway station looking for sex, and sometimes I'll come out 2 or 3 times before I can settle down in a cubicle and wait, hoping a gay guy will take the cubicle next to me. When one finally does, I get turned on but I am so scared sometimes I shake. I want him to do me and then to get out of there as fast as possible. I guess the other guy feels the same way. Sometimes you run into a bastard who will have you do him and then he takes off before you are satisfied. I get mad but I know how he feels.

Social learning approaches have been among the most influential in treatment programs. Not only have most treatments in sexual anomalies been directed to homosexuality, but the behavior modification approach based on learning theory has been used. This will be discussed later under treatment. Summarizing the previous theories in terms of the stimulus response matrix, they conclude that the homosexual male reacts to males but prefers females. His gender behavior is feminine and he prefers anal intercourse with men but also vaginal intercourse with women. Anxiety prevents him engaging in the latter.

Organic Theories

A final set of approaches may be broadly called organic theories. The homosexual male has been described as an intersex, a "female brain in a male body". It is assumed that the male homosexual may be reacting like a woman. He prefers men sexually and tends to be effeminate. This behavior may be due to his heredity, his blood chemistry, his brain chemistry and/or brain structure. Whereas some physical abnormalities may be evident in some cases, such as Klinefelter's syndrome, the majority seen in psychiatric clinics have superficially normal male bodies. However, this does not mean that they do not have unusual brains with female receptors that may induce them when they are physically mature to desire male sex partners. Nor does it rule out the possibility that they have peculiar genes, the part of sexual make up that carries all heredity.

The genes exist in 46 chromosomes of the human body cells. Two of these chromosomes determine sex. Half come from the mother and half from the father. The sex chromosomes are labeled X or Y. If X from mother pairs with X from father, a girl is born; if X pairs with a Y chromosome, a boy. Sometimes an extra chromosome is present, for example XXY, producing among other things, sexual abnormalities of the genitals (Chapter 14). However, it is possible to show that the external body can look normal and genital sex be appropriate but differ from the chromosomal sex. A second possibility is that the homosexual's hormone chemistry, which is related to sexual behavior in a complex way, may be different. Perhaps they have female hormones rather than male ones, or at least, more of them than heterosexual men do. Perhaps they have a different interaction of the hormones than other men do. This can be studied by analyzing the blood of homosexual versus heterosexual men.

One intriguing hypothesis is that the fetus is subject to unusual hormone activity from the pregnant mother. In particular, there is an excess of female hormones (estrogens) or a reduction of male hormones (androgens) in the blood occurring at a *critical* period of development in the womb. When the fetus is subjected to this unusual hormonal condition, his "brain is feminized" but his genitals and blood chemistry appear normal[133]. As mentioned earlier, such a phenomenon has been demonstrated in lower animals by experimental manipulations of hormone levels in the fetus and this could conceivably happen naturally to humans.

We now turn to the experimental data. Many of the postulates that have been described are based on nonsystematic clinical observations or on speculations with no empirical support. Some of these formulations will be better than others. Some clearly need to be dismissed.

THE EXPERIMENTAL EVIDENCE

An enormous amount of literature is available on homosexuality and the interested reader may wish to turn to source readings[25] [31] [51] [189]. Generally, however, controlled studies pertinent to the origin and treatment of homosexuality are few in number.

Aversion to females and intercourse-phallometric studies. There have been several claims that homosexual men desire the female body in reality but fear operates to induce them to seek a surrogate in the male. They really desire intercourse, perhaps incestuous intercourse, but anal intercourse with a man serves as a substitute outlet. Only a few studies have been conducted using penile plethysmography and standard sex history questionnaires but all of them oppose such an interpretation. First, Freund and his colleagues[54] have shown that the homosexual male's response to females is an inversion of the heterosexual's response.

A paradigm experiment is to show two groups of men pictures of males and females in the nude. One group is heterosexual and the other homosexual, by their own admission and sexual history. The pictures depict males and females standing smiling at the viewer. The age range of photographic subjects is from 6 years to 25 years old. Most important, a set of neutral pictures is included, that is, pictures that are devoid of obvious sexual content or sexual symbols. Penile tumescence changes are recorded by a penile plethysmograph, the phallometer (see Chapter Two). Figure 4.1 shows the

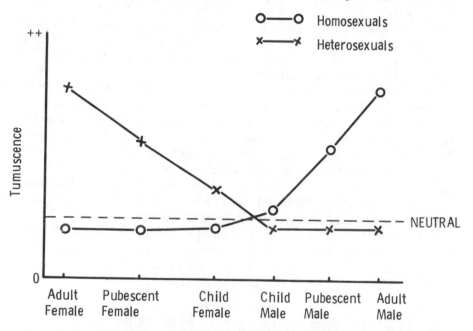

FIG. 4.1   Penile tumescence reactions of homosexual and heterosexual men to male and female sex stimuli.

outcome of such a study. As expected, heterosexual men respond with the largest increase in penile tumescence to mature females. Since pubescent girls are similar in many ways to the adult female, the men react to these girls but not as much as they do to the adult female. Psychologists know this as stimulus generalization. Finally, they react to the child because of her female body as well, but the reaction is smaller still. The smallest reactions occur to the neutral stimuli as predicted. Some reactions occur from expectations of the subjects that they will see erotic pictures, or as attention reactions, or, as simple random variation due to penile volume changes from uncontrolled or unknown sources. It is therefore important to include neutral stimuli to control for such measurement errors. In this study, we know that normal men respond more to the 6-year-old female than to the neutral pictures even though the reactions are small. This result is statistically significant but if neutral pictures were not included, we would not know that fact. Note also that all the reactions of heterosexual men to nude males of all ages are in the neutral zone and, in fact represent only random variation. This suggests that the male body has a very low, or no erotic valence for heterosexual men. This profile for normal men is typical and has been repeated many times in laboratory tests.

Now, examining the homosexual men's responses, we see almost a mirror image of the heterosexual profile. Their largest responses are to adult males, secondly to pubescent boys and least to male children. Unlike heterosexuals' reactions to female children, homosexuals' responses to male children are closer to the neutral zone. The same explanation of stimulus generalization can be applied again. Note also that the homosexuals' responses to females are only random variations in the neutral zone as well. Classifying men as either hetero– or homosexual on this test is highly discriminating because approximately 95% are correctly identified by statistical analysis. Much of the 5% error is due to research participants reacting indiscriminately to all stimulus materials or not reacting at all. One could say they are "polymorphous perverse" but apparent "expectation set" of seeing "pornographic materials" causes overreactivity. One normal research participant in another study noted, "I feel stupid now. I was so excited about seeing sexy movies I couldn't restrain myself. I realized I overdid it when I had an erection to the first picture of a nude male. Overall, the pictures were dull, but I really felt stupid when I had an erection to that first landscape."

McConaghy[121] basically reproduced the above research findings using similar procedures but his prediction of hetero– and homosexuality was only 85%. Although this is still satisfactory, some difference in results may be due to scoring of penile reactions, and to use of his rapid presentation of stimuli, which may not allow detumescence to occur between subsequent stimulus presentations. Both studies suggest that there is very little overlap in reactions of homosexual men to males versus females. So if there is any erotic reaction to females on the part of homosexual men, it is generally so small that we cannot detect it by this method.

It can be argued that fear would reduce any reaction to females and we would not detect it here. If, however, the homosexual men were sexually aroused and were shown a female, they might show an aversive or fear reaction. Freund and his colleagues investigated this question in three experiments. In the first study, groups of heterosexual and homosexual male volunteers were compared[54]. All were sexually prearoused by stimuli that they preferred. When they were prearoused to a predetermined level of penile tumescence, they were shown one of the following sets of pictures: adults of the nonpreferred sex (for example, females for homosexual subjects), pubescents of the nonpreferred sex, neutrals and, to have clearly aversive stimuli, color pictures of skin diseases (cancer, leprosy, etc.). Penile detumescence was measured and research participants' reports of disgust were recorded. Both groups of volunteers responded in the same way. There was a large decrease in penile volume to the skin disease stimuli and they were rated by the experimental subjects as quite disgusting. Reactions to the nonpreferred sex pictures were no different from reactions to neutral stimuli. The homosexual men did not rate pictures of females as disgusting but the heterosexual men did find pictures of males disgusting, although not as disgusting as the pictures of skin diseases. This study did not support the aversion theory of homosexuality. Possibly, the anxiety is only aroused by the vulva itself as Melanie Klein indicated. Another study investigated this issue[59].

The same experimental paradigm was used in a second study but only homosexual subjects were used and the stimuli differed. The latter were parts of the female body, namely, the face, breasts, and the fully exposed vulva as well as neutral stimuli of landscapes. Whereas there were no differences in penile reactions to the stimuli, prearoused homosexual men rated the vulva as more disgusting than anything else but the breasts were also considered disgusting. If one accepted the verbal report of the participants, one could conclude that the theory was supported. If one accepted the penile reactions, it would not. At least their verbal report of their reactions did not affect their physiological responses to the stimuli. These results parallel the heterosexual ratings from study one. Unfortunately, no heterosexual controls were used for comparison in this study.

Finally, it is possible that intercourse itself would produce some reaction. In a third study[55], homosexual men were prearoused again to criterion tumescence and then they heard audiotaped descriptions of five classes of stimuli. Four of these were the progressive stages in courtship: searching for a female partner, pretactile interactions with her in a courtship, foreplay, and heterosexual intercourse. The fifth was, as usual, neutral statements. The surprising results were that homosexual men responded to intercourse and foreplay significantly more than to the other stimuli. The prearoused men continued to respond with increased tumescence rather than showing an aversive decrease in penile volume. In contrast, their verbal reports indicated that they found intercourse and foreplay quite disgusting. Even so, no aversive physiological reactions occurred. It is possible to be disgusted and sexually aroused at the same time. Heterosexual men who are having homoerotic contact note this sort of experience. However, a recurrent theme in studies employing penile plethysmography is that verbal reports do not agree with penile reactions in many instances.

The discrepancy may simply mean the subjects are lying, are unaware, or, are careless about reporting. This seems unlikely in volunteer subjects who are well instructed on what to do in the study. There are at least two other possible explanations. First, when working in the range of mild sexual arousal, the penis may react before the subject is aware of it, that is, there is a lag in recognizing physiological reactions. In fact, the erotic profile in Fig. 4.1 may be obtained from subjects who are unaware of reacting at all[53]. Some penile reactions are subliminal but show the direction of erotic preference anyway.

A second possible explanation is that the cognitive appraisal of erotic arousal is more complex than the physiological one. Other extraneous factors may enter a decision to consider a situation erotic. It seems the presence of a disgusting situation reduces the positive valence of a potentially erotic situation. Oral genital heterosexual interaction is an instance of a sexual act that is usually highly stimulating but considered disgusting nonetheless by some college students[47]. One might expect that research subjects will rate it as disgusting but be sexually aroused and show penile tumescence to such stimuli. On the other hand, positively presented stimuli may enhance the erotic valence of a given stimulus. A beautifully colored and aesthetic picture of a mature female may arouse the same males more than a plainer less attractively presented one. Such parameters have not been well studied to date but they may offer some explanation of differences in self reports and penile reactions.

In the preceding studies, aversive reactions were clearly shown by penile detumescence to grotesque pictures of skin diseases but not to pictures of female bodies, to their vulvas, or to intercourse. This certainly weakens the theories that anxiety is an important factor in homosexuality although verbal reports of disgust may be construed as offering some support. However, the theory must contend with the self reported disgust reactions of heterosexuals to the nude male body.

My colleagues and I[99] examined the aversion theories in a *therapy analogue study*. Treating patients is a complicated business and it is not always easy to control an experimental laboratory situation. However, it is possible to study some of the important variables in treatment in analogue studies on either normals or on patients in a laboratory experiment. One common method used to study fear is to examine the effect of anxiety reduction procedures on snake phobia in normals. For example, a therapist may argue that the sequencing of two procedures is important. He can vary them in the laboratory with the fear of snakes in normal volunteers to determine if he is correct.

A study on homosexuality would be conducted in analogue form as follows. If homosexuals are afraid of females, then fear reducing procedures should be effective in changing their behavior toward women. Reduce fear and the homosexual male should respond more to females erotically. In our study[99], homosexual and heterosexual men were compared in their reactions to pictures of nude men and women, and to neutral pictures. Penile circumference was measured and verbal reports of physical sexual arousal were obtained. The two groups of men were compared under three experimental conditions: under relaxation, under increased general arousal, and under an untreated control condition. In the relaxation condition, the participants were seated in a quiet room in a lazy boy chair with lowered light level. They heard a taped instruction in Jacobson's[85] progressive relaxation, (see Chapter 3) which is used in reciprocal inhibition therapy and which helps many people to relax, some to a point where they may fall asleep. The other experimental condition, increased arousal, was used as a point of reference. A loud static noise was presented to each subject to increase his general level of alertness. This latter experimental manipulation was ineffective and we can ignore it here.

The aversion theories would predict that the relaxed homosexual should react more to the female and less to his surrogate stimulus, the male. In fact, the homosexual subjects did not react to females differently from neutral pictures under any condition. Nor did they report differential reactions. Contrary to theory, they reacted more to males when relaxed than they did in the control condition. The analogous result occurred for the heterosexual subjects as well. They reacted more to females under relaxation than in the control condition but not at all to males or neutrals. One might conclude that such a treatment procedure would be ineffective with homosexual patients. In any event, it did not support the aversion theories of homosexuality.

Sex history studies. The sex history questionnaires of exclusive homosexual versus exclusive heterosexual men may be examined to see if they support any of the theories. When my colleagues and I[98][137] examined homosexuals' self reports of erotic behavior we found that they rated sexual interaction with men as pleasant and not disgusting. The most common behaviors were kissing, mutual masturbation and fellatio. Eight in 10 homosexual research volunteers said they desired to fellate a male and 9 in 10 wanted to be fellated. They averaged 8 partners whom they fellated and who fellated them. Seven in 10 desired anal intercourse and were not disgusted by it. They averaged 2–3 partners who reciprocated in anal intercourse, about 1/3 of the number with whom they reciprocated fellatio. Manosevitz[109] also found that homosexual men preferred mutual masturbation and fellatio. Kinsey[90] found anal intercourse is practiced by homosexual men about half as often as fellatio and mutual masturbation. He maintained that they do not find anal intercourse particularly arousing and only an occasional individual can climax in this way. The heterosexual research participants in our study[137] on the other hand, were less likely to try anal intercourse with women. Perhaps this reflects an unwillingness of the female since 5 in 10 are not disgusted by it, but on the average it has been tried only once or not at all. Thus whereas anal intercourse is more common in homosexuals than in heterosexuals, it does not emerge as a particularly dominant behavior. Its etiological significance may therefore be questioned.

Masters & Johnson[116] described anal intercourse as pleasurable for their homosexual research participants and also note that the love making observed in their laboratory revealed a much greater concern to please sex partners. They observed a tenderness of homosexuals for their long term partners not observed in heterosexual partners who tended to be "task oriented." However, they presented no quantitative data.

When we[137] questioned exclusive homosexuals, about half admitted to desires for vaginal intercourse and half were not disgusted by it. In contrast, only 2 in 10 heterosexuals admitted to a desire for homosexual relations and 8 in 10 were disgusted by it. One could argue that heterosexuals show more homosexual aversion than the converse. Freund[51] describes the attempts of homosexual men at vaginal intercourse as curiosities, as attempts at social conformity, or, trying to "go straight". This curiosity appears to parallel homosexual experiences in heterosexual men.

Finally, we[98] [137] found an unusual behavior occurring frequently in homosexual men; outdoor masturbation with no one around. This act is more common to exhibitionists and may reflect narcissism and/or exhibitionistic tendencies. This will be discussed again under exhibitionism.

Homosexuality and neurosis. Phallometric and Sex History studies have not supported unequivocally any of the aversion theories. Perhaps a broader frame of reference would offer support. Clinical data on psychiatric problems in homosexuals would be informative. Of course, seeing only patients who are homosexual can be misleading. If only heterosexual psychiatric patients were seen, one could conclude that heterosexuals are all sick. Should the clinician generalize this conclusion to the community at large? It is difficult to know the incidence of psychiatric problems in homosexual men since social ostracism prevents many of them from identifying themselves[3] [134]. Moreover, there may be hostility to mental health workers because we have not helped their cause and, in fact, may have harmed it by our theories. We may solve this dilemma in two ways.

First, we can examine clinical cases of homosexuality and see if there are any signs of anxiety, especially toward females. If diagnoses of neurosis are prominent, then the theory would have some support. We cannot accept just any pathology but only diagnoses in which anxiety is the critical element. Since people come to clinics because they have problems, one has to expect some pathology but not necessarily anxiety. Second, we can search for "healthy homosexuals". If we manage to obtain the help of homosexual men in the community who have never been hospitalized for a psychiatric illness and who seem normal in other respects, for example, they are adjusted socially in the sense of having a steady job, friends, and enjoy the basics of life, we can determine if they still show pathology in psychological tests. Unfortunately, this question has been embroiled with a political issue[132][150].

The Gay Liberation Movement has its proponents who are eager to show that homosexuals are normal and are not sick, so the reason for equal rights is all the more important. Some researchers and the gay activists have examined the members of homosexual clubs whereas clinically based individuals and groups who maintain that homosexuality is a sickness which needs to be treated[173] continue to examine their clinical samples. Thus both groups may bias the outcome of their studies in expected directions.

Hart and his associates[73] have reviewed problems of nonpatient research participants and of research methodology in studies of homosexuality. They note the experimenter bias just described. Design problems that they discuss have been noted throughout the chapter and will not be repeated here. When research participants are recruited through clubs and agencies other than psychiatric hospitals, the studies show that the homosexuals are variable in their personality characteristics but they fall within normal limits as one might expect.

Hooker conducted perhaps the most famous controlled study[82]. She compared homosexuals from homophile organizations with heterosexuals from other community organizations matched for age, education, and intelligence quotient. She then had clinicians rate the participants blindly on their adjustment. The experienced clinicians could not discriminate the two groups. Saghir and Robins[156] did a similar study with the same outcome.

Loney[105] studied a sample of male and female homosexuals who were acquaintances, friends or customers at a bar. The research volunteers were unselected for psychiatric history or gay liberation club membership. Thirty-two percent of the homosexual men had had some form of therapy for homosexuality per se. An additional 10% had therapy for some other reason. One has to wonder if this truly represents a higher incidence of psychiatric consultation than that in the general population. Since homosexuality is considered a problem, some men may seek treatment or at least advice. Length of time in treatment varied from 1 session to 3 years. Unfortunately, Loney does not give us an average time in treatment. Two other controlled studies[34][164] on nonclinical cases of homosexuality showed that adjustment was generally satisfactory and significant pathology absent.

One of the major supporting studies of psychoanalytic theory suggesting homosexuals are neurotic was carried out by the Biebers and their associates[19][20][22]. One hundred homosexual men undergoing psychoanalysis were examined by their therapists on a questionnaire that investigated developmental history and parent child relationships. It was concluded that the patients were in fact suffering from a neurotic condition. One might expect support since the Biebers asked psychoanalysts' opinions on what their patients were like rather than asking the patients themselves[18][182]. Although a control group was used, the questionnaire employed was not assessed for validity and only superficially for reliability.

Two studies by the present writer and his associates also examined the issue of neurosis in homosexuality. In the first study[98] a group of community volunteer homosexuals and a group of homosexual patients were compared with two groups of transsexuals, and a group of normal heterosexuals. The patient group of homosexuals presented considerable emotional disturbance on the MMPI (Minnesota Multiphasic Personality Inventory) and evidence of other clinical pathology such as increased thoughts of suicide and attempts at suicide. They displayed psychotic features on the MMPI whereas the normal homosexual group did not. The most prominent scales were depression and schizophrenia as one might expect in an inpatient sample. The results were not influenced by naive lying, responding in a socially desirable way or by education and IQ. This study represented both sides of the political controversy and came up with the results of both groups. Patients were emotionally disturbed but nonpatients were normal. Note, however, that neurosis was not a significant factor in the results suggesting that the psychoanalytic theory was not supported in a clinical sample. The second study was also interesting although it examined only clinical cases of various sexual anomalies. The homosexual sample consisted of patients who presented with psychotic or other emotional disturbances and those who were seeking advice about "coming out" or about altering their homosexuality because of social pressure. Even within this group, there were cases without evident pathology. Thus the studies in total did not support the findings that neurosis or other pathology is a necessary component of homosexuality.

Stoller[177] raised the question whether homosexuality is a diagnosis in itself. He argues that a diagnosis is a syndrome or constellation of signs and symptoms shared by a group of people. The signs are visible to the observer and have underlying dynamics. Homosexuality does not satisfy this definition. Because there is only a sexual preference, it is not a constellation of signs or symptoms, and different people with homosexual preferences have different psychodynamics underlying their sexual behavior. Quite different life experiences can cause these dynamics and behaviors. He therefore recommended homosexuality be removed from the American Psychiatric Association nomenclature.

In summary, controlled studies show that, with the exceptions of a tendency to increased femininity, homosexual men do not have a consistent MMPI or clinical profile and do not manifest anxiety as their major problem[30 34 56 73 82 95 98 105 111 156 164 165 178]. Bell and Weinberg[13] suggested there are "homosexual types." This appears to be misleading. One can expect as much diversity in the personalities of gay men as one finds in the general population, although certain settings or cultural subgroups may present a higher frequency of certain personality traits than other groups would. Moreover, statistical methods of cluster analysis like those used by Bell and Weinberg in their study are fraught with serious methodological difficulties[35 170]. Although some groupings will emerge from any cluster analysis, their replicability and validity is seldom ascertained. Profiles of homosexual patients are as varied as those of the general psychiatric population, suggesting that homosexuality co-occurs by chance with various psychiatric problems. Second, "healthy homosexuals" can be found who do not manifest psychiatric problems unless, of course, the homosexuality itself is considered a problem. In any case, the postulated dynamics are not observed when systematic studies are done.

Parent child relations of homosexual men.   Another approach to studying the possible emotional disturbance of homosexual men has been to examine parent child relationships during childhood. Unfortunately this must involve retrospective reports of research participants. The Biebers' book stirred up interest in this problem in their study of homosexuals in psychoanalysis. They asked therapists to answer questions about their patients and the homosexual was characterized as having a poor relationship with father and a close binding intimate relationship with mother. Although a control group was used, the data were one step further away from a retrospective report since the therapists rather than the patients answered the questions. One again has to ask whether the fact that the research participants were patients in addition to being homosexuals is important.

Evans[39] improved the Biebers' et al study by developing the questionnaire for self administration and he used it with heterosexual and homosexual male groups. He described his findings as remarkably similar to the Biebers but disagrees that a pathological relationship was evidenced in the experimental group. Research participants did describe themselves more often than heterosexuals as frail and clumsy as children, less often athletic, more often fearful of physical injury, avoided physical fights, played with girls, and were loners who seldom played baseball or competitive games. They described typical mothers more often as puritanical, cold to men, as insisting on being the centre of attention, as making sons their confidant; were seductive to them, allied against fathers, openly preferred sons to fathers, interfered with heterosexual activities in adolescence, discouraged masculine attitudes, and encouraged feminine ones. Nevertheless, the combination of close binding intimate mother and paternal hostility with detachment was not observed as often as Bieber et al. suggested. Only 28% of the sample had such a combination and 11% of the controls were presumably did not become homosexual had it as well. Evans notes that many of the homosexual relationships appeared to be warm and as good if not better than heterosexual ones. The results were replicated in another study by Evans[40] and in a different setting on nonpatient homosexual males by Thompson and his colleagues[183] with basically the same outcome. However no one checked the scale for validity or reliability.

Three additional studies based on clinical interviews of patients provided contradictory results. In the first study, Buhrich and McConaghy[26] found little evidence of pathological relationships for homosexual patients with their mothers. In the other two studies, Freund[60] and Gebhard and their associates[64] found homosexual men had a significantly poorer relationship with father than heterosexuals and more often were closer to mother. Parent child relations and degree of feminine gender identity were not correlated in the Freund et al's study.

The mounting evidence appears negative for the theories. Nonetheless, all the above studies on parent child relations had a serious limitation in that no standardized test was used in any case. The Bieber questionnaire and its self administered expanded version were never checked for validity and only a few items were checked for reliability. Thus the questions asked may be poor, bias the research participants to respond in an expected way and/or they may not give the same answers on two occasions.

Three other studies used a standardized parent child relationship questionnaire with some demonstrated reliability and validity. In the first study Paitich and I[136] administered homosexual patients the Clarke Parent Child Relations Questionnaire (PCR), which contains a variety of measures: mother's aggression to respondent, father's aggression to respondent, respondent's aggression to mother, to father, mother's aggression to father and father's aggression to mother; mother's competence, father's competence, mother's affection, father's affection, mother's strictness, father's strictness, mother identification, father identification, mother's indulgence and father's indulgence on the respondent. Relationships with fathers were most prominent. The research participants said they exchanged hostilities more often with fathers who were low in affection and the sons in turn did not identify with them. Fathers were also considered hostile to mothers who in turn indulged their sons. Heterosexual nonpatients on the other hand reported low aggression to father. Very similar results were obtained by Bene in a second controlled study using the projective Bene-Anthony Family Relations Test[15] with nonpatient homosexuals and heterosexuals.

In the third study Paitich, Steiner and I[98] compared patient and nonpatient homosexuals, and transsexuals to heterosexual nonpatients on the Clarke PCR. Interestingly, mother indulgence occurred only in the homosexual patient group who also considered fathers' competence and affection to be low and their sons identified less with them. The nonpatient homosexuals were not different from normals. The scales of the questionnaire used were shown to be unbiased by IQ, naive lying, or by responding in a socially desirable way. Therefore, to some extent, it controls for community volunteer versus patient status differences present in other studies of homosexual groups. Overall, it seems the parent child relations of homosexual men can be normal and if they are pathological, it need not be linked to homosexuality per se.

Femininity and feminine gender identity.   Only one feature is consistent in the findings on homosexuality—increased femininity and/or increased feminine gender identity[56 96 98 103 109 110 160 178 190]. A distinction can be made between femininity and feminine gender identity. The former implies taking on female behaviors and/or enjoying female activities and tasks in a given culture. Many educated men, for example, enjoy plants, the theater, ballet, and so forth, activities that are considered generally to be feminine interests. Such men would feel nonetheless that they are men and not women. Gender identity, on the other hand, implies a desire to be one sex or the other. Some men not only enjoy female activities and interests but think that psychologically, they are women and may wish to be changed physically into women. Whereas femininity itself in men is not usually a problem, cross gender identification often is. Many normal heterosexual men show some femininity but few show feminine gender identity. Education and femininity may interact in complex ways that are not well understood at present[110 120]. On the other hand, about 2/3 of homosexual men show some varying degrees of femininity or feminine gender identity and at some point in their lives, wished they were women[57 62]. We do not know at present the intensity or duration of their cross gender identity. Freund et al[58] found that the rate of homosexual development and the extent of heterosexual experience are weakly related to the degree of feminine gender identity. Earlier onset of homosexual interest was correlated with less heterosexual experience and a higher degree of feminine gender identity. This finding supports the psychoanalytic theory of increased feminine gender identification in homosexual men. However, it does not explain the 1/3 who have normal masculine identification. If gender confusion or identity is a precursor of homosexuality, how can 1/3 not be feminine identified? Moreover, the degree of feminine gender identity in the homosexual male seems to be mild compared to the extreme feminine gender identity that occurs in the transsexual who seeks an operation to change his anatomical sex. Less than 3% of the homosexual males score in the range of the transsexuals on a feminine gender identity scale[62]. The case of causality of gender identity in homosexuality seems rather weakened by this finding. Nevertheless, the two are linked and there are several explanations why this is so.

Some theorists, especially those working with children (see Chapter 6), assume that feminine gender identity *causes* the male sex object preference, or assume the latter is an integral aspect of gender identity. The child first cross gender identifies and/or takes on feminine behaviors. His parents may encourage this in one way or another, either by positively reinforcing female behaviors and/or punishing male behavior. Being attracted to the male body is a segment of female behavior, albeit a special segment. The male child, therefore, develops a preference for sexual interaction with men as part of his gender identity. Research with effeminate boys, although limited in quantity, has shown that some such boys do later become homosexuals. If one could change gender behavior in childhood so that the treated boys do not develop later sexual interest in males, the causal link of gender identity to homosexuality would be supported to some degree.

The opposite theory, although plausible, does not seem to be feasible. That is, sex object preference for males may cause feminine behavior or feminine gender identity. Since genital sexual behavior is only obviously manifested at puberty, such a theory seems less likely. However, sex play does occur in the preschooler, including attempts at intercourse[87]. Among the most prominent theories of human development, Freud's theory specifies a "sexual" period of development before 5 years of age. A preference for male bodies may develop at this early stage or earlier, perhaps reflecting a genetic or organic factor. Female behaviors of the homosexual later in life may be a convenient and/or desirable way of attracting male attention in a world that is so emphatically heterosexual. Another possibility is that homosexual men are less bound by conventional sex roles and freely adopt bits and pieces of whatever roles are congruent with their personalities. Note that the tendency to increase feminine gender identity is weak in this group and may be a transitory speculation on the dilemma of being at odds with a heterosexual society.

The final possibility is that sex object preference for males and feminine gender identity are independent and co-occur, perhaps by chance. The vast majority of heterosexual men are male identified and prefer women. Nevertheless, it is possible to find all combinations of object preference and gender identity in men. Consider Table 4.1, which simplifies the situation for illustration. Assume that gender identity (GI) is dichotomous as male or

TABLE 4.1
A Comparison of Gender Identity and Sex Object Preference

| | | Object Preference | |
		Men	Women
	Male	A Homosexuals	B Heterosexuals Normals
Gender Identity			
	Female	C Homosexuals Transsexuals	D Transvestites Transsexuals

female and similarly, sex object preference is either for men or women. This 2 × 2 combination allows four possibilities: A. Male GI and prefer men; B. Male GI and prefer women; C. Female GI and prefer men; D. Female GI and prefer women. If gender identity caused sex object preference or vice versa, one would not expect to fill all four cells of the Table but only the 2 pertinent ones, that is, male GI would result in a sex object preference for women, female GI in a preference for men. One should not find cases in cells A and D. In fact, all four cells can be filled.

As noted above, about 1/3 of homosexual males are male identified, 2/3 female identified in varying degrees, occupying cells A and C in Table 4.1. Normal heterosexuals occupy cell B but transvestites and transsexuals (Chapter 6) occupy cells C and D as well. Transsexuals show extreme feminine gender identity and want an operation to be changed into females. One would assume a homosexual orientation in such men and in fact many are. However, some are also heterosexual and erotically prefer the female body over the male body (see Chapter 6). An example is *Mr. K*, who applied for surgery to be changed into a woman. He also had phallometric testing which clearly indicated reactions to women but little to men. When confronted with the findings, he said:

Mr. K: Oh yes, I know I like women's bodies sexually; I'm not attracted to men at all.

Doctor: Why then do you want an operation to become a female.

Mr. K: Because I am a woman. I feel comfortable dressed as a woman. When I come home from work, I change into my dress and I just relax like that.

Doctor: But if you had your penis removed, how would you relate to women sexually?

Mr. K: I guess that would make me a lesbian. Yes. That's what I want to be, a lesbian.

The transvestite shows a marked heterosexuality and vehemently denies any homosexual interest, perhaps because of the focus of clinical examination on his interest in female clothes. His object preference is for women—after himself masturbating in female attire. Yet, there is a strong if sexually focused interest in the feminine that suggest feminine gender identity. Unfortunately, researchers have only begun to investigate this question.

Gender identity has been discussed as if it were a unitary entity but this may not be so. Many facets are contained in femininity and many measures of it are poor and/or clearly multidimensional[67][106]. Perhaps the feeling of "feminine" is different in homosexuals than in women. The idea of male role and female role in sexual interaction must either be parodied or absent when two men interact sexually. Their interaction may be completely different but more information is needed on this question.

Bem[14] has offered a new approach to the problem in using the concept of androgyny. The term assumes "masculinity" and "femininity" are independent dimensions and men and women possess varying degrees of both. Although the idea is promising, there is no satisfactory measure of androgyny available. The widely discussed Bem Sex Role Inventory or Androgyny scale has been shown to splinter into many factors[187] that masculinity and femininity items tend to be bipolar[166] and the scale has other statistical problems[193] including a tendency for research participants to respond in a socially desirable way[14]. In examining androgyny in homosexual men, there were no statistical significant differences in my unpublished data but Hooberman[81] found gay university students scored lower on masculinity, higher on femininity and higher on androgyny compared to heterosexuals. The gays also scored higher than heterosexuals on Freund's et al FGI scale but did not differ from them on a measure of self esteem. Perhaps a better measure of androgyny would produce consistent results but this remains a question for future research. At present, the androgyny measure available has the same problems as masculinity–femininity measures.

Biological Factors in Homosexuality. Another set of theories suggests that homosexual men differ from heterosexual men on some organic factor.

Heredity. If heredity differed, the genes of homosexual men would differ. The genes carry our total heredity but the development of this genetic material can be influenced by many environmental factors, including the uterine environment provided by the mother for her fetus. There is a considerable volume of material available on organic and hereditary issues in homosexuality but the reader should be cautioned that methodology is frequently poor when it comes to ascertaining the homosexual status of the research participants.

Usually self report of homosexuality is all that is used in the investigation. No sexual history is taken to determine the exclusiveness of the homosexual behavior or to determine if any other sexually anomalous behavior is present. Men who have a significant amount of homosexual experience will answer ads requesting research volunteers but further questioning may indicate that their preference is heterosexual. In one extreme case in our laboratory, a heterosexual male who had over 20 female sex partners and who had sexual contact only 5 times during one weekend with another male sincerely applied for the advertisement we posted around the university asking for "homosexual volunteers." In many of the studies we are not privileged to know if they even have that much experience and are simply accepted at their word that they are homosexual. In some of my research projects up to 50% of applicants have been screened out based on a thorough procedure, which in perspective makes self report and a small number of cases appear inadequate. A proper study should have some validation of the participants' reports that they are in fact homosexual. They may mean something different from what the researcher does. In the patient population, a wide range of sexually anomalous behavior may co-occur with the homosexual behavior. Since a considerable number of normal men engage in homosexual acts at some point in their lives, it is to be expected that patients will do so too. A *preference* for the homosexual behavior must therefore be established as discussed in Chapter Two.

To illustrate the problem, one of the earlier reports using a large sample size[94] examined prison records for "homosexual activity". Some of these men were married and possibly heterosexual according to the author, but he had no other criterion at the time. A later genetic study[139] used "homosexual patients" but they ranged from 1 to 6 on the Kinsey scale indicating some were predominantly heterosexual. No further explanation is offered for this incongruity. Often individuals doing such research are trained in physiology or genetics rather than in psychology, psychiatry or sexology. This limits their appreciation of the complexities of homosexuality. An inter-disciplinary collaborative study would be beneficial in answering the questions in this area of research.

A second important consideration is that genetics and biomedical science is an evolving field and knowledge seems to grow in leaps and bounds. Often studies have poor methodology from our perspective because a discovery has outdated previous findings. This can happen in 5 or 10 years.

We now know for example, that earlier studies that examined the urine of homosexual and heterosexual men for hormone differences were poor studies because the newer radioimmuno assay procedures measuring the same hormones in the blood are much more precise (See [153] for example).

A third problem in studying hereditary factors is that large samples are needed and they should be representative of the population. Traits have to be judiciously studied. If a certain trait appears once in a million times in the population and we expect to find it in homosexuals who appear in 4% of the population, we can be looking for a needle in a hay stack because it should only occur by chance four times in 100 million. Moreover, it is usually impossible to know if we have a representative sample of homosexual men. They volunteer their services for our research and we cannot know who does not volunteer. Other problems which pervade the whole area of research are also present and Bell[12] has suggested we go back to the drawing board to research homosexuality. I suggest the reader treat the findings skeptically and with caution.

Some earlier work reviewed by Money[133] suggested that homosexual men had mothers and/or fathers who were older at the time of their son's conception. Moreover, they had more older brothers[1] [167] [168] [179]. Perhaps a change in the mother's ova with aging or with repeated births was a factor in developing homosexual offspring. A logical link between femininity in homosexual men and a greater number of brothers is not clear for developmental theories. It could be argued that an all female environment would encourage feminine gender identity in a young male but an all male environment would not.

Kallman[88] also found greater occurrence of homosexuality in twins than would be expected by chance. His ingenious approach to studying heredity was to compare identical and fraternal twins and nontwin sibs. It is expected that hereditary traits would be most evident in the identical twins who presumably have identical heredity. With increasing genetic distance through fraternal twins and nontwin sibs, the discrepancy would be greater. Allen[4] criticized Kallman's study because there was a 100% concordance of homosexuality between identical twins. A perfect finding in any of the social and biological sciences raises suspicion and Kallman later retracted his results[4]. Serious methodological problems in his study made any results highly suspect. Money notes that current research evidence suggests that even cytogenetically identical twins may not have the identical number of chromosomes, illustrated by certain cases of mongolism and Turner's syndrome. That is, as far as sexual heredity is concerned, identical twins may not be as identical as we thought 30 years ago.

Other studies have provided inconsistent ratios of brothers and sisters to a point where Money suggests it probably represents statistical random variation. However, the suggestive finding remains that homosexuals are the later children of aging mothers.

If the heredity of homosexual men differed from average heterosexual men, the logical place to expect differences would be in the chromosomes carrying sexual heredity. Unfortunately, the few studies done have not demonstrated signifiant differences between homosexuals and heterosexuals[139 143 147 152 153]. Two of these studies have searched for the so called Barr body which was earlier discovered to be present in the cell nucleus of female mammals but not in males. Although Pritchard[143] examined the chromosomes themselves, the latter being the better technique, Money[133] has criticized these studies in a review paper indicating that too few research participants were used and positive findings were associated with the presence of some other abnormality. When homosexual men with no physical abnormality are studied, they do not differ from normal heterosexuals. However, Money suggests that a chromosome count of a large number of homosexuals might disclose some hereditary difference. In the meantime, there is no proven basis for a genetic theory of homosexuality.

The genetic studies also confused femininity and object preference. The homosexual is often viewed as the intersex between a man and a woman and to be effeminate. This is not necessarily so. It may be best to separate out the gender identity component and the object choice component of their behavior. This is why research studies have looked to male versus female differences in behavior rather than differences in heterosexual versus homosexual men. Some other contrast in these two groups in terms of heredity may be important.

Heredity is complex and possible differences may appear but they have not been found in sex related chromosomal matter or the Barr body to date. Allen[4] has suggested that homosexuality can be treated and this proves it is not genetic. However, it is erroneous to equate changeability with environment and unchangeability with heredity[5]. For example, an incision into the occipital area of the brain (environmental) produces irreversible blindness whereas cretinism or dwarfism is a hereditary condition, which responds to thyroid gland treatment in many cases.

Prenatal environment.   One can also examine the prenatal environment for unusual features in homosexuals. Although this has not been investigated in humans, it has been shown in lower animals that altering hormonal chemistry can produce physically normal looking animals that show cross-sex mating behavior[133]. This interesting hypothesis is difficult to investigate in humans, because we cannot go back in time to reconstruct the abnormal transitory hormonal state the mother may have experienced during her pregnancy. Nor at present can we properly examine the hypothalamus, the part of the brain most likely influenced by this state. Moreover, generalizing from lower animals to humans is often questionable.

Human society complicates our animal existence greatly so that even the theory of evolution is defied. Man does not adapt to his environment anatomically to survive, rather, he changes his environment to meet his needs. We do not grow fur in cold climates, we build fires and wear clothes. This does not mean that humans are uninfluenced by their animal existence but that the human case is complex and we should be cautious about generalizing from lower animals to humans. A hope for testing the theory of a transitory hormonal state in the fetus may come from some residue either in the brain or blood sex hormones. Perhaps that abnormal fetal state permanently altered the fetus's brain receptors and when technology is developed to the point where we can examine it, we will know.

Brain waves and intelligence of homosexual men.   Very few studies have examined the actual brains of homosexual men. In one controlled study that examined brain waves or electroencephalograms of homosexual and heterosexual men, Papatheophilou, James and Orwin[138] found both groups were normal. This measure is fairly poor, however, since approximately 20% to 30% of EEGs are abnormal in the general population. This makes it difficult to scrutinize small differences between groups. More recent technological developments in the area of brain scans and in examining the brain chemistry of the intact brain may be more fruitful. These studies remain to be done.

An interesting corollary of the feminizing of the homosexual brain is the postulate that homosexuals should be more intelligent than the nonfeminized male. Weinrich[188] has reviewed eight studies and half did not perform statistical tests of significance but he concluded that homosexuals tended to be brighter. Selection criteria in the remaining studies were poor and the conclusion of an overall trend of homosexual men to be brighter should be treated with caution. Weinrich offers several hypotheses why homosexuals are more intelligent: unintelligent people do not recognize their sexual anomaly; homosexuals are ostracized by peers as children and work harder at school as a result; or intelligent children are ostracized and become gays; since homosexuals have both male and female components, they combine the male spatial and female verbal ability to score higher overall; and prenatal hormones may affect both IQ and sexual orientation. Most of these are untenable and lack rigorous empirical support. It has yet to be established that homosexual men are above average in intelligence generally. It is especially difficult to know if one has a representative sample of all homosexuals so the question would appear to be a moot one. In one controlled study Raboch and Sipova[148] examined the Raven Standard Progressive Matrices, which is heralded as a culture fair test of intelligence. The research participants were feminine and nonfeminine homosexuals, male transsexuals and eunuchoids as well as normal heterosexuals. All results were within normal limits although the authors argued that the homosexuals tended to be brighter. Even the normal subjects in this group scored four points above average. Although there was no statistical test performed, enough information was provided to do one. The homosexual groups did not differ significantly from controls overall. Moreover, there was no difference in the feminine groups and more masculine groups. We are not told how participants were classified into these groups either.

The myth remains that homosexuals are the creative geniuses of society throughout history. Oscar Wilde[49] admitted to being homosexual in a Victorian society that was quite punitive to such behavior. His works stand out in literature as a measure of his ability. Other claims have been made that Shakespeare was also homosexual[17] and had a love affair with his patron, the Earl of Southampton. His attitude to women and men in his literary works is noted as a reflection of his homosexuality. Similarly, Leonardo da Vinci who ranks among the greatest geniuses of all time was thought by some writers to be homosexual. Pacion[135] asks in his report if Leonardo was an active or a latent homosexual, or perhaps just impotent. We do not know and the whole suggestion that he was homosexual is simply surmise.

Even if these geniuses were homosexual, it does not indicate that all great men are homosexual or that there is a link between the two. Systematic study of this point is difficult because it is almost impossible at present to adequately sample the homosexual population to see what the average intelligence of the group is. Research studies often conducted at universities are based on students who tend to be above average intelligence anyway and the results are biased. At this point in time, the association of unusual brain structure, intelligence and homosexuality remains only a hypothesis without supporting facts.

Hormone profiles.   In the meantime, hormones have been more extensively studied in homosexual research participants but results have not clarified our knowledge[130] [152] [161]. Based on male–female distinctions one might expect homosexual men to have lower levels of "male sex hormones", namely, testosterone, and/or higher levels of female hormones, estrogens, leutinizing and follicle stimulating hormones. If research studies are examined, they are confusing and inconsistent. Based on existing reports, one can expect every possible outcome, that is, homosexual men have more, less and similar amounts of male hormones compared to heterosexuals.

Meyer-Bahlberg[130] has reviewed the present literature and has summarized the many problems that make the results of these studies inconclusive. In addition to the poor validation criterion noted at the beginning of this section, there are the added problems of using only a few cases, poorly matching the control participants for age, time at which blood is drawn, and, in the assay procedure used. As noted earlier (Chapter 2), it is preferable to draw blood than to sample urine for hormones and it is preferable to take several samples rather than one[129] [141]. Quality control should be assured by splitting samples and using standards for comparison. Radioimmunoassay procedures seem best at present. A medical examination should be conducted to rule out other physical abnormalities, especially endocrine abnormalities. The participants should be healthy and blood tests of liver functioning are advisable. The psychological health of the participants is important since some psychiatric abnormalities may be associated with hormonal abnormalities. Participants should be screened for drug use and medication since these may also influence hormone levels. When these criticisms are taken into account, no study remains untouched.

The results are suggestive that the predominantly male hormone, testosterone itself is not related to homosexuality but some other hormone or combination of hormones might be. Dorner and his colleagues[36] [37] indicate that homosexual men may differ from heterosexuals in showing a positive estrogen feedback effect. The authors injected participants with estrogen and found that serum leutinizing hormone decreased significantly in the homosexual men and increased above the initial level afterwards. While the decrease was observed in the heterosexual participants, it did not subsequently rise above the initial level afterwards.

An interesting finding that appears in two studies was the difference in homosexual and heterosexual men in the ratio of two hormones, androsterone and etiocholanolone[41] [112]. Evidently, the endocrine chemistry is very complex and there are many more possibilities that need investigation. A clear methodological study needs to be done and now the technology and knowledge are available to do it. It involves considerable effort but with greater experimental controls and better study designs, this may offer support for an organic theory of homosexuality.

Conclusion - The Homosexual Stimulus Response Matrix

Available evidence (Table 4.2) presents the following erotic profile of the *typical* homosexual (See also [2] for a summary). The stimuli he responds to are the mature male body and to a lesser extent the developing and immature male body. He does not respond to females but does not appear to have a great aversion to them. He tends to be somewhat feminine in in-

TABLE 4.2
Summary of Evidence for Theories of Homosexuality

Theory	Experimental Support
1. Aversion to female body	Negative
2. Aversion to intercourse	Negative
3. Diagnosis of neurosis	Negative
4. Disturbed parent child relations	Positive in patients but negative in nonpatients. Not necessarily close binding intimate mothers.
5. Increased femininity and feminine gender identity	Positive
6. Youngest son of aging mother	Mixed outcome, needs more work
7. Genetic predisposition	Negative
8. Female hormone profile	Mixed results; no adequately controlled study
9. More intelligent than average	Positive but poorly studied

terests/behaviors and shows moderate degrees of feminine gender identity. The features of his male sex partners other than body shape have not been studied well. There is no evidence for dominance–submissiveness, sadism–masochism, or activity–passivity, being generally important in partner choice. His desired responses to his preferred stimuli are mutual masturbation, fellatio, and anal intercourse. There is a significant incidence of outdoor masturbation with no one around. The meaning of this behavior is not clear at present but may reflect narcissism.

Homosexuality is not consistently associated with any psychiatric abnormality. With the exception of femininity and feminine gender identity, there is little support for any of the psychoanalytic, or social learning theories. Some organic theories have yet to be tested in humans although there are available interesting studies on lower animals.

Of all the sexual anomalies, most investigation and theorizing has been on homosexuality. This may reflect its large frequency among the sexual anomalies or social concern and aversion to it. The American Psychiatric Association changed homosexuality from the status of 'disease' to 'disturbance' in 1973[171][177]. This naturally influences treatment considerations.

TREATMENTS

Some authors think we should not be concerned with changing homosexuality per se. Freund[52] notes that there is little evidence that we can alter erotic preferences in homosexual men and it is unfair to raise false hopes of cure. Masters & Johnson[116] on the other hand, think that conversion to heterosexuality is possible and that the individual should make the choice to change or not. This offers maximum freedom and one should not be denied any opportunity for treatment.

The whole debate on therapy for homosexuality confuses the questions *can* we and *should* we change homosexual men into heterosexuals? This section is devoted to asking can we in fact change them and what criteria should we use for successful therapy? This is a more complex question than it initially seems.

Therapy success has most often been defined in terms of changes in overt sexual behavior. The patient says after treatment that he can react erotically to women and perhaps has had sexual intercourse. We should not be surprised that this is possible. In laboratory studies, it has been shown that homosexual men can be aroused by audio descriptions of heterosexual intercourse[59]. No training was required.

An interesting therapy example in this respect is *Mr. L*, who was concerned about his homosexuality. He took an incidental remark of the therapist as a challenge. From phallometric testing and sex history, he appeared to be exclusively homosexual in preference:

Mr. L: I'm concerned about heterosexuality. I mean, all I've done is homosexual stuff. I'm wondering if I'm ok.

Doctor: You've never tried heterosexual intercourse and you are wondering if you are homosexual?

Mr. L: Um . . . ya . . . I've never tried it . . . (pause) . . . Is that normal?

The following session:

Mr. L: Well I tried it this week . . . intercourse that is.

Doctor: How did you go about that?

Mr. L: It was easy. I picked up a girl at the singles bar and we went to her place and had sex.

Doctor: How did you find it?

Mr. L: It was ok, I guess. I mean I had an erection and came and everything. She seemed to like it . . . but it wasn't as exciting as sex with a man. It was kind of like masturbating . . . no feeling there. Do you know what I mean?

Such men are likely spontaneously aroused by a wide range of other erotica as well. This would parallel the reactions of heterosexual men who may engage in homosexual acts even to the point of orgasm and who can react to a wide range of socially deviant sexual stimuli[61][90][97][145]. However, as discussed in Chapter Two, all these men would show a clear erotic preference for one activity or the other.

In light of these facts, it would seem insufficient merely to be able to train the homosexual patient to respond to females overtly. Changing preference and reactivity to the female body over the male is a more satisfactory criterion but it may be much more difficult to achieve. The latter will reflect a greater personal satisfaction for patients because when they are spontaneously erotically aroused, their new preference would be for sexual intercourse with a woman and they would not be bothered by urges for their previous anomalous behavior.

In this section, treatments will be scrutinized for effecting changes in orgasmic preference. In my opinion, it stands out as the most satisfactory criterion of therapy success. A less satisfactory outcome would be attainment of coitus without disgust or distress even though the patient still had homosexual urges. Particularly, in the case of married homosexuals, both actual and desired orgasms should be considered first. Such men may perform with their wives but desire men nonetheless. *Mr. J.*, who had undergone aversion therapy was disillusioned because he was still having homosexual fantasies after 40 sessions of 20 trials during which he had experienced considerable pain. He was married but had clandestine washroom affairs, which involved risk of imprisonment at the time. He had dropped out of treatment thinking the aversion therapy was not working but believed something would change his homosexual thoughts that kept bothering him. He was questioned about intercourse with his wife.

Doctor: How do you find intercourse with your wife?

Mr. J: It's Ok. She is a wonderful woman and a fine mother to our children. We do lots of things together and I really love her. If only I could not be unfaithful to her with all this sex in the washrooms. If she ever knew, she'd die.

Doctor: Do you enjoy intercourse with her?

Mr. J: It's alright. It is not as exciting as sex with a man. When we were first married her naked body against mine was arousing and I could come inside her. Now I have to use fantasies of men to get aroused or I may think of a recent washroom contact and that gets me through it.

Doctor: You make it sound like a chore.

Mr. J: I guess it is most of the time and I thank God I'm (Roman) Catholic (smiles).

Doctor: I don't get the connection.

Mr. J: Well according to our religion rhythm is the only form of birth control we can practice so that is one week of the month we cannot have sex. Then her period takes up another week. So I'm free two weeks of the month.

There are two additional criterion that I wish to suggest are effective as a minimum standard in accepting any therapeutic approach. First, it should make theoretical sense and second, the follow-up should be adequate. Each sexual anomaly is described in some theoretical terms. We have seen that many of the theories of homosexuality are wanting. The treatment should be based at least on a theory that does not have considerable counter evidence. The treatment should then be consistent within a logical framework. Learning theory underlies most behavior therapy approaches, at least that is the claim made. Nevertheless, some methods clearly violate these principles and should not be used on these grounds. For example, anxiety relief conditioning and simple positive classical conditioning to enhance heterosexual responsiveness (Chapter 3) are ineffective and can be rejected for current clinical application. In this way many ineffective and inappropriate procedures can be abandoned.

The second criterion, follow-up of a patient, is very important because one wants to know that the "cure" is relatively permanent. Most studies in the professional literature do not give the reader the benefit of that information. The danger of inadequate follow-up is acceptance of an ineffective method of treatment and application to unsuspecting patients. Rarely do we know if something goes wrong. The reader should be cautious of short term "cures".

Behavior Therapies

Most behavior therapy treatments of sexual anomalies reported in the professional literature have been devised for homosexuality. They also appear as the most frequently reported of all approaches to treating homosexuality. The methods used can be conveniently divided into aversion therapy, heterosexual enhancement techniques and multitreatment approaches.

Chemical and electrical aversion therapy.   Historically the first case of aversion therapy for sexual anomalies reported in professional literature was the treatment of a homosexual male. Max's study[117] of classical conditioning used pictures of males followed by electric shock to reduce the strength of homosexual response in his patient. He claimed that the homosexual fixation was broken up. The assessment of this patient was inadequate from present standards since we do not know his erotic preferences or even how frequent the homosexual acts were. We are not told if he was exclusively homosexual or had any heterosexual experience. Follow up was short.

One of the most extensive studies done to date on homosexual men was ironically one of the earlier studies carried out by Freund[50], who followed up 67 homosexual men for as long as 8 years. He used a chemical aversion method of classical conditioning. Pictures of men were presented when the patient had been administered nausea producing agents, apomorphine and emetine. With repeated presentations, men should be associated with nausea instead of erotic arousal. Hopefully, these results would not generalize to men in all situations but only in erotic contexts.

In order to enhance heterosexual responsiveness, the patients were administered testosterone propionate to increase sexual arousability. They were presented pictures of females several hours later, once the testosterone had taken effect. Some patients reported being sexually aroused to females for the first time in their lives. The initial results were encouraging and patients were enthusiastic about their new found heterosexuality. Some even married, later to be divorced or have unhappy marital situations because of their returned homosexual yearnings and desires (See [7] and [109]). About a fifth remained changed in overt behavior but less than 5% stopped all homosexual activities.

It is likely that no patient really changed his erotic preference or failed still to have homosexual desires. It may also be that the wives of such patients have a need to maintain a neurotic relationship that undermines her husband's treatment[74]. Very little work has been done on wives of homosexual men and any influence they may have on treatment. Frigidity and/or general sexual inadequacy of the wives may be logical avenues to investigate.

In the 20 years following the first report by Max, scattered cases appeared in the professional literature, all of them uncontrolled studies using classical conditioning. This handful of therapists used pictures of males followed 100% of the time by electric shock or reinforcement on a variable interval/ratio schedule. Some used anxiety relief conditioning described earlier[174]. These cases have been reviewed by Feldman[42] and most of them add nothing to the existing literature except additional cases.

One of the reports by McGuire and Vallance[128] is interesting in that the patients could set their own shock level and could treat themselves in their own home, using a portable shock apparatus. Whereas this seems promising since the number of sessions could be increased and the environment in which it occurs could be broadened, a fear was expressed that patients would set their own shock level too low and that they might become adapted to it as part of a masochistic outlet. In any case the overall outcome was not different from the other treatment approaches.

A later and more popularized treatment of homosexuality was undertaken by Feldman, MacCulloch, Mellor and Pinschof[45] who introduced an operant method, avoidance conditioning. In this procedure a picture of a male would be followed by electric shock after a delay of 5-to-10 seconds. In the interim, the patient could *avoid* shock by removing the picture of the male usually either by pressing a hand switch or a foot pedal. Feldman and MacCullough attempted to incorporate important properties of learning theory into this method. On a third of the conditioning trials a partial reinforcement schedule was used, that is, no shock followed pictures of men. In animal studies, this has been found to produce more effective learning than administering shock on every trial[89]. Avoidance of shock has been found to be more resistant to extinction than passive classical conditioning, that is, the effect of treatment will last longer, at least in animals. A third of the trials were like this. Finally, a third were of the classical conditioning type since patients could avoid shock two thirds of the time and this would be ineffective learning.

Each avoidance trial was followed by an anxiety relief conditioning trial. That is, a slide of a female followed the termination of electric shock. This presumably was to enhance reactivity to the female by associating her at least with relaxation or relief of pain. As noted in Chapter 3, this procedure is logically inconsistent with learning principles and may be reducing the effectiveness of the avoidance trials. Nevertheless, this method has been widely imitated in practice and used with a variety of other anomalies[6 27 30 42 71 100 107 180]. All of these latter studies suffer the same problems as the Feldman and MacCulloch studies and their presentation here would be unnecessary repetition.

Feldman and MacCulloch's results were impressive in terms of a 60% "cure rate". In summarizing treatment[43] of 43 cases of mixed homosexuals and pedophiles, they indicated that a prior history of heterosexual interaction and of self referral for treatment are prognostic of successful therapy outcome. Nevertheless, they did not use a detailed sex history assessment or any phallometric assessment of erotic preferences.

In the later studies copying the Feldman and MacCulloch's avoidance conditioning method, many married "bisexuals" and even some pedophiles, rather than exclusive homosexuals were treated. All were casually labeled "homosexuals". Assessments were poor, phallometric measurement was almost never done and follow ups were either not done at all or were very short. The reports are usually case studies. Two reports however are noteworthy since they are controlled studies.

Birk and his colleagues[23] compared aversion treatment plus unspecified group therapy to group therapy alone. Five of eight aversion therapy cases showed "homosexual response suppression" according to the authors, whereas none of the latter group did. This offers some support for the effectiveness of the aversion procedure since none of the remaining studies use a control condition, including the original Feldman and MacCulloch procedure or any of the reports previously described. Birk and his associates[23] thought the combination of aversion therapy to suppress homosexual outlets and psychotherapy to open heterosexual modes of response was essential.

A second report by Tanner[181] is also illustrative of the contrast between controlled studies and untested clinical speculation. In the clinical lore, the "booster" session is supposed to be effective in maintaining the gains made in aversion therapy. Just as the allergic patient must have intermittent shots of antigen to control his allergy, so the homosexual should have intermittent booster shots of aversion therapy to maintain his aversion to homosexual outlet. There is only one systematic study on this hypothesis and Tanner has done it.

He compared five men with and five without booster sessions after a course of aversion therapy in the manner of Feldman and MacCulloch. Moreover, he measured erectile responses to slides of nudes one year after treatment. From the report, it is not clear what the outcome of aversion therapy was although the author claimed it was effective. However, he did compare the booster and no booster conditions by statistical test. There were no differences in the two groups suggesting that the fuss over booster sessions is unwarranted[44].

The Feldman and MacCulloch procedures have aroused controversy about the nature of avoidance conditioning[108] [184]. The dispute is a rather technical one about differences between classical and operant conditioning. The two are not clearly distinct to many theorists[89] and this debate adds little to our knowledge of effective treatment. McConaghy carried out several experiments, which suggested that this debate was purely academic. He did considerable work in investigating the aversion treatment of homosexuality and he carried out some of the few controlled studies in the literature.

First, he asked if conditionability was a factor in outcome of aversion therapy. Since individuals differ in their conditionability, those who are more responsive should condition better and show greater effects of treatment. Using groups of heterosexual and homosexual men, McConaghy[123] tried to classically condition them by presenting pictures of red circles and nude women to the heterosexuals and green triangles followed by nude men to the homosexuals. He measured penile volume changes. After repeated pairing of the stimuli the heterosexuals should start to respond to the red circle alone and the homosexuals to the green triangle alone. This in fact happened in most cases.

A comparison of the two groups' reactions to male versus female nude pictures showed they reacted most to their preferred sex. The homosexuals reacted to nude men and showed no reaction or a negative reaction to female nudes. McConaghy then compared these results with independent outcome measures after aversion therapy[122 125]. He asked patients to report on their changes in intensity of heterosexual and homosexual feelings. He also reassessed their penile reactions to the pictures of nudes. The patients who said they had changed were compared with those who had not. There was no difference in the two groups in conditionability to male nudes. This suggests conditionability is unrelated to aversion therapy outcome. McConaghy notes this in a later paper[124] but also adds that his patients did not experience aversion outside treatment when exposed to pictures similar to those used in therapy. The treatment did not generalize to everyday life. More important, a conditioned reaction was not set up by the therapy in spite of reported changes in homosexual behavior.

This study illustrates an important advantage of behavior therapy; the means to examine if a learning phenomenon is in fact occurring. Behaviorists refer to the learning curve which is a graphical plot of task performance over time or learning attempts. For example, one could indicate the number of falls from a bicycle with attempts at riding it. So with the treatment of homosexuality. When the erotic arousal to men is being extinguished or suppressed and the response to females is being enhanced, a graph can be plotted of penile reactivity to the female and male pictures. As treatment progresses, the penile reaction to males should gradually diminish and that to females gradually increase so the plot of the latter has a lazy *S* shape. If this does not occur then conditioned learning likely is not occurring. If any future studies are attempted in this area, the inclusion of this data would tell the experimenter at a glance what is happening. Surprisingly, few have taken this seriously. Perhaps because it is too time consuming.

McConaghy has made another significant contribution to this area of research since he conducted one of the very few controlled comparisons of two treatment methods[122]. He compared the apomorphine chemical aversion described earlier by Freund with an electrical aversion method of classical conditioning. One of the reasons that electrical aversion had become popular was the impreciseness of the chemical method. One never knew when the patients would become nauseous and the critical timing necessary between the pictures of nude men and the nausea could not be controlled. Another addition to the McConaghy study was the measurement of penile reactions to treatment, again a rarity in this area of research.

He found that both methods of treatment were effective but the unsuccessful cases of patients who had electrical aversion were more likely to resume homosexual relations earlier. However, the unpleasant apomorphine treatment can leave the patient physically drained at the time of the assessment, in this case, two weeks later. About half of the patients showed an increase in reactivity to females and a decrease in reactivity to males, which was maintained throughout follow up at least one year later[123], and even several years later[124]. Only a quarter had ceased homosexual activity and a quarter, not necessarily the same individuals, had commenced or increased heterosexual activity. However, all patients were still aware of some homosexual feelings.

When McConaghy's studies are taken together, they suggest that the relationship of aversion therapies to conditioned reflex learning is a tenuous one. The patients who conditioned best in an independent experiment did not necessarily show the best outcome of aversion therapy. Second, the more precise electrical aversion therapy was no more effective than the imprecise chemical aversion therapy indicating either that the learning principle is amiss or the procedure is not classical conditioning. As McConaghy noted, the effectiveness of aversion therapy still needs to be established.

He recently[126] extended his earlier work to conduct the largest study yet on the aversive conditioning of 157 male homosexual patients. He reported four controlled studies. In the first, he replicated his earlier report comparing chemical aversion therapy, aversion relief and the classical conditioning modes of treatment on 40 patients. In the second study, he compared chemical aversion therapy with the Feldman and MacCulloch avoidance conditioning on 40 separate patients. In the third study, he compared 46 patients on classical, avoidance and backward conditioning. The latter is theoretically not supposed to work and thus serves as a placebo control treatment. In the fourth study of 31 patients, he compared classical aversive electrical conditioning with a positive conditioning in which pictures of nude women were associated intially with pictures of nude men and later with pictures of heterosexual relationships. The latter was designed to enhance heterosexual reactivity. About half of the patients in each study had previous heterosexual relationships and all were subjected to the phallometric assessment described in his earlier studies. At 3-to-4 weeks after treatment and at follow up a year later, about a quarter of patients in all treatments reported an increase in heterosexual feelings and about half reported a reduction in homosexual feelings. The exception was the positive conditioning group in Study 4 in which only a quarter of the patients initially reported a reduction in homosexual feelings. At follow-up a year later, the groups were more or less comparable.

Immediately after treatment, 75% of all patients reported no homosexual acting out but a year later this dropped to 25%. When penile reactions to pictures of men and women were assessed, all patients showed a shift in the direction of increased heterosexuality but most remained significantly homosexual.

An ironic and interesting finding is that there was no evidence of positive conditioning in Study 4 and McConaghy concluded that it must have served as a placebo condition. Nevertheless the patients undergoing this treatment shifted in the same direction on the phallometric test and to a comparable extent as the aversion treatment patients. This casts doubt on the validity either of the treatment or of the phallometric score he used. If this score is examined carefully in his studies, it can be seen that about a fifth of the homosexual patients score in the range of heterosexuals before any treatment was initiated. This may reflect the fact that many have had heterosexual experience to begin with.

The shift in scores with treatment, especially with the placebo, suggests that this test has considerable unreliability or that patients change spontaneously with attention rather than specifically with treatment. When only the group showing scores on the phallometric test clearly in the homosexual range are examined, the change is very little or none. This offers empirical validation that in the aversion therapies the "homosexuals" showing the most change are "bisexuals" or heterosexuals to begin with. The exclusive homosexual changes little with any treatment. The studies also show that the theoretical debate over the relative effectiveness of classical and operant conditioning was unwarranted since both methods had little differential empirical impact on actual homosexual behavior outside the treatment setting.

Feldman has criticized the whole area of aversion therapy for homosexuality[42] noting that the reports are marked by a rather moralistic overtone, which in conjunction with chemical aversion therapy, or even electrical aversion I might add, could render the whole therapeutic situation so unpleasant that the patient is "forced into health". Many reports have an inadequate psychiatric description of patients even though some psychopathology from depressive psychosis to chronic personality disorders is apparent. Moreover, details of follow-up and outcome are extremely scanty. Follow-up should be at least several months and in this author's opinion, at least one year for this behavior. Feldman noted the inappropriate over representation of case studies. This can be misleading especially since single case failures are not usually reported. Finally he argues that there is a very strong need for an objective evaluation of the direction of sexual interests before and after treatment that is independent of clinical data. In short, there should be an assessment of erotic preferences, which only McConaghy has done to any degree. Presumably penile tumescence measures would be used.

Ignoring the problems of poor assessment of erotic preference, of short inadequate follow-up and of poor reporting on exactly what the nature of the behavior being treated is, how does the method fare in terms of outcome? The present author estimated[95] that in about 50% to 60% of cases, the deviant behavior "disappears" for a 3-to-6 month period. Beyond that, we often do not know what happens although Lazarus[102] suggested that it reemerges as strong as ever. Some patients who have been subjected to this method indicate that they seem to lose all interest in sex of any kind for a short period of time and then one day their homosexuality reemerges and they act out. Some say that they are only affected in the treatment unit and not outside. For example, *Mr. M* noted:

> *Mr. M:* When I approach the treatment unit I can feel my stomach tighten up.. When I get to your office I am visibly tense as you can see. I may shake a bit until that first shock hits me. Then I seem to gain my composure. When it is all over I feel relieved knowing it won't happen again for another week. But I will leave here and walk down the street and see a handsome man and feel turned on.

Bancroft[7] has reviewed several studies of chemical and faradic aversion therapy and from a total of 299 cases, 41% showed some improvement. This is based on those completing treatment. Note, however, that 23% refuse aversion therapy and 14% dropped out. It is important to determine how many will accept treatment since a high refusal rate will reduce the general utility of the method. Moreover, when examining treatment outcome, those who have elected to participate may be peculiar in some respect.

Covert sensitization. The more recent developments in aversion therapies have not been used as often on homosexuals, at least have not been reported in the literature. Covert sensitization appears to be a cheap and safer alternative to the use of faradic aversion therapies. In this method both the conditioning stimuli, for example, men, and the aversive stimulus, in this case pain, vomiting, and so forth, are imagined. Expensive equipment is therefore unnecessary and original reports suggest it is even more effective than shock aversion[28]. A drawback of the procedure at the same time is that the therapist has no control over the stimuli since they are all imagined. Curtis and Presly[33] suggest that the patients' imagination be tested prior to treatment. One of course must use cooperative patients in this method. The same criticism applies to all imagery methods like hypnotism and systematic desensitization.

There are several reports in the literature on eight cases of homosexuality treated with covert sensitization[11 27 33 65 84 162]. Seven out of the eight cases appear successful but there are short follow up, the longest being for one year.

When using anxiety provoking stimuli in any therapy, care must be taken to ensure that the patient is not so anxious that the treatment makes the problem worse. On the other hand, the patient may habituate to punishment. In one homosexual client known to the writer, covert sensitization was employed. The patient imagined approaching an attractive man for sex. As he came close, he felt nauseated and vomited over this imagined person until he ran away. The first two sessions were quite effective in reducing urges to act out. The patient was visibly shaken and said he did not have urges to act out in his everyday life. However, on the third session, he seemed quite relaxed to the therapist and when questioned about this, he said he was liking the treatment and found it sexually arousing to imagine touching the other man's penis covered in vomit. This may be viewed as masochistic but the change in the anxiety state of the patient was also noteworthy.

In another case, the chronic anxiety level of the patient was raised. A 19 year old male charged with a variety of crimes, mostly theft, presented as homosexual and wished to be treated for it. The aversive conditioning sessions were quite traumatic for him. After only a few sessions, there was a dramatic increase in his homosexual desires and acting out. He reported being more tense all the time. Treatment was terminated and the homosexual acts and anxiety declined in frequency and intensity to their former level. Such cases suggest that caution and careful measurement during aversion treatments be used.

Although aversion therapy per se has received some criticism (See Chapter 3) the aversion treatment of homosexuality specifically has received a barrage of criticism[8 75 86 91 92 93 142]. Considering the pain involved for the patient and risk especially in the case of chemical aversion therapy or complex cases of high anxiety[185], some writers are eager to find safer and more pleasant alternatives to treating the condition. The most important criticism is that similar results can be obtained with nonaversive methods like systematic desensitization.

The claim that desensitization was as effective as aversion was based on a few case studies but one report was a systematic comparison of the two forms of therapy. James[86] used anticipatory avoidance conditioning in twenty cases and desensitization in another twenty cases. The latter method also involved hypnotism, which is not standard for this procedure. Patients in each treatment were subdivided into two groups: heterophobic (fear of heterosexuality) and those who were not. It was expected that the heterophobic patients would benefit more from desensitization and the nonanxious would benefit more from aversion. Results showed that all patients responded better to desensitization than to aversion. Sixty percent of the aversion cases reported no improvement whereas only 20% of the desensitization cases were unchanged. There were no differences in heterophobic and nonheterophobic cases.

Heterosexual enhancement procedures.   Many methods have been used to enhance heterosexual responsiveness and most of them appear to be directed to homosexuals. Aversion methods have been criticized as incomplete since they leave the patient with no sexual outlet[9 102]. In fact, the patient is not homosexual in outlet nor is he heterosexual. This is the lull noted earlier when all sexual urges seem to be suppressed (See also [122] and [174]). In response to this problem, attempts have been made to enhance heterosexual responsiveness as adjuncts to aversion therapies. Anxiety relief conditioning and use of testosterone have been noted. The methods have been reviewed by Barlow[9].

Reciprocal inhibition therapy aims to relieve anxiety. It has been widely used in the treatment of phobias. If we examine the major theories of homosexuality, anxiety about heterosexual intercourse and/or about women in general was important. The most frequent treatment has been to raise anxiety level to homosexual outlet through aversion therapy. This seems contrary to common sense. If someone is anxious, one tries to remove the anxiety. Reciprocal inhibition therapy would therefore seem like the most logical and humane choice. By reducing anxiety to intercourse and to women in general, a few reports have indicated successful outcome. Unfortunately, these studies[83][176] suffer the same poverty of methodology, evaluation and follow up as the aversion studies. At least they are theoretically logical. It appears in the long run, erotic preference is not altered by these methods either. The anxiety and disgust associated with heterosexual relations appear to diminish but there remains little pleasure in the act.

This is illustrated by *Mr. N*, a handsome middle aged university professor, who desired to be heterosexual. He had unsuccessfully tried various therapies over a 15 year period, including 8 years of psychoanalysis. He preferred men in his sexual fantasies but he had no physical contact with men or women. In the course of 8 desensitization sessions to intercourse with women (See Chapter 3), he was able to have heterosexual fantasies without distress. An in vivo approach to women was discussed. A female who was eager to relate sexually to him was not difficult to find. In fact a staff member in his department openly indicated her attraction to him. He found her appealing and enjoyed her company. He described his encounter with her:

> *Mr. N:* It was a lovely evening. We dined at my favorite restaurant and saw a really enjoyable comedy at the theater. We walked and talked afterwards. Then she suggested we go to her place for a nightcap. We talked on her sofa for a while and started to neck. I realized I really liked her although I don't know if I'm in love with her; it's more like friendship—a close friendship. I undressed her and she was naked. I still had my clothes on. My shirt was undone and she felt the hair on my chest. But I couldn't go on. When I touched her breasts and again when I touched her between the legs, I didn't feel anything. I wasn't sexually aroused and I wasn't afraid or disgusted. I just didn't feel anything. I stopped and got dressed. She was perplexed and disappointed but not as much as I was. I've spent 15 years in therapy to achieve that evening, only to find I didn't want it after all!

A similar outcome might be obtained in training a willing heterosexual to become homosexual.

Positive classical conditioning.   A simple classical conditioning treatment to enhance heterosexual responsiveness has been devised in which pictures of women are conditioning stimuli and pictures of men are the unconditioned stimuli. Since the homosexual patients already react to men with penile tumescence, the pictures of women should become arousing by repeatedly preceding the pictures of men. Although such studies are only experimental in nature, they do seem to work to some extent[76] [126]. The major problem is that the reaction to the female is always smaller than that to the male. This is in the nature of classical conditioning. Moreover, the reaction to the female may remain subliminal, or below the threshold of awareness of the patient. No matter how prolonged the treatment, the reaction to the woman would always be a small anticipatory reaction to the male.

Fading.   A more effective operant method has been devised by Barlow and Agras[10] called fading. The homosexual patient is required to view slides of males. Penile circumference is monitored. Gradually a slide of a female is phased in by means of a rheostat attached to the projector while the picture of the male is faded out. That is, the relative brightness of the two images is varied. The pictures are manipulated so the patient maintains 75% full erection at all times. Eventually the female picture is on the screen at full brightness and the picture of the male is completely removed. The homosexual patient at the end of treatment should find himself sexually aroused in the presence of a female sex stimulus. Only a few single cases have been reported but the method seems promising. Barlow and Agras note, however, that homosexual arousal remains high after treatment and their patients tended to be confused and depressed.

Fading might be useful in the case of pedophilia as well, in which the image of a child could be faded out and the image of a mature female phased in. It would be interesting to see if the patient's erotic preferences changed when this treatment was completed. At least in this method, we know that something happened in the erotic sphere, more than we know in many cases. Once again, however, we must be careful to note that a change in reactivity does not mean a change in erotic preference. All this method has done for sure is to create a penile reaction to females, presumably where there was none before. The patient should still react to men and in fact may still prefer to have sex with men. One is forced to look at orgasmic outlet and the patient's satisfaction with those outlets. McCrady[127] has argued that the reverse sequence of slides should be used and penile erection gradually incremented. While he argues that this is an improvement over Barlow et al.'s method, the treatment apparently failed and there was no generalization of gains in therapy to other stimuli.

Positive operant conditioning. Another operant conditioning procedure has been reported by Quinn and his associates[144] in which penile reactions to slides of female nudes have been enhanced by rewarding a thirsty patient with small amounts of liquid. The homosexual patient in the investigation was asked to abstain from liquids for 18-to-24 hours prior to treatment. Chemicals were also administered to enhance thirst. Penile circumference was monitored while the patient looked at the slides. When penile tumescence occurred, no matter how little at first, a small amount of liquid was given. Gradually the size of the penile reaction increased before reinforcement was given. Eventually the patient was having full erections to the pictures of the females. Aversive conditioning was also used. The reported outcome was successful.

I[95] used this method with one patient who was not considered cured in spite of penile changes. No chemicals were used to enhance thirst and aversive conditioning was not employed. In five sessions, a 26 year old male who had been exposed unsuccessfully to a variety of methods over a 7 year period was having full erections to nude female stimuli for the first time in his life. He was pleased. In the next session, he indicated that it was hard work having the erections. In the seventh session, he was having quick full erection but said during the session to the therapist, "Oh my God, my penis is moving but there is nothing going on in my head!" Presumably the patients who appear for treatment want something in their head changed as well, something perhaps related to erotic preferences. This split of penile and cognitive reaction appears again and again throughout the reports of sexual anomalies. Can the two be dissociated? It seems everyone does dissociate the two at least at some point. Early morning erections are frequently reported by patients and nonpatients alike but the feeling need not be erotic, rather they may only feel a need to empty their bladders. Other contexts in which this occurs will be discussed again later.

Orgasmic reconditioning has also been used to create heterosexual responsiveness. In this procedure, the patient masturbates to homosexual fantasies or slides[113] and just prior to climax, a heterosexual fantasy or slide is substituted. The repeated pairing of heterosexual stimuli and orgasm reinforces heterosexual patterns. Some therapists simply ask their patients to masturbate in private to heterosexual fantasies. Thorpe, Schmidt and Castell[186] used this procedure in having a homosexual patient masturbate to a picture of a female until he ejaculated. After 11 sessions, the patient remained homosexual and the treatment was terminated.

In my experience patients find orgasmic reconditioning very difficult, and as discussed earlier, the logical end of this experience according to theory should be a diminution of pleasure in the total fantasy. This in fact is reported by some patients. *Mr. O* described his experience vividly:

Mr. O: When I masturbate to my favorite fantasies, it is nice and it is a real turn on. Doing what you told me changed that. I've tried it a few times like you suggested. The first time at the end, when I switched to a female and imagined having sex with her, it was like someone hit me with a hammer. Now I've done it 3 or 4 times. I have to work at it to get turned on. My old fantasies are just not as exciting but neither are the new fantasies of the women. They still don't turn me on.

Perhaps the patient becomes aware that he values his anomalous sexual behavior more than he realized.

Multitreatment approaches.   A final set of behavior therapies for homosexuality involves an eclectic and multitreatment approach to the behavior. One may use covert sensitization and systematic desensitization and/or assertive training to overcome the multiple problems presented by the patient[102]. Responsiveness to males may be reduced by aversion therapy and/or desensitization and shyness in approaching females in vivo is reduced and heterosexual abilities enhanced by assertion therapy. Many other combinations of treatment can be devised in this fashion. Hopefully, the limitations of one treatment will be overcome by the accompanying and complementary treatment. Single method treatment failures have been attributed to the fact that each of the methods alone has some inadequacy but together they may be powerful and have more lasting effects.

Stevenson and Wolpe[176] reported two cases of homosexuality treated by assertiveness training, desensitization and "environmental manipulations" with some success. Rachman[149] in a discussion of the cases postulated that the improvement was due to nonspecific factors that improved the patients' mental health generally. If this is so, one has to wonder what purpose the learning theory overlay to treatment serves. McConaghy's controlled studies showed that it did not matter what form of aversion therapy or of positive conditioning was used, patients improved. Thus any form of professional attention may have produced similar results.

A difficulty with multitreatment case studies is the number of unreported or reported but confounded treatments concurrently administered to the patient. For example, one case study reported by Latimer[101] received in vivo desensitization, assertiveness training but not the environmental manipulations described by Stevenson and Wolpe. Since the treatment was successful in the single case reported, it would offer support for the hypothesis that the environmental manipulations may be unnecessary since similar results were obtained without it. Although this is a dangerous assumption to make for any case study, it is especially difficult because the patient has other concurrent treatment.

He was given Diazepam, or Valium, a common tranquilizer during the relaxation training to reduce his anxiety. This would confound any interpretation one could place on the effect of the relaxation training itself. Then he was given a course in the "pleasuring approach" of Masters and Johnson, designed to increase his heterosexual responsiveness and pleasure in doing so. Assertiveness training was used to improve his heterosocial skills to the point that he dated a girl and asked if she would have intercourse. He told her he was nervous but she agreed and all went well. He was apparently transformed into a heterosexual at that point although he may have been one initially since he never had homosexual relationships but only fantasies. No assessment is reported. He was lost to follow up after four months. One may also wonder if assertiveness training or one other procedure alone is effective and the remaining methods are necessary. We do not know what is the necessary ingredient for success and the reports on multiple treatments are considerably poorer in terms of assessment and follow up than the previous reports using one method of behavior therapy. Moreover the multiple treatment approaches do not always offer a logical explanation for the inclusion of a treatment.

In a case report by Shealy[163], a homosexual male was treated with a combination of behavior therapy and "cognitive therapy" or rational emotive therapy, devised by Ellis. In the latter method, one seeks to remove illogical thoughts that maintain a patient's neurotic behavior. In the present case, the homosexual client was to increase his thoughts of sexual adequacy. Fusing this with behavior therapy, he was told to retain his urine as long as possible and when he began to go, to repeat to himself "women find me very attractive". However he was also told to discontinue using males as masturbation fantasies and to use females. The approach appears to be an unsystematic orgasmic reconditioning procedure so that in the first week of treatment the patient could use male fantasies to become aroused and then switch to female ones. In the second week he eliminated the male stimuli completely. Then the male stimulus was paired with the female so that if he had fantasies of sex while looking at men on the street, he was to imagine them as women, with breasts, long hair, and so forth. The logic was to enhance the neutral female's erotic valence by pairing her with the male. This would seem to be simple classical conditioning or even a home made version of fading noted earlier. However, it would appear to be presented in the wrong order as backwards conditioning suggesting that it should not work. The third method was the typical procedure of covert sensitization used to reduce the potency of the male stimulus and make it aversive. After 15 one hour sessions, his erotic homosexual fantasies were reduced to about 25% of their pretreatment level. No follow-up or assessment is reported.

Other similar studies have been reported but leave the same lingering doubts that anything effective has been done[68] [72] [104] [158]. A few cases have used penile assessment[114] [157]. Freeman and Meyer[48] reported a paradoxical improvement in nine cases although two relapsed after an 18 month follow-up. Their method was a combination of instructions, simple positive classical conditioning and aversive conditioning. Patients were told to abstain from homosexual behavior, masturbate only with heterosexual fantasies, not to frequent gay spots, to girl watch and report progress to the therapist. Simple classical conditioning involved pairing pictures of females with males. Eighty slides were presented at each session usually three females and one attractive male. The subject stimulated himself during viewing and had to climax before the end of the session. One may wish to postulate an operant conditioning element to this treatment. The aversive conditioning followed the positive conditioning. There were 45 trials during which the patient reported when the slide was sexually arousing. Shock was delivered on each trial.

The method may be considered ineffective for two reasons. Since the patient had climaxed before aversive conditioning began, it is possible that he would find it difficult to become sexually aroused at all. Second, the two procedures counteract each other. The male slide is used as the arousing unconditioned stimulus in part one of the session and it is the conditioning stimulus in the second aversive part of the session. So as the treatment progresses, the unconditioned stimulus in part one, the male, loses its potency since it is associated with shock. Thus aversive conditioning should counteract the gains made in positive conditioning and render it ineffective. However, the patients were all having full erections to male slides before treatment and some erections to females as measured by penile volume. After treatment the reverse was the case suggesting a change in erotic reactivity to males and females. The follow-up did not involve penile measurement but the authors indicated that seven men maintained their heterosexual adjustment, after one year. Six were exclusive homosexuals prior to treatment and all were changed at one year follow-up. Then two relapsed after 18 months. The three nonexclusive patients were apparently married to start suggesting that their heterosexuality may have been masked in the results. They may be as adjusted as they were before treatment but have stayed away from "gay spots".

Although the outcome of Freeman and Meyer's study appears promising, the treatment is inconsistent and the reader should be skeptical. The study illustrates one difficulty of multiple treatments; the various operations may be inconsistent with each other and caution should be exercised. The same could result from a combination of aversion therapy and assertive training. If the valence of homoerotic stimuli is too strong and one is using assertiveness too early to enhance heterosocial skills, the patient may be too uncomfortable and drop out of treatment. This may have happened in one of two cases treated by Sandford, Tustin and Priest[157] with a differential reinforcement procedure.

The two patients in their study were shown pictures of males and females. When women were shown, the patient was encouraged to be aroused and increments in penile circumference were reinforced with a small amount of water. This would be rewarding since the patient fasted from liquids for 24 hours prior to the session. This method was basically used by Quinn, Harbison and McAllister[144] in operant shaping of penile erections. Slides of the male were followed by electric shock as in aversive conditioning. Since both were used concurrently, it was differential reinforcement, that is, the procedure in which one rewards appropriate behaviors and punishes inappropriate ones.

The first patient wished to discontinue after five sessions when there was only a 40% difference in erections to females over males. The second patient who stayed in treatment considerably longer finally showed full erections to females and none to males. The differential response is impressive and both patients reported that they did not desire homosexual contact and they were "involuntarily aroused by females". The author was skeptical of his results and suggested the method was valuable as a means of facilitating heterosexual arousal. One may wish to treat the results of penile measures with some skepticism at this point. Two other studies suggest this is appropriate.

Herman and Prewett[78] used a differential reinforcement or feedback method in which the patient was simply told by means of a flashing light, when he was having erections. Then he was tested in terms of penile reactions to male and female slides. He learned to react more to both sexes over the sessions. In other words, he could create erections via this feedback method. Other reports of voluntary control over erection have appeared and are discussed in Chapter 3. After treatment, the patient reported increased heterosexual masturbation fantasies and dated. However, he relapsed soon after that. One has to wonder at those reports which do not measure penile erections and only ask patients what is happening. Nevertheless immediate post treatment data would appear to indicate a successful case.

Herman and his colleagues[77] conducted another study that suggests the importance of social desirability variables in treatment and suggests that the expectations of both patient and therapist may play an important part in outcome. Four patients were simply exposed to explicit erotic stimuli of males and of females separately. Patients were told it was a new treatment which had "ups and downs" and to be trusting. Patients all showed the appropriate and expected changes. Reactions to females grew larger with treatment and those to males became smaller or remained unchanged at a lower level. The stimuli used varied in their erotic valence to the extent that they may have influenced outcome. All patients attempted heterosexual behaviors in their lives outside the treatment unit but all had considerable difficulties. Although the authors of this study suggest that a differential reinforcement method like positive and aversive conditioning may be needed, the amount of change elicited with simple exposure is noteworthy. Treatment study outcomes may be biased by such factors and immediate post measures of arousal and attempts at heterosexual adjustment may be suspect.

Summary of behavior therapy methods. Collectively the multiple behavior modification procedures seem the most promising of the behavior therapies offered. However, they have been the least carefully executed studies and present the complicating factor that one method may interfere with the other. Moreover, follow-up using these methods is poorest among the behavior therapy studies and it remains to be shown in a systematic study that they are more effective than use of a single method such as assertive training or desensitization alone.

The behavior therapies as a group of treatments have offered the best details and controls over procedure of any methods reported in the literature. The goals of treatment are usually clear and the criterion of success specified. Other methods in contrast suffer many deficiencies in this respect.

In summarizing the mass of information on behavior therapy, it is to be noted that the more careful the assessment and the longer the follow-up of patients treated, the more modest the claims. Adams and Sturgis[3], have shown this by providing an informative report of studies on the treatment of homosexuality by behavior modification methods. They conveniently divided cases into uncontrolled versus controlled and into group versus single case reports. Overall about 3/4 of the cases showed some "improvement" and one quarter did not change. However when this was examined in terms of the frequency of coitus, only 1/5 showed this behavior. Four in ten were having homosexual urges, and 1/3 were acting out. One has to wonder what the criterion "improved" entails. A breakdown of the type of study is informative. The highest rate of cure, 91%, comes from the uncontrolled case studies and the lowest from the controlled group data 62%, and uncontrolled group data close at 64%, with controlled single cases in between at 79% improved. The difference in reports of coitus are even more discrepant; uncontrolled single cases 57%, controlled single cases 25%, uncontrolled group data 37% and controlled group data 3%. An interesting contrast also appears in the use of penile measurement. The controlled studies used it in 71% of group cases and 64% of single cases whereas in the uncontrolled cases it was used for 33% of group studies and only 15% of single cases. The differences in outcome are important and Adams and Sturgis further note that the "control" is relative since even the controlled group studies are characterized by a lack of experimental rigor and appropriate controls. So conclusions of all studies should be viewed tentatively. They further state that the procedures used do not yet have the sophistication or validity that allows a clinician to place much faith in them so he may use them competently with some assurance of success.

Hypnosis

Hypnosis has been introduced in the treatment of homosexuality with striking success but only in a few cases. In this method, subjects who are suggestible are placed in a deep trance and told that homosexuality is undesirable and aversive whereas heterosexuality is desirable and attractive. Krafft-Ebbing (See [151]) in the last century used this method with homosexuals, claiming some success in outcome. It was felt even at that time that those patients who achieved "deep" hypnotic trances responded better to change. Research on this question was described in Chapter 3.

Roper[151] described the typical hypnotherapy procedure for homosexuals as follows. The patient is asked to lie on a couch and a trance is induced by suggesting that the eyes open and close, while looking at the ceiling light. He is told the eyelids would gradually become heavy to open and as this occurred, feelings of sleepiness would follow. Finally a desire for deep sleep would be felt. The patient's response to suggestion and post hypnotic amnesia were used to gauge the depth of trance. Various suggestions were made, for example, physical changes in sensation; feelings of strength in an arm and hand.

Once successfully hypnotized, feelings of self confidence, assertion and masculinity were suggested. As acceptance of these increased, further suggestions were offered such as change in sexual orientation, or attraction to women and aversion to men. They were told about the onset of their homosexuality based on facts previously obtained. It was noted that a certain degree of sexual uncertainty was normal in growing up but it has been prolonged in their case and their homosexuality has become a habit. Post-hypnotic suggestions were also made that the feelings of change would continue. As these were accepted, further reinforcing suggestions were made. For some, this meant looking at former homosexual behavior with distaste even to the point that they would experience an unpleasant taste in their mouths. The taste would be changed into something pleasant when they looked ahead at heterosexual relations. Thus the method seems to incorporate the logic of behavior therapy methods in forming an aversive association to homosexual behavior and a positive association to heterosexual behavior.

Roper reported a varied number of sessions as short as six over a few weeks to scattered sessions over a period of years. This is not clearly specified but he notes that the number of sessions varies greatly. In some cases the change in sexual orientation was reached early after only a few weeks.

About half of the cases showed a marked improvement defined as reduction in homosexual inclinations and behavior, and an increase in heterosexual inclinations and behavior. It is noteworthy that several of Roper's cases were nonexclusive homosexuals and in fact may have been heterosexual to begin with. Many of the marked improvements were associated with some pre-treatment attraction to women and some patients even reported heterosexual intercourse in their experiential background. One has to wonder if a "bisexual" label would not be better applied to these individuals.

The depth of trance was associated with improvement but this is a circular criterion. The depth of trance is defined as responding to suggestion. The more suggestible the patient, the more likely he will improve. The method seems powerful but it may in fact be limited since suggestible individuals may be few in number. One also has to ask if erotic preference has been changed. This was not adequately reported.

Roper noted the detrimental effect of doubt on treatment outcome. Some patients had been told that there was no possibility of changing their homosexuality and that they simply had to live with their problem. An unspecified "many" had almost given up hope of treatment in spite of an apparent great desire to do so. The contemporary move to acceptance of homosexuals in the community may promote such a position that one should not attempt to change homosexuality and some therapists may point out the many treatment failures. If one seeks out help without looking for success, treatment is not likely to have much impact.

Psychotherapy

Psychoanalysis and psychotherapy are terms used as if there were one underlying common process used by all individuals in practice. This is misleading to assume because there are many forms of psychotherapy[140]. It is easy to assume the treatments are complex and difficult to specify to the layman. This may be the case. Psychoanalysts are usually required to undergo analysis themselves before they become full fledged practitioners. This may take a period of years. The subtleties of analysis are perhaps too elusive to be read from a book or simply described in a treatment procedure. Nevertheless the literature on treatment by psychotherapies is vague and cannot possibly communicate to practitioners the procedures undertaken and the outcome of therapy. Often the reports describe case studies rather than systematic data as well, making comparisons even more difficult. For example in one psychotherapeutic study of homosexuality by Woodward[192], the term prognosis is used without referrent. Neurosis and homosexuality are mentioned and it is noted that there is not necessarily an overlap. "Psychotherapy" was undertaken in most cases treated. No further information is given. A claim is made that in 60% of the cases of incarcerated homosexual men, the homosexual impulse was lost. We have no idea how this was assessed. With 40% of patients dropping out of treatment and with a lack of follow up in 83% of the remaining cases, the results are highly suspect. It is doubtful if the best trained psychotherapist would have any idea what treatment was actually applied. The author notes that there was a disproportionate number of exclusive homosexuals and psychopaths among the drop outs. Interestingly, about half of the patient sample who scored as heterosexual on the Kinsey scale, were still treated as though they were homosexuals. One can only guess at the reasoning of the author. Moreover the author subcategorizes the "degree of change" and ends up with more cases than the total. Perhaps a typographical error or a casualness in reporting.

It may seem unfair to select one author. Let's turn to another. In examining 100 cases of homosexuality, Curran and Parr[32] reported that treatment consisted of a mixture of "physical, psychological, social and environmental measures including in-patient care usually associated with some psychiatric condition such as alcoholism." About a quarter of the patients had "psychotherapy in the broad sense of further psychiatric interviews of any number or type including analysis". Most simply discussed the problems at an initial interview, were counselled, were prescribed medication or discussed environmental adjustments. Since about half of the sample was considered free of personality disorder, psychosis or neurosis, does this simply represent counselling about adjusting to the community as a homosexual? Those patients receiving psychotherapies were compared with those not so treated and followed-up over 4 1/2 years. Only 60% could be followed-up and of these 80% showed no change in orientation. Interestingly, the short counselling sessions were as good as the longer psychotherapies in changing personal feelings of satisfaction and adjustment to the community.

Some psychotherapists are clear in their goals and outcomes of treatment. Hadfield[69] notes that he defines "cure" *not* just in terms of control of homosexual desires, nor in terms of loss of homosexual desires but loss of interest and propensity to own sex and acquiring a sexual interest directed to females. In short, a change in erotic object preference is his criterion of successful therapy. He considered homosexuality to be a neurosis with traumatic origins in childhood. The recovery of the childhood experience and the feelings associated with it cure the homosexuality.

In one illustrative case, his patient had a sensuously disposed mother who aroused sexual feelings in the child. She died and he then had a strict aunt who was unaffectionate. He was lonely. He craved affection and turned to homosexual experience for it. Analysis served to revive his repressed sexual feelings toward his mother and once released, his heterosexual feelings developed normally as if they had never been repressed. Over a thirty year follow-up, the patient married and remained heterosexual. Hadfield describes several other cases with equally impressive results.

However, he is casual as many other psychotherapists are about the classification of patients. He described a total of four cases treated over 30 years and of these, two were bisexuals and two exclusive homosexuals. Two may have been pedophilic and one of them a sadistic and pedophilic mixture. Nevertheless all were cured. He recommends that the prevention of homosexuality like that of all other neuroses seems to lie in right parenthood but he does not specify what that means.

Hadfield's patients displayed some neurotic behavior and were evidently in need of some care for other problems than homosexuality. Whereas we may wish to assume that homosexual and neurotic behaviors are independent, some psychotherapists assume it is a unitary and neurotic entity. The weight of experimental evidence suggests this is not the case. Therapists may be exposed only to homosexuals who are also neurotic and/or psychotic. The constant association of the two leads to a theorizing that the two are connected. When data like Hadfield's are reported, one has to wonder if homosexuality may not have multiple etiologies. In fact, is the neurotic homosexual performing some surrogate activity whereas the healthy one is not? One would have to try to change the neurosis independently of the homosexual behavior to find out. After all, over a third of the male population at large engages in homosexual behavior during their lifetime; some of them may be doing so for neurotic reasons. This does not mean that homosexuality per se is neurotic. A more recent report by the Biebers[21] suggests that the neurosis is independent of homosexuality.

Once again we are faced with vagueness but the authors note that "most" homosexuals in therapy do *not* become heterosexual but "most" resolve many problems in their lives such as those related to self esteem, assertiveness, work effectiveness, and social relationships. A substantial number do change they claim, from 30% to 50%. They hasten to add that a shift to heterosexuality does not mean that the potential for homosexual arousal has been totally extinguished. In other words, such patients have had a heterosexual adjustment but may still have a homosexual preference. Since most are now "adjusted" but remain homosexual, it seems that the neurotic behavior and homosexuality are unrelated. Hadfield's fewer cases suggest the two are related.

The Biebers note that their method is psychoanalysis and psychoanalytically oriented psychotherapy. They view it as a cognitive therapy, which delineates and evaluates irrational beliefs and belief systems associated with fears of injury that cause symptoms and functional disturbances. This makes their approach sound like Ellis' rational emotive therapy[38].

The Biebers and their colleagues[22] do us a disservice in labeling their book "Homosexuality" and talking about "Male Homosexuality" as though it were the core of a neurotic disorder. Rather they are talking about treatment of neurotic symptoms in homosexual patients. The homosexuality does not change in the majority of cases with improvement by psychotherapy. The Biebers focus their energies on disturbed family relations in homosexual patients and many of the disturbed relations appear to be characteristic of neurotic and character disordered patients in general. The fear of injury by a male and the close binding intimate relationship with the mother may result in a neurotic cluster of symptoms in adulthood that clinicians are familiar with. Socarides[172] also noted he treated 44 overt homosexuals with psychoanalysis and 45% developed full heterosexual functioning. It is not clear how many were females or what criterion of heterosexual functioning were used.

Ellis[38] reported on 28 homosexuals treated with psychoanalytically oriented psychotherapy. He does stress the importance of the following techniques: providing an accepting and noncritical relationship for the patient; not insisting the patient overcome all their homosexual tendencies but accepting many of them as normal and idiosyncratic; showing the therapist is favorably prejudiced to heterosexuality; focusing on the patient's general feelings of inadequacy and overcoming this as a major goal of therapy; and finally, persuading him to engage in sexual relationships with females. About 3/4 showed improvement after varying numbers of sessions from 5-to-220. Unfortunately we do not know how he assessed outcome or how long he followed up his patients. A number of other psychotherapy and group therapy studies have been reviewed by Hinrichsen and Katahn[79] and add little to our conclusions. Psychotherapists themselves[119] have complained about the inadequacies of their studies but little has been done to date to change this situation.

In the final analysis, it seems that psychotherapies are about as successful as behavior therapies. A review study by Bancroft[7] showed that about 40% of psychotherapy patients improve with treatment. The length of follow-ups, however, have been impressive in contrast to the behavior therapies but the description of methodology and assessment have been considerably poorer. There are no controlled studies. Adjustment to the community as a goal of treatment in homosexual men seems possible without a change in sexual orientation and it seems possible in few sessions rather than by extensive analysis that may run into years. The long term psychotherapies are expensive and therefore tend to cater to the rich and the select. If one is seeking a change in object choice, they do not appear to offer much hope of doing so. Homosexuals with neuroses seem to have as good prognosis as heterosexuals with neurosis.

It is interesting to contrast the behavior therapies and the psychotherapies. The former developed out of psychology and has had a research orientation for at least 50 years. The stress has been on data collection and its interpretation. Psychoanalysis has its roots in medicine in which a history of techniques has been handed down with theory. Authority and precedence is prominent in medicine and research methodology has only recently been stressed in the discipline of psychiatry. This perhaps explains the poverty of description and data from the psychotherapists and the details from the behavior therapists. Hopefully, there is a trend to change. Both treatments offer only limited hope of altering erotic desires. All are promising but show little satisfactory systematic evidence that they are effective. Taken at face value, they can help almost half of applicants for therapy make a heterosexual adjustment and to perform heterosexually but not necessarily change their erotic preferences.

Masters and Johnson Method

The treatment program offered by Masters and Johnson[116] for homosexuals' is one of the very few that explicitly presents alternatives. Over a period of ten years, they have studied homosexual interactions and have offered treatment. Basically the homosexual who applied for treatment because he was having difficulties interacting with his male partner was treated in an analogous fashion to the heterosexual dysfunctional male (Chapter 15). The techniques seemed to be highly satisfactory in this respect. They reported about an 80% success rate in such cases. However, they also treated a second group of dissatisfied homosexuals who wished either to become heterosexual or to have their heterosexuality restored. Their methods may be described as enhancing heterosexual responsiveness much in the style of behavior therapy methods.

Results of treatment were satisfactory. In the male group, 75% success was reported even after follow-ups of 1-to-5 years. This is far more impressive than any other technique to date. Their clinic may offer the homosexual a sense of freedom that heretofore was not available. As Masters and Johnson stress, the choice to be a functional heterosexual or homosexual should be the client's and not the therapist's.

The optimism derived from reading their book must be mitigated by many of the same criticisms leveled at other studies. The Kinsey scale was used to evaluate the patient's heterosexuality–homosexuality and this scale is a poor measure. Based on both psychological reactions and overt experience, individuals rate as follows:

0. Exclusively heterosexual with no homosexual
1. Predominantly heterosexual, only incidentally homosexual
2. Predominantly heterosexual, but more than incidentally homosexual
3. Equally heterosexual and homosexual

4. Predominantly homosexual, but more than incidentally heterosexual
5. Predominantly homosexual, but incidentally heterosexual
6. Exclusively homosexual

The psychological reactions and the overt experience are blended into one but may be quite distinct. For example, a male may feel himself to be an exclusive homosexual and to have no desire for females whatsoever. Nevertheless, he may have only had the opportunity for heterosexual intercourse, perhaps instigated by some female in his past. How would he rate himself? How do individuals weight this? We do not know and this uncertainty nakes it difficult to ascertain erotic preferences from the questionnaire. Some measures like the Sex History Questionnaire in Appendix I separate out overt experience and desires and a profile can be constructed for the individual.

In the Masters and Johnson sample, about 3-in-5 homosexuals desiring heterosexual restoration/conversion were married. The authors note that exclusive homosexuals were not as motivated to change. Only about 5% of their sample were exclusively homosexual on the Kinsey scale. Sixty percent were rated 4. Two individuals were even rated 2, predominantly heterosexual. One does not know in essence what proportion of the subjects would have an erotic preference for men and it is difficult to ascertain from the book. We know from other studies that previous heterosexual experience is important in 'converting' to heterosexuality. We still do not know if the patients in the Masters and Johnson's method changed their erotic preference. Many may have been heterosexual to begin with. It was important to have a committed partner for acceptance into the program as well. So the selected patients may have biased the results in the successful direction. Haynes[75] has suggested the use of fem. le surrogates as an alternative to the use of a committed partner. He notes that such a method has been used successfully with cases of impotence and may be useful in cases of homosexuality. Unfortunately he presents no data on its effectiveness.

The reader is further cautioned about the Masters and Johnson's program. The failure rate is satisfactorily low when considered in terms of those patients who were accepted into treatment, completed it and were followed-up. About 3 out of 4 were satisfactorily treated, or as Masters and Johnson prefer to say, only 1-in-4 failed. However, note the "successes" in terms of the overall number of applicants:

Total number of applicants	70	100%
Rejected by therapists	16	23%
Drop outs or treatment failures	11	16%
Follow up failures	4	6%
Lost to Follow up	16	23%
'Successful' cases	23	33%

The percentage add up to slightly more than 100 because of rounding error but one can see in these terms that if you apply for the program you have only a 1-in-3 chance of coming out of it successfully based on what is known.

About a quarter of the patients could not be traced. Masters and Johnson make the unwarranted assumption that some of their lost cases were successful. A lost case is not in the control of the therapist but the assumption that treatment losses will show the same proportion of successes as those the therapist can find is problematic. The lost cases may not want to be followed up because the treatment was a failure, because they are angry about the treatment or are in therapy somewhere else.

It is a noteworthy contrast that the dysfunctional groups fared much better and were more willing to take part in treatment than the dissatisfied group. This may suggest that leaving homosexuals as homosexuals is the best course of action. Finally, we should note that we have no index of how the successes were assessed and there are no ratings to indicate the assessment was reliable and valid. This would be a definite asset in giving the study, which is long and comprehensive some substantive value.

Treatment of Choice

A number of therapies assume that homosexual males are sick, disturbed individuals and yet the empirical facts deny this formulation. If a homosexual patient is neurotic or psychotic, the neurosis and psychosis need psychiatric attention but the homosexual aspect of his behavior need not be a part of treatment. It has been my experience in dealing with emotionally disturbed homosexuals that progress is made much more rapidly when homosexuality is not a part of the therapy. If sexual orientation is the only presenting problem, often in the case of "coming out", a few sessions in self acceptance and introduction to homosexual services in the community may be all that is required for a satisfactory adjustment. Some recent reports[118][191] advocate such an approach and one systematic study compared two methods of enhancing homosexual functioning; assertive training and counselling/guidance. Both were considered satisfactory[154].

The debate on the pathological status of homosexuality continues and viewpoints are polarized. The Task Force on Homosexuality of the New York County District Branch of the American Psychiatric Association[173] concluded that homosexuals may be as well adjusted as heterosexuals in terms of academic achievement, vocational success and gratification in social relationships. The committee did not take exception with this conclusion nor with the fact that there were homosexual individuals of superior accomplishment. However it did object to the contention that homosexuals were as well adjusted and compensated as heterosexuals and it objected to equating "adjusted" with normality or lack of pathology.

On the other side of the argument, individuals maintain that the homosexual does not differ from any other troubled minority group. The issue in therapy is acceptance of himself as a homosexual. Such acceptance is blocked by the antihomosexual attitudes of society[80] [169]. Nonetheless it is possible to have the homosexual patient adjust to his anomalous behavior in society.

The controversy appears to be resolving in the direction of removing homosexuality from treatment considerations since the American Psychiatric Association changed homosexuality to a sexual orientation disturbance in 1973[171]. Spitzer has suggested that in some cases homosexuality may be useful in the understanding of dynamics of certain cases of mental illness.

Rekers[150] has berated both sides of the controversy for not being scientific and confusing a priori values and scientific data. He argues that terms like illness, health, gay and homosexual pathology are perjorative and imply unestablished relationships. Moreover he notes that some individuals would like the American Psychological Association (APA) to assert that the homosexual is not sick, which is unscientific as well. We cannot prove that something is not the case (the null hypothesis) only that no relationship has been established.

An interesting survey was conducted in 1971 on a sample of 163 professionals who were canvassed about their attitude toward homosexuality[46]. The mental health workers were from the San Francisco Bay area and may be unusual. However, 9-in-10 had treated homosexuals and almost all said they would treat some goal other than changing sexual orientation, namely, self acceptance, self assertiveness or improved interpersonal relationships. When asked directly if they would treat a homosexual with the aim of changing sexual orientation, about 4-in-10 said they would. Seven-in-10 thought they could change sexual orientation. Three quarters of the sample supported a diagnosis of *personality disorder* for homosexuals although 8-in-10 would label it a *sexual deviation*. A quarter thought homosexuality should disqualify an individual from security sensitive federal employment but almost all the respondants were opposed to treating homosexual acts between consenting adults as a criminal offense. Almost all felt it was possible for homosexuals to function effectively. Ironically 3/4 of the respondents had used group therapy with homosexuals although only 14% considered it the treatment of choice. The latter was not specified in the report. It is surprising that there are so few studies of group therapy in the professional literature to date and one has to wonder at the extensive use of aversion therapy for homosexuality.

Table 4.3 summarizes the outcome of treatments for homosexuality. It has been the "bisexual" male who has been the most successful candidate for heterosexual adjustment in all the therapy approaches discussed. A heterosexual responsiveness was already in his erotic repertoire so

TABLE 4.3
Summary of Treatment Effectiveness for Homosexuality

Method	Results
1. Chemical and Electrical Aversion Therapies	40% to 60% cease homosexual behavior for 3 to 6 months. "Bisexuals" do best. Logical and theoretical basis for this treatment are questionable according to controlled studies.
2. Covert Sensitization	Limited application but successful in case studies. Suffers same problems as other aversion therapies. No controlled research on the method.
3. Reciprocal Inhibition Therapy	Logical fit to theories of homosexuality as a problem of anxiety. Limited application but it is as effective as other methods.
4. Positive Classical Conditioning	Theoretically and practically unsatisfactory. Limited use.
5. Fading	Problematic in few cases reported. Patient may respond to females but continues to react to males.
6. Positive Operant Conditioning	Limited use with mixed results.
7. Orgasmic Reconditioning	Results in loss of sexual pleasure but substitute behavior is not evident. Limited use.
8. Multitreatment Approaches	Seems effective in few reported case studies. Uncertain what effective ingredient(s) are.
9. Hypnosis	Comparable to other methods in limited number of reported cases.
10. Psychotherapies	Poor assessment of outcome compared to behavioral methods but much longer follow ups. Comparable success rates of 40%.
11. Masters & Johnson Method	Reported 75% success rate but when patient selection and drop outs etc. are accounted for, it is 33%, comparable to other methods. Success rate for homosexual dysfunction is much higher and a more appropriate method.

treatments may alter the relative strength of his hetero– and homosexual response rather than change his basic make up. As we will discuss in the next chapter on bisexuality, this also has its problems.

In spite of the claims of "cures" there has been no adequate demonstration that it is possible to alter erotic preferences as opposed to overt behavior in exclusive homosexual males[52]. Is it sufficient to have a man live a sex life that is ego dystonic even if it generates no anxiety? Whatever the conviction of the therapist, this is not a growth experience for the individual. It creates a sham for him and teaches him to deny a part of himself that is very real and present and is likely to be present for the rest of his life. A homosexual does not choose to have an erotic preference for men any more than heterosexuals can choose to prefer women. We would not agree to training a man with aphasia that he is really no different from everyone else though therapeutic efforts have failed to change his inadequate language functioning. Rather we attempt to train such individuals to live with dignity and within the frame of their existing abilities, peculiarities and their sexuality. Homosexual men represent the full gamut of human personality and talents, from poets and scientists to ministers of church and state to laborers and mechanics. To have their whole life degenerated because they are homosexual seems like poor therapeutic practice.

Mr. A represents the possible contrast in therapeutic approaches. He was an American citizen who moved to Canada in adulthood. As a resident in Florida, he experienced a traumatic event. While working in a bank as a teller, there was a holdup and one of the gunmen made him lie on the floor and put the gun to his head. The gunman said, "One false move out of you and I'll blow your brains out". He felt at that moment his life would end. He had to be treated for an anxiety state by a Florida psychiatrist but migrated to Canada before the course of treatment was completed. While in his new home, he found it difficult to relate to the homosexual community and tried to make a heterosexual adaptation. He joined a group therapy program that met weekly. He felt he was not coming to logger heads with either his homosexuality or his depression and anxiety, although he claimed his anxiety was not so bad anymore, it was depression. He felt his previous group therapy sessions had not dealt with either. He also started individual therapy but did not find that satisfactory. He thought the therapist wanted him to change into a heterosexual but was unsure. In fact he was so passive he did not know what to expect or where he was going. He came to our clinic "inquiring about homosexuality":

Doctor: Are you a homosexual?

Mr. A: I, no, I don't know—that is, I want to find out about it.

Doctor: Are you attracted to men?

Mr. A: Well yes, but I'm attracted to women too.

Doctor: Which do you find more attractive?

Mr. A: Well, it's easier to be aroused by men. I have to work at being aroused by women.

Doctor: Have you had any sex experience with men and women?

Mr. A: Only with men, although I've kissed women on dates.

Doctor: How do they compare?

Mr. A. The women don't do anything to me unless I really work at it. I find the men exciting right away. I can get excited looking at a man on the street. Is that abnormal?

Doctor: Sounds like you have a homosexual preference but you can't accept it.

Mr. A: But homosexuality is abnormal, isn't it?

Doctor: We really don't know what causes homosexuality but most research evidence at present suggest that a homosexual man can lead a normal productive life as a homosexual and he need not have psychiatric problems. In fact at present, it is probably the simplest and best solution to being a homosexual. Accept and enjoy it.

Mr. A: But what will people say? I just can't go out and tell everyone I'm a homosexual. They wouldn't accept it.

Doctor: That may be true. Everyone won't accept it. Perhaps even some close friends won't accept it either. But you need not advertise your sex life. Most heterosexuals don't go around telling everyone, "Hey, I'm heterosexual," or telling even close friends what they do in bed with their wives, girl-friends and lovers. Reserve sex for sexual situations. Live the rest of your life in an enjoyable way as you would if you were heterosexual.

Mr. A: Now that I feel it is out in the open about being homosexual, I can admit a lot of things to myself. I know in my heart that I really don't like girls and that it has been difficult trying to date them. They are so eager to carry on some sexual involvement and I can't do it. I can admit to myself that I have been really phoney with them.

Doctor: You will feel a lot better if you try to meet your needs rather than try to conform to something that is not you. Under the law, homosexual acts in this community are acceptable providing they are done between consenting adults in private . . . . the same law that applies to heterosexuals.

Mr. A: You know, suddenly I don't feel depressed. I haven't felt this good in years. There are still problems which I would like to discuss but I don't feel depressed right now and it is good.

Doctor: I'm glad you feel that way and that I could help. When you come to your next appointment, we can discuss those problems.

The extent of emotion felt by *Mr. A* is not as intense in many cases of homsexuality but "coming out" can be quite traumatic for young people and if handled in the above fashion, a few sessions can change the patients dramatically. In fact the treatment of choice is no treatment of homosexuality per se but a short course in self acceptance.

BIBLIOGRAPHY

1. Abe, K., & Moran, P. A. Parental age of homosexuals. *British Journal of Psychiatry,* 1969, *115,* 313–317.
2. Acosta, F. X. Etiology and treatment of homosexuality: A review. *Archives of Sexual Behavior,* 1975, *4*(1), 9–29.
3. Adams, H. E., & Sturgis, E. T. Status of behavioral reorientation techniques in the modification of homosexuality: A review. *Psychological Bulletin,* 1977, *84*(6), 1171–1188.
4. Allen, C. *A textbook of psychosexual disorders.* London: Oxford University Press, 1969.
5. Anastasi, A. *Differential psychology.* New York: MacMillan, 1958.
6. Bancroft, J. Aversion therapy of homosexuality: A pilot study of ten cases. *British Journal of Psychiatry,* 1969, *115,* 1417–1431.
7. Bancroft, J. *Deviant sexual behavior.* London: Oxford University Press, 1974.
8. Barlow, D. Aversive procedures. In W. S. Agras (Ed.), *Behavior modification: Principles and clinical application.* Boston: Little, Brown & Co., 1972, 87–125.
9. Barlow, D. Increasing heterosexual responsiveness in the treatment of sexual deviation: A review of the clinical and experimental evidence. *Behavior Therapy,* 1973, *4,* 655–671.
10. Barlow, D., & Agras, S. *An experimental analysis of "fading" to increase heterosexual responsiveness in homosexuality.* Paper presented at the 17th Annual Meeting of the Southern Psychological Association, Miami Beach, Florida, 1971.
11. Barlow, D., Agras, S., & Leitenberg, H. *A preliminary report on the contribution of therapeutic instructions to covert sensitization.* Paper presented at the Annual Meeting of the Association for Advancement of Behavior Therapy, Florida, 1970.
12. Bell, A. P. Research in homosexuality: Back to the drawing board. *Archives of Sexual Behavior,* 1975, *4*(4), 421–431.
13. Bell, A. P., & Weinberg, M. S. *Homosexualities.* New York: Simon and Schuster, 1978.
14. Bem, S. L. The measurement of psychological androgyny. *Journal of Consulting and Clinical Psychology,* 1974, *42*(2), 155–162.
15. Bene, E. On the genesis of male homosexuality: An attempt at clarifying the role of the parents. *British Journal of Psychiatry,* 1965, *111,* 803–813.
16. Bergler, E. *Homosexuality: Disease or way of life?* New York: Hill & Wang Co., 1957.
17. Besdine, M. Shakespeare: The homosexual element in the life of a genius. *Medical Aspects of Human Sexuality,* 1971, *5*(2), 158–183.
18. Bieber, I. Homosexuality—a psychoanalytic study of male homsexuality. *British Journal of Psychiatry,* 1965, *111,* 195–198.

19. Bieber, I. Homosexual dynamics in psychiatric crisis. *American Journal of Psychiatry,* 1972, *128*(10), 1268–1272.
20. Bieber, I. A discussion of "Homosexuality: The ethical challenge". *Journal of Consulting & Clinical Psychology,* 1976, *44*(2), 163–166.
21. Bieber, I., & Bieber, B. Male homosexuality. *Canadian Journal of Psychiatry,* 1979, *24,* 409–421.
22. Bieber, I., Dain, H., Dince, P., Drellich, M., Grand, H., Gundlach, R., Kremer, M., Rifkin, A., Wilbur, C., & Bieber, T. *Homosexuality: A psychoanalytic study of male homosexuals.* New York: Basic Books, Inc., 1962.
23. Birk, L., Huddleston, W., Miller, E., & Cohler, B. Avoidance conditioning for homosexuality. *Archives of General Psychiatry,* 1971, *25,* 314–323.
24. Bond, J., & Hutchison, H. Application of reciprocal inhibition therapy to exhibitionism. *Canadian Medical Association Journal,* 1960, *83,* 23–25.
25. Brewer, J., & Wright, R. (Eds.). *Sex research: Bibliographies from the Institute of Sex Research.* Phoenix: Orxy Press, 1979.
26. Buhrich, N., & McConaghy, N. Parental relationships during childhood in homosexuality, transvestism and transsexualism. *Australian & New Zealand Journal of Psychiatry,* 1978, *12,* 103–108.
27. Callahan, E. J., & Leitenberg, H. Aversion therapy for sexual deviation: Contingent shock and covert sensitization. *Journal of Abnormal Psychology,* 1973, *81*(1), 60–73.
28. Cautela, J. R. Covert reinforcement. *Behavior Therapy,* 1970, *1,* 33–50.
29. Cavenar, J., Spaulding, J., & Butts, N. Autofellatio: a power and dependency conflict. *Journal of Nervous and Mental Disease,* 1977, *165,* 356–360.
30. Clark, D. F. A note on avoidance conditioning techniques in sexual disorder. *Behavior Research & Therapy,* 1965, *3,* 203–206.
31. Cooper, A. J. Etiology of homosexuality. *In Understanding Homosexuality: Its Biological and Psychological Bases.* Loraine J. A. (Ed.). Lancaster, England: Medical & Technical Publishing Co. Ltd., 1974.
32. Curran, D., & Parr, D. Homosexuality: An analysis of 100 male cases seen in private practice. *British Medical Journal,* 1957, *1,* 797–801.
33. Curtis, R. H., & Presly, A. S. The extinction of homosexual behavior by covert sensitization: A case study. *Behavior Research & Therapy,* 1972, *10,* 81–83.
34. Dean, R. B., & Richardson, H. Analysis of MMPI profiles of forty college educated overt male homosexuals. *Journal of Consulting Psychology,* 1964, *28*(6), 483–486.
35. Domoney, D. W. *Multivariate Cluster Analysis: A Monte Carlo Study of Some Basic Parameters,* Ph.D. Thesis, University of Toronto, Toronto, 1975.
36. Dorner, G., Rohde, W., Stahl, F., Krell, L., & Masius, W. A neuroendocrine predisposition for homosexuality in men. *Archives of Sexual Behavior,* 1975, *4*(1), 1–9.
37. Dorner, G. Hormones and sexual differentiation of the brain. In *Sex Hormones and Behavior.* Ciba Foundation Symposium 62 Amsterdam: Excerpta Medica, 1979.
38. Ellis, A. The effectiveness of psychotherapy with individuals who have severe homosexual problems. *Journal of Consulting Psychiatry,* 1956, *32*(3), 191–195.
39. Evans, R. B. Childhood parental relationships of homosexual men. *Journal of Consulting & Clinical Psychology,* 1969, *33*(2), 129–135.
40. Evans, R. B. Parental relationships and homosexuality. *Medical Aspects of Human Sexuality,* 1971, *5*(4), 164–177.
41. Evans, R. B. Physical and biochemical characteristics of homosexual men. *Journal of Consulting & Clinical Psychology,* 1972, *39*(1), 140–147.
42. Feldman, M. P. Aversion therapy for sexual deviations: A critical review. *Psychological Bulletin,* 1966, *65*(2), 65–79.

43. Feldman, M. P., & MacCulloch, M. J. *Homosexual behavior: Therapy and assessment.* Oxford: Pergamon Press, 1971.

44. Feldman, M. P., & MacCulloch, M. J. Avoidance conditioning for homosexuals: A reply to MacDonough's critique. *Behavior Therapy,* 1972, *3,* 430–436.

45. Feldman, M. P., MacCulloch, M. J., Mellor, V., & Pinschof, J. The application of anticipatory avoidance learning to the treatment of homosexuality. III. The sexual orientation method. *Behavior Research & Therapy,* 1966, *4,* 289–299.

46. Fort, J., Steiner, C., & Conrad, F. Attitudes of mental health professionals toward homosexuality and its treatment. *Psychological Reports,* 1971, *29,* 347–350.

47. Freeman, R. J. *The role of subject, context, and stimulus variables in determining evaluative and behavioural reactions to explicit depictions of human sexual behavior.* Master of Arts thesis, University of Waterloo, 1976.

48. Freeman, W., & Meyer, R. A behavioral alteration of sexual preferences in the human male. *Behavior Therapy,* 1975, *6,* 206–212.

49. Freemon, F. R. Oscar Wilde: Poet, novelist, playwright, homosexual *Human Sexuality,* 1971, *5*(6), 113–124.

50. Freund, K. Some problems in the treatment of homosexuality. In H. J. Eysenck (Ed.), *Behavior therapy and the neuroses.* London: Oxford Press, 1960.

51. Freund, K. Male homosexuality: An analysis of the pattern. In J. A. Loraine (Ed.), *Understanding homosexuality: Its biological and psychological bases.* Lancaster, England: Medical & Technical Publishing Co. Ltd., 1974, 25–81.

52. Freund, K. Should homosexuality arouse therapeutic concern? *Journal of Homosexuality,* 1977, *2*(3), 235–240.

53. Freund, K., Langevin, R., & Barlow, D. Comparison of two penile measures of erotic arousal. *Behavior Research & Therapy,* 1974, *12,* 355–359.

54. Freund, K., Langevin, R., Cibiri, S., & Zajac, Y. Heterosexual aversion in homosexual males. *British Journal of Psychiatry,* 1973, *122,* 163–169.

55. Freund, K., Langevin, R., Chamberlayne, R., Deosora, A., & Zajac, Y. The phobic theory of male homosexuality. *Archives of General Psychiatry,* 1974, *31,* 495–499.

56. Freund, K., Langevin, R., Laws, R., & Serber, M. Femininity and preferred partner age in homosexual and heterosexual males. *British Journal of Psychiatry,* 1974, *125,* 442–446.

57. Freund, K., Langevin, R., Satterberg, J., & Steiner, B. Extension of the gender identity scale for males. *Archives of Sexual Behavior,* 1977, *6*(6), 507–519.

58. Freund, K., Langevin, R., Wescom, T., & Zajac, Y. Heterosexual interest in homosexual males. *Archives of Sexual Behavior,* 1975, *4*(5), 509–518.

59. Freund, K., Langevin, R., & Zajac, Y. Heterosexual aversion in homosexual males: A second experiment. *British Journal of Psychiatry,* 1974, *125,* 177–180.

60. Freund, K., Langevin, R., Zajac, Y., Steiner, B., & Zajac, A. Parent-child relations in transsexual and nontranssexual males. *British Journal of Psychiatry,* 1974, *124,* 22–23.

61. Freund, K., McKnight, C. K., Langevin, R., & Cibiri, S. The female child as a surrogate object. *Archives of Sexual Behavior,* 1972, *2,* 119–133.

62. Freund, K., Nagler, E., Langevin, R., Zajac, A., & Steiner, B. Measuring feminine gender identity in homosexual males. *Archives of Sexual Behavior,* 1974, *3*(3), 249–260.

63. Gardner, R. A., & Gardner, B. T. Early signs of language in child and chimpanzee. *Science,* 1975, *187,* 752–753.

64. Gebhard, P. H., Gagnon, J. H., Pomeroy, W. B., & Christenson, C. V. *Sex offenders.* New York: Harper & Row, 1965.

65. Gold, S., & Neufeld, I. A learning approach to the treatment of homsexuality. *Behavior Research & Therapy,* 1965, *2,* 201–204.

66. Goldberg, A. A fresh look at perverse behavior. *International Journal of Psychoanalysis,* 1975, *56,* 335–342.

67. Graham, J., Schroeder, H., & Lilly, R. Factor analysis of items on the social introversion and masculinity-femininity scales of the MMPI. *Journal of Clinical Psychology,* 1971, *27*(3), 367–370.

68. Gray, J. J. Behavior therapy in a patient with homosexual fantasies and heterosexual anxiety. *Journal of Behavior Therapy & Experimental Psychiatry,* 1970, *1,* 225–232.

69. Hadfield, J. A. The cure of homosexuality. *British Medical Journal,* 1958, *1,* 1323–1326.

70. Hadfield, J. A. Origins of homosexuality. *British Medical Journal,* 1966, *1,* 678.

71. Hallam, R. S., & Rachman, S. Some effects of aversion therapy on patients with sexual disorders. *Behavior Research & Therapy,* 1972, *10,* 171–180.

72. Hanson, R. W., & Adesso, V. J. A multiple behavioral approach to male homosexual behavior: A case study. *Journal of Behavior Therapy & Experimental Psychiatry,* 1972, *3,* 323–325.

73. Hart, M., Roback, H., Tittler, B., Weitz, L., Walston, B., & McKee, E. Psychological adjustment of nonpatient homosexuals: Critical review of the research literature. *Journal of Clinical Psychiatry,* 1978, *39*(7), 27–31.

74. Hatterer, M. S. The problem of women married to homosexual men. *American Journal of Psychiatry,* 1974, *131*(3), 275–278.

75. Haynes, S. N. Learning theory and the treatment of homosexuality. *Psychotherapy: Theory, Research & Practice,* 1970, *7*(2), 91–94.

76. Herman, S. H., Barlow, D. H., & Agras, S. An experimental analysis of classical conditioning as a method of increasing heterosexual arousal in homosexuals. *Behavior Therapy,* 1974, *5,* 33–47.

77. Herman, S. H., Barlow, D. H., & Agras, S. An experimental analysis of exposure to "explicit" heterosexual stimuli as an effective variable in changing arousal patterns of homosexuals. *Behavior Research & Therapy,* 1974, *12,* 335–345.

78. Herman, S. H., & Prewett, M. An experimental analysis of feedback to increase sexual arousal in a case of homo- and heterosexual impotence: A preliminary report. *Behavior Research & Experimental Therapy,* 1974, *5,* 271–274.

79. Hinrichsen, J. J., & Katahn, M. Recent trends and new developments in the treatment of homosexuality. *Psychotherapy: Theory, Research and Practice,* 1975, *12*(1), 83–92.

80. Hoffman, M. What outcome can be expected in psychotherapy of homosexuals? *Medical Aspects of Human Sexuality,* 1971, *5*(12), 95–96.

81. Hooberman, R. E. Psychological androgyny, feminine gender identity and self esteem in homosexual and heterosexual males. *Journal of Sex Research,* 1979, *15*(4), 306–315.

82. Hooker, E. The adjustment of the male overt homosexual. *Journal of Projective Techniques,* 1957, *21,* 18–31.

83. Huff, F. W. The desensitization of a homosexual. *Behavior Research & Therapy,* 1970, *8,* 99–102.

84. Ince, L. P. Behavior modification of sexual disorders. *American Journal of Psychotherapy,* 1973, *27,* 446–451.

85. Jacobson, E. *Progressive relaxation.* Chicago: University of Chicago Press, 1938.

86. James, S. Treatment of homosexuality II. Superiority of desensitization/arousal as compared with anticipatory avoidance conditioning: Results of a controlled trial. *Behavior Therapy,* 1978, *9,* 28–36.

87. Johnson, W. R. *Human sexual behavior and sex education.* Philadelphia: Lea & Febiger, 1968.

88. Kallman, F. Comparative twin studies on the genetic aspects of homosexuality.

Journal of Nervous & Mental Disease, 1952, 20, 55-59.

89. Kimble, G. A. Conditioning and learning. New York: Apple Century Crofts, Inc., 1961.

90. Kinsey, A. C., Pomeroy, W. B., & Martin, C. E. Sexual behavior in the human male. Philadelphia: W. B. Saunders Co., 1948.

91. Kraft, T. Treatment for sexual perversions. Behavior Research & Therapy, 1969, 7, 215.

92. Kraft, T. A note on aversion therapy. Psychological Reports, 1970, 27, 165-166.

93. Kraft, T. Systematic desensitization in the treatment of homosexuality. Behavior Research & Therapy, 1970, 8, 319.

94. Lang, T. Studies on the genetic determination of homosexuality. Journal of Nervous & Mental Disease, 1940, 12, 55-64.

95. Langevin, R. The modification of human sexual behavior. Proceedings of the National Symposium on Medical Sciences and the Criminal Law. Toronto: University of Toronto Press, 1973, 40-53.

96. Langevin, R., Paitich, D., Freeman, R., Mann, K., & Handy, L. Personality characteristics and sexual anomalies in males. Canadian Journal of Behavioral Science, 1978, 10(3), 222-238.

97. Langevin, R., Paitich, D., Ramsay, G., Anderson, C., Kamrad, J., Pope, S., Geller, G., & Newman, S. Experimental studies in the etiology of genital exhibitionism. Archives of Sexual Behavior, 1979, 8(4), 307-331.

98. Langevin, R., Paitich, D., & Steiner, B. The clinical profile of male transsexuals living as females vs. those living as males. Archives of Sexual Behavior, 1977, 6(2), 143-154.

99. Langevin, R., Stanford, A., & Block, R. The effect of relaxation instructions on erotic arousal in homosexual and heterosexual males. Behavior Therapy, 1975, 6, 453-458.

100. Larson, D. E. An adaptation of the Feldman and MacCulloch approach to treatment of homosexuality by the application of anticipatory avoidance learning. Behavior Research & Therapy, 1970, 8, 209-210.

101. Latimer, P. A case of homosexuality treated by in vivo desensitization and assertive training. Canadian Psychiatric Association Journal, 1977, 22, 185-189.

102. Lazarus, A. A. Behavioral therapy for sexual problems. Professional Psychology, 1971, 2, 349-353.

103. Lester, D., McLaughlin, S., Cohen, R., & Dunn, L. Sex-deviant handwriting, femininity, and homosexuality. Perceptual and Motor Skills, 1977, 45, 1156.

104. Levin, S. M., Hirsch, I. S., Shugar, G., & Kapche, R. Treatment of homosexuality and heterosexual anxiety with avoidance conditioning and systematic desensitization data and case report. Psychotherapy: Theory, Research & Practice, 1968, 5(3), 160-168.

105. Loney, J. Background factors, sexual experiences, and attitudes toward treatment in two "normal" homosexual samples. Journal of Consulting & Clinical Psychology, 1972, 38(1), 57-65.

106. Lunneborg, P. W. Dimensionality of MF. Journal of Clinical Psychology, 1972, 28, 313-317.

107. MacCulloch, M. J., & Birtles, C. J. Anticipatory avoidance learning for the treatment of homosexuality: Recent developments and an automated aversion therapy system. Behavior Therapy, 1971, 2, 151-159.

108. Mac Donough, T. S. A critique of the first Feldman and MacCulloch avoidance conditioning treatment for homosexuals. Behavior Therapy, 1972, 3, 104-111.

109. Manosevitz, M. Early sexual behavior in adult homosexual and heterosexual males. Journal of Abnormal Psychology, 1970, 76(3), 396-402.

110. Manosevitz, M. Education and MMPI Mf scores in homosexual and heterosexual males. *Journal of Consulting & Clinical Psychology*, 1971, *36*(3), 395–399.

111. Manosevitz, M. The development of male homosexuality. *Journal of Sex Research*, 1972, *8*(1), 31–40.

112. Margolese, M. Homosexuality: A new endocrine correlate. *Hormones & Behavior*, 1970, *1*, 151–155.

113. Marquis, J. N. Orgasmic reconditioning: Changing sexual object choice through controlling masturbation fantasies. *Journal of Behavior Therapy & Experimental Psychiatry*, 1970, *1*, 263–271.

114. Marshall, W. L. The modification of sexual fantasies: A combined treatment approach to the reduction of deviant sexual behavior. *Behavior Research & Therapy*, 1973, *11*, 557–564.

115. Martinson, F. M. Eroticism in infancy and childhood. *The Journal of Sex Research*, 1976, *12*(4), 251–262.

116. Masters, W. H., & Johnson, V. E. *Homosexuality in perspective*. Boston: Little, Brown & Co., 1979.

117. Max, L. Breaking up a homosexual fixation by the conditioned reaction technique: A case study. *Psychological Bulletin*, 1935, *32*, 734.

118. May, E. Discussion of "Recent trends and new developments in the treatment of homosexuality" by James J. Hinrichsen and Martin Katahn. *Psychotherapy: Theory, Research & Practice*, 1977, *14*(1), 18–20.

119. Mayerson, P., & Lief, H. Psychotherapy of homosexuals: A follow up study of nineteen cases. In J. Marmor (Ed.), *Sexual Inversion*. New York: Basic Books Inc., 1965, 302–344.

120. McCarthy, D., Anthony, R., & Domino, G. A comparison of the CPI, FRANCK, MMPI, and WAIS Maculinity-Femininity indexes. *Journal of Consulting & Clinical Psychology*, 1970, *35*(3), 414–416.

121. McConaghy, N. Penile volume change to moving pictures of male and female nudes in heterosexual and homosexual males. *Behavior Research & Therapy*, 1967, *5*, 43–48.

122. McConaghy, N. Subjective and penile plethysmograph responses following aversion-relief and apomorphine aversion therapy for homosexual impulses. *British Journal of Psychiatry*, 1969, *115*, 723–730.

123. McConaghy, N. Penile response conditioning and its relationship to aversion therapy in homosexuals. *Behavior Therapy*, 1970, *1*, 213–221.

124. McConaghy, N. Aversion therapy. *Seminars in Psychiatry*, 1972, *4*(2), 139–144.

125. McConaghy, N. Aversion therapy of homosexuality. *Current Psychiatric Therapies*, 1972, *12*, 38–47.

126. McConaghy, N. Is a homosexual orientation irreversible? *British Journal of Psychiatry*, 1976, *129*, 556–563.

127. McCrady, R. E. A forward-fading technique for increasing heterosexual responsiveness in male homosexuals. *Journal of Behavior Therapy and Experimental Psychology*, 1973, *4*(3), 257–261.

128. McGuire, R., & Vallance, M. Aversion therapy by electric shock. A simple technique. *British Medical Journal*, 1964, *1*, 151–153.

129. Mello, N. K., & Mendelson, J. H. Alcohol and human behavior. In L. L. Iverson, S. D. Iverson, & S. H. Snyder. *Handbook of psychopharmacology* (Vol. 12). New York: Plenum Press, 1978, 235–317.

130. Meyer-Bahlburg, H. F. Sex hormones and male homosexuality in comparative perspective. *Archives of Sexual Behavior*, 1979, *8*(2), 101–120.

131. Miller, M. Why are women's fashions and hairstyling industres dominated by homosexuals? *Medical Aspects of Human Sexuality*, 1971, *5*, 61–67.

132. Mitchell, S. A. Psychodynamics, homosexuality, and the question of pathology. *Psychiatry,* 1978, *41*(3), 254–263.
133. Money, J. Sexual dimorphism and homosexual gender identity. *Psychological Bulletin,* 1970, *74*(6), 425–440.
134. Myrick, F. Attitudinal differences between heterosexually and homosexually oriented males and between covert and overt male homosexuals. *Journal of Abnormal Psychology,* 1974, *83*(1), 81–86.
135. Pacion, S. J. Leonardo da Vinci: A psychosexual enigma. *Medical Aspects of Human Sexuality,* 1971, *5,* 35–41.
136. Paitich, D., & Langevin, R. The Clarke parent-child relations questionnaire: A clinically useful test for adults. *Journal of Consulting & Clinical Psychology,* 1976, *44*(3), 428–436.
137. Paitich, D., Langevin, R., Freeman, R., Mann, K., & Handy, L. The Clarke SHQ: A clinical sex history questionnaire for males. *Archives of Sexual Behavior,* 1977, *6,* 421–436.
138. Papatheophilou, R., James, S., & Orwin, A. Electroencephalographic findings in treatment-seeking homosexuals compared with heterosexuals: A controlled study. *British Journal of Psychiatry,* 1975, *127,* 63–66.
139. Pare, C. M. Homosexuality and chromosomal sex. *Journal of Psychosomatic Research,* 1956, *1,* 247–251.
140. Patterson, C. H. *Theories of counseling and psychotherapy.* New York: Harper & Row, 1966.
141. Perloff, W. H. Hormones and homosexuality. In J. Marmor (Ed.), *Sexual inversion.* New York: Basic Books, 1965, 44–69.
142. Phillips, D., Fischer, S., Groves, G., & Singh, R. Alternative behavioral approaches to the treatment of homosexuality. *Archives of Sexual Behavior,* 1976, *5*(3), 223–228.
143. Pritchard, M. Homosexuality and genetic sex. *Journal of Mental Science,* 1962, *108,* 616–623.
144. Quinn, J. T., Harbison, J. J., & McAllister, H. An attempt to shape human penile responses. *Behavior Research & Therapy,* 1970, *8,* 213–216.
145. Quinsey, V. L., Chaplin, T. C., & Varney, G. A comparison of rapists' and non-sex offenders' sexual preferences for mutually consenting sex, rape and sadistic acts. *Behavioral Assessment,* 1981, *3,* 127–135.
146. Quirk, D. A follow up on the Bond-Hutchinson case of systematic desensitization with an exhibitionist. *Behavior Therapy,* 1974, *5,* 428–431.
147. Raboch, J., & Nedoma, K. Sex chromatin and sexual behavior. A study of 36 men with female nuclear pattern and 194 homosexuals. *Psychosomatic Medicine,* 1958, *20,* 55–59.
148. Raboch, J., & Sipova, I. Intelligence in homosexuals, transsexuals and hypogonadotropic eunuchoids. *The Journal of Sex Research,* 1974, *10*(2), 156–161.
149. Rachman, S. Sexual disorders and behavior therapy. *American Journal of Psychiatry,* 1961, *118,* 235–240.
150. Rekers, G. A. A priori values and research on homosexuality. *American Psychologist,* 1978, *33*(5), 510–512.
151. Roper, P. The effects of hypnotherapy on homosexuality. *Canadian Medical Association Journal,* 1967, *11,* 319–327.
152. Rose, R. Testosterone, aggression, and homosexuality: a review of the literature and implications for future research. *Topics in Psychoendocrinology,* Sachar, E. J. (Ed.) New York: Grune & Statton, 1975.
153. Rosen, I. *The pathology and treatment of sexual deviation: A methodological approach.* London: Oxford University Press, 1964.

154. Russell, A., & Winkler, R. Evaluation of assertive training and homosexual guidance service groups designed to improve homosexual functioning. *Journal of Consulting & Clinical Psychology,* 1977, *45*(1), 1–13.

155. Sagarin, E. Prison homosexuality and its effect on post-prison sexual behavior. *Psychiatry,* 1976, *39*(3), 245–257.

156. Saghir, M., & Robins, E. *Male and female homosexuality: A comprehensive investigation.* Baltimore: Williams & Wilkins, 1973.

157. Sandford, D. A., Tustin, R. D., & Priest, P. N. Increasing heterosexual arousal in two adult male homosexuals using a differential reinforcement procedure. *Behavior Therapy,* 1975, *6,* 689–693.

158. Salter, L. G., & Melville, C. H. A re-educative approach to homosexual behavior: A case study and treatment recommendations. *Psychotherapy: Theory, Research & Practice,* 1972, *9*(2), 166–167.

159. Saul, L. J., & Beck, A. T. Psychodynamics of male homosexuality. *International Journal of Psychoanalysis,* 1961, *42,* 43–48.

160. Schatzberg, A. F., Westfall, M. P., Blumetti, A. B., & Birk, C. L. Effeminacy, I. A quantitative rating scale. *Archives of Sexual Behavior,* 1975, *4*(1), 31–41.

161. Schiavi, R. C., & White, D. Androgens and male sexual function: A review of human studies. *Journal of Sex & Marital Therapy,* 1976, *2*(3), 214–228.

162. Segal, B., & Sims, J. Covert sensitization with a homosexual: A controlled replication. *Journal of Consulting & Clinical Psychology,* 1972, *39*(2), 259–263.

163. Shealy, A. E. Combining behavior therapy and cognitive therapy in treating homosexuality. *Psychotherapy: Theory, Research & Practice,* 1972, *9,* 221–222.

164. Siegelman, M. Adjustment of male homosexuals and heterosexuals. *Archives of Sexual Behavior,* 1972, *2*(1), 9–25.

165. Siegelman, M. Psychological adjustment of homosexual and heterosexual men: a corss-national replication. *Archives of Sexual Behavior,* 1978, *7*(1), 1–11.

166. Sines, J. O., & Russell, M. A. The BSRI, M, F, and androgyny scores are bipolar. *Journal of Clinical Psychology,* 1978, *34*(1), 53–56.

167. Slater, E. The sibs and children of homosexuals. *Symposium on Nuclear Sex,* Smith, D. R., & Davison, W. M. (Eds.). London, 1958.

168. Slater, E. Birth order and maternal age of homosexuals. *Lancet,* 1962, *1,* 69–71.

169. Smith, J. Ego-dystonic homosexuality. *Comprehensive Psychiatry,* 1980, *21*(2), 119–127.

170. Sneath, P. H., & Sokol, A. A. *Numerical Taxonomy.* San Francisco, Freeman Co., 1973.

171. Socarides, C. W. The sexual deviations and the diagnostic manual. *American Journal of Psychotherapy,* 1978, *3*(2), 414–426.

172. Socarides, C. W. *Homosexuality.* New York: Jason Aronson, 1978.

173. Socarides, C. W., Bieber, I., Bychowski, G., Gershman, H., Jacobs, T. J., Myers, W. A., Nackenson, B. L., Prescott, K. F., Rifkin, A. H., Stein, S., & Terry, J. Homosexuality in the male: A report of a psychiatric study group. *International Journal of Psychiatry,* 1973, *11*(4), 461–479.

174. Solyom, L., & Miller, S. A differential conditioning procedure as the initial phase of the behaviour therapy of homosexuality. *Behavior Research Therapy,* 1965, *3,* 147–160.

175. Spitzer, R. L. The diagnostic status of homosexuality in DSM III: a reformulation of the issues. *American Journal of Psychiatry,* 1981, *138*(2), 210–215.

176. Stevenson, I., & Wolpe, J. Recovery from sexual deviations through overcoming non-sexual neurotic responses. *American Journal of Psychiatry,* 1960, *116,* 737.

177. Stoller, R. J., Marmor, J., Bieber, I., Gold, R., Socarides, C., Green, R., & Spitzer, R. A symposium: Should homosexuality be in the APA nomenclature? *American*

Journal of Psychiatry, 1973, *130*(11), 1207–1216.

178. Stringer, P., & Grygier, T. Male homosexuality, psychiatric patient status, and psychological masculinity and femininity. *Archives of Sexual Behavior,* 1976, *5*(1), 15–27.

179. Suarez, B. K., & Przybeck, T. R. Sibling sex rates and male homosexuality. *Archives of Sexual Behavior,* 1980, *9*(1), 1–12.

180. Tanner, B. A. Shock intensity and fear of shock in the modification of homosexual behavior in males by avoidance learning. *Behavior Research & Therapy,* 1973, *11,* 213–218.

181. Tanner, B. A. Avoidance training with and without booster sessions to modify homosexual behavior in males. *Behavior Therapy,* 1975, *6,* 649–653.

182. Taylor, F. K. Homosexuality. *British Journal of Psychiatry,* 1965, *111,* 195–198.

183. Thompson, N. L., Schwartz, D. M., McCandless, B. R., & Edwards, D. A. Parent-child relationships and sexual identity in male and female homosexuals and heterosexuals. *Journal of Consulting and Clinical Psychology,* 1973, *41*(1), 120–127.

184. Thorpe, G. L. Learning paradigms in the anticipatory avoidance technique: A comment on the controversy between MacDonough and Feldman. *Behavior Therapy,* 1972, *3,* 614–618.

185. Thorpe, J. G., & Schmidt, E. Therapeutic failure in a case of aversion therapy. *Behavior Research Therapy,* 1964, *1,* 293–296.

186. Thorpe, J. G., Schmidt, E., & Castell, D. A. A comparison of positive and negative conditioning in the treatment of homosexuality. *Behavior Research & Therapy,* 1963, *1,* 357–362.

187. Waters, C. W., Waters, L. K. & Pincus, S. Factor analysis of masculine and feminine sex-typed items from the Bem sex-role inventory. *Psychological Reports,* 1977, *40,* 567–570.

188. Weinrich, J. On a relationship between homosexuality and IQ test scores: A review and some hypotheses. In *Medical Sexology: The Third International Congress.* Forleo, R., & Pasini, W. (Eds.), Littleton, Mass.: PSG Publishing Co., 1978.

189. West, D. J. *Homosexuality re-examined.* Minneapolis: University of Minnesota Press, 1977.

190. Westfall, M. P., Schatzberg, A. F., Blumetti, A. B., & Birk, C. L. Effeminacy. II. Variation with social context. *Archives of Sexual Behavior,* 1975, *4*(1), 43–51.

191. Wilson, G. T., & Davison, G. C. Behavior therapy and homosexuality: A critical perspective. *Behavior Therapy,* 1974, *5,* 16–28.

192. Woodward, M. The diagnosis and treatment of homosexual offenders. *British Journal of Delinquency,* 1958, *9,* 44–59.

193. Yonge, G. D. The Bem sex-role inventory: Use with caution if at all. *Psychological Reports,* 1978, *43,* 1245–1246.

5 Bisexuality

There is very little theoretical literature on bisexuality per se. Most often it is considered as a special facet of homosexuality. I think the topic merits discussion in its own right for three reasons. Most of the "successes" in treatment of homosexuality were actually cases of "bisexuality", that is, patients were married or had heterosexual experience at the start of treatment. Little more is said about treatment outcome in their cases and generally we do not know what their initial erotic preferences were. Therapy is more important if it can change a man who prefers men or who is truly ambisexual and prefers both men and women into a heterosexual. Second, theoretical papers are divided on the belief in the existence of the bisexual. If one uses overt behavior as a criterion, bisexuality appears to be quite prevalent. However, if one uses erotic preferences or reproductive functioning it seems to be nonexistant. The third reason a special chapter is devoted to bisexuality is that clinically at least, they are considered to be less disturbed than exclusive homosexuals. In contrast I have found these men to be much more emotionally disturbed than exclusive homosexual patients and I believe the usual treatments applied to changing them into heterosexuals are not only misguided but antitherapeutic.

THE THEORIES

The word bisexual is ambiguous and at least three overlapping meanings have been applied to the term: relating to both sexes in overt behavior, in erotic preferences, and in reproductive functioning.

Overt behavior.   Freud himself discussed a constitutional predisposition to bisexuality. As he originally used the term, it applied to mental life generally and *all* men had the potential to be bisexuals. However, he was skeptical of the existence of bisexuality and noted that proof rested in biological experimentation. This did not hamper his followers and the term has been so broadly used, according to Rado,[28] that it is almost meaningless. Any relationship between two men, any dominance or submissiveness, competition or friendly cooperation is a manifestation of homosexuality perhaps only in unconscious or latent form. Any "femininity" defined as psychoanalytically labeled "sex symbols" in fantasy, dreams or in manifest culturally stereotyped female behavior represents latent homosexuality whether it is ever orgasmic or not.

Salzman[32] has attempted to clarify the concept of latent homosexuality. He noted that "latent" means either dormancy or potentiality. Dormancy implies that homosexuality is present in seeming heterosexuals as a fully developed and mature function but is inactive for whatever reason. By way of anology, a previously developed ability to ride a bicycle may be considered dormant while we are not using it. In the same way our homosexuality is dormant and in fact may never surface. Potentiality implies possibility of homosexuality developing given adequate stimuli and circumstances. Similarly, for example, one may not know how to ride a bicycle, but given a normal healthy body, the desire and a bicycle, he/she can learn. Many men who are deprived of women in prison or on long voyages, engage in homosexual behavior. If it is their first sexual experience, they may become homosexual according to Sagarin[31]. The two meanings of latency are not really clear cut but Salzman notes that Freud's original meaning was dormancy which lacks operational meaning, so, it cannot be clearly pinned down to some observable behavior.

Some of Freud's followers at least have been critical of the term, latent homosexuality, and have rejected it. Others continue to be fascinated by the idea of unconscious homosexuality. The idea emerges especially in studies of the relationship between homosexuality and paranoid delusions, which is one of the few testable postulates of psychoanalysis, according to Lester[20]. Some psychotic patients, manifest feelings of hostility and fear because they claim they are being persecuted. These paranoid patients were construed by Freud and others to be defending against the unconscious homosexual desires that had become manifest during the psychosis[30]. All individuals have these desires but most are never aware of them because effective psychological defense mechanisms prevent it. The paranoid individual's wishes surface to consciousness but he may project them on to others whom he believes wish to make homosexual advances to him. It may also reflect feelings of insecurity about his masculinity. He may show preoccupation with homosexuality and when the whole process occurs over a short period of time, it is labeled homosexual panic[12][20]. *Mr. A* was brought to the clinic by his family in an acute homosexual panic. He was very effeminate in his mannerisms and gait, presenting the layman's stereotype of the homosexual. He had not yet "come out" and did not indicate to the therapist he was homosexual, if in fact he could admit it to himself. He was an extremely sweaty and agitated individual:

> *Mr. A.* Doctor, tell me why I'm having these awful thoughts. They scare me and I don't understand them. It started happening a week ago Saturday. I found myself looking at men in the supermarket and they looked at me with sexual desire in their faces. They wanted to have me. I was scared to death they would attack me and force me to have sex with them. A couple of days later, it happened again on the street and last night, it was so bad I became hysterical. I couldn't stand it and my mother and sister brought me in. Why are those men looking at me like that?

Ovesey[26] agrees that latent homosexuality is not a useful concept but introduces the term pseudohomosexuality. Some heterosexually oriented men are bothered by homosexual ideation or dreams that are motivated by striving for power and dependency. These pseudohomosexuals misinterpret their striving as homosexual in nature but their feelings are not truly sexual. As Freud observed, the striving may manifest itself as delusions of persecution, jealousy, erotomania or megalomania. Jealousy results from the belief that the male cannot hold a woman against the competition of stronger men. He fantasizes these rivals with the misinterpretation of homosexual interest. Erotomania, or an exaggerated display of sexual feelings and response, serves to compensate for failed masculinity by sexual conquest of women. Megalomania is an attempt at ego inflation when self esteem is low.

Mr. J presented as a pseudohomosexual. He came from an extremely deprived background involving a drunken abusive father. Facing an incest charge involving his 8-year-old daughter, his wife on whom he was excessively dependent divorced him. He described his homosexual yearnings:

> *Mr. J:* Mary was always too busy for sex or too tired and I would go for months without it. It got so bad she wouldn't touch me because she figured I wanted sex. I love her and I don't want to lose her so I would never be unfaithful. But sometimes I just had to get some sex. I knew where to go for a blow job. I'd go down to the gay theaters and see a show. I would get a blow job in the washroom and sometimes in the theater. I would have liked to go to bed with my wife instead but at least it was some release and I wasn't unfaithful to her.

> *Doctor:* How are things now that you're divorced?

> *Mr. J:* Well, I'm dating anyway (smiles). I asked out the office dreamgirl and she agreed to go out. All the guys want to take her out but I'm the

first one she's accepted. So I paraded her down the aisle at the office for
our date so all the guys could see. I thought, "Eat your hearts out, guys!"
(laughs).

Stoller[33] has clearly outlined the problems of the psychoanalytic use of
the term, bisexual. Freud believed in a constitutional bisexuality that influenced both object choice and degree of masculinity/femininity.
However, in humans at least, masculinity can be established in early life by
psychological forces in opposition to biological states, for example in hermaphrodites, transsexuals, and effeminate homosexuals. As noted in the
last chapter, sex object choice versus masculinity–femininity and gender
identity may also be independent. Psychoanalysts continue to mix the
terms. They also continue to associate active with male and passive with
female. Salzman[32] has noted that Masters and Johnson's research on actual
behavior during sexual intercourse casts serious doubt on this notion. Males
and females can vary in the degree of activity so that intercourse is best
described as an exchange of active and passive behavior for both sexes. Of
course all the confusion about exclusive and nonexclusive homosexuality
discussed in Chapter 4 applies here as well. Basically the idea of erotic
preferences and transient sexual behavior is confused in discussion of the
bisexual, which makes it difficult to understand this anomaly.

Erotic preference.   The second meaning of the term bisexual, as an
erotic preference, is not used as widely as it should be. If overt "bisexual"
behavior is restricted to incidences of orgasm with both men and women;
the Kinsey studies[16] show that a third to a half of the male population
display "bisexuality" at some time in their lives. It is unknown at present
how many of these men show a sexual preference for both men and women
such that they are truly ambisexual. Freund[9] doubts the existence of truly
bisexual persons. While many men of heterosexual preference engage in
homosexual acts, they do so because the preferred female is unavailable.
They are shy and unable to approach a suitable female or they are simply
curious. The male with a homosexual preference may engage in heterosexual acts for analogous reasons. In addition, social pressure to conform to a
heterosexual society may drive many homosexual men to adapt even to the
point of marriage and having a family[9]. When erotic preferences are ascertained, men either prefer males or females but not both[9,35].

Freund[9] distinguished "bisexuality proper" from the overt sexual
behavior that is more commonly labeled bisexual. He used erotic preference
as a criterion of bisexuality proper and measured it as a preference for the
body characteristics of males versus females. Other behaviors that may be
critically arousing for the bisexual have not been systematically investigated. Some aspect of both male and female behavior or some sexual
act may be important to the bisexual.

The gender behavior of bisexals has not been extensively discussed in the literature other than as a contrast to exclusive homosexuals. If bisexuals' gender identities were ambivalent they may need to play both male and female roles, with sexual outlets being incidental. Perhaps they respond to effeminate behavior in both men and women. Possibly, they have a preference for anal intercourse, which can be performed on either sex. The anus of men and women are not too clearly distinguishable in photographs and only the curvature of the female hips gives away her profile to the casual observer. One may speculate that other behaviors are also important.

Mr. G illustrates the possible range of important factors. He was in love with a woman and was worried about marrying her because of his homosexual desires. He was a rather easy going, good looking Irishman with a good sense of humor. His outstanding clinical features were indecisiveness and passivity, which were reflected in his sexual behavior. Phallometric testing for erotic preference failed to produce significant reactions because *Mr. G* found the pictures "duller than hell". He was questioned about his sexual behavior:

Doctor: Tell me how you go about meeting men for sex.

Mr. G: Well, I don't really meet them. They meet me. Somehow they know I'm game and they approach me. I'd just be standing on the street corner watching people go by and along would come some fellow who'd start talking to me. In no time at all he'd start talking about sex and we'd go to his place for a good time.

Doctor: Does this happen all the time? Do you meet men in other ways?

Mr. G: It happens quite often. They seem to appear out of the woodwork. I don't know how they can tell. Other times I meet men at lectures at the university, but mostly on the street.

Doctor: What sort of things do you do sexually?

Mr. G: Everything and anything. Everything you can do and anything he wants to do to me. I just let him go ahead and do his thing.

LATER......

Doctor: Tell me how you met your girlfriend.

Mr. G: She saw me one day at a talk down at the university and came over and sat beside me and said hello. It sounds like I don't do much in any of my affairs!—But I liked her and she liked me. She knows about the homosexual thing and she doesn't like it. She said if it were another woman, she'd beat me to a pulp.

Doctor: That sounds pretty aggressive.

Mr. G: She can be a rough one. She likes to rough it up; we wrestle and she can belt me a good blow but she is kind and thoughtful under all the roughness. It's very pleasant to be with her. The hours fly past when we're together.

Doctor: Tell me about sex with her.

Mr. G: It's everything and anything too. It's wild and she is usually the aggressor. She bites and scratches. Look at me, I'm black and blue (lifts his pant leg to expose his calf covered in bruises and cuts).

It's sort of embarrassing to say, but she likes to have me orally. What do you call it? Fellatio? I thought only homos liked to do that.

Doctor: How do you feel about that?

Mr. G: Well, like I said, it's embarrassing to talk about but it feels good. Real good.

Bisexual reproduction.   Rado[28] has discussed bisexuality in the sense of reproductive functioning and he has concluded that the concept is not useful in understanding human sexual behavior. He noted that the sex organs of both male and female have a common source in the embryo so that the young fetus is bisexual. The selective action of the prenatal environment and heredity produces either male or female and in rare cases anatomical bisexuals or hermaphrodites who show genital abnormalities in the form of diminutive or partial organs of both sexes. However, the latter is rarely associated with homosexuality and its explanatory value in bisexual behavior is too limited.

Krafft Ebing (in [15]) deduced that if the reproductive system was "bisexual" then the associated neuropsychological or central brain circuitry may also be bisexual. Dorner[7] currently subscribes to such a theory. Whereas homosexual and bisexual men's reproductive organs seem normal, their brains may be feminized in varying degrees, explaining their overt behavior.

Dorner theorizes that the brain is sex hormone dependent and is differentiated as male or female in part by neurotransmitters. Early prenatal environmental influences by systemic hormones mature and fix the sexual orientation and gender role throughout life. Changes in amounts of neurotransmitter or duration of their presence for the fetus may fix a lifelong pattern of anomalous sexual behavior. Rado points out that there is no evidence to support the assumption that brain sex functions are independent from genital functioning or are independently influenced by developmental disturbances. However, some experiments on animals do show that "homosexual" behavior can be created in animals with normal genitals by selectively changing the uterine sex hormone balance.

Some animals also show reproductive bisexuality. The oyster, certain snails and mollusks (gastropoda and pteropoda) have complete male and female sex organs and can fertilize in both ways. However, this is not so in humans because the two reproductive potentialities are mutually exclusive.

The growth of male functions impedes or destroys the female functions and vice versa[28]. Since Rado considers this the only legitimate use of the term "bisexual", it does not exist in humans.

Other theorists attempted to link bisexuality to organic factors. Everything genetic, hormonal or constitutional that applies to homosexuality applies here as well. Of course one may expect that effects would be less pronounced than those in exclusive homosexuals because the bisexual has "more normal," more heterosexual, features. One can imagine a continuum of organic factors influencing male to female development:

Heterosexual Male
Bisexual
Homosexual
Transsexual
Heterosexual Female

It has been suggested that females are more likely than males to show bisexuality because it tends to occur throughout the animal kingdom and because the female is passive, her role is more pliant. One may wish therefore to place the bisexual male closer to the female in the above sequence. Some authors warn about generalizing from animals to humans and data on human studies should be carefully examined.

The Experimental Evidence

The ambiguity of the term bisexual is not helped by the dearth of studies on the topic. There are only two phallometric studies that examine erotic preferences of bisexual men. Both studies suggest that there is no bisexuality in reactions to the body characteristics of mature males and females.

Penile reactions to men and women.   Freund and I[10] compared the self reported bisexuality of androphiles or men who erotically prefer mature male partners with those of pedophiles. The androphiles were sorted into bisexual and nonbisexual based on whether they had intercourse with a mature female more than five times in a 2 week period or less. A second group of androphiles were selected on the softer criteria of whether they had ever fallen in love with a mature female or had desired intercourse with one. The pedophiles either faced charges of sexually molesting a child or admitted an erotic preference for children. They were sorted into bisexual and nonbisexual groups based on their self report of attraction either to both sexes or only to boys.

The phallometric test of erotic preference (Chapter Two) was used to compare reactions of the groups to pictures of men and women, boys and girls. One would expect that the bisexual groups would respond more to females than the nonbisexual groups but this was true only for the pedophiles. They reacted to 6-to-8-year-old girls most, less to 8-to-10-year-old girls and like the remaining groups not at all to pubescent and mature females. When the ratio of responses to males versus females is compared as a "bisexuality index", they were the only ambisexual group. All of the androphiles showed a disproportionate reaction toward males over females. Thus if bisexuality exists in this population, it occurs only in men who erotically prefer children. The men who interact sexually with adults of both sexes showed a clear preference for men. The second study was similar in its results.

McConaghy[23] compared penile reactions of married and single men who came to his clinic conscious of homosexual feelings and who wanted these feelings eliminated or reduced. Some had experienced intercourse with women and some had not. When the men were compared on an index of sexual orientation derived from phallometric measures to pictures of men and women, all patients were clearly in the homosexual range. That is, once again, bisexuality did not appear to exist in terms of physiological reactions to body characteristics of men and women. As noted elsewhere, psychic appraisal of sexual arousal and physiological reactions do not always agree. In most people they are congruent but in the bisexual they are not. Possibly the phallometric test is amiss in these cases. Possibly the patients are acting as heterosexuals for other than sexual reasons. For another perspective on their erotic preferences we can examine sexual histories.

Sex history of bisexual men.   If the bisexuals are truly ambisexual, they should show comparable experience with both men and women rather than the imbalanced responses to pictures they showed in the phallometric tests just noted.

In a controlled study by Paitich and his associates[27] bisexual men were compared to other sexually anomalous groups and to heterosexual controls on the Clarke Sex History Questionnaire scales. To be considered bisexual, an individual had five or more sexual contacts with males 16 or older and two or more instances of intercourse with a woman. For simplicity, they will only be compared to exclusive homosexuals and exclusive heterosexual controls. Figure 5.1 shows the relative frequencies of sexual acts with various age groups of males and females. A Z score of 0 is average for the sample, whereas positive scores are above average, negative scores below average. It is clear that none of the 3 groups had contact with children or pubescents of either sex, otherwise, they would have been classified as multiple anomalies or as pedophiles. However, when the reactions to male youths and adults are compared, the bisexuals appear to be "super homosexual". They have considerably more experience than the exclusive homosexuals who were comparable in age and education. The heterosexuals, as expected, had less than average experience with adult men. When sexual experiences with the

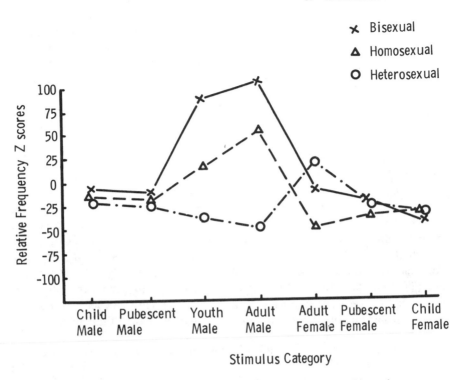

FIG. 5.1   Frequency of homosexual and heterosexual outlets in bisexual men.

adult female are compared, the bisexuals are in between heterosexual and homosexual groups but are slightly below the average of all the groups in the study. When the bisexuals' experience is divided into type contact with females, they are more likely than heterosexuals to engage in anal intercourse. They did not differ significantly from homosexuals on frequency of anal intercourse with men. They show greater desire and less disgust for homosexual relations than they do for heterosexual relations. All the information taken together suggests a preference for homosexual over heterosexual outlet so their "bisexuality" is rather imbalanced in the homosexuality direction once more.

Wolff[37] reported a comparative study of male and female bisexuals and similar conclusions may be drawn from her data. The male bisexuals tended to have slightly more male partners than female partners. Her selection criterion for bisexuality was self report with neither use of standardized instruments not cross validation. Nevertheless similar results emerged. Although it is possible that some as yet undiscovered dimension of behavior is prominent in the bisexual's attraction to men and women, other clinical reports suggest that the bisexual is really a clandestine homosexual who is adapting to the heterosexual world perhaps out of fear or for social convenience.

"Coming out" in bisexual men.   Roesler and Disker[29] studied "coming out" in homosexual male youths, the period during which they became aware of their homosexual impulses and attempted to fill their sexual needs by meeting and revealing themselves to other homosexual men. Coming out was quite emotionally disturbing since almost half of the sample visited a psychiatrist and a third made significant suicide attempts. Pertinent here is that almost a third described themselves as bisexual and it was this group which was slower to "come out". Almost half of the bisexuals had not come out compared to only 13% of the exclusive homosexual group. The present writer tested this difference statistically and found it significant but we are missing necessary information to show that the difference is not due to age or other factors. Other suggestive findings were that, of the youths who had not "come out" yet, 61% thought they had a fair to good chance of becoming "straight" or exclusively heterosexual. Only 27% of youth who had come out over a year previously thought this was a possibility. Unfortunately, we do not know which ones were bisexual. Nor can we link suicide attempts to bisexuality or fear of "coming out" from the data. The report is, however, interesting because in contrast to other studies, the research participants were self labeled bisexuals rather than described as such by the writer.

Some bisexual men never really "come out" and have secret affairs with men in washrooms, even remaining unknown to their sex partners. The "bisexual" *Mr. S* describes his typical washroom encounter as follows:

Mr. S: There is a washroom hangout that is known for fast sex. One of us will get down on his knees and stick his dink under the partition or if you're lucky there is a blow hole in the wall and you can stick it in there for a job. When we are finished, one of us waits a few minutes to leave so that we cannot identify each other.

Doctor: Do you know any of the people that you have sex with?

Mr. S: You never see their face, it's strictly for sex.

Doctor: Have you ever run into someone you did have sex with?

Mr. S: Ah...there was once about ten years ago. I had seen this man leave the cubicle in a washroom out west. I never thought I would see him again but he turned up in town at a mutual friend's place for dinner one evening while he was vacationing. We never let on that we knew each other and I never saw him again.

Bieber and his associates[4], examined their therapy cases for bisexuality. Twenty eight percent were bisexuals since they had sustained heterosexual relationships even to the point of marriage. The concern about disclosure of homosexual behavior occurred in 90% of the cases but no comparison of bisexuals and homosexuals was made. However, their study suggests that fear and clandestine relationships were the rule. An aversion to being identified as homosexual is illustrated by *Mr. H* who was married and had a respectable position in his community. He was extremely cautious where he had sexual encounters but his suspiciousness was reflected in his behavior in a different way from *Mr. S.*

> *Mr. H:* I usually go away from my area to have sex and I don't go back to the same place too often in case someone is watching. You never know if there are police staking you out. When I do meet someone we go to his place; naturally my wife wouldn't approve of me bringing him home; or we go to a motel for the night. I don't have sex with the same person twice in case people get suspicious.
>
> *Doctor:* Are there any characteristics you look for in your partners?
>
> *Mr. H:* I like young men but I'm not so good looking myself. I have some choice but often you take what is available. One thing I do avoid is the obviously effeminate looking man. I wouldn't want to be seen on the street with someone who looked gay since it would surely arouse suspicion.

Freund[9] has described clinical cases in which there is a shift from heterosexual to homosexual behavior. He notes that the opposite shift rarely occurs spontaneously. Most frequently, the shift occurs around the time of puberty. In his study, he found 18% of the homosexual men indicated that until age 15, they were exclusively attracted to females. One has to wonder how well defined sexual attraction is for the prepubertal boy. Attraction may mean common interest or preferring the company of girls. The results do suggest the potential for bisexuality in homosexual males.

Bieber and his colleagues[4] came to this conclusion in their study of homosexual patients undergoing psychoanalysis. They felt a basic heterosexual potential was evident in bisexuals by the inclusion of women in their social lives, attempts at heterosexual intercourse and the occurrence of frankly heterosexual dreams. The bisexual male has been construed to be an intersex between homosexual and heterosexual males. On this basis, Bieber et al tested the notion that bisexuals, being more masculine, would prefer the insertor role rather than insertee role in anal intercourse with men. This expectation was not confirmed. The equation of masculine with active and feminine with passive is considered simplistic by some analysts[28] and does not fit the facts of homosexual or heterosexual exchanges[21] [22].

The evidence at present is at best suggestive but it points to the conclusion that bisexuality is an attempt to adapt to the heterosexual world. The theory that there is no such individual who has a bisexual erotic preference would appear to be more readily testable but to date, there are only two systematic phallometric studies. Freund[9] indicated that he has searched in vain for bisexual men, that is, men who react erotically to both the mature male and female bodies in a phallometric test. He does discuss cases of masochism and transvestism in which there is high sexual arousal to both men and women but noted they reacted phallometrically to the body characteristics of women and not to men. His results suggest that erotic preferences for bodies of both men and women do not appear to exist but other features and behavior of the stimulus persons remain to be studied.

Latent homosexuality. The unconscious component of our bisexual nature has been most often studied in the latent homosexuality of the paranoid psychotic state. Freud and his followers maintained that all heterosexual men had a dormant homosexual component to this nature. The proof of this theory has rested on demonstrating that latent homosexuality becomes manifest in *all* paranoid psychotic states. Lester[20] who has reviewed the literature on this question, points out that psychoanalytic theory makes this a clear unambiguous prediction. We know that exclusive homosexuals are not usually paranoid. One can argue that they have adapted to their sexual behavior and delusions were unnecessary. Many therapists believe homosexuals generally have heterosexual potential. The theory suggests the converse, that all paranoid psychotics have homosexual concerns.

The typical study has compared paranoid and nonparanoid psychotic or other patients on the incidence of overt homosexual acts, desires, preoccupations as manifested in their delusions or on projective psychological tests. Overall the results were negative. Paranoid delusions can occur in the absence of significant homosexual impulses either conscious or unconscious. Klaf and Davis[17] for example found that approximately a third or less of paranoid schizophrenic patients in general had previous homosexual experience, preoccupations, or delusions with sexual content. Since two thirds did not, this weakens the case for the association of paranoia and latent homosexuality. Habitual homosexuality occurs in 3% of paranoid patents, about the same percentage (4%) found in the general population in the Kinsey studies[16][30]. This suggests that the paranoid symptoms co-occur with manifest exclusive homosexuality by chance.

The studies that Lester reviewed are methodologically very poor. There were no assessments, phallometric or otherwise, of erotic preferences in the patients studied. There was no validation of diagnoses in groups where unreliability is common. So we do not know if we are dealing with homosexuals or heterosexuals, paranoid or other psychotic states. The measures of "unconscious homosexuality" are vague conceptually. They are poorly described and typically have no reported reliability or validity. The studies used either psychiatric judgments, projective tests or unvalidated experimental procedures.

Aronson[1][2] has studied the problem of latent homosexuality using the Rorschach Wheeler signs and the projective Blacky test to examine the hypothesis of an association of paranoia and latent homosexuality. He found a positive relationship between the two but Meketon and her associates[24] were unable to replicate the findings with the Rorschach. In particular they found considerably fewer of the Wheeler homosexuality signs than Aronson did. Goldfried[13] thought the diagnosis of homosexuality could be made from the Rorschach but concluded that only 6 of the 20 Wheeler signs were "probably good" in validity, 6 were "unquestionably poor" and the other 8 were of "ambiguous validity". The "good" signs are interesting because they also appear ambiguous to the present author and Meketon et al commented on their unreliability and invalidity. The signs were: contorted monster or threatening figure (Card 4), human or human-ized animal such as Bugs Bunny (Card 5), depreciated female (Card 7) and on any card, human or animal anal detail, humans or animals seen back to back, and feminine clothing. The focus on the anus as a homosexual preoc-cupation reflects a misconception that anal intercourse is the main mode of sexual outlet for homosexuals. This is also evident in some homemade stimuli testing the hypothesis[8]. The interest in female clothes also mirrors the confusion of feminine gender identity or femininity and object choice in homosexual men. Other reports are only case studies or collections of case studies, such as Gardiner's report[11]. They suffer all the problems of the foregoing attempts at controlled studies and the uncertain results on a single individual. The original validation data on the Wheeler signs[36] is poor and based on only a few cases. One has to wonder why they have received so much attention.

Only two studies examined physiological measures to validate homosex-ual or heterosexual object choice. Koegler and Kline[18] measured sweating, heart rate and respiration responses to films of heterosexual, homosexual and neutral content and to a film about subincision. The sample size was small but results were paradoxical since overt homosexuals, paranoid schizophrenics and normal heterosexuals differed in unexpected ways in their reactions. Normals responded less to the heterosexual film than the other two groups whereas the latter did not differ in their reaction to the homosexual film. Perhaps a larger sample would produce different results but measurement of physiological reactions other than those of the penis are suspect as indices of erotic preference. Disgust for the film on subinci-sion may have distorted results as well. Only Freund[9] examined phallo-metric reactions in 14 patients with persecutory delusions and 30 with neuroses. Pictures of men, women, and children were shown to the patients while penile volume changes were monitored. There was no evidence of "bisexuality" according to the author but no statistical analyses were reported. Moreover, the paranoid group was very heterogenous and the control group of neurotics is less appropriate than comparable schizophrenics or psychotics without paranoid delusions.

While the results of studies attempting to link paranoia to homosexuality are mixed, a methodologically sound study remains to be done. Lester has pointed out that homosexual men may find the heterosexual environment very stressful and they might develop heightened suspiciousness as a result. Paranoid ideation may reflect his concern about concealing and disavowing his homosexuality. Carr[5] has noted that negative results that fail to demonstrate homosexual preoccupation in paranoia do not conclusively rule out the possibility. Especially since these patients are suspicious, their homosexuality may not come out till some later date. Perhaps the techniques to assess it are inadequate and other methods would reveal it at some time in the future. Nevertheless support for the hypothesis is lacking.

Animal bisexuality.   All types of bisexuality can be found in the animal kingdom if not in man. There are organisms which can function reproductively as both male and female but this case clearly does not apply to humans[28]. Overt bisexual behavior can be demonstrated in the form of mounting or characteristic male sex behavior and as reception or lordosis, the typical posture of the receptive female laboratory rat in which the rear end is raised, the back arched, and the head raised back.

It has been suggested that female animals in general are typically "more bisexual" than males[14]. Some writers have pointed out that human females are also "bisexual" more than males[35]. It has been further suggested that the male or female sex behavior is under hormonal control. The amount of bisexuality that develops depends on the kind and amount of steroid (sex) hormone present in the growing fetus[14] [25]. The evidence linking bisexuality to ambiguous sex organs is negative as Rado noted. At best it is uncertain and need not occupy us here (See Chapter 14). To our knowledge the overwhelming majority of men who are bisexual, like the homosexual, have normal male genitals. If there is some central nervous system abnormality, it has yet to be discovered. More recently it has been found that the brain, behavior and the genitals in animals at least may be differentially influenced by hormones contrary to what Rado suggested[28]. Denniston[6] also notes that homosexual behavior occurs in a wide variety of animals and seems related to conditioning for social dominance rather than to unusual endocrine conditions. He feels the conditioning is directive and the hormones serve a general activating role. All these viewpoints are speculations which have not been tested in humans.

West[35] has discussed the general issue of animal research on homosexuality. Some authors like Weinrich[34] think homosexual behavior is widespread among wild animals but West notes that homosexual behavior appears to take place much more readily when animals are deprived of the opposite sex. This appears to be true of humans as well. He notes that an exclusive homosexual preference seen in humans on the other hand, does not seem to occur among wild animals, although a certain degree of "bisexuality" comes naturally. West further notes that sexual gestures relate to dominance and submissiveness and one has to wonder to what degree it is truly erotic. In many of the animal studies, mounting and receptiveness are discussed, but not ejaculation, orgasm or erotic preferences. As West notes, mounting may occur as a natural response to sexual excitement and a male may turn to any available mate in order to reach a climax. When mounted by another animal for example, male rats almost invariably refuse to reciprocate. However, some behavior does seem bisexual since the male who responds to another male receptively appears to vigorously mount females when they are available. Kinsey et al.,[16] have argued that injection of male hormones generally increases the frequency and intensity of an animal's sexual response but there is no evidence it affects its object choice of a male versus female partner. It would seem that erotic behavior in lower animals and humans is quite fluid and considerable bisexual behavior can be demonstrated but it is uncertain whether a bisexual orgasmic preference exists in most species. The presence of free choice is an important ingredient in examining whether a real preference for both sexes exists.

Psychopathology in bisexual men.   A final issue concerns mental health. Bieber et al[4] maintain that bisexuals are less pathological than exclusive homosexuals because they have engaged in heterosexual activity more often, are less likely to be effeminate, were less likely to be "lone wolves", were more assertive, less often had mothers who were close binding and intimate, and were more sexually potent with women. It is noteworthy that several of these signs involve heterosexual outlet. Contrary to their contention, the weight of evidence suggests homosexuals are not necessarily mentally disturbed. Moreover, in contrast to their results on bisexuals, the one controlled study in the literature using standardized instruments suggests that bisexuals are *more* emotionally disturbed than a clinical sample of homosexuals.

My colleagues and I[19] found that bisexuals scored significantly higher than exclusive homosexual patients on the psychotic scales of the MMPI: paranoia, psychasthenia, schizophrenia and mania whereas there were no differences in femininity. On the Cattell 16 Personality Factors Test (16 PF) which is less satisfactory than the MMPI, the bisexuals showed a picture that reflected our general clinical impression of them. Compared to the homosexual patients, they were less trusting, more shrewd and calculating and more socially controlled and precise. These bisexuals seemed overconcerned with social conformity and perhaps their heterosexual behavior was also a way of conforming.

It is interesting that the bisexuals were more paranoid than exclusive homosexuals, which may reflect the concealing of homosexual feelings and leading a double life. Possibly some of the test patients in the latent homosexuality studies were this type of individual. The "latency" of their homosexuality may be more apparent than real because of their public admission of their socially unacceptable impulses.

Table 5.1 summarizes the limited evidence for theories of bisexuality.

TABLE 5.1
Summary of Evidence for Theories of Bisexuality

Theory	Empirical Support
1. Ambisexual Erotic Preference	Negative. Phallometry shows they respond to men usually, occasionally to women but *not* to both.
2. Overt Behavior reflects adaptation to heterosexual world	Positive. Their sex history is that of a 'super homosexual'. They are clandestine, 'come out' late and are suspicious. Response to females is secondary.
3. Latent Homosexuality is evidence of universal bisexuality	Negative. Most individuals are monosexual in object choice. Psychological studies are poor methodologically. Association of homosexuality and paranoid psychosis seem to be a chance relationship.
4. Biological bases of bisexuality	No evidence.
5. Psychopathology is less in bisexuals than in homosexuals	Limited evidence suggests the opposite to be the case. Suspiciousness and conformity are prominent personality traits in bisexual men.

Speculations and the Stimulus Response Matrix of Bisexuals

Clinical cases of bisexuality are quite emotionally disturbed and some of that disturbance may be due to playing a heterosexual role which does not fit. In their eagerness to conform, they make serious attempts to be heterosexual. They carry over homosexual practices, particularly anal intercourse because it bridges male and female. The rear end in itself is not a very distinctive part of the mature anatomy. It makes sex with a woman easier.

However, the pretense is overwhelming for them. The fear of their homosexual activities being revealed and the phoniness of their lives can be unbearable and it shows up in their clinical profile. The hollowness of life for such men is illustrated by *Mr. B.*

Mr. B: I like to pretend, especially with heterosexuals who can be so cruel to gays, pardon me, queers. Last weekend, I met this vain university graduate who was so full of himself I wanted to retch. I said his university was a good "small town" school and that I was an Oxford man myself and name dropped like mad. He bought the whole story not knowing I've never even been to England. As he "oh yes'd" and "really'd", I could hardly contain myself. When I left, I thought what a jerk he was but at the same time, I felt bad because I had a new lie to live and keep straight in my head.

A local homophile organization official commented to me on the altered social reality of such individuals and of homosexuals in general. They may perceive everyone's behavior as acting in a staged play. Life can be difficult under these circumstances since they are alienated from social roles that the average heterosexual takes for granted and spontaneously accepts without thinking. The official noted "Did you ever wonder about that 'village queen', Down By The Old Millstream?"

The sparse existing literature involves clinical cases of bisexuality. We know nothing of possible normal cases. Perhaps some healthy men have a true ambisexuality which is reflected in sex object preference, gender identity or other facets of sexual behavior. Hopefully, this group will be more carefully studied in the near future.

TREATMENT

There are no unique treatments for bisexuality which have not been applied to homosexuality described in Chapter 4. The interested reader may wish to review these methods at this point.

The overall finding was that bisexual men were most likely to change regardless of the procedure used and exclusive homosexuals were least likely to change. Success has been defined in terms of ability to engage in heterosexual foreplay and ultimately coitus. Only the exceptional writer spoke of erotic preferences and when the results of those studies are reexamined for bisexuals, they seem rather empty.

The bisexuals were capable in many cases of engaging in heterosexual intercourse before treatment. They continue to do so after treatment and usually we do not even know if this result represents a significant increase in the frequency of intercourse. A more crucial question is "did he not enjoy coitus before treatment and did he genuinely enjoy it after treatment?" We do not know from available information.

A clinically worrisome feature of bisexuals, besides their gross emotional disturbance, is the tendency to be phoney and conforming. If you want to hear that they are heterosexuals, that may be exactly what you will hear, regardless of their true feelings. They may seek treatment voluntarily or otherwise because in contemporary Western cultures, one is constantly bombarded with the ideal of romantic love and marriage. When a patient does not desire these things, he may feel that there is something wrong with him or he feels left out and angry. The pressure to be Mr. Average is even greater when the patient realizes he has sexual desires that are against the law and if he acts on his desires, he may spend time in jail. The Bible calls homosexuality an abomination which should be punished by death (Leviticus 20: 13). Faced with these social values, no wonder many "bisexuals" and homosexuals want treatment to change to the norm.

This places a tremendous burden on the individual to whom the bisexual may turn for help in changing. The therapist has the key to change and has a great responsibility to his patient. For this reason, it is especially important that he not hold out false hope to his patient. Often the burden is greater on the therapist who has a liason with the law. The court orders him to treat the homosexual client and change him in lieu of a prison term. This situation is not conducive to trust and can strain the therapeutic relationship to the point of making it ineffective. Bancroft[3] considers the medical (psychiatric) attitude to treating homosexuality hypocritical because it reinforces negative social attitudes toward homosexuality while presenting the illusion of free choice in changing to heterosexual or remaining gay.

If the therapist chooses to use the many methods described for homosexuality, he is faced with a dilemma. Do any of them in fact work? Some clinicians do not care that erotic preferences are changed. Rather if the frequency of overt behavior, i.e., acting out, can be reduced so that the patient can stay out of trouble with the law, this is quite satisfactory. This will relieve the legal responsibility he has and it will make it easier for the patient to cope with a heterosexual society. Even marriage to a woman may be considered desirable because it will even further normalize his situation and offer more constraints, which keep him out of trouble. Sex is not everything and marriage can offer many other satisfactions even to a homosexual man.

On the other hand, the act of sexual union with a woman may not be attractive after all, once the homosexual can do it. This parallels human experiences in which an ideal or goal is esteemed and sought after but once it is attained, it simply does not suit the needs or tastes of that individual. Faustus in the poem by Christopher Marlowe sells his soul to the devil in order to have any wish he desires throughout his life. One of his longings is to see Helen of Troy from the famous legend by Homer. When he sees her, he says with evident disappointment, "Is this the face that launched a thousand ships?" Similarly disappointment and anger can arise in patients who are at odds with social mores.

Treatment of Choice

Self acceptance in the face of pressure to conform is the main goal of treatment for the bisexual. He is capable of both homosexual and heterosexual behavior, but he knows what he prefers. He needs help to accept that fact. The presence of serious complicating psychiatric factors including paranoia need attention as well. In contrast to the exclusive homosexual, object choice cannot be ignored in this group. Since hiding their sexual preference among other things, is part of their life style, they must learn to cope with it and to be honest with themselves and important others in their lives. *Mr. M* was married at the time he first came to our clinic and he was both depressed and angry. He was married for 22 years but his wife had no knowledge of his homosexual activities. He did not trust therapists in general and contacted our clinic via a gay hotline in the community. He had few friends and his interpersonal relationships at work were superficial and businesslike. He complained about depression and about the meaninglessness of his existence.

> *Mr. M:* I have to muster up my energy to get going in the morning and each day is a chore. I'm unhappy with my marriage and I don't know what to do about this homosexual thing. I'm drawn to the gay life but it is such a bind at the same time. I know you understand what it means to me but other people don't. Everytime there is a joke about queers I laugh too but I hate them telling it and I hate myself for laughing. I wonder, "Do they know about me and talk behind my back?" Sometimes I think they do. I always pretend I'm in a good mood even when I'm not. I might lose my job if they knew how I really feel. That bothers me too.

> *Doctor:* What would they do if they found out about you?

> *Mr. M:* (Pause) Actually nothing would change. I don't know that they like me now and I guess they wouldn't like me then. All it would do is confirm that they don't like me.

> *Doctor:* Why don't they like you now?

> *Mr. M:* I don't give them a chance. No one knows me really and I don't allow them to know me because I'm afraid they will find out about the real me and my life would go down the tube. Strange. It is down the tube now and they don't know that I'm gay or anything else. What can I do? I'm so depressed.

> *Doctor:* People get depressed when they are not getting the rewards from life that they should. You are unknown to people around you in your

daily life. It looks like you will have to open up to them and take the risk that they may not like you. Perhaps they like you more than you realize or would like you more if they could know what you are really like. If they know you are angry or sad, you don't have to be phoney, as you said, pretending you feel good when you don't. If they can share life with you including your ups and downs, then you have a friend. If not, you never had them as a friend in the first place.

Self acceptance is also aided by a proper assessment of erotic preferences. Often the patient knows his preference but the confirmation by the therapist that he is gay (or heterosexual but usually gay), helps him to be more accepting of himself. Then some of the principles used with exclusive homosexuals in self acceptance can be applied. Improvement can be remarkable if the patient is persuaded not to live a phoney life and to "come out".

Since the bisexual already has heterosexual experience or interest, the temptation for the therapist is to adapt him to heterosexual outlets. However it is usually clear that the homosexual potential is generally greater in the bisexual and that training him for behavior contrary to his erotic preference is likely to exacerbate his problems since he will continue to be phoney. He needs to be ego syntonic and free.

BIBLIOGRAPHY

1. Aronson, M. L. A study of the Freudian theory of paranoia by means of the Rorschach test. *Journal of Projective Techniques,* 1952, *16,* 397–411.
2. Aronson, M. L. A study of the Freudian Theory of Paranoia by means of the Blacky pictures. *Journal of Projective Techniques,* 1953, *17,* 3–19.
3. Bancroft, J. Modification of homosexual preferences: some ethical considerations, in *Medical Sexology: The Third International Congress.* Forleo, R., & Pasini, W. (Eds.), Littleton, Massachusetts: PSG Publishing Co., 1978.
4. Bieber, I., Dain, H. J., Dince, P. R., Drellich, M. G., Grand, H. G., Gundlach, R. H., Kremer, M. V., Rifkin, A. H., Wilbur, C. B., & Bieber, T. B. *Homosexuality: A psychoanalytic study.* New York: Basic Books, 1962.
5. Carr, C. A. Observations on paranoia and their relationship to the Schreber Case. *International Journal of Psychoanalysis,* 1963, *44,* 195–200.
6. Denniston, R. H. Ambisexuality in animals, in *Sexual Inversion: The Multiple Roots of Homosexuality.* Marmor, J. (Ed.). New York: Basic Books Inc., 1965.
7. Dorner, G. Hormones and sexual differentiation of the brain. *Sex, Hormones & Behavior,* Ciba Foundation Symposium, N.Y., 1979.
8. Eriksen, C. W. Perceptual defense as a function of unacceptable needs. *Journal of Abnormal & Social Psychology,* 1951, *46,* 557–564.
9. Freund, K. Male homosexuality: An analysis of the pattern. In J. A. Loraine (Ed.), *Understanding homosexuality: Its biological and psychological bases.* Lancaster, England: Medical & Technical Publishing Co. Ltd., 1974, 25–81.
10. Freund, K., & Langevin, R. Bisexuality in homosexual pedophilia. *Archives of Sexual Behavior,* 1976, *5*(5), 415–423.

11. Gardner, G. E. Evidences of homosexuality in one hundred and twenty unanalyzed cases with paranoid content. *Psychoanalytic Review,* 1931, *18,* 57–62.

12. Glick, B. S. Homosexual panic. *Journal of Nervous and Mental Disease,* 1959, *129,* 20–28.

13. Goldfried, M. R. On the diagnosis of homosexuality from the Rorschach, *Journal of Consulting Psychology,* 1966, *30*(4), 338–349.

14. Goy, T. W., & Goldfoot, D. A. Neuroendocrinology: Animal models and problems of human sexuality. *Archives of Sexual Behavior,* 1975, *4*(4), 405–420.

15. Harwich, A. Aberrations of sexual life. *After the Psychopathia Sexuales of Dr. R. von Kraft-Ebbing.* London: Staples Press, 1959.

16. Kinsey, A. C., Pomeroy, W. B., & Martin, C. E. *Sexual behavior in the human von Krafft-Ebing.* London: Staples Press, 1959.

17. Klaf, F. S., & Davis, C. A. Homosexuality and paranoid schizophrenia: A survey of 150 cases and controls. *American Journal of Psychiatry,* 1960, *116,* 1070–1075.

18. Koegler, R. R., & Kline, L. Y. Psychotherapy Research: An approach utilizing autonomic response measurements. *American Journal of Psychotherapy,* 1965, *19,* 268–279.

19. Langevin, R., Paitich, D., Freeman, R., Mann, K., & Handy, L. Personality characteristics and sexual anomalies in males. *Canadian Journal of Behavioural Science,* 1978, *10*(3), 222–238.

20. Lester, D. The relationship between paranoid delusions and homosexuality. *Archives of Sexual Behavior,* 1975, *4*(3), 285–294.

21. Masters, W. H., & Johnson, V. E. *Homosexuality in Perspective,* Boston: Little, Brown and Company, 1979.

22. Masters, W. H., & Johnson, V. E. *Human Sexual Inadequacy.* Boston: Little, Brown and Company, 1970.

23. McConaghy, N. Heterosexual experience, marital status, and orientation of homosexual males. *Archives of Sexual Behavior,* 1978, *7*(6), 575–581.

24. Meketon, B. W., Griffith, R. M., Taylor, V. H., & Wiedeman, J. S. Rorschach homosexual signs in paranoid schizophrenia. *Journal of Abnormal & Social Psychology,* 1962, *65,* 280–284.

25. Money, J. Sexual dimorphism and homosexual gender identity. *Psychological Bulletin,* 1970, *74*(6), 425–440.

26. Ovesey, L. *Homosexuality and pseudohomosexuality.* New York: Science House, 1969.

27. Paitich, D., Langevin, R., Freeman, R., Mann, K., & Handy, L. The Clarke SHQ: A clinical sex history questionnaire for males. *Archives of Sexual Behavior,* 1977, *6*(5), 421–436.

28. *Rado, S. A critical examination of the concept of bisexuality, in Sexual Inversion: The Multiple Roots of Homosexuality,* Marmor, J. (Ed.), New York: Basic Books Inc., 1965.

29. Roesler, T., & Deisher, R. W. Youthful male homosexuality. *Journal of the American Medical Association,* 1972, *219*(8), 1018–1023.

30. Rossi, R., Delmonte, P., & Terracciano, P. The problem of the relationship between homosexuality and schizophrenia. *Archives of Sexual Behavior,* 1971, *1*(4), 357–362.

31. Sagarin, E. Prison homosexuality and its effect on post-prison sexual behavior. *Psychiatry,* 1976, *39*(3), 245–257.

32. Salzman, L. "Latent" homosexuality, in *Sexual Inversion: The Multiple Roots of Homosexuality.* Marmor, J. (Ed.). New York: Basic Books Inc., 1965.

33. Stoller, R. J. The "bedrock" of masculinity and femininity: Bisexuality. *Archives of General Psychiatry,* 1972, *26,* 207–212.

34. Weinrich, J. D. Homosexual behavior in animals: a new review of observations from the wild, and their relationship to human sexuality, in *Medical Sexology: The Third International Congress.* Forles, R., & Pasini, W. (Eds.). Littleton, Massachusetts: PSG Publishing Company, 1978.

35. West, D. J. *Homosexuality re-examined.* Minneapolis: University of Minnesota Press, 1977.

36. Wheeler, W. M. An analysis of Rorschach indices of male homosexuality. *Rorschach Research Exchange,* 1949, *13,* 97–126.

37. Wolff, C. *Bisexuality: A Study.* London: Quartet Books, 1977.

6 Transsexualism and Transvestism

INTRODUCTION

Transsexual males appear at psychiatric clinics for an operation to change them into women. They express a persistent wish to be a member of the opposite sex; which is epitomized by the desire for sex reassignment surgery. Their external anatomy is usually normal and male, although many have already received some form of hormonal treatment and electrolysis for hair removal to be more convincingly feminine. Transsexuals argue that they are really females trapped in male bodies; that nature made a mistake. They often stick to their conviction rather firmly. They simply want a psychiatrist to approve an operation to have their penises and testicles removed and to create artificial vaginas. At times they may be very convincing females, such as *Mr. A*. His psychiatrist described their first encounter as follows:

> I was tired that Monday morning. I had been on call and had responded to an emergency at 4:00 a.m. I was developing a cold and thought I would be better off going to bed than meeting a client. I stepped off the elevator at my floor feeling miserable and as I entered the reception area to my office, there was one patient sitting waiting for me. I momentarily forgot that I was seeing a transsexual and that "she" was as male as I was. "She" was dressed in a fashion some other clinicians have referred to as "midnight whore". "She" had a clinging black dress with a plunging neckline and a slit up the side. "Her" shape was convincingly female, with full round breasts and hairless legs. She had long red hair and an alluring smile. This was the woman of my wildest erotic fantasies and I couldn't help myself—I was turned on—for a moment. I found myself treating her like a woman, opening doors and lighting "her" cigarette. I was really taken in, and then "he" spoke. The illusion was shattered.

On the other hand, some patients who appear for sex change surgery are the most unconvincing females. They may come to the clinic dressed in male attire or as a female but with black facial beard showing under heavy rouge and lipstick and a body build that suggests they might make a good football player.

It is often difficult to ascertain what, if any, genital gratification is obtained in the act of being a woman for transsexuals. Many do interact sexually with men in what can be labeled "homosexual behavior", but the operation they request would diminish their ability to respond sexually to men. In fact, hormone treatment with estrogens to promote breast growth may reduce sex drive, although some patients say this is not so[92]. What then is going on in the transsexual?

Transvestites cross dress like transsexuals but they clearly have genital gratification associated with the act of dressing in women's clothes[155]. This is often done in private and their sexual act is either a solo activity or done with a cooperative wife or girlfriend. *Mr. P*, a 30-year-old married businessman, illustrates the typical behavior of transvestites.

> "My wife goes out to her bridge club one night and visits her family another and I am alone those evenings. I have a collection of underclothes and dresses which I use on those nights. I used to use my wife's clothes sometimes but she would get annoyed because I stretched them out of shape. So I just use my own clothes now which I continually supplement with new ones. My wife and I may go shopping while I'm dressed up (as a woman) to pick out new things.

> When I'm alone I savour each item. I will stand nude in front of our full length mirror and apply make up. Then I will feel the panties I am about to put on. I will rub them all over me, but especially on my penis. I will do the same with my bra. When I have on my corset, slip and dress, I enjoy the transformation. When I was younger, I would get so excited, I would come without touching my penis. Now I masturbate to come and sometimes I will have sex with my wife dressed like this and at other times I just like to dress up without any climax".

Transvestites may also wish to be changed into women and some theorists argue that, in later years, they do become transsexuals[170]. The transvestite presents a different yet connected set of questions. What is there about dressing in female clothes that provides the erotic excitement that makes it their preferred sexual act?

The Problem of Definition

Each sexual anomaly seems to have its own peculiar clinical or conceptual problem. The most evident issue to be settled in the study of transsexualism and transvestism is simply one of definition. It has long been assumed that a sex object preference for men or women is an integral part of gender identity. Therefore transsexuals should all erotically prefer men. The existence of "heterosexual" transsexuals is therefore puzzling and confusing. Transvestism has been assumed to be fetishistic since orgasm accompanies crossdressing. It is the clothes themselves that are erotic. It has been assumed transvestites erotically prefer women over men. So its presence in "homosexuals" has been problematic[30].

To solve the dilemma, a host of diagnostic labels [58][108][155][157] has been offered that are only names and add nothing to our knowledge about the problems. Nevertheless, there is some consensus today that the transsexual is usually "homosexual" and the transvestite is usually "heterosexual"[32][58][155][157]. The reader will find the use of the terms homosexual and heterosexual confusing in the context of crossdressing. The male transsexual denies he is homosexual and some writers have attempted to accommodate them by using other labels such as heterogendral[125]. I feel this only adds to the confusion. What is needed are terms to separate out erotic object preference and gender identity. Homosexual implies a mixture. Therefore *androphilic* (literally lover of men) will be used to imply an erotic object choice for men without reference to gender identity. Similarly heterosexual also mixes gender identity and erotic object choice for women so *gynephilic* will be used to express an erotic object choice for women without implying gender identity. Freund[53] has used the terms in this fashion. It is my thesis that *erotic object choice and gender identity are independent factors in sexual behavior.* When this assumption is made, the incongruities and diagnostic difficulties presented by transsexualism and transvestism are greatly diminished. Thus the reader who is somewhat familiar with the topic of this chapter will find the stress on findings, is aimed at supporting this thesis.

Table 6.1 illustrates currently accepted features, which distinguish transvestism and transsexualism. The bottom of the Table also shows the relationship of erotic object choice and gender identity to transvestism and transsexualism. Cells A and D are presumed to be empty but in fact are not. We will come back to this later.

One has to be cautious in studying both transvestism and transsexualism as described here. Historically, both terms were labeled only as transvestism. Often writers used transvestism to cover both terms and one must ask which is being discussed. Sometimes it is not clear[7][81][162]. Even those authors who make the seemingly simple definitional distinction made in Table 6.1 will talk of transvestism meaning both transvestism and transsexualism. Harry Benjamin[12], a pioneer in the use of sex reassignment surgery, discusses three categories of patients that represent an evolution of transvestite into transsexual. The precise differences in the groups have still not been sorted out. Current writings on this topic show there is still much conceptual confusion possibly due to the shortage of facts about these anomalies. For the sake of clarity, first transsexualism is discussed, then transvestism.

TABLE 6.1
Currently Accepted Differences in Transsexualism and Transvestism

	Transsexualism	Transvestism
1. Fetish for female garments	No	Yes
2. Erotic object preference	Men	Women
3. Crossdressing	Yes	Yes
4. Crossdressing with masturbation	No	Yes
5. Gender identity	Feminine	Masculine/ Bisexual

		Gender Identity	
		Masculine/Bisexual	Feminine
Erotic Object Choice	Male	A	B Transsexuals
	Female	C Transvestites	D

TRANSSEXUALISM

The Theories

The transsexual as androphilic.   Freund and his colleagues[55] have argued that the transsexual is basically a "homosexual" in the extreme form. Therefore everything that applies to homosexuality (Chapter 4) applies here as well. The two groups have been aligned because both show: preference for male sex partners, a tendency to feminine gender identity, and narcissism. Each feature is exaggerated in the transsexual.

Desire for gynephilic partners.   Not only does the transsexual want a male sex partner, he wants a "heterosexual" one and he wants to relate to him as an anatomical woman. In fact, the transsexual may want sex reassignment surgery in order to attract gynephilic men. Benjamin[12] notes that the transsexual does not like "homosexuals". He may even have an aversion to his own penis and that is why he wants it removed. As a female, he could relate to a gynephilic male in a passive and stereotypic way. He may not be able to cope or may not desire the sexual demands of another androphilic man. *Mr. S* was very sensitive about the use of the term "homosexual" and about reference to him other than as a female. Medical examination showed he was a normal male.

> Mr. S: I've had sex with other men but I'm not a homosexual. That is quite disgusting to me, men having sex with men. I am really a woman and that makes all the difference in the world.

The typical androphile enjoys and expects mutual masturbation and fellatio (See Chapter Four). Since the transsexual wants his penis removed, he may not use it in sexual relationships with androphilic men. This makes reciprocal enjoyment and satisfaction difficult and can be disruptive to a continuing relationship or even to repeated casual sexual encounters. His excessively feminine behavior may also be unattractive to androphiles who, after all, prefer men[97] [98] [99].

Feminine gender identity. Whereas many androphilic men wish at some time that they were women or have displayed behavior and attitudes typical of women, the transsexual often claims that he has always felt that way. The totality and extremeness[155] [157] of the feminine gender identity manifests itself in a desire for a female body. *Mr. J* appeared at the clinic as a partially feminized male. Hormone therapy had produced breast enhancement and he appeared seductively dressed. He described his history:

> Mr. J: As long as I can remember I've wanted to be a girl. I was three years old when I started dressing as a girl much of the time. Mother took me to our family doctor who thought it was a passing phase and I would outgrow it but I didn't. I felt good about being dressed that way even though some of the kids laughed at me. I had a doll and tea set and would rather be with the girls playing house than doing anything else. I knew even then that my body was a mistake but I really started to want surgery when I was 13 and that desire has stayed with me to date.

Not all authors are agreed that the conviction of femininity in the transsexual is so long lived and firmly established. Person and Ovesey[126] note that the transsexual's feminine gender identity may be superficial and stereotypic in spite of a seemingly exterior copy of the feminine anatomy. The "conviction" of being a female in a male body may be *confusion*. *Mr. B* presented such a picture.

He first came to our clinic at age 13 as a behavior problem and later as a candidate for sex change surgery. He was a confused individual but not psychotic according to his psychological tests. He had earlier been considered schizophrenic but this diagnosis was not accepted at his current assessment. He was a muscular 19 year old when evaluated for sex reassignment surgery. He appeared dressed in male clothes with exaggerated masculine features. He wore jeans with a large leather belt and a buckle with a Mack truck on it. His hair was short cropped, military fashion. He carried a series of tools attached to the belt including a knife. On the bulging bicep of his right arm, was a tatoo of an eagle with flaring talons. He said:

> *Mr. B:* I've felt like a woman for a long time. I'm more relaxed when I'm dressed in a nightie and female panties. Women have an easier time meeting men too than the other way around. They are asked if they want a seat or a drink and men are always looking at them. I think I would really like that. It would solve my problems.
>
> *Doctor:* When do you wear the female clothes?
>
> *Mr. B.:* I'm wearing them right now. I have female panties on and a bra under these clothes. It helps me to get through the day.
>
> *Doctor:* What about the tatoo and the tools and all the male things you like to do. Would you miss them if you were a woman?
>
> *Mr. B:* I don't know. (Pause). I don't think so. I'd be much happier as a woman.

Phallometric testing to ascertain whether he preferred to react to men or women showed an overwhelming and clear reaction to adult females. Reactions to men were no greater than those to neutral stimuli. Note that *Mr. B* would be considered gynephilic but he is transsexual nonetheless, according to the definition given above. This fact has been repeatedly documented but is difficult to accept[7 13 30 57 70 72 73 108 120 127 152 158]. The confusion has led to a plethora of unnecessary psychiatric diagnostic labels which I noted earlier. It is possible that gender dysphoria is *the* problem in transsexualism, regardless of any preference for the male or female body shape.

Stoller and Newman[157 158] have suggested individuals like *Mr. B* are bisexual in gender identity and may remain so after surgical intervention. As noted in Chapter 5, some "bisexuals" adapt to a "heterosexual" world by "faking it" and conforming to expected role behavior. The transsexual may do this in a different way. He copes with the same problem by becoming a woman and in this sense is inconspicuous and conforming. *Mr. A* described such a feeling this way:

> *Mr. A:* I want to be a whole woman. I am a woman. I've felt like a woman and with the operation, I will be a whole woman. I don't want to spend my life associating with gays or pretending to be a woman. I want the satisfaction of having a full female body and finding a real straight man to share myself with. I'm tired of pretending and being discovered and having to move from place to place. It will be so nice to lead a normal life.

Narcissism. The third parallel of transsexualism to androphilia is in narcissism. This term was discussed in Chapter 3 but it merits amplification here. There are at least two meanings of the term. The first meaning indicates a preoccupation with oneself as a sexual object. Thus a male who can be sexually gratified solely by his reflection in a mirror or by looking at his own body can be called a narcissist. A second meaning of the term implies admiration by another in a dyadic relationship. Eric Fromm[60], humorously noted: The narcissist's lover says to him, 'Oh darling, I love you' and the narcissist replies, 'Oh darling, I love me too'. The narcissist may require the involvement of another admirer to satisfy his need. The two forms of narcissism are worth distinguishing. For clinical purposes the transsexual, *Mr. L,* was photographed in the nude and in his favorite female attire. He chose to wear a see-through blouse so his surgically enhanced breasts were clearly visible to the observer. During the photographic session the patient was quite evidently sexually excited and continued to be so just after it was all over. The photographer noted: "He really got off on having his picture taken. It sure wasn't me that turned him on. I felt like a stage prop".

Neither type of narcissism need be erotic and some transsexuals have been considered asexual[13][67]. The gynephilic *Mr. D* was like this. He claimed that he never masturbated in the female attire and in fact rarely masturbated at all. A low sex drive may occur in some transsexuals because of the hormone treatment they undergo. It has also been argued that their gratification is nongenital[11]. They are aroused and satisfied *cerebrally* by the sole fact of being a woman. This may take the problem of transsexualism out of the realm of erotic preferences.

Mr. D described his late evening walks alone dressed completely as a female.

Mr. D: I will sit and watch TV all dressed in female clothes and feel really relaxed. Late at night when no one is around I will walk the streets in the cool evening air, nervous that someone will see me and at the same time hoping men will see me and take me for a woman.

Doctor: Do you hope for sexual contact with a man?

Mr. D: No. I like the feeling of being treated and taken as a woman. I don't particularly want sex.

Asexuality may be more apparent than real in this anomaly because they are not interested in other sex partners but are preoccupied with their own bodies. In this sense, they may parallel the female who is considered to be narcissistic in her preoccupation with her own body and she too does not usually derive erotic gratification from this activity. At least neither transsexuals nor females derive erotic gratification from their own bodies in a solitary form of narcissism, that is, from self admiration and self stimulation, but they both may derive narcissistic satisfaction in an interpersonal context, like being admired by another person, in both cases, by a male.

Transsexuals as exhibitionists.   Transsexualism has been identified with exhibitionism[102] in that the transsexual derives pleasure from being accepted as a woman and dressing in public in female attire like *Mr. B.* The exhibitionist, (Chapter 10) however, usually wishes to have his penis admired and may masturbate while doing so. This is uncharacteristic of the transsexual who conceals any male features he possesses.

The masochistic wish.   The removal of male features may be more than a desire to appear feminine. It may be a masochistic wish. Not only do transsexuals appear at clinics for sex conversion operations but they may mutilate themselves by castration or by cutting off their penises[55] [102]. This may be an aversion to their own penises noted earlier or reflect masochistic tendencies or both. Note that this does not appear to represent masochistic *sexual* gratification as discussed in Chapter 13 under masochism and sadism. Rather, it reflects a more general tendency for self destruction and not a compelling association of sexual satisfaction with pain or humiliation. In this vein, castration for the transsexual may be an escape from *all* sexual impulses rather than a wish to be a female[12] [102]. He may be threatened by all sexual activities including masturbation. He holds only a distorted concept of what a true female is like. Thus there need be no incongruity between an androphilic desire for men and a desire to have a woman's body by removal of his penis. The loss of libido by castration would be a relief rather than a worry. However, transsexualism may reflect true masochism as a desire for humiliation. *Mr. N* noted his favorite if infrequent sex fantasy:

Mr. N: I dress up as a woman—completely. Then I imagine a man is making love to me. He forces his penis into my mouth and makes me suck it. When he comes, he ejaculates right in my face.

Doctor: How do you feel about that?

Mr. N: It feels good.

Doctor: Do you masturbate or come yourself?

Mr. N: No just him. But I feel satisfied too.

Family background of transsexuals.   The long standing and strong desire of the transsexual to be a woman may have come about because his parents rejected his masculinity from a very early age. This may be outright rejection in the form of such statements to the child as "I really wanted a girl'' or ''Why weren't you a girl?'' Consequently, the parents may encourage the child to adopt female behaviors. Alternately, they may cause the development of sadomasochistic attitudes in the child to his own genitals, which are the obvious cause of his parents rejecting him. Hiding the genitals from the parents under a dress may be the source of transvestism and the desire for complete removal of the sex organs the start of transsexualism.

Some parents of the transsexuals are not so overtly hostile to the child's sexuality but crossdress him in female attire and subtly encourage him to do so on his own[157] [162]. Some mothers seem fascinated by the transformation of the male child to female[66]. As a result, he may later develop a desire to be permanently female. Some parents of transsexuals may have either psychiatric problems or sexual conflicts of their own, so it is not surprising that they develop sexually confused children[22] [166].

Another way parents may encourage the development of transsexualism is by dressing up their son as a girl for punishment, which may become a *traumatic fixation*[61]. When an individual is faced with overwhelming anxiety, he may develop stereotyped behavior that may seem bizarre but which is a product of the attempt to react to the extreme anxiety. This traumatic fixation may develop in the transsexual when the boy fears he will be castrated especially while he is dressed like a girl since in his mind, girls have had their penises cut off. So he repeats the stereotyped female behavior until it becomes a fixed habit. The original punishment by the parent is reenacted in his crossdressing and in his cognitions about himself. This theory could be applied equally to transvestism suggesting a common etiology in the two conditions.

Finally, the parents may offer the female role a favored status. Even though the male child is not particularly encouraged to crossdress, he perceives the family benefits of being female and attempts to copy such behaviors. *Mr. K* illustrates this theory.

> *Mr. K:* I really dislike my sister. She gets everything and I get nothing. Sometimes I go into the other room to eat my dinner while she hogs the conversation and has Mom and Dad running here and there for her, doing her bidding. If I try to say something, I'm ignored but the minute she opens her mouth, it's ''Oh really Jane? How nice'' and ''What do you think of this?'' and on and on until I feel like just getting up and leaving. Sometimes, I do. I go and watch T.V. while everyone else is eating in the dining room.

Organic basis of transsexualism.   Finally, transsexualism has been viewed as a biological problem, just as homosexuality has. Therefore, all that has been said about an organic basis for homosexuality (Chapter 4) applies here as well. Both have been called a form of intersexuality—a bridge between males and females. Possible genetic, constitutional and hormonal differences have been postulated. The interested reader may wish to review these theories in Chapter 4. Transsexualism has attracted much theoretical attention and some combinations of the above factors have been used to explain it. These multiple causation theories are not elaborated here because they add no new information. (See [102] for details and an excellent review of earlier literature and [123] for some of the problems of genetic research in gender behavior).

The Experiments on Transsexualism

A parallel of transsexuals to androphiles has been suggested because they both prefer male sex partners, show high feminine gender identity and are narcissistic. There are only four phallometric studies in the professional literature which makes the evaluation of these theories difficult[6 7 29 55]. The research investigators cannot take all the blame this time. The transsexual does not want anyone investigating his penis, he just wants it removed. Even when they are cooperative and will permit phallometric testing, self administration of hormones or perhaps mental set prevents any significant erotic reactivity from being measured in the laboratory. Perhaps some are truly asexual and a lack of penile reactivity should be expected. Transvestites on the other hand are reluctant to appear at psychiatric clinics unless they "become transsexuals" and want an operation.

Transsexualism and androphilia. Three phallometric studies have attempted to determine if transsexuals are more aroused by men or women. The procedure for doing so has been described in Chapter 4. Basically penile reactions are compared to stimulus movies of male and female children and adults and to neutral stimuli. Freund and his associates[55] compared transsexual and nontranssexual androphilic men. They found transsexuals clearly prefer mature males. Transsexuals reacted less to immature males than androphilic controls did. The verbal report of the transsexuals indicated that they preferred partners in their twenties but not younger. An interesting question is whether they prefer their sex partners to be older than themselves. Typically females in our culture prefer their male mates to be older than themselves. If the male–to–female transsexuals also had this preference, it would parallel the normal female pattern. However this question was not asked. In another study of 13 transsexuals who had been surgically reassigned to female, Money and Brennan[113] found that seven had established relationships with men. Contrary to the expected pattern in our culture, five of the seven "females" were older then their male partners. In the Freund et al., study[55] little or no reaction to females was evident in the transsexuals indicating that they were not "bisexual" in erotic object choice nor were they gynephilic. However, this may simply reflect the subject selection procedure. Nine percent of the individuals who were gynephilic were excluded from the results. Thus, this study presents a biased picture that there are no transsexuals who erotically prefer women over men[108] [170].

Barr, McConaghy and their associates examined penile reactions to males and females in three further studies[6] [7] [30] [31]. One report is an elaboration of another illustrating two cases of "apparent heterosexuality" in applicants for sex reassignment. Overall, the results support those of Freund et al that transsexual applicants for sex reassignment are generally androphilic preferring mature male partners. Nevertheless, they found some gynephilic transsexuals too.

There may be only a few gynephilic transsexuals who present themselves for surgery because they are screened out by physicians or mental health workers before they reach a gender identity clinic, perhaps because of obvious "confusion", for example, they are married and have children or claim to like women, and so forth. Moreover, some transvestites later become transsexuals and request sex reassignment surgery. They have been reluctant to come to psychiatric clinics and we are just beginning to find professional reports on this group.

Bentler[13] assumes without question that transsexuals may be gynephilic, androphilic or asexual and devised a typology of transsexualism based on that distinction. He examined 42 post-surgical transsexuals and was surprised to find about 1/3 fell into each of the three groups. Patients were classified on the basis of answers to five questions: (1) before surgery I was homosexual; (2) heterosexual; (3) ever married as a male to a female; (4) had pleasant and successful intercourse with a woman; (5) number of women with whom he had intercourse as a male. Classification was quite discrete except for the asexual group all of whom never had successful intercourse with a woman and about half said they were "heterosexual".

To highlight the terminological confusion that can result in this area, I will just note that almost all Bentler's patients said that after surgery, they were "heterosexual". This represents a complete reversal in self concept for the androphiles according to Bentler. What we do not know is whether they are judging their preference for men or women *as* women or *as* men. One can appreciate that meetings at gender dysphoria clinics must be quite confusing at times for the staff!

Other demographic information suggests that the transsexual can be either gynephilic or androphilic but is predominantly androphilic. Up to half of various samples marry and have children[75] [93] [109] [128]. They may report they are attracted to the female body and perhaps most important for treatment, they may not be satisfied with a female body when they do get one as will be discussed later[102]. The best one can conclude from this available information is that androphilic transsexuals seem to be more numerous than gynephilic ones. However, it would be false to conclude that gynephilic transsexuals do not exist. Their small but persistent numbers suggests that something is amiss in the parallel of transsexualism to androphilia.

Preference for gynephilic male partners.   Freund et al[55] found that androphilic transsexuals reported less gynephilic experience than nontranssexual androphilic controls. Early androphilic development was associated with less subsequent gynephilic experience. This agrees with the claim of transsexuals that they have always felt like women and thus would have little desire for sex relations with women, even from an early age. Ninety-eight percent of the transsexuals compared to 14% of the androphiles preferred "heterosexual" male partners. Results also showed that about a sixth of the transsexuals had experienced heterosexual intercourse in contrast to about a quarter of the androphilic controls. An interesting finding was that about 4 in 5 transsexuals imagine during heterosexual intercourse that they are the female and their partner, the male. All the androphiles who had intercourse with a woman indicated that they fantasized that she was also a man.

Transsexualism and feminine gender identity.   Freund and his colleagues examined gender identity in transsexuals by means of a questionnaire which includes a Feminine Gender Identity Scale[54 55 57]. The questionnaire was administered to a transsexual group and to control groups of androphilic and gynephilic males who were not transsexuals. They found that transsexuals scored significantly higher than androphiles on feminine gender identity. Score overlap between the two groups was minimal. No androphile was misclassified as transsexual and only 2% of transsexuals were misplaced into the androphilic group in statistical analysis. There was no overlap of transsexual and gynephilic group scores but one third of the androphile group scores overlapped with the gynephiles' scores.

In a second study my colleagues and I used the masculinity–femininity scale of the MMPI[93]. Although results were in the same direction, they were not as clear cut. Transsexuals tend to be more feminine than androphilic groups supporting the theory of a parallel in the two groups. Derogatis, Meyer and Vazquez[42] found transsexuals scored higher on femininity and lower on masculinity than gynephiles did on the Bem Androgyny Scale. All results support the theory of increased femininity in transsexuals. Buhrich and McConaghy[33] compared transsexuals, transvestites, neurotics and general hospital patients. The transvestites were members of a club whereas the rest were patients. They found increased femininity on the California

Personality Inventory Femininity Scale and the Draw-a-Person Test among other tests including the Wechsler Adult Intelligence Scale (WAIS). The groups were recategorized on degree of feminine gender identity into strong and moderate. Unfortunately no reliability for the groups' classification was reported. As expected, the "strong" group scored higher on the Femininity test. There were no differences on intelligence scores. One has to wonder at this point what proportion of sexually anomalous males in general have high feminine gender identity and/or a fetishistic attraction to clothing of the opposite sex. Perhaps the combination of fetishism and transvestism–transsexualism is a chance cooccurrence of two behaviors and they have no etiological connection. On the other hand, the dichotomy of "heterosexual fetish" and "homosexual crossdresser" to characterize the transvestite versus the transsexual may be too simpleminded.

Fleming and his colleagues[48] studied transsexualism using the Bem Androgyny Scale, which measures traditional male and female behaviors and a difference score of the two. As expected, male-to-female transsexuals were more feminine and less masculine than Bem's normative sample but social desirability scores were the dominant factor. Whereas this too can be interpreted, it confounds the results and indicates problems with the Bem scales[10][166].

Mirror complex—narcissism.   Only one study examined narcissism in transsexuals. Freund et al[55] used phallometric testing to examine if transsexuals are narcissistic. Penile reactions of transsexuals to pictures of themselves in the nude and in female attire were compared to reactions to pictures of men and women. The patients did not react more to their own bodies than to female stimuli, that is, they reacted apparently at the neutral level. This suggests that mirror complex narcissism is not present in transsexuals. However, we do not know if they are sexually aroused by interpersonal narcissism, that is, by admiration from others. Thus the only strong support for the parallel of transsexualism and androphilia occurs to some degree in feminine gender identity and in a preference for male sex partners.

Transsexualism and other sexual anomalies.   There are only two controlled studies of transsexualism using a standardized psychometric sex history questionnaire[42][93]. In the first study Steiner, Paitich and I compared five groups: transsexuals who applied for surgery at a gender identity clinic and who for at least one year had lived consistently as females. A second similar group had lived as males throughout their contact with the clinic. Two further control groups were androphilic; those who had been patients and those who had never been patients at a psychiatric hospital and looked clinically "normal." Finally, a normal gynephilic control group was used.

The research participants were compared on the Sex History Questionnaire in Appendix One. There were no cases in any group of: pedophilia, exhibitionism, voyeurism, frotteurism, rape or toucheurism. The only differences were in androphilic and gynephilic outlet and crossdressing. Note, however, that this questionnaire does not ask about masochism and such differences may have gone undetected.

Transsexuals as asexual.   In our study the gynephilic controls had more sexual experience with women than the other four groups as one would expect but the transsexual groups had even less experience than either androphilic group. The last groups claimed less disgust than transsexuals for gynephilic contact but it should be noted that no subject had had intimate sexual contact with a female, that is, intercourse, except the gynephiles.

The gynephilic controls had less androphilic experience than any of the other groups. Normal androphilic males had the most experience and indicated the most desire and the least disgust for such acts. The androphilic patients were not far behind in experience and feelings. Next in line with less experience were the transsexuals living as males. They not only had less experience but indicated that they had less desire and more disgust for sexual contact with men. They liked handling the male genitals less or kissing men on the lips and indicated they were more likely to find the handling of another male's genitals disgusting. The transsexuals living as women had less experience with men again but did desire such contact and did not display the incongruity of the transsexual group living as males.

The two transsexual groups differed from the androphilic groups in the frequency with which their own penises were used in sexual interactions. One might expect that since the transsexuals wanted their penises removed, they might show less involvement of their own genitals in sexual acts. Both transsexual groups were less likely to have fellatio performed on them by males and had less handling of their penises by other males. Nor did they perform anal intercourse since their penises would also be involved. There was also an incongruity again for the transsexuals living as males. They had significantly more fellatio performed on them than their counterparts living as females. They wanted to become women but were somewhat disgusted by sex with a male. Their own penis was involved in sexual behavior to a significant degree but they wanted it removed. It should be noted, however, that both transsexual groups appeared to enjoy orgasm via their penises to a significant degree both in having their penises handled and in being fellated by a male. The assertion that transsexuals are asexual is not the case. One may then wonder why they are so eager to have their genitals removed.

By separating out gender identity and sex object choice, the behavior of the transsexual living as a male is clearer. His desire to be a woman is for his own satisfaction and his gender needs. He may prefer body characteristics of either male or female and if the latter, he may be digusted by sex with a man.

Derogatis and his colleagues[42] have reported similar findings. They compared male transsexuals and gynephilic controls on the Derogatis Sexual Functioning Inventory, the Brief Symptom Inventory and Bem's Sex Role Inventory or Androgyny Scale. The Derogatis scale provides standard psychological assessment of a range of sexual functioning. It showed that the transsexuals had considerable sexual experience but it was in a restricted range of behaviors compared to the heterosexuals. As expected, they engaged less frequently in heterosexual intercourse than controls but as well, showed less active involvement of their penises in sexual acts such as mutual fellatio. In addition, transsexuals had less sex information and lower drive level although 7 in 10 reported masturbating and drive level may be counfounded with range of sexual experience on this scale. Sexual fantasies tended to be androphilic and transvestitic.

While Derogatis et al's results on sexual experience and use of penis in sexual behavior supports our study, their research participants had undergone considerable more screening prior to surgery than our candidates do and so they may be a more select group. Nevertheless, about half of their transsexuals had experienced heterosexual intercourse indicating some gynephilic interest.

Masochism.   The next feature of transsexualism that may be pathologically significant is masochism. The desire for penis ablation is seen as a critical factor in the anomaly. Freund and his colleagues[55] have examined this question. Research participants were asked 10 questions about masochism, which asked whether the respondant was sexually excited by being humiliated, embarrassed or physically injured. Three quarters of the androphilic controls indicated no masochism at all. Only half of the transsexuals answered the questions and of these, less than 5% indicated any masochism whatsoever. This argues against masochism as a factor in transsexualism. Since half of the subjects in the study did not answer the questions, one may ask if they were concealing information or whether the questions were seen as irrelevant. When candidates are applying for surgery, they may be very careful of what they say. However, the existing information suggests that masochism is not a major factor in transsexualism. Another approach to the question was to ask transsexuals to rank desire for female body versus penis ablation. Seven items were included but the subjects overwhelmingly chose to have the female body first. Almost 90% chose to have the total female body rather than mere penis ablation (penectomy). This suggests that an aversion to his own penis was not a prominent factor but in order to have a female body, the penis would have to be removed. However, these results are not clear cut. There could be both an aversion to the penis and a desire for a female body. It would be very difficult to ascertain which is which.

Fetishism for female garments.   Finally, Freund and his colleagues asked whether female garments had a fetishistic component for transsexuals. Less than 10% of the androphilic transsexuals indicated that the female clothes were erotically attractive. Bentler[13]found that among surgically sex reassigned men, 50% of "heterosexuals", 23% of "homosexuals" and 18% of "asexual" cases were sexually aroused while crossdressed. Although it has been argued that transsexuals are androphilic and not fetishistic, a small number of them do seem to be fetishistic. Buhrich and McConaghy[29] [30] [32] argue that there are two discrete syndromes in *transsexualism,* one comprising a fetishistic arousal to female garments, the other not. The fetishists are more likely to be gynephilic in orientation and experience, that is, they seem to be transvestites. Existing studies confuse crossdressing and sex object preference. In addition, they never examine the "fetishism" phallometrically but beg the question by saying the fetishists masturbate in female attire. It is noteworthy that their transsexuals' sexual fantasies were predominantly of being a woman whereas their female sex partner was a man.

Although Buhrich and McConaghy have mixed transsexualism and transvestism, Freund et al[58] have attempted to polarize differences in the two groups. The latter claim that transvestism cooccurs exclusively or almost exclusively with female erotic object choice. Transsexualism rarely or never accompanies female erotic object choice and is usually associated with male erotic object choice. Since clinical evidence contradicts these assumptions, they then proceed to describe a host of diagnostic labels that define gender dysphoria in both androphiles and gynephiles, adding to the existing confusion. A clear controlled study has yet to be done which shows that fetishism is the important component in transvestism and that it is not important in transsexualism. Data exist that both crossdressing and feminine gender identity occur in both gynephiles and androphiles. It is a fruitful question to ask why transsexualism is more prominent in males of androphilic versus gynephilic orientation but not to deny its existence in gynephiles.

It is noteworthy that fetishism has been poorly assessed in general. The patient is asked if he has been sexually aroused while crossdressing. If he says yes, he is a fetishist. However, a fetish implies an inordinate erotic reaction to *inanimate objects themselves* such as clothes or leather (See Chapter 7). The transvestite may be aroused to himself dressed as a woman rather than to the garments per se. This would seem like typical gynephilic arousal albeit to a special female, namely, themselves crossdressed. It is not usually clear what the fetish comprises and the results of reports should be considered with caution.

Only Freund and his associates[58] separate out fetishism for inanimate objects and orgasmic crossdressing. They labelled the latter cross gender fetishism which involves fantasizing during "fetishistic" activity that one belongs to the opposite sex. Freund et al found that both gynephiles and androphiles could be transsexuals. If the heterosexuals displayed fetishism, they were labeled transvestite. If they showed greater feminine gender identity and less fetishism, they were "heterosexual borderline transsexual". An analogous set of terms were applied to androphiles. However, it seems fetishism may be present in both transvestism and transsexualism. Unfortunately the wording of Freund et al's[58] key question to sort patients into "fetishistic" versus "nonfetishistic" still leaves ambiguity about the sexual arousal value of garments themselves. A clear empirical statement has yet to be made on the importance of fetishism in the two anomalies.

Transsexualism and psychiatric disorders.   Little attempt has been made to study other important facets of transsexualism systematically. Stoller and Newman[158] note the importance of sorting out psychotic and other non-transsexual individuals but one may well ask how pathological are "true" transsexuals themselves?

Hoenig and his associates have presented the most thorough psychiatric evaluation of the question[75][76]. They note that a high incidence (70%) of psychiatric disorders accompany transsexualism, but the anomaly itself lends to no diagnostic classification. Work adjustment was poor in half their cases and almost half had criminal records. A third were prostitutes. Finney and his associates[47] and Rosen[143] in uncontrolled studies supported the findings of pathology. The former found a preponderance of hysterical personalities but the latter found no consistent profile.

The research literature using the MMPI as the major assessment tool in both controlled and uncontrolled studies has been mixed[83][143][154][163]. Some report the absence of pathology even when MMPI profiles are examined and control groups are used. However there are several problems with these results. Studies generally have examined MMPI *average* scores that can mask pathology in a number of patients. For example Tsushima and Wedding[163] reported an average T-score for the transsexuals of 66 on the schizophrenia scale, which is close to the clinically significant $T = 70$ used as a cutoff for pathology. A sizable number of their patients must have scored in the pathological range to obtain that average. No one has claimed that *all* transsexuals are psychotic or emotionally disturbed but some clearly are. Another problem with the MMPI studies of transsexuals is the lack of reporting of other significant information, such as psychiatric diagnosis, suicide attempts or criminal history. The total information may present a different picture than the MMPI alone. Finally one must contend with selection of patients for surgery. Some clinics screen out psychotic men so the results showing no pathology may be biased.

In a controlled study of transsexuals by my colleagues and me[93] , emotional disturbance and criminal records were examined. The transsexuals living as males manifested more emotional disturbance as measured by psychometric instruments whereas those living as women were more likely to have criminal records. Leavitt and his co-workers[95] found similar results on the MMPI but also suggested self administration of hormones differentiated the two groups. However, the use of hormones and "living as a female" may be very difficult to separate in practice. Length of time on hormones was also weakly correlated with 4 MMPI scales but the relative contribution of hormones and "living as a female" to the results were not statistically separated. Since the MMPI contains mainly historical trait items that are unresponsive to short term state changes, character differences in the two groups may better explain the results.

Derogatis et al[42] have also conducted a controlled study of transsexual and normal males. Using the Brief Symptom Inventory, they found that in transsexuals there was more suicidal ideation, increased interpersonal sensitivity, depression and paranoid ideation. These results indicated they were sensitive to manipulating people and felt inferior and self conscious. They also were more likely than controls to fear crowds and to experience negative mood. One may postulate that such symptoms relate to living their lives in a disguise, to dissatisfaction with being a male and to fear of discovery.

Newman and Stoller[120] suggested that the pathological cases be excluded from sex reassignment surgery and some studies indicate that many applicants should be refused. Unfortunately, this has not always been the case. One can expect to see considerable pathology in applicants for sex reassignment surgery, especially if they are not prescreened.

Parent-child relations of transsexuals.   It has been suggested that family dynamics may be similar in transsexuals and androphiles and such a finding would offer some, albeit weak, support for the theory connecting the two anomalies. Freund et al[56] compared transsexual, androphilic and gynephilic men on the incidence of loss of father and mother and on ratings of closeness to each parent. There were few differences between transsexuals and androphiles and between androphiles and gynephiles. However, transsexuals were closer to mother than gynephiles and they reported more unreplaced loss of mothers.

My colleagues and I have done the only controlled study of parent child relations in transsexuals using a standardized instrument. In our study[93], transsexuals living as males, as females, normal androphiles, androphilic patients and gynephilic controls were compared. There were no significant differences in family constellations in terms of number of brothers and sisters, birth order or death/absence of a parent. On the standardized Clarke Parent Child Relations Questionnaire, 4 of 16 possible scales were significant. Mothers were more indulgent than average to androphilic patients and transsexuals living as males. Both transsexual groups reported father as less competent and affectionate than androphiles and gynephiles did and they identified less with him. There were no group differences in the exchange of aggression among mother, father and son. There was thus mixed support for the theory.

Genetic and endocrine factors in transsexualism. There are only a few genetic studies on adult transsexuals[5 34 78 133], and two cases were mislabeled by currently accepted definitions of transsexualism and transvestism. Barr bodies and chromosomes were normal male. Rekers and his colleagues[133] studied 12 gender disturbed children in the age range of 4 to 13. All were found to have normal chromosomes and to be physically normal except for one boy with an undescended testicle. These results reduce the possibility of a genetic factor being present in transsexualism. Buhrich, Barr and Lam-Po-Tang[34] reported an unusual finding that one case of transvestism and one of transsexualism presented with *XYY* chromosomal patterns which are clinically presumed to be associated with aggressiveness and criminal histories (See Chapter 14).

Hoenig & Torr[78] reviewed foreign language publications with their own presentation of data. Karyotyping of the transsexuals in their report and other genetic studies all found the research participants to be normal. Recent interest has developed in the H-Y antigen which is a cell surface component present in all male tissue but not in females. Eicher et al.,[44] reported there was a reversal of sex patterning of H-Y antigen in transsexual males and females. Although the typical male has H-Y antigen positive, 4 of 7 male transsexuals were negative and 5 of 7 females were positive. The authors however express concern about the influence of oestrogen hormone therapy on the outcome of the results. The findings are only suggestive because of the methodological difficulties just noted, the reliability of assays, and due to the lack of an appropriate control group for comparison.

In suggestive case studies of familial comparisons, transsexualism was reported in male twins[84 107]. McKee, Roback and Hollander[107] have identified other case reports that must remain suggestive until large scale studies can be done. *XY* chromosomes were normal in these cases indicating that some other genetic or environmental factor might be important. Constitutional studies indicate transsexuals are physically normal males. A few cases with organic etiology are different and are discussed in Chapter 14. Hormonal assays indicate normal male profile[150]. However, all of the assay problems noted in Chapters 3 and 4 apply here, and a study with adequate controls remains to be done[111]. Overall theories of transvestism-transsexualism are not popular and have found little support in research findings. The added problem of self administered sex hormones in transsexuals also complicates data collection and interpretation.

Hoenig and Kenna[74] reviewed studies on electroencephalogram (EEG) abnormalities in transsexuals and included foreign language publications. There was some general suggestion that temporal lobe or general dysfunction of the brain is related to transsexualism. Of the 35 men and 11 women they studied themselves, 48% showed EEG abnormalities and another 24% showed borderline abnormalities. Moreover, of the abnormal EEGs, 45% were in the expected temporal lobe area. Other case reports also indicate brain pathology but Hoenig and Kenna note some of the confounding factors in interpreting the results. Fifty four percent of the patients had some personality disorders and the incidence of EEG abnormalities is higher in this group than average. Self administered drugs may also influence the EEG recording (cf. [91]) but we do not know the extent to which research participants have been screened on this variable. No control group was used and the study was not done blind. This is especially important in EEG studies when the clinical art of interpretation is employed rather than the use of spectral analysis that is more precisely done by a computer.

An important study was done by Kolarsky and his colleagues[89] because they examined an unselected group of 86 epileptic patients. They found sexual abnormalities in 22%, in particular, voyeurism, exhibitionism, fetishism, sadism, masochism, frotteurism and pedophilia. The sexual anomalies mostly involved the temporal lobe. They were more likely to happen if the brain pathology was already present in the first year of life. It seems there is some connection between temporal lobe dysfunction and sexual anomalies but a well controlled study has yet to be done. It should involve EEG spectral analysis on patients free of drugs and should have a control group. The results then can be analysed blind so that no bias in interpretation is present. A researcher familiar with sexual anomalies should be involved to insure correct categorization of transsexual versus transvestite. Many of the existing reports do not, so that there is considerable ambiguity even about the actual presence or absence of a sexual anomaly.

Hoenig and Kenna found that low sex drive was associated with EEG abnormalities in their patients. However only frequency of masturbation was analysed rather than total outlets in this group going on 30 years of age when it is expected that sexual interactions with others would be more frequent than masturbation. The evidence on hyposexuality in temporal lobe pathology is controversial according to these authors but the larger better documented studies suggest this is the rule in such disorders. It appears to be an important facet of behavior to analyse in EEG studies, although low sex drive per se may not be an important sign of transsexualism. If the patient claims he is asexual and transsexual then a neurological test may be positive. One useful clinical finding was that EEG abnormal transsexuals were discovered earlier by family than EEG normal ones.

Hunt and Hampson[82] reported the only study of transsexualism using the neuropsychological Reitan test battery which measures behavioral correlates of brain functioning. All mean scores were within normal limits, except the Tactile Performance Test scores which were marginally significant. All WAIS IQ scores were in the normal to bright normal range. Their results rule against neurological impairment but EEG and behavior tests of impairment do not necessarily agree and the question is worth further investigation.

The transsexual stimulus response matrix. A summary of the results testing theories of transsexualism appears in Table 6.2. The majority of transsexuals appear to prefer the body characteristics of the mature male who is heterosexual and masculine in his gender behavior. However, a minority are attracted to the female body shape and/or appear to be fetishistic. It is unknown whether they are masochistic or have a need for some form of submissive dominance relationship. The preferred response is to be a passive female in heterosexual intercourse. Perhaps this is immaterial since they are willing to accept an operation to remove the ability to respond sexually. They are less likely to use the penis in sexual relationships with men but they do use it, supporting the androphilic pattern of behavior. They want to crossdress and it is not known if this has an interpersonal narcissistic element to it. It does not appear to be mirror complex narcissism, that is, arousal to their own body per se. One can expect to find a significant number of emotionally disturbed individuals in this group.

TREATMENT OF TRANSSEXUALISM

Although there is a dearth of professional reports on the treatment of transsexualism by means other than surgery, it is assumed that the anomaly is very resistant to any behavior therapy or psychotherapy treatment[11][12][130]. However, there are no systematic studies comparing different treatments on this group.

Behavior Therapy

Among the behavior therapy methods, Barlow's is the only study using operant conditioning procedures to modify transsexual behavior in a 17-year-old male[4]. Initially, an attempt was made to change sexual arousal patterns by "fading" described in Chapter 3. This failed and the focus of

TABLE 6.2
Summary of Evidence for Theories of Transsexualism

Theory	Experimental Support
1. They are androphilic	Yes, generally, but some are gynephilic
2. Prefer "heterosexual" male partners	Yes, if they are androphilic themselves
3. Feminine gender identity	Yes, strong
4. Parent/child relations disturbed	Yes, limited support for poor father relations as in clinical cases of androphilia
5. Traumatic fixation	Untested
6. Aversion to their own penis	No, but only one study done
7. Aroused by own body (automonosexualism)	No, but only one study done
8. Narcissistic in an interpersonal context	Untested
9. They are asexual	No, in fact they use their own penises substantially
10. They are exhibitionists	No
11. Other sexual anomalies present	No
12. They are masochists	No, but only 1 study done using self report
13. Organic cause – brain damage, genetic, constitutional, endocrine	Some positive findings but evidence is limited
14. Personality Pathology	Yes, frequently associated with other psychiatric disorders
15. They are *not* fetishists	Generally no, but some may be. Not clearly established to date

treatment shifted to feminine behavior. The boy said that as long as he could remember, he thought of himself as a girl. His masturbation fantasies were of himself as a girl having intercourse with a man.

The male and female components of behavior were subdivided for treatment. First sitting, standing and walking were altered. Male behavior was modelled and videotaped feedback was used. Successful male behavior was praised and verbal feedback was given on errors. Ridicule by others in social situations was a source of embarrassment for the patient and change in the effeminate behavior was rewarded by his being more at ease in social situations where he was no longer ridiculed. Next, social behavior and vocal characteristics were modified. Finally, sex fantasies were again approached and successfully altered by praising male sex fantasies and by positive classical conditioning in which pictures of female nudes were followed by pictures of male nudes. Aversion therapy, both electrical and covert sensitization (Chapter 3) were used successfully to reduce androphilic arousal. At one year follow-up, gains in treatment were maintained and the patient was dating a girl and engaging in light petting. The patient's baseline frequency of behavior was recorded and systematically altered by reinforcement. Some reversals were demonstrated when the reinforcer was removed. Nevertheless, it is a single case and the single case experimental design has serious problems (see Chapter 3). It is an improvement over the uncontrolled case study but group data are desirable.

Behavior modifiers appear to have assumed that the adult transsexual is resistant to change and the best course of treatment is prevention in childhood[73]. A number of investigators have attempted to alter the atypical feminine behavior of boys in the hope of preventing later transsexualism and homosexuality. The assumption in this case is that feminine gender/sex role behavior causes androphilia or androphilia is one part of feminine gender behavior. As we have already discussed, gender identity and sex object choice may be independent.

The feminine boy may experience a wide range of problems from peer rejection to intrafamilial tensions. Yet the most prominent aspect of his effeminacy appears in his play. Normal boys tend to play with male sex typed toys, but the atypical ones play with female sex typed toys[8 66 140 168 169 173]. This play activity may be influenced by the presence or absence of strangers, male versus female observers, among other factors[131] but in spite of these variations, changing cross sex play is a potent enough procedure that it serves as one major avenue in which to modify effeminate behavior generally.

Green and his associates[68] have carried out the most extensive research in the area. Their treatment is complex and involves the development of a close trusting relationship between a male therapist and the boy, stopping parental encouragement of feminine behavior, interrupting the excessively close relationship between mother and son, enhancing the role of father and son, and generally promoting the father's role within the family. Therapy includes the whole family but the therapist takes an active part in treatment by encouraging masculine behaviors in the boy and at the same time actively disapproving of his feminine behavior. Thus he serves as a model for the child and as a differential reinforcer handing out positive and negative reinforcements. The treatment is intended to pervade the child's life and the therapist even taps the fantasy life of the child and discourages feminine thoughts. Green and his associates argue that it is important to work not only with the child but with the family as well, which is often advisable in childhood problems. Moreover, the earlier and more intensive the treatment, the better. Part of the procedure is to train the parents as behavior modifiers. These techniques are common among school psychologists who intervene in a wide range of behavior disorders. By using parents as therapists, treatment may be carried out during most of the child's day rather than being restricted to a 1 or 2 hour session per week with his psychiatrist or psychologist.

Green and his colleagues found that a considerable amount of retraining of the boys was necessary, but the results are encouraging. Four of five boys stopped crossdressing and manifesting other signs of femininity. The fifth body continued to show signs of crossdressing and feminine gesturing but did so less often than before treatment.

The authors conclude that, first, the therapist should be male because he provides a male model to identify with and may fill the gaps left by the absent or psychologically inaccessible father. Second, the implicit or explicit approval of parents for feminine behavior must be stopped. Parents often dismiss the behavior as "cute" or "nothing to be concerned about". It may develop into a major problem if unchecked. Punishment of feminine behavior must be paired with a substitute reward for masculine behavior. Often the role of father is undermined by mother and seen by the child as second best. The passivity of father must be changed. Some boys not only play with female toys and express a wish to be a girl but manifest feminine gestures. This is brought under voluntary control in Green's method by sensitizing the child to it. Both therapist and parents point out to the boy when he is doing it. He may be given actual instructions in modifying these behaviors.

Rekers and his associates [131] − [141] have presented a series of case studies of effeminate behavior in boys treated by operant conditioning. In their method, the child is differentially reinforced for playing with boys versus girls toys. A typical example[137] is one in which an aunt and uncle observed their 7-year-old effeminate nephew at play. They were cued to smile and compliment him for playing with male toys. When he played with female toys, he was ignored or the relatives picked up a magazine to read. The authors consider the latter to be extinguishing the behavior rather than suppressing or punishing it. In practice, this may be difficult to separate although extinction would appear from animal studies to be more effective than punishment[87]. In any case their method was effective in altering the frequency of play behavior to the masculine direction. In addition, a self monitoring procedure was employed. The child was given a wrist counter and told by a "bug-in-the-ear" to press the wrist counter when he played with the masculine toys. Later the prompt was faded out and the child was told to be self reinforcing. He was followed up after a year and evidenced no feminine behaviors. One may fear that only toy selection is influenced by treatment but the authors report that the patient was "quite relaxed and more responsive and socially relevant" than prior to treatment. He was "nonfeminine", participated in sports and was happy to be identified as a boy. His bedroom was typically male and he himself showed no conspicuous evidence of feminine gestures or mannerisms. Even the context of his speech was not marked by the previous feminine expressions.

The influence of treatment on the patient's everyday behavior was remarkable. The method was simple compared to the complex procedure used by Green and his associates and to that used in some of Rekers' other work[136]. One may wonder how much the complexity is necessary in treatment. Effeminate behavior may be easier to change in some boys than in others. Rekers and his associates[136][146] recognize these differences and distinguish gender behavior disturbance and cross gender identification. The former is evidenced only by feminine behavior and the boy presumably is satisfied being male. The cross gender identified boy, however, evidences this behavior but also wants to be a woman or believes that he is in fact female. Although there is no research evidence on the question, Rekers and his associates think the behavioral disturbance might be easier to change. It may change spontaneously on its own for all we know. The two in fact may not be as easy to distinguish as the authors indicate[173]. A thorough assessment is essential to ascertain the degree of gender disturbance before implementing treatment.

When the Rekers team treated what they labeled a "transsexual prepubescent boy", their method approached the multifaceted techniques used by Green and his associates[68]. The child of the study[135] manifested feminine gestures and behavior. He preferred to play with girls' toys and was ostracised by his male peers. He was unhappy when initially seen in assessment. The operant procedures were used to change his feminine speech content and feminine speech inflections. This was ineffective when used only in the laboratory and the child's mother was called in to work on his behavior in the home. More than a feminine toy preference was modified. They attempted to change finger extension in female fashion, hand gestures, limp wrists, flutters of the forearm, palming, hands on hips, feminine gait; role playing feminine behaviors, feminine play with sister, as well as voice inflections, and feminine speech content. After one year, there was no evidence of feminine behavior or cross gender identification. He had more friends but still preferred uncompetitive, less physically demanding and more passive activities. He continues to have a close relationship with his sister. He is considered reasonably happy by his parents. The authors have presented other studies[134][138][139][141] supporting the efficacy of such a technique in treating effeminate behavior in boys. The potency of these methods may rest in their early intervention in the behavior. One has to wonder how old the patient can be and still submit to effective treatment. Barlow's case report involved a 17-year-old. Perhaps also, some transsexuals are more amenable to behavior treatment than others. There are no systematic data on this question.

Femininity has been associated with several sexual anomalies, transsexualism, transvestism and homosexuality. By extinguishing cross gender behavior, these sexual anomalies may be prevented from developing. This would certainly offer support for the theory that feminine gender behavior causes the anomalies. However, it is not conclusive evidence because many boys (1/3 of androphilic men judging from adult samples of men) will develop an androphilic orientation and yet not manifest any cross gender behavior. They are never examined in a clinic and if they were, the assumption would have to be made that they are normal judging from their play, mannerisms, and so forth. Nevertheless, it would be valuable to know that altering feminine behaviors in boys can prevent later sexual anomalies. The techniques seem powerful in the case studies reported in the professional literature and are logically congruent with learning theory principles.

An unfortunate problem with this clinical approach is the length of follow up required to answer the question. Since they are in essence longitudinal studies, it requires years to know what the outcome is. Followups have been short in general, typical of behavior modification approaches. Moreover, the studies were uncontrolled since there were no comparison or control groups of untreated effeminate boys. Nevertheless, the Green and Rekers studies appear to be the single most promising approach to the problem of transsexualism and promise to offer insights into some of the basic factors in the development of adult sexual behavior.

It is interesting to note that Green and his associates point out that we have much early evidence in children of cross gender identity but considerably less information on harbingers of later androphilia. Three followup studies of these boys at puberty suggests that the link to androphilia is positive but considerable uncertainty remains.

Zuger[174] provided a follow-up study of 16 "untreated" boys presenting feminine behavior. Sixty percent were homosexual. Only two of them were transsexual or transvestite. It is noteworthy that three of the homosexual boys later attempted suicide and one transsexual actually carried it out. The latter was a drug addict preparing for sex reassignment surgery when he suicided. This should alert the clinician to the problems associated with gender dysphoria. As we have already noted, although many transsexuals appear "normal", emotional instability is a major factor associated with this anomaly. Green and Money examined 11 untreated effeminate boys and Money and Russo[115] later continued the longitudinal study on them into adulthood. Much data was lost, but eight of nine children later established a homosexual role. To date, none is known to be transvestitic or transsexual.

Green[65] reported on variable numbers of boys followed into "early to mid-adolescence". Actual ages were not reported. Of 11 who masturbated, none had exclusive homosexual fantasies, four had both homosexual and heterosexual fantasies, four were exclusively heterosexual whereas three had no fantasies. No descriptions of fantasy categories or reliability ratings are provided. Twelve boys had viewed male nudes, 18, female nudes. We do not know how the two groups overlap but of the 12, three were usually aroused by males, five sometimes and four were not. Of the 18, six were usually aroused by females, nine sometimes, one rarely and two never. We do not know the context in which arousal occurred. Nine boys had experienced intercourse or heavy petting, one with males only, five with both sexes and three with females. Green considers some of the boys homosexual and some bisexual, supporting the connection of effeminacy in childhood and later sexual orientation disturbance.

Zuger[174] has provided the clearest report to date on effeminate boys but there are many problems with all the studies. Most important, we are unsure about erotic preferences. Adolescent males undergo many changes and homosexual acting out is not uncommon in the inexperienced youth. Nevertheless he may prefer females and a later exclusive heterosexual pattern will emerge. The use of the concept of bisexuality is problematic and, as discussed in Chapter 5, there appears to be no bisexual erotic preference. Men prefer either women's or men's body characteristics so the large group of "bisexuals" in Green's[65] report leaves much ambiguity about what is happening. Effeminacy in childhood appears to be a good criterion of later sexual disturbance but it will miss about a third of androphilic men since this proportion report no effeminacy in childhood (Chapter 4). Moreover, of the effeminate boys followed up, about a third, perhaps more, seem to be normal heterosexuals. So while effeminacy seems to be a useful criterion to select boys with sexual orientation disturbance, there is still strong support for the thesis that erotic preference is independent of gender identity.

Sex Reassignment Surgery

The major treatment of adult transsexualism presented in the psychological literature over the past 20 years has been management by surgical intervention. Although some writers oppose sex reassignment surgery, it is still widely available[49] [102]. It is therefore important to examine the existing literature for the problems that have emerged in this area.

Comprehensive programs have been worked out to prepare a transsexual for sex reassignment surgery[67] [100]. In one such program developed by Steiner and her colleagues in our hospital[153], the patient undergoes an elaborate screening. If he is either a gynephile or has a severe psychiatric disorder, he is dropped from the program. It is believed such persons would adapt poorly to the female role and/or are confused.

After extensive psychological and psychiatric examination as well as a physical examination, the patient is told to try living as a female. Continuous contact with the clinic is undertaken for at least a year, and 2 1/2 years pass on the average before the actual operation takes place. In the first year, the patient undergoes supportive psychotherapy and is told to live as much as a woman as possible to see how they adapt to the role. It is interesting to note that no attempt is made to suggest he adapt to a "homosexual" orientation. Many patients claim they have already tried it and do not like it.

If the patient survives the first year and still wants surgery, steps can be taken to change names legally to female ones if this had not already been undertaken by the patient prior to coming to the clinic. However, this process is simpler legally after surgery. Oestrogen hormones are administered resulting in decrease of body hair, permanent change in voice and breast growth. This is also believed to result in a reduction if not a loss of sex drive. Breast implants may be requested by the patients. Many candidates for sex reassignment are already taking hormones prior to application for the operation.

The next step in the procedure is to perform castration and penectomy. This is the final irreversible step in the sequence of becoming a woman. After castration the artificial vagina is contructed. Several operations may be necessary if there are complications. The latest techniques are relatively sophisticated since part of the penis is retained to become part of the new feminine sex organ. In some cases the bowel is cut and it is used to become the vagina[104]. There are problems of rejection of the new vagina and of infections, which demand close medical supervision. A perennial problem is the vagina coming out and Jayaram, Stuteville and Bush[85] recommend placement of a bakelite dilator for at least a year after surgery to prevent this from happening. Patients and professionals alike discuss the ability of the postsurgical transsexual to have orgasm. Since there are no nerve endings in the artificial vagina and since the patient is on oestrogens that supposedly reduce sex drive, one has to wonder how orgasm is possible. There are no systematic studies to show if in fact this is the case.

Surgery itself may present problems[77] but techniques are improving[171]. Any major operation involves a degree of risk but even if surgery is uncomplicated, the artificial vagina is difficult to achieve. The pelvic opening of the male may be too small to construct a satisfactory vagina. Randell[130] notes that heterosexual intercourse quite often will not be satisfactory because there may just not be enough space in the male pelvis for adequate penetration. Partial sex reassignment such as castration or hormone therapy alone may be unsatisfactory for the patient. When oestrogen hormone therapy is used to increase breast size, there may be a risk of malignancy. In two cases, carcinoma of the breast was attributed to the massive hormone imbalance caused by castration and administration of oestrogens (See [77] and [160]). Both patients also had breast enhancement by implants. In two other cases, oestrogen therapy in male transsexuals was linked to a pulmonary embolism[96] and to cerebrovascular occlusion[40]. Although some authors report the use of oestrogens in male transsexuals is satisfactory[12] [121], they recommend that it be used conservatively. Hoenig recommends that all patients undergoing surgical or hormonal treatment should be kept *indefinitely* under medical surveillance. Although lack of follow-up of such patients testifies that this recommendation is not heeded; the cost to the individual and/or the state would be great if surveillance were indefinite. Hormone therapy is risky and can be dangerous. Few writers have weighed these health factors against possible benefits that might be derived for the patient.

There is one other serious limitation of surgery. Although it has improved over the past ten years, the final product, even if it does not collapse, does not look convincingly like a vagina in this writer's opinion (See Jones [86] for pictures). However, technology is improving.

The entire sex reassignment process is complicated and long, pointing out the strength and endurance of the transsexual's wish to be a female. Even a simple procedure such as changing name may be complicated[64] [112] [118]. Usually, a lawyer is employed to have a legal name change. If the patient has not progressed sufficiently in assuming the female role, the judge may deny the request because there is insufficient reason. The courts are concerned that the change of name may be for the purpose of committing a crime, such as fraud. Since a number of transsexuals have criminal records, the courts may view the name change with suspicion. Even with the legal change, they may experience great difficulty in changing their birth certificate, which designates sex at birth. Some states/provinces do not permit it. The candidate for surgery must also then change his name and/or sex on driver's license, passport, social security/insurance, school records and degrees, professional licences and maybe, citizenship papers. Should the transsexual wish to marry, there may be great difficulty encountered since most laws consider marriage an act between a man and a woman. The validity of transsexual marriages has not been litigated widely. The marriage may be of doubtful validity[64]. If the patient is already married and has sex reassignment surgery, this may provide grounds for divorce. Finally, the transsexual may be accused of an attempt to commit an indictable offense while disguised. One solution to this dilemma is to have the transsexual carry a letter from his psychiatrist stating he is to live and function in the chosen female role.

Two issues have concerned clinicians in the surgical treatment of transsexualism. First, selection of particular candidates for surgery rather than accepting all requests for treatment has been a problem. Second, the exact criteria to use in assessing outcome of surgery have been debated. Stoller[156] was uneasy about these issues in 1973 and may well remain uneasy today because the number of outcome studies is limited[151]. Surgery has been indiscriminately granted to many.

Patient selection for surgery.   The transsexual announces his own diagnosis and physicians accept this simply because they request surgery. Some patients may be unhappy postoperatively but follow-up is so poor we do not know. According to Stoller, a desire for surgery is insufficient for the diagnosis of transsexualism. There should be evidence for lifelong femininity, inability to live as males, and the capacity to pass effortlessly and continuously in society as members of the opposite sex[67] [125]. Newman and Stoller[120] suggest prognosis for sex reassignment is best for individuals who meet their criteria but little systematic research study is available to support this theory.

Newman and Stoller[120] and others[108] [127] [130] [152] have noted that "non-transsexual men" apply for sex reassignment namely, "transvestites, homosexuals and schizophrenics". Stoller considers the transvestite to be too attached to the male social role and uses his penis too often for sex reassignment surgery to be effective. They think the "fetishistic crossdressers (transvestites) with transsexual yearnings" are frequently misdiagnosed as transsexuals. Newman and Stoller suggest that administration of female oestrogen hormones in small dosages may quieten temporarily these patients with intense gender distress. In contrast to these groups, the true transsexual hates to use his penis for erotic gratification and is uncomfortable in the male role. As we have seen in the first section of this chapter, this assertion has not been empirically supported. The transsexual does use his penis rather frequently and the distinction between transvestite and transsexual is not so clear cut.

Newman and Stoller further argue that many androphiles fantasize sex change, especially "queens" who enjoy dressing "in drag" (as females) for an evening. Few seek surgery because their sense of identity as androphiles is greater than their sense of femaleness. If they do desire surgery, crisis oriented psychotherapy with a sympathetic therapist is recommended to change their desire. Such therapy stresses the value a patient places on his penis, his maleness and his identity as an androphile. It is noteworthy that some authors consider this patient to be *the* transsexual[55] [57]—the extremely feminine identified androphile. The boundary between the two is therefore not as clear cut as it seems initially. Perhaps for both gynephiles and androphiles, if there is great emphasis on the use of the penis in sexual interactions, surgery is counterindicated, regardless of sexual orientation. In practice, however, gynephiles often have been denied surgery.

Finally, a desire for sex reassignment may develop as a result of a psychotic episode. Newman and Stoller describe the case of a married father in his forties. Prior to admission, he became increasingly withdrawn and experienced fear without cause. At one point he believed he was Christ's new representative on earth and Christ was a "cryptowoman". His wife was puzzled by his gentle behavior that had an effeminate tinge to it. He started then to put on her clothes. He did this because he believed he was the reincarnation of Mary Magdalen. This was presumably not for erotic pleasure, in spite of his choice of a prostitute identity. He was uncertain but he heard he was to become a woman. This patient was diagnosed as schizophrenic and treated as such. Most transsexuals are not considered psychotic in spite of their belief that they are women. As Lukianowicz[102] pointed out in 1959, they *feel like* women but *know* full well they are anatomical men. The schizophrenic just described would not know that. He would *fully believe* he was Mary Magdalen and thus would not be in contact with reality. Unfortunately, the feeling of being a woman may be a persistent conviction in psychotic patients that make the distinction of psychosis from transsexualism difficult.

Person and Ovesey[126] disagree with Stoller's assertion about the transsexual's conviction of femininity. They feel that the transsexual is not convinced about his feminine gender identity, rather, he is confused. They feel it is more accurate to state that he has an ambiguous gender identity that may blur the boundary between psychosis and transsexualism.

Criteria of success and the outcome of sex reassignment.   When one examines research reports, the description of the transsexual population is generally poor and no outcome criteria are described other than to say the patients were "satisfied" or "adjusted". A report has yet to appear in the professional literature that uses a reliable and validated index of such "adjustment". There are almost no controlled studies and therefore the following results should be considered with caution.

Implicit in Stoller's selection of patients for surgery is satisfactory outcome criterion. If applicants for surgery are gynephilic, do not have strong and persistent feminine gender identity, use the penis orgasmically or are mentally ill, the outcome of surgical sex reassignment will be poor.

Various other criteria of success have been used in evaluating the outcome of surgical sex reassignment for transsexualism. Most reports note the "satisfaction" of the patient in contrast to all other psychological therapies in which the therapist notes his own satisfaction with the treatment outcome, that is, some improvement in psychological symptoms and/ or social adjustment. The transsexual would be satisfied because he has been given exactly what he wanted but is he now psychologically adjusted?

Money[112] offers five criteria for examining sex reassignment: patient's expressed satisfaction, employment, police record, psychiatric record and marriage. He reported on 17 male cases as well as 13 female cases. All the males are certain they did the right thing for themselves.

Money thinks psychiatric problems are basically independent of transsexualism. If they need treatment before surgery they still need it after. However in a sample, which is not clearly demarcated in his report, he notes that in a total of 24 cases including females, none needed psychiatric treatment for the first time postsurgically. Two needed treatment before and after surgery but 10 who needed it before did not need it after surgery. Twelve did not need or receive treatment at any time. One case postoperatively needed urgent help for attempting suicide and subsequently succeeded in accomplishing it. Money notes it was not a new suicide attempt; it was a continuation of other attempts. However, we cannot know if the surgery exacerbated the symptoms to generate the suicide. Money believes the psychiatric needs of the transsexual, including finalizing femininity with surgery does not solve the life problems that may be attendant on gender identity confusion. It does not abolish suicidal depression, psychopathic delinquency or schizophrenic thought disorder.

In eight of the 17 cases, job status remained unchanged and still varied widely in prestige. No one was unemployed. Some patients improved their employment status even graduating from university and preparing for a professional career. Two were housewives and one was legally married. Two were prostitutes, one full time. The latter according to Money raised a few medical eyebrows but he thinks it is not an issue for medicine to decide whether society should have prostitutes. In any case, "she was able to be a more effective prostitute" following surgery.

Six of the 17 males had police records prior to reassignment for impersonating a female, soliciting, and robbery. Two were charged after reassignment on at least two occasions for soliciting. Money states that the salient point is that *no patient* acquired a police record *for the first time* following reassignment. He thinks overall the amount of crime decreased.

Nine of the 17 males married, and Money concluded that there is a tendency for sex reassignment to favor stability of sexual partnerships. These results suggest that the major outcome from sex reassignment is the satisfaction of the patient but the other goals that might be of greater concern to society were less likely to be affected, that is, psychiatric record, unemployment, and crime. Although there was some decline in crime in his patient group, a more careful study following police records is necessary for more definite conclusions. There is a stabilizing trend to marriages but there may be many legal obstacles preventing this from occurring.

Meyer and Reter[110] have performed one of the best studies to date on surgery outcome. They compared 15 patients who had undergone surgery and 35 awaiting it. They basically examined the criteria Money discussed but found no objective advantage over waiting list patients in social rehabilitation even though it was subjectively satisfying for the patient to have the surgery. However over 50% of the sample was lost to follow-up, and the measures they used in their assessment have questionable validity (See Fleming, Steinman and Bocknek, [49]). In a clinical report on 16 patients from a total of 125 sex reassignment applicants, Lothstein[100] found evidence of depression. He recommended that a better counselling program be established before operations. No systematic data are provided.

In a follow-up study Hunt and Hampson[82] examined 17 male-to-female transsexuals before surgery and an average 8.2 years after. They report on MMPI and their own unvalidated but reliable measure of economic, sexual and interpersonal adjustment, psychopathology and family reactions. There were no differences on MMPI scores but this test is relatively insensitive to changes due to treatment. Personality style was not changed and the only noteworthy change on the other measures was an improved sexual adjustment. Almost a quarter of the group continued to express a strong need for further surgical procedures although they described previous surgery as extremely beneficial. There were no psychotic breakdowns but two patients attempted suicide at one and at six years after their operations respectively. The study shows that surgery can be satisfying for selected patients but the unvalidated scale they used needs elaboration and further development to pinpoint problems of the transsexual patient.

Randell[130] has also discussed the psychiatric status of the transsexual as an outcome criterion. He noted that legally it may be unacceptable to operate on a transsexual only to make living as a female more comfortable. There must be some medical indication to the effect that the operation is necessary to *preserve* the mental health and *prevent* serious deterioration in the patient. He believes the surgery does contribute to mental stability. In 37 of 52 patients (44 males and 8 females) whom he followed after surgery, the majority were "improved" on clinical evaluation. Twenty-nine showed excellent or good "adjustment" compared to four who did prior to surgery. However, twelve were poorly adjusted, four were worse and two suicided. Unfortunately, neither Money nor Randell present sufficient definitions of their terms nor do they offer systematic data evaluating their measures for reliability and/or validity.

Hoenig and his colleagues[77] reported on 6 male cases treated by surgical reassignment. They looked at social and work adjustment, criminal record, the patients' and the therapists' evaluations. Prior to surgery, four of the six had poor work records due to the transsexualism and all had poor *social* adjustment. Only one was a prostitute but four of the six had criminal records. Five had personality problems. Five patients had penis, scrotum and testes removed. One patient had brain surgery, a leucotomy and it did not change the transsexualism. Three had operations to create an artificial vagina but *with poor results,* which may be a major factor in the outcome of the study. At follow-up varying from 2-to-10 years, one could not be contacted but only two were described as having a satisfactory work record. This included one housewife. Two were on welfare, one had been reconvicted. Four of five said they were satisfied with surgery but three were not positively evaluated by the clinicians. In this study the outcome of surgery was mixed. It is one of the few studies which examines a range of outcome criteria. Unfortunately, it is not a controlled study with established reliable measures. It is noteworthy that one of the patients was gynephilic prior to surgery and he was not among the treatment failures. This questions the selection criteria for surgery and raises doubts about the current definition of the transsexual as an androphilic person.

Walinder and his associates[165] compared five failures and nine successes in surgery and outlined a long list of contraindications for surgery. Among the contraindications were complicating psychosis, dementia or mental retardation, serious alcohol and drug abuse, and in contrast to Money's assertions, repeated criminal acts.

Walinder et al suggested that physical characteristics of the applicant should be compatible with the new feminine role and the individual should not possess an emotionally unstable personality. Excessive distance to the therapist's office and long interruptions of hormone therapy further indicated poor prognosis. Secondary factors were inadequate self support and excessive heterosexual experience. Patients who were older at first request for sex reassignment were among those dissatisfied with the outcome. Overall, only 5% of 100 cases of men and women in Sweden treated over a four year period were dissatisfied. This would suggest that surgery is a relatively powerful method in the management of transsexualism.

Steiner and her colleagues[151] reported on 27 male-to-female surgical reassignments and noted that all patients were satisfied at postsurgery and none wished to revert back to their biological gender after an average 2.9 years. Patients generally showed improved adjustment from pre to post surgery. Using the Walinder et al criteria, they found that prognostic of poor adjustment were inadequate self support characterized by poor work history, criminal record and personality problems such as impulsiveness, mood swings and unstable interpersonal relationships. Interestingly, inadequate family support was *not* predictive of poor adjustment. Unfortunately, this was a preliminary report presented at a convention at the time of writing and a more detailed analysis is yet to be reported.

Pauly[125] summarized reports on surgical outcome up to 1968 and included his own and Benjamin's cases. He found satisfactory outcome occurred in 68% of cases, 7% were unsatisfactory and 25% were uncertain. His criteria were unspecified improvement in social and emotional adjustment. Although postoperative transsexuals were not free of emotional conflict, they were improved. Dissatisfaction was more likely if the individual's legal status could not be changed. It should be noted that all of the cases Pauly summarized were uncontrolled individual or group studies. This kind of study tends to inflate success rates as noted earlier perhaps simply because they would not be published if they were unsuccessful. Follow-ups were variable in length. The status of the literature is unchanged at the time of this writing with no controlled studies reporting on the treatment of this sexual anomaly.

Benjamin's[11] and Pauly's[125] outcomes differ substantially. Benjamin followed 151 patients for 5-to-6 years after surgery. Patients rated themselves as "good" or "satisfactory" in outcome in 86% of cases. A third were satisfied in all respects, whereas half were satisfied but lacking in one area of their lives. Pauly reported on 100 patients of whom 48 had undergone surgery. Forty-two percent were considered satisfactory with only one case in eight unsatisfactory. However, half the sample was lost to follow-up. This is a common problem but the contrast in Benjamin's results and Pauly's is noteworthy. If a systematic and reliable rating was carried out, so we had a clear idea of what 'satisfactory' means, the difference might be explained.

Hore and his associates[80] have reported 6-to-18 month follow-up on 16 male transsexuals who underwent successful surgery. They note medical complications, but 2/3 considered themselves to have benefited from the operation since they feel more feminine and are more confident in their new role. A third of them was not satisfied, most over surgical complications. But two who had successful surgery still did not regard themselves as fully female. Thus, it seems that surgery did not improve the symptomatic complaints in these patients. The following surgical complications occurred: Urethral stricture in four patients (later satisfactorily corrected); rectovaginal fistulas occurred in four of the patients (most cases corrected 2-to-3 months later by additional surgery); urethral fistulas in two patients (this too appears correctable); infection in failure of a skin graft in one patient, (corrected); deep vein thrombosis in two patients, possible pulmonary embolus, (patient recovered); vaginal stenosis in one case also required additional surgery. Obviously surgery has its risks and it is noteworthy that surgery failed to satisfy two patients in this small sample and their psychological symptoms remained. This sample appears to satisfy the criterion suggested for sex reassignment. All were androphilic on the Kinsey scale although several had both androphilic and gynephilic experience. None claimed to be fetishistic for female clothes. Half of the patients had previous psychiatric contact, mainly for depression. A quarter were unemployed at the time of referral and 2/3 were considered socially stable, while 1/8 were prostitutes.

Bentler[13] has presented data on 42 transsexuals, which is contrary to all current theorizing and treatment selection procedures. It is not clear when the patients underwent surgery but they divided into "heterosexual", "homosexual" and asexual with approximately a third of the patients in each group. No statistical analyses are performed and a number of the questions are ambiguous as reported.

About half of the "homosexual" and asexual groups indicated "having sex with a male" as the basic reason for surgery but only 10% of the "heterosexuals" did. The latter group appear on the average most concerned about avoiding male expectations or requirements. However, these data are presented ambiguously. Twenty-seven percent of the "homosexuals" but none of the other groups found life as a woman was "not up to expectations".

It seems then that one of the cardinal criteria for approving sex reassignment surgery was not validated in this project. The gynephilic and perhaps the asexual groups would usually be denied surgery but they were least likely to show post surgery dissatisfaction! The three groups were apparently comparable in duration of presurgical administration of hormones (1-to-1 1/2 years) and proportion of individuals living as women presurgery (about 60 to 70%).

Almost all patients said they would undergo surgery again, but there were postoperative problems and pain in 20-to-40% of cases, most being in the "homosexual" group. However, the present writer tested Bentler's outcome data statistically and the differences in the three groups were nonsignificant. A number of patients requested additional cosmetic surgery beyond penectomy and castration. A quarter of the "heterosexuals", a third of asexuals and half of the "homosexuals" had nose alteration (rhinoplasty). Less frequent were face lifts, skin peel, larynx shaving, ear changes and breast implants. Thus another criterion "can pass convincingly as a female" was violated.

A paradoxical finding is that 64% of "homosexuals", 86% of asexuals and 50% of the "heterosexuals" claimed they experienced greater sensitivity in the genital area following surgery. Moreover, orgasm as a female was more pleasing than as a male in 50% "homosexuals", 67% of asexuals and 86% of the "heterosexuals" than as a male. Bentler notes that it is difficult to believe a physiological basis exists for these claims and suggests further investigation.

Money and his associates[114] reported that some post operative problems may emerge as a result of family or community rejection of the transsexual.

They indicate the need for deception, and defiance or defensiveness led to unhappiness so their patients felt they were scheming and manipulative. The authors suggest that a formal public declaration of change of sex would be advantageous in transsexual rehabilitation. However, in their own and other cases, family rejection may occur because of the knowledge of the transsexualism or of the operation in addition to outside community pressure.

What if the patient desires to marry? Can they conceal the fact of the operation from their husbands? This would seem difficult and inadvisable. However, the family may reject the patient in contrast to Money et al's group in which the community seemed to be at odds with the family who were accepting of the patient. In my hospital's gender clinic a transsexual who passed as an acceptable female and who was dating males regularly, enjoyed the new found femininity as well as a career. A follow-up highlighted the family problems:

Doctor: Is there anything you would like help with at present?

Patient: Well, everything is fine. I'm really happy at work and dating but I would like to know how to change my parents' attitude to me. They tell me I'm a freak and they refuse to see me. My father said he had raised a son and as far as he was concerned, I was still his son but if he was going to live this masquerade, as far as he was concerned, his son was dead and he did not want to see him again. What can I do? (Cries) I want to see them. Can't they accept me as a woman? As I really am inside?

The family remained unapproachable and loneliness is one real possible undocumented outcome that the transsexual may experience.

Summary of sex reassignment surgery effectiveness. In attempting to offer an overall evaluation of sex reassignment surgery, we have little systematic research on which to base it. Working in this area gives one the unpleasant feeling he/she is deluding himself into accepting surgery as *the* answer to transsexualism. More cautious workers in the field describe surgery as "management" rather than treatment. Lurking in the background is the suspicion that the problem of transsexualism remains after sex reassignment surgery which is a procedure with its own dangers. Stoller and Newman[158] have suggested in two case reports that the transsexual may be "bisexual" and that after all the operations and female hormones, a male part remains untouched within them. A whole issue of the *Archives of Sexual Behavior* in July 1978 was devoted to the fourth international conference on gender identity and a cursory skimming of the issue reveals that little has changed in the area (See for example Lothstein [101]). There are no systematic studies although there is a plea for controlled measures to be used[103]. The most interesting article is one by Virginia Prince who has adapted to the female role as a tranvestite–transsexual. She speaks out against surgery as the solution to the transsexual's problem and states that it is possible to shift one's gender identity away from the genitals and into the head so surgery is superfluous. For the very effeminate "homosexual" she suggests psychiatrists encourage them to forget about surgery and set about becoming happy "homosexuals". She also recommended that professionals learn to distinguish between the concept of sexual urges and of gender that may reflect different motivations.

As often happens in the mental health sciences, ideas come round robin and repeat themselves. Lukianowicz[102] in 1959 pointed out that surgical treatment was unsound because it was irreversible, had no sound ethical rationale and was physically dangerous. Once the patient has his penis removed, it cannot be given back. Lukianowicz noted one case in which the patient who was castrated and legalized as a woman, came back as a man, very unhappy, wishing to be changed again into a man. He had "lost his illusions". The lack of ethical rationale is noted in that the patient may have a morbid psychic imagination, that is, he may be mentally ill. Childs[38] reported a case in which he believes sex reassignment surgery precipitated a psychotic reaction. Money and Wolff[116] also reported a male to female transsexual who subsequently reverted to the male role, apparently satisfied in the end.

Lukianowicz also noted that the argument for surgery can be reduced to absurdity: "If a patient had a wish to die, should the physician actively comply? Or if a patient wished his eyes removed because they commit sins, should he remove them?" Whereas such a point of view may have seemed clearer 20 or 30 years ago, it is not today. Some would argue that if a person wanted to die they should be given the opportunity. Nevertheless, the role of medicine has been traditionally to heal, and sex conversion surgery may seem like it is feeding the problem of the patient rather than solving it.

Finally Lukianowicz noted the danger inherent in sex change surgery. Any major surgery presents some risk; a greater risk than walking down a street. He described one case in which a patient suddenly died from a pulmonary embolus after a successful castration and penectomy. Fourteen years later, Stoller[156] pointed out that attitudes to sex change have become increasingly liberalized but we still know very litle about the number receiving it, the frequency of postoperative complications, the morbidity and mortality rate, the nature and frequency of psychiatric complications and how many individuals benefited. He suggests sex reassignment be restricted only to the most feminine men and that more scrupulous follow-up and careful considerations of requests for surgery be undertaken. However all the cardinal selection criteria for suitable candidates have been violated without apparent serious consequence.

The Harry Benjamin International Gender Dysphoria Association[17] has presented guidelines for standards of care for transsexuals and other gender dysphoria persons. They suggest improvement in standards of treatment and professional conduct but at the same time they widen the net of individuals who may undergo sex reassignment surgery. For example schizophrenics who have first been treated for their psychiatric disorder may presumably be candidates if they meet other criteria. Reflecting DSM III, either gynephilic or androphilic individuals may be labeled transsexual and undergo surgical sex reassignment even though theoretically they are not all suitable candidates and even though there is still no adequate research on the value of such surgery.

Few have spoken out against the trend to surgery in the management of transsexualism or to have doubted the assertion that transsexualism is not treatable by psychotherapy or behavior therapy. For whatever reason, this appears to have been accepted in spite of an absence of sound empirical studies or even systematic descriptive studies reported in the professional literature. Why is transsexualism seen as so incurable and transvestism and homosexuality seen as modifiable by seemingly superficial techniques used by behavior therapists? Perhaps the availability of surgical techniques congruent with the patients' wish is a clue why this has occurred. Transsexuals are very insistent that they are females trapped in male bodies and surgery is the only answer to their dilemma. They do not care to hear what the therapist has to say and any suggestion that they are "sick" may result in therapy termination. They will seek out someone else who will give them what they want.

The layman may consider it sheer determination. Why not then try surgery? It is what they want and they will not accept psychotherapy. This resistance to therapy occurs with other sexual anomalies in clinical settings. Especially when there is a criminal charge, sexual offenders often will be angry and resist any treatment. In fact they want to retain their anomaly and resent any effort to alter it. Should the social order be changed to accommodate them as well? Androphilia was once an offence and has been so accommodated in some countries. Reform groups are on the rise for pedophilia[18] and perhaps others will arise. Some prominent cities have sadomasochism clubs[148] that might well develop into the same sort of movement. Therefore, why not legalize sadomasochistic acts between consenting adults in private? Such questions horrify the traditionalist and the liberal adds "why not?"

Treatment of Choice

Only two methods to treat transsexualism have been reported (Table 6.3). The existing literature suggests that the best treatment is early identification

TABLE 6.3
Summary of Treatment Effectiveness for Transsexualism

Method	Results
1. Behavior Therapy-Operant Methods	Positive in children, untested in adults. No controlled studies.
2. Sex Reassignment Surgery	Uncertain for patients although most are "satisfied". No apparent effect on psychiatric problems or antisocial behavior. No controlled studies.

of the condition and preventive therapy. The operant methods described for children appear to be effective in spite of follow-up problems, and seems the best approach to use at present. Extremely and persistently effeminate boys are likely to develop gender disturbances in later life. A reversal of the behavior including family involvement appears to prevent the condition from emerging. Once the transsexual is an adult, surgery has been the major approach used and its outcome is uncertain at present. If social goals are of concern, that is, reduction in psychiatric and criminal problems; surgery does not appear to help. It does not seem to improve the psychiatric condition of the patient and one has to determine if this is acceptable and ethical. In spite of the attention transsexualism has received in the last 20 years, it is still not well understood and conceptual confusion abounds. The assessment of surgical outcome is not satisfactory at present and operations may best be limited to systematic outcome studies.

Controlled studies using psychotherapy and behavior therapy may be started if willing subjects could be found. Although many patients do not want to change, it does not mean that there are none willing to try. We do not treat exhibitionism or pedophilia this way and there is no reason to treat transsexualism that way either. Perhaps we can be more skeptical of the convictions of the patient. Certainly much more work is needed to understand gender identity and behavior. Perhaps a conviction on our part that transsexualism can be treated would change the perceptions of the patients as well. Genital exhibitionists are also very resistive to treatment and yet a wide range of programs have been attempted. Some of the techniques of persuasion to involve a patient in therapy could be applied to the transsexual.

TRANSVESTISM

The Theories

Since many authors originally identified transvestism as a general concept covering what today is called transsexualism, the same theories have been applied to both anomalies. In this section, only new theories have been specifically applied to transvestism and seem to cover the current meaning of the term will be reviewed.

The transvestite as fetishist and narcissist.   The major hypothetical difference of transvestites from transsexuals is the use of the penis in sexual acts. The transvestite usually masturbates to climax while wearing the female attire. The main theoretical and conceptual reason postulated for this behavior is that they have a *fetish* for female attire. That is, the clothes have an erotic valence far above their usual value for males and the objects are capable of eliciting complete sexual satisfaction for transvestites. It is possible that conditioning and masturbation habits produced such an inordinate attraction to the garments. This is discussed in Chapter 7 under fetishism.

The term "Mirror Complex" has been used to describe transvestism. It is viewed as autoerotic and narcissistic since the individual derives total satisfaction from admiring himself before a mirror. In some individuals, the mirror complex may be fused with a fetishistic attraction to the texture and sometimes to the smell of the female garments.

Mr. D was a 23 year old graduate student who was about to be married but was concerned about his crossdressing. He found it more stimulating than sex with his fiancee and worried that it might interfere with his marriage. He said sex with her was satisfying but he really enjoyed the clothes. He had a collection of female underclothes. He would dress in them, look at himself in the mirror and masturbate to climax.

Doctor: Can you tell me what you are feeling and thinking when you are dressing up?

Mr. D: I get sexually excited as I take the clothes out of my drawer. I love the feel of the silk panties. Texture is very important to me in all of my dressing up. When I slip the panties on, I run my hands down them next to my skin. It feels so good. Then I take out the brassiere and feel it before I put it on. I enjoy watching myself in the mirror. It gets more and more exciting and I start to masturbate and then it is all over. I feel kind of silly.

Doctor: Do you feel anything else?

> *Mr. D:*   Sometimes I feel I would enjoy being treated as a woman by others but not all the time.

He also described dreams in which he was a woman or his sexuality was ambiguous; that is, he was unsure if he was male or female. However, he was disgusted by "homosexuals" and any reference to him being effeminate brought forth anger.

If the transvestite were simply a fetishist, the confusion between it and transsexualism may not exist. However, it seems that the transvestite also has a desire to appear as a female and may in the course of his sexual development desire surgical sex reassignment[108]. Let us ignore these facts for a moment and just examine the fetish. It is not as simple as it first appears. The transvestite not only masturbates in the presence of the female clothes, he *puts them on* to do so. Why?

Psychoanalytic theory suggests that the hidden penis is the main source of erotic gratification. The transvestite enjoys the pretence of being a woman and his pleasure in the deception is only exceeded in the moment he surprises his audience by showing the hidden penis. This whole act develops around castration anxiety[59]. The masquerade as a female with a penis assures him he still has it and this relieves his anxiety that he too may be castrated. Thus his maleness is an essential ingredient in his masquerade. He is not effeminate usually, he enjoys his penis and it is only in the sexual act of transvestism that he fuses male and female identity. It may be that this particular defense against anxiety distinguishes the sexually anomalous from the psychotic[88]. His ego is split so that he parcels out and isolates his sexual behavior from reality. In other respects than sex, he seems normal.

Another variation of the psychoanalytic theme is that the transvestite is allowed a period in early life to develop and establish masculine identity. Then there is that phase in the oedipal period when females are irritated by male gender identity. During this time, a female attacks him and crossdresses him. This helps to establish his pattern of behavior. Such behavior may become quite pervasive and the transvestite who appears in public may have had, in addition, disruptive relations with a father who was distant and passive. Thus the father is not likely to intervene on behalf of his son or to promote a model of masculine behavior. This development contrasts with the transsexual whose feminine gender identity emerges in the preoedipal period and is maintained later.

The transvestite's miniature society.   Buckner[25] has presented an interesting interpretation of transvestism. He argues that there is both sexual and social satisfaction from crossdressing. Transvestites are more than fetishists. Such men establish a miniature society within themselves. They internalize both the male and female roles and act them out, all for their self satisfaction.

They might be considered bisexual in gender identity since they are both male and female at the same time. This may also make him asexual to the outsider in that his total sexual needs are contained within himself. *Mr. J* is such an individual. He noted:

> *Mr. J:* I feel like there are two persons in me, a man and a woman. At work during the day, I am the man and at night when I come home, I will dress up for "us" so that I am the perfect woman and wife. I will unwind by putting on my best clothes for us. As the "she" in me unfolds in front of the mirror, I can feel the tension drain from me. After a nice meal, I will come (masturbate) in front of the mirror.

This arrangement provides the perfect marriage; no arguments, no threats to masculinity, no fear that one partner will not be sexually satisfied. Why should he turn outside himself to a real female? Buckner thinks that these are important considerations in the development of transvestism. He thinks such men are passive and lack social drive early in life and are low in libido. Between 5 and 14 years of age, female clothes are associated with erotic gratification. It becomes a familiar pattern to fall back on when interpersonal difficulties occur. These difficulties occur at the time of puberty and they may be real or imagined. The transvestite may fear that marriage is unobtainable because he is a perfectionist and has an exaggerated notion of the requirements of the male role. This involves an extreme fear of failure and he may in fact fail at almost any task he undertakes, which then becomes a self fulfilling prophesy.

He has blocked "heterosexual" outlets because of his attitudes and he does not turn to "homosexuality" perhaps because of a socially conditioned aversion to it. So he turns inward to his established fantasies and elaborates them so they become very complex. His sex life is separate from his everyday male self, which is largely a symbolic manipulation of male role behaviors. Since his own sexual behavior is so highly predictable, he cannot fail. Nevertheless he may marry, not for erotic reasons, but because his ideal of a successfully functioning "heterosexual" male is one who is married. He may feel that when he is married and has a regular sexual outlet, his need to crossdress will diminish. However, his fantasy world is often more important and vital than his real marriage.

This is a rather complex anomaly that is more than a fetish, cross gender identity or a fusion of the two; it involves the whole personality and its interpersonal problems. It has been postulated that the transvestite has an obsessive compulsive personality whereas the transsexual is "homosexual". At times, the personality disorder may develop into a psychosis and delusions may be present.

According to Lukianowicz[102] *transvestites* may want so much to be women that they will believe they are menstruating and tell their doctors they are having regular periods. Some desire to bear children. However, the desire to be a woman is not necessarily a delusion. The individuals involved are quite aware that they are anatomical males, they simply "feel like a woman", as Lukianowicz[102] has noted, and they are not delusional at all. However, the case in which an anatomical male claims and believes he is menstruating would be a delusion. The same argument of course applies to transsexuals.

A multifaceted theory of transvestism.   A rather complex theory has been proposed by Gutheil[69] who claimed that six factors are important in the development of transvestism: latent or manifest "homosexuality", sadomasochism, narcissism, scoptophilia (voyeurism), exhibitionism and fetishism. "It is fetishistic because female clothes are overvalued; it is homosexual because he desires to be a woman; it is exhibitionistic because he desires to show himself as a woman and it is masochistic because of a persistent desire for castration". Unfortunately, we cannot be certain he means the same things we do when using the terms in this book. However, he argues that the various components are represented in each individual in varying degrees. Perhaps only some combinations are present and other elements almost completely absent. This theory mixes a number of concepts but illustrates the difficulty we have in conceptualizing a person who is a gynephilic male, but who wants to be a woman or act like a woman. Latent "homosexuality" emerges again as an empirically untestable postulate (See Chapter 5) and is associated with unresolved castration anxiety. It seems, moreover, that femininity or feminine gender identity is confused with an object preference for men. It is interesting how strong our cultural and experiential associations are. "Androphiles must be effeminate or have feminine gender identity" is implicit in many theoretical assumptions. Since the transvestite dresses and acts like a woman, he must therefore be androphilic, even if only latently so. However, as noted throughout this chapter, gender identity and sex object preference may be independent concepts. History and culture are so varied in the depiction of the male and female roles that Mother Nature may have found it unwise to tie reproductive function inextricably to transient gender roles.

Experiments on Transvestism

The most popular theoretical concept of transvestism is that he is a gynephilic fetishist. Although it is not spelled out clearly, it is assumed that the clothes have an erotic valence above that which is usual for men. He is masculine gender identified but may enact both male and female roles in his "miniature society" when he crossdresses in solitude for his own gratification. He may have strong feelings of inadequacy and difficulties in making a heterosexual adaptation.

Unfortunately controlled studies of transvestites' sexual history and penile reactions are nonexistent. The best available is a large but uncontrolled study by Prince and Bentler on 504 cases of transvestism[128]. The participants in the study were subscribers to a transvestitic magazine so the sample may be biased. On the other hand, the sample size is noteworthy. As the authors indicate, it is larger than the total cases in all the world's medical and psychological literature combined. This testifies to the lack of systematic studies but also to the difficulty of obtaining transvestites for research and clinical investigation. Three quarters of their sample had no previous psychiatric consultation and about an equal number were college educated.

Fetishism and object choice.   About nine in ten of the Prince and Bentler sample claimed they were "heterosexual" and about three in five were married. A quarter had "homosexual" experience but most preferred women sexually. One in seven were currently interested in having a sex change operation. Seven in ten thought they were men with a feminine side seeking expression and when they were dressed as a woman they felt like they were a different personality. Interestingly, only one in eight described themselves as fetishists rather than transvestitic or transsexual. One would expect fetishism to be more prominent since it is so often clinically implicated in this anomaly. The incidence of fetishism, as obtained by self report, is similar to that in transsexuals as noted earlier[7][13][58]. This suggests first that fetishism may not be prominent in the two anomalies and second, that it makes a poor distinction between transsexualism and transvestism.

In a later study, Bentler[13] found that men who applied for sex reassignment surgery indicated they were fetishistic or at least that they were sexually aroused while cross dressed in 23% of "homosexual" cases and 50% of the "heterosexual" cases but only in 18% of the asexual cases. It is not clear if the garments themselves were sexually arousing but the incidence of sexual arousal while dressed in the clothes was greater in heterosexuals than in homosexuals. Possibly, the sexual arousal means different things to the two groups. It may be a fetish for one and not for the other. This remains to be established. The androphilic crossdresser has at least a more socially congruous picture of himself than the gynephile.

It is commonly accepted that sex object preference must be part of gender identity, that is, wanting sex with a man is part of the female gender role. The androphilic transsexual prefers men and wants to be a woman so it fits for him. Perhaps his stereotypic conformity to feminine norms reflects a greater desire to conform to the behavior pattern. The gynephilic transsexual on the other hand is aware that he responds erotically to the female body and at the same time desires to be a woman. He may develop skills at playing both roles of men and women as Buckner suggested. He does not require surgery as often as the androphilic transsexual since he has all he needs in himself. It may be the imbalance of sex object needs and gender identity needs that produce the various combinations of surgery applicants seen clincially. This question is discussed again later.

Steiner and her colleagues cast doubt on the clear cut absence of gynephilic transsexualism and on its distinction from transvestism[152]. They examined a group of 21 transvestites defined as men who crossdressed and experienced orgasm in so doing. These men were clearly gynephilic according to their sex history questionnaires (Appendix One). The authors noted that the problem of diagnosis in these men becomes somewhat confusing. Because they all request sex change surgery, that is, they are willing to give up the 'insignia of masculinity', namely, their male genitalia, they would be excluded from any traditional definition of transvestism. On the other hand, their marital status, the existence of erotic pleasure with their penises (heterosexual coitus, masturbation, etc.) as well as other factors would rule out a diagnosis of transsexualism. It seems the alignment of transvestite with gynephilic object choice and transsexual with androphilic object choice is premature and needs rethinking.

The Prince and Bentler findings support the clinical contention that most transvestites are gynephilic[128], but contradict older findings, which suggest that about a third are androphiles, a third gynephiles and a third bisexual. Of course the distinction between transsexualism and transvestism was not made earlier. An additional difference was that Hirschfeld and Hamburger[70 71 72] who reported the earlier results both offered these figures and in addition indicated that about a sixth were bisexuals, a sixth automonosexuals or self satisfied by orgasm, and a few cases were asexual. Unfortunately these interesting findings are not supported by current workers but then there are no systematic studies on the subject and perhaps judgment should be reserved about what is going on.

A further suggestion that transvestites are gynephilic is the frequency with which they both marry and have children. Marriage is no guarantee that patients are gynephilic since many reasons are evident for marriage other than sexual outlet. Nevertheless, 64% of the Bentler and Prince sample were married and of them, 74% were fathers.

The theory that transvestites play both roles socially for themselves has not been tested to date. Buckner[25] derived this theory from the Prince & Bentler data, which indicated that 78% of the sample reported that they felt like a different personality when crossdressed. The nature of this feeling remains to be empirically studied.

Personality pathology.   The transsexuals as a group evidence much clinical pathology and it is an important consideration in their treatment. Little comparative data is available on transvestites but it seems that they are better adapted than the transsexuals[13 14 15 23 128].

The Bentler and Prince studies[14] [15] [16] suggest that their subjects had adjusted to their sexual anomaly and did not require psychiatric intervention. They did use psychometric instruments with the group and with normal controls. They found nonsignificant results on the Differential Personality Inventory, the Holtzman Inkblot Test, and Jackson's Personality Research Form. However, the transvestites did present themselves as more controlled in impulse expression, more inhibited in interpersonal relationships, less involved with others and more independent.

These studies were conducted on a subsample of the larger study reported earlier. In the total sample, participants were asked if they had ever sought psychiatric help. Seventy six percent had not, and of those who had, half indicated that it was of no help to their transvestism.

It may be difficult to ascertain the incidence of pathology in transvestites because they are reluctant to come to clinics but also because they are rarely accepted for surgery. It seems, however, that there is an increasing trend to accept them. Newman and Stoller have warned about ruling out pathological cases who may seek sex reassignment and only "true" transsexuals should be accepted. A history of living as a convincing female is an important criterion for acceptance. This would also bias the answer to the question of the incidence of psychiatric problems in transvestites-transsexuals. By definition, they become something else and yet the desire to be female may be quite strong and persistent.

Meyer[108] examined clinical variants among applicants for sex reassignment and noted the range of problems that can occur. There were 87 applicants over a period of three years. Among these were a group of transvestites who came to the clinic in middle age, depressed and suicidal; some anxious to the point of depersonalization and some with homicidal impulses. The happy intraindividual society of man and woman had become unsatisfactory and the patients wanted resolution by becoming a woman totally. A younger transvestite group appeared to be more intact but details are lacking to be sure. Another group consisted of masochists who enjoyed humiliation, beatings and bondage, and experienced sexual arousal to pain and suffering. Other groups were stigmatized homosexuals, polymorphous perverse applicants, schizoid persons, and eonists as well as miscellaneous cases. The eonists may be considered the 'true transsexuals' as defined here.

Steiner and her colleagues[152] examined a group of 21 male transvestites. Overall, a diagnosis of depression emerged for the group and although standardized tests were used in the assessment, no control group was employed.

Other older reports suggesting pathology in transvestism are unsatisfactory because they confuse transvestism and transsexualism and often may lump together the two groups making it difficult to clarify the issues raised here. One of the early studies, a review article by Lukianowicz[102], however, has to be one of the clearest existing papers written in this author's opinion.

Similar problems arise here as with homosexuality. There may be healthy and sick individuals who have a sexual anomaly. We do not see the healthy ones. If Prince and Bentler's study had not been conducted, only clinical reports would be available and we would not know. However, it seems that psychopathology need not accompany transvestism in general although one may expect it at a psychiatric clinic where people come, after all, because they have psychological problems.

Some famous cases in history appear to have led productive lives. Among them, George Sand, a female who had a prolonged affair with Chopin, lived on and off as a male and as a female[28]. In the middle ages, transvestite saints were favored. Especially females would be encouraged to crossdress and take on male roles. St. Joan of Arc is noteworthy[35]. The males, however, lost status if they crossdressed as women. In modern times, Gandhi may have had transvestitic or transsexual yearnings coupled with guilt over normal sexual intercourse. It is known that he preferred to be called "she" in his later years. Whether this was a cognitive religious decision or reflected his more basic sexual needs is not known[124]. Ernest Hemingway who suffered several depressions[172] was also fascinated with female roles[2]. While he in part created the image of the twentieth century male as cool, aggressive and impassive, he apparently crossdressed with his wife and/or styled his clothes and hers so they were almost identical. In his diaries which came out after his death, he appears preoccupied with transvestism.

The institution of berdache which occurred among Plains Indians of North America[52] may have served a personal and social function that appears to be mainly nonorgasmic. In berdache, the individual might assume the dress, role and status of the opposite sex, usually a male assuming the female role. They could be highly valued. It is not clear that orgasmic needs are an essential part of this role. The extreme and aggressive demands of the male role in Plains Indian cultures may have encouraged the berdache which includes transvestism. It provides the male with social status in spite of the sex role change. Forgey[52] notes that the berdache was not necessarily androphilic although some were sought out by tribesmen for sex relations. Although these case studies are fascinating, they offer little insight into the nature of the transvestism. We cannot trust anecdotal and historical reports, but it is noteworthy still that some of the individuals reported appeared to have little or no pathology.

Parent child relations.   There are no controlled studies of family patterns in transvestism but Spendsley and Barter[149] examined the clinical files of 18 adolescents who dressed in women's clothes. The label transvestism was used to describe the boys but categorization was inconsistent. All were certain of their masculine identity but at one point two were labeled polymorphous perverse, one transsexual, one homosexual and two un-classified. Only five masturbated while crossdressed so that the group looks like a mixture of transvestites, transsexuals and miscellany. Masturbation for the boys was secondary to appearing female in 92% of the cases. In 100% of the cases the mother preferred the sister or other female relatives over her son. She showed no hostility to the female but was aggressive to males. She had an intense interdependent interaction with her son whom she subtly encouraged to crossdress. Only one of the 18 mothers showed any hostility to crossdressing whereas 14 fathers expressed no reaction, three ridiculed it and one was puzzled. The fathers were always present in the family in a passive or distant way and were fearful of family relationships. The results suggest that envy of the female is a dynamically important factor in creating gender disturbances but the outcome should be treated cautiously because clinical files were used that were not validated or checked for reliability. The inconsistency in diagnosis and 100% figure are also suggestive that the study be replicated with better controls before treating it seriously.

Biological factors. In examining organic and genetic factors in transvestism, we are left with a small number of case reports on which to base a judgment. The poverty of methodology generally in this area is to be noted again and all results should be treated with extreme caution.

One case report indicated that there may be a constitutional factor in transvestism since it appeared independently in father and son[27]. This may be a chance occurrence and a controlled study needs to be undertaken.

It has been suggested that transvestism may be related to temporal lobe brain disorders. Some cases have been observed in which crossdressing started with the onset of temporal lobe dysfunction[1 21 45]. Perhaps more properly, limbic or hypothalamic dysfunction which appears to be involved in sexual behavior may be implicated. We are unable with present technology to examine limbic sites satisfactorily but their dysfunction often is reflected in frontal and temporal lobe disorders. In the series of case presentations offered in the literature, we are at a loss to know how much other confused behavior is present and to know the incidence of cases in which temporal lobe dysfunction is not associated with sexual anomalies.

Blumer noted that in a series of 60 cases treated in his clinic, only three had sexual anomalies. Two were homosexual and one was considered "transvestism related". The latter patient was sexually aroused by wearing his baby sister's diaper which is not a typical transvestitic behavior. Blumer also examined the electroencephalograms (EEG) of 15 *transsexuals* and found they were within normal limits. So temporal lobe dysfunction may be related in a few cases to sexual anomalies but because the individual is transvestitic or transsexual, it does not automatically mean he will show brain pathology in the temporal lobe. In fact, the connection is a tenuous one and the degree of overall confusion especially for epileptic patients should be noted rather than bizarre dressing behavior alone which may be erroniously labeled transvestism. A good study in the area has yet to be done.

Walinder[164] reported EEG results of 26 patients he labeled transvestites. Thirty-eight percent of their EEGs were abnormal and of these 60% involved disorders of one or both temporal lobes of the brain. This suggests an important connection between transvestism and brain damage in pertinent areas of the cortex. However their study was not controlled and the diagnostic classification was confounded to a point that fetishists, transvestites and transsexuals were mixed in the group so it is impossible to determine which is which. He described in detail a case which illustrates the striking connection between cerebral damage and transvestism. The case is atypical in that the crossdressing started after brain insult which was associated with an accident at the age of 23. It is not clear if this case is typical of those in Walinder's sample or is unusual. Although brain pathology may result in unusual sexual behavior, the opposite is not necessarily true: unusual sexual behavior may not reflect brain pathology. Walinder did point out an important confounding factor in temporal lobe disorders that has not been discussed by other authors in connection with sexual anomalies. He noted that there may be an accompanying disorder in gonadal functioning. Hypogonadism and involuntary sterility may be implicated. Endocrine disorders associated with temporal lobe damage in sexual anomalies has yet to be carefully examined in a controlled study.

Housden[81] reviewed earlier case studies of biological factors in transvestism. However most cases were likely transsexuals as popularly defined. Overall, 75 cases were observed by 22 authors, including 11 cases of Housden's own. Most were biologically normal males. Only one tenth had female physiques and less than 5% had body and facial hair characteristic of the female. All had normal male sex organs. Endocrine functions were within normal limits and chromosomes were normal. In general, the presence of organic and constitutional factors appears to be unlikely, based on the existing evidence. However, the confusion of androphilic–gynephilic, of transvestism and transsexualism remains. The poor technology and methodology may have also played a part in the outcome.

Conclusion—The Transvestite Stimulus
Response Matrix

Most theories of transvestism noted in Table 6.4 are untested so conclusions must be speculative. Transvestites tend to prefer the female body shape according to self reports but there are no phallometric experiments to support

TABLE 6.4
Summary of Evidence for Theories of Transvestism

Theory	Experimental Support
1. They have a fetish for female attire	Mixed, untested
2. Mirror complex narcissism	Untested
3. Interpersonal narcissism	Untested
4. Enjoys pretense and revealing hidden penis	Untested
5. Fusion of male and female identity	Untested
6. Forms minature society of man and woman in one person	Untested
7. Bisexual gender identity	Untested
8. Blocked gynephilic outlet	Untested
9. They are latent homosexuals, sadomasochists, voyeurs and exhitionists	Untested
10. Sex object choice	Female, no controlled study. Some prefer men
11. Biological factors	Some temporal lobe brain pathology. Not adequately tested. Physically normal.

this. It is not clear if they desire feminine behavior from sex partners or if they want to relate to women as women in a pseudo lesbian relationship. They may want to relate to themselves alone as both male and female in an orgasmic way. Fetishism is supposed to be important but there are no phallometric studies. The one self report study on a sizable sample tends to minimize the fetishistic element in transvestism and support the idea of a dual personality containing male and female elements that is self satisfying and orgasmic. Thus the transvestite may be characterized as asexual or automonosexual. It is not known to date if the transvestite is more aroused to the female body characteristics or to the clothes she wears or if he identifies with her in a narcissistic way. If he has truly a fetish for the clothes, intercourse with a woman may be attainable only because she is wearing the garments. She may be an unnecessary prop. Alternatively he may be aroused to both the body of the female like normal men as well as to the clothes. We do not know at present which is the case. The narcissistic *identification* may involve the male imagining himself as the female sex partner rather than actually responding to her female body. Just as the exhibitionist may imagine a woman in a pornographic magazine is exposing the way he likes to, so the transvestite may imagine he is the female lover being admired by himself. It is not known to what extent masochism and dominance submissiveness are elements in transvestism. Although he appears to enjoy intercourse, the subcumbus position (woman on top) is often demanded according to clinical reports. It is unknown how often exhibiting, peeping, rape, frottage, masochism, sadism or obscene phone calls are correlated with transvestism. Since the latter often come to our attention in clinical settings, it appears that they may be unrelated. Overall the research information is very limited and unsatisfactory.

TREATMENT OF TRANSVESTISM

Transvestism has generally been considered amenable to treatment and a variety of methods have been applied albeit to a limited number of cases. The earliest clinical reports used faradic aversive conditioning. The basic principles described in Chapter 3 involve pairing the sexually arousing transvestitic behavior with electric shock or nausea inducing agents.

Behavior Therapy

Chemical aversion therapy.   In chemical aversion therapy, the patient is first administered nausea inducing drugs. When he indicates that he feels sick, his favorite female clothes used for crossdressing are presented. He should touch them and look at them as best as he can. Then he is overwhelmed by the need to vomit. The clothes are withdrawn and the procedure repeated several hours later. In the four reports using chemical aversion[3][63][117][159] three were case studies and the fourth an uncontrolled group study together totaling treatment of 16 cases. About 60% gave up crossdressing. In Glynn and Harper's[63] study, charges had been laid that may have predisposed the patient to success. Follow-up was short, a matter of months. All of the problems inherent in short follow-up of course apply here.

Electrical aversion therapy.   Electrical aversion studies offer greater control over the timing of crossdressing and the aversive shock which follows shortly after. Barker[3] compared chemical aversion therapy of one patient to electrical version of a second. While he noted the above advantageous features of electric aversion therapy it appears the one who received it was a treatment failure whereas the one treated by chemical aversion was not.

Marks and Gelder[105][106], have established an electrical aversion procedure which has been copied by Rosen and Rehm[145]. They used penile measurement during treatment and have the longest follow up of any studies in this area; two years. In their procedure, shocks were delivered during the cross-dressing itself as well as in fantasies of doing it. Shocks were given at random 1-to-120 seconds after dressing started, and, on a quarter of the trials, none was given, thus using an effective partial reinforcement schedule. Garments were dealt with individually, that is, imagining the pleasure felt when putting on stockings then shoes, and so forth. Their earlier patients[105] were selected because they had "well integrated personalities" but this term is not described further.

Marks and Gelder started with five cases and added to their sample in later reports. In their last report[106], nine patients were described as simple transvestites and seven more as being transsexual-transvestites since they were not always sexually aroused by garments and had a desire to have a female body.

A total of 33 cases have been treated with faradic conditioning, including Marks and Gelder's patients. About 60% reported cessation of crossdressing[3 19 20 23 39 46 51 94 122].

Unlike all the other studies using this method, Marks and Gelder had access to an untreated control group. They were not convinced that it constituted a satisfactory control group since the patients were select. However, in the control group of 12, 17% were much improved and 25% improved indicating respectively a 50% and 25% reduction in crossdressing. The treatment may therefore be having some effect but spontaneous change is frequent enough that uncontrolled studies should be considered with extra caution.

Covert sensitization. Only one other study is a controlled experiment. Callahan and Leitenenberg[36] used a single case experimental design to compare covert sensitization and faradic conditioning. In the former, the crossdressing and the aversive stimuli following it would both be imagined. All patients received both treatments during which penile circumference was monitored. Mixed sexual anomalies were treated but one patient was a transsexual-transvestite. He responded best to treatment and indicated that electric shock stopped the crossdressing but he did not feel it was permanent until covert sensitization was used. Thus the two treatments interacted.

This illustrates the problem of a within person design. Because all patients had both treatments, we do not know which had the lasting effect. If different people were given only one or the other of the treatments, the answer may be clearer. Moreover, the two treatments may interact as they did with this patient. Both appeared to affect his perception of satisfactory change in his behavior. After eight months, the patient was still free of urges to crossdress and the frequency of intercourse with his wife increased. Pretreatment he had 35% to 72% of full erection to crossdressing but after conditioning only 4%. However, erection to intercourse was approximately the same at 10% to 15%.

The patients who have transsexual features respond to treatment more poorly than those who do not. This is true even though they are apparently predominantly gynephilic. For example, in Marks and Gelder's study, 67% of the "simple" transvestites were much improved with treatment but none of the transsexual-transvestites improved at all.

It is paradoxical that so much attention has been devoted in the literature to distinguishing the transvestite from the transsexual and these pragmatic behavior therapists rather matter of factly mix the labels because that is what they see and treat clinically. A difference in treatment outcome may be due to the fact that transvestism is associated with an orgasmic drive and the gynephilic transsexualism is not. One can interpret this to mean that transsexualism may not be a sexual disturbance but a social or interpersonal one. The simple transvestite's activities are focused on one isolated aspect of his life, namely sexual release while the transsexual's activity encompasses a wide range of his life, making treatment less generalizable and his behavior more difficult to change.

One may also interpret the finding to mean that short term effects are expected when sexual behavior is punished as noted in Chapter 4. All sex drive is suppressed but it comes back in 3-to-6 months. With the short follow-up in most case reports, treatment failure may be less evident in the simple transvestism group.

These studies illustrate one additional problem. Some transvestites may be emotionally disturbed and present difficulties in treatment. Oswald[122] reported a case study in which the patient appeared to be schizophrenic. Treatment failed. Blakemore and his associates[19] presented another case study in which the patient apparently made a satisfactory recovery and lost the transvestitic symptoms. Unfortunately in a follow-up article within a year[20], it was noted that the patient attempted suicide and was most unhappy. Is this coincidental to the transvestism as Money noted psychotic symptoms are coincidental to transsexualism? Blakemore et al inferred a close link and warned against the simplistic approach to the problem.

Shame aversion therapy.   A newer variant of aversive conditioning called shame aversion therapy[147] was used on a transvestite. In this treatment, the patient was required to crossdress before a disinterested group of men and women who watched him without reaction or comment. Like other forms of aversive conditioning, the logic of the treatment is to associate the sexual anomaly with an unrewarding and/or unpleasant experience following arousal. In this case, shame replaces electric shock. In the filmed version of this method which the author saw at an American Psychology Association (APA) convention, the patient was evidently experiencing shame. He was in tears as he crossdressed and had a look of anguish on his face. He attempted suicide the following day according to the investigator. The two preceding studies would appear to warn against the use of aversive methods with transvestism. Shame aversion therapy has the limitation of being applicable only for a few sessions. Some patients may enjoy what they are doing before an audience so treatment becomes ineffective. Perhaps only certain individuals can undergo such treatment. Those with "exhibitionistic tendencies" may be poor candidates.

The aversive conditioning methods are especially problematic for the transvestitic person who is basically gynephilic. If one assumes a fetish is operational and one is attempting to remove that aspect of his behavior, presumably results should be satisfactory. However, if one assumes he is playing roles of both male and female in his crossdressing behavior, the object of punishment is less obvious and satisfactory. If one punishes such role playing, the male role playing may also be suppressed, leaving the patient with no behavior in a sexual context. If he feels punished by society and feels inadequate and must play both roles himself, this may leave him feeling even more inadequate. This may be why there were two attempts at suicide among the few cases reported in the literature in contrast to the lower incidence of suicide attempts in reported cases of other anomalies treated by aversive conditioning therapy. Perhaps it simply reflects concurrent psychopathology which was not evident at the time of treatment or which was not assessed in the treatment program. Behavior therapists have not troubled themselves with such speculations but have simply focused on the overt behavior pattern.

Biofeedback.   In another behavior therapy approach, Rosen and Kople used biofeedback in the treatment of a "transvestite-exhibitionist"[144]. Marital counselling was also used for a poor sexual relationship due to an inorgasmic wife. The transvestitic behavior was described as fetishistic presumably since erotic sensations were generated by touching undergarments. However, the patient also enjoyed crossdressing for men and exposed his penis in the female attire in the back seat of his car. The patient suggested he might be a "latent homosexual" but reported no acting out in this respect. Careful baseline data for frequency of behavior were collected before any treatment was undertaken. The patient faced a criminal charge of indecent exposure and was presumably cooperative in treatment. The biofeedback method was similar to "fading" developed by Barlow (Chapter 3). The patient was shown a heterosexual film and heard a videotape of his transvestitic-exposing behavior. He was allowed to maintain full erection during the heterosexual film but only 50% erection to the audiotape of the anomalous behavior. A penile circumference mercury in rubber stain gauge was used to monitor erections. In a series of 12 sessions, the criterion erection allowed was gradually reduced by 10% decrements until only 5% full erection was permitted. Exceeding this criterion limit was signalled by a feedback alarm sound so the patient would know it. Obviously, a cooperative patient is necessary for this procedure. Moreover, it is surprising that the patient did not satiate with the repetition of the heterosexual film as commonly happens in laboratory studies[142]. One could argue that such a decrement is expected and is confounded with the treatment condition. However, it did not happen with the film. As it turned out, the patient responded to treatment and was followed up for 16 months. Fortunately for the author and us, the patient was caught engaging in his anomalous behavior which he never really gave up in the first place. He and his wife confessed that they had deceived the therapist all along. This stresses the importance of follow-up and the need for criterion measures that are often neglected in the literature. Since behavior therapists usually have a short follow-up, we never really know if treatment had any lasting effect. In the rare study like the one just described, we can see the polished clinical picture usually painted and at the same time we can see we have been deceived. The honesty and courage of the therapists involved is to be commended. They postulated that the patient may have been unwilling to disappoint the therapist and may have worried about further intensive therapy which could result in a job loss due to time away from work. The authors note the unreliability of self report data but also point to the therapists' expectations as a factor in outcome. Written permission to publish the case may have conveyed to the patient the expectation of successful outcome and may have aroused the desire not to disappoint the therapist. It is also possible that the patient did not really want to change his behavior and simply went along with the therapists. This is commonly encountered with forensic cases.

Multiple treatment methods. Aversion therapy itself has been considered limited because it does not increase the frequency of desirable heterosocial behavior[4]. Multiple behavior techniques have been applied in case of sexual anomalies to overcome this problem with some apparent success[41,50]. Foa's[50] patient had a history of exhibiting as well as crossdressing with masturbation and of wearing concealed female clothes in social situations. He had had heterosexual intercourse. The goals of treatment were to enhance his satisfaction with coitus, to improve his general interpersonal relations as well as to extinguish his deviant habit. Assertive training, desensitization and behavior rehearsal were used to enhance his heterosocial comfort. Covert sensitization and later, faradic conditioning were used to create an aversive reaction to crossdressing. After seven months, the patient was symptom free and normal heterosexual activity was maintained. The author notes the order of treatment was important. Earlier therapy using only aversive conditioning failed to elicit the patient's cooperation.

Gershman[61] treated a transvestite with thought stopping, covert sensitization and aversive shock. The case is interesting because Wolpe and Goldstein commented on it during its exposition. Some of the inherent problems of multiple treatment methods are brought out in the discussion and in this case there appeared to be no logic in applying the three aversion methods other than "the more treatments the better". An interesting feature of the transvestitic activity was that it apparently allowed the patient to get through intercourse with his girlfriend to the point of climax. One would expect then that by making crossdressing aversive, it would hinder his heterosexual relationships rather than helping them. This is pointed out by the commentators. It seems the procedures allowed the patient to control when the images of crossdressing occurred whereas they were uncontrollable prior to therapy. Nevertheless he chose to use the transvestitic images during intercourse and at other times as well. Apparently the treatment did not satisfactorily resolve the problem and the follow-up was left in the patient's hands. He had not called the therapist after six months. No news is good news but the therapist should have contacted the patient.

Dengrove[41] treated a 35-year-old married transvestite-transsexual by aversive conditioning via a portable shock box and with systematic desensitization. He also had a number of problems related to assertiveness in interpersonal situations which were helped by therapy. He was seen ten times and said his desires to crossdress were gone but there was still difficulty in approaching his wife.

Positive methods.   The question may be raised if all of the multiple therapies were necessary. We cannot say anything based on this limited data. However, some therapists argue that positive control alone is an alternative to aversion therapy. Moss, Rada and Appel[118] reported on two cases of transvestism. One received only faradic aversion therapy and the other was only offered advice on improving his heterosexual repertoire without crossdressing of course. Both cases were successful in reducing crossdressing behavior but the patient treated by aversive conditioning failed to improve his marital situation and his general level of adaptation deteriorated slightly according to the authors.

Carr[37] reported another successful case study using positive control. The patient in the study engaged in multiple sexual anomalies including transvestism. It is not clear what was the individual's preferred orgasmic outlet. Normal gynephilic behavior was enhanced and chances to act out the anomalous behavior were decreased.

Although there are only these two studies using positive control, they suggest that treatment can be sucessful without aversion therapy, even though the latter has been the one most frequently used with transvestites.

Orgasmic reconditioning. Lambley[90] used orgasmic reconditioning in one case of transvestism. The patient was also given in vivo exercises in order to increase heterosexual encounters. After five weeks he met an old girlfriend with whom he had sex on one occasion successfully. He managed to imagine seducing her while he wore his female clothes during masturbation and orgasm. The difficulties experienced with heterosexual intercourse were treated like sexual dysfunction (Chapter 15) and some improvement was evident. However after six months the patient still desired to crossdress although he said intercourse was a primary interest.

The present author has used orgasmic reconditioning in one unpublished case. In behavior therapy fashion, a baseline of behavior was recorded for gynephilic outlet and crossdressing with orgasm. The patient was living with a female and had opportunities for intercourse. However, he crossdressed as frequently as he had intercourse in spite of his own efforts to stop it. He was instructed to use his transvestitic fantasies as usual and to masturbate as usual in the privacy of his own home but at the last moment when orgasm was inevitable, he was to switch to a fantasy of intercourse with his girlfriend. After one week, he said the procedure did not affect his crossdressing although it was a little harder to get turned on at all. In the next week, the fantasy of intercourse was to occupy more time before climax was inevitable. He tried this three or four times and stopped, claiming it was not working. The goal of this treatment, as explained to the patient, was eventually to replace the transvestitic fantasy by the gynephilic one while he masturbated. He said the heterosexual fantasy was not exciting but neither was the transvestism and in addition he lost interest in masturbating. As discussed in Chapter 3, this, in theory, is the expected outcome of treatment rather than the increased heterosexuality reported in the literature. The patient discontinued treatment and did not give up his transvestism.

Other Treatments

Surgery. Some transvestites who are considered to be gynephilic fetishists develop "transsexual yearnings". I think they are not distinct in gender dysphoria from androphilic transsexuals who are more likely to receive surgery. This group of transvestites may be older when they apply for sex reassignment surgery and have been labeled "aging transvestites". One may wonder why androphiles are younger when they apply for surgery. There are at least two possible reasons. In androphilic men, the high degree of femininity and an object preference for men are congruent with the surgery. The gynephile, in contrast, is attracted to women as well as crossdressing and the incongruity as well as his gynephilic desires may cause him to hesitate about surgery. A second possible factor is that androphiles may be rejected by the gay community because of their prescribed sexual interactions. That is, the transsexual does not like his penis involved in sexual interaction to the degree that another androphilic man may wish. Moreover, the extremeness of femininity, including the "female masquerade" may annoy them. Thus possible rejection by homosexuals may encourage them to seek surgery earlier than gynephiles who are accepted by females and who enjoy using their penises in heterosexual intercourse.

Surgical sex reassignment is not offered frequently to the gynephilic group because they seem confused about their gender identity. They may prefer heterosexual interactions or they may use their penises in transvestitic activity and they are therefore excluded. This argument is spurious because the androphilic transsexuals also use their penises considerably. To remove it surgically can also produce problems for the androphilic transsexual. As one "successful candidate" who underwent sex reassignment claimed: "I'll never be a real woman. I'll always just be a castrated man." If in fact gender behavior and object choice are independent, transsexuals may satisfy their gender behavior needs but orgasm with their preferred sex object may be permanently removed. It does not seem any more incongruous to create a lesbian.

If one thinks surgery should be performed at all, the limited empirical data suggest that gynephilic transsexuals fare as well as, if not better than, androphiles after sex reassignment surgery. Hoenig[77] reported one successful case and Bentler[13] indicated that in a study of 42 transsexuals, "heterosexual" and "asexual" postoperative patients were more satisfied than "homosexuals" who are presumably *the* ideal group for successful sex reassignment.

Transvestites generally do not come to the attention of the psychiatric community unless they want surgery. They do not break any laws by engaging in their behavior in private. Available data suggest they generally do not have severe psychiatric problems. Should we therefore be concerned with treatment? Would an attitude of acceptance for their private life change our perceptions of transvestism? Our knowledge is limited and so little has been tried in the way of treatment.

Psychotherapy.   Individual reports of other treatments have appeared irregularly over the past thirty years. Deutsch[43] treated a married man with multiple sexual anomalies including voyeurism and transvestism. An unspecified short psychotherapy was used. Deutsch noted the critical role played by the wife in treatment change. She agreed to help her husband and was present when he crossdressed. However she insisted that he do it before a mirror. He did not like his female appearance and felt greatly relieved. He appreciated his wife's efforts and became more affectionate to her. Her continued support and nondominant way carried him through to a continued heterosexual adjustment after six months.

Hora[79] treated a 27-year-old college graduate via psychoanalysis. The transvestism was revealed to symbolize the following: the transvestism act itself was intercourse with mother; fetishism was denial of castration; passive homosexual attitude was denial of male competitive desires and masochism-castration was punishment for incest. The patient resolved the complex of problems but no follow-up was reported.

Hypnotherapy.   Beigel[9] and Wollman[171] successfully treated a few cases of transvestism with hypnosis. The former noted the use of hypnotism served several functions: to influence the individuals' ideas about the nature of their crossdressing which permitted a belief in changing it; to motivate them to change to a normal sex role; to enable them to uncover the course of their sexual orientation like psychoanalysis does; to reduce the overestimation of the importance of female activities and to find substitutes; to make it easier to give up the crossdressing; and make the goals of heterosexuality desirable. Although the procedures are similar to behavior therapy conditioning (Chapter 3), Beigel is employing the technique much as a psychoanalyst would use other means at his disposal, that is, free association or art therapy, to reveal the primal scene which started the transvestism. In four of five cases reported, the anomalous behavior appeared to stop. In one of Beigel's cases, results were not so clear cut although the author argues that hypnosis had some impact. The patient had relapses after treatment but decided 3 months after therapy determined to "stop the silly performances". A controlled assessment of hypnosis has yet to be done.

Miscellany.   Brierley[23] has reviewed the many and varied other approaches to transvestism, most of which are of dubious therapeutic value. Electroconvulsive therapy (ECT) has been used in a few cases of transvestism and the outcome was uncertain. The patients involved suffered other psychiatric illnesses which responded to ECT but the crossdressing may not have been affected. The same is true for antipsychotic medication and hormone therapy. A few cases are reported with inadequate descriptions of the transvestism and of outcome. If any of these methods are worthwhile, an adequate demonstration of their effectiveness is still forthcoming.

Treatment of Choice

Treatment effectiveness is summarized in Table 6.5. Transvestites are even less understood than transsexuals. The former are less demanding of

TABLE 6.5
Summary of Treatment Effectiveness for Transvestism

Method	Results
1. Chemical Aversion Therapy	60% success. Physical dangers. Poorly studied
2. Electrical Aversion	60% success. Less danger but also poorly studied
3. Other Aversion Methods	Mixed success. Only a few cases. Suicide risks
4. Other Behavior Therapy Methods (Biofeedback, multiple methods, orgasmic reconditioning, positive control)	Mixed success. Only case studies
5. Surgery	Some success but not adequately evaluated
6. Psychotherapy	Two cases, one positive outcome
7. Hypnotherapy	80% success but only few cases. No controlled studies
8. Miscellany (ECT, Drugs)	Transvestism not affected but psychosis/depression relieved

psychiatric services than transsexuals who request an operation. Transvestites do not seem distressed about their behavior and perhaps we should not attempt to change them. All existing procedures have not been adequately assessed in the treatment of transvestism and they must be considered experimental. The *patient's desire* to change should be paramount in any treatment. Foremost, an emphasis on self acceptance and on their interpersonal strengths in other areas of their lives are important. Once they are able to accept themselves as individuals they can view their sexual anomaly as an isolated aspect of their make up rather than the totality of their being. The latter is often assumed.

The Seahorse Club in Australia and the Full Personality Expression Club in the United States are two transvestitic groups that offer the individual acceptance and normalize his experiences[26]. The Australian club has over 250 members, publishes its own quarterly magazine and allows the family to attend meetings. This suggests that society can learn to adapt to and accept the transvestite's behavior.

Before any treatment is established, it would be well to ascertain if in fact transvestism is the "fetish" it is claimed to be. There is no systematic or empirical evidence to suggest it is, other than clinical theory. The transvestite's claim that they feel like another person when crossdressed may be crucial to the anomaly. This may reflect a gender identity problem rather than a fetish. Viewed in this way, it makes sense that some of them will develop feminine gender identity stronger than their gynephilic orgasm needs just as the androphilic transsexuals do. The transvestite illustrates how gender identity can splinter, how it may be bisexual or nonsexual. If research efforts are directed in this area, our understanding will increase. In the mean time, it is perhaps best to leave their sexual behavior alone and focus on counselling for life problems.

Speculations

The current state of clinical knowledge on transvestism and transsexualism is very confused. A variety of labels and clinical subgroups are emerging, likely without good reason. The confusion may be clarified and labels become unnecessary by sorting out gender identity and erotic object preference. Consider Table 6.6. For simplicity, a two by three celled table has been constructed. Assume for the time being that object preference is

TABLE 6.6
Gender Identity and Erotic Object
Preferences in Transsexuals and Transvestites

Preferred Sex Object Choice	Preferred Gender Identity		
	Masculine	Bisexual/Neither	Feminine
Male	Homosexual	Bisexual Homosexuals	Homosexuals Transsexuals
Female	Heterosexual Normal	Transvestites	Transvestites Transsexuals

dichotomous as preferring male or female. Gender identity, however, is divided into three although in reality, it is likely a continuum from very masculine to very feminine. The three groups are masculine identified, bisexual/neutral and feminine identified. Assume the two dimensions are independent and let us not be swayed by the numbers of subjects in each cell. By far the largest cell is masculine identified and female object choice in which we cast the masses of heterosexual normals. All the remaining cells are small, some smaller than others. The population of androphilic (homosexual) males will run across the top three cells some in each group. At the extreme will be the transsexuals who are very feminine identified and prefer males. This is the group some writers claim are the "true" transsexuals. However, transsexuals also appear on the bottom row preferring the female body shape but still being extremely feminine identified. Thus if we accept that preferred gender identity and object preference are independent, it is more readily accepted that transsexuals can appear on both lines of the table. If we assume that transsexualism is a problem of gender identity and has little to do with sex object preference, the picture is even clearer. This also explains why the social aspect of crossdressing is so important to the transsexual. He feels "comfortable" crossdressed and will do so without orgasmic satisfaction. It may be associated with his orgasmic behavior but is larger than it and encompasses it only in one facet of his life—sexual interactions. It seems too narrow to limit the crossdressing behavior to orgasm and if we treat the problems more generally and not assume gender behavior has to be consistent with orgasmic outlet, our difficulties in understanding it diminish. Prince[127] and Bruce[24] distinguish sex and gender but it is not clear whether "sex" implies sex drive reduction or object choice. In any case the overriding influence of gender is emphasized. The common assumption that dissatisfaction in the transsexual is related to a conflict in object choice and gender identity may be misleading. Object choice may be relatively unimportant and dissatisfaction may be due to vascillating gender identity. This possibility has yet to be investigated satisfactorily.

The transvestite, popularly defined, fits mainly on the bottom line of the table and is labeled as preferring the female body shape and being either feminine identified or bisexual/neither. Some patients who masturbate in female attire and prefer the female body shape want an operation to change them into women, as incongruent as it may seem. Since it would eliminate their erotic behavior, it is a reasonable assumption that the feminine gender identity is a powerful and overriding element in their make up. It is this element which may change over the years—the transvestite may become more feminine and desire to become a woman[108]. The erotic object preference remains constant and there is little evidence to indicate that it changes with time[76] although sex drive level may decrease. If he is bisexual, that is, equally male and female in gender identity, one component may win over the other. What may happen in the gynephile is that erotic object choice balances or outweighs gender feelings so that sex reassignment surgery is not desired in the young transvestite. However, as sex drive level decreases with age, the gender component becomes stronger so the "aging transvestite" does want surgery. The androphile, in contrast, has a more congruous picture of himself from the start; he wants to be a woman and desires sex with a man and so he may seek surgery at a younger age. Early and extensive sex experience with gay men and rejection by the gay community may also prompt him to seek sex change surgery. However, the greater dissatisfaction of the androphile with sex reassignment surgery (as in Bentler's study, [13]) may result from the loss of libido. Perhaps the androphile has a greater narcissistic element than gynephiles from the start since it comes not only from gender feelings but, as theorized in Chapter 4, from androphilia itself.

This brings us to the last group of transvestites—the bisexual/ neither group. Many transvestites described themselves as having a feminine side seeking expression. One may view this as a significant but isolated feminine gender identity element or as a split in their personality with two large elements, one male, the other female. If the female element is evenly balanced with the male, such an individual may act out bisexually or assume both roles equally. Alternatively the valence to be male and female may cancel each other out so he does not know how to behave. Since neither male nor female behavior is impelling, he may seem asexual and cannot describe to the clinican what "turns him on".

The bisexual gender identity appears to characterize the typical group studied by Prince and Bentler and by Buckner. The individual plays both male and female roles for himself to his satisfaction perhaps because he is bisexual in gender identity and can genuinely feel both the female and male elements in his character. He is self satisfied and needs no outsiders including psychiatrists. This would form a means of adjustment which perhaps reduces personality pathology and personal failure in the real and external world. One may postulate a counterpart in the "bisexual-homosexual" of which we know so little.

What we may be seeing clinically are gradations of feminine gender identity combined with male versus female object preference. When the patient is androphilic in object preference and wants to be a woman, this makes sense to us and an operation seems suitable. When we see the gynephile who wants the same operation, it does not make sense because it is difficult to associate such gender behavior with gynephilia. It would perhaps be an improvement to drop the terms transvestism and transsexualism and talk only of gender dysphoria, an unhappiness with being one's anatomical gender.

It would be interesting if we could examine the idea of bisexual gender identity but there are no instruments available to do so. The Kinsey scale mixes too many components. A recent development, the Bem Sex Role Inventory which measures "androgyny", assumes all individuals possess a male and female element in them in varying degrees[10]. For some individuals, the male balances the female as suggested here in the bisexual/neither category. Unfortunately, the scale is biased by a tendency to respond in a way that makes one look stereotypically good for their anatomical sex[10]. Moreover, the test splinters into many subfactors which are weak and unreliable[167]. While the idea is promising, the one measure in the area is not satisfactory. A new measure of bisexual gender identity would be an asset in answering the many questions raised by transsexualism and transvestism.

One final speculation about both transvestism and transsexualism. The fact that the anomalous male *himself* is crossdressed may be *the* critical element in his behavior. Transsexuals want to be "super females", they often want big breasts, to be the seductive "midnight whores", to be prostitutes, to be "perfect females". The transvestite avoids all interpersonal difficulties. He is *the* ideal female for him. All these behaviors may reflect narcissism, either as a preoccupation with themselves or as an inability or unwillingness to depend on others for interpersonal and sexual needs. Perhaps the presence of temporal lobe dysfunction in many cases indicates an inability on their part to "decenter" and take the role of others (egocentrism). Their "sex partners" may often be addendums or props for their own behavior. These hypotheses are untested but they suggest interesting avenues to explore in the two anomalies.

BIBLIOGRAPHY

1. Ball, J. R. A case of hair fetishism, transvestism, and organic cerebral disorder. *Acta Psychiatrica Scandinavica,* 1968, *44,* 249–254.
2. Baker, C. (Ed.) *Ernest Hemingway Selected Letters 1917–1961.* New York: Chas. Scribner's Sons 1981.
3. Barker, J. C. A comparison of pharmacological and electrical aversion techniques. *British Journal of Psychiatry,* 1965, *111,* 268–276.
4. Barlow, D., Reynolds, J., & Agras, W. Gender identity change in a transsexual. *Archives of General Psychiatry,* 1973, *28,* 569–579.
5. Barr, M. L., & Hobbs, G. E. Chromosomal sex in transvestites. *The Lancet,* 1954, *1,* 1109–1110.
6. Barr, R. F. Responses to erotic stimuli of transsexual and homosexual males. *British Journal of Psychiatry,* 1973, *123,* 579–585.
7. Barr, R. F., Raphael, B., & Hennessey, N. Apparent heterosexuality in two male patients requesting change-of-sex operation. *Archives of Sexual Behavior,* 1974, *3*(4), 325–330.
8. Bates, J. E., Skilbeck, W. M., Smith, K. V. R., & Bentler, P. M. Gender role abnormalities in boys: An analysis of clinical ratings. *Journal of Abnormal Child Psychology,* 1974, *2*(1), 1–16.
9. Beigel, H. G. Three transvestites under hypnosis. *Journal of Sex Research,* 1967, *3*(2), 149–162.
10. Bem, S. L. The measurement of psychological androgyny. *Journal of Consulting and Clinical Psychology,* 1974, *42*(2), 155–162.
11. Benjamin, H. Transsexualism and transvestism as psychosomatic and somato-psychic syndromes. *American Journal of Psychotherapy,* 1954, *8,* 219–230.
12. Benjamin, H. Transvestism and transsexualism in the male and female. *The Journal of Sex Research,* 1967, *3*(2), 107–127.
13. Bentler, P. M. A typology of transsexualism: gender identity theory and data. *Archives of Sexual Behavior,* 1976, *5*(6), 567–584.

14. Bentler, P. M., & Prince, C. Personality characteristics of male transvestites: III. *Journal of Abnormal Psychology,* 1969, *74*(2), 140–143.
15. Bentler, P. M., & Prince, C. Psychiatric symptomatology in transvestites. *Journal of Clinical Psychology,* 1970, *26,* 434–435.
16. Bentler, P. M., Sherman, R. W., & Prince, C. Personality characteristics of male transvestites. *Journal of Clinical Psychology,* 1970, *26,* 287–291.
17. Berger, J. C., Green, R., Laub, D. R., Reynolds, C. L., Walker, P. A., & Wollman, L. *Standards of care: The hormonal and surgical sex reassignment of gender dysphoric persons.* Prepared by the founding committee of the Harry Benjamin International Gender Dysphoria Association, 1979, University of Texas Medical Branch, Galveston, Texas, 77550.
18. Bernard, F. An enquiry among a group of pedophiles. *Journal of Sex Research,* 1975, *11*(3), 242–245.
19. Blakemore, C., Thorpe, J., Barker, J., Conway, C., & Lavin, N. The application of faradic aversion in a case of transvestism. *Behavior Research & Therapy,* 1963, *1,* 29–34.
20. Blakemore, C., Thorpe, J., Barker, J., Conway, C., & Lavin, N. Follow-up note to: the application of faradic aversion conditioning in a case of transvestism. *Behavior Research & Therapy,* 1963, *1,* 191.
21. Blumer, D. Changes of sexual behavior related to temporal lobe disorders in man. *Journal of Sex Research,* 1970, *6*(3), 173–180.
22. Bradley, S. J., Doering, R. W., Zucker, K. J., Finegan, J. K., & Gonda, G. M. Assessment of the gender-disturbed child: A comparison to sibling and psychiatric controls. In *Childhood and Sexuality,* Sampon, J. (Ed.), Montreal: Editions Etudes Vivantes, 1980.
23. Brierly, H. *Transvestism: A handbook with case studies for psychologists, psychiatrists and counsellors.* New York: Pergamon Press, 1979.
24. Bruce, V. The expression of femininity in the male. *Journal of Sex Research,* 1967, *3*(2), 129–139.
25. Buckner, H. T. The transvestic career path. *Psychiatry,* 1970, *33,* 381–389.
26. Buhrich, N. A heterosexual transvestite club: Psychiatric aspects *Australian and New Zealand Journal of Psychiatry,* 1976, *10,* 331–335.
27. Buhrich, N. A case of familial heterosexual transvestism. *Acta Psychiatrica Scandinavica,* 1977, *55,* 199–201.
28. Buhrich, N. Transvestism in history. *Journal of Nervous and Mental Disease,* 1977, *166*(1), 64–66.
29. Buhrich, N., & McConaghy, N. Can fetishism occur in transsexuals? *Archives of Sexual Behavior,* 1977, *6*(3), 223–225.
30. Buhrich, N., & McConaghy, N. The clinical syndrome of femmiphilic transvestism. *Archives of Sexual Behavior,* 1977, *6*(5), 397–412.
31. Buhrich, N., & McConaghy, N. The discrete syndromes of transvestism and transsexualism. *Archives of Sexual Behavior,* 1977, *6*(6), 483–495.
32. Buhrich, N., & McConaghy, N. Two clinically discrete syndromes of transsexualism. *British Journal of Psychiatry,* 1978, *133,* 73–76.
33. Buhrich, N., & McConaghy, N. Tests of gender feelings and behavior in homosexuality, transvestism and transsexualism. *Journal of Clinical Psychiatry,* 1979, *35*(1), 187–191.
34. Buhrich, N., Barr, R., & Lam-Po-Tang, P. R. Two transsexuals with 47 XYY Karyotype. *British Journal of Psychiatry,* 1978, *133,* 77–81.
35. Bullough, V. L. Transvestites in the middle ages. *American Journal of Sociology,* 1974, *79*(6), 1381–1394.
36. Callahan, E. J., & Leitenberg, H. Aversion therapy for sexual deviation: Contingent

shock and covert sensitization. *Journal of Abnormal Psychology,* 1973, *81*(1), 60–73.

37. Carr, J. E. Behavior therapy in a case of multiple sexual disorders. *Journal of Behavior Therapy & Experimental Psychiatry,* 1974, *5,* 171–174.
38. Childs, A. Acute symbiotic psychosis in a postoperative transsexual. *Archives of Sexual Behavior,* 1977, *6*(1), 37–44.
39. Clark, D. F. A note on avoidance conditioning techniques in sexual disorder. *Behavior Research Therapy,* 1965, *3,* 203–206.
40. deMarinis, M., & Arnett, E. N. Cerebrovascular occlusion in a transsexual man taking mestranol. *Archives of Internal Medicine,* 1978, *138,* 1732–1733.
41. Dengrove, E. Behavior therapy of the sexual disorders. *Journal of Sex Research,* 1967, *3*(1), 49–61.
42. Derogatis, L., Meyer, J., & Vazquez, N. A psychological profile of the transsexual. *Journal of Nervous & Mental Disease,* 1978, *166*(4), 234–254.
43. Deutsch, D. A case of transvestism. *American Journal of Psychotherapy,* 1954, *8,* 239–242.
44. Eicher, W., Spoljar, M., Cleve, H., Murken, J., Richter, K., & Stangel-Rutkowski, S. H-Y antigen in trans-sexuality. *The Lancet,* 1979, *2,* 1137–1138.
45. Epstein, A. W. Relationship of fetishism and transvestism to brain and particularly to temporal lobe dysfunction. *Journal of Nervous & Mental Disease,* 1961, *133,* 247–253.
46. Feldman, M., MacCulloch, M. J., & MacCulloch, M. C The aversion therapy treatment of a heterogenous group of five cases of sexual deviation. *Acta Psychiatrica Scandanavica,* 1968, *44,* 113–124.
47. Finney, J. C., Brandsma, J. M., Tondow, M., & Lemaistre, G. A study of transsexuals seeking gender reassignment. *American Journal of Psychiatry,* 1975, *132*(9), 962–964.
48. Fleming, M., Jenkins, S., & Bugarin, C. Questioning current definitions of gender identity: implications of the Bem Sex-Role Inventory for transsexuals. *Archives of Sexual Behavior,* 1980, *9*(1), 13–26.
49. Fleming, M., Steinman, C., & Bocknek, G. Methodological problems in assessing sex-reassignment surgery: a reply to Meyer and Reter. *Archives of Sexual Behavior,* 1980, *9*(5), 451–456.
50. Foa, E. B. Multiple behavior techniques in the treatment of transvestism. In J. H. Eysenck (Ed.), *Case histories in behavior therapy.* Boston: Routledge & Kegan, 1976.
51. Fookes, B. H. Some experiences in the use of aversion therapy in male homosexuals, exhibitionism and fetishism—transvestism. *British Journal of Psychiatry,* 1969, *115,* 339–341.
52. Forgey, D. G. The institution of berdache among the North American Plains Indians. *Journal of Sex Research,* 1975, *11*(1), 1–15.
53. Freund, K. Male homosexuality: an analysis of the pattern. In *Understanding Homosexuality: Its Biological and Psychological Bases.* Lorraine, J. A. (Ed.), Lancaster, England: Medical and Technical Publishing Co., 1974, 25–81.
54. Freund, K., Langevin, R., Satterberg, J., & Steiner, B. Extension of the gender identity scale for males. *Archives of Sexual Behavior,* 1977, *6*(6), 507–519.
55. Freund, K., Langevin, R., Zajac, Y., Steiner, B., & Zajac, A. The transsexual syndrome in homosexual males. *Journal of Nervous & Mental Disease,* 1974, *158,* 145–153.
56. Freund, K., Langevin, R., Zajac, Y., Steiner, B., & Zajac, A. Parent-child relations in transsexual and non-transsexual homosexual males. *British Journal of Psychiatry,* 1974, *124,* 22–23.
57. Freund, K., Nagler, E., Langevin, R., Zajac, A., & Steiner, B. Measuring feminine

gender identity in homosexual males. *Archives of Sexual Behavior,* 1974, *3*(3), 249–260.

58. Freund, K., Steiner, B., & Chan, S. Two types of cross gender identity. *Archives of Sexual Behavior,* 1982, *11,* 49–63.

59. Friend, M. R., Schiddel, L., Klein, B., & Dunaeff, D. Observations on the development of transvestism in boys. *American Journal of Orthopsychiatry,* 1954, *24,* 563–575.

60. Fromm, E. *The art of loving.* New York: Harper & Row, 1956.

61. Gershman, H. The role of core gender identity in the genesis of perversions. *American Journal of Psychotherapy,* 1966, *20,* 58–67.

62. Gershman, L. Case conference: a transvestite fantasy treated by thought stopping, covert sensitization and aversive shock. *Journal of Behavior Therapy and Experimental Psychiatry,* 1970, *1,* 153–161.

63. Glynn, J. D., & Harper, P. Behavior therapy in transvestism. *Lancet,* 1961, *1,* 619.

64. Green, D. Legal aspects of transsexualism. *Archives of Sexual Behavior,* 1971, *1*(2), 145–151.

65. Green, R. Childhood cross gender behavior and subsequent sexual preference. *American Journal of Psychiatry,* 1979, *136*(1), 106–108.

66. Green, R., Fuller, M., Rutley, B. R., & Hendler, J. Playroom toy preferences of fifteen masculine and fifteen feminine boys. *Behavior Therapy,* 1972, *3,* 425–429.

67. Green, R., & Money, J. *Transsexualism and sex reassignment.* Baltimore, Md.: The Johns Hopkins Press, 1969.

68. Green, R., Newman, L. E., & Stoller, R. J. Treatment of boyhood "transsexualism". *Archives of General Psychiatry,* 1972, *26,* 213–217.

69. Gutheil, E. A. The psychologic background of transsexualism and transvestism. *American Journal of Psychotherapy,* 1954, *8,* 231–239.

70. Hamburger, C. The desire for change of sex as shown by personal letters from 465 men and women. *Acta Endocrinologica,* 1953, *14,* 361–375.

71. Hamburger, C., Sturup, G. K., & Dahl-Inversen, E. Transvestism; hormonal, psychiatric and surgical therapy of a case. *Nordisk Medicin,* 1953, *49,* 844–848.

72. Hirschfeld, M. *Sexual anomalies and perversion.* London: F. Alder, 1936.

73. Hoenig, J., & Kenna, J. The nosological position of transsexualism. *Archives of Sexual Behavior,* 1974, *3*(3), 273–287.

74. Hoenig, J., & Kenna, J. C. EEG abnormalities and transsexualism. *British Journal of Psychiatry,* 1979, *134,* 293–300.

75. Hoenig, J., Kenna, J., & Youd, A. Social and economic aspects of transsexualism. *British Journal of Psychiatry,* 1970, *117,* 163–172.

76. Hoenig, J., Kenna, J., & Youd, A. A follow-up study of transsexualists: Social and economic aspects. *Psychiatrica Clinica,* 1970, *3,* 85–100.

77. Hoenig, J., Kenna, J., & Youd, A. Surgical treatment for transsexualism. *Acta Psychiatrica Scandanavia,* 1971, *47,* 106–133.

78. Hoenig, J., & Torr, J. B. Karyotyping of transsexualists. *Journal of Psychosomatic Research,* 1964, *8,* 157–159.

79. Hora, T. The structural analysis of transvestism. *Psychoanalytic Review,* 1953, *40,* 268–274.

80. Hore, B., Nicolle, F., & Calnan, J. Male transsexualism in England: sixteen cases with surgical intervention. *Archives of Sexual Behavior,* 1975, *4*(1), 81–88.

81. Housden, J. An examination of the biologic etiology of transvestism. *International Journal of Social Psychiatry,* 1965, *11,* 301–305.

82. Hunt, D. D., & Hampson, J. L. Follow-up of 17 biologic male transsexuals after sex-reassignment surgery. *American Journal of Psychiatry,* 1980, *137*(4), 432–438.

83. Hunt, D. D., Carr, J. E., & Hampson, J. L. Cognitive correlates of biologic sex and gender identity in transsexualism. *Archives of Sexual Behavior,* 1981, *10*(1), 65–77.

84. Hyde, C., & Kenna, J. C. A male M X twin pair, discordant for transsexualism, discordant for schizophrenia. *Acta Psychiatrica Scandanavia*, 1977, *56*, 265–275.

85. Jayaram, B., Stuteville, O., & Bush, I. Complications and undesirable results of sex reassignment surgery in male-to-female transsexuals. *Archives of Sexual Behavior*, 1978, *7*(4), 337–345.

86. Jones, H. Operative treatment of the male transsexual in *Transsexualism and Sex Reassignment*. Green, R., & Money, J. (Eds.), Baltimore: Johns Hopkins Press, 1969.

87. Kimble, G. A. *Hilgard and Marquis' Conditioning and Learning*. New York: Apple Century Crofts Inc., 1961.

88. Klein, M. *Psychoanalysis of Children*. London: Hogarth Press, 1932.

89. Kolarsky, A., Freund, K., Machek, J., & Polak, O. Male sexual deviation. *Archives of General Psychiatry*, 1967, *17*, 735–743.

90. Lambley, P. Treatment of transvestism and subsequent coital problems. *Journal of Behavior Therapy and Experimental Psychiatry*, 1974, *5*(1), 101–102.

91. Lang, S. C., & Julien, R. M. Re-evaluation of estrogen-induced cortical and thalamic paroxysmal EEG activity in the cat. *Electroencephalography and Clinical Neurophysiology*, 1978, *44*, 94–103.

92. Langevin, R., Paitich, D., Hucker, S., Newman, S., Ramsay, G., Pope, S., Geller, G., & Anderson, C. The effect of assertiveness training, provera and sex of therapist in the treatment of genital exhibitionism. *Journal of Behavior Therapy & Experimental Psychiatry*, 1979, *10*(4), 275–282.

93. Langevin, R., Paitich, D., & Steiner, B. The clinical profile of male transsexuals living as females vs. those living as males. *Archives of Sexual Behavior*, 1977, *6*(2), 143–154.

94. Lavin, N., Thorpe, J., Barker, J., Blakemore, C., & Conway, C. Behavior therapy in a case of transvestism. *Journal of Nervous and Mental Disease*, 1961, *133*, 346–353.

95. Leavitt, F., Berger, J., Hoeppner, J., & Northrop, G. Presurgical adjustment in male transsexuals with and without hormonal treatment. *Journal of Nervous and Mental Disease*, 1980, *168*(11), 693–697.

96. Lehrman, K. L. Pulmonary embolism in a transsexual man taking diethylstilbestrol. *Journal of the American Medical Association*, 1976, *235*(5), 532–533.

97. Levine, E. M. Male transsexuals in the homosexual subculture. *American Journal of Psychiatry*, 1976, *133*(11), 1318–1321.

98. Levine, E. M., Shaiova, C., & Mihailovic, M. Male to female: the role transformation of transsexuals. *Archives of Sexual Behavior*, 1975, *4*(2), 173–185.

99. Levine, E. M., Grunewald, D., & Shaiova, C. H. Behavioral differences and emotional conflict among male-to-female transsexuals. *Archives of Sexual Behavior*, 1976, *5*(1), 81–85.

100. Lothstein, L. M. The psychological management and treatment of hospitalized transsexuals. *Journal of Nervous & Mental Disease*, 1978, *166*(4), 255–262.

101. Lothstein, L. M. The postsurgical transsexual: empirical and theoretical considerations. *Archives of Sexual Behavior*, 1980, *9*(5), 547–564.

102. Lukianowicz, N. Survey of various aspects of transvestism in the light of our present knowledge. *Journal of Nervous & Mental Disease*, 1959, *128*, 36–64.

103. MacKenzie, K. R. Gender dysphoria syndrome: towards standardized diagnostic criteria. *Archives of Sexual Behavior*, 1978, *7*(4), 251–262.

104. Markland, C., & Hastings, D. Vaginal reconstruction using bowel segments. *Archives of Sexual Behavior*, 1978, *7*(4), 305–307.

105. Marks, I. M., & Gelder, M. G. Transvestism and fetishism: Clinical and psychological changes during faradic aversion. *British Journal of Psychiatry*, 1967, *113*, 711–729.

106. Marks, I. M., Gelder, M. G., & Bancroft, J. Sexual deviations two years after electric aversion. *British Journal of Psychiatry,* 1970, *117,* 173–185.

107. McKee, E. A., Roback, H. B., & Hollender, M. H. Transsexualism in two male triplets. *American Journal of Psychiatry,* 1976, *133*(3), 334–337.

108. Meyer, J. K. Clinical variants among applicants for sex reassignment. *Archives of Sexual Behavior,* 1974, *3*(6), 527–558.

109. Meyer, J. K., Knorr, N. J., & Blumer, D. Characterization of a self-designated transsexual population. *Archives of Sexual Behavior,* 1971, *1*(3), 219–230.

110. Meyer, J. K., & Reter, D. J. Sex reassignment. *Archives of General Psychiatry,* 1979, *36,* 1010–1015.

111. Meyer-Bahlburg, H. F. Sex hormones and male homosexuality in comparative perspective. *Archives of Sexual Behavior,* 1977, *6*(4), 297–325.

112. Money, J. Prefatory remarks on outcome of sex reassignment in 24 cases of transsexualism. *Archives of Sexual Behavior,* 1971, *1*(2), 163–165.

113. Money, J., & Brennan, J. G. Sexual dimorphism in the psychology of female transsexuals. In R. Green, & J. Money (Eds.), *Transsexualism and sex reassignment.* Baltimore: The Johns Hopkins Press, 1969, 116–136.

114. Money, J., Clarke, F., & Mazur, T. Families of seven male-to-female transsexuals after 5-7 years: sociological sexology. *Archives of Sexual Behavior,* 1975, *4*(2), 187–197.

115. Money, J., & Russo, A. Establishment of homosexual gender identity/role: Longitudinal follow-up of discordant gender identity/role in childhood. Paper presented at APA Annual Meeting, Toronto, August 1978.

116. Money, J., & Wolff, G. Sex reassignment: male to female to male. *Archives of Sexual Behavior,* 1973, *2,* 245–250.

117. Morgenstern, F., Pearce, J., & Rees, L. Predicting the outcome of behavior therapy by psychological tests. *Behavior Research & Therapy,* 1965, *2,* 191–200.

118. Moss, G. R., Rada, R. T., & Appel, J. B. Positive control as an alternative to aversion therapy. *Journal of Behavior Therapy & Experimental Psychiatry,* 1970, *1,* 291–294.

119. Nelson, C., Paitich, D., & Steiner, B. Medicolegal aspects of transsexualism. *Canadian Psychiatric Association Journal,* 1976, *21*(8), 557–564.

120. Newman, L., & Stoller, R. Nontranssexual men who seek sex reassignment. *American Journal of Psychiatry,* 1974, *131,* 437–441.

121. Orentreich, N., & Durr, N. P. Mammogenesis in transsexuals. *The Journal of Investigative Dermatology,* 1974, *63,* 142–146.

122. Oswald, I. Induction of illusory and hallucinatory voices with considerations of behavior therapy. *Journal of Mental Science,* 1962, *108,* 196–212.

123. Ounsted, C., & Taylor, H. *Gender difference: Their ontogeny and significance.* Edinburgh: Churchill-Livingstone, 1972.

124. Pacion, S. J. Gandhi's struggle with sexuality. *Medical Aspects of Human Sexuality,* 1971, *5*(1), 73–93.

125. Pauly, I. The current status of the change of sex operation. *Journal of Nervous & Mental Disease,* 1968, *147,* 460–471.

126. Person, E., & Ovesey, L. The transsexual syndrome in males. *American Journal of Psychotherapy,* 1974, *28*(1), 4–20.

127. Prince, V. Transsexuals and pseudotranssexuals. *Archives of Sexual Behavior,* 1978, *7*(4), 263–272.

128. Prince, V., & Bentler, P. M. Survey of 504 cases of transvestism. *Psychological Reports,* 1972, *31,* 903–917.

129. Randell, J. Transvestism and trans-sexualism. *British Medical Journal,* 1959, *2,* 1448–1452.

130. Randell, J. Indications for sex reassignment surgery. *Archives of Sexual Behavior,*

1971, *1*(2), 153–161.

131. Rekers, G. A. Stimulus control over sex-typed play in cross-gender identified boys. *Journal of Experimental Child Psychology*, 1975, *20*, 136–148.

132. Rekers, G. A. Assessment and treatment of childhood gender problems. In B. Lahey, & A. Kazdin (Eds.), *Advances in clinical psychology* (Vol. 1). New York: Plenum Press, 1977, 267–306.

133. Rekers, G. A., Crandall, B. F., Rosen, A. C., & Bentler, P. M. Genetic and physical studies of male children with psychological gender disturbances. *Psychological Medicine*, 1979, *9*, 1–3.

134. Rekers, G. A., & Lovaas, O. I. Behavioral treatment of deviant sex-role behaviors in a male child. *Journal of Applied Behavior Analysis*, 1974, *7*, 173–190.

135. Rekers, G. A., Lovaas, O. I., & Low, B. The behavioral treatment of a "transsexual" preadolescent boy. *Journal of Abnormal Child Psychology*, 1974, *2*(2), 99–116.

136. Rekers, G. A., Rosen, A. C., Lovaas, O. I., & Bentler, P. M. Sex role stereotype and professional intervention for childhood gender disturbance. *Professional Psychology*, 1978, *9*(1), 127–136.

137. Rekers, G. A., & Varni, J. Self-monitoring and self-reinforcement processes in a pre-transsexual boy. *Behavior Research & Therapy*, 1977, *15*, 177–180.

138. Rekers, G. A., & Varni, J. Self-regulation of gender-role behaviors: A case study. *Journal of Behavior Therapy & Experimental Psychiatry*, 1977, *8*, 427–432.

139. Rekers, G. A., Willis, T. J., Yates, C. E., Rosen, A. C., & Low, B. P. Assessment of childhood gender behavior change. *Journal of Child Psychology & Psychiatry*, 1977, *18*, 53–65.

140. Rekers, G. A., & Yates, C. E. Sex-typed play in feminoid boys versus normal boys and girls. *Journal of Abnormal Child Psychology*, 1976, *4*(1), 1–8.

141. Rekers, G. A., Yates, C. E., Willis, T. J., Rosen, A. C., & Taubman, M. Childhood gender identity change: Operant control over sex-typed play and mannerisms. *Journal of Behavior Therapy & Experimental Psychiatry*, 1976, *7*, 51–57.

142. *Report of the Commission on Obscenity and Pornography.* Washington, D.C., U.S. Government Printing Office, 1979.

143. Rosen, A. Brief report of MMPI characteristics of sexual deviation. *Psychological Reports*, 1974, *35*, 73–74.

144. Rosen, R. C., & Kople, S. A. Penile plethysmography and biofeedback in the treatment of a transvestite-exhibitionist. *Journal of Consulting & Clinical Psychology*, 1977, *45*(5), 908–916.

145. Rosen, A. C., & Rehm, L. P. Long term follow-up in two cases of transvestism treated with aversion therapy. *Journal of Behavior Therapy & Experimental Psychiatry*, 1977, *8*, 295–300.

146. Rosen, A., Rekers, G., & Friar, L. Theoretical and diagnostic issues in child gender disturbances. *Journal of Sex Research*, 1977, *13*(2), 89–103.

147. Serber, M. Shame aversion therapy. *Journal of Behavior Therapy and Experimental Psychiatry*, 1970, *1*, 213–215.

148. Spengler, A. Manifest sadomasochism of males: results of an empirical study. *Archives of Sexual Behavior*, 1977, *6*(6), 441–456.

149. Spensley, J., & Barter, J. T. The adolescent transvestite on a psychiatric service: Family patterns. *Archives of Sexual Behavior*, 1971, *1*(4), 347–356.

150. Starka, I., Sipova, I., & Hynie, J. Plasma testosterone in male transsexuals and homosexuals. *Journal of Sex Research*, 1975, *11*(2), 134–138.

151. Steiner, E. W., Bernstein, S., & Muir, C. *Gender identity: New perspectives and outcome in a decade of change.* Paper presented at the Annual Meeting of the Canadian Psychiatric Association, Vancouver, 1979.

152. Steiner, E. W., Satterberg, J., & Muir, C. Flight into feminity: The male menopause? *Canadian Journal of Psychiatry*, 1978, *23*, 405–410.

153. Steiner, E. W., Zajac, A., & Mohr, J. A gender identity project: The organization of a multi-disciplinary study. *Canadian Psychiatric Association Journal*, 1974, *19*, 7–12.

154. Stinson, B. A study of twelve applicants for transsexual surgery. *The Ohio State Medical Journal*, 1972, *68*, 245–249.

155. Stoller, R. J. The term "transvestism". *Archives of General Psychiatry*, 1971, *24*, 230–237.

156. Stoller, R. J. Male transsexualism: uneasiness. *American Journal of Psychiatry*, 1973, *130*(5), 536–539.

157. Stoller, R. J. *The transsexual experiment*. London: The Hogarth Press, 1975.

158. Stoller, R. J., & Newman, L. E. The bisexual identity of transsexuals: Two case examples. *Archives of Sexual Behavior*, 1971, *1*(1), 17–28.

159. Strzyzewsky, J., & Zierhoffer, M. Aversion therapy in a case of fetishism with transvestitic component. *The Journal of Sex Research*, 1967, *3*(2), 163–167.

160. Symmers, W. Carcinoma of breast in transsexual individuals after surgical and hormonal interference with the primary and secondary sex characteristics. *British Medical Journal*, 1968, *2*, 83–85.

161. Taylor, A., & McLachlan, D. Clinical and psychological observations on transvestism. *New Zealand Medical Journal*, 1962, *61*, 496–506.

162. Taylor, A., & McLachlan, D. Transvestism and psychosexual identification. *New Zealand Medical Journal*, 1964, *63*, 369–373.

163. Tsushima, W. T., & Wedding, D. MMPI results of male candidates for transsexual surgery. *Journal of Personality Assessment*, 1979, *43*(4), 385–387.

164. Walinder, J. Transvestism, definition and evidence in favor of occasional derivation from cerebral dysfunction. *International Journal of Neuropsychiatry*, 1965, *1*, 567–573.

165. Walinder, J., Lundstrom, B., & Thuwe, I. Prognositc factors in the assessment of male transsexuals for sex reassignment. *British Journal of Psychiatry*, 1978, *132*, 16–20.

166. Weitzman, E. L., Shamoian, C. A., & Golosow, N. Family dynamics in male transsexualism. *Psychosomatic Medicine*, 1971, *33*(4), 289–299.

167. Whetton, C., & Swindells, T. A factor analysis of the Bem sex-role inventory. *Journal of Clinical Psychology*, 1977, *33*(1), 130–133.

168. Whitam, F. Childhood indicators of male homosexuality. *Archives of Sexual Behavior*, 1977, *6*(2), 89–96.

169. Whitam, F. The prehomosexual male child in three societies: the United States, Guatemala, Brazil. *Archives of Sexual Behavior*, 1980, *9*(2), 87–99.

170. Wise, T., & Meyer, J. The border area between transvestism and gender dysphoria: transvestite applicants for sex reassignment. *Archives of Sexual Behavior*, 1980, *9*(4), 327–342.

171. Wollman, L. Surgery for the transsexual. *The Journal of Sex Research*, 1967, *3*(2), 145–147.

172. Yalom, I. D., & Yalom, M. Ernest Hemingway—A psychiatric view. *Archives of General Psychiatry*, 1971, *24*, 485–494.

173. Zucker, K., Doering, R., Bradley, S., & Finegan, J. Sex-typed play in gender-disturbed children; a comparison to sibling and psychiatric controls. *Archives of Sexual Behavior*, 1982, in press.

174. Zuger, B. Effeminate behavior present in boys from childhood: Ten additional years of follow-up. *Comprehensive Psychiatry*, 1978, *19*(4), 363–369.

7 Fetishism

INTRODUCTION

Fetishism is an orgasmic preference for, or an inordinate and persistent sexual arousal to, inanimate objects or parts of the body. Often the fetishes are related to the human body, for example, to female or male clothing, although other objects have been described. An outstanding feature in the study of fetishism is the number of attempts that have been made to classify the fetishes. Krafft-Ebing (in Raymond [39]) divided the fetishes into parts of the female body, her clothing, special materials and animales. Epstein[15] noted that objects with certain surface characteristics such as glistening (wetness or rubber), metallic shining, leathery, silky, and velvety or those objects with unusual accentuation of shape such as high heels; often serve as fetishes. Balint[3] claimed that many fetishes are objects which can serve as receptacles in the fetishist's acts, for example, shoes, corsets, and so forth, and even in one case the hollow part of an artificial leg was used. The receptacle of course symbolizes the vagina and the womb so the use of the penis in contact with these symbols is understandable.

Gebhard[18] has devised a typology of fetishes. They are either inanimate objects or some physical attribute of a person (partialism). One may be partial to redheads for example and find them more erotic than persons with other colors of hair. The degree of arousal differs between individuals from mild to strong and for some men it is strong and the stimulus is essential. Thus one may like redheads but he can react to other females or males as well. However if one could *only* react to redheads, this would be a necessary fetish according to Gebhard. We are all fetishists in this sense since we display some idiosyncratic sexual arousal to a wide range of stimuli. Normal heterosexual men usually show a marked reaction to the pubic area of the female, and somewhat less reactions to the breasts and rear end[17]. One could say these are socially acceptable fetishes. However, in so doing, the term fetish becomes so broad as to be useless. Therefore arousal to body parts must be normatively defined, that is, the arousal must be contrasted with the usual pattern of sexual arousal in a community. Consider *Mr. A* who had a foot fetish.

He was a married man who stated that he liked everything about women but especially their feet. He tended to classify people according to the shoes they wore, their cleanliness of their feet and the way they moved their feet when seated or walking. He noted:

> *Mr. A:* "People's feet differ as much as their faces and there are beautiful feet and ugly feet. Some people move with grace and rhythm and others are awkward or do not care how they move. I like beautiful feet just like some men like beautiful breasts".

Phallometric testing showed he reacted most to feet; far above any other body part including the pubic area of the female. This is atypical since men usually react most to the pubic area and the feet are almost neutral, that is, have very little or no erotic valence. Only the unusual pattern of arousal like *Mr. A's* is discussed here as a "partialism" fetish. Inordinate arousal to in-animate objects is usually better definable clinically. The objects themselves may be so overvalued it is difficult to connect them to people.

Mr. B, for example, was sexually excited by stealing female panties, usually from clothes lines. He would rub them against his penis while he masturbated. He did not care to whom they belonged but only that they were worn. While they are obviously associated with females, the object itself seems to override any value the female body might have for this man. He was single and apparently not interested in women. In fact arousal to the female in the panties may have been more difficult for him than to the fetish alone.

Gebhard subtyped inanimate fetishes into media and form. Media means substances and their texture like leather and rubber while form defines the shape of the object, like high heel shoes and girdles. The media fetishes may be soft such as lingerie or hard like metal or leather. According to Gebhard, the sadomasochist is often involved in a hard media fetish or form fetish such as constricting garments, shoes or boots. This provides a criterion to distinguish sadomasochism and pure fetishism.

The fetishes are usually considered to be symbolic of loved or longed for individuals. Thus parts of the body may be similar to those of mother or an object may be associated with her; for example, her apron or shoes or pan-ties. For some writers, the fetish need not be sexual but can be any object with excessive personal value. Amulets or fertility idols are often referred to as fetishes. The delusions of psychotic patients have an obsessive quality to them and certain objects may be greatly overvalued. These delusional activities and/or objects have also been described as fetishes, although their sexual qualities may be absent or only symbolic[38]. Such meanings make our task of understanding sexual fetishism so broad that progress is difficult. Unless the fetish object has the capacity to arouse the male to orgasm, it will be excluded from consideration in this discussion.

Theories

Castration and separation anxieties.   The most natural question to ask about fetishism is why an inanimate object becomes so important that it displaces the usual sexual stimuli in attractiveness. Freud[16] claimed that the fetish was a substitute for the imagined female penis, particularly that of the mother. The fetishist denies the reality of the world and refuses to recognize that women have no penis. This is his solution to a fear of being castrated. Bak[2] stated that the object chosen symbolizes the penis and it may be the object from the last moment in which the woman could still be regarded as having a penis. Thus an apron or corset would serve this purpose because when they are removed, the vagina may be evident.

The fetish develops in the prephallic stage when the child shows inordinate separation anxiety from the mother. The anxiety results in increased clinging to her either totally or to a substitute part of her. The child reaches out to her constantly which leaves him with eroticized hands that are so important in the fetishist's desire to touch.

Mr. C described the development of his fetish in terms that support this theory. He first recalls following his mother to the laundry room and playing with the clothes as she took them from the clothes dryer. He liked the soft and warm feeling of her panties and rubbed them against his skin. They made him feel good and excited at the same time. Later he used to take them to the privacy of his room and masturbate, all the time concentrating on the soft texture of her panties.

Fixation in pregenital stages is also evidenced by anal eroticism and by an inordinate interest in smelling. Some writers have noted an association of coprophilia (lit. love of feces) with fetishism as support for this theory. Balint[3] agreed that the fetish should have a smell which suregly signifies feces but behind this symbol is the much strongly repressed mother's vagina which he noted, also smells.

When the fetishist identifies with his penisless mother, he also wishes to give up his own penis which creates conflict for him. He alternately identifies with a phallic and penisless mother so his "ego is split." The fetish is his defense and compromise. Fetishism, transvestism and homosexuality are different phases of this compromise so one may expect a frequent association or overlap of the three.

Mr. E illustrates this theory. He recalled that the fetish he had for jeans first developed at three or four years of age. He later reenacted the following primal scene in masturbation fantasies. His mother wanted to wash his jeans but he wanted to keep them on. He was adamant that he would keep them on and he feared she would wash the life out of them. Just as she pulled the jeans from him and threw them into the wash, he would climax. While the patient did not make a connection of "jeans" and "genes", he did specify that it was important that the clothes had been worn by someone to increase their sexual arousal value to him. "Washing the life out of them was also exciting". This could be viewed as castration anxiety since part of the life in his penis would be destroyed. Later, as a teenager, he would secretly use boy's jeans for masturbation. He experienced some erotic attraction to young boys as well who appeared to represent himself in a narcissistic identification.

According to Freud, if the fetish is removed, overt homosexuality might emerge, and Stekel said it would in any case[39]. The parallel of fetishism to homosexuality also suggests that feminine gender identity may be as important in the former as in the latter. Some theorists claim the fetishist identifies with an object which impairs full masculine gender identity[14] and others note a fusion of male and female[41] or an increased tendency to feminine identification[36]. Caution must be advised in acceptance of these theories because fetishism is poorly delineated and as in many other sexual anomalies, no attempt is made to determine orgasmic preferences or empirically validate claims. Many transsexuals and transvestites are considered to be fetishists. However, existing studies, as poor as they are, indicate that less than half of transsexual men can be called fetishists. Transvestites may have a fetish for female clothes but this has yet to be established as fact. They are sexually aroused while dressed as women but we do not know if the clothes or being a woman or some other fantasy is important in their anomaly (See Chapter 6).

Fetishism as a conditioned response.   Behavior theorists have proposed two possible explanations of fetishism. First it may be developed by simple conditioning. Binet first defined fetishism as a sexual idolatry and indicated the fetishist had a general nervous hyperasthesia, which is an unusual capacity for forming conditioned responses[39]. The fetish develops by accidental conditioning. Ellis (in Raymond [39]) also later described fetishists as sensitive, nervous, timid and precocious but the origin of their behavior was some sexually emotional episode in early life. Rachman[37] suggested that any stimulus could be eroticized by association with an unconditioned erotic stimulus. Thus by pairing gloves or boots with attractive females, the former can take on an erotic valence. This is classical conditioning described in Chapter 3. Since anything can become a fetish by accidental association, one need not look for special classes of objects as fetishes. Presumably the fetish can be unlearned in the same fashion it is acquired.

In a similar vein, masturbation fantasies may stamp in unusual sexual behavior via operant conditioning. Marquis[31] suggested that fantasies are important in learning and unlearning sexual behavior. One may ask, however, why the particular fantasy is chosen in the first place, for example, why a wet shoe instead of making love to a woman.

Fetishism as a sadistic act.   Karpmann[22][23] and others[36][41] considered fetishism to be sadistic. It is frequently associated with kleptomania, a compulsion to steal[23]. The detachment of the object from the lover ensures chastity to the fetishist lover. This serves as a self imposed punishment for his cruel fantasies and attitudes. He wants to depreciate his sex partner and to flee from him/her at the same time. Thus we see again contradictory explanations of the behavior—a desire to fuse with the loved one and a desire to injure and flee. Balint[3] described fetishism as an undisturbed possession of a love object. The fetish is lifeless and usually can easily be away from its owner, for example, a garment. This ensures that the loved one will not criticize or abandon him or in other ways interfere with the enjoyment of his sexual release.

Epstein[14][15] has noted the power of objects with wet or glistening surfaces to evoke erection and ejaculation in a chimpanzee and erection in a baboon. However, he postulates that even in these animals, the surface quality of objects may be related to primitive body parts or markings. The objects are symbols by which one identifies with the owner of the object or incorporates him/her.

Brain pathology.   Finally, fetishism has been linked to organic problems, in particular, to malfunctions in the temporal lobe of the brain. The unusual attraction to objects found in fetishism and transvestism may reflect a problem in the "sex centres" of the brain test measured at present by electroencephalogram (EEG) or brain scans (e.g. the CT-scan).

Epstein[14] thought that the development of brain pathology alters the neural system so that fetishistic behavior can make its appearance. He noted that the fetish object evokes a stereotyped discharge in the brain analogous to the reflexive discharge of epilepsy. He related it to a conditioned reaction but it sounds much like the stereotyped behavior characteristic of imprinting in animals. In the latter, a characteristic behavior, such as a baby bird following its mother, occurs with great persistence and intensity early in life. This learning phenomenon appears to be irreversible later and may have wide ranging influence including an effect on sexual behavior. Epstein even talked of "release phenomenon" such as fetish associations or memories which trigger the act much as the "releaser stimulus" triggers instinctive behavior including imprinting in animals. Blumer[6] and Kolarsky and his associates[24] thought that the sexual, aggressive and paroxysmal (motor discharge) behavior of seizures in epileptics were related. They suggested that a brain lesion needs to be present since early childhood to be a significant causal factor in development of sexual anomalies.

The Experimental Evidence

Fetishists are so rare in clinical settings that even case study data is hard to obtain. Curran[11] found only five cases of fetishism as a primary problem in a sample of 4,000 patients and none were facing criminal charges.

There is not a thorough descriptive study available but there are three controlled clinical analog studies using penile measurement that offer some answer to the question whether fetishism is acquired as a conditioned response and whether any stimulus can have inordinate erotic valence.

Fetishism as a conditioned response. Rachman[37] first tested these hypotheses in an experimental study of classical conditioning. He used pictures of boots as conditioning stimuli and pictures of females as unconditioned stimuli for normal men. By repeated pairing of the two, the boot should become arousing in itself. This in fact happened supporting the theory.

In a second study, McConaghy[33] used a similar paradigm pairing pictures of red circles and nude females for heterosexuals and green triangles with nude men for homosexuals. Once again, conditioning occurred but the effects in both studies were small. Moreover some stimuli used may have had prior sexual association value which could explain the small effects reported.

In a third study, my colleague Michael Martin and I[28] varied the erotic valence of the unconditioned stimulus so there were two levels of arousal potential. Random polygons with no association value were used as conditioning stimuli. Pictures of nude females were used as unconditioned stimuli and the individuals sorted them into three arousal levels: none, moderate and strong. The mild and strong ones were used for the conditioning experiment. The strong stimuli in fact elicited significantly greater levels of penile tumescence than the moderate ones in the heterosexual volunteers, as expected. However the conditioning stimuli did not differ when they should have. A stronger unconditioned stimulus should produce a stronger conditioned response. Possibly both sets of erotic slides were not sufficiently arousing to have the desired effect.

In a further experiment a more powerful unconditioned stimulus, erotic movies, were used. However results were similar. Overall the results of the two studies showed the conditioning stimulus was not affected by the erotic valence of the unconditioned stimulus as it should have been. The "conditioned reactions" only occurred about half the time and of a magnitude close to random variations about baseline penile volume. The conditioned reactions were 25 times smaller than the stronger unconditioned erotic movie stimuli. In fact the results were so weak we did not think they provided a satisfactory explanation of the sexual learning phenomena nor could they be the basis of a useful treatment procedure. In effect, the conditioned reaction to the fetish must always be smaller than the unconditioned reaction to the female if this were the case. However, we define fetishists as having larger reactions to objects than to females. Some other principle must be operative.

Fetishism, transvestism and homosexuality.   One other question has been examined empirically, the association of fetishism, transvestism and homosexuality (See Chapter 6). Unfortunately, transvestites have been asked the ambiguous question "Do you masturbate while crossdressed?" (cf. [8]). In a study by Bentler[5], about half of gynephilic transsexuals did so whereas about a quarter of androphilic transsexuals did. However, we do not know if the garments themselves, the fantasy life or other behavior while crossdressed were erotic. Fetishism seems to bear a chance relationship to crossdressing and homosexuality. However, more information is clearly needed (Chapter 6).

Fetishism and sadism.   Snow and Bluestone[42] have reported three cases in which they linked fetishism and homicidal impulses. They argued that the fetish is a defense against the feeling that a live female will injure him and against his own impulse to injure or kill. However, only one of their three cases could be considered a fetishist and even he was a voyeur as well. The first case involved rape, transvestism and obscene calls and the patient was aware of his impulses to overpower women. He raped and murdered an elderly woman. The second case was a voyeur fetishist who was aroused by leather gloves which he would steal by breaking and entering. He also drove around in search of women in leather gloves. He would watch them from a distance and masturbate. It was during one of the break and enter episodes that he killed an older woman alone in her home at that time. It is not clear that the murder was sexualized or due to panic at being surprised and caught engaging in a criminal act while on parole. The third case involved a toucheur who impersonated a physician and fondled the bare breasts of a female patient in a waiting room. No violence was evident in this schizophrenic man but he requested a psychiatric examination since he feared he would commit mass murder of women. He had married eight times but could not consumate the marriages since he was orgasmic only by fondling, kissing and sucking female breasts. One might wonder if he suffers from premature ejaculation but sufficient detail was not provided to know.

Since rape and other sexual aggression such as toucheurism are more clearly associated with violence toward women (See Chapter 12), it seems unnecessary to find an explanation of the homicidal impulses of Snow and Bluestone's cases in fetishism. The general criminality of one patient particularly offers an alternative and perhaps better explanation of violence than fetishism does. There seems little convincing evidence to date that fetishism per se is associated with violence.

Brain pathology. Only one other theory has any supporting empirical data, the association of temporal lobe brain dysfunction and fetishism. Most are case studies[6] [13] [14] [15] [21] [25]. In most reports, the sexual behavior was inadequately assessed. A patient, described by Mitchell[35], would commence an epileptic fit at the sight of a safety pin. Orgasm or even erection is not described in connection with the safety pin but he received "thought satisfaction" from it. His seizures and his "fetish" were relieved by brain surgery, a temporal lobectomy. Epstein[14] presented data on twelve cases. Of these, eight had abnormal brain tracings (EEGs), two had seizures and four showed evidence of brain disease. These results suggest an important link of fetishism and temporal lobe damage in the brain. Kolarsky and his colleagues[24] in Czechoslovakia have conducted the best study to date on the question of brain pathology and sexual anomalies. From 115 men who had been diagnosed as epileptic from a neurological examination including an electroencephalogram (EEG), 86 (75%) volunteered for the study. The research participants were screened by judges for sexual anomalies and a selected few were also administered the phallometric test of erotic preference. They found a wide range of sexual anomalies in 19 men (22%). Only 58% of them had been diagnosed previously as sexually anomalous. Hyposexuality was prominent but transvestism and fetishism occurred in a minority of cases. The authors noted that the majority of these cases showed temporal lobe lesions which developed before 3 years of age. This suggests that brain pathology be carefully examined in conjunction with sexual anomalies.

It would be premature to conclude that brain dysfunction caused fetishism or any other sexual anomaly since we know temporal lobe damage is not *always* associated with fetishism. It would be important to examine a large number of fetishists for the incidence of brain pathology. Possibly all fetishists have brain pathology and because of their rarity we must study them rather than all temporal lobe disorders. One diagnostic feature seems important: A very early onset of fetishism may be organic in origin since most sexually anomalous behavior is only prominent about the time of puberty[20].

The Fetishist's Stimulus Response Matrix

In the case of fetishism we are faced with an unknown. It is very rare in pure form. It has been associated with masochism, sadism, transvestism, coprophilia and homosexuality. Most theories are untested (Table 7.1) and since there are so few fetishists seen in clinics, the theories may remain untested.

TABLE 7.1
Summary of Evidence for Theories of Fetishism

Theory	Experimental Evidence
1. Castration Anxiety	Untested
2. A conditional reaction: anything can serve as a fetish	Three supportive analog studies. Effect is very weak and cannot explain inordinate arousal value of objects.
3. Fetishism is associated with homosexuality and transvestism	Perhaps a chance relationship. The question has not been adequately researched.
4. It is a sadistic act	No convincing evidence.
5. Brain Pathology	Positive relationship, especially if there is temporal lobe damage early in life. More research needed.

My own intuitions with a handful of cases is that the fantasy life surrounding the fetish object is more important than the surface or physical qualities of the objects. Feelings of inadequacy or inferiority have also been prominent. Brain pathology may also be important but it needs adequate research.

TREATMENT

A full range of treatments has been used in case studies. No group descriptive studies or controlled group studies have been reported.

Behavior Therapy

Chemical aversion therapy has been reported in a few cases. The earliest was Raymond's[39] report of a 33 year old married patient treated with aversive conditioning. The patient had masturbated to fantasies of handbags and babycarriages. This later escalated into damaging the carriages with his motorcycle or by scratching them with his hands. He was facing several charges because of his malicious damage. The attacks, however, were not associated with orgasm. The anomaly was first manifested when he was sailing his boat as a boy in the park and it accidentally struck a baby carriage. He was impressed by the feminine consternation shown at the time. As a boy he had been sexually aroused by his sister's handbag. He found during psychoanalysis that the objects were "sexual containers" for him but he continued to act out after this insight.

Chemical aversion therapy was employed and emetine hydrochloride with apomorphine served to induce nausea. Just as the nausea attack developed, he was presented handbags, carriages and colored illustrations of these. By repeated pairing, the fetishes should take on aversive qualities and the frequency of the behavior decline. This procedure was repeated every two hours at first and later given irregularly. The patient wrote an account of his behavior and how it was ruining his life. He improved with treatment and was given a booster session at six months although he said he did not need it. After 19 months, he was still doing well and sex relations with his wife had improved. He did not require fetish fantasies to be aroused during intercourse. He had not been in trouble with the law although it seems he was rarely reported or apprehended for his behavior in any case.

Raymond and O'Keefe[40] later used the same procedure successfully in a more questionable case of a "pin up" fetish. The patient was a 23 year old married man who collected pictures of nude or scantily dressed females which he hid about the house. The pictures upset his wife as they had upset his rather puritanical mother. He claimed that intercourse was satisfactory but his wife said he did it just for the sake of it without feeling. Often he was too tired or lazy to do it and it usually depended on her initiative.

In treatment, pictures of nude females were presented just before nausea ensued from apomorphine injections. Subsequently he lost interest in the pin up pictures but increased the frequency of intercourse with his wife. After 22 months the gains were maintained. However, the results seem illogical. His interest in nude females should be reduced because of treatment and therefore his interest in his wife should also decline. Appropriate heterosexual stimuli were punished and yet the frequency of intercourse increased. According to learning theory, this should not happen. Moreover, one might wonder why he lacked interest in his wife but not other women.

Often marital difficulties are reflected in reduced frequency of intercourse. Therapy should have explored this more fully. The existence of a fetish is also questionable since he appeared to enjoy the body characteristics of attractive females that men usually do.

Cooper[10] treated an impotent transvestite whom he considered to be a fetishist. Chemical aversion was used but stress to the right ventricle of the patient's heart was noted and it required 4 weeks of treatment. This is a very real danger of chemical aversion and its use today is rarer. The patient was later treated by reciprocal inhibition therapy (Chapter 3) for his impotence with his wife but the procedure was atypical. The wife was told about the nature of reciprocal inhibition theory and she agreed to cooperate. The patient was to lie in bed beside his wife naked with no intention of doing anything sexual. He found that he would relax and eventually have coitus. After nine months, the couple were having intercourse about once a week. He was not crossdressing although his conditioned aversion to it had diminished. There are further suggestions that treatment was unsuccessful.

The patient hinted to the therapist that sexual arousal to the clothes was returning. The frequency of intercourse also seems rather low for a 25 year old newly wed male. A further hint that his erotic preference was unchanged was that "his failure in intercourse was usually followed by practicing his abnormal behavior" which the author considered to be both a sexual outlet and to reduce anxiety. The patient had a loss of libido for 3 weeks after treatment which is characteristic of aversion therapy cases. It is noteworthy that the lack of interest in the wife is labeled impotence. If this principle is followed every sexual anomaly in which there is not manifest interest in coitus with a mature female could be considered impotence. The term should be reserved for inability to perform sexually with a preferred sex object (See Chapter 15).

Clark[9] used a similar chemical aversion therapy to treat a 29-year-old married man who was labeled a fetishist. He masturbated while wearing various female garments but especially a girdle and stockings. Eventually he wore the clothes all the time during the day to help him relax and the label gynephilic transsexual would seem more appropriate then fetishist.

Photographs of his most sexually stimulating garments were used as conditioning stimuli and Raymond's[39] earlier procedures were copied. After three months, he was symptom free and enjoying a normal sex life. The patient occasionally thought wistfully of his former pleasures but did not want to wear the girdle. It is unfortunate that follow up was not longer because it is this type of patient which Marks and Gelder (Chapter 6) found least likely to change in their series of transvestitic and transsexual cases. Aversion therapy can reduce all sexual desire for a brief period but when it returns, the old preferences do as well. A case by Kusher[27] illustrates this problem.

Electrical aversion therapy.   He treated a 33-year-old man who had a 20 year history of masturbation while wearing stolen female panties. Instead of chemical aversion, the more exactly timed and controllable faradic aversion therapy was used. One may note this is another case of transvestism and possibly transsexualism but it was labeled fetishism.

The conditioning stimuli were pictures of women wearing panties which were followed by the unconditioned stimulus, electric shock. The shock level was set so the patient found it so uncomfortable, he wanted it stopped. In addition to seeing pictures, he was instructed to handle panties and to imagine himself wearing them. After 41 sessions, he said he was no longer troubled by the "fetish" but a month later, it spontaneously recovered. The patient likely confused his lack of sexual interest with lack of interest in the "fetish." When he came to the clinic for a booster session two days later, he said he was not having urges. Nevertheless, two booster sessions of the faradic conditioning were used. Then his "impotence" was dealt with by reciprocal inhibition therapy. He was told his unsatisfactory heterosexual life was due to his high anxiety in heterosocial situations.

This treatment resulted in quick improvement and gains were maintained after 19 months. He married, has a family and only has fleeting thoughts of the "fetish." Occasionally, when either fatigued or sexually unexcited by his wife, he resorted to fetish fantasies to attain climax during intercourse. It would seem the "fetish" was still an integral part of his sexual life but he had made a heterosexual adaptation.

Thorpe and his colleagues[43] used faradic aversion therapy with anxiety relief in the treatment of a 32-year-old motorcycle fetishist. He derived erotic satisfaction from stealing motorcycles and driving them away at high speed, having an erection and emission in the processs. The patient was described as ignorant of sexual matters and had a history of blacking out when the topic of female genitalia was discussed or when he read sexual material. This suggests possible brain pathology which has been considered important in fetishism. He was also apparently homosexual although no further details are described. The conditioning stimuli were sexual words related to the anomaly and they were followed by electric shock. The relief stimuli after shock were words relating to socially acceptable sexual behavior. The patient improved and started losing his interest in motorcycles. Homosexual fantasies decreased and concurrently heterosexual behavior increased. Treatment was in progress and incomplete when reported. However the procedure should be used with caution since anxiety relief conditioning reduces the effectiveness of aversive conditioning (See Chapter 3).

A few other patients have been treated with aversive conditioning either with the classical variety in which the fetish object is paired with shock or with the operant variety in which sexual arousal response are shocked. The main problem with these studies in general is that it is usually not clear exactly what the anomaly is. The "fetish" may be associated with cross-dressing in which case it may more appropriately be labeled transvestism and even transsexualism since orgasm is not always associated with the act of crossdressing[4 29 30 34] and feminine gender identity may be evident. It may even be related to masochism[30]. Often one cannot tell what is happening. Treatment usually seems unsuccessful and follow-up is short. Most reports have no assessment of erotic preferences or penile measurement during treatment to indicate change. Patients frequently have said they reverted to their fetish behavior during times of stress or "think of it now and then", or only use it when having intercourse with their wives. If they are satisfied with that outcome, the therapist should not be. The anomalous sexual preference has not been altered substantially after subjecting patients to pain and to the risk of physical injury.

One of the dangers in mislabeling fetishism is that fetish-like behavior can be part of more serious sadistic behavior and rape. Kolvin[25] describes a case of fetishism which I would be inclined to call toucheurism, if anything. The 14-year-old mentally dull boy faced three charges of indecent assault during which he would "feel compelled" to run after women in skirts and put his hand up under her clothes. It is not clear if this behavior was associated with orgasm at anytime even later during possible fantasies. It is uncertain what the conditioning stimuli were but covert sensitization appears to have been used. The sexual fantasies were followed by aversive images of falling which the patient had described currently in his unpleasant dreams. There were seven sessions in three weeks. He improved and maintained gains after 17 months. Thirteen months after treatment he had accused a neighbor's wife of an illicit affair. The author suggested that this may be a different manifestation of a sexual problem and the case merits prolonged follow-up. Since the patient had a criminal record for theft and since there were other posssible unreported indecent assaults, he has features in common with rapists and sexually assaultive men noted in Chapter 12. It would seem important to distinguish solitary innocuous fetishistic acts from aggressive interpersonal acts like those shown by this boy since he may be a danger to the community at large.

Multiple treatment methods.   Marshall[32] has criticized early attempts to treat fetishism as generally simplistic. He described fetishism as complex and he suggested that a multifaceted approach to the problem was necessary. His patient was a 21-year-old university student who engaged in three main fetishistic related behaviors: physical contact with trousers while masturbating, fetish fantasies which occurred during and apart from masturbation, and overt behavior aimed at procuring trousers for masturbation.

Penile circumference was used to measure arousal to the fetish materials, to heterosexual slides and to neutral materials. Electrical aversion therapy was paired with thought stopping. The patient brought some of the trousers with him and was shocked while reaching for them, touching them, feeling, smelling and placing them against his body. In addition, the patient was also told after a number of faradic trials, "Stop that!" along with the shock and eventually the command was given on its own. Finally the command alone was given on 75% of the trials and shock alone on 25%. In a three week period, over 1,000 trials were given. Just after treatment the patient still had 41% of full erection to the fetish materials, significantly more than he did to neutral stimuli. Then orgasmic reconditioning was initiated. The patient was given materials describing heterosexual activities along with pictures. He was to use this during masturbation but could use the fetish to be aroused initially. Then the heterosexual material occupied more of the masturbation time, displacing the fetish until finally the total time including climax only involved heterosexual fantasies. This was used for four weeks and at this time the heterosexual materials produced as much erection as the fetish did, about 45% full erection. In a third treatment, the patient carried smelling salts with him so that every time he began to have a fetishistic fantasy, he would inhale the salts. He used them on 90% of appropriate occasions but after two weeks, he continued to have fantasies even though the penile measurement showed only 18% arousal to the fetish and 56% to heterosexual materials. The patient was not cured but was considered to be improving all the time. His only difficulty was in maintaining heterosexual fantasies during masturbation in the period between initiation and ejaculation.

The behavior therapies have had mixed success with fetishism. Since only a few uncontrolled case studies have been reported with limited follow-up, the overall impression of outcome is uncertainty. A significant problem in evaluating treatment is that fetishism has commonly been misdiagnosed. A satisfactory evaluation of these techniques must await further research.

Hypnosis has been used by Glick[19] in the treatment of a "clothing fetishist" who may better be labeled a transvestite. He was attracted to a range of female clothes and he masturbated when in contact with them. It is not clear whether he put them on himself. Glick used a combination of behavior therapy and hypnosis which highlights their similarities. The patient was first instructed under hypnosis to become nauseated when the therapist clapped his hands. Then he visualized erotic scenes about clothes but they were tainted with aversive images from the start. The slip or panties in his images would be stained with urine or covered with feces. Thus the conditioning stimulus was aversive and not neutral or positive in its valence. Then in a classical conditioning procedure, the therapist clapped to induce nausea. The author advised against using the procedure with psychotic patients but did not say why. He also noted the timing between conditioning stimulus and aversive unconditioned nausea was "at best a crude affair" which is the same problem with the imprecise chemical aversion therapy. Since all stimuli in hypnosis are in the patient's head, one has to wonder how well timed anything is or whether the parallel of hypnosis and classical conditioning is only a superficial and inaccurate similarity. In any case, after six sessions, the patient showed "marked improvement" which was maintained after nine months. It is not clear, however, that the "fetish" was gone.

Psychotherapy

The few cases of fetishism treated by psychoanalysis illustrate Freud's theory that the patient identifies the fetish with the "female penis" and thus denies castration. Kronengold and Sterba[26] reported two cases in which analysis was incomplete but sufficient to change the fetish. In the first case, a 30-year-old man stole rubber aprons and wrapped them about his nude body like a diaper and in so doing climaxed. He traced this interest to seeing his baby foster sister changed on a rubber sheet when he was only four years old. Soon after, the smell of rubber excited him and he noticed pleasurable sexual sensations when he smelled or touched the rubber. At this age, he also had ample opportunity to notice that his sister had no penis. Later, he found that the painted velum loincloth on statues of Christ reminded him of rubber and it too became sexual. The fetish was interpreted as follows: When he stole the rubber apron from women, it symbolized the man robbing the woman of her penis. He masochistically identifies with the woman by placing the apron over his own penis. So he then represents the phallic woman and at the same time she is sadistically robbed of her penis, the apron. The Christ in the loincloth also symbolized the female being martyred.

In the second case, masochism was more evident than fetishism. The 24-year-old patient tied his ankles and passed the ropes over his penis and often bound his arms and hands as well. By stretching his legs, he exerted pressure on his penis via the rope and climaxed. Usually there were welts on his body. He seemed to be homosexual and also enjoyed binding other men for sexual gratification. Although the rope may be seen as fetishistic and obviously serves as a phallic symbol, it was more evidently instrumental to bondage. These two cases were incomplete and the outcome is uncertain.

However, the dynamics were considered to be similar to transvestism and masochism. Our knowledge of these various anomalies is too primitive to draw such broad general conclusions.

Anonymous, Chambers and Janzen[1] presented an eclectic multiple therapy of a shoe fetishist. The case is particularly interesting because one author is the patient who comments on his feelings during treatment. He was a university student who stole women's shoes. He was seen in unspecified psychotherapy and also was given covert sensitization which he was to use on himself whenever the fetishistic urges arose. He would think of his fetish and then the aversive events related to being caught by the police, being charged, and so forth. Gestalt dialogues were also used. The patient in this technique has two chairs, one for himself and one for the part of him that wanted to steal the shoes. In the dialogue he switched chairs and offered arguments for and against maintaining his fetish. He found some of the psychotherapy difficult but he thought the aversion therapy was effective. The Gestalt dialogue let him know that the fetish side of him was not all wrong but needed satisfaction too. Psychotherapy had its period of resistance and the patient wanted to quit and/or feed the therapists false data. However, he subsequently realized that the line between normal and abnormal was a fine one and he started to improve from that point. It was assumed that heterosexual difficulties motivated the fetish. In the course of treatment, he started a series of relationships with women and his fetish ceased to be a motivating factor in his life. It should be noted he continued to have "abnormal" fantasies but he did not feel guilty about them anymore. The exact frequency of urges or fantasies is not reported nor is the duration of follow-up. However, the main purpose of the study was to scrutinize the therapist patient interaction so this information may have been considered incidental.

Woody[44] used both aversion therapy and psychotherapy in the treatment of two patients. The first was a heterosexual transsexual who displayed the unusual behavior of binding one leg when he crossdressed. Operant punishment was used as aversion therapy. He either crossdressed or imagined doing it and was shocked over 26 sessions whenever he indicated to the therapist that he was sexually aroused. He also underwent 12 sessions of unspecified psychotherapy during which he discussed many of his problems and attitudes. Woody believed the patient entered well into the therapeutic relationship and made excellent progress. At five month follow-up, he said he was no longer excited by the binding of the female leg but he still thought that he would like sex reassignment surgery.

The second patient had a fetish for rubber goods. He traced this interest to an incident when he was five years old. He had to wear rubber sleeves for eczematous arms at the time and during the following year, he saw his father engaging in sexual activities with both his mother and a female friend. He wrapped the rubber around himself for comfort. He received sexual pleasure from the rubber during childhood and later used them for masturbation. He also had 26 sessions of aversion therapy but only 11 of psychotherapy. He hoped treatment would fail because he was only there since his wife would divorce him otherwise. After four months, he had occasional fantasies of rubber but did not act on them. It seems the fetish was no longer a problem.

Woody found the two treatments he used were complementary in producing change. It should be noted that both patients appear to have retained important parts of their sexual behavior even after the short follow-up.

Collectively, the psychotherapy case reports of fetishism are among the most interesting and creative studies of sexual anomalies but they are also the poorest methodologically. In addition, they lack the extensive follow up characteristic of psychotherapy reports. This renders their general utility in treating fetishism uncertain.

Brain Surgery

Crossdressing and fetishism and other sexual anomalies have been associated with temporal lobe malfunctions of the brain, sometimes due to epilepsy or tumors[12][14][21][35]. However, the few case reports involving corrective brain surgery have poorly documented sexual history information. One is generally uncertain what has been treated, although the surgery usually eliminates the bizarre sexual behavior. The status of normal sexual outlets is not typically well described, if at all mentioned. The major problem with these studies is that the incidence of sexually anomalous men with temporal lobe epilepsy and vice versa is basically unknown. Blumer[6] examined 12 temporal lobe epileptic men which casts some light on the problem. More then half were hyposexual that is, sexual response or arousal occurred less than once a month and, in most, less than a year. This suggests epilepsy might be associated with sexual dysfunction but not especially with fetishism. When seizure activity decreased, there was a statistically significant improvement in sex drive. Only two of Blumer's cases displayed anomalous sexual behavior. Two with homosexual behavior prior to surgery failed to show it after[24]. It is difficult to know whether the change in sexual behavior was part of the general lethargy, withdrawal or emotional dulling noted in some cases of psychosurgery or reflected a change in erotic preference (See Breggen [7]). While reported cases are dramatic, it must be noted that at present there is no compelling association between brain pathology and fetishism. Nevertheless the question merits serious investigation by sex researchers in collaboration with neurologists. It would seem most important in the assessment and treatment of fetishists to rule out possible brain pathology.

Treatment of Choice

A choice is difficult to make when no systematic evidence exists to support any theory and when so few cases have been reported in the literature. In the handful of cases I have had the opportunity to treat, the fetish has been a powerful sexual behavior and no patient was truly anxious to give it up. There was in fact a cooperativeness and yet a paradoxical contrariness which is both a barrier to communication and a denial of the desire to change. The fetish appeared to be laden with symbolism which lends itself

TABLE 7.2
Summary of Treatment Effectiveness for Fetishism

Theory	Experimental Evidence
1. Aversion Therapy	Cases poorly defined but success rate seems comparable to other anomalies. Only case reports.
2. Multiple Treatments	Limited success.
3. Hypnosis	Apparently positive in a case report.
4. Psychotherapy	Multiple sexual anomalies treated. Positive results but needs better research.
5. Brain surgery	Positive when pathology linked to onset of fetishism behavior.

to psychoanalysis or other interpretative psychotherapy. In this sense, it seemed unique among the sexual anomalies although many writers have found symbolism in all sexually anomalous behavior. Rather than being an identification with the phallic woman, the behavior has appeared as a dissociation of sex from people, either out of anger or feelings of inferiority. In this sense, fetishism may be similar to transvestism in which the male plays both male and female parts in sex, thus being totally self satisfying and avoiding disappointment or failure. This may be one reason the two anomalies have been associated. However feminine gender identity appears to play an important role in transvestism while gender identity may be either impaired altogether or masculine in fetishists. Although transvestites have been labeled "fetishists", this hypothesis remains to be verified empirically with appropriate questions and phallometric testing. Research effort might be directed to documenting the erotic stimulus response profile of fetishists.

Therapy may be unnecessary when the fetishism is a solitary innocuous act. Such cases can be counseled to accept fetishism as an isolated aspect of their lives while appreciating their other nonsexual behaviors. This will increase their self esteem. All other treatment must be considered experimental.

BIBLIOGRAPHY

1. Anonymous, J., Chambers, W. M., Janzen, W. B. The eclectic and multiple therapy of a shoe fetishist. *American Journal of Psychotherapy,* 1976, *30*(2), 317–326.
2. Bak, R. C. Fetishism. *Journal of American Psychoanalytic Association,* 1953, *1,* 285–294.
3. Balint, M. A contribution on fetishism. *International Journal of Psychoanalysis,* 1935, *16,* 481–483.
4. Bancroft, J. *Deviant Sexual Behavior.* Oxford University Press, 1974.
5. Bentler, P. M. A typology of transsexualism: gender identity, theory and data. *Archives of Sexual Behavior,* 1976, *5*(6), 567–584.
6. Blumer, D. Changes of sexual behavior related to temporal lobe disorders in man. *Journal of Sex Research,* 1970, *6*(3), 1173–1180.
7. Breggen, P. Lobotomies: an alert. *American Journal of Psychiatry,* 1972, *129*(1), 97–98.
8. Buhrich, N., & McConaghy, N. Can fetishism occur in transsexuals? *Archives of Sexual Behavior,* 1977, *6*(3), 223–235.
9. Clark, D. F. Fetishism treated by negative conditioning. *British Journal of Psychiatry,* 1963, *109,* 404–407.
10. Cooper, A. J. A case of fetishism and impotence treated by behavior therapy. *British Journal of Psychiatry,* 1963, *109,* 649–652.
11. Curran, D. Sexual perversion. *Practitioner,* 1954, *172,* 440–445.
12. Davies, B., & Morgenstern, F. A case of cysticercosis, temporal lobe epilepsy and transvestism. *Journal of Neurological and Neurosurgical Psychiatry,* 1960, *23,* 247–249.
13. Entwhistle, C., & Sim, M. Tuberous sclerosis and fetishism. *British Medical Journal,* 1961, *2,* 1688–1689.
14. Epstein, A. W. Fetishism: A comprehensive view. In J. Masserman (Ed.), *Dynamics of deviant sexuality.* New York: Grune & Stratton, 1969, 81–87.
15. Epstein, A. W. The fetish object: Phylogenetic considerations. *Archives of Sexual Behavior,* 1975, *4*(3), 303–308.
16. Freud, S. *Collected papers* (Vol. 5). London: Hogarth Press, 1956.
17. Freund, K., McKnight, C. K., Langevin, R., & Cibiri, S. The female child as surrogate object. *Archives of Sexual Behavior,* 1972, *2*(2), 119–133.
18. Gebhard, P. Fetishism and sadomasochism. *Science and Psychoanalysis,* 1969, *15,* 71–80.
19. Glick, B. S. Aversive imagery therapy using hypnosis. *American Journal of Psychotherapy,* 1972, *26*(3), 432–436.
20. Hoenig, J., & Kenna, J. EEG abnormalities and transsexualism. *British Journal of Psychiatry,* 1979, *134,* 293–300.
21. Hunter, R., Logue, V., & McMenemy, W. H. Temporal lobe epilepsy supervening on longstanding transvestism and fetishism. A case report. *Epilepsia,* 1963, *4,* 60–65.
22. Karpman, B. The obsessive paraphilias. *Archives of Neurology & Psychiatry,* 1934, *32,* 577–626.
23. Karpman, B. *The Sexual Offender and His Offences.* New York: Julian Press, 1957.

24. Kolarsky, A., Freund, K., Machek, J., & Polak, O. Male sexual deviation: association with early temporal lobe damage. *Archives of General Psychiatry*, 1967, *17*, 735-743.
25. Kolvin, I. 'Aversive imagery' treatment in adolescents. *Behavior Research & Therapy*, 1967, *5*, 245-248.
26. Kronengold, E., & Sterba, R. Two cases of fetishism. *Psychoanalytic Quarterly*, 1936, *5*, 63-70.
27. Kushner, M. The reduction of a long-standing fetish by means of aversive conditioning. In L. Ullman, & L. Krasner (Eds.), *Case studies in behavior modification*. New York: Holt, Rinehart & Winston, 1965, 239-242.
28. Langevin, R., & Martin, M. Can erotic responses be classically conditioned? *Behavior Therapy*, 1975, *6*, 350-355.
29. Marks, I. M., & Gelder, M. G. Transvestism and fetishism: Clinical and Psychological changes during faradic aversion. *British Journal of Psychiatry*, 1967, *113*, 711-729.
30. Marks, I. M., Rachman, S., & Gelder, M. G. Methods for assessment of aversion treatment in fetishism with masochism. *Behavior Research Therapy*, 1965, *3*, 253-258.
31. Marquis, J. N. Orgasmic reconditioning: changing sexual object choice through controlling masturbation fantasies. *Journal of Behavior Therapy and Experimental Psychiatry*, 1970, *1*, 263-271.
32. Marshall, W. L. A combined treatment approach to the reduction of multiple fetish-related behaviors. *Journal of Consulting and Clinical Psychology*, 1974, *42*(4), 613-616.
33. McConaghy, N. Penile volume change to moving pictures of male and female nudes in heterosexual and homosexual males. *Behaviour Research and Therapy*, 1967, *54*, 43-48.
34. McGuire, R., & Vallence, M. Aversion therapy by electric shock: A simple technique. *British Medical Journal*, 1964, *1*, 151-153.
35. Mitchell, W., Falconer, M. A., & Hill, D. Epilepsy with fetishism relieved by temporal lobectomy. *Lancet*, 1954, *2*, 626-630.
36. Payne, S. M. Some observations on the ego development of the fetishist. *International Journal of Psychoanalysis*, 1939, *20*, 161-170.
37. Rachman, S. Sexual fetishism: An experimental analog. *Psychological Record*, 1966, *16*, 293-296.
38. Rappaport, E. A. The resolution of a delusional hair fetish. *Psychoanalytic Review*, 1971, *57*, 617-626.
39. Raymond, M. J. Case of fetishism treated by aversion therapy. *British Medical Journal*, 1956, *2*, 854-857.
40. Raymond, M., & O'Keefe, K. A case of pin-up fetishism treated by aversion conditioning. *British Journal of Psychiatry*, 1965, *111*, 579-581.
41. Romm, M. Some dynamics in fetishism. *Psychoanalytic Quarterly*, 1949, *18*, 137-153.
42. Snow, E., & Bluestone, H. Fetishism and murder. In S. Masserman (Ed.), *Dynamics of deviant sexuality*. New York: Grune & Stratton, 1969, 88-100.
43. Thorpe, J., Schmidt, E., Brown, P., & Castell, D. Aversion-relief therapy: a new method for general application. *Behavior Research and Therapy*, 1964, *2*, 71-82.
44. Woody, R. H. Integrated aversion therapy and psychotherapy: Two sexual deviation case studies. *Journal of Sex Research*, 1973, *9*(4), 313-324.

8 Heterosexual and Homosexual Pedophilia

The term pedophilia literally means love of children and the pedophile attends a psychiatric clinic either because he is bothered by sexual desire for children or has been charged with a sexual offence involving a child. Superficially the anomaly seems straight forward but there are several practical problems that create considerable ambiguity in understanding this behavior. First, there is uncertainty about the definition of "child". Age may be used to distinguish the child from the adult but various authors suggest 12, 13, 15 and even 18 years of age as a cutoff point. Others indicate puberty as the end of childhood or use age differences between the offender and victim as a criterion. A spread of 7-or-10 years and as few as 4 years age difference have been suggested to define pedophilia. Thus research and therapy on pedophilia covers a very heterogeneous group of men.

A second confusing factor is that research samples are a mixture of incest offenders and pedophiles. In fact in some studies "pedophiles" may have been convicted for incest, indecent assault, statutory rape, or carnal knowledge. The incest offender is peculiar in violating a double taboo in our culture by sexually interacting both with a minor and with his own kin. For this reason the group should be kept separate.

A third confounding factor is the mixing of heterosexual and homosexual pedophiles. The two groups may have different etiologies and certainly have different erotic profiles which merit study in their own right. Moreover, treatment goals of necessity are very different, as we will discuss later.

A fourth complicating factor is mixing men who erotically prefer adults with those who prefer children and calling them all "pedophiles". Some men act out with children under duress or circumstance and are unlikely to recidivate. Others show a spontaneous erotic preference for children and it is this latter group which needs careful study and attention in treatment. If one again applies the criterion of erotic preferences, considerable clarity is imposed on the research literature. The phallometric test of erotic preference described in Chapter 2 is invaluable in establishing if there is greater erotic reactivity to the child and even to pubescent youths than to the adult.

So much confusion exists in the literature because of the different purposes of the authors. Offender research may focus on the type of charge rather than on the sexual anomaly. I believe that to understand the phenomenon it is necessary to define the preferences and perhaps first study men who have an obvious attraction for immature partners, that is, attraction to those with no pubic or axillary hair, smaller genitals, and lack of swelled breasts in females or lack of chest hair and beard in males. Then the more subtle differences in preferences for emerging adults could be studied. It is also important to distinguish heterosexual from homosexual pedophiles before attempting to define common features. This had not been done in practice so that theories and data combine both groups.

THE THEORIES

Regression to childhood. Since the pedophile prefers to engage in sex with children, it has been postulated that he is fixated at an infantile stage of development. He exposes and the child does likewise in what some psychiatrists call the "show and tell stage of sexual development", characteristic of 4-or-5 year olds. They look and touch and fondle. Intercourse is usually not possible with the child and rarely occurs. The pedophile has the gentleness and curiosity characteristic of the preschooler's sexuality.

According to psychoanalytic theory, fixation results from castration anxiety. Every normal boy wishes to possess mother and replace father but is afraid to do so lest he be castrated. He therefore develops an aversion to mother as the incest taboo. However the pedophile's anxiety is so general that he fears to possess any mature female since they all symbolize mother. So he settles for an immature female as his own instead.

Aversion to adult females. Castration anxiety may manifest itself in a phobia for pubic hair of the adult female, which a child lacks, or as a general aversion to the mature female body. A 30-year-old parolee, *Mr. A,* noted his difficulty:

> *Mr. A:* "I've been staying away from the kids although it has been difficult at times. I have a very understanding girlfriend now and she is very pa-

tient with me. We even pet and I can get quite excited but when I see her crotch all covered in hair I lose my erection. I like her but quite frankly her pubic hair disgusts me''.

Mr. B. illustrates a more general aversion to mature females. A teacher and a practicing pedophile for almost 20 years he noted:

> *Mr. B:* "I'm just not interested in women. I find the thought of intercourse with them quite disgusting and I know I couldn't do it. Women are interested in me; I don't know why, and I don't mind being friends but when they show signs of getting romantic, it puts me right off''.

The aversion to females however must be considered in the same fashion as the homosexual's supposed aversion to females (Chapter 4). Is the pedophile's repulsion for the mature female any different from that expressed by heterosexuals for homosexual acts? In pedophilia, as in homosexual androphilia, a lack of interest and/or arousability to mature females has been interpreted as anxiety and impotence but it may be no more than disinterest. *Mr. C* compared his experience of intercourse with a mature female to pedophilia.

> *Mr. C:* "I must say from the outset that adult female breasts do nothing at all for me. They may as well not be there. When I had intercourse with a girlfriend a few years ago, it was out of curiosity. I didn't love her the way I can love a child, something is always missing. We did have intercourse which she apparently enjoyed but to me, it was nothing. I had an erection and finally came but it was not as exciting or as high as I get with a child, even without ejaculating''.

Mental and emotional retardation.   A further reason the pedophile may engage in infantile sexuality is because he has regressed to or is fixated at this stage of development due to senility or mental and emotional retardation[49][63]. Some writers have stressed the occurrence of pedophilia in senile dementia among the mentally retarded and in schizophrenia (cf. [49]) where the patient's confusion may explain his inappropriate sexual behavior with children.

Mr. D was a retarded obese dishevelled 18-year-old charged with homosexual pedophilic acts on a 6-year-old boy. He freely admitted to fellating the boy and giving him candy for the favor. He seemed oblivious to his foul body odor and dirty clothes along with an extreme case of acne.

> *Doctor:* "Have you dated girls your own age?''
>
> *Mr. D:* "I tried a couple of times but they don't seem to like me''.
>
> *Doctor:* "Why do you think that?''

Mr. D: "I don't know. They always say they are busy. So I wanted a friend
and met Gary (the victim) and he liked me".

The pedophile as unassertive.   Freud has described the pedophiles as
"cowardly" but preferable contemporary terminology might be "unassertive". The typical case has been described as immature, passive and suffering from feelings of inferiority[37]. For this reason he finds it difficult to relate to the adult female and if he attempts to do so he may be impotent. This
was the case with *Mr. A* and *Mr. B* noted earlier. The ignorance and inexperience of the child prevents the impotence and deficiencies from being obvious so the pedophile can perform[29][34][73]. However the impotence may only
represent lack of interest in the mature female and an erotic preference for a
different object.

Some pedophiles do have intercourse with mature females and even
marry but nevertheless continue to be interested sexually in children. This
suggests a parallel to the bisexual androphile (Chapter 5) who marries for
the social acceptability and rewards of marriage but continues to manifest
desire for a culturally taboo sex object.

The feelings of inferiority may also be the result of violating social norms
rather than being the cause of the anomaly. *Mr. E,* a 30-year-old homosexual pedophile who came for treatment on his own accord, illustrates the
former possibility:

Mr. E: "When I'm alone and do my thing with kids, it feels good. I don't
care about anything at that moment. It feels great but when it is over I immediately feel guilt and want to get the hell out of there. I worry that the
kid will tell and that someone will find out.

(later)

When I'm out with people and they seem to like me, I often withdraw
from a close relationship because I think if they knew what I was really
like they'd hate me."

The passivity and immaturity ascribed to the pedophile may reflect no
more than the nature of the sexual act, namely, fondling and exposing
rather than the "more active and mature" intercourse. Pedophiles may
show an inordinate interest and fascination with children and their behavior
and thus be labeled as immature. *Mr. B* taught handicapped children and
his employer's report described him as having "extraordinary sensitivity to
the needs of the children" which was coupled with "an intelligent and
creative approach to teaching such that the children respond with enthusiasm and even joy." *Mr. B's* own perception of his behavior was:

Mr. B: Some people think I'm peculiar because I'm so interested in the
children. I can get right into their games at their level. I really enjoy

watching their response and their play and I think pedophiles must perceive children differently from the average person. Maybe it's the sexual element. I can tell Breugel (the painter) was a pedophile just the way he painted them. It's the same fascination with children that I feel."

The unassertive nature ascribed to the pedophile can be interpreted in at least two ways. On the one hand, he may be unable to relate to mature females and seeks the child as a surrogate. On the other hand his lack of assertiveness in pursuing adults may be really indifference.

Pedophilia as homosexuality.   Noyes and Kolb[52] described pedophilia as a variant of homosexuality. Both anomalies involve a disturbed mother relationship which results in a substitute sex object choice, either in the child or in the adult male. One might therefore expect the two anomalies to cooccur frequently. Both the homosexual pedophile and androphile who prefers mature men can be described as narcissistic because they see themselves mirrored in the preferred sex object and because they identify more with mother than father. Thus homosexual pedophiles should show greater femininity and feminine gender identity like their androphilic counterparts. However the homosexual pedophile wants to act toward the male child in the way he desires his mother to act toward him. *Mr. F* described his sexual fantasies of boys as follows.

> *Mr. F:*   "I imagine an idealized child who is being indulged by his mother at bedtime. His every wish is being anticipated and met. He is very content and happy. I may imagine I am that child."

Pedophilia and exhibitionism.   Narcissism may also be evident in the association of pedophilia with exhibitionism. Often the pedophile exposes to children and may do so exclusively. Mohr, Turner and Jerry[49] noted that typically the pedophile knows the child at least as an acquaintance whereas the exhibitionist picks a stranger. Moreover pedophilia involves close contact with the child including body contact, whereas exhibiting does not and is usually done from a distance. However the frequent co-occurrence of the two anomalies has suggested a common etiology. The interested reader may wish to examine theories of exhibitionism in Chapter 10 since they are not reviewed here.

Other anomalies in pedophilia.   Other behaviors co-occur with pedophilia but not as frequently, namely fetishism and sadism. Newspapers give considerable coverage to sadism, sexual molestation and murder of children. However, the child may be murdered to prevent reporting of the offence rather than as a sadistic act in itself[34]. These cases are atypical of the pedophile but are of great concern. The need to play a dominant role may be evident in a benign form in pedophilia, especially in the homosexual pedophile. In its extreme form, the dominance can assume sadistic proportions when the pedophile needs complete control over his victim even to taking his life. Since such men lack closeness to their fathers, they assume a pseudopaternal role to the victim, evidenced by gift buying and treats. The element of control or dominance may be paramount to the sexual act. *Mr. G* who was a 36-year-old married businessman indicated what he liked best about sex with an 8-or-9-year-old boy:

> *Mr. G:* "I treat them to hot dogs and chips. We go in amusement halls on Main St. and play the pinball machines so the boy is having a great time. Then when we are alone, I teach him about sex and persuade him to take down his trousers. I will rub my penis against his bottom but the really exciting part is buttering him up with compliments and persuading him to get those pants down. That's when I get really excited and I enjoy it more than anything else."

The element of dominance may be crucial to sexual excitement and performance in all the pedophile's relationships including those with adult females. *Mr. H* was married but was a confirmed pedophile. He was 35 and worked as a casual laborer. He clearly was aware of the importance of dominance in his sexual relations:

> *Mr. H:* "I usually cannot have sex with my wife unless we have a fight and she is apologetic and at my mercy. When she is in tears at my feet, then I can get aroused and we have sex. With the kids I can be aroused right away. I am bigger and stronger than them and I can't keep my hands off them."

Heterosexual versus homosexual pedophilia.   Little has been said in the literature of differences between heterosexual and homosexual pedophilia. Although the two are discusses collectively, the most frequent clinical cases are heterosexual pedophiles which outnumber homosexual cases about 2-to-1[30][56]. Only a small proportion are bisexual or undifferentiated pedophiles. Psychoanalysts have suggested homosexual cases were narcissistic whereas heterosexuals seek a mother surrogate in the female child. The ages of the victims appear to differ in the groups with homosexual pedophiles engaging slightly older ones and preferring inner crural (between the legs) or anal intercourse. The heterosexual pedophiles prefer to fondle and expose to younger victims[49]. A further difference in the two groups may occur in parent child relations. Heterosexual pedophiles do not identify with father or with mother who did not meet her son's immature dependency needs. The homosexual pedophile on the other hand was closer to mother and distant from father so that the son later assumes a pseudopaternal role with his victims to compensate for the lack in his own father. In all cases of pedophilia, the mother is stronger and more competent than the father. Karpman[34] noted that all pedophilia is a sign of serious neurotic conflict in which the father is feared and identification with him is inadequate so that the son is later unable to cope with the adult female. The pedophile also seeks out the child as revenge on his mother who rejected him.

The child as a surrogate.   Karpman[34] distinguished erotic preference for children and surrogate activity with the child. In the former the pedophile always craved children because of some emotional fixation in childhood. In the case of surrogate activity the offender suffers an uncontrollable impulse which happens to be acted out on children.

A 48-year-old dentist was described to the author by a colleague. The man had recently lost his wife and was extremely depressed but immersed himself in his work to overcome his sorrow. A 9-year-old girl who had a series of dental appointments told her mother he was "putting his dinky in my mouth". The mother was reluctant to believe it at first but when the dentist was confronted with the child's statements he broke down in tears and confessed to the acts which were completely out of character for him. Prognosis in such cases is very good but I will return to this later.

The bisexual or undifferentiated pedophile reacts erotically to both boys and girls which suggests that body characteristics other than the child's small size may not be important to the pedophile. Little has been said of bisexual pedophilia in the literature but its existence suggests that homosexual and heterosexual versions of the anomaly may share a common root.

The Experimental Evidence

Aversion to adult females.   Freund reported the first controlled phallometric studies of pedophilia and unfortunately most were done at the time when he was developing his standard test of erotic preference[18] [19] [20]. Some of the slides were inadequate since a few of the photographic subjects were older adults so physical attractiveness may have been confused with age preference. In others the extent of physical development may have been atypical of the chronological age. There were too few slides in each sex age category and no neutral stimuli were used so that baselines of nonerotic reactions of the penis were difficult to distinguish. Unfortunately few studies have been done since Freund has developed a more refined test[23].

In spite of these problems, it is clear from Freund's data that pedophiles reacted more to the child of the preferred sex than controls did. In the earlier version of the standard phallometric test, over 90% of pedophiles and controls could be correctly identified as such based on penile reactions to slides of males and females at various ages ranging from 4-to-41 years of age. An idealized profile of heterosexual pedophiles and normal controls is depicted in Fig. 8.1. Neither group reacted differently to males and to neutral slides. However they did show a reversal of reaction patterns to females. Normal men reacted positively to the female child as young as 6-years-old. As the stimulus female increased in age, penile reactions were larger. All responses to females were significantly larger than those to neutral stimuli[23]. In contrast, as the stimulus female became older, the heterosexual pedophile's reactions *decreased* in size so the smallest reactions

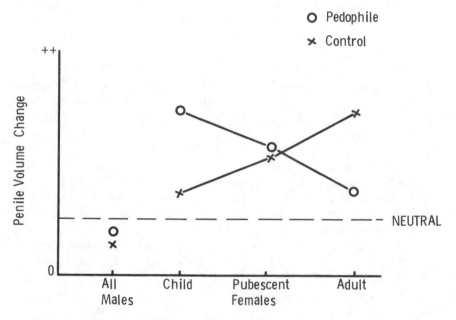

FIG. 8.1   A comparison of penile reactions in heterosexual pedophiles and gynephilic controls.

were to adult females. If one changes the labels "male" and "female" on the horizontal axis of Fig. 8.1, it shows the idealized comparison of homosexual pedophiles and homosexual androphiles. The reaction to adults of the preferred sex for both pedophilic groups is small but greater than responses to neutral stimuli. This suggests that aversion to the adult is not an operative factor or the response would be negative or at the neutral level at least. Rather, it looks like stimulus generalization in which there is some positive reaction to the adult by virtue of his/her similarity to the child. However this evidence is only suggestive and the phobic theory of pedophilia has yet to be tested directly.

Demographic and sex history data also oppose the phobic theory. First, a substantial number of pedophiles marry. Mohr, Turner and Jerry[49] found 65% of heterosexual and 47% of homosexual pedophiles were married. The heterosexuals' marriages tended to last longer than the homosexuals' did. Both groups tended to marry late compared to the general population, perhaps reflecting their retarded maturity. In other samples 40% to 50% of pedophiles characteristically marry (see [16] [49] [50]) although Bernard[6] reported only 8% among a group of nonpatient homosexual pedophiles did so. Marriage does not mean that the pedophiles prefer mature women but it does imply that they can function satisfactorily with adults which raises doubts about the phobic nature of their interactions. Some theorists imply that impotence would be a problem in the pedophile's marriage because it is a phobic situation but Mohr, Turner and Jerry[49] did not mention sexual dysfunction as an important factor in their sample of pedophiles.

Second, Paitich and his colleagues[54] found that the sexual experience of heterosexual pedophiles with adult females on the Clarke Sex History Questionnaire (Appendix 1) was not distinct from that of a normal heterosexual control group. Pedophiles in this sample were subdivided according to whether they had sexual relations with boys or girls 12 and younger since they were 18 themselves or had sexual relations with boys and girls 13-to-15 since they were 21 themselves. Few differences in the groups emerged and they were collapsed into one group of heterosexual pedophiles and one of homosexual pedophiles.

The pedophiles' sexual interaction with children typically involved exposing as well as victim contact. The heterosexual pedophilic group were passive and more likely to attempt to induce the female to touch them or they would engage in frottage rather than attempt intercourse or touch the female in a sexual way with their hands. They were less interested than the control group in sex with mature females but when they did so they were more inclined to engage in a range of behavior, including oral, genital and anal interactions.

Bisexuality.   In reality, pedophiles are quite heterogeneous in their reactions. Some appear to react without distinction among female age groups but remain unreactive to males[19]. For others the pubescent youth may be preferred so that the erotic profile in Fig. 8.1 for a pedophile is an inverted "V" with the peak reaction to adolescents. It is the normal heterosexual who generally reacts less to the child than he does to the adult female. Maybe he has learned to inhibit his reactions to children whereas the pedophile has not. Usually the normal male's penile responses to children are subliminal but positive nonetheless and this is possibly because the reactions have been suppressed or inhibited.

A unique feature of pedophilia is that bisexuality appears in both overt behavior and in stimulus preferences. In Chapter 5, it was noted that bisexuals who had sexually interacted with both mature men and women reacted with penile tumescence only to the body characteristics of men. It was suggested that these "bisexuals" had adapted to a heterosexual world by performing with and even marrying a woman but that their erotic preferences were usually for men. However pedophiles who say they are bisexual may react to the body characteristics of both boys and girls. In the only two comparative studies in the literature, Freund and his colleagues[25][26] administered the standard phallometric test to bisexual and monosexual androphiles and homosexual pedophiles. In the first study, the bisexual pedophiles reacted more to female children than any other group did and when the ratio of reactivity to males and females was computed as a "bisexuality index", they stood out from all the other groups as most bisexual. The second study replicated the first. Freund and his associates[26] suggested that pedophiles may erotically differentiate the sexes solely on the basis of genitalia whereas a range of signs are used by nonpedophiles. On the other hand, the pedophile may respond mainly to some part of the child's body other than the genitals or only bisexual pedophiles may be unusual in their reactions. No real resolution of the hypotheses was offered in the two studies and the unusual finding needs further investigation. Genitalia of the children would seem to be secondary since they are so different but perhaps small size or immature facial features are important. If control and/or dominance is an important aspect of the bisexual pedophiles' erotically preferred behavior these features reflecting immaturity might be most arousing, regardless of the child's sex. Overall one can make the generalization that as a group they react more phallometrically to children than controls do and this can serve as a diagnostic aid (See also [22]).

The pedophile as homosexual.   One further fact is clear. In none of Freund et al's study was there a reaction of heterosexual pedophiles to males which was different from those of controls, suggesting that the general link of pedophilia to homosexuality is not supported. The homosexual pedophiles of course did respond to mature men but not as much as they did to children. This would be expected from the mere similarity of boys' and men's bodies but there were no reactions to females.

Homosexual pedophiles had more sexual experience with men than either controls or heterosexual pedophiles. The latter do not differ in the extent of homosexual experience. It is perhaps the tendency of earlier writers to discuss the pedophilias collectively which led to the hypothesis that they are a variant of homosexuality. This may also have produced the incorrect assertion of laymen that androphilic men are pedophiles. Although homosexual androphiles may have sex relations with children and adolescents as peers, they generally are not different from gynephilic men, the normal heterosexual, in their experience with children.

Homosexual pedophiles have had more contact with men than heterosexual controls have but less than homosexual controls. They have the most experience with boys, their preferred sex object. The heterosexual pedophiles outnumber their homosexual counterparts 2-to-1 suggesting pedophilia is predominantly a heterosexual anomaly.

The homosexual pedophiles were much more similar to the homosexual androphilic controls than the corresponding heterosexual groups were[24]. There was comparable degree and type of outlet. The only real difference was in terms of the object, adult versus child. The homosexual pedophile was unlikely to have much heterosexual experience like his heterosexual counterpart.

Quinsey and his colleagues[59] did a study which supported Freund's[25] [26] results, using a mixed group of heterosexual, bisexual and homosexual pedophiles, nonsex offenders and nonpatients. The pedophilic group may be considered unusual because 10% were psychotic and 30% were mentally retarded. Penile circumference, skin conductance responses and verbal reports were measured to slides of male and female children, pubescents and adults, to violence, and to heterosexual petting between a man and a woman. Skin conductance measures failed to distinguish the groups. However penile measurement showed expected differences. Heterosexual and bisexual pedophiles peaked on responses to female children whereas homosexual pedophiles reacted most to male children. The bisexual pedophiles once again reacted more to both sexes although predominantly to girls.

An interesting additional finding in Quinsey et al's study was that all groups responded greatly to heterosexual petting. This may mean that pedophiles are heterosexually inclined but such stimuli are often ambiguous. Normal heterosexual men react to a range of anomalous stimuli, such as two lesbians petting, but this does not mean they prefer lesbianism. Stimuli of intercourse are much more complex than they initially seem and it is difficult to know exactly what the patient is reacting to. At the very least it suggests that the heterosexual reactivity of pedophiles would appear to be substantial, without any treatment.

Pedophilia and other anomalies. In the analysis of Sex History Questionnaires by Paitich and his associates[54], heterosexual pedophilia and exhibitionism were correlated to each other but not to homosexuality. The main distinction of pedophilia from exhibitionism was in the age of the victim and the type of contact. Exhibitionists did act out with female children but their most frequent acts were with physically mature females. They had no body contact with the victim and, in fact, if the female wanted such contact, many would not have it (See Chapter 10). The pedophile, on the other hand, acted out most with the child to whom he exposed while inducing her to touch him. Although body contact with children was much rarer for exhibitionists, in practice, some individuals do have it so distinctions between the two anomalies may be difficult to make. Assessment of erotic preferences in cooperative patients usually helps to sort out whether one is dealing with a pedophile or an exhibitionist.

Collectively the above data did not support the theories indicating that pedophiles show fear and aversion for the mature female, fixation at an immature stage of development, and inability to relate to mature women. An interesting phallometric finding which has received little attention and theorizing is that pedophiles may be truly bisexual. Often there is a somewhat greater reaction to one sex over the other but nevertheless bisexual pedophiles react to both sexes more than to neutral stimuli and this is unique among all the sexual anomalies.

The phallometric test of erotic preference has an invaluable diagnostic function in this respect. Some men show greater reactivity to the female child but also comparatively larger responses to mature females than to mature males. A therapy program to adapt such men to a relationship with a woman seems feasible. However in the male who prefers boys, the odds are high that he will react more to men than to women so that a therapy program to adapt him to mature men would seem more practical. The varying bisexual cases that fall in between these two extremes can also be judged accordingly.

Senility, retardation and brain pathology. Some theorists have suggested that a disease process is operative in pedophilia, either as senility or mental retardation. Most of the formulations are based on case studies rather than on systematic experiments or on the use of standardized psychological tests. Mohr, Turner and Jerry[49] reviewed the existing literature up to the early 1960's and noted the frequency with which conclusions about senility and mental retardation were based on clinical judgments alone. In studies based on IQ tests, the pedophiles are usually similar to the general population with a tendency to show more cases at the lower end of the distribution perhaps reflecting their poorer educational achievement levels. Mohr et al's own data on the Wechsler Adult Intelligence Sale (WAIS) and our own[39] from the same setting are essentially in agreement with these findings. The pedophile is unlikely to be retarded or senile.

Swanson's[73] study of offenders charged for sexual involvement with 3-to-14-year-old children is an example of uncontrolled evaluation. There was no control group and 32% of the prisoners were incest cases. Half may not have erotically preferred children and were experiencing conflict or loss of the usual source of sexual satisfaction due to separation, illness, and so forth. Results are therefore ambiguous but only 16% were suffering from chronic brain syndrome or mental subnormality with 4% borderline schizophrenic reaction. Contrast a nonclinical sample of pedophiles studied by Bernard[6]. He found that 62% had never seen a psychiatrist and that 90% did not "want to be rid" of their pedophilia. The sample was unusual since 21% had a university degree. However his results serve to remind us that clinical samples may be biased toward finding pathology which is not an inherent part of the sexual anomaly and that there may be well adjusted pedophilic individuals in the community. The Working Group on Pedophilia, part of the Dutch Association for Sexual Reform on which Bernard reports, and groups like "PIE", Pedophilic Information Exchange, in Great Britain may bring forth into the community other clandestine pedophiles who lead normal lives while their erotic preference remains a secret.

Generally, mental retardation and senility have not proven to be satisfactory explanations of pedophilia. Brain pathology has been associated with a range of sexual anomalies but the evidence is not convincing yet (e.g. [61]). Base rates of the brain pathology and of the sexual anomaly are usually not reported and when they are, the results have been disappointing. Brain pathology, especially to the so called association areas of the brain, the frontal and temporal lobes, can be related to a wide range of bizarre behavior including unusual sexual behavior. Whether this is a chance co-occurrence or a causal relationship remains to be established. Clearly, however, many pedophiles and other sexually anomalous men have no obvious brain pathology. Nevertheless so little systematic work has been done on brain pathology in pedophiles that the hypothesis of organic factors in this anomaly should be explored.

There are no genetic studies of pedophilia per se and only one study of hormones[60] which showed that pedophiles plasma testosterone levels were within normal limits.

Personality pathology. Emotional retardation, immaturity, passivity and feelings of inferiority have been considered etiological factors in pedophilia[76]. Few studies have been done and a major problem of earlier reports on this question was their tendency to mix pedophiles in with sex offenders generally. Mohr, Turner and Jerry reviewed these earlier studies and concluded that the work in the area had not developed to a stage where generalizations could be made.

Toobert and his colleagues[74] conducted one of the earlier controlled studies using the MMPI. Pedophiles whose sex object choice was children 12 years of age, or under, were compared to prisoners in general. No statistical test results were reported but both groups showed only clinically significant T scores over 70 on the psychopathic deviate scale which measures rebelliousness and nonconformity. The average scores of the pedophiles on femininity (Mf scale) and paranoia (Pa scale) were significantly higher than those of controls, but all average scores were within normal limits. The authors developed their own scale of pedophilia from the MMPI which correctly identified 75% of pedophiles in a cross validation sample. According to the authors, the results reveal the pedophile to be weak and inadequate, with low self esteem, supporting the theoretically predicted personality. However, to date their scale has not been validated to show that, in fact, it measures these traits.

Atwood and Howell[2] compared imprisoned heterosexual pedophiles to nonsex offenders on the MMPI using a special "sex deviation" scale. Although the two groups were significantly different on this unvalidated scale, the pedophiles were not distinct from neurotic or psychotic patients.

In a personality study of homosexual and heterosexual pedophiles, normal heterosexuals and homosexuals, among other groups, my colleagues and I found some support for the stereotype of the pedophile[39]. The heterosexual pedophiles were tense, reserved, and among the shyest of all the groups. They also tended to be shrewder, less emotionally stable, and less group dependent. The homosexual pedophiles presented as much more emotionally disturbed with significant Depression, Schizophrenia, Psychopathic Deviate, Paranoia and Social Introversion scores on the MMPI. The groups of pedophiles were mixed outpatients and incarcerated men awaiting trial.

In two studies, Fisher and Howell[14] [15] compared heterosexual and homosexual pedophiles to other prisoners and to the normative data of the Edward's Personal Preference Schedule, a multi-scale personality inventory. Pedophiles' victims were generally under 10 years of age but did range up to 17-years-old and included incest cases. Heterosexual pedophiles compared to other prisoners scored significantly higher on deference, succorance, abasement and lower on achievement, autonomy, change, heterosexuality and aggression supporting the theoretical personality type.

In the second study, Fisher and Howell[15] compared two pedophilic groups to normative data. The heterosexual pedophiles scored higher than homosexual pedophiles on order and endurance but lower on nurturance and, paradoxically lower on heterosexuality. The authors suggested that the result indicated malingering which questions the validity of the whole study.

Howells[32] compared heterosexual pedophiles and controls on a version of the Kelly Repertory Grid. An interesting comparison was made between the constructs "adult" and "child". Children were seen as less forceful, pushy and domineering than adults by the pedophiles. This perception of children may relate to the pedophile's lack of assertiveness with adults or it may be a quality, differentiating children and adults. Howells thinks dominance plays a role in the pedophile's view of people and may reflect an inability to control the social environment.

McCreary[47] compared MMPI profiles of first offenders and recidivist pedophiles in prison. Repeated offenders scored higher on Psychopathic Deviate (Pd), Hypochondriasis, Hysteria and Schizophrenia (Sc) scales reflecting more overall pathology. However only Pd and Sc scales were in the range considered clinically significant (T score greater than 70). It is not clear how many were heterosexual and how many homosexual but there were no differences in femininity as reported earlier by Toobert, Bartelme and Jones[74]. The postulated personality profile of the pedophile was not obtained.

Virkkunen[79] found that when mixed pedophilic prisoners are sorted into antisocial and other groups, the former were less shy, timid and less childish for their ages. They were also incorrectly reported to be more intelligent. When I reanalysed their data I found, in fact, that a number of the findings were incorrectly reported. Derivation of the item scores used were also ambiguous and unvalidated so the conclusions must be treated with caution.

Frisbie and her colleagues[11] [27] [77] compared pedophiles from prison with those in hospitals for self evaluation reactions on the semantic differential. They found that the results reflected the hospital versus prison setting more than individual differences. Good stereotypes and acceptable facades were typical and there was no overall pedophilic profile which emerged. Their study emphasizes the importance of validating data collected on pedophiles, especially prison samples where individuals may be looking for paroles.

Quinsey[56] noted that the picture of the pedophile as an unassertive individual who may be guarded, moralistic and guilt ridden may reflect attempts to convince prison staff of their normality. It should also be noted that if these traits are common to pedophiles they may be the result of society's reaction to the anomaly rather than a causal factor in its etiology. Clearly more extensive and better controlled studies need to be done to verify the personality traits common to the pedophile. It should be ascertained that an erotic preference for children exists and that there are not multiple sexual anomalies involved which may color the personality traits associated with pedophilia itself. To date only one study has done this[39] and hopefully more are forthcoming.

It is noteworthy that pedophilia has been linked to homosexuality, femininity, and feminine gender identity. Freund et al[26] compared heterosexual and homosexual pedophiles to corresponding control groups who preferred mature partners on the Feminine Gender Identity Scale. They found that both pedophilic groups did not score significantly different from heterosexual controls and that all groups scored lower in feminine gender identity than homosexual androphiles. MMPI results noted earlier also failed to support the femininity hypothesis and, even the homosexual pedophilic group did not show the characteristic high femininity scores typical of androphilic homosexuals. If anything, pedophiles are strongly masculine identified.

Parent child relations. There is only one controlled study of parent child relations in pedophiles using a standardized instrument and it does not support the hypothesis that there is stronger mother identification. Surprisingly the theoretical literature does not adequately distinguish the parent child relationships of the homosexual and heterosexual pedophile. Paitich and his colleagues[53] found that pedophiles generally showed less mother identification than heterosexual controls and other sexually anomalous men. Their mothers were also reported as more strict and less affectionate. Father relationships and identification were within normal limits. The same profile was characteristic of incestuous men who also engage immature victims or partners. The results of the one controlled study in the literature are contrary to theory. It is perhaps the *lack* of mother identification which promotes pedophilia. Since she is the prototype of mature females and since she is not a satisfactory person to relate to, the pedophile seeks out immature partners.

In Gebhard's[28] prison sample, mixed pedophiles and sex offenders were compared to controls on three questions: How he got along with mother, with father during 14–17 years of age, and, which parent he got along with better. Results were unremarkable although use of force and acting out with immature partners were associated with poorer adjustment to both parents.

The Pedophile's Stimulus Response Matrix

Pedophiles differentiate generally into three groups, heterosexual, homosexual and bisexual. The most important feature is the young age of the preferred sex object. Peculiar to this anomaly is the erotic reactivity of some pedophiles to the body shape and characteristics of both boys and girls. This suggests either that some stimulus characteristic like relative size of pedophile to partner, absence of secondary sexual characteristics, or emotional immaturity of the partner are important to the pedophile. An alternative possibly is that the stimulus is relatively unimportant compared to the responses. The tendency of heterosexual pedophiles to exhibit to their victim may reflect narcissism and a desire to be watched or paid attention to. The "teacher" role and "benevolent father" played by both heterosexual and homosexual pedophiles may also reflect the same trait or a need for dominance and control over the victim. These facets of pedophilia remain generally unstudied.

Another feature of the heterosexual pedophile which may reflect narcissism is his inducing the child to touch him rather than vice versa, although the latter occurs. This may be no more than self gratification but it could also reflect his desire to have his powerful and important part admired by the child.

One can expect usually to see a gentle person clinically in the pedophile and his attachment to children may be very resistant to alteration. However a number of men charged with indecent acts may be sexually normal. Phallometric assessment and a detailed sex history usually reveal whether his acts are isolated events or a perennial pattern. First offenders may be difficult to assess particularly if they are nonadmittors. Violence associated with some cases of pedophilia is not well understood (See Shoor, Speed and Bartelt, [66] for example). There is little in the way of systematic research on pedophilia generally (See Table 8.1).

TABLE 8.1
Summary of Evidence for Theories of Pedophilia

Theory	Experimental Evidence
1. Pedophile is fixated at an infantile stage of development	Untested
2. Pedophile has an aversion to all mature women	Negative but only very limited evidence is available
3. Pedophiles are mentally or emotionally retarded	No but they do tend to show IQs at the lower end of the normal range
4. Pedophiles are shy, passive and unassertive	Some positive support. More controlled studies needed on the question
5. Pedophilia is a variant of homosexuality	Negative
6. Pedophilia and exhibitionism tend to occur together	Yes and they may be difficult to separate in individual cases
7. Pedophiles are sadists, fetishists or need to play the dominant sex role	No evidence but more controlled studies needed
8. "True" bisexuality occurs in the pedophiles as a stimulus preference for both male and female children	Positive but the nature of the preference is unexplained at present
9. Heterosexual pedophiles do not identify with either parent but homosexual pedophiles are closer to their mothers	Both groups show only less mother identification. Mothers were considered strict and unaffectionate
10. In many cases, the child serves as a surrogate for adult females under unusual circumstances so a true erotic preference for children does not exist	No systematic investigation but clinical impression suggests it is true and should be systematically studied

TREATMENT

The most frequent treatment of sexual anomalies has been some form of aversive conditioning, and the treatment of pedophilia is no exception. The professional reports are almost all uncontrolled case studies with a few uncontrolled group studies. In contrast to treatment reports of homosexuality, the number of reports is small for what has been considered an important social problem.

Behavior Therapies

Aversion therapy presents special problems in pedophilia. In the normal heterosexual male there is substantial responsiveness to females of all ages, although the largest responses are to adults. The same ranging responsiveness holds true for heterosexual pedophiles. In fact variation is pronounced in this group, such that the largest responses may be elicited by the mature female, particularly by pseudopedophiles, who show a normal erotic profile but who act out under extenuating circumstances with a child. In most of these cases treatment for pedophilia per se is unnecessary as they are unlikely to repeat their offence.

Some pedophiles react equally to the adult female and the child and others react to the child first and secondarily but substantially to the adult female. This may be due to stimulus generalization, that is, due to the physical similarity of the adult and child bodies. If one attempts to extinguish or suppress the pedophile's responses to the child, by the very nature of stimulus generalization, reactions to the mature female will also decrease. This is depicted in Fig. 8.2. Before therapy, the patient is more likely to act out sexually with the child and less likely to act out with the adult. It is hoped with treatment that the potential to act out with the child will drop below the action threshold so he rarely has urges to do so. However, out of necessity the whole range of responses to females will drop proportionally so that the weaker tendency to respond to the adult is pushed well below the action threshold making adjustment to the adult female difficult. The situation may be even more problematic when the pedophile responds most to the pubescent female who may have most of the adult female's body features but lacks her emotional maturity. A suitable treatment must use one of two procedures. First one can differentially reinforce adult and child stimuli so response strength is maintained to the adult whereas it is lost to the child. Second, one may differentially increase the reaction potential to the adult so it is stronger than that to the child, the latter simply being ignored or later suppressed by aversive conditioning when positive reactions to adult females will remain. The existing studies generally have not employed either procedure and have used simple aversion therapy. In fact

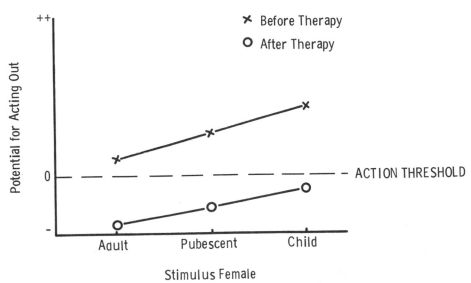

FIG. 8.2   Effect of therapy on the heterosexual pedophile's potential to act out.

we usually do not know if the men treated even had an erotic preference for children.

The case is complicated for homosexual pedophiles who prefer males and children. Typically the amount of responsiveness of homosexual men to females in general is of such a small order that it is not distinct from reactions to neutral stimuli. There is some positive reaction to the adult male so that adapting the homosexual pedophile to the androphilic role might be the most successful course of action in locales where homosexual acts between consenting adults are not criminal offenses. Only two reports to date have attempted such a course of treatment[36] [65]. In trying to adapt the homosexual pedophile to heterosexual relations with an adult female, one has a double task. All of the problems inherent in treating homosexuality noted in Chapter 4 as well as the problems of pedophilia are present and must somehow be dealt with.

Aversion therapy. The earliest reports of aversion therapy for pedophiles used electric shock in a classical conditioning fashion. Pictures and/or fantasies of children were the conditioning stimuli, which were followed soon after presentation by unpleasant electrical shock.

Bancroft and Marks[4] reported on four cases and Mellor (in Bancroft[3]) on 12 cases respectively. The former did not consider aversion therapy sucessful because only one of the four showed any limited improvement. Mellor was more successful in eight of the 12 cases although the criterion of success, the SOM measure (Sexual Orientation Method) of Feldman and

McCullough[13] is of questionable validity. Bancroft concluded that pedophiles often engage in deceiving themselves and others, which makes treatment evaluation difficult. He did not think there was any obvious prognostic criterion of success in treating pedophiles.

Rosenthal[64] varied several parameters of operant conditioning in the aversion therapy of a heterosexual pedophile. First he punished the occurrence of an erotic response and varied both shock intensity and duration. When the patient indicated he was aroused to pictures, he was shocked unpredictably for 1 to 6 seconds and with unpredictable intensity. This procedure was not effective and a second approach was used. The latency to react erotically was punished so the patient received stronger and longer shocks to quick erotic reactions and weaker shorter shocks for reactions that took a long time to develop. The patient appeared to respond to this method. Booster sessions were given after five months although they seemed unnecessary. After 32 months the patient had not acted out. Although the patient's verbal signal was used to indicate sexual arousal, this study seems ideally suited for penile measurement.

Wijesinghe[80] varied another parameter of conditioning to successfully treat four cases, two heterosexual and two homosexual pedophiles. Massed practice sessions were used without explanation. This is unusual because learning studies show that learning trials distributed over time are more efficient and lasting than massed trials or those occurring closely together in time[35]. There were six 1 hour sessions in 1 day involving 30 minutes of shock trials using pictures of children as conditioning stimuli and then 20 minutes of viewing adult females as relief stimuli. The two heterosexuals were followed up without further therapy at 5 years and at 18 months without recidivism. However the one patient, although now married, was taking minor tranquilizers for free floating anxiety. The two homosexual pedophiles also fared well after 18 months and 2 years respectively although the first patient was seen "on a supportive basis" for 2 months after aversion therapy. All four patients were treated with unspecified "subsequent support" after aversion therapy. Since the treatment is contrary to learning principles and other unspecified treatment was employed, the results should be treated with caution. Heterosocial adjustment only appeared satisfactory in one married heterosexual pedophile.

Steffy and his colleagues[69 70 71] used a variety of current theory to develop their aversion therapy technique, which they considered to be an adjunct to other ongoing treatment, namely to milieu therapy, dynamic group therapy and didactic content-oriented group projects. The latter were not specified in detail. They adapted the operant avoidance conditioning developed by Feldman and McCullough[13] to treat pedophiles. This method has an advantage over simple classical conditioning in being more resistant to extinction. Shock is administered on a partial reinforcement schedule, that is, on the majority of trials as opposed to continuous reinforcement or shock on every trial. Animal studies have shown partial reinforcement to be the more effective[35].

Steffy and Gauthier[69] [70] [71] argued that it is important to punish the pedophile's approach behaviors to the child rather than the actual "point of attacking a child". Inhibition developed early in the chain of approach behavior to the child should prevent temptation. This of course is in opposition to the procedure used by Rosenthal in which the actual erotic response is punished. Both authors however make valid points based on learning theory: Shock should be contingent on a response to be eliminated and shock should be given earlier in a chain of behaviors to be most effective.

Steffy and Gauthier further enhanced their treatment by varying the pattern and intensity of shocks. The logic was to create as much uncertainty as possible since it seems to be essential to the development of anxiety that inhibits acting out with children. The remaining procedure is basically the avoidance conditioning of Feldman and McCullough[13] described in Chapter 3 and 4. Slides were followed after 10 seconds by shock which could be avoided by pressing a footpedal. Shock termination was followed by presentation of a slide of a female.

The authors developed a Sexual Attractiveness Scale (SAS) for periodic assessment of erotic interest. The scale consists of slides of adults and children of both sexes in varying states of undress and nude. Galvanic Skin Responses (GSR) were measured to determine anticipatory anxiety to each class of stimuli. Unfortunately the GSR appears also to be used as an index of erotic arousal so the two are confused.

A rarity in the area of behavior therapy is a prediction of treatment outcome. However Steffy and his colleagues predicted in accord with learning theory that the men who showed the best conditioning should show more evidence of generalization on the SAS after treatment as well as less acting out after release from prison.

Of 43 men treated and followed up over a 4 year period, 11 had recidivated or were suspected of acting out but were not caught. This represents a 75% success rate. The interpretation of conditioning data is complex but there were no clear differences in success and failure groups on GSR reactivity to the SAS. Failed patients showed more overlap of verbal attractiveness ratings of children and adults while successful ones reported greater attraction to children. McConaghy[46] also found that conditionability was not related to treatment outcome for homosexual patients (Chapter 4). One must question whether in fact conditioning is occurring in aversion therapy.

The Steffy and Gauthier study represents the largest number of cases of pedophilia reported to date. It is unfortunate they did not use penile measurement in their study. Quinsey et al[59] compared pedophiles, other prisoners and community volunteers on penile circumference changes, skin conductance and verbal reports of erotic arousal to pictures of males and females at various ages and to neutral scenes. Skin conductance (SC) is related to but not identical with GSR. Both SC and verbal ratings failed to distinguish pedophilic and control groups while penile measurement did.

Quinsey, Bergersen and Steinman[57] further used these three types of measurement to investigate therapy outcome in an uncontrolled group study. Ten pedophiles; five heterosexual, three homosexual, one bisexual and one unspecified case were given a course of 20 sessions of classical conditioning although some who did not respond favorably were given more. There were eight shocks given to 10 slides of children. Penile circumference changes before, during and after therapy failed to discriminate adult and child slides although both were distinct from neutral stimuli. Thus differences in response to child and adult were minimal so one may wonder about a pedophilic preference in the study group. Skin conductance responses did discriminate adult and child slides, the largest reactions being to children. However, as in Steffy's study, these reactions existed before therapy and did not change with treatment. There was no report of follow up or in fact if the prisoners were released after treatment. In a further study they did examine released individuals.

In the subsequent study Quinsey, Chaplin and Carrigan[58], compared response contingent shock (operant conditioning) and biofeedback, in part, because the classical conditioning method they used in the earlier study was unsatisfactory. Therefore when penile reactions were above criterion to children, a shock was administered. In the biofeedback procedure, colored lights were used to tell the patient prisoner when tumescence was increasing to adult females and decreasing to children. Twenty-one patients received treatment, eight had only the punishment while the rest had both and the order of treatments for the latter was varied. Biofeedback was found relatively ineffective whereas aversion therapy was effective. A follow up of 30 pedophilic patients including some of the 21 in this study showed 20% redicivated within 28 months. Repeated offenders showed larger penile reactions to children after treatment than successful cases. The authors note that data are preliminary and the sample size is small but the diagnostic significance of the results is promising.

Nolan and Sandman[51] treated a heterosexual (bisexual ?) pedophile with an aversive conditioning procedure they labelled "biosyntonic therapy". Rather than monitor reactions to erotic stimuli, they attempted to identify the pattern of physiological reactivity characteristic of the individual patient. They noted that such patterns are highly idiosyncratic so each person should be treated individually. Heart rate, peripheral vasomotor activity, respiration and skin potential were used and once the pattern of reactivity to the child was identified it was punished by electric shock in traditional operant fashion. However reactions to mature females were differentially and positively reinforced with money in a second phase of the study. At six month follow up the patient had not recidivated. The biosyntonic aspect of the treatment however remains dubious. The relationship of penile reactions to other physiological events is a poor and uncertain one (Chapter Two). Moreover identifying these patterns is time consuming and expensive. The simple use of phallometry is much cheaper and clearer.

Levin and his colleagues[41] treated a 39-year-old married heterosexual pedophile who was also incestuous. There were 32 one hour sessions with three variants of aversive conditioning used in this thorough report. Initially, covert sensitization was used in which fantasies of sexual arousal to children were conditioning stimuli and imagined nausea was the unconditioned stimulus which followed. Aversion relief was next in which the patient imagined being attracted to women. This procedure had limited effectiveness and the second set of aversion trials was similar only valeric acid, a foul smelling chemical, served as a tangible aversive stimulus to accompany the imagined nausea. Finally psychologically unconditioned aversive stimuli were used which depicted past unpleasant consequences of sexual misbehavior, for example, being caught by wife, or ridiculed by police.

Both self report and penile tumescence were measured to slides of adults and children before and after treatment. Both measures indicated improvement. Penile arousal to children decreased from 62% full erection before treatment to 3% after, while reactions to adults increased from 5% to 30%. The authors note that the greatest changes occurred when valeric acid was used but its individual effectiveness could equally be explained by its order in the sequence of methods. The authors were careful to check that there was generalization from material used in treatment to non therapy slides and it did. At the 10 month follow up, phallometric testing was again used and reactions were much more variable. The patient said he lacked interest in children and he reacted to slides of them only with 3% to 17% full erections, averaging 10%. However only 6% to 48% penile tumescence, average 20%, was given to adults leaving doubt that his reactivity to them was enhanced. Moreover he only had limited opportunity to act out since he was an inpatient during those 10 months.

The outcome of aversion therapy for pedophilia is comparable to other sexual anomalies. Unfortunately the same problems and inadequate controls are also evident (See Chapter 3 for details). It has not generally been clear if the pedophiles were homosexual or heterosexual, married or single, what the age range of children involved were, if there was an erotic preference for children and how penile reactions to mature females compared with those to children. The very few studies examining penile reactions after treatment indicated that there was little change, raising the question of exactly what, if anything, was altered.

Peculiar to the aversion therapy of pedophilia is the number of reports attempting during treatment to examine physiological reactions other than penile responses. Generally the measures have not been useful because they reflect general arousal which is only weakly related to sexual arousal[21]. Since these physiological measures are also laborious to score and/or expensive as well as ineffective or unproven, it would seem best to use penile measurement at present.

Quinsey[55] has reviewed methodological issues in evaluating aversion therapy for imprisoned pedophiles. He especially noted malingering as a problem and the fakability of results including phallometric testing. The variables of therapeutic import assume a different meaning for men seeking a ticket to freedom. Setting one's own shock level at "painful" or "unpleasant" and using fantasies can be particularly problematic. Quinsey concludes that the success rate of aversion therapy is not high enough to permit confidence in deciding whether an individual should be released into the community.

Multiple Treatment Approaches

A few reports have combined several therapy procedures on the same person. The perceived advantage of the multiple treatment approach is that since patients usually have many problems, a variety of methods should be applied, each to the appropriate problem. The pedophile is attracted to children and aversive conditioning could be used to reduce the frequency of his urges. He may experience difficulty relating to women in heterosexual relationships and assertion therapy or reciprocal inhibition might be useful to help him overcome that difficulty, and so on.

Marshall[43] used multiple procedures to treat a bisexual pedophilic prison inmate. Avoidance conditioning, after Feldman and McCullouch's method, served to aversively reduce arousal to children. Details are not specified but there were 30 sessions over a 3 week period. Then at the end of this program desensitization of heterosexual anxiety (Chapter 3) was started in conjunction with social skills training. The latter was applied to relations with females and involved role playing, coaching and modelling. Fifteen 45 minute sessions were conducted over 2 months. The patient changed masturbation fantasies from children to exclusively adult female images. He also reported a reduction in anxiety to brief contacts with female office workers but he was not released on parole. This is a serious limitation in testing any treatment on pedophilia. Because prison authorities are very reluctant to release such offenders into the community, we cannot know if they act out again with children.

Prison serves three functions: Retribution for crime, deterring the offender from further offences and rehabilitating him to a new and hopefully normal life upon release into the community. Social pressures to fulfill the first two functions can interfere with the rehabilitative goals of therapy. The lack of substantial evidence that therapy procedures are effective in other noncriminal anomalies are ample reason for the hesitancy of prison authorities to test out treatment effectiveness in the community.

Marshall[44] also used avoidance conditioning with orgasmic reconditioning in a mixed group of sexual anomalies which included two heterosexual, two homosexual and one bisexual pedophile. The unique feature of his study, for pedophilia at least, was the pre-and-post-treatment asessment of penile circumference changes to children and adults. Generally reactions to children decreased whereas those to adults increased. One homosexual pedophile did recidivate but that still represents an 80% success rate after 3-to-16 months.

In another multiple treatment study Forgione[17] used mannequins in a novel way to both assess and treat a 17-year-old single heterosexual pedophile and a 56-year-old married bisexual pedophile. In effect, patients acted out their pedophilic behavior and fantasies with life sized mannequins while being photographed. Treatment involved aversive conditioning, family counselling and assertion training. The younger patient was also subjected to orgasmic reconditioning. First in classical aversive conditioning pictures of the mannequin children and patients interacting were followed by inevitable shock. This sequence was followed by slides of adult or pubescent females and of heterosexual couples. This served as anxiety relief conditioning. Then the patient could escape shock by saying "no more" or "take it away". Finally this was changed to 30 trials of avoidance conditioning in which the patient could avoid shock by removing the pictures of children within 3 seconds after they were presented.

Two sessions of family counselling was designed to relieve fears about future acting out and to teach everyone involved with the patient to reinforce his assertive behavior. Assertion training was taught for 1 hour by a female therapist. Three monthly booster sessions of avoidance conditioning and counselling the family to deal with changes also were used. Three year follow up of the heterosexual pedophile and 2 years for the bisexual showed they had not acted out again. The bisexual had some fantasies of children but they were easy to control. Forgione argued that the use of mannequins permitted the therapist to use conditioning stimuli that were more realistic than could be provided otherwise.

Kohlenberg[36] presented a unique and instructive report on the treatment of a homosexual pedophile. The therapist attempted to adapt the pedophile to homosexual relations with mature men rather than the typical attempts at adaptation to adult females. Since the homosexual pedophile is more responsive to adult men than adult women generally such an adjustment would seem to be a practical and attainable goal of therapy[24][25]. The

34-year-old patient had two arrests for sexual involvement with 6-to-12-year-old boys. He also peeped at them as a more general means of acting out and had a rich fantasy life.

Initially classical aversive imagery conditioning was employed. The patient imaged scenes involving children and signalled when the image was vivid at which time shock was delivered. There were four sessions of 11 pairings of images and shocks after which this method was terminated. The author thought the aversion therapy was not effective since the frequency of pedophilic thoughts in the patient's daily life was not decreasing from baseline. Judging from Kohlenberg's graph of the data, pedophilic thoughts may even have been on the increase. The author suggested that the number of pairings may have been insufficient or the shock may not have been strong enough. However rather than test these hypotheses he switched to a Masters and Johnsons type therapy for sexual dysfunction. A sexual partner who was a friend of the patient's took part in the treatment. They were to give each other sensate pleasure in any form of body contact but touching of the genitals and anus. Sexual arousal was *not* a goal of the session. Rather, the anxiety of close encounters to males was to be reduced. At first the patient was tense but later relaxed and in so doing became sexually aroused. At follow up 6 months later he had not acted out again either in peeping at children or in seeking sexual contact with them. He was however engaging more in sexual outlet with men. Because of the novelty of the approach, comments on the study were invited. Davison and Wilson[10] noted that although many therapists might object to the treatment on ethical grounds, that homosexual androphilia is a viable lifestyle and treatment goal (See also [72]). However they criticized the treatment program.

They noted that the analysis of the pedophilia was inadequate. They objected to aversion therapy being used first especially since the man was anxious with adults. They indicated that there is no evidence to suggest that the unwanted behavior, the pedophilia in this case, has to be interrupted before a new behavior can emerge. Work on other sexual anomalies suggests that effective change can be obtained without aversion therapy and that the outcome is just as effective.

The success of the case study is marred by the fact that the patient had a history of sexual activity with men to begin with and the frequency of his acting out with children was rather low. A much longer follow up would therefore be necessary to conclude that treatment was effective. Apparently his contact with men after treatment was only two or three times a month which is rather low for a 34-year-old man. It would be important to know that this was satisfactory for him in meeting his sexual needs. As Davison and Wilson noted, was he happy now?

Related to the problems Davison and Wilson raise is the fact that treatment was not based on any theory of pedophilia. Treatments are tried and in the case of multiple treatments, one is never certain which is having its effect or if all are in fact necessary. The therapy can become a shotgun approach which is time consuming and expensive and in the long run, one still wonders if it was effective and if so, how it had its impact on changing behavior.

Edwards[12] reported a case of homosexual incest involving three sons ages 13, 9 and 5 over a ten year period. It started when the patient discovered his wife having an extramarital affair so the issue of revenge against his wife rather than a true erotic pedophilic interest may be raised.

The patient had spent a year in psychoanalysis but although it helped him feel better about himself, his incestuous behavior continued. In the current treatment, thought stopping and assertion therapy were used. The exact procedure was not specified for thought stopping but an example might be: (1) Thought of sex with a child enters his mind, (2) He interrupts this with a loud "No!" or "Stop that!". This is repeated every time the thought occurs. His "pedophilic" thoughts decreased to once or twice a week and sexual relationships with his wife improved. He then left the country for a month and upon return he was engaged in assertive training, reading *Your Perfect Right*. This improved his relationship with his wife in which he exercised greater control over their relationship. At 4 month follow up there was no relapse. Although the case is atypical it was nonetheless effective without electrical aversion therapy.

Positive Behavior Therapy Procedures

It has been noted in the treatment of homosexuality (Chapter 4) that positive heterosocial enhancement procedures like assertion training and systematic desensitization can have as effective an outcome as aversion therapy. The same may be true for pedophilia. However there are only a few test cases.

Laws[40] adapted Barlow's fading procedure for homosexuals to treat a 44-year-old heterosexual pedophlic prisoner with a history of acting out with 8-to-10-year-old girls and to treat a 22-year-old homosexual pedophile with a history of acting out with 12-to-13-year-old boys. In the fading method an arousing stimulus is first presented, in this case, of children. The patient must maintain arousal, usually 75% full erection, while the picture of an adult is faded in and the child faded out. Slides are selected by the patient so the children are arousing and the adult females are neutral or at least not aversive. By juggling the images to maintain the erection, eventually the patient finds himself with an erection before the adult female slide alone.

Laws did this but in addition faded adult to child in a "mild covert sensitization procedure." Patients imagined themselves in a sexual situation with the adult female. If aroused, they were allowed to see the slide of the child fade in while telling themselves "Why am I attracted to this kid? It isn't as much fun as adults and I get in trouble. I will stop it. I don't want to be excited by kids". Then the adult was faded in again so they could become sexually aroused, telling themselves "This is better. She (or he) is much more attractive than that kid".

No follow up is reported on these two prisoners but the findings are interesting because this is one of the three studies in the literature that uses fading and it did not work. Laws used probe stimuli of solitary children and adults periodically to determine how well the patients were doing. There was virtually no change with the largest penile reactions still to the children rather than to adults.

The covert sensitization procedure was comparatively more effective but it failed to generalize to probe stimuli and the patients continued to show largest reactions to children. The heterosexual pedophile showed a transitory reversal in which he reacted more to the adult but at the end of treatment there appears to have been a general suppressing effect on all sexual arousal to male or female. This may be satiation with the slide material or the general temporary reduction in sexual arousal found in aversion therapy. It also seems similar to the loss of interest in patients doing orgasmic reconditioning. Their preferred object, children in this case, as well as the nonpreferred adult, all lose appeal. Perhaps discrimination learning could prevent this from happening. Laws likens the covert sensitization method he used to aversion relief and it too may have the same ineffective results because it is theoretically unsound.

Too few studies have been reported to make any clear statement on the effectiveness of positive conditioning procedures for pedophilia. Judging from their use with other sexual anomalies, they can be as effective as aversion therapy and since they are more humane and less dangerous, they should be tried more often on pedophiles.

Group Therapy

Several writers have recommended that pedophilia, like exhibitionism, is best treated by group therapy[67]. This may be particularly the case for pedophiles because often they are in prison where economic and practical limitations on personnel resources dictate the necessity of using group treatment.

Smith[67] used group therapy and dismissed individual psychotherapy as untested and too demanding for staff and dismissed chemotherapy and physical methods like ECT and castration as undesirable without clearly stating why. He thought group therapy is the method of choice because it allows patients with similar problems to share experiences and hopefully, gain insight and learn to control their socially unacceptable impulses. The patient can find a degree of acceptance in these groups which may facilitate development of interpersonal relationships.

Several criteria may be used to determine the inmate's or patient's suitability for return to the community: Development of strong conditioning against repeating his offense, insightful dissipation of neurotic distortions, gaining concern for others, maturing in attitudes and social responsibility, divesting himself of hostility and resentment, and enhancing self image as a mature adult who recognizes sex involves responsibility as well as pleasure. The criteria seem rather general and Smith offers no data on their reliability or validity. He presents three cases, two of exhibitionism and one of homosexual pedophilia. The latter was diagnosed as a sociopathic personality and in prison, he began to develop symptoms of paranoid psychosis. No real evaluation of a group therapy program is offered.

Marshall and McKnight[45] described a program for sex offenders, including pedophiles, who fall under Canadian legislation sentencing them as "dangerous sex offenders". Group therapy was employed but the emphasis was on laboratory based behavioral modification assessment and treatment, including aversion therapy, training in social skills and a ward program involving a graded introduction to social interaction. One heterosexual and two homosexual pedophiles were subjected to the avoidance therapy. The patients also experienced anxiety in the presence of adults and to reduce it, systematic densensitization was used while modelling and role playing were used to improve appropriate social behaviors. The ward based program was tied into social skills training and aimed to introduce them to an individual social contact interaction. This was gradually expanded. Group therapy focused on discussion of current difficulties and was reality-oriented. Interpretations of problems were not offered so this may not have constituted traditional psychotherapy.

Treatment was 4, 5, and 8 months long for the three patients respectively. The heterosexual pedophile was not released although all three patients showed immediate post therapy improvement. One homosexual case recidivated after 18 months in the community but the other had not after 8 months. As in the multiple behavior therapy programs, it is difficult to know what, if any, element of treatment is most important in outcome.

A number of writers have discussed group therapy approaches with pedophiles[31 42 62 65 75] but only Hartman[31] has presented any outcome results. Seven heterosexual pedophiles were treated with 90 minute weekly analytically oriented group psychotherapy for 4 years. The treatment aimed at long term character changes and six of seven could be regarded as "having recovered from the pedophilia". This may mean "at least controlling their infrequent pedophilic urges". Thus we do not know if their erotic preferences have changed and one may wonder if a shorter course in behavior therapy would not be as effective as this long treatment.

Serber and Keith[65] described an interesting group therapy approach in which a sexual retraining program was used with homosexual pedophiles. It included desensitization and education of prison staff, cooperation with local gay groups and sexual retraining of the homosexual pedophiles in the direction of adult homosexual behavior. This would seem like the most readily attainable goal of therapy for homosexual pedophiles and the initial report is glowing but no outcome or follow up data are reported.

Quinsey[56] reviewed group therapy studies of pedophilia indicating that it remained the most widely used treatment for this anomaly. He criticized the studies as being based on contradictory premises and the method used being so generally described that replication would seem impossible. There is little data to indicate that changes occur within the groups nor has the effectiveness of group therapy been compared to other treatments. Collectively group therapy studies of pedophilia has been poorly delineated without reference to direction of treatment or theoretical characteristics of the pedophile which are the targets of treatment. Follow ups were short and assessments so general that the effectiveness of this procedure is uncertain. The poor outcome of group therapy with exhibitionism (Chapter 10) which could be traced might serve as a guide to the use of this approach.

Individual Psychotherapy

Only a few case reports are available on the treatment of pedophiles with psychotherapy methods. They have been reviewed by Mohr, Turner and Jerry[49] (See also for examples, [7] [37] [38]). As in group therapy, writers have talked about the approach to use with pedophiles but have presented no data. Karpman[33] presented a detailed report of a heterosexual pedophile "cured" by psychoanalysis. The free association and analysis of dreams was extensively reported. The start of pedophilia was traced to an aversion to the pubic hair of the adult female when the offender was 7-years-old. An adult female neighbor had undressed him and herself and forced intercourse. He emphasized how hairy she was and how it frightened him. Presumably reliving his experience and breaking through the anxiety to the adult female ended his pedophilic desires but little information is provided and this must be inferred. Bell and Hall[5] also reported over 1300 dreams of a pedophile but they were not concerned with treatment. The interested psychoanalytic reader may find it useful.

Conn[8] used brief psychotherapy and included hypnotherapy for some cases treated for pedophilia and other sexual offences. Two pedophiles are discussed and, in one case especially, unassertiveness appeared to be a major problem which was improved by therapy. It is unclear from the two cases whether there were still pedophilic urges after treatment.

Corsini[9] used psychodrama to treat an incarcerated pedophile who suffered from an "inferiority complex". The patient had fondled a young girl but indicated that he never had the slightest pedophilc desire previously and his behavior was a mystery to him. Psychodrama revealed that the crime against thc child was not due to "any perversion" but was due to a desire to be punished for having wished his father was dead. Once again the outcome of the case is uncertain so that the total effectiveness of psychotherapy methods with pedophiles remains unknown.

Chemotherapy

The use of antiandrogens in treatment of sexual anomalies has increased in popularity but very limited work has been done generally. Van Moffaert[78] reported two cases treated with cyproterone acetate, provera and psychotherapy. One case was a homosexual pedophile which is inadequately described and the other a case of an exhibitionist-fetishist. The pedophile had previously received estrogens and psychotherapy without success. He was then given cyproterone and later, provera, a less effective but potent agent, was substituted. After a year of treatment he was not seeking out boys and his leisure interests involved social contact with adults.

There are two problems at least with such a treatment program in pedophiles. First, the patient must be kept on the drugs indcfinitcly since urges to act out are pervasive whereas exhibitionism is a more seasonal outlet which means drugs could be administered on a demand basis. The second problem stems from the first. Long term use of both antiandrogen drugs has undesirable side effects. Cyproterone may cause the testicles to atrophy whereas provera may lead to infertility by hyaliniation of the tubuli seminiferi[78]. Other side effects, noted in Chapter Three, indicate overall that the physical sequelae of these drugs may far outweigh social benefits derived.

Spodak and his colleagues[68] reported seven cases treated with Depo-provera, up to a maximum of 500 milligrams per week. Five cases were pedophilic; four homosexual and one heterosexual. No time span of treatment or follow up was indicated but two homosexual pedophiles were arrested again but the other three were doing well. The heterosexual patient was able to have sex with his wife but the two homosexual patients appear to have had no sexual outlet. This would be an intolerable situation to many men. It is generally accepted, among behavior therapists at least, that a substitute sexual outlet must replace the anomalous one. The antiandrogens affect only the arousal component of sex behavior and not its direction. Once the drug is no longer administered, the original preferred object of sexual gratification is sought out. At best then, chemotherapy is an adjunct to treating the sexual anomaly. It may help to temporarily reduce urges to act out while other therapy is used in attempts to change the sex object choice.

Castration

The permanent removal of sexual urges comes to mind when pedophilia or violent sexual offences are discussed. The topic has been discussed in Chapter Three and only a cursory note is made here. It is an unproven method and penile arousal is still possible after castration. Recidivism rates seem low in reported studies but generally it is difficult to know to whom the data refers. "Offenders" rather than pedophiles or rapists are superficially described. Since recidivism rates are so low for sex offenders who are not castrated, it becomes a questionable procedure. Physical health problems and perhaps mental health ones too are of great concern as an outcome of castration. The patient may not be happy and he may continue to be troublesome socially as well as be a burden on the health care system which has to deal with the physical consequences of castration. Castration of pedophiles has not been specifically reported but the interested reader may wish to see general results described in Chapter Three.

Treatment of Choice

Treatments used on pedophiles are summarized in Table 8.2. Selection of a best treatment for pedophilia is hampered by the poor reporting of cases in the literature. There is an important distinction between homosexual and heterosexual pedophile which is often glossed over. Both groups may be mixed together, and simply labelled "pedophiles". Men who are bisexual are rarely assessed phallometrically. The heterosexual group shows considerable reactivity to adult females and a program aimed at heterosexual adaptation seems reasonable. However the homosexual pedophile reacts first to boys, secondly to adult males and not at all to females. A treatment aimed at homosexual adaptation with adults would therefore seem more likely to succeed. In light of social changes and the new professional perspective on homosexuality, this would be a humane and ethical treatment goal.

Bisexual pedophilia is a singular anomaly to date since there are erotic reactions to body characteristics of the male and female. Most often erotic reactions to the sexes are not identical and a predominant reaction to girls or to boys, is evident. As a correlate of these findings, a greater reactivity to adult women or to men may also be evident. From phallometric testing, the therapist can decide whether a heterosexual or homosexual adaptation to adults is more feasible.

TABLE 8.2
Summary of Treatment Effectiveness for Pedophilia

Method	Results
1. Aversion Therapies	Success comparable to other anomalies. Unknown if erotic preference for children has been changed and in fact it is not usually assessed systematically. No controlled study available
2. Multiple Behavior Therapy	Positive in case studies. Same problems of multiple treatment as in other anomalies: what are effective ingredients
3. Positive methods: assertion therapy, systematic desensitization, Masters and Johnson method	Case studies positive. One unique treatment adapted homosexual pedophile to androphilia
4. Group Therapy	Poorly evaluated, mixed programs in general. Outcome ambiguous
5. Psychotherapy	Only a few case reports. Some positive outcomes
6. Antiandrogens	Generally positive results but patient usually on high doses of drugs. Physical risks become problem of concern. No controlled study
7. Castration	Outcome positive but no controlled study of pedophilia per se. Only a few cases may have been treated

Two other groups are confused with pedophiles, normal men and incestuous men, also making evaluation difficult. The "child" involved may be a minor under the law which can mean 16 or even 18 years of age. When the offender is 17 or 19 years of age, and the victim 16 years old, the meaning of pedophilia is suspect and likely inappropriate. Usually we do not know the preferred age of partners for the pedophile. Phallometric testing would clarify age preferences greatly and sort out normal men who need little or no treatment. Even in those cases where the "child" is clearly immature, for example, 6 or 8 years old, the "pedophile" may be acting in an atypical way due to situational stress and may show a normal erotic profile on the phallometric test. Recidivism is rare in such cases. Generally it is low among sex offenders, about 20%[48], so little intervention is necessary other than probation, counselling and perhaps a change in their living conditions[56]. It is the repeated offender who requires therapeutic attention.

In incest cases, many offenders appear to prefer the mature female body, and very few are true pedophiles. Incestuous pedophilic men doubly transgress social norms by sexual involvement with a child and with a family member. Pedophiles are usually not incestuous.

Now assuming we are talking about "true" pedophiles, some goals of treatment can be suggested. It is important for the patient to feel you are on his side and for him to know that you are aware how important his object preference is to him. This basic acceptance can greatly enhance his self esteem. Lewis Carroll has been considered pedophilic and yet he offered much joy to the world. Adachi[1] has noted that " . . . . interpreting Carroll has become one of the psychoanalytical games of this century, achieving—if nothing else—a sobering diminution of his reader's pleasure". Hopefully we will not do this to our patients. The major goal of therapy is keeping the patient out of trouble with the law. Stressing social consequences of being caught and of imprisonment can help. Then use of masturbation to reduce sex drive and control over his environment to eliminate opportunities to act out may be valuable to him as well. A change in the route to work or daily habits may be helpful in reducing the number of opportunities to act out.

The presence of mental retardation and disease processes may be a complicating factor in any sexual anomaly but these factors have been of particular concern to theorists working on pedophilia. They do not occur more frequently in this anomaly but when they do, treatment is complicated. Disease processes must be controlled concurrently. Quinsey[56] has suggested that in cases of mental retardation direct teaching of sexual skills and of Masters and Johnson's direct instruction method used in sexual dysfunction may be applicable. Given a supportive relationship, different methods can be experimentally tested to adapt the patient to adults if he so wishes. It must be experimental because there is no satisfactorily proven method to change him to date.

In many cases the physical attributes of the child cannot be important, for example, pubescent victims. Rather the victim's immaturity and/or inexperience seem noteworthy. The benevolent teacher role played by the patient in such contexts or his need to dominate and control his victim would be interesting treatment targets for either psychotherapy or behavior modification. It seems that the very features of the child which deter normal men, such as innocence and emotional immaturity, are attractive to the pedophile. Etiological and therapy investigation may do well to examine these unexplored areas.

BIBLIOGRAPHY

1. Adache, T. On Lewis Carroll. Toronto Star, January 19, 1980.
2. Atwood, R., & Howell, R. Pupillometric and personality test scores of female aggressing, pedophiliacs and normals. *Psychonomic Science,* 1971, *22*(2), 115–116.
3. Bancroft, J. *Deviant Sexual Behavior.* London: Oxford University Press, 1974.
4. Bancroft, J., & Marks, I. Electric aversion therapy of sexual deviations. *Proceedings of the Royal Society of Medicine,* 1968, *61,* 796–798.
5. Bell, A. P., & Hall, C. S. *The personality of a child molester,* Aldine Atherton Ltd., 1971.
6. Bernard, F. An enquiry among a group of pedophiles. *The Journal of Sex Research,* 1975, *3,* 242–255.
7. Cassity, J. H. Psychological considerations of pedophilia. *Psychoanalytic Review,* 1927, *14,* 189–199.
8. Conn, J. H. Brief psychotherapy of the sex offender. A report of a liason service between a court and a private psychiatrist. *Clinical Psychopathology,* 1949, *10,* 347–372.
9. Corsini, R. J. Psychodramatic treatment of a pedophile. *Group Psychotherapy,* 1951, *4,* 166–171.
10. Davison, G. C., & Wilson, G. T. Goals and strategies in behavioral treatment of homosexual pedophilia: Comments on a case study. *Journal of Abnormal Psychology,* 1974, *83*(2), 196–198.
11. Dingman, H. F., Frisbie, L., & Vanasek, F. J. Erosion of morale in resocialization of pedophiles. *Psychological Reports,* 1968, *23,* 792–794.
12. Edwards, N. B. Case conference: Assertive training in a case of homosexual pedophilia. *Journal of Behavioral Therapy and Experimental Psychiatry,* 1972, *3,* 55–63.
13. Feldman, M. P., & McCullough, M. J. *Homosexual Behavior: Therapy and Assessment.* Oxford: Pergamon Press, 1971.
14. Fisher, G. Psychological needs of heterosexual pedophiliacs. *Diseases of the Nervous System,* 1969, *30,* 419–421.
15. Fisher, G., & Howell, L. Psychological needs of homosexual pedophiliacs. *Diseases of the Nervous System,* 1970, *31*(9), 623–625.
16. Fitch, J. H. Men convicted of sexual offences against children. *British Journal of Criminology,* 1962, *3,* 18–27.
17. Forgione, A. G. The use of mannequins in the behavioral assessment of child molesters: Two case reports. *Behavior Therapy,* 1976, *7,* 678–685.
18. Freund, K. Diagnosing heterosexual pedophilia by means of a test for sexual interest. *Behavioral Research & Therapy,* 1965, *3,* 229–234.
19. Freund, K. Diagnosing homo- or heterosexuality and erotic age-preference by means of a psychophysiological test. *Behavioral Research & Therapy,* 1967a, *5,* 209–228.
20. Freund, K. Erotic preference in pedophilia. *Behavioral Research & Therapy,* 1967b, *5,* 339–348.
21. Freund, K. Psychophysiological assessment of change in erotic preferences. *Behavioral Research & Therapy,* 1977, *15,* 297–301.
22. Freund, K., & Chan, S., Coulthard, R. Phallometric diagnosis with 'nonadmitters'. *Behavioral Research & Therapy,* 1979, *17,* 451–457.

23. Freund, K., McKnight, C. K., Langevin, R., & Cibiri, S. The female child as a surrogate object. *Archives of Sexual Behavior*, 1972, *2*, 119-133.

24. Freund, K., Langevin, R., Wescom, T., & Zajac, Y. Heterosexual interest in homosexual males. *Archives of Sexual Behavior*, 1975, *4*, 509-517.

25. Freund, K., & Langevin, R. Bisexuality in homosexual pedophilia. *Archives of Sexual Behavior*, 1976, *5*, 415-423.

26. Freund, K., Scher, H., Chan, S., & Ben-Aron, M. Experimental analysis of pedophilia. Unpublished manuscript. Clarke Institute of Psychiatry, Toronto, 1981.

27. Frisbie, L. V., Vanasek, F. J., & Dingman, H. F. The self and the ideal self: Methodological study of pedophiles. *Psychological Reports*, 1967, *20*, 699-706.

28. Gebhard, P., Gagnon, J., Pomeroy, W., & Christenson, C. *Sex Offenders*, New York: Harper & Row, 1965.

29. Glueck, B. C. Psychodynamic patterns in the homosexual sex offender. *American Journal of Psychiatry*, 1956, *112*(8), 584-590.

30. Groth, W., & Birnbaum, H. *Men Who Rape: The Psychology of the Offender*. New York: Plenum Press, 1979.

31. Hartman, V. Notes on group psychotherapy with pedophiles. *Canadian Psychiatric Association Journal*, 1965, *10*(4), 283-288.

32. Howells, K. Some meanings of children for pedophiles. In *Love and Attraction*. Cook, M., & Wilson, G. (Eds.). London: Pergamon Press, 1978.

33. Karpman, B. A case of paedophilia (legally rape) cured by psychoanalysis. *Psychoanalytic Review*, 1950, *37*, 235-276.

34. Karpman, B. *The Sexual Offender and His Offenses*. New York: Julian Press, 1957.

35. Kimble, G. A. Hilgard and Marquis' *Conditioning and Learning*, New York: Appleton Century Crofts Inc., 1961.

36. Kohlenberg, R. J. Treatment of a homosexual pedophiliac using in vivo desensitization: A case study. *Journal of Abnormal Psychology*, 1974, *83*(2), 192-195.

37. Kopp, S. B. The character structure of sex offenders. *American Journal of Psychotherapy*, 1962, *16*, 64-70.

38. Kurland, M. L. Pedophilia erotica. *Journal of Nervous & Mental Diseases*, 1960, *131*, 394-403.

39. Langevin, R., Paitich, D., Freeman, R., Mann, K., & Handy, L. Personality characteristics and sexual anomalies in males. *Canadian Journal of Behavioral Science*, 1978, *10*(3), 222-238.

40. Laws, D. R. Non-aversive treatment alternatives for hospitalized pedophiles: An automated fading procedure to alter sexual responsiveness. Paper presented at the meeting of the American Psychological Association, New Orleans, September, 1974.

41. Levin, S. M., Barry, S. M., Gambaro, S., Wolfinsohn, L., & Smith, A. Variations of covert sensitization in the treatment of pedophilic behavior: A case study. *Journal of Consulting and Clinical Psychology*, 1977, *45*(5), 896-907.

42. Marcus, A. *Nothing is My Number*. Toronto, General Publishing Company, 1971.

43. Marshall, W. L. A combined treatment method for certain sexual deviations. *Behavioral Research & Therapy*, 1971, *9*, 293-294.

44. Marshall, W. L. The modification of sexual fantasies: A combined treatment approach to the reduction of deviant sexual behavior. *Behavioral Research & Therapy*, 1973, *11*, 557-564.

45. Marshall, W. L., & McKnight, R. D. An integrated treatment program for sexual offenders. *Canadian Psychiatric Association Journal*, 1975, *20*, 133-138.

46. McConaghy, N. Penile response conditioning and its relationship to aversion therapy in homosexuals. *Behavior Therapy*, 1970, *1*, 213-221.

47. McCreary, C. P. Personality differences among child molesters. *Journal of Personality Assessment*, 1975, *39*(6), 591-593.

48. Mohr, J. Evaluation of treatment. In *Sexual Behaviors: Social, Clinical and Legal Aspects.* Boston: Little, Brown and Company, 1972, 412–426.

49. Mohr, J., Turner, R. E., & Jerry, M. *Pedophilia and Exhibitionism.* Toronto: University of Toronto Press, 1964.

50. Nedoma, K., Mellan, J., & Pondelickova, J. Sexual behavior and its development in pedophilic men. *Archives of Sexual Behavior,* 1971, *1,* 267–271.

51. Nolan, D. J., & Sandman, C. "Biosyntonic" therapy: Modification of an operant conditioning approach to pedophilia. *Journal of Consulting and Clinical Psychology,* 1978, *46*(5), 1133–1140.

52. Noyes, A. P., & Kolb, L. C. *Modern Clinical Psychiatry.* Philadelphia: Saunders and Company, 1958.

53. Paitich, D., & Langevin, R. The Clarke parent child relations questionnaire: a clinically useful test for adults. *Journal of Consulting and Clinical Psychology,* 1976, *44,* 428–436.

54. Paitich, D., Langevin, R., Freeman, R., Mann, K., & Handy, L. The Clarke SHQ: A clinical sex history questionnaire for males. *Archives of Sexual Behavior,* 1977, *6,* 421–436.

55. Quinsey, V. L. Methodological issues in evaluating the effectiveness of aversion therapies for institutionalized child molesters. *The Canadian Psychologist,* 1973, *14*(4), 350–361.

56. Quinsey, V. L. The assessment and treatment of child molesters: A review. *Canadian Psychological Review,* 1977, *18*(3), 204–220.

57. Quinsey, V. L., Bergersen, S. G., & Steinman, C. M. Changes in physiological and verbal responses of child molesters during aversion therapy. *Canadian Journal of Behavioral Science,* 1976, *8*(2), 202–212.

58. Quinsey, V. L., Chaplin, T. C., & Carrigan, W. F. Biofeedback and signaled punishment in the modification of inappropriate sexual age preferences. *Behavior Therapy,* 1980, *11,* 567–571.

59. Quinsey, V. L., Steinman, C. M., Bergersen, S. G., & Holmes, T. F. Penile circumference, skin conductance, and ranking responses of child molesters and "normals" to sexual and nonsexual visual stimuli. *Behavior Therapy,* 1975, *6,* 213–219.

60. Rada, R., Laws, D., & Kellner, R. Plasma testosterone levels in the rapist. *Psychosomatic Medicine,* 1976, *38*(4), 257–268.

61. Regestein, Q. R., & Reich, P. Pedophilia occurring after onset of cognitive impairment. *The Journal of Nervous and Mental Disease,* 1978, *166*(11), 794–798.

62. Resnik, H. L. P., & Peters, J. J. Outpatient group therapy with convicted pedophiles. *International Journal of Group Psychotherapy,* 1967, *17,* 151–158.

63. Revitch, E., & Weiss, R. G. The pedophiliac offender. *Diseases of the Nervous System,* 1962, *23,* 73–78.

64. Rosenthal, T. L. Response-contingent versus fixed punishment in aversion conditioning of pedophilia: A case study. *The Journal of Nervous and Mental Disease,* 1973, *156*(6), 440–443.

65. Serber, M., & Keith, C. G. The Atascadero Project: Model of a sexual retraining program for incarcerated homosexual pedophiles. *Journal of Homosexuality,* 1974, *1*(1), 87–97.

66. Shoor, M., Speed, M. H., & Bartelt, C. Syndrome of the adolescent child molester. *American Journal of Psychiatry,* 1966, *122,* 783–789.

67. Smith, C. E. Correctional treatment of the sexual deviate. *Journal of Psychiatry,* 1968, *125*(5), 615–621.

68. Spodak, M. K., Falck, Z. A., & Rappeport, J. R. The hormonal treatment of paraphiliacs with depo-provera. *Criminal Justice and Behavior,* 1978, *5*(4), 304–313.

69. Steffy, R. A. A plan for an aversive conditioning behavior therapy for pedophile

offenders. Lakeshore Psychiatric Hospital, New Toronto, Ontario. Delivered to the meeting of correctional psychologists, Montreal, August 29, 1965.

70. Steffy, R. A. Progress report on the treatment of the pedophile sex offender: Development of the sexual attractiveness scale (SAS). Lakeshore Psychiatric Hospital. Paper delivered to the Alex G. Brown Memorial Clinic Fourth Annual Conference on addictions and on sexual deviation at the A.G. Brown Clinic, Mimico, Ontario, April 28, 1967.

71. Steffy, R. A., & Gauthier, R. Psychophysiological factors in aversive behavior therapies: A contrast between successfully and unsuccessfully treated pedophile offenders. Paper delivered to the OPA Annual meetings, Kingston, Ontario, February 5, 1970.

72. Strupp, H. H. Some observations on the fallacy of value-free psychotherapy and the empty organism: Comments on a case study. *Journal of Abnormal Psychology,* 1974, *83*(2), 199–201.

73. Swanson, D. W. Adult sexual abuse of children. *Diseases of the Nervous System,* 1968, *29,* 677–683.

74. Toobert, S., Bartelme, K. F., & Jones, E. S. Some factors related to pedophilia. *International Journal of Psychiatry,* 1959, *4,* 272–279.

75. Turner, R. E. The group treatment of sexual deviations. *Canadian Journal of Corrections,* 1961, *3,* 485–489.

76. Tuteur, W. Child molesters and men who expose themselves—An anthropological approach. *Journal of Forensic Science,* 1963, *8,* 515–525.

77. Vanasek, F. J., Frisbie, L. V., & Dingman, H. F. Patterns of affective responses in two groups of pedophiles. *Psychological Reports,* 1968, *22,* 659–668.

78. Van Moffaert, M. Social reintegration of sexual delinquents by a combination of psychotherapy and anti-androgen treatment. *Acta Psychiatrica Scandanavica,* 1976, *53,* 29–34.

79. Virkkunen, M. The pedophilic offender with antisocial character. *Acta Psychiatrica Scandanavica,* 1976, *53,* 401–405.

80. Wijesinghe, B. Massed aversion treatment of sexual deviance. *Journal of Behavior Therapy and Experimental Psychiatry,* 1977, *8,* 135–137.

9 Incest

There is almost universal prohibition against sexual relations between certain individuals who are kin. The nuclear family of mother, father, brothers and sisters are prohibited sexual interaction by the taboo but other relatives like uncles, aunts, cousins and steprelatives are also included. Beyond the nuclear family, the exact kin forbidden sexual relationships appear to be culturally determined. All mother's clan may be off limits for example. There are notable exceptions to the incest taboo, for example, the pharoahs of Egypt inbred to keep the royal blood pure[34].

The meaning of incest can be ambiguous. Incest proper usually involves evidence of familial intercourse with orgasm although it may include sex contact such as fondling and touching without vaginal penetration. The latter category is so broad that it can be overinclusive, for example, any kind of intentionally arousing contact to the sexual organs by a family member may be labelled incest[15]. Some theorists believe children have sexual fantasies toward their parents and a wide range of behaviors may be interpreted as sexual. Once again the criterion of orgasmic outlet clearly defines this sexual problem. However, the presence of a criminal charge may be a more practical criterion of incest since it reflects the existence of a family problem. Moreover incest need not involve a sexual anomaly. In almost 80% of reported cases, intercourse takes place between father and pubescent or post-pubescent daughter[53]. Only some fathers are pedophilic and have had sexual contact with children other than their own. The second largest reported number of incest cases are between brother and sister (about 20%) whereas mother-son, father-son and multiple relationships explain a minor 2%-to-3% of cases[28 40 41 43]. It would seem that incest usually involves appropriate sex stimuli and responses. It is the socially defined relationships which makes it a problem.

A number of reports have speculated on the incidence of the various incest relationships, arguing that father-son or brother-sister incest is common[11] or that the overall incidence is higher than reported[15] [53]. We cannot know the incidence of unreported or undetected behavior. It would therefore seem unfounded to make statements like "brother-sister incest is more common than it is reported." To date only Finkelhor[16] has offered any perspective on this notion. In surveying 796 university students, he found that 15% of the females and 10% of the males reported some familial sibling sexual experience. Unfortunately we do not know exactly what is implied by "sexual experience". It at least includes exhibiting, fondling, touching, intercourse and attempted intercourse. Less than 2% of the sample engaged in attempts at intercourse or completed the act. The two types of activities are not distinguished in the report. Therefore in the only empirical study addressing the question, the postulated higher incidence of sibling incest was not found.

Generally incest has been treated as a social familial problem[23] [36] [53] and it is doubtful in many cases whether a sexual anomaly is involved. However, the presence of the latter is often implicit in discussions of incest and for this reason, the topic has been included in the book.

THEORIES

The primal horde. A major question which occupied Victorian and early twentieth century anthropologists is why the incest taboo exists at all. Freud (in Henderson [23], See also Rist, [44]) speculated that in primal hordes of early men, rivalry for women was so common that young men inevitably banded together to murder the tyrant father who kept all the women to himself. The subsequent fighting among the young brothers was so disruptive to the social organization that the incest taboo was developed. This rather fanciful hypothesis is without foundation in fact (no one was around at the time of the primal horde) and is based on rather poor anthropological methods and overgeneralizations characteristic at the time. Similar seemingly plausible explanations were offered for a number of social and technological inventions. For example, one may speculate that the bow and arrow was invented one day, while a primitive man was bending a bush's branch and noticed how it snapped back. From this, he learned to make bows. The plausible but nonfactual explanations have been satirized by contemporary anthropologists who consider such notions premature and unacceptable.

Functional and biological basis of the incest taboo.   The incest taboo may be functionally described as fostering the child's dependency needs and allowing him/her to develop independence and to fulfill a role outside the family[24][44]. Perhaps this function and the protective nature of parenting more than anything else serves to prevent incest.

A biological basis for incest has been suggested by Lindzey (in [23]) and the Franceses[17]. Inbreeding is maladaptive in the long run, at least in terms of physical fitness and resistance to disease. So in the Darwinian sense of survival of the fittest, outbreeding is more likely to be naturally selected than inbreeding. However Karpman[25] and Ferracuti[13] argue that incest is strictly a cultural taboo and is not antibiological per se since normal procreation can result from the incestuous union. Bluglass[5] has reviewed the few studies which examine the children of incest. Up to 61% of the children had abnormalities and/or died in some studies but the largest controlled study on 161 Czechoslovakian children found very few abnormalities and their incidence was comparable in a control group[45].

Family dynamics.   The second question which has concerned theorists is determining which factors contribute to the breakdown of this powerful taboo. Sociological theory has dominated contemporary thinking. Incest is conceptualized as a collusion usually between father, mother and daughter,[23][44][53][54]. The whole family fears abandonment and uses incest to reduce anxiety and promote perpetuation of the family. Mother feels hostile to the daughter and forces her into the role of wife and lover, at the same time avoiding her own unwanted role with her husband. She may be sexually dysfunctional and incest relieves her worry over sexual matters. The daughter feels that without incest, there would be no family at all. A number of reports have been devoted to the daughter victims of incest who suffer later psychic trauma[3][7][10][22][23][48]. Sloane and Karpenski[46] noted that the daughter acts out her conflicts by indulging in promiscuous relationships instead of developing neurotic symptoms. Incest would then appear to be a defense against neurosis. Gordon[20] described it as an act of revenge against a depriving mother, which would be congruent with a character disorder in the daughter. Meiselman noted that there is no characteristic MMPI profile of female incest victims but they do experience various kinds of sexual problems in later life. While mother appears to be the villain in this theory, father and daughter also satisfy their needs in cooperating[15].

Mr. A was charged with carnal knowledge for oral genital sexual relations with his 9-year-old precocious daughter and he illustrates the family complicity in incest:

Mr. A: "Sex hasn't been good for the past couple of years. The wife works days and I work nights so we never get together. When we do, she is too tired or has a headache. I don't think she is really interested anymore."

Doctor: "Have you discussed separation?"

Mr. A: "I don't believe in that. I never had much of a family life myself and I want to keep ours together. I love my wife and daughter and I wouldn't hurt them for the world. That's why I feel so bad about this mess. I don't know what will happen now."

Doctor: "What do you do for sexual satisfaction now?"

Mr. A: "When Mary wouldn't give me any sex, I used to go down to the gay spots. It is easy to get a blow job. I feel disgusted after but if feels good while I get it. With us both working all the time I haven't even been able to do that. I have to mind Cindy and that's how it all started. You may not believe me but she started it. She knows a lot for a nine year old and wanted to come into the washroom when I was there. The lock is broken and she came in even when I said no. She asked me if she could touch it (penis) and one thing led to another. We have been at it for about six months. I feel guilty but in some ways it is better than sex with my wife. I feel close to my daughter."

It is interesting that the daughter is often viewed by the father as provocative just as the child is by the pedophile. However, this may simply represent the male's fantasy, perception, or justification of his own behavior rather than intentional behavior on the part of the child.

Lustig and his colleagues[29] noted five factors which result in the violation of the incest taboo: (1) The daughter is a central figure in the family replacing mother; (2) husband and wife are sexually incompatible such that father has unrelieved sexual tension; (3) father will not seek a sex partner outside his family; (4) all members fear family disintegration or abandonment and incest wards this fear off; (5) the mother unconsciously sanctions the incest. Other writers have proposed similar reasons[15]. The last point is noteworthy because mothers in incest cases often express horror when the father and daughter are finally discovered. Her complicity is therefore labeled "unconscious." Public knowledge of the incest often results in divorce and family dissolution[53].

Critical ages of family members.   The age of family members has been considered an important variable[23]. The father is in his late thirties or early forties during which period marital stress is most likely to develop and when death, separation and divorce more often occur. With a frustrating marriage and an attractive adolescent daughter, fathers are most likely to act out. However the age of father may be coincidental to incest. Since men charged with incest marry on the average at 22 to 24 years of age[18], the father would have to be at least 37 to have a 14 year old daughter, assuming the wife became pregnant immediately after marriage and the first child was a girl. This more parsimonious explanation may be the only reason for the ages of the incest participants.

Personality disturbance in incest offenders. Some writers have speculated that the father is "borderline", paranoid with unconscious homosexual strivings and that intellectual deficiency and constitutional inferiority may play a part in *some* cases. Cavallin[8] described the incestuous father as paranoid and unconsciously hostile to the helpless daughter in whom he acts out his primitive genital impulses. The fusion of alcoholism in incest and the association of incest with rape by some writers[15] supports the notion that it is a hostile act. Karpman[25] on the other hand and defined incest as a consenting relationship whereas rape is different and involves force. Weiner[53] noted the capacity of incestuous fathers to rationalize their behavior and to avoid guilt feelings.

Weinberg[51] describes three categories of incestuous fathers: introverts, psychopathic personality and pedophiles. All have poor sexual adjustments and their marital relations are devoid of affection. Karpman points out that homosexuality is an element in incest as one might expect from strong mother identification. However the unconscious reasoning is "If I cannot have sex with mother no one else will." Thus in homosexual relations with a man he prevents one further possible approach of a male to his mother.

As a group, incestuous fathers have been described as tyrannical, dominating their wives and families, and behaving without regard for feelings of other family members whom they intimidate. They are often violent and as part of their pattern of behavior, force themselves on their daughters. However some are shy, inhibited, ineffectual in social relations and depend on their wives for emotional and even financial support. All incestuous fathers feel inadequate as males and are angry toward women. All of these features are clinically inferred since systematic controlled studies are almost nonexistent[15].

Family background of incest offenders. According to psychoanalytic theory we all have unconscious desires for our opposite sexed parents so the problem of incest reduces to understanding why the desires break through to consciousness and overt acts in some cases. Kaufman, Peck and Tagiuri[26] postulated that a history of desertion anxiety is important. The wives of incestuous men have mothers who are stern, demanding, cold and hostile because their husbands deserted them. Their hostility was displaced to the daughters who became as a result hard, infantile, and later married men similar to themselves in character and who became incestuous later in life. The incest victim, the daughter, treated with hostility by mother, was lonely and fearful and accepted father's sexual advances as affection, tacitly encouraged to do so by mother.

Weiner considered incestuous fathers to have a disturbed relationship with their own fathers who were harsh and authoritarian. The sons both hated and admired their own fathers resulting in a passive homosexual longing for him and paradoxically satisfying this longing through an incestuous relationship with their daughter[35]. On the other hand, some theorists describe the mother as important in developing the incestuous behavior[25]. The father is either absent or not a strong character and this allows the mother to dominate. She extravagantly admires her son and spoils him to think his passive body is omnipotent. As a consequence the son does not develop the perception of himself as able to respond in a sexually adult manner. His overidentification with mother fosters his later incestuous behavior. One might label this the "God's Gift to Women Syndrome."

Incest as holding the family together. An important problem for psychoanalytic theory is the universality of incestuous desires as casual factors in a wide range of sexual anomalies. It remains to be explained why one anomaly rather than another develops. No clear answer has been offered to date. This theory must face the paradoxical postulate that both the incest taboo and acting out incestuously serve to keep the family together. The members avoid desertion anxiety and family dissolution by tacit participation in the incest act. However Freud's original postulate suggested that the incest *taboo prevented* family disintegration. This contradiction also needs resolution.

The role of social class, poverty, and alcohol in incest. Sociological variables have been implicated in incest: Lower social classes, rural homes, poverty, inadequate housing with crowding and poor sanitary facilities. All promote physical proximity of family members and isolation from the community. The fathers have backgrounds that promote social deprivation, poverty, inadequate education, occupational instability and broader criminal tendencies. Some writers[9] [23] [53] noted that sampling bias may account for some of these results. Alcohol plays some role since about 50% of incest offenders are alcoholics or heavy drinkers[15]. Disinhibition by alcohol may explain the sexual advances to a forbidden object, the daughter. The refusal by the wife to have intercourse with her husband may be due to his drinking and/or impotence.

The Experimental Evidence

Empirical evaluation of incest is difficult, first because there are very few controlled studies with standardized interviews or questionnaires used[32] and second, because incest is difficult to prove and the family members protect each other[43]. Meiselman has offered a critical review of the many problems of incest research and the interested reader may wish to consult her book[32]. This section only concerns incestuous fathers. Excellent reviews of the literature on sociological-anthropological factors and on the mother-daughter characteristics have been done by Henderson[23], Weiner[53], Weinberg[51] and Ferracuti[13]. A Forensic review has been reported by Bluglass[5]. First we examine the evidence indicating whether incestuous fathers are pedophilic and/or homosexual.

Incest, pedophilia and homosexuality. Gebhard[18] presented 147 cases of imprisoned incestuous fathers. Of these 56 (38%) involved offenses against prepubertal children under 12 years of age. Among the 56 only 4% admitted to a preference for girls as young as 12-to-15-years-old. None of the remaining offenders who were involved with older victims admitted to a preference for less than a 16-year-old female. This is a prison sample which may be biased by sentencing practices in the courts but the low incidence of pedophilic preference agrees with Weinberg's survey suggesting that pedophilia is not a major factor in incest. A sample of 27 incestuous cases from my hospital[38] suggests similar lack of pedophilic interest and experience. There is only one phallometric study published to date to validate these findings.

Quinsey and his associates[39] compared 16 incestuous and 16 non-incestuous sex offenders who had interacted with girls 14-year-old or younger. The two groups were matched on age of victim. They found that, in spite of victim's age, the incestuous group had an appropriate (normal) erotic profile, with largest reactions to adults whereas the nonincestuous groups were more characteristically pedophilic (See Chapter 8).

Homosexual interest and experience in the incest offenders studied by Gebhard[18] are comparatively low in contrast to controls. This was also true of our sex history data since there were no significant differences in homosexual experience on any other item between incest cases and normal controls. The absence of other sexual anomalies as well suggests that these men display a normal erotic profile. A search for unusual erotic stimuli provoking the incestuous behavior or a preference for nonconventional erotic responses would seem unwarranted.

The personality of incestuous fathers. Contradictory traits have been postulated to explain the incestuous father's character and acts. He may be shy, introverted and socially inadequate or he may be hostile, aggressive, psychopathic and violent. He may be alcoholic and lack a sense of masculine adequacy. The latter may be due to overidentification with mother and one may expect femininity in incestuous fathers, a feature they theoretically share with homosexuals.

Gebhard's data[18] and my own[27] suggest they are generally shy and introverted rather than aggressive. Alcoholism is also quite prominent. Virkkunen[49] reported 50% to 80% in various studies he reviewed, were chronic alcoholic while Kaufman[26] reported 72% and Gebhard[18] describes 8% to 23% as alcoholic and 20% to 30% as frequent drinkers. Drug usage was unremarkable and incest cases seem conventional in this respect. In Gebhard's sample criminality was a significant factor since 28% to 50% of his samples had three or more convictions. In other samples this was not the case and the trend was for incestuous fathers to be noncriminal[9] [27] [53]. Tormes[47] reported violence in 13 of 20 incest cases and in seven of the 13 cases it was *constant*. Chronic alcoholism is also implicated but the study is not controlled on these measures. Virkkunen[49] also linked the violence in incest cases to alcohol abuse. However, violence is often vaguely described or is undefined in these studies. Validation and reliability ratings of exactly what constitutes violence would be an asset in these studies. It would also be useful to know if the "hitting or abuse" is any different from that exercised by nonincest cases in the same communities from which incest samples were drawn.

In Gebhard's samples 12% to 14% used force whereas 9% to 17% used threat. Gebhard noted the difficulty in distinguishing parental authority from threat. In any case the majority of incidences involved neither force nor threat. However these minority of cases may well represent rape as described in Chapter 12. It would seem important to work out ground rules for discriminating the two types of cases. The retrospective fantasies of incest victims may make this task difficult. There are only three available reports of MMPI results on groups of incestuous men. Cavallin[8] presented an uncontrolled group study without statistical analyses but my colleagues and I[27] and Anderson[2] used controlled group comparisons.

It is noteworthy that incestuous cases in our sample did not differ from controls in masculinity–femininity, contrary to prediction. As a group they scored highest on MMPI depression and paranoia or suspiciousness. This supports uncontrolled reports in the literature but neither feature was atypical of individuals facing charges for sexual offences.

Cavallin[8] reported on 12 incest cases in which paranoia was prominent. Although he claimed, as other writers have, that psychosis was not a factor, two of his 12 cases were psychotic. Weiner[52] had similar conclusions and one in five of his reported cases had a psychotic break. Confusion and personality disorder then plays some role in incest. According to psychoanalytic theory paranoid psychosis should be associated with homosexuality (Chapter 5) rather than incest. Wahl[50] described two cases of mother-son incest which he associated with loss of control due to alcohol and schizophrenia. Perhaps any unusual sexual behavior in psychotic individuals may simply be stimulus confusion[27].

Anderson[2] compared 14 incestuous families and 14 control families on the MMPI and on demographic variables. The control families were seen at a clinic for problems unrelated to incest. Only the average T score for the Psychopathic Deviate (Pd) scale was statistically significant. Sixty four percent of incestuous fathers had pathological scores (T score over 70) compared to 20% of control fathers. Most incestuous fathers were alcoholic and half had criminal records. "Many" of them were physically abused as children themselves.

The outstanding feature of incestuous men on the MMPI and 16 PF scales in our study was introversion. They were reserved, shy, conscientious, conservative and guilt prone. They were the least assertive of all clinical sexually anomalous male groups studied. The numbers of individuals who were psychopathic or aggressive, polymorphous, perverse were few in number but this may reflect sampling bias in our clinic. The picture of an individual who is family centered and unable to seek gratification outside it best fits our data. Discovery of the incest often resulted in divorce and family dissolution[53].

Family history of incest. A possible explanation of the incest is that father is perpetuating a pattern of behavior promoted in his own family of origin. Perhaps some early sexual contact with an adult established the pattern. In Gebhard's[18] prison sample there were no noteworthy differences between controls and the incest groups in prepubertal sexual contacts with adults. Over 90% had no heterosexual contact and over 80% no homosexual contact when they were children. Our own clinic data is similar. The research participants were asked a number of direct questions about sex and sexual play with their sisters, brothers, mother, father, other boys and figures and other adults while they were a child. There were no statistically significant differences between incestuous men and normal heterosexual controls. However more incestuous men had seen their own mothers nude and seminude than controls had. Their fathers were more concerned that the incest offenders keep their privates clean and there was a tendency for their mothers to be the same way. However there was no handling of the boy's penis in a sexual way or washing it by either parent to a greater extent than control participants' had. Therefore early childhood seduction does not appear to be a major factor in incest. Overall they seem normal sexually. This suggests that the etiology of incest lies in social and personality factors.

The Parents of Incestuous Men

Family background was thought to be significant in developing incestuous fathers. Broken homes, desertion, overidentification with mother, absent father, anger to father, and longing for father are described. In Gebhard's prison sample of incestuous offenders there were no remarkable findings related to family background which distinguished incest offenders from other groups. Between 61% and 82% of their parents were reported to have fair to good adjustment whereas a control sample of nonsex offenders indicated 78% of their parents had such adjustment and community controls had 84%.

Broken homes are more frequent in prison groups with nonsex offenders at 54%, incestuous groups 44% to 60% but community controls indicated only 31%. Thus there is a higher incidence of divorce and separation in the incest offenders' family of origin but it is difficult to assign this variable causal significance in his behavior because it occurs as often in nonincestuous prisoners.

Parent–child relations are varied in Gebhard's groups. When the victim was pubescent or mature, the offenders described good relationships with their own parents. When the victim was a child, the offenders said they had a better relationship with their mother than their father although both relationships were poor.

Paitich and I[37], compared incest offenders and other groups on 16 scales of the Clarke Parent Child Relations Questionnaire, which examines intrafamilial hostility; affection, strictness, indulgence and competence of parents and the child's identification with each parent. In 27 cases of incest, there was an absence of aggression between parents and the incest offender. Both parents were judged to be competent. However incest offenders scored lowest among all sexually anomalous groups in mother affection and identification and highest on mother strictness, contrary to expectation. Relationships and identification with fathers were unremarkable. The results contradict Gebhard's to some extent and differences in sampling and use of standardized scale may be important in the results. Both controlled studies agree that the father is not particularly significant in creating an incest offender and perhaps further systematic work should examine mother son relations.

Miscellaneous factors.   A range of sociological variables relating social class, poverty, rural home, age of offender, and education, among others, have been considered important in incest. The offender does tend to be older than the average sex offender. As noted earlier, this may be a circumstantial factor, that is, he has to be older to have a teenage daughter. However he does tend to be less educated than other sex offenders generally and in some cases less intelligent but overall in our data bank, they were of average intelligence but of poorer education generally. The importance of a rural setting for incest has been overestimated and it can occur anywhere[23] [53] [54]. The closeness of the incestuous family and perceived social isolation however may be important factors in the act.

The Incest Offenders' Stimulus Response Matrix

There is little evidence to suggest that incestuous men have other than a normal erotic profile (Table 9.1). They generally prefer physically mature females and desire the normal range of sexual interactions with them. Their choice of female is socially deviant and this may reflect their social introversion, shyness and disinhibition from excessive use of alcohol in many cases.

TABLE 9.1
Summary of Evidence for Theories of Incest

Theory	Empirical Evidence
1. Rivalry for females in the primal horde	No evidence, mere speculation
2. Protective role of parenting prevents incest	Untested
3. Biological theory-inbreeding is maladaptive	Mixed support
4. Collusion of family members promotes incest to keep them together and avoid separation anxiety	Untested
5. Mother is sexually dysfunctional, father lonely and shy or is aggressive and alcoholic	Limited support on fathers. Systematic and controlled studies needed
6. Ages of family members are critical	No definitive study but ages may be a coincidental factor
7. Incest offenders have disturbed relationship with their fathers	Contrary to theory, the limited evidence suggests a disturbed mother relationship
8. Incest offenders have a passive homosexual longing for their fathers	Negative
9. Incest holds family together and the taboo holds it together	These contradictory psychoanalytic postulates have not been investigated empirically. Discovery of incest by non family usually results in dissolution of family
10. Social class, poverty and incest are important conditions supporting incest	Positive but these factors support a host of problems and are not peculiar to incest
11. Incest offender is pedophilic	Negative, he prefers physically mature females

Family dynamics involving mother complicity, lack of sexual interest and desire of the daughter and father to keep the family together appear to be important. Nevertheless, little systematic work has appeared in the professional literature to support this theory.

Speculations.   There are two previously unrecognized factors which may explain the incest taboo. The first is familiarity of participants in a sexual interaction. We know from controlled studies that erotica loses its arousal value with repetition[42]. Clinical patients with sexual anomalies often indicate that they need novel stimuli to sexually arouse them and that they seek new places with new women to act out. Marital partners satiate with one another to some degree so that their sexual outlet become perfunctory and "task oriented"[31]. New partners or extramarital affairs can relieve the monotony of repetitious behavior. Familiarity may also operate to produce the incest "taboo" as well. Parents see their child in a helpless dependent state over a prolonged period of time. In incest, that protective parenting role breaks down but normally it does not, perhaps because the prolonged exposure to the child extinguishes any sexual desire for them by the time they are physically mature and capable of sexual response. Thus the "taboo" may only be a lack of interest in most cases because curiosity about the potential sex partner has been totally dissipated. The incest offender may therefore be a desperate man craving any form of affection he can get. Stepdaughters may often be victims of incest because they are relatively unfamiliar to the offender to begin with so she may have more arousal value than a natural daughter to whom father usually has longer exposure. Alternately alcoholism may disinhibit the offender so he engages in a range of inappropriate behavior. A study of the factors which influence curiosity, especially sexual curiosity, may be invaluable in understanding incest[4].

Some writers indicate that the absence of the father for a period of time is a factor in promoting incest. That absence can help to reduce the familiarity of the victim. Just as erotica will satiate an individual and become unarousing, father's absence for a period of time and reintroduction results in increased arousal again.

The second factor that may explain the infrequency of mother-son and brother-sister incest is a size-dominance factor in sexual partners. Usually the male sex partner is bigger, stronger and, in humans, slightly older than the female. In birds other factors are also important; the male is brightly colored and the female is not. It has been shown that territoriality is also important. Size is particularly important because if, for example, a female fish is nourished so that she is big and the male is undernourished so he is small, they will reverse sex courting ritual, the male taking the female part. The Franceses[17] note that among lower animals who show bonding behavior there is an equivalent to incest. Among the howler and rhesus monkeys, males depart from the family of origin before puberty often to the accompaniment of aggressive behavior from adult males. However the female children remain and father-daughter incest is most likely to occur, and mother-son incest is avoided. The authors further note that dominance which is size related plays a role which limits the occurrence of incest.

Abernathy[1] has shown that incest occurred in a chimpanzee when the son was finally larger than his mother and could beat her up so she submitted. In unpublished studies conducted with university students and staff, Freisen and I found that the size (height and weight) of partners along with their age and strength were the most important factors in sexual attractiveness. The male ideally has to be bigger, older and stronger to arouse the female. Sex organ size and secondary sex characteristics were less important and varied with individual tastes. These factors would preclude a mother-son liason even if women were not generally less prone to such socially unacceptable behavior.

The son of necessity is always younger and for a prolonged period he is smaller and weaker than his mother. It would also follow that in families with a boy and a girl, half the cases by chance would involve an older girl and younger brother who might be smaller and weaker as well. This would be expected by chance in two children families about 25% of the time. In contrast, father-daughter relations almost always satisfy the size relationship. He is always older, bigger and stronger except in rarer cases. Thus, if the size-dominance variable is operative, by chance father-daughter incest is possible in 100% of cases, brother-sister incest in 25%, mother-son in none. Homosexual incest would involve a rarer difference in erotic preference. The actual percentages are about 78%, 19% and less than 3% (including miscellany), fairly close to expected proportions of reported cases. This factor could readily be examined in cases of sibling incest. The combined factors of familiarity and size may be parsimonious variables which are prominent in the incest taboo and in other sexual behavior. They also lend themselves to easy empirical test.

Treatment

A major obstacle to any treatment of incest offenders is that its discovery very often results in divorce or separation, making recidivism very unlikely[9]. Henderson[23] noted the complexity ascribed to the etiological factors in incest and concluded that treatment must consequently be complicated. Some authors[9][30] stress that family therapy be used since incest is a symptom of family maladjustment. Machotka and his associates[30] suggested that therapy should focus on the pervasive denial of incest by family members and on dysfunctional relationships. However neither author presents any data on this approach or its outcome. The single case report is particularly suspect in evaluating outcome of the treatment of incest. Whereas sexual anomalies in general have a recidivism rate of 10% to 20%, authors describe repeated incest as "rare" or happening "almost never." One must therefore examine a large number of cases to detect even a few repeated offenders. This would appear to be unrealistic. A different criterion is more appropriate: maintaining the family intact with each member adjusted in that environment. Ethical issues may be raised about the soundness of this goal and about the protection provided to the minor involved. Separation of family members may be the most feasible goal.

Behavior Therapy

There are only two behavior therapy case reports in the research literature[6] [21] conducted by the same research group. In both cases covert sensitization was used. The imagined conditioning stimulus was sexual interaction with the daughter. It was followed by an unconditioned aversive stimulus that ironically described guilt related scenes of discovery of the behavior and loss of family contact and/or respect. According to several authors, incest offenders supposedly deny guilt. The pragmatic therapists took advantage of their patient's actual guilt prone tendencies.

One patient was also treated concurrently for genital exhibitionism by covert sensitization. Penile circumference was monitored and reactions to incest decreased over treatment sessions in both cases, whereas self reported arousal to incest only declined in one case.[6] An in-therapy measure of penile arousal to nondeviant stimuli was not obtained in either case and this would be invaluable in showing that incest declines but normal sexual reactions do not. It is particularly important in the case of incest because the sex object chosen, the adult female, is normal. Conditioning must be very specific and make intercourse only with the daughter aversive while intercourse with other women, in particular the wife, remains strong and positive. In both patients this apparently happened but validation by phallometric test would be more satisfactory. One patient was followed up only for 11 weeks and the undesirable behavior had not recurred. In the other case followed for 6 months, fantasies of incest recurred after 3 months but disappeared again when better and more appropriate social relations with the daughter were strengthened.

Although these results seem promising, caution is advised because the studies involve single cases. Moreover the problem of generalized aversion to all females and not just the daughters was not fully assessed and could be an undesirable outcome of this method.

It is interesting that assertion therapy has *not* been applied to incestuous men. Other sex offenders such as exhibitionists have been described as shy and unassertive whereas in fact they are not, as determined by controlled studies. However incest offenders best fit the description of unassertiveness and this treatment may signficantly improve their adjustment. They cannot relate to their wives and tell them their feelings. Perhaps they act out of sheer loneliness in the incest act, just for some body contact (See Fink [14], and Nathan [35]). They cannot establish role boundaries in the family, all perhaps through lack of assertiveness and inability to express their feelings appropriately. It would be interesting to see this approach used on incest offenders.

Family Therapy

A reading of the psychotherapy literature on incest shows that a mixture of formulation of hypotheses, assessment, and some treatment are reported without clear details on what was done in therapy. It is difficult to draw any conclusions and follow up is poorly recorded. Machotka and his colleagues [30] reported four cases of incest treated by family therapy and individual therapy. The outcome of the cases is uncertain although one daughter had a psychotic breakdown for a brief period. The therapists suggested that family dynamics be the focus of treatment rather than the current or historical sexual activities of the family. The sexual behavior is likely incidental to disordered and confused family role functioning. By treating the family as a whole it helps to distribute the responsibility, place guilt in perspective, and prevent the recurrence of incest. The inappropriate role assignment of the daughter and the denial of a problem should be the focus of treatment.

Eist and Mandel [12] presented a more detailed case history but once again the outcome was uncertain and follow up was not specified. They used a male and female co-therapist for the family. They argued that the advantage of this approach is that two observers are better than one; it offers a broader range of alternatives to deal with the family's multiple problems; gender roles and models are provided to handle differences of viewpoint in the family in a respectful and nonshaming way; the therapists can help each other develop their own point of view; and they can support each other and keep up their morale. An attempt was made to provide the family with a positive growth experience promoting extrafamilial relationships. It was made clear to the family that the unacceptable behavior was to discontinue and that the development of new channels of communication between mother and daughter were to be developed which would prevent a recurrence of the incest. Individual family members' separation, differentiation and responsibility were accomplished by insisting that members speak for themselves and accept ownership of their own productions. There was a great deal of limit setting on shaming and scapegoating of others in the family and of parental indulgence of negative behavior and disrespect for others. Where there were legal scrapes, the therapists insisted the involved party "face the music." Development of respect for others and their rights was considered very important since it was hypothesized that its absence was instrumental in causing the incest in the first place. This procedure sounded like assertion therapy which, as noted earlier, seemed appropriate for the fathers. Apparently all family members improved; mother's depression lifted and her self esteem increased. Husband's rage diminished and mother became more involved with him socially and sexually. Apparently the children's fears of abandonment diminished and a new pattern of behavior was established which mitigated against further incest.

The Justices[24] have offered a do-it-yourself prevention guide to avoiding incest but offer no data whatsoever to back up the effectiveness of their suggestions. They propose that incest and other problem behavior in the family can be avoided if parents learn to meet their own needs and learn how to handle stress. Keeping the amount of stress in one's life manageable is important in prevention of problems. This is not the total answer however and professional help may be an important facet of prevention.

The best described and documented approach to the problem of incest is the Child Sexual Abuse Treatment Program (CSATP) in California developed by Henry and Anna Giarretto and Suzanne Sgroi[19]. They have treated and discharged over 600 families and there has been no recidivism. Children are returned to the family sooner than they were prior to the program, 90% within the first month after discovery. Treatment is provided soon after detection rather than deferring it until father is released from jail. The results of their program are encouraging since normal father-daughter relations have been achieved in "most families." The authors indicated that the involvement of the criminal justice system is important. It provides a powerful authority incentive for changing the family structure and prevents treatment drop outs.

Therapy usually begins with individual counselling for family members, followed by joint counseling of the mother and daughter. Subsequently other children in the family join into the group counseling sessions and eventually the father is included in the group. Marriage counseling for husband and wife is also started when the therapist considers them ready for it. In treatment, the child victim is convinced she is not to blame for the incest but the adults are. She must hear from both mother and father that they are to blame and the father must apologize. She must know sexual feelings are normal and good so she will not be turned off sexually to other men.

The mother will not see her daughter as a rival after absolving her of the blame. Rather she sees her as an innocent bystander in a dysfunctional marriage. The mother must decide whether she wants to salvage the marriage and if she does, a special couples group helps to improve the marriage rather than just make it bearable. The father accepts the full responsibility for the incest but at the same time, hope must be fostered in him that the family can be maintained intact with treatment. The incest is never condoned and it is stressed to him how destructive it is to the family. Using humanistic psychology throughout, an attempt is made to deal with his loneliness and to teach him to express his positive feelings toward his wife.

In group therapy sessions they meet other incestuous groups and generally they feel relieved to know that they are not alone. The help group teaches a model of good parenting and supports individuals to keep them involved. The overall program is impressive in outcome and in the efficiency of its methods. It is inexpensive because group therapy is used and self help groups are formed of the incestuous families themselves. The method is described for father-daughter incest but they do handle other forms of sexual abuse of children. The program has expanded rapidly in a very few years and has been enthusiastically received. It is therefore difficult to cast a sour note but the assessment of the program needs to be improved substantially. There is no standardized measurements or interviews reported in their study and there are no control groups of other methods or of untreated cases. Their evaluation of treatment is only superficially reported. So at this juncture in time, all one can say is that the program seems logical to the problem and looks promising. I am eager to see its full evaluation.

Treatment of Choice

A major question to be settled before choosing a treatment (Table 9.2) is the feasibility of keeping the incestuous family intact after discovery. Some

TABLE 9.2
Treatment Effectiveness of Incest

Method	Results
1. Covert sensitization	Positive in 2 case studies
2. Family therapy	Uncertain outcomes. Writers appear more concerned with describing methods
3. Child Sexual Abuse Treatment Program	Highly successful but no systematic data

writers think the discovery is a breaking point signaling that incest no longer can hold together a pathological family. Perhaps divorce is a reasonable alternative and the emotional sequelae of facing the participants in that irreversible act is too great a burden to bear. Perhaps social attitudes could be altered to incest.

If the family splits up, no treatment for incest per se is necessary. The court usually gives custody of the children to the mother and recidivism of incest is rare. The reports of the victims of incest appear to have considerable difficulty later in life and they should have some treatment after the discovery of incest whether the family dissolves or not. Certainly treatment directed to changing the father's erotic preference is unnecessary in most cases since his stimulus response matrix is apparently normal.

Family therapy directed to changing members' roles would seem to be appropriate and logical but its success has yet to be fully established. It would be important to show that each member is happy within the family and that potential incest is not a constant worry. In cases of force, violence, and alcoholism, it would be difficult to establish a natural family environment.

The impact on the daughter victim has not been discussed fully in this chapter but there are important issues that need systematic investigation. She may be pregnant with father's baby; she may suffer the emotional sequelae characteristic of rape victims; she may be mentally ill either before incest or as a consequence. She may be retarded or suffer some brain damage prior to the incest (See Weiner [53], and Henderson [23]). Can such girls be placed again in the family environment? We need answers to the questions and we need controlled studies to determine the direction treatment should take.

BIBLIOGRAPHY

1. Abernathy, V. Dominance and sexual behavior. *American Journal of Psychiatry,* 1974, *131*(7), 813–817.
2. Anderson, L. A. *Personality and demographic characteristics of parents and incest victims.* Paper presented at the Eleventh Annual MMPI Symposium, Minneapolis, Minnesota; March 1976.
3. Bender, L., & Blau, A. The reactions of children to sexual relations with adults. *American Journal of Orthopsychiatry,* 1937, *7*, 500–518.
4. Berlyne, D. E. *Conflict, Arousal and Curiosity.* New York: McGraw Hill, 1960.
5. Bluglass, R. Incest. *British Journal of Hospital Medicine,* 1979, *22*, 2–15.
6. Brownell, K. D., & Barlow, D. H. Measurement and treatment of two sexual deviations in one person. *Journal of Behavior Therapy and Experimental Psychiatry,* 1976, *7*, 349–354.
7. Browning, D. H., & Boatman, B. Incest: Children at risk. *American Journal of Psychiatry,* 1977, *134*(1), 69–72.
8. Cavallin, H. Incestuous fathers: A clinical report. *American Journal of Psychiatry,* 1966, *122*(10), 1132–1138.
9. Cormier, B. M., Kennedy, M., & Sangowicz, J. Psychodynamics of father-daughter incest. *Canadian Psychiatric Association Journal,* 1962, *7*, 203–217.
10. De Rascovsky, M. W., & Rascovsky, A. On consummated incest. *International Journal of Psychoanalysis,* 1950, *31*, 42–47.
11. Dixon, K. N., Arnold, E., & Calestro, K. Father-son incest: Under-reported psychiatric problem? *American Journal of Psychiatry,* 1978, *135*(7), 835–838.

12. Eist, H. I., & Mandel, A. U. Family treatment of ongoing incest. *Family Process,* 1968, *7,* 216–232.
13. Ferracuti, F. Incest between father and daughter. In *Sexual Behaviors: Social, Clinical and Legal Aspects.* Resnik, H., & Wolfgang, E. (Eds.). Boston: Little, Brown & Company, 1972.
14. Fink, P. J., Nathan, R., Rosen, R., Walker, H., & West, H. Sex and loneliness. *Medical Aspects of Human Sexuality,* 1971, *5*(2), 99–131.
15. Finkelhor, D. Psychological, cultural, and family factors in incest and family sexual abuse. *Journal of Marriage & Family Counseling,* 1978, *4,* 41–49.
16. Finkelhor, D. Sex among siblings: a survey on prevalence, variety and effects. *Archives of Sexual Behavior,* 1980, *9*(3), 171–194.
17. Frances, V., & Frances, A. The incest taboo and family structure. *Family Process,* 1976, *15*(2), 235–244.
18. Gebhard, P., Gagnon, J., Pomeroy, W., & Christenson, C. *Sex Offenders.* New York: Harper & Row, 1965.
19. Giaretto, H., Giaretto, A., & Sgroi, S. Coordinated community treatment of incest in Burgess, A., Groth, A., Holstrome, L., & Sgroi, S. (Eds.). *Sexual Assault of Children and Adolescents,* Lexington, Mass., Heath & Co., 1978.
20. Gordon, L. Incest as revenge against the pre-oedipal mother. *Psychoanalytic Review,* 1955, *42,* 284–292.
21. Harbert, T. L., Barlow, D. H., Hersen, M., & Austin, J. B. Measurement and modification of incestuous behavior: A case study. *Psychological Reports,* 1974, *34,* 79–86.
22. Heims, L. W., & Kaufman, I. Variations on a theme of incest. *American Journal of Orthopsychiatry,* 1963, *33,* 311–312.
23. Henderson, D. J. Incest: A synthesis of data. *Canadian Psychiatric Association Journal,* 1972, *17,* 299–313.
24. Justice, B., & Justice, R. *The broken taboo.* New York: Human Sciences Press, 1979.
25. Karpman, B. *The Sexual Offender and His Offences.* New York: Julian Press, 1957.
26. Kaufman, I., Peck, A. L., & Tagiuri, C. K. The family constellation and overt incestuous relations between father and daughter. *American Journal of Orthopsychiatry,* 1954, *24,* 544–554.
27. Langevin, R., Paitich, D., Freeman, R., Mann, K., & Handy, L. Personality characteristics and sexual anomalies in males. *Canadian Journal of Behavioral Science,* 1978, *10*(3), 222–238.
28. Langsley, D. G., Schwartz, M. N., & Fairbairn, R. H. Father-son incest. *Comprehensive Psychiatry,* 1968, *9*(3), 218–226.
29. Lustig, N., Dresser, J. W., Spellman, M. W., Murray, T. B., & Wash, T. Incest. *Archives of General Psychiatry,* 1966, *14,* 31–40.
30. Machotka, P., Pittman, F. S., & Flomenhaft, K. Incest as a family affair. *Family Process,* 1967, *6,* 98–116.
31. Masters, W. H., & Johnson, V. *Homosexuality in Perspective.* Boston: Little, Brown and Company, 1979.
32. Meiselman, K. C. *Incest,* San Francisco: Jossey-Bass Publishers, 1978.
33. Meiselman, K. Personality characteristics of incest history psychotherapy patients: a research note. *Archives of Sexual Behavior,* 1980, *9*(3), 195–197.
34. Middleton, R. Brother-sister and father-daughter marriage in ancient Egypt. *American Sociological Review,* 1962, *27,* 603–611.
35. Nathan, R., Rosen, R., Walker, H., & Franklin, H. W. Sex and loneliness. *Human Sexuality,* 1971, *4*(2), 99–131.
36. Neu, J. What is wrong with incest? *Inquiry,* 1976, *19,* 27–39.

37. Paitich, D., & Langevin, R. The Clarke Parent-Child Relations Questionnaire: A clinically useful test for adults. *Journal of Consulting and Clinical Psychology,* 1976, *44,* 428–436.
38. Paitich, D., Langevin, R., Freeman, R., Mann, K., & Handy, L. The Clarke SHQ: A clinical sex history questionnaire for males. *Archives of Sexual Behavior,* 1977, *6*(5), 421–435.
39. Quinsey, V., Chaplin, T., & Carrigan, W. Sexual preferences among incestuous and nonincestuous child molesters. *Behavior Therapy,* 1979, *10,* 562–565.
40. Raphling, D. L., Carpenter, B. L., Davis, A., & Kan, T. Incest. *Archives of General Psychiatry,* 1967, *16,* 505–511.
41. Raybin, J. B. Homosexual incest. *The Journal of Nervous and Mental Disease,* 1969, *148*(2), 105–110.
42. Report of the Commission on Pornography and Obscenity. Washington, D.C.: U.S. Government Printing Office, 1979.
43. Rhinehart, J. W. Genesis of overt incest. *Comprehensive Psychiatry,* 1961, *2,* 338–349.
44. Rist, K. Incest: theoretical and clinical views. *American Journal of Orhtopsychiatry,* 1979, *49*(4), 680–691.
45. Seemanova, E. A study of children of incestuous matings. *Human Heredity,* 1971, *21,* 108–128.
46. Sloane, P., & Karpinski, E. Effects of incest on participants. *American Journal of Orthopsychiatry,* 1942, *12,* 666–673.
47. Tormes, Y. *Child victims of incest.* Denver: The American Human Association, Children's Division, 1968.
48. Tsai, M., & Wagner, N. N. Therapy groups for women sexually molested as children. *Archives of Sexual Behavior,* 1978, *7*(5), 417–427.
49. Virkkunen, M. Incest offences and alcoholism. *Medicine, Science, And The Law,* 1974, *14*(12), 124–128.
50. Wahl, C. W. The psychodynamics of consummated maternal incest. *Archives of General Psychiatry,* 1960, *3,* 188–193.
51. Weinberg, S. *Incest Behavior.* New York: Citadel Press, 1962.
52. Weiner, I. B. Father-daughter incest: A clinical report. *Psychoanalytic Quarterly,* 1962, *36,* 607–632.
53. Weiner, I. B. On incest: A survey. *Exerpta Criminologica,* 1964, *4,* 137–155.
54. Westermeyer, J. Incest in psychiatric practice: a description of patients and incestuous relationships. *Journal of Clinical Psychiatry,* 1978, *39*(8), 643–648.

III RESPONSE PREFERENCE ANOMALIES

10 Exhibitionism

INTRODUCTION

Genital exhibitionism is usually an act performed by a male who shows his naked genitals in a more or less public place to an unsuspecting and/or unwilling female. He may or may not masturbate to climax. About half do so. The occurrence of such behavior in females is rare and when it occurs, it has usually been asssociated with mental retardation or mental illness[36][37]. Some men, especially exhibitionists, may argue that women expose but it is socially acceptable. The traditional burlesque strip show usually presents a host of females who disrobe for a predominantly male audience. Moreover, women in general are allowed to show varying amounts of their breasts in public places without penalty as well. Some patients have expressed anger over this apparent injustice. *Mr. N,* a university student charged for the first time with indecent exposure opened his initial clinical interview:

> *Mr. N:* I'm here because I exposed and it's damn unjust! She could show me her body but I can't do it. It's ok for her to have her dress cut so low it leaves nothing to your imagination and she can walk the streets but let me do it once and wham! Into jail I go. You tell me why they should get away with it and I can't!
>
> (LATER)......
>
> Tell me, are strippers exhibitionists? I think they are and the law protects them. I'm an upright citizen but it doesn't protect me!

Indecent exposure is among the most common sexual offenses but the severity of this problem is viewed differently in various locales and times[87]. Frequently, it is considered a nuisance rather than a serious crime. It is unclear how often it is even reported. It constitutes about one third of sexual offences appearing before the courts,[62 72 85 86] making it major in the area of sexual anomalies. However, outside Europe and America, it appears nonexistent[87].

Some forensic cases seem to be angry and unwilling participants in clinical assessment and/or treatment. In contrast, for some, their anomalous desires are an affliction they would very gladly have you remove, if that were possible. Why do they do it? Is there something special they derive from exposing which cannot be obtained from a consenting partner in private? There are many speculations about what is happening but there are few facts.

THE THEORIES

Exhibitionism and pedophilia.   There is disagreement among theorists about the class of stimuli to which the exhibitionist responds erotically. The most frequent victims of his acts seem to be the physically mature female but it is also well known that it is difficult, in practice, to distinguish the pedophile or "child molester" from the exhibitionist[72 78]. Mohr, Turner and Jerry[72] suggested that the pedophile is interested in physical contact with the child whereas the exhibitionist only wants to be seen, with no physical contact desired. Even those men who appear to prefer the mature female do act out with children. The age of the stimulus person seems unimportant in some cases. *Mr. A* was charged with exposing to a 23-year-old female. He was asked:

Doctor: What is the youngest and oldest person you have exposed to?

Mr. A: The oldest would be around 40 and the youngest, maybe 8. Usually they are about—13 or 14 to 20, 22. That's the age I like best!

Doctor: What do you do to them? Does it change with the age group?

Mr. A: No. It's usually the same. I show them my penis and masturbate. That's it.

Doctor: Do you like them to react in any special way?

Mr. A: No. I just want them to watch and get a kick out of it. If it's a turn on for them, that's nice.

Doctor: Is age important for you in any way?

Mr. A: No. As long as they are female, I'll expose!

Unconscious homosexuality as a motive.   A number of writers have postulated that the exhibitionist is basically homosexual, albeit in some cases, an "unconscious homosexual"[18 43 82 83]. Interestingly, paradoxical postulates appear in the study of sexual anomalies. Homosexuals who show no obvious interest in women are considered heterosexual in preference. Now a group that seems predominantly heterosexual is asssumed to be homosexual. This latter hypothesis is as difficult to test as many psychoanalytic postulates are. The incidence of homosexual behavior and the reaction of exhibitionists to the male body shape has not been extensively reported in the experimental literature. From such hypotheses, one might expect in some cases at least, that it would be substantial. Such a theoretical position is illustrated by *Mr. B* who was a voluntary patient concerned about his exposing and his potential for homosexuality. He had some heterosexual experience and while he was living with a female at the time of treatment, he was a naive and suggestible person.

> *Mr. B:* I don't really know what I want from exposing. I did it for my girlfriend once. She clapped, cheered and said, "Get it up! Get it up!" and I climaxed. I felt good but kind of silly too. What I really wonder is if I'm homosexual.

> *Doctor:* Why do you wonder that?

> *Mr. B:* Well, all these guys make advances at me when I'm driving my (taxi) cab. They ask if they can pay for the fare with sex. They think I'm gay. There must be something about me. Maybe they know what I don't.

> *Doctor:* Have you ever had sex with a man?

> *Mr. B:* No, but I wonder what is would be like. The guys down at the pub say what I really need is a man to give me a good screw up the ass. Maybe they're right!

Autoeroticism. It is noteworthy that many males with homoerotic preferences "expose" in public places albeit to other males, and share with heterosexual exhibitionists the practice of "outdoor masturbation with no one around"[51] [78]. Homosexual males and exhibitionists may both also display autoeroticism. The homosexual *Mr. F* described earlier (page 81) illustrates this. *Mr. C,* a heterosexual and an exhibitionist, who was in his late twenties, did not date either sex. He was reflecting on the development of his anomaly and noted:

> *Mr. C:* When I was younger just being nude was so exciting, I found it difficult not to masturbate. Going to the beach was embarrassing. Even coming out of the change room in a bathing suit made me have an erection when I didn't want it. It was very embarrassing.

Mr. D, who was a voyeur and exhibitionist, also exposed and described trying to fellate himself when he was 14-years-old. The act proved impossible and frustrating for him. The question arises in these cases whether their own bodies are the source of erotic stimulation. Is the female an unnecessary prop? Exposing outdoors alone also suggests autoeroticism and/or narcissism.

This question has a long history and Kraft-Ebbing discussed autoeroticism and presented detailed and extreme cases that he labeled automonosexualism[33]. He reported one case in which the male involved was totally absorbed in his own body as a sexual outlet. He would stand naked before the mirror, admire his body, kissing his reflection and masturbating or even ejaculating without masturbation. He showed no interest in either male or female and seemed totally satisfied with his own body.

Co-occurrence with voyeurism. The most frequent question asked about exhibiting has been: "What is the person engaging in the act trying to accomplish?" One theory is that the exhibitionist is totally absorbed in the act of seeing and being seen by a female and that tactile contact is not really desired. Freud[41] first noted this in saying "certain components of the sexual instinct which are normally contributory agents leading to the final act, are singled out to replace it." The frequent co-occurrence of voyeurism and exhibitionism noted by clinicians support such an interpretation[28] [62] [82] [83]. This is illustrated by *Mr. A* noted earlier, who had been charged with an incident bordering on rape. He seems to have been acting out his fantasies:

> *Mr. A:*   When I was coming into town, I saw a nice young girl about 18, hitchhiking. She said she wanted to go to town and I said sure. On the way, I said I had to pick up my little brother and was it ok with her. She said sure. I went off a sideroad where I knew no one was around. I know that area by the lake. I pulled up at an abandoned house and said I'd be back in a minute. I went into the house and came out nude. She screamed when she saw me. I told her to do what I said; I was an exhibitionist and wouldn't hurt her. I told her to take down her jeans and pants to her knees. I watched her and masturbated. I said she could do the same but she didn't want to. Then I got dressed and drove her where she wanted to go.

Exposing as a courtship disorder.   A more general theory has been suggested by Freund[28] who has postulated that voyeurism, exhibitionism, toucheurism and rape are various modes of a common underlying courtship disorder. He conceptualizes the normal male-female erotic interaction in four phases: searching for a partner, pretactile interaction (mainly a verbal exchange in humans), tactile interaction (the prelude to intercourse), and genital union. Although these four stages may overlap substantially, they can be separated for theoretical purposes. This theory unifies four sexual anomalies in postulating that each represents an exaggerated or distorted phasing or sequence of courtship. Table 10.1 shows this relationship. The

TABLE 10.1
Relationship of Disordered Phrases of Courtship and Exhibitionism,
Voyeurism, Toucheurism, and Rape

	Search	Pre Tactile	Tactile	Intercourse
Voyeurism	X			
Exhibitionism		X		
Toucheurism			X	
Rape				X

voyeur who only looks and masturbates shows a distorted search phase of courtship. His acts of looking do not progress beyond looking before he climaxes. Excessive sexual energy appears to be invested in looking. The exhibitionist, on the other hand, has an exaggerated or distorted pretactile phase of interaction in this sequence and the remaining phases of tactile interaction and genital union are either fully omitted or appear only in a vestigial way. Presumably, the exhibitionist is enacting this sequence when he exposes. The "blockage" or exaggeration at the tactile phase and intercourse represent courtship disorders of toucheurism and rape respectively, exemplifying the same exaggerated investment of sexual energy in one phase of courtship. The frequent co-occurrence of these four behaviors noted in clinical cases suggests some relationship. Exhibitionists are often voyeurs as well. Toucheurs often progress to rape. *Mr. C,* charged with indecent exposure was asked:

Doctor: How do you know if you will expose or peep?

Mr. C: I'll expose if I can but if it is getting late and nothing has happened, I go to laneways and alleys looking for windows where someone is undressing and watch.

Fear of females and of intercourse. More recently, Kolarsky and his associates[45] have postulated that a female's courtship behavior inhibits the exhibitionists sexually, but her noncourtship activity does not. This may be opposite to the normal pattern. One would expect from this theory that exhibitionists would react differently to intercourse than controls. One might also expect their marital relations to be adversely influenced. Implicit in this point of view is that a distorted courtship sequence leading to genital union is acted out in exposing. Systematic information is lacking to resolve the question but the idea that the exhibitionist, like the homosexual, is afraid of women, generally, or of intercourse in particular, is commonly held. *Mr. D,* a voyeur and exhibitionist, described earlier, was asked:

Doctor: How do you feel about having sex with a woman?

Mr. D: I've thought about it and I guess I should want it more than I do, but when I get alone with my girlfriend, I get all knotted up inside and can't get an erection. She is more than willing to do it but I am not turned on. I know then there is no way I can do it. Most of the time I just don't care to have it. Do you think that is abnormal?

The fear exhibited, as Taylor notes[97], is of not being able to assert his masculinity, of failing and of being impotent. However, in many cases, disinterest may be evident rather than fear. *Mr. E*, a handsome, well dressed young executive, who came with his attractive wife for counselling because he lacked interest in intercourse spent hours each night peeping and exposing when the opportunity arose. He stated:

Mr. E: Sex with my wife is ok and it's ok with other women but they turn me off. My girlfriend (a former national beauty pageant winner) said she would do anything, even lick my boots if I stayed with her. I don't go for that crap. Exposing, now that's exciting!

Narcissism.   In another theoretical approach, Karpman[43], in his classic compendium, suggested that exhibitionism is narcissistic because (1) is has elements of autoeroticism since the exhibitionist derives pleasure from seeing himself in the nude; (2) he sees himself as conferring a service, or kindness in exposing; and (3) he wishes to be envied for the possession of his penis. The first point has been discussed above as automonosexuality. The second point is commonly observed in desire for the female to "get a kick out of" or "be turned on" by exposing. *Mr. F*, who was basically a vagrant and managed to survive by part time jobs across the country, preferred both exposing and intercourse, and noted:

Mr. F: I think women are more interested in men exposing than they will admit. When I was all alone last week at the bus stop early in the morning, there was this woman waiting for the bus—just the two of us. So I opened my fly and let my privates hang out. She didn't notice at first and I made it seem accidental. She kept looking at it and then would look away. She did it again and again. I pretended I didn't notice. She sure looked a lot. I think she really liked it.

The third point is embodied in the psychoanalytic theory of the unresolved oedipal conflict and its attendant castration anxiety that surfaces as feelings of inferiority which can manifest themselves in many ways. Some focal feelings of inadequacy about the penis are noteworthy. *Mr. A* in reply to a direct question said:

> *Mr. A:*   I think my penis is smaller than average. Maybe that's why I expose.
> I show women an erect penis as if to say, "see, it is big". Maybe they
> won't like me if they see me without an erection.

Physical examination showed *Mr. A* to have a flaccid penis over 5 inches in length indicating his ignorance of "average" and his unrealistic ideas of female expectations. One might then postulate a "more basic underlying reason" for these feelings of inferiority-castration anxiety. Bejke[11] described exhibitionists as regressing to an infantile practice. They have a strong mother fixation and their victims are "mother images." One may wonder then why pubescent and immature girls are so often victims of the act rather than more mature women who could more likely serve as mother images. However, some other facet of the victim may provoke memories of the mother. The mother and father are both considered punitive toward the child's masturbation acts and/or toward his cleanliness surrounding toilet functions both urinary and fecal. However, the mother being more tender hearted, is more forgiving and the child comes to treat her punishment less seriously. The father, on the other hand, is stricter and since he sees less of the child and plays with him less, the punishment is considered more severe. Bejke surmised that children who have intestinal bacteria problems may have more foul smelling feces so the parents are more eager to maintain cleanliness around toilet functioning. Since the child is unable to discriminate masturbatory and toilet functions, he confuses the two. He develops guilt about masturbation.

Bejke further surmised that foul smelling feces may be associated with a high meat, low carbohydrate diet and that vegetarians are less likely to develop this problem. He noted that Trobriand Islanders have a fish and vegetable diet and are free of the problem of exhibitionism. However, he failed to note that the rest of the world outside North America and Europe is free of it too[87]. In any case, one can expect a great concern with cleanliness in exhibitionists and the desire to expose may be almost masochistic since it is associated with mild punishment from the mother and the victims are mother surrogates.

Exposing as a sadistic act.   Exhibiting has been described as a substitute act of a *sadistic* kind by other authors[3,21,33]. As Glover[31] noted this "sadism" need not be the brutal kind envisaged by the layman but rather, may be expressed generally as an attempt to exploit, enslave, frustrate or humiliate another person. It takes place against the will of the victim and it is "an attack, surprise, assault, a violation." *Mr. F* is an example for support of such a theory. In discussing the kind of women he preferred to expose to, he noted:

> *Mr. F:*   I pick out the sleazy ones who can't handle their sexuality. Some
> young girls think they are pretty great and know what they are up to.

They wear clothes they think are sexy; low cut dress, slit up the side of the skirt, you know the type I mean; but they can't handle it. They look cheap. I figure I'm going to teach them a lesson. I expose to them and they are shocked. They run away, they can't handle it. I think *that* will teach them a lesson.

Doctor: What do you enjoy most about exposing like that?

Mr. F: Their reaction of shock. I think I am giving them the punishment they deserve.

Such behaviors may be expected to take on even more active punishing qualities in blatant sadism. Some writers[86] think it is not unusual for exhibitionists to commit common assaults at some stage. The blending of exposing and rape would be such an instance, illustrated by *Mr. G,* who was apprehended for rape after terrorizing a community for several months. Finally, the crimes were linked to this one youth. At first, he would jump out of bushes late at night to unsuspecting females wearing only a stocking over his head and carrying a rifle. He would masturbate and this seemed to be basically an exhibiting act. However, he started to follow women into underground garages late at night. He would drive around the neighborhood in the nude and when he saw a woman going into underground parking, he would follow quickly before the doors closed and would corner these women and force them to perform oral sex and anal intercourse as well as vaginal intercourse. He was finally apprehended when a man drove into the garage and the woman involved screamed. Such cases illustrate the theory but it would seem such transitions are less typical of exhibitionists[72][100].

Hypersexuality.   Exhibitionists may be considered "hypersexual" that is, have an excessive need for sex outlets[21]. If this is so, they may respond to so many things, that the "critical stimuli and/or behavior" in such acts may be difficult to define. There is evidence that this is so since they act out with children; they often engage in other sexual behavior that occurs infrequently in the general population, for example, peeping and toucheurism. *Mr. H,* a 23-year-old vagrant, who engaged in a wide range of sexually anomalous behavior was predominantly an exhibitionist.

Doctor: I see you have reported engaging in quite a range of sexual behavior on the sex history questionnaire. First can you tell me about sex with other men.

Mr. H: I like to go down to the gay steam baths. I have a massage and lie there half asleep until some queer comes along to blow me off. It's ok but I don't want to do it to them. If they ask, I show them my fist.

Doctor: How about involvement with children?

Mr. H: Oh, I've fucked some 12, 13-year-olds. I was in on a gang rape of a 14-year-old retarded girl once. I punched her face and she bled all over. The bitch bit my cock.

Doctor: Any younger children involved?

Mr. H: Tried once with a 9-month-old baby I was babysitting. It didn't fit in her cunt or ass. Finally I stuck it in her mouth. Wasn't much fun.

If the exhibitionist has an orgasmic pretactile courtship phase of interaction in his exhibiting, this may also represent heightened sexual arousability. A first avenue to investigate for hypersexuality is sex hormones. It is well known that injecting testosterone into males produces sexual arousal[106]. If exhibitionists naturally have excessive levels of testosterone in their blood stream, this may make them hypersexual. Although this seems like a relatively straight forward hypothesis to investigate, little work has been done to test it out.

The exhibitionist as shy and unassertive. More complex explanations of exposing have been suggested by personality theorists. The exhibitionist is afraid of intercourse, it is assumed because of his basic character. He is shy and unassertive and although he is masculine identified, he cannot act in the normal fashion because of feelings of inferiority[5 67 68 72 92 98 107]. This inferiority focuses on his sexuality, and in particular, on his penis. Witzig[107] noted that it may be important to distinguish those who act out with "no genital gratification" (masturbation) from those who do so. The one who masturbates is regressing to an adolescent practice. It proves he is aggressive and it protects him from the fact that he may prove impotent in actual physical involvement with a female. This is why exposing occurs where direct sex contact is not possible. What woman in her right mind is going to have intercourse with a total stranger in the middle of a public street?

This does not mean that the male involved may not desire intercourse no matter how unrealistic it may seem. *Mr. H* illustrates this viewpoint. He indicated:

Mr. H: What I really would like is some nice young thing to expose to me too and then maybe we could go somewhere and have sex.

Doctor: Do you think that will happen?

Mr. H: I don't know.

Doctor: You have been exposing since you were 15 on the average of 4–5 times a week and that means you have exposed over 1600 times now. Right?

Mr. H: Um Hum. Ya. Gee, I guess so!

Doctor: Has a woman ever offered you sex or exposed to you?

Mr. H: (long pause)----No, but one might!

On the other hand, cases like the following are difficult to incorporate into such a theoretical framework. *Mr. I* was a handsome but inadequate person with many feelings of inferiority. He had an extensive criminal history including common assault. He had numerous affairs and considerable experience with females. On the ward, there was an ongoing romance which supported his history as a "lady's man". When asked why he exposed, he said:

> *Mr. I:* Because I'm stupid. Seriously, I don't know what I get out of it but it gets me into trouble. To show you how crazy it is, let me tell you what I did about a month ago. I usually spend my Saturdays in the bar and this week, I had a date that evening with a nice girl. When I was in the bar, I picked up this other girl and we went to her place and had sex. Then I went out with my date that evening and had sex with her too. Would you believe I exposed on the way home? Now, that's stupid!

Taylor[97] noted that those exposing without orgasm are shy and unassertive. This theoretical formulation presents a paradox—the shy, unassertive exhibitionist will show his genitals in a public place to a stranger. This seems assertive enough, and may be construed even as aggressive but it is perhaps something that the normal assertive male would not do even if the desire were present.

Marital problems of the exhibitionist. Finally, one may expect marital difficulties to be common for exhibitionists but the theoretical literature is divided on this point. Bastani[10] claimed that deprivation of intercourse may play an important part in the etiology of exhibitionism, but Mohr, Turner and Ball[71] cautioned that exhibiting may result from a dissatisfaction and anxiety aroused by sex relations rather than by a lack of them. Bastani[10] discussed marriage as a "prophylaxis against exposing" but no data are presented by any authors. Maybe regular sexual intercourse reduces the need for exhibiting. Possibly, those who marry are a select group with less "need" to expose. If Freud is correct, the exhibiting (scoptophilia) replaces the act of genital union and one may expect marital, especially sexual discord. The hypothesis of a courtship disorder might also predict a reduction of exhibitionism in married men since they receive genital gratification and presumably, they also adequately complete the courtship sequence in the normal way. On the other hand, certain exhibitionists may have a preference for the "disordered" courtship sequence over the normal sequence. *Mr. O,* a 40-year-old married teacher, described his ambivalence about exposing versus intercourse as follows:

Mr. O: My wife and I had a lovely evening last Saturday. We were both drinking and feeling good. We sat on the sofa in the living room listening to the stereo and started to pet. She would look at my penis and smile. I found myself exposing to her. Then we would get back to petting and I would start to lose my erection. It went back and forth like that for a while until we finally had sex and it was all over. I guess I was disappointed I couldn't just expose to her.

The very same thing happened on our honeymoon. She was sitting before a fireplace in a see-through negligee and I came into the room totally nude and with an erection. She thought I was turned on by her but I was really exposing.

Bejke[11] considered exhibiting a compromise act resulting from sexual deprivation by the wife and from a desire for new sex partners. He described the typical exhibitionist as a faithful male who does not engage in promiscuous acts. If he does have sexual relations with many women, he will have one partner before going to another and will not be unfaithful to anyone. In the same way, he has a sense of obligation to his wife and although he may desire other women, he is faithful.

However, once his wife does not want more children and is unwilling to have some form of birth control, he must practice coitus interruptus or withdrawal before ejaculating. This is apparently typical of the exhibitionist's wife and is very frustrating so he starts to look outside his marriage for satisfaction. He will not have an affair with another woman because he fears making the strange woman pregnant, finds it difficult to make the contact, fears venereal disease and infecting others. So he contents himself with the sexual contact at a distance and with self release by masturbation in front of the stranger. It almost appears in this theory as if the marriage difficulties trigger off the exposing. However, one must ask why it occurs earlier before marriage. The desire for strangers or new sex stimuli is not exclusively an aspect of the exhibitionist's make up. Novelty is an apparent facet of many sexual anomalies and of normal heterosexual relations. Kinsey found that 50% of married men had extramarital intercourse by the age of 40. The desire for novelty does not seem peculiar when examined in this light. The attitude of the wives about intercourse and birth control along with the exhibitionist's attitudes about fidelity and cleanliness seem too circumstantial to explain exhibitionism in general. Needless to say, Bejke presented no statistical data to back up his claims.

Some of the theoretical speculations are examined in this chapter. There is little systematic data to support any of the theories described in this introduction but the few studies which have been done indicate that most of the theories are wanting.

THE EXPERIMENTAL EVIDENCE

The exhibitionist as homosexual and pedophilic. Examining the stimulus response matrix, it is clear that theorists are confused over what class of stimuli the exhibitionist responds to. He may be homosexual, pedophilic or a normal heterosexual. This question can be examined in two ways: first by determining if the exhibitionist responds phallometrically to these varied stimuli or only to one class and, second, by determining if the sex history of exhibitionists differ from normal control research participants in experience with children and men. Most of the available literature consists of case studies which, as we can see from the theory section, can illustrate any theoretical position one chooses. My colleagues and I have conducted the only controlled study to date in the professional literature[51].

Exhibitionists were compared to normal heterosexual research participants on penile tumescence reactions to movies of men and women, boys and girls in a standard test as discussed previously (Chapter 2)[29]. Neutral stimulus materials were included. There were no statistically significant penile volume reactions that distinguished the two groups. Reactions to females were in the predicted direction. All subjects reacted to female children but the reactions were larger to the physically mature female than to the child. Neither group showed significant reactions to any age of male. So in this respect, the exhibitionists appear to be normal.

When the two groups are compared on their sex history questionnaires for incidence of sexual acting out with males versus females and adults versus children, the results are again negative. Homosexual acts, desire for them and disgust for them are not different in the two groups. The exhibitionists have most of their experience with the physically mature female. They tend to select women between 16 and 30 although children are also the target of indecent exposure. Nevertheless, pedophilic acts in which there is some form of body contact with the child are not commonly a part of their repertoire. The immature female appears to be the victim of varied sexual offences but there appears to be nothing peculiar about her body shape which is especially attractive. Perhaps something else about her behavior is important. This point is discussed later.

Exhibitionists' reactions to their own bodies. A second stimulus may be important as a turn on for the exhibitionist—his own body. He may be autoerotic or he may need an audience. A female audience would seem unnecessary if he is autoerotic. Only one study approaches this question[51].

Using phallometric measurement, exhibitionists were compared on penile volume changes to nude females, nude males, neutral slides, and themselves in the nude, partially dressed in underwear, and clothed. The only reactions greater than those to neutral stimuli involved penile tumescence to physically mature females. The study was terminated with only four subjects used and a larger sample might support this theory. However, the idea that their own body was stimulating was a surprise to these four subjects. It seemed some sort of audience is necessary for the act to be satisfying, much as an actor needs his audience.

Interpersonal narcissism.   Although the actor usually does not interact directly with the audience, their presence is important for his continuing to act. *Mr. J,* who was a musician, compared his exposing to his performance on stage:

> *Mr. J:*   I'm different when I'm on stage. For one thing, I'm dressed up in a fancy costume and the audience are in everyday street clothes. I'm above them; the stage is usually several feet above the level of the tables where they sit. They have to look up to me. The lights are on me; their eyes are focused on me. They watch what I do. I play the music. I carry the ball so to speak. They applaud what I do; I don't return the applause. I'm the total focus of their attention, they have come to be entertained. Those are the things I enjoy about playing in a band and I like a lot of the same things about exposing. I want the woman watching me to be rapt in awe; to watch me in selfless adoration.

This may seem different from the reactions of the average man. In our study we attempted to determine if the exhibitionist is more excited by women attending to his genitals than the average man[51]. Two groups were compared; 10 exhibitionists and 10 controls, on penile volume reactions to 14 categories of stimuli. These stimuli were audiotaped statements about exposing with varying reactions of mature females, and about intercourse and peeping. We return to the other stimuli later and focus on the exposing for the moment. The advantage of these audio stimuli over pictures is that one is never sure using the latter that the research participant is responding to the visual features you want, for example, how does one portray admiration in a picture in a way every man will appreciate? In an audiotape, one simply says, "She is admiring you", whatever that may be for the individual. A sample tape from this experiment is as follows:

1. It is a warm summer day. You are walking along the beach alone.
2. There is a good looking young woman lying on a blanket not too far away. She is wearing a tiny bikini.
3. You take off your bathing suit and start walking towards her.
4. She sees your nude body and sits up. She starts to smile.
5. She looks at your penis and tells you that it is so big and beautiful.

6. She stares at your face and tells you that you are very handsome.

7. She looks at your shoulders and chest and says you must be very strong.

8. She stares at your penis and tells you that she wishes she had one like yours.

9. She stares at your thighs and legs and says you are very manly.

10. She examines your entire nude body and smiles warmly.

Each of the 10 segments lasts 10 seconds and with penile volume measurement, one can determine if there is a sudden change in arousal to one segment over the others. The narcissism interpretation of exhibitionism might predict a sudden increment in arousal to segment 5 of the last excerpt (she looks at your penis and tells you that it is so big and beautiful). However, the results did not differentiate controls and exhibitionists. All participants did respond more to this statement than to a neutral one so one might conclude that all were erotically aroused and narcissistic. However, not everyone engages in public genital exhibitionism so there must be some difference. The exhibitionists may have a much stronger need for narcissism, which is not measured by this test. Maybe different stimuli would support the theory.

Another interpretation is that normal individuals will respond to a wide range of sexually anomalous stimuli only in the lab. We know they react erotically to female children, to exposing, as well as to peeping and rape, and reports of reactions to rape scenes in books or movies have been anecdotally described. These results suggest that the average male in experiments of this sort are polymorphous in their sexual response but they do not act out in an orgasmic way and are much more inhibited in this respect. The relative amount of erection in these studies is therefore limited and erectile response must be considered in conjunction with orgasm. This latter criterion clearly differentiates most exhibitionists and normals and should be the criterion of preference in thinking about sexual anomalies.

Exhibitionism as a courtship disorder. Another approach to understanding exhibitionism is to ask patients directly what they want from exposing themselves. Much theorizing indicates that the activity focuses on intercourse. It has been maintained that they in fact want it as an outcome but at the same time, they are afraid of it. However, they simply may not be interested. Two samples of exhibitionists[51] were asked, what would happen if they were invited by the female to whom they are exposing to have intercourse. About half did not desire sex relations with the victim and less than 10% always or almost always desired intercourse or some form of sex contact. Only about a fifth of them ever even attempted to have intercourse. Even if the female were receptive to sex relations, only about half would be willing to do it. This may represent fear or lack of interest.

The exhibitionist may seem less interested in intercourse because he suffers from a courtship disorder. When courtship between man and woman is considered in terms of four phases (search for a partner, pretactile contact, tactile interaction and intercourse). Freund has suggested that the exhibitionist displays an exaggerated or unusual phase of pretactile interaction[28] and that the usual courtship behavior of the female turns him off but excites the normal male.

Freund and his colleagues[28] compared exhibitionists and controls on penile volume changes to statements depicting the four stages of courtship and to neutral statements. All subjects showed a greater reaction to intercourse and foreplay than to searching and pretactile interaction but the postulated difference between the two groups on pretactile interaction was not found. One significant result that can only be considered a trend, was the greater reaction of exhibitionists than the controls of foreplay or tactile interaction. This study represents the only attempt in the literature to test this theory.

One other study by Kolarsky and his associates[45], compared penile tumescence reactions of normals and of exhibitionists and toucheurs to scenes of movie clips showing the same female in seductive poses and in nonseductive ones. Overall, the results were nonsignificant and there are many designs and statistical problems with this study, but the authors indicated that the results suggest the anomalous group may be aroused both by a woman whose actual behavior is nonerotic but it stripping, as well as by her seductive behavior. Normals, however, did not react as much to the nonerotic stimuli. This result is surprising and better control of age of experimental and control groups and use of better stimuli might change this result. The study does suggest that exhibitionists and other sexually anomalous males react to both normal courtship overtures as well as to the body shape of females.

Other results from the sex histories of exhibitionists[51], indicate that they have a heterosexual and dating experience profile that falls within normal limits. Moreover, they are not different in marital frequency and divorce/separation rates from the general population or controls in research samples. Nor do they appear to differ from controls in marital adjustment. Although more work is needed in this area, the evidence does not support an interpretation that the exhibitionist is afraid of intercourse; is incapable of relating to females, or is incapable of executing the normal courtship sequence in a way that a normal female would accept. If he has an aversion to intercourse, it is very subtle and difficult to detect in empirical studies.

Narcissism versus the desire for intercourse. When compared to narcissistic interests in exposing, intercourse takes second place. In two samples of exhibitionists[51] about half said they hope the females to whom they expose will enjoy seeing the penis and about 30% hope the female will be impressed by its size. When the desire to be seen and the desire for intercourse are compared, the former relates more to masturbation frequency during exposing and to the total frequency of exposing. Although the desire for intercourse is related to total exposure frequency, it is poorly related to orgasmic behavior during exposing.

Outdoor masturbation.   One behavior that is common among exhibitionists and which offers support for the narcissism theory is outdoor masturbation with no one around. Such acts may be carried out on the deserted street where, one can postulate, he hopes to be seen by a female who just happened to come on the scene. On the other hand, this act may be done in the woods with no one as close as 20 miles and the possibility of being seen is rather remote. Such acts are rare among heterosexual normals but do occur among other sexual anomalies, in particular, among pedophiles and homosexuals, as reported on the Sex History Questionnaire[78]. The exact significance of this behavior has not been systematically studied but certainly reflects a lack of the social inhibitions which constrain the average person. There may also be something peculiar about the outdoors which is stimulating. It is possible that narcissism and automonosexuality may be elements in it. *Mr. K,* who was a real estate salesman, said that he enjoyed selling and it was particularly enjoyable when he had a client who was diametrically opposed to his view, and whom he convinced of his own viewpoint and sold the property. On one such occasion, he did so and remarked:

> *Mr. K:* I had just made this big deal and was really pleased with myself. The house was out of the way and there was no one around. The clients had just left in their car and I stayed behind and got into my car. I felt so good I decided to masturbate.

At times, men who are charged may suggest they were engaging in such acts but a woman "just happened" to come along and they were caught. One may suspect they are faking to deny the charges but in some instances the naivety of the individual may be an element. *Mr. L,* who was apprehended for indecent exposure was incensed that he was charged. He noted:

> *Mr. L:* No one ever comes through that park at that time of day. I was all alone and decided to masturbate. She just happened to come along and see me. I didn't want her to see me especially.

Sadism.   It has also been theorized that exhibitionism is a sadistic act with the intent of shocking or humiliating another person, in this case, a female. Only one controlled study addresses the question[51] of whether the exhibitionists have a history of sadism.

In two samples, the results were negative and no differences were elicited from exhibitionists versus controls in sexual history on such items. They were asked if they had ever experienced sexual arousal and/or orgasm to physically hurting someone, humiliating or embarrassing them, threatening or frightening someone, or beating them, having any of the above done to them or seeing someone unconscious or unable to move. None of these behaviors were related to strength of orgasmic behavior in exposing.

Sadism was also examined in a phallometric study with the audio stimuli described earlier in tests of the narcissism theory of exposing. Fourteen categories of stimuli were used: exposing with the female becoming sexually aroused, exposing with the female admiring him, exposing and the female becomes angry and insulted, exposing with the female unreactive, with her embarrassed and shocked, and finally with her fearful and in his power. Intercourse was described under three conditions: male initiated, female initiated, and mutual initiation. Other situations involved peeping at a sole female undressing and at intercourse/fellatio, watching a female expose, and violence against a female with no sexual contact. Of course, neutral control statements were also included. An example of the stimulus illustrating shock and embarrassment is:

1. It is a lovely spring afternoon. You are walking through the woods. No one is around.

2. As you walk you notice a young woman sitting on a bench by herself.

3. She is wearing tight shorts that reveal her long legs, and her blouse is unbottoned in front.

4. She hasn't seen you yet. You start to unzip your pants as you walk towards her.

5. When you are close you hold out your penis and get her attention.

6. She turns and looks at your exposed penis. Her mouth opens and her eyes widen with surprise.

7. She stares at you. She cannot take her eyes off your penis. She is shocked.

8. She begins to blush and you can tell she is really embarrassed but she continues to look at your penis.

9. She stands perfectly still, staring at your penis and blushing red.

10. She starts to walk away, occasionally looking over her shoulder, still shocked.

Penile volume changes were measured. Interestingly, again there are no significant differences between nonpatient controls and exhibitionists. They all react about the same to the exposing and significantly more than they do to neutral statements and to violence with no sexual contact. In fact, a wide range of reactions is acceptable to both groups and is still sexually arousing. We are faced with the same dilemma as discussing narcissism. Are all the controls sexually anomalous or do many normal men respond to sexually deviant stimuli? The controls were well screened in this study by interview and psychological tests. So the former is a less likely hypothesis. It would seem a wide range of sexual stimuli are arousing to a general population of males but few are orgasmic and preferred orgasmically. Maybe the stimuli were not adequate as tests of the sadism theory in this experiment. This is certainly a possibility and further work should be done. However, the sexual history information does not support the sadism theory of exhibitionism and these results are at least negative.

Voyeurism.   Freud has argued that the sexual energy of exhibitionists is invested in seeing and being seen and not in intercourse. This would suggest that voyeurism and exhibitionism would go hand in hand. Freund has postulated that there are four interrelated courtship disorders: voyeurism, exhibitionism, toucheurism and rape, representing successive disturbances in the courtship sequence. Numerous studies have suggested an association of these four but most are descriptive[62 72 82] and none are systematic.

In two samples we compared the sex history questionnaires of exhibitionists and non patient controls to a multiple sexual anomaly group to examine these questions[51]. Using the multiple anomaly group serves to control for patient status, and for having some sexual anomaly other than exposing. By polarizing the exhibitionists between these two control groups, we can determine what is peculiar to them.

Only peeping was linked to exposing with any strength of bond. None of the respondents had raped. Touching a female stranger was marginal in significance for the first sample and nonsignificant for the second one. Only 7% of exhibitionists in the first sample had done it more than five times. This behavior was not associated with orgasm. Many of these incidents appear to be accidental events in crowded buses and subways. Peeping was prominent and Freud's theory was supported in part. About half of the exhibitionists had peeped but only a tenth had peeped more than five times. The association of peeping and orgasm was not ascertained in this sample but was in the second one. In the second sample, a similar number had peeped but unfortunately, so had controls. In both groups, about a third of controls and multiple anomaly controls had peeped. When orgasm associated with peeping is examined, it clearly separates out the groups. None of the normal controls had reported climaxing while peeping but about a third of the exhibitionists had done so compared to a sixth of the other sexually anomalous men. Thus this orgasmic behavior offers weak support for the theory that peeping and exhibiting go hand in hand. Why do they go together? Freud only said the act of looking replaces the act of intercourse in "scoptophilia" or love of looking. This does not tell us why the two are associated. It simply restates the facts. There are two unresearched explanatory clues which may be pursued.

First, the exhibitionist wants the female to whom he exposes to "get a kick out of his act". Although intercourse offers mutual enjoyment for both partners, the female object of exhibiting gets nothing out of it unless she is sexually turned on or enjoys it in some way. In the case of *Mr. A,* he forced a female to undress and wanted her to masturbate while watching him and vice versa. Thus, he may have enjoyed watching "being watched". This may be the parallel to a mutually consenting sexual interaction between man and woman leading to intercourse—the man is more turned on if he has some sign that the woman is enjoying the sexual exchange. A second facet of this act is the clinical statement of some exhibitionists who see pornographic pictures of females as acts of exposing. It is not clear if the average man focuses on this possible interpretation of the pictures or simply enjoys the body characteristics and fantasied intercourse, and so forth, with her. The exhibitionists may identify with the cover girl as an exhibitionist, one who not only gets away with it legally but gets paid for it. Peeping may be justified in this way: if they leave their blinds up while they are undressing, they really want you to see them; they are in fact exposing. All this remains speculation and future research may provide clearer answers to these issues. The links between exhibiting and the other sexual anomalies of rape and toucheurism were not supported in this study. Further studies of orgasmic preferences and outlets may offer evidence to support the theory.

Hypersexuality and testosterone.   The exhibitionist may actually act out his desires that normals appear to have only in the laboratory because he is hypersexual. He may act out with children, expose, peep, act out with men or desire to do so, may be sadistic, narcissistic, and so forth; certainly wide ranging in behavior theoretically, and hypersexuality may be a factor. If one injects testosterone in a normal male, he tends to focus his energies on sexual matters and seems overresponsive. Although it may not be a parallel situation, excessive natural levels of testosterone in exhibitionists may be one reason they are acting out the way they are, that is, possible hypersexuality. Only one study examined this question[51]. Normals and exhibitionists were compared on serum testosterone levels and on penile volume output. The latter is the sum penile volume change of the six largest reactions to erotic pictures used in the standard phallometric test described earlier (Chapter 2)[29]. While this is a crude index, it offers some idea of the extent to which the research subject is responding to the stimuli. A hypersexual person might be expected to react a lot during the session.

An early morning blood sample showed that there were no significant differences in the two groups. If anything, there was a trend to lower serum testosterone in exhibitionists than in controls—opposite to expectation from the theory. In fact it was almost abnormally low. However, the controls for age of participants in the two groups was not satisfactory and the time period over which the samples were spread was large. In a second study, this was adequately controlled and there were no significant differences in the two groups, and all testosterone levels were within normal limits. When penile volume output was compared for the two groups, there were no significant differences either, although testosterone and the output measure were weakly related. A study involving repeated blood samples from the same individual has yet to be done.

Married exhibitionists may be peculiar in some respect. Intercourse is part of marital duties, so if it provokes anxiety or fear of rejection, or if it is distasteful in some way, this should be reflected in the exhibitionists' marriages. The female partners may be unhappy. There may be more divorce, and lack of marital satisfaction for exhibitionists who must cope with the anxiety and stress generated by the situation in which they are always proving themselves or trying to avoid stress. In the one study addressing the question, there were in fact no differences in frequency of divorce or separation compared to control subjects[51]. Marital adjustment measured by a Marital Relations Questionnaire[76] indicated there were no meaningful differences in overall marital adjustment, willingness to compromise, marriage satisfaction, affectional compatibility, common interests, and strength of marriage bond. However, the number of cases was small and the self-reports of the patients were used. Their wives may feel differently although our clinical interviews suggest this is not the case. Nevertheless, this type of information is not to be trusted, and systematic studies on the wives need to be done.

Some theorists indicate that marriage should reduce the desire for exposing; that it is a prophylaxis against exposing[10]. Presumably, one form of sexual outlet is as good as another. Maybe, marital sexual outlet increases the exhibitionists' feeling of adequacy which detain them from exposing. On the other hand, the anxiety engendered in marriage and the stress to have intercourse may provoke exposing. As noted earlier[71], it is not the lack of intercourse that causes the exposing, rather, the inability to cope with the demand to have it that may provoke the act. Only one study ascertains whether married exhibitionists in fact expose less or more than single ones[51]. When single and currently married exhibitionists were compared on sexual history, it was found that the married group reported exposing more in their lives, and did so more often with an erect penis and masturbated more often than the singles group. Moreover, there was no difference in the recency of exposing. This might appear to support the theory that marriage is a stressor and drives the exhibitionist to expose. However, the married exhibitionists had more varied heterosexual outlets than the single exhibitionists; namely intercourse, cunnilingus, anal digitation; and they feel less desire for additional sex partners or greater frequency of intercourse. One might expect that married men would have more opportunities than single ones to do so. In addition, the married subjects were 7 years older than controls on the average (29 versus 22) which may account for a substantial amount of the experience accumulated. In a second sample, the age difference was 7 years again but the overall sample was 3 years older—25 for singles and 32 for married exhibitionists. This time, there was no difference in exposing history, frequency or recency. Married men did want the female to enjoy the exposing more than the singles did. There were no differences in heterosexual history in this case. It is possible that a day to day diary for a month would reveal differences in single and married groups, or that correlating deprivation from intercourse and exposing behavior would reveal support for the theory, but this study did not.

Lack of assertiveness.   Another facet of exhibitionism is the reported shyness, lack of assertiveness and feelings of inadequacy as a male and about his own body. In two controlled studies, my colleagues and I[49][51] used personality inventories and found that exhibitionists are not different from non patient controls in assertiveness, using a wide range of current measures that are reliable and valid. They do tend to be shyer and more masculine but results were inconsistent. In the first study[49] which examined MMPI and 16 PF profiles of exhibitionists as well as other sexually anomalous and control subjects, the exhibitionists were more masculine on both tests. On the MMPI, they also tended to be more nonconforming and to have more family difficulties (Pd scale). On the 16 PF, they were sober and shy. The 16 PF, however, is now a rather suspect instrument[38] and results should be treated with extreme caution.

In a second study with a different set of measures[51], the results did not confirm those of the last study. The MMPI was used again but also the Edwards Personal Preference Schedule, the BEM Androgyny Scale and the Feminine Gender Identity Scale, all measuring gender identity and/or masculinity/femininity. Exhibitionists did not differ from controls on any measure. Nor did they appear as shyer or more introverted as in previous suggestive work. This study also compared exhibitionists and normals on two behavioral observation studies measuring assertiveness and androgyny and results were either negative or inconsistent. There were, however, no differences in masculine behavior or in dominance. Results simply failed to support the theories. In most respects, the exhibitionists looked clinically normal. With the exception of their indecent exposure, they would not be distinguishable from normal.

Masturbation during exposure.   Maybe the exhibitionists who masturbate while exposed are different from the ones who do not. About half do have orgasmic outlet with exposing. It has been postulated that the shy, unassertive exhibitionists are the ones who do not have genital gratification when exposing. One control study addresses the question. Exhibitionists in two separate samples were subdivided into two groups on the basis of their sexual histories[51] as masturbators versus nonmasturbators while exposed. Although there were significant results, they did not support the theory. In the first sample, the MMPI and 16 PF were used and only the MMPI Mania scale related negatively to erection while exposed but not to masturbation when exposed. In other words, the more often they had an erection when exposed, the less overall energy they had. This relationship was weak and should not be taken too seriously in light of the number of tests which were done. In the second sample, masturbation when exposed related to being more masculine and more confused in their thinking. However, the results are suspect since the validity scales of the MMPI related as much to the outcome as the other clinical scales. Other samples with other scales may support the theory. However, the available results suggest that there are no important personality differences in the two groups.

Feelings of inferiority about the penis.   One study addresses the question[51] that exhibitionists have feelings of inferiority about their bodies, in particular, about the penis. We asked research participants:

1. Have you ever been ashamed to appear in a bathing suit?
2. Have you ever felt you would like to change your physical appearance in some way?
3. Have you ever felt you would like to be taller?
4. More muscular?
5. Stronger?
6. Heavier?
7. Have a more athletic build?
8. Be more athletic?
9. Do you think that you are reasonably attractive to the opposite sex?
10. Have you ever been ashamed to appear in the nude with persons of your own sex around?
11. Have you ever wished you had a larger penis?
12. Do you think that your penis is smaller than average?
13. Have you ever been afraid that something was wrong with your private parts?

14. Were you ever thought of as a sissy or weakling?

15. Have you ever felt you would like to be more forceful than you are?

16. Have you ever felt that you would like to be better looking?

17. Do you think you are more feminine or more masculine in your appearance?

18. Do you think you are more feminine in your personality or more masculine in your personality?

19. Have you ever felt inferior because of your build or shape for any reason?

20. Was your mother concerned about your private part that you should keep it clean and take care of it?

21. Was father?

22. Do you remember that your mother used to wash it for you with her hand?

23. Did father?

24. Can you remember your mother handling your private parts with her hand in a sexual way?

Exhibitionists, other heterosexual anomalous nonexhibitionists, and nonpatient controls were compared. The exhibitionists differed from non patient controls only on six items. If one only examined these two groups, it could be concluded that exhibitionists have some feelings of inferiority about their bodies. They would like to be more athletic, have a more athletic build, have a larger penis, and be better looking than controls would. They more often felt there was something wrong with their penis and their fathers were concerned that they take care of it and keep it clean. However, when the other respondents with sexual anomalies are included, they are also different from controls in the same way except for two items: the exhibitionists differ from both the controls and other patients in wanting to have a more athletic build and to be more athletic. Thus if there are general feelings of inferiority about the body and concerns about cleanliness in the patient sample, they are not specific to exhibitionists. The theory can only be considered partially supported. A hypothesis could be restated: Males with sexually anomalous behavior are more likely than controls to report some feelings of inferiority about their bodies and some concern about cleanliness.

Parent child relations.   Only one study in the literature examines parent child relations in a systematic study of exhibitionists[77]. Using the same design just noted, Paitich and I found that exhibitionists did not differ in a remarkable way from controls in terms of mother relationships but they judged fathers as more strict than controls did. However, exhibitionists' scores tend to fall between the extremes of controls and other sexually anomalous men indicating that their parent child relationships may be disturbed but not as greatly as in other anomalies. In conjunction with the notion of a concern about cleanliness, this finding offers some support for the psychoanalytic theory. However, the findings should be replicated in a purer sample of exhibitionists.

Little has been said about alcohol because it is not a prominent factor in this anomaly[72]. Some earlier work indicated alcoholism was a frequent associate of indecent exposure, but when more general samples are examined, it becomes a less significant factor. Clinically exhibitionists present as hard working individuals with a good work record. About 1-in-4-or-5 have a previous sexual offence and about 1-in-4 also have a previous nonsexual conviction. The recidivism rate is about 13 to 17% in various studies so most offenders are appearing in court for the first time[72]. Since there is also little evident psychopathology in these men, the therapist can focus on exhibiting itself without worrying about a host of extraneous factors that are prominent in other anomalies like rape.

Conclusion and Speculations on the Exhibitionist's Stimulus Response Matrix

The evidence summarized in Table 10.2 seems overwhelming that the stimulus of choice for the exhibitionist is the physically mature female. Any substantive evidence of homosexual orientation is absent in controlled studies. To postulate latent homosexuality raises a question which is difficult to test. However, there does appear to be some overlap in the age range of female victims of indecent exposure and pedophilia, suggesting a link of the two. Children are often implicated and it is an open question why this is the case. It seems exhibitionists' penile reaction to female children is within the normal range of response. It may be puzzling then why female minors, especially pubescent girls, are the victims of exposing. It should be noted that they are not the sole victims of exhibitionists but tend to attract a wide range of multiple anomalies as well. Therefore, it may be inappropriate to ask why exhibitionists per se rather than sexually anomalous males in general are attracted to this age group. Two suggestive answers emerge: Avoiding getting caught and getting the reaction they want. Teenage girls can be as physically mature as adults but lack the social maturity. They are less likely to know how to react to exposing and in fact may give the exhibitionist the reaction, or at least some form of attention that he wants. This may be something an older woman would not do. She may look away in disgust or alarm rather than be attentive and smile or even watch with interest, something which a teenage girl who is curious and naive might do. Moreover, this group may be less likely to report the offence. Children are often perplexed as to what to do. They may or may not tell

TABLE 10.2
Summary of Evidence for Theories of Exhibitionism

Theory	Experimental Support
1. Exhibiting as latent homosexuality	Negative
2. As pedophilia	Same age range of victims but no body contact for the exhibitionist. No inordinate penile reactions to immature females
3. Turned on by their own bodies	Negative
4. Turned on by admiration from females	Mixed support. A likely hypothesis to investigate
5. As a courtship disorder	Negative but more work needed
6. Desire for intercourse in exposing	Negative but needs more investigation
7. As a sadistic act	Negative
8. Associated with voyeurism	A weak but positive link
9. As hypersexual	Negative
10. Marriage is a prophylaxis against exposing	Negative
11. Exhibitionists are shy and lack assertiveness	Negative
12. Those who masturbate during exposure differ from those who do not	Negative
13. They suffer feelings of inferiority about their penis	Negative
14. Fear females and intercourse	Negative
15. They are sexually aroused by physically mature females	Positive. Similar to normal controls.

their parents. When asked for important details and descriptions, they may not be able to give them. *Mr. M* preferred to expose to young girls and would drive around schools at the start and end of the school day. Having exposed for 20 years in this environment, he was alarmed one day:

> *Mr. M:* One of the girls I exposed to was so good I just had to drive around the block again for another turn. When I came around the school yard, she was standing there with a pencil and pad trying to see my license plate, and she scared the hell out of me. That had never happened before and I did not think it was possible. I got out of there as fast as I could.

Interestingly, *Mr. M* had not exposed again two years later. Whether this was because of the scare or because he was getting up in years (he was 35 then) is not known.

Of course the relationship of exposing and the female victim's age may be a matter of chance. Any female may do as long as she shows some interest and watches. Does an actor select the age and characteristics of his audience? If a 12-year-old is available and is interested, that is fine; if she is 40, that's fine too.

When we examine the response side of the matrix, only three responses are prominent: masturbation while exposed, peeping and intercourse. The typical exhibitionist in the controlled studies reviewed here, has a normal dating and heterosocial sexual experience profile. Many are married and appear to enjoy intercourse. Thus a penile preference for the mature body shape of the female and enjoyment of intercourse are connected. It is doubtful, but far from conclusive that the exhibitionist wants intercourse when he exposes. He does not seem to be afraid of it either. It simply seems irrelevant. What he seems to want most is to be watched while he masturbates with no physical contact. It would be more satisfying if the female also enjoyed exposing and masturbated at the same time. Then, there would be a parallel to the mutually enjoyable intercourse that normal males prefer. Intercourse is more stimulating when the female shows interest and enjoyment. So for the exhibitionist, it would be nicer if she enjoyed exposing too. Unfortunately for him, that is not the case. Mutual enjoyment pervades many human needs—a game of poker is more exciting than a game of solitaire. Is it peculiar that this should be present in sexual behavior? Peeping is the only sexual anomaly consistently but weakly associated with exhibiting. This may find an explanation in the association that peeping may be "watching someone else expose". It is possible that the voyeur places himself in the role of the female exposing unwittingly (or otherwise) to him and he can pretend she sees him too and they are both enjoying it.

The strip show is a haven for the exhibitionist. This may be the case for similar reasons. He is watching someone expose. Some men have interpreted the pornographic pictures of females as exposing. They do not enjoy them solely for their body shape or as a fancied sex partner. As the reader is aware now, we are engaging in speculations. Many of the questions raised here are testable. The next few years of research should provide interesting answers to the hosts of questions presently unanswered.

The clinician who sees an exhibitionist can expect to meet a relatively normal looking person. If the indecent exposure were not revealed, he might label the individual a normal control subject. Once the clinician does know about the sexual anomaly, some form of personality label is attached; usually character disorders or immature personality, inadequate personality, and so forth. There is little support for such labels in standardized psychometric testing. One has to struggle to find any personality differences between the exhibitionist and the normal. Maybe there are none. Maybe we need to look no further than the sexual behavior itself. Personality is a global concept and much of human behavior may be situational or at least parcelled out to the aspect of life for which it is relevant.

Few of the theorized differences in personality were found in controlled studies. On the other hand, I have attempted to provide an example of each theoretical position with case studies. When a number of exhibitionists are examined, the same personality traits should emerge. If they do not, we have a theory for each person and we ascribe a host of etiologies to exhibitionism. One can speculate on chance occurrence of traits with exhibitionism and develop a large number of theories but this is not parsimonious. It would tell us no more about the exhibiting behavior itself.

The studies of sexual history and penile reactions in the exhibitionist have provided more information about what is happening and now the clinical speculations seem irrelevant. If any traits should be investigated, they would be those of narcissism or more currently, the borderline syndrome of which narcissism is a major part. This has received no attention in the professional literature and only one measure is remotely pertinent—the narcissometer[40]. This test is a measure of the extent of time a person spends looking at themselves as opposed to the environment. Unfortunately, narcissism seems more complex than that. The extreme narcissist may need no outside input to his behavior but most need an audience to admire them. One may find out if exhibitionists are generalized narcissists or only sexual narcissists. The former may be much more difficult to treat for their exposing tendencies because the underlying cause is so pervasive. *Mr. O*, noted above, appeared to be a general narcissist. In one instant he described, he was asked by his men's club to thank a guest speaker:

> *Mr. O:* I thanked the speaker at some length, perhaps for 5 minutes. One of the other men at the head table hinted I should stop. He asked me after why I went on for so long. I told him it was a great talk. But, the real reason was that I enjoyed hearing myself talk and having all those people watching me!

The exhibitionist may react with penile tumescence to display activities in a wide range of social contexts, even those with no obvious sexual component. These would provide interesting hypotheses to test in experiments. For the present, we can say he seems normal in most respects with the exception of his exhibiting. He reacts to females of all ages but mostly to physically mature ones. He can enjoy intercourse but also has a preference to show his genitals to an attentive female and sometimes to masturbate. No more seems desired.

TREATMENT

The preceding sections have shown that there is no agreed upon theory of exhibitionism today and treatment methods reflect this. One can expect to see a host of unsystematic case studies using a variety of methods. However, in the case of this anomaly, therapists have shown a particular concern with the patients' unwillingness to be treated. Since exhibitionists often face criminal charges, they may be forced into treatment as an alternative to prison. Denial of any problems is considered prominent in exhibitionism[30] [32] [62] [64] [65] [107]. Moreover, prisoners' compliance to treatment may be for the purpose of either getting out, getting passes or discontinuing contact with the therapist and legal system permanently. The "cure" may be more apparent than real. *Mr. P,* who was incarcerated for a third time and had a genuine change of heart about treatment noted:

> *Mr. P:*   I was playing games with you the other times. I never really stopped having the urge to expose. I was doing it everywhere, in shopping centers on Saturday afternoons, on the bus, you name it. I was laughing up my sleeve every time I came in here telling you I may have had an urge or two or 'no, I didn't have any urges this week'. I was making fun of you but I was mad too. I'm sorry now because I see I was the real victim of the joke.

Police records cannot tell you this sort of thing is going on; only the truth from an honest reformed patient can.

Some men are very adept at avoiding detection such as *Mr. H,* who described exposing over 1600 times and was never caught. One day he happened to be exposing outside our clinic door, saw our sign and thought to himself, "This isn't normal. I'm going in to get help." Another patient, *Mr. Q,* had been exposing for 20 years around town but especially outside a prominent plaza in the city and he was never incarcerated. He noted that the high school girls seemed to enjoy his antics and they called him "Flash." No one seems to have taken the trouble to report him. How often does this happen? What are the odds of getting caught? Although authors belittle the value of self report, it ultimately must be our criterion of success. Perhaps a change in our expectations will make accurate reporting by such patients more reliable.

The reoccurrence of exposing behavior has been implicitly assumed to be the criterion of treatment success. No one talks of changing the exhibitionist's "erotic preference". Some theorists see homosexuality as so unusual that an erotic preference may be discussed, but the act of exhibiting seems more superficial and even as a distorted form of seeking intercourse or as a means of avoiding intercourse. Nevertheless, an unusual erotic preference for exposing may be present and one must ask if all desire for these outlets is removed with treatment.

BEHAVIOR THERAPY

Aversion therapies.   One of the most prominent treatments used in the research literature has been aversive conditioning described in Chapter 3. The advantage of the method is that it is atheoretical. The undesirable behavior, in this case indecent exposure, is associated in the laboratory via slides or audiotapes with an unconditioned unpleasant stimulus such as electric shock. With repeated presentations and pairing of the two, the urge to expose should decline in frequency. A traditional avoidance conditioning procedure used on homosexuals was adapted to a 12-year-old exhibitionist by MacCullough, Williams, and Birtles[61].

In this method, the subject of treatment attends to pictures or statements. As he becomes aroused, he is faced with giving up the arousal and removing the slides by pressing a button or receiving an electric shock. Thus, the avoidance aspect of the procedure. One might expect that the conditioning stimulus would be pictures or statements about exposing and the unconditioned stimulus to be electric shock. However, in this case the 12-year-old boy was presented with slides of women, 20 years of age and older, and then faced electric shock. Age appropriate but physically immature female peers were associated with relief from shock as used in anxiety relief conditioning. Although the patient had some form of unspecified psychotherapy concurrently, it was considered that the effective ingredient in treatment was the aversive conditioning. There were a total of 18 sessions, 20 minutes long and after 5 months, the patient reported a reduction in exhibitionistic behavior, in his masturbation fantasies, and in his sexual orientation to older women.

As discussed in Chapter 3, anxiety relief conditioning does not have a theoretical basis and may be detrimental to treatment. Moreover, one has to wonder why age of stimulus subject was punished instead of exposing. If, in fact immature females were associated with anxiety relief, would not pedophilia result? It seems the attraction to the physically mature female body would be a healthy feature of the child's behavior. No theoretical reason was presented why the older female was the key in changing exposing behavior.

Abel and his colleagues[1] offered one of the very few studies in which penile measurement was taken during treatment as an index of sexual arousal. They reported treatment of three exhibitionists in which the subjects' own descriptions of the deviant act were used in the aversive procedure. Each description was divided into three segments and initially the last segment was paired with electric shock. Later the second and finally the first segments were paired with shock. In some of the presentations at each session, the patients could avoid shock by verbalizing normal sexual behavior in place of the anomalous behavior. Tapes of normal sex were also used and treatment produced a reduction in penile arousal to the deviant stimuli while reactions were maintained to the normal stimulus sequence.

At 18 week follow up there was no recidivism in the patients but some showed an overall reduction in erotic arousal to normal stimuli in the laboratory as well. As the authors noted, the results are promising but additional studies with greater numbers of both experimental and control cases and long term follow ups are necessary.

Although there are scattered individual case studies in the literature,[25][47], Evans was one of the first[23][24] to report a systematic study of aversive conditioning with exhibitionists. He postulated that the fantasy life of the patient was an important facet of the anomaly. The actual act of exposing was only a take off point for the patient to masturbate, perhaps later, in the privacy and safety of his home. After McGuire, Carlisle and Young's theory[69], Evans argued that fantasies followed by masturbation reinforce the exhibiting habit in the manner of operant conditioning. Bancroft[7] has noted that this reasoning in circular since the fantasies may be the result of the sexual anomaly rather than the cause. This, however, is an open question.

From the patients' descriptions of exposing, Evans derived statements that were used in the aversive conditioning. Slides of the statements were made which would elicit the erotically arousing images and fantasies of the patient. For this reason, the procedure was called *emotive imagery deconditioning*. At each of ten sessions and later periodic booster sessions over a 2 year period, this slide material was paired with an electric shock. It is noteworthy that all patients were voluntary clients at a private behavior therapy clinic. It is uncertain if criminal charges were involved. Shock was not presented at a single high voltage as it usually is, but gradually increased in intensity until the patient could not stand it anymore. At that point the patient pressed a foot pedal which terminated shock. It is not known if this novel method produces any different results from shock used at a single high intensity. Animal research suggests it would be less effective[93].

Patients were divided into 2 groups; those whose masturbation fantasies were to normal heterosexual intercourse and those whose fantasies were of exposing. In the former group, conditioning took effect quicker and none of the five patients were exposing after a 6 month follow up. Two of the five who had masturbation fantasies of exposing, continued actively to expose after 6 months. However, a later analysis of the data by the present author in cooperation with Evans showed that the pretreatment frequency of exposing was higher for the group with exposing fantasies. If the patient was having lots of urges to expose during treatment, his prognosis was poorer than patients who had infrequent urges to expose irrespective of fantasy content. As noted in Chapter 3, this is an important consideration in assessing treatment outcome. The relation of masturbation fantasy content to treatability would still seem to be an open question.

Hackett[32] used a form of aversive conditioning in the classical conditioning mode but he also used a variety of other methods some of which he considered crucial to treatment, namely, methods involving the expression of anger. We will return to this later. Because he used a variety of methods, we do not know which was having effect or if in fact some combination of methods was important.

Only one other study besides Evans's using aversive conditioning was a controlled study. Rooth and Marks[88] used a "Latin square" experimental design to compare three treatments on 12 exhibitionists. In this design each person received all three treatments for 1 week but the order in which he received them was varied and balanced across individuals so that all possible orders of the three treatments was used. Moreover, the same treatment cannot appear twice in the same position order. Thus for three treatments A, B, C; one Latin square would be: A, B, C and B, C, A and C, A, B. By this procedure, the effect of order of presentation is controlled to some degree but it is assumed treatments do not interact in any way. Rooth and Marks used aversion therapy, self regulation and relaxation.

The aversion therapy was the classical conditioning kind in which imagining or rehearsing indecent exposure in front of a mirror was always followed by electric shock. The patient signaled imaging and the therapist administered shock on each of 15 trials during one session. "Aversion relief" was also employed in the form of conversation with the therapist. Subsequently, patients administered the treatment themselves with a portable shock box an unspecified number of times. Seven patients reported marked tension during this treatment and three reported marked anger. This could adversely influence treatment (see Chapter 3).

The relaxation therapy was Jacobson's[39] method described in Chapter 3 in which patients were trained in deep muscle relaxation during one session. Then they were told to carry the exercise out daily on their own and when they went into tempting situations, they should counteract incipient tension by attempting to relax as trained. All patients enjoyed this treatment.

Self regulation involved a method described by Bergen[12] in which the chain of stimulus cues leading to exposing were identified and a repertoire of alternative behaviors like smoking or reading were used to interrupt the sequence in its early stages. However, this method was complicated by use of self administered covert sensitization and what seems like assertiveness training. This method produced shame, depression and embarrassment in seven patients and anger in two patients.

The authors used patient's self report but argued that it is better than penile plethysmography since many exhibitionists do not have erections to exposing anyway, and ultimately we must rely on self report. All patients were subjected to each of the three treatments in different orders, and they evaluated aversion therapy as having the most effect of the three. This conclusion is questionable because the three treatments may have interacted to produce the result. The order of presentation is inextricably confounded with treatment method and it could have interacted significantly in unknown ways which may have produced the outcome observed. There was a 6 month follow up during which a variety of procedures were used intermittently with selected patients. Seven of the 12 relapsed, four were convicted after 14 months. Whereas exposure rate was reduced after treatments, it was still substantial. Perhaps longer therapy time and administration of only one treatment to each patient would have produced different results.

Shame aversion therapy.   The largest number of cases treated with an aversive conditioning method was carried out by Wickramsakera[104][105] who reported on 25 cases of chronic offenders and followed them up for a period of 3 months to 7 years. It is not known how many were incarcerated. His method was a variant of shame aversion therapy (see Chapter 3) called, *aversive behavior rehearsal.* In this procedure, the patient was permitted to expose in a controlled environment before a group of unreactive and disinterested staff, both male and female. Some patients who refused this treatment did it vicariously by watching another exhibitionist do it on videotape.

When the patient must face his victims in this way, it resulted in shame and embarrassment which acts as a punishment or negative reinforcer for him. Thus the frequency of exhibiting should decline. Although the procedure seems straight forward, Wickramsakera described an elaborate preamble with the patients which precedes the actual aversion therapy.

The initial sessions were for information collection, history, and so forth. Then the therapist attempted to ascertain who was appropriate for the therapy by administering a psychophysiological test in which a cap pistol was discharged behind and close to the patient's head. Imaging ability was tested and the patient was encouraged to disclose his deviation to important others, such as wife or parents. Finally, there were two 40 minute aversion sessions. The therapist opened the session in a kind but grave manner, then became progressively more obnoxious and confronting by rapid questioning and by ordering the patient to expose and masturbate before staff. He was repeatedly asked to expose and get dressed. Often at this point, the patient was in tears, trembling, weak and nauseous. The team was dismissed and the main therapist again became warm and kind, expressing admiration at the patient's courage.

Thus the procedure is much more than straight forward conditioning. One of the claims of behavior therapy is the simplicity of methodology. This makes it cheap and efficient. Training of new therapists is relatively easy. However, from this description of aversive behavioral rehearsal, the actual procedure is more complex than meets the eye in its title. It approaches the complexity of role playing and psychotherapy methods. One has to wonder how much the inventor of this method has to do with its success. Sometimes a prominent therapist can be more successful at his method than anyone else. Generalizability to other therapists and settings is an important consideration in evaluating outcome.

Wickramsakera reports 100% success rate with his method although there was a 20% drop out rate. An additional sixth of the cases would only undergo vicarious treatment but this was apparently as effective as in vivo treatment. These are impressive results. Note also that only 1-to-4 sessions were used for each patient. Although the method may seem abhorrent to the sensitive individual, some exhibitionists who are eager to be rid of their anomaly might undergo such a procedure knowing it would only involve a short period of time. Patients would have to be selected judiciously because as Serber[91] who invented shame aversion therapy noted, if more than a few sessions are used, the patient can begin to like it. Moreover, in the few cases reported by Serber, one patient attempted suicide the day after treatment. Generating higher levels of shame and guilt in individuals who may already be pathologically depressed and be experiencing excessive guilt may push them to the brink of suicide.

In spite of any optimism generated by Wickramsekera's results, conclusions should be tempered by the fact that it was not a controlled study. We are not informed of procedures usual in behavior modification techniques, such as baselines of exposing behavior prior to treatment or current urges to expose. There is no control group of untreated exhibitionists or of a group treated by some other method. We do not know the criminal history of the patients treated. It is unusual for exhibitionists to be sent to prison these days unless they are more than exhibitionists, that is, pedophiles, toucheurs, rapists or they have concurrent records for other offenses of a violent and/or nonsexual nature. We do not know how central exhibiting is to their sexually anomalous repertoire nor if the patient is engaging in some other outlet which is less detectable by the law enforcement agencies. Many exhibitionists will for instance engage in peeping as well as exposing. *Mr. R,* who had served time for theft as well as indecent exposure, indicated that he still had urges to act out but he was sticking to the safer peeping:

> *Mr. R:*   When you expose, there is always the chance the dame involved will squeal on you to the cops. I think I'm pretty good at telling who will report you and who won't. But now, I'm tired of prison and I don't really care to go back so I'm sticking to peeping. It's not as good as exposing but most of the time, no one knows you are there and I can take my time and come (climax).

The most important consideration is the fact that the Wickramsakera's study was conducted on offenders and without a control group. Patients were also preselected. It is possible that the prison experience alone was sufficient to deter the exhibitionist from further acting out or that they would lie about their current behavior at follow up to avoid further contact with the prison. The best candidates were those with high manifest anxiety, with fundamentalist religious background and high motivation. From the foregoing review, this would appear unusual among exhibitionists but it may explain the apparent success of the method. At least the use of a control group would provide us some information on these factors. Use of police records for follow up would be another validation of the patient's report.

Several authors have discovered the shame aversion method independently about the same time[81] [91] [96] [103] and there are slight variations in the procedure. Serber told the patients only to observe themselves and be aware of being observed before the staff audience. Patients are preselected so they are ashamed of the act and desire not to be observed in its execution. They must be aware of the antisocial nature of the act. Two exhibitionists were treated and followed up for 6 months without repetition of the act. Like Wickramsekera, self report was used in follow up. Reitz and Keil[81] treated one other case similarly but also had him observed by nursing staff. After a 19 month follow up, he was symptom free as well. The final case was treated with a method similar to Wickramsakera's and the patient was symptom free after one year. Unfortunately, each of these case reports suffers the same problems of the larger number of cases in Wickramsakera's study.

What appears to be a variant of shame aversion therapy was developed in New Zealand by Wardlaw and Miller[103] and labeled "a controlled exposure technique." This method involves the patient deliberately exposing in a nonrisk situation. The authors noted that most of these "practice or controlled exposures" occurred at home or at work. In each act, the patient would open his trousers, expose the penis and count to ten before zipping up. The exposing would be done regularly at planned time, usually hourly, throughout the waking day. The critical element in treatment was each patient imagining how stupid he felt and in general, experiencing all the negative feelings he normally did *after* the exhibiting.

Although some patients report feeling "stupid and embarrassed" after exposing, it is too late to have any impact on their behavior. The timing between a conditioned and unconditioned stimuli, in this case exposing and feelings of guilt and shame, need to be precisely timed to be effective according to learning theory[44]. Animal studies have suggested that even a short delay is ineffective. Punishing the events at the start of a deviant act or those events leading up to the deviant act is more effective than punishing the actual behavior itself after it occurs. The method of controlled exposure may be making the timing of shame more contingent on the exposing and thus preventing future acting out.

The authors noted that in this method, sexual excitement does not accompany the act of exposing so that in effect, the exposing behaviors may be extinguished since they go unrewarded. It has been argued that extinction is more effective than punishment (cf. Chapter 3, and [48] and [93]). It would be an interesting study to compare the control part of this method with the aversive part to determine which is more effective.

Three patients were treated and all showed improvement. They did not expose after a 4 year follow up in two cases and after a 3 year follow up in the third case. Two patients had no subsequent urges and reported having satisfactory sexual relationships in their marriages. A third patient noted he had tried to expose on three occasions but felt so foolish that he did not. Two cases showed no police involvement, the third case was out of the country and could not be checked. This is quite a dramatic change since each patient reported exposing at least several times a month. Nevertheless, one should be suspicious of uncontrolled studies and in this one it is clear something is amiss since data were carefully reported.

The authors counted frequency of exposing and other sex outlet data before, during and after treatment and they attempted a *reversal procedure*. In this latter technique, it is assumed that if the deviant behavior is being influenced by the treatment method and it is discontinued for a brief period, the frequency of the deviant behavior should increase again. In only 1-of-the-3 cases is there any trend to recovery of the urges and actual exposing does not reappear at all. Moreover, in 2-of-the-3 cases, there were no acts of exhibiting during baseline in spite of patients' reports that they were acting out several times monthly. The frequency of acting out may have been determined by some other factor which eliminated it before the "controlled exposing technique" began. In the third case, the exhibiting behavior started at a low frequency and disappeared rather quickly. It is possible that some extraneous factors were again operative. It is also possible that the patients were exposing erratically over time although they did expose several times a month just prior to treatment. Incarceration can serve as a deterrent in many cases and some patients with whom the present author has had contact noted that they may not have urges to act out for months or years after being caught, even though no treatment is initiated.

Covert sensitization is an aversive procedure that involves exclusive use of imagined stimuli. The conditioning stimulus, in this case exposing, and the unconditioned stimulus, nausea or pain, are all imagined. Brownell and Barlow[14][15] used this method on a patient who was exposing and who was involved in an incestuous relationship with his stepdaughter. A card sort comparison was made of arousing thoughts of exhibiting, sexual contact with his stepdaughter, sexual contact with his wife and with other women. Frequencies of these behaviors were recorded as well. Initially, the patient was having many thoughts of other women and relatively few of wife, and stepdaughter or of urges to expose. The aversive scene was derived from the subject's own fears rather than by use of some standard stimulus situation which is assumed to be aversive for all individuals. This is an important consideration. Even electric shock which seems to be painful to many of us may not elicit any reaction from some patients or they may adapt to it quickly. The patient involved in this study selected three aversive situations: being caught exposing by his wife and the subsequent divorce; being caught by his younger children and losing the rights to see them; being burned to death in the closed room where the anomalous acts occurred. These would be paired with the sexual acts as in the following example:

> You have the urge to expose when you see a next door neighbor. You rush to your window and stand there naked. As she watches, you begin to play with your penis—it feels good. You can feel your hand on your penis and suddenly the door opens and your son and daughter walk in. They see you in front of the window and begin to cry hysterically. They run out of the house and you begin to feel panic. You dress and chase them but the police come to get you. You are in court and are told you may never see your children again. Later you hear they have to leave town because the other kids are taunting them about having a perverted father. You feel empty inside; there is nothing worth living for.

Common features with shame aversion therapy is evident. The patient was followed up for 11 weeks and received marital counselling which concentrated on improving communication within his marriage. Results showed that sexual thoughts of wife increased while the thoughts of anomalous behavior remained low in frequency, and thoughts of other women declined in frequency. Once again, the authors present detailed frequency data which offer the reader insight into what is happening. The actual frequencies of anomalous behavior are low before any treatment and remain low. However, sex appropriate behavior does increase in frequency. Perhaps that is all that is necessary in any treatment: to alter the relative frequency of sexual behavior patterns rather than eliminate an anomalous one. In this case, the anomalous behavior did not change its frequency all that much but the appropriate behavior, such as sexual thoughts of his wife did increase dramatically with treatment. The follow up was too short. We do not know if the anomalous behavior would reappear in time or why he showed such a low frequency of exposing urges at baseline. He had 12 to 15 exposure incidents in the 3 months prior to admission. He was also concurrently on lithium which might affect his mood and sexual acting out. He may have been a sporadic exposer, that is, he could go for months and years without doing it. This confounds our interpretation of the data and we are left with one more doubtful case study.

A similar procedure was used on a combined sadist-exhibitionist patient by the same researchers, but with clearer results[34]. Using a 2 week daily treatment program, penile erections to deviant stimuli were reduced to 0% full erection for exhibiting and 20% for sadism although the patient maintained 75% erection to normal heterosexual stimuli. Gains were maintained during an 8 week follow up but we are not told if the patient acted out. The exhibiting was atypical in this case, showing a late development at 25 years of age in *contrast* to his sadistic behavior that developed at puberty.

Maletzky[63] used covert sensitization with 10 exhibitionists but assisted the unconditioned aversive images with the foul smelling valeric acid. He used the acid because of patient complaints that imagined aversive scenes were not strong enough. Patients exposed from 2-to-11 times per month. There were 11-to-19 treatment sessions during which there were 3-to-5 presentations of the stimuli. Unique to the study was an in vivo test of acting out. The therapist hired actresses to tempt the patients after treatment and at a 1 year follow up. Actresses dressed in a fashion considered to be the most provocative for each patient. The "temptation" occurred in the patients' favorite haunts for exposing. Only 1 patient failed. With booster sessions, he too passed a subsequent in vivo test. Urges declined from an average 16.5 per month (range 6-29) to 0.6 (range 0-2) after treatment. Acting out declined from 5 per month (range 1-11) to 0.1 (range 0-1). It did not appear to matter that patients were forced into treatment. There were no drop outs. With such impressive results, it is unfortunate that a control group was not used.

The aversive therapies collectively ignore any dynamic interpretation of exhibiting. Some behavior modifiers think that this is best but dynamics are important in at least 2 ways. First, it is assumed that anger and anxiety are prominent factors in exhibiting. Punishing an angry or anxious person can paradoxically increase the frequency of undesirable behavior. Since many exhibitionists are angry and deny a need for treatment, caution is advised in using this method. They may develop an aversive reaction to the whole therapeutic setting and they may lie or recidivate out of spite.

Mr. J, described earlier, illustrates this problem. He was charged with indecent exposure and granted probation provided he receive treatment at our clinic. He was not a cooperative patient and soon dropped out of treatment. Approximately 2 years later, he returned voluntarily for treatment and noted:

> *Mr. J:* I wasn't serious about treatment when I was here last. I was angry because I was caught and have to come to see you. I was determined that there was no way you were going to get through to me. Now I'm here because I want to be here. I'm tired of my life and I want to stop exposing.

There was a noticeable difference in working with him as well. In his first forced appearance at our clinic, he rarely followed instructions; he missed appointments because he was "sick" or "lost the appointment slip." He never did his homework, and so forth. In the second voluntary treatment program, he was reluctant to end sessions, he worked avidly at reading materials, he did not miss appointments and if the therapist cancelled, he called to arrange another appointment. There was honesty and a rapport which was never obtained in the first forced attendance at our clinic.

Second, if exposing is a desire for intercourse, can we carefully and selectively punish this deviant approach to sexual intercourse, without at the same time punishing appropriate behaviors? This is unknown at present. The advantage of the Brownell and Barlow[14] [34] studies is that they were careful to ensure that appropriate sources of arousal were not hampered by an association with punishment of deviant arousal (generalization). It may be difficult in fact to selectively punish exposing. No investigations to date have examined the question.

Systematic evidence supporting the effective use of aversive conditioning with exhibitionists is very limited. Any program set up using this method should be careful to build in an evaluative dimension using a suitable research design.

Reciprocal inhibition therapy was applied to 1 case of exhibiting. Bond and Hutchison[13] theorized that exhibiting occurred after some environmental stress which constituted a challenge to the patient's sense of adequacy or was provoked by an encounter with a female "of specified age and physical appearance." It is not clear if this female represented an erotic encounter or a stressor. Exhibiting was viewed as an act to reduce anxiety cued off by these stimuli. The patient also engaged in voyeurism and obscene telephone calls. The exhibiting was preceded by a feeling of sexual excitement and dread. The patient had faced 34 charges and 11 convictions with nine prison terms of 4 months to 1 year. He had undergone previous treatment: individual and group psychotherapy and CO_2 abreaction therapy. He wore a chastity belt at one point which his wife locked in the morning and unlocked at night. He was charged with indecent assault while wearing it; he grabbed a woman in a crowd. He then underwent hypnosis but did not benefit although he found the relaxation part beneficial. The similarity to reciprocal inhibition likely prompted the therapist to use the method.

The patient was seen 4 times weekly and his wife accompanied him so he did not expose on the way to the clinic. Relaxation exercises (described in Chapter 3) were used and a hierarchy of exposure provoking stimuli were developed, for example, type of female, her physical attributes and the place of exposure. He was trained to be relaxed in the presence of these stimuli. The patient was able to be in formerly provocative situations without arousal when accompanied by his wife. When out alone, he attempted to expose on one occasion and had an "involuntary relaxation" reaction causing him to lose his erection. He felt foolish and went home. After 29 sessions, he recidivated. However, he lost urges in the following two months.

This study is interesting from two perspectives. The "attributes" which aroused urges to expose in the patient appears to be no more than those of a desirable mature female. It would seem that they would arouse sexual desires rather than anxiety in many men. The association of relaxation with the exposure situation presumably interfered with sexual arousal. This assumes that sexual arousal and general or autonomic arousal are on a continuum. It is not uncommon for psychological theorists to assume that all arousal is the same in its effect on the brain. Thus if sexual arousal and anxiety are combined up to some point, they will add together to produce more sexual arousal. However, there have been very few empirical tests of this theory. In one experiment[52], it appeared that the relaxation exercises used in reciprocal inhibition therapy increased sexual arousal to preferred sex objects in both heterosexual and homosexual men. In the case of the exhibitionist, it would be expected that the patient should become more excited by the exposure situation with treatment. Thus, on theoretical and empirical grounds, the treatment should not work. If anything, urges to expose should increase.

The second interesting facet of this case is that it was followed up by Quirk[80] several years later as a failure case. A biofeedback method of relaxation therapy was instituted involving the galvanic skin response or GSR. Basically, the GSR measures sweating. When the patient becomes more tense, he sweats more and this is recorded on a polygraph. By giving him feedback on his GSR activity via changing slides, he learned to relax to provocative stimuli. This treatment was employed and seen as successful at first, but I had the opportunity to talk to Quirk at a later date and the patient had again recidivated. No treatment had a lasting impact on his behavior. Moreover, the patient appeared to expose sporadically at irregular intervals.

Many exhibitionists are troubled by summer time when there is much more sexual stimulation out of doors. Possibly there are changes in hormones too which make the male more sexually excitable[106]. One research study showed that patients were more likely to recidivate when released in summer than when released in winter[51]. Some individuals will go for years without exposing again and follow up must be long before a failure is detected.

Hypnosis

Hypnosis has been used in a few cases in a way described by Roper[89]. It may be considered a form of classical conditioning similar to covert sensitization since all stimuli are imagined and the therapist associates exposing in this case with some unpleasant event or with the suggestion that it is no longer interesting[46]. Wickramsakera[104] suggested that there is a similarity between the trance-like state some exhibitionists enter unknowingly before exposing and the trance of hypnosis. The parallel suggests that hypnosis may be a fruitful intervention technique.

Roper treated three patients who had exposed for at least 5 years and each had one conviction. It was suggested to the patient while in a deep trance that exhibitionism be viewed as a habit pattern that had become established. Since he now understood why he exposed, it no longer had the same control over him as previously and he would not need to do it. This procedure was repeated until the patient agreed with the statements. He was also given suggestions to increase his self confidence. Sessions were an a hour to hour and a half long at weekly intervals for as long as deemed necessary. However, only a few sessions were necessary and 2 of the 3 patients lost the urge to exhibit after the first session. The cases have been seen from 3-to-6 years later without recidivism. This appears to be a powerful method but the study only offers uncontrolled case reports. The three cases may be peculiar since they were suggestible enough to be hypnotized. We do not know their baseline of exposing prior to treatment although the behavior had been eliminated at follow up. They may have been ready to "burn out" anyway. It has been noted that most exhibitionists are in their teens and twenties. Since three fourths of exhibitionists are under 30, and only about 5% are over 40, it is reasonable to assume they "burn out" or stop exposing spontaneously[72]. Therefore, what seems to be effective treatment may be no more than burning out. Roper's cases were 22, 25 and 26-year-olds. The first is likely to continue exposing for 5 years after treatment but the others maybe in the processing of burning out at 5 year follow up. Nevertheless, the treatment appears to be powerful and inexpensive and a systematic study of its effectiveness is warranted.

Psychoanalysis and Psychotherapy

Psychoanalysis and psychotherapy have been used in a few cases of exhibitionism but a unified treatment approach and theory of exhibiting have not been presented. The few case studies in the literature have assumed that the oedipal conflict is a significant factor in exposing. Sperling[94], thought the patient she treated was orally frustrated placing the origin of the exhibitionist's conflict at an earlier stage of development. She noted he had been frustrated and teased by his mother who refused to give him her breast and gave it to a younger sibling. By exposing this patient would show his penis to a strange female on the street and refuse to give her his penis in the same fashion mother refused him the breast. This could be conceptualized as getting back at mother. However, the case was not so clear cut and the patient's problem was also seen as involving severe anxiety, defence against depression, castration anxiety, sadism, latent homosexuality and incestuous cravings. This patient was in treatment for 14 years and it is uncertain that he was "cured" of his cravings to expose after that time. This certainly makes any benefits derived time consuming and expensive.

Peck[79] used psychoanalysis in another case report and the patient was only seen for 2 months, but daily during the first month. He was considered to have a compulsion to expose which developed as a result of a sexual trauma occurring when he was 6-years-old. An older girl exposed him to a group of children. He was humiliated but paradoxically, he later suggested they both do it alone. Exposing behavior was intensified by his moving to the Orient where he was socially isolated. He had not exposed for 3 years after treatment.

The other cases[4] [11] [16] [19] [42] [98] are similar in format and as noted earlier about psychotherapy studies in general, it is usually not clear what exactly is being treated or what the goals of therapy are. This makes reporting the case material difficult and it makes it almost impossible for another psychotherapist to read the report and repeat the procedure himself. Perhaps each person is unique and psychotherapy remains an art which must evolve with each therapist for each patient. In terms of the criterion, change in exposing behavior, this method has not fared well.

In one better described case study[108], Zechnich assumed that a lack of privacy in childhood was critical to exhibiting. The treatment program involved 6 steps:

1. Providing adequate privacy by letting the patient reveal what he wants when he wants. He is encouraged to withhold thoughts as well.

2. Focus on the arrest and the avoidance of success in his life. A *contract* not to get arrested is made and subsequently a contract not to expose.

3. Give him permission to succeed and counteract his injunction to fail. The patient was encouraged to take a well paying responsible job.

4. Ignore case history and symptoms.

5. Include patient's wife in treatment so she cannot maintain his "neurotic" behavior outside treatment and perhaps most important,

6. Encourage legitimate showing off.

The patient in this study was encouraged to resume his previous interest in singing. The patient was "successfully treated" although we were not told what this means and no follow up was reported.

Group Therapy

In terms of the number of cases, group therapy appears to be a method of choice for exhibitionists although the reason for the choice is not clear. Barnett[9] reported a case study in which both group and individual therapy were used. He does not indicate the composition of the group or the therapeutic approach used. However, the patient's problem was his sexual naivety. The act of exposing was conceptualized as a desperate attempt to communicate with women and assert his masculinity. Anger was prominent in this case although egocentric and controlling behavior were more important and when the latter changed, the patient improved. Therapy lasted 13 years. This would seem to add little in economy over individual psychotherapy.

Hackett[32] used a trial and error method of finding out what would be effective in treating exhibitionists. He used aversive conditioning, various behavior modification methods, and psychotherapy and then group therapy which was divided into three phases. In the first, *enthusiastic endorsement,* patients welcomed the opportunity for treatment and spoke freely and intimately about their lives. They attended regularly without any acting out. When the impulse to expose emerged, the therapist suggested masturbation to avoid acting out. This was insufficient so inducing pain was added: burning self with cigarette, biting cheek—anything to induce pain. The second phase was a *sector analysis* of precipitating events and motives leading to exposure. Here anger not only to women but to other men and employers was revealed to be an important source of exposing urges. The third phase began after the connection of anger and exposing was established. It concerned alternative ways of coping with anger and the desire to expose. "Sublimation" was tried unsuccessfully, that is, exposing to a wife or girlfriend. Then venting anger in socially acceptable ways was tried successfully. Physical strenuous exercise was suggested, for example, punching a bag or jogging. Style of exposing was altered so the penis was covered to hide movement. Patients also learned to anticipate desire to expose and might stay with family members until it passed. Pervading all phases was a general "psychotherapy" which was not described in other terms.

He treated 37 cases of incarcerated exhibitionists and he was successful in 34 of the 37 cases. He followed them up for varying periods of 6 months to 14 years after release. He thought that the discharge of anger was critical to the success of treatment. The exhibitionists are hostile to women and once this surfaces, the need to expose should disappear. It is necessary to have the patient committed to treatment, according to Hackett, and forcing him by law is one method. However, this has doubtful utility in a general clinical setting. Moreover, prisoners are adverse to psychiatric facilities and may resent professional intervention. This generally makes treatment difficult if not impossible and the veracity of patients' reports of exposing doubtful. The success of the mixture of methods used by Hackett is surprising and may reflect his character and rapport with the patients. They were certainly willing to try a variety of methods over a prolonged period, even burning themselves with cigarettes, as an aversive conditioning method. Therapists express mixed opinions about forced treatment and we will return to this problem again.

Mathis and Cullens[64][65] described the enforced group treatment of exhibitionists and note the "self destructive mechanism of denial of the illness" in their characters which, they believe, has led practitioners to avoid accepting exhibitionists as patients. They proposed a 6 stage group therapy program. The stages were: denial, acceptance, anger, disappointment, upward movement and separation. The patient may experience shame and guilt the first few times he exposes but soon these feelings are denied access to consciousness. Even after arrests and fines, he denies a problem exists. He may construe the act of exposing as manliness. He enters treatment as an alternative to legal consequences. The denial not only is present in reference to the charges but reflects his whole life style. He shows little awareness of his everyday emotions and has a poverty of relationships. He remains isolated in treatment for a 4-to-6 month period, and denies his need of the group, in contrast to Hackett's patients who enthusiastically endorsed treatment. With constant confrontation by group members who are past this phase, he changes. Any interpretation of behavior during this period has little effect.

The second phase of *acceptance* happens when the patient can admit he has a part of his make up which is immature and destructive. He will begin to relate to the group and its members. This stage of treatment is accompanied by a tendency to overidealize the therapists and group members, a stage not uncharacteristic of other groups in therapy. This idealization is gradually and gently deflated and the third stage, *anger* develops.

The patient is frightened by overt anger, not because he fears retaliation but he fears being overwhelmed by his infantile rage. He may equate rage with masculinity and exhibiting may reflect his hostile feelings toward the female. Anger emerges gradually, first as outbursts against the law or other social groups, then against group members and finally against important females in the patient's life; his mother, wife or girlfriend. This newly awakened feeling may result in actual violence and the authors report two instances in which a patient knocked his wife unconscious and another who smashed a window with dishes. Mathis and Cullens noted that family members may need support and reassurance at this time.

Once the patient works through his expression of anger, he enters the phase of *disappointment*. He may be proud of his manly expression of anger but he is disappointed that he still has the urge to expose. He sees this as a lack of progress. Group leaders and members assure him that it is expected and that now his impulse is conscious and therefore subject to control and this reflects a sign of personality growth. This stage is short and he moves into the phase of *upward movement*. This usually does not occur until at least 1 year after the start of the group. Since these exhibitionists were usually underachievers, change in socio-economic status was easily noted. This process is approached cautiously and after considerable discussion and support. Once the patient makes the change, it reflects, according to Mathis and Cullens, the most important indicator of improvement.

The final stage is *separation* which may be difficult for men who are experiencing the first close peer group attachment in their lives. Some men were placed on "consulting status" which meant they could return to the group at varying intervals of 2-to-6 weeks to report what was happening in their lives. They also served as an encouragement to other members who were newer to the group. A modest fee of $5 was charged for each session, one advantage of group therapy. Both male and female co-therapists were used.

There were 45 men seen in all but 13 (28%) dropped out of treatment because "the legal hold on them was dropped before the mechanism of denial was eliminated." Fifteen men were discharged to consulting status and 17 are still in treatment. None completing treatment or currently in treatment have recidivated, but two of the drop outs had. It is not reported if anyone is having urges or acted out and did not get caught.

A report on "urges to expose" is important in any outcome study of exhibitionism. We do not have this information in Mathis and Cullen's report but their study is interesting from another perspective. The authors see it as an advantage that the patients were "sentenced" to treatment. If there was no legal commitment, patients quickly dropped out of treatment. Those forced to stay in treatment might distrust and resent the therapist at first but soon they were trusting and dependent on the group. Nevertheless, they noted that a 3 month period was inadequate to force members to remain in treatment and even 6 months might be too short for some. Group members later thought that even this was an inadequate length of time. How much would be adequate for the average patient? This suggests it may be more effective to treat willing patients.

Earlier reports by Turner[99] and Paitich[75] involved group therapy and later individual therapy. A unique aspect of this approach was the involvement of the wives in a parallel treatment program[75]. The wives were seen in a complementary group because their attitude played a vital role in treatment. There were five characteristics of the group dynamics: *permissiveness* to talk feelings in this inhibited group; *support* for expressing feelings and support for other group members in trouble; *stimulation* to express fears, ignorance and problems in the permissive and supportive atmosphere provided by therapist and other members; *verbalization* of feelings rather than just acting them out; and *reality testing* by others in the group. The group was involved in 84 sessions over a 4 year period. Ten patients were discharged and relieved of their symptoms and were considered "cured". Only two committed further offences, one sexual and one nonsexual. There was one drop out who left the city. Current contact with Drs. Turner and Paitich suggests that in the long run, treatment was ineffective and most patients recidivated.

Witzig[107] also reported on the enforced group treatment of exhibitionists. He was initially skeptical about such an approach but found that in spite of discomfort with therapy, patients usually kept their appointments and displayed enough anxiety to promote the therapeutic process. All 25 men in the study later agreed it took the heavy hand of the law to force them into treatment. The therapist did not threaten to report them for missing sessions but indicated that "if their probation officer asked if they were attending, the therapists would be forced to tell the facts." About half were first offenders and while the author noted that recidivism rate is low in this group (10-20% according to Mohr[70]), he thought they needed some treatment for behavior which can lead to a "disastrous habit." About 60 to 70% of the patients were seen on an outpatient basis without risk to the community. Witzig thought the patients should be assessed via social history and in suspected cases of psychotics or sociopathic character disorders, with psychological testing and psychiatric evaluation. He divided exhibitionists into several groups: those with neurological impairment, psychotic or prepsychotic, those with neurotic use of denial, the "pervert" who cannot achieve satisfaction in ways other than exposing and a group displaying other forms of antisocial behavior. No data are presented on the frequency with which one can expect these various groups but from detailed work of other investigators, all except the "pervert" would appear clinically rare.

Witzig further divided his patient group into those who exposed with genital gratification and those who did not. He maintains that, in almost every instance of exposure without genital gratification (masturbation), the act follows a period of intense conflict over some personal problem. One case was described of an enlisted man having career difficulties because of authorities; another of a student who exposed when he found the curriculum too difficult. Group therapy did not attempt to get at deeper underlying causes of exhibitionism but confronted the patients with questions like, "Why expose when you are caught in a frustrating conflict?" When the patient became aware of the precipitating dilemma, he could also become aware that he had alternatives besides exposing, and could take other courses of action.

The theory that exhibiting follows stress appears repeatedly and once again there is no empirical evidence to suggest that this is in fact the case. An exhibitionist, *Mr. S* seemed initially to this writer to offer support for the notion that stress produced acting out. However, after his third charge which involved losing his job and almost resulted in divorce, he said in both dejection and anger:

> *Mr. S:*   I'm tired of this business, I must leave another good job. Everyone in town is talking about me because they printed my name in the paper with the details of the trial. What can I do? I've been in analysis, behavior therapy, assertive therapy—everything for 8 years and I'm still exposing. I've read everything on exhibiting and I still don't know why I do it. It was supposed to be after stress at work or at home but I don't believe that any more. It happens when I feel plain horny! What can I do about that?

Witzig notes that the exhibitionist may be narcissistic, have difficulty with aggressiveness and may be trying to prove to himself he is more aggressive than he really is. The male who exposed with genital gratification, does so in a context in which intercourse is impossible so he does not have to worry about failing to penetrate a woman. A stimulus to treatment according to Witzig is to present the patient with the discrepancy between his public exposure and the rest of his character. He noted for example that most exhibitionists find the thought of a nudist camp repulsive but nevertheless expose in public places. This discrepancy between their exposing and the rest of their personality can be a stimulus to treatment. Unfortunately, there is no empirical data to suggest that exhibitionists generally in fact have an aversion to nudist camps.

No other details are given about the therapy process. Only 1-in-25 recidivated over a 2 1/2 year period. Others were suspected but denied the charge during the treatment. Two exposed after treatment (8%). Interestingly, one quarter of the men had fewer than eight sessions and have not recidivated. The authors noted that the one legal scrap very likely was enough to help them control exhibiting. Why then was group therapy necessary? Did it have any impact? The typical patient attended 20-to-30 sessions and some had as many as 60. The program was seen as economical since the average cost of maintaining a prisoner was estimated at $10,000 per year per person in 1968 and the number of prisoners was reduced from 2.5 to 0.5 charged with indecent exposure who were serving time.

This study points out the importance of segregating first offenders and repeated offenders. As Mohr noted, the likelihood of them repeating their offence is about 10–20%. Witzig had an 8% failure rate, close to that expected. We do not know if these are first offenders recidivating. It would seem uneconomical to include them in a treatment program since the act of being caught in itself is sufficient to deter most. If they wish treatment, it should be voluntary. Most, I would guess, will refuse.

Rosen[90] reported in some detail the actual sessions of an analytic group therapy treatment with a mixed patient population consisting mostly of exhibitionists and exhibitionist-pedophiles. He noted that initial remarks were usually addressed to the therapist who in turn addressed these remarks to the group as a whole. In this way, an attempt to encourage social relationships was fostered in place of narcissistic gratification. In the first few sessions, they discussed theories of why they exposed themselves and how they should be treated. Rosen elaborated how he further encouraged transference to the group as a whole rather than to the therapist. Social relationships developed between members of the group and they were encouraged to exchange information including that on exposing. The patients seemed to stop acting out when they could reach a certain level of ability to verbalize their urges and could feel secure in the therapeutic relationship.

Subsequently, aggression became a prominent issue which was interpreted as a defence against feminine identification and against homosexuality. When overt homosexual feelings became prominent, the group dissolved. It is noteworthy that there was a homosexual mixed in the group and perhaps he created too much anxiety and disruption. According to Rosen, the use of a group with common diagnoses was valuable because it created a greater ease with which polarities of identification and differences in personality traits can be delineated. It also intensified group transference in affective terms as well as establishing clear goals for the group.

In this treatment as in Hackett's and Mathis and Cullens', exhibiting was equated with aggression and it was possible to deal with their sexual problem much of the time by dealing with their aggression. The results of follow up are not clear because the author noted that some patients labeled "satisfactory" may have had urges to expose or may still be exposing. He had the same problems as other authors since once the legal hold was dropped, patients stopped treatment. Only two patients are reported as recovered and one as relapsed from two groups of 24 patients in total. On the average, there were 23 sessions. Follow up averaged 20 months and at that time there were no reconvictions. Nevertheless, it was concluded that treatment should have been longer than 6 months.

Assertion Therapy

A behavior therapy technique that has been hinted at by the group therapists and individual cases as a logical method for exhibitionists has been reported anecdotally by Lazarus[58] and systematically investigated by the present author and his colleagues[50]. Exhibitionists are described as shy and unassertive. They are uncommunicative with females, they attempt to assert their masculinity by exposing. They are unaware of their emotional life. They do not know how to relate to their peers. Lazarus first noted that assertiveness training would be an effective treatment for patients with these characteristics as well as for other sexual anomalies such as fetishism, voyeurism, transvestism and pedophilia. However, he presented no data. Hackett's group therapy appeared to be rather effective in that approximately 92% of his patients did not recidivate. He indicated that expression of anger was critical to successful therapy. Mathis and Cullens and Rosen also described anger expression as an important stage of treatment. Assertiveness training would appear to be an effective method of doing this economically.

An assertion training program was initiated for 33 exhibitionists which focused on communication with females but also on other interpersonal problems. All patients were treated with assertion training and 15 of them were administered provera, an antiandrogen drug to reduce sex drive. All patients were repeated exposers with at least two incidences of exposing but only 23 had charges at the time of treatment.

After an initial assessment, there were 15 weekly sessions of one hour duration that involved: feedback on the appropriateness of behaviors in terms of eye contact, duration of response, latency of response, loudness of speech, fluency of speech, compliance to demands, requesting new behaviors and overall assertiveness[22]; discrimination of assertive, aggressive and unassertive responses; practice in these; development of a belief system of his personal rights and those of others; readings or listening to, "I Can If I Want To"[60] and "Your Perfect Right"[2]; initiating conversations, giving and receiving complements and training subjects to elicit "loving and caring" responses[59]. They were coached on their own behavior and offered a model of behavior during treatment. Half the patients had a female therapist and half a male. All therapy sessions were recorded and audio playbacks were used to enhance assertiveness training. Many patients did not know the difference between assertiveness and aggressiveness but then again neither did normals[51]. In fact, theorists may be confused as well in trying to empirically discriminate the two[6][66]. In any case, they learned our meanings of the terms and discriminated what we suggested. The procedure attempted to tackle every facet of their behavior: their appearance, whether they spoke out or not in a given situation, especially with women; the content of their speech, and how they expressed themselves. According to the dominant theories of exhibitionism, release of their hostility to women, asserting their masculinity to women and being able to overcome shyness with women are the key to relieving them of their exhibiting symptoms. The loving and caring responses are not just asserting one's own feelings but takes into account the feelings of others. This tends to promote positive interpersonal reactions.

Forty-five percent of the patients dropped out of treatment before the 15 week period was up. This was not affected by the sex of therapist but was influenced by use of the drug provera. Sixty seven percent of the drug group dropped out compared to 28% of the nondrug assertion training group. Dropouts tended to be younger and have the desire to expose come on them more suddenly than nondropouts. About half of the patients recidivated at the time of writing the project report and only 30% had not recidivated or dropped out of treatment. Only three individuals or 9% of the total sample were not having urges to expose. After 3 1/2 years, all but two of the patients have recidivated.

An interesting sign that recidivism was coming, was the frequency of exposure during therapy. Recidivists averaged 11 of the 15 weeks of treatment during which they had urges and/or acted out. The nonrecidivists only averaged 5 weeks, or less than half the frequency of urges. Since the nonrecidivists had a lower frequency of urges to act out initially, they may show more progress with treatment because they do not have as strong a habit to overcome. Perhaps the act of incarceration effectively lowered the desire to expose. Maybe they were lying.

There were few other meaningful differences between the two groups. All patients liked the treatment, felt they benefited from it, and it did not matter whether the therapist was male or female. Assignment was random. Ninety five percent of the patients thought the treatment helped them overcome their problems. However, it did not affect the frequency of their exposing. They felt treatment was about the right length of time and it offered them a better understanding of themselves and they were now more able to communicate as would be expected from assertion training.

Results relied on self report of the patients, but with a difference. They were told that if they were in trouble with the law to call one of the team therapists at any time. This would ease the pressure of the police and courts on them. Moreover, they were told to let us know if their urges were getting out of hand so that the anomaly would not develop into an offence again. They were also told that "two treatments which are considered to be effective are being compared. We did not have any vested interest in one or the other but wanted to know which was more effective. Thus be sure to let us know if it isn't working and tell us exactly what is going on. It will help you and/or others in future with your problem." In all but two cases, the therapists thought the patients were being honest and in fact they all did report recidivating although there were no further charges for any patient to date. This illustrates one limitation of the use of police records and the advantage of patients who have a vested interest in informing the therapists of actual recidivism.

Chemotherapy. Chemicals have been applied to exhibitionists not necessarily with the aim of changing the desire to expose, but to reduce the frequency of sexual desire generally. So the drugs would not change erotic preferences, they simply lower sex drive for all erotic stimuli. Once the drug is removed, the original urges emerge again.

A number of drugs have been suggested as useful. The phenothiazines[10] especially thioridazine, may be useful since it depresses sex drive in high dosages. Antidepressants are useful for the underlying depression (if the patient happens to be pathologially depressed) and to reduce acting out. The long term use of such drugs is questionable. The neuroleptic drugs like phenothiazines have long term effects such as tardive dyskenesia and short term effects making them undesirable except in extreme circumstances. Rarely is the exhibitionist psychotic or so depressed as to require such medication for the primary illness.

Feminizing hormones have also been used because they reduce sex drive in the male. However, they may have undesirable side effects such as infertility or at least decreased production of sperms; decreases in erection levels, in ejaculation volume, in sexual dreams and fantasies; and increases in weight, fatigability, sleep requirements and mood disturbance. Less frequent side effects are loss of body hair, hot and cold flashes and temporary breast development[95] [101]. Cyproterone acetate is one such antiandrogen that is available in Europe but not in North America. It may never become available because it results in testicular atrophy due to reduction of gonadotrophins, even when administered in 100 mg. daily dosages[10].

Davies[20] treated a case of exhibitionism with cyproterone. He indicated that the patient was reluctant to try the therapy but did so for his wife's sake. He stopped treatment after 2 months because he was angry at being deprived of his sexual pleasures and complained of headaches. However, he did not act out during that time.

Van Moffaert[101] reported using cyproterone on a 36-year-old fetishist-exhibitionist. Unfortunately the patient also had an unspecified psychotherapy and occupational therapy. His urges to expose disappeared but no follow up was reported.

The Laschets[53] [54] [55] [56] [57] also reported using cyproterone in 11 cases which were "mainly exhibitionists" although they also treated an unspecified number of pedophiles, indecent assaults, incest, fetishists and cases of "sodomy." Parameters of treatment and follow up are not reported but the authors stated that even when the induced effects of cyproterone are reversed, the patients did not revert to their former deviation. The Laschets summarized foreign language publications using antiandrogens, all apparently successful.

The implication of their reports is either that the drug altered erotic preference, reduced sex drive permanently or ideally, by having a period with reduced sex drive, cyproterone only altered anomalous desires and not normal desires. However, since all sexual functioning presumably returned, only anomalous erotic behavior must be affected. The Laschets' results are surprising and contrary to other North American reports[73] [95]. If the drug is used, the patient must be on it permanently or at least use it on a demand basis. Since exhibitionism is often more tempting in summer, in colder climates therapists may use it only then and not in the colder winter. This is preferable since there may be long term side effects.

The only other study of a drug therapy for exhibitionists was the study by the present author and colleagues comparing assertiveness therapy and provera (medroxyprogesterone) on 33 cases of exhibitionism noted earlier. Provera is not as potent as cyproterone when compared in animal studies but reduces sex drive nonetheless. Twenty patients who had the drug were administered 100 to 150 mg. per day or every second day in order to "titrate" the amount for the individual. It was desirable to take the "edge" off their sex drive so they did not have urges to act out and were not constantly thinking about sex. On the other hand, it was not desirable for them to have erectile difficulties, especially if they were married. The ideal case was that of *Mr. T.* Initially at 100 mg. everyday, he experienced erectile difficulties and reported this after 2 weeks. The amount was reduced to 100 mg. every 2 days and the difficulties disappeared. He felt comfortable with the treatment and noted:

> *Mr. T:* I never think about sex. I'm busy now anyway and it is good not to be bothered by urges to expose. My wife gets annoyed sometimes because I'm not interested in her either but once we are together in bed and I feel her body next to mine, I get turned on and everything goes well from there.

Each patient had his provera "titrated" in this way for his individual needs. Nevertheless, as noted earlier, the dropout rate from treatment was more than double for provera when combined with assertion therapy than for assertion alone. Many patients felt uncomfortable with the drug. Some said they felt out of control, that they were no longer the masters of their fate. Some feared being demasculated. Initially, the treatment program was intended to compare provera alone with assertion alone and with the two treatments in combination. However, all 5 patients started on provera alone dropped out of treatment for reasons just noted and it was discontinued for ethical reasons. The use of drug therapy alone for exhibitionism had a poor prognosis. Some patients did not like having their sex drive reduced. Some were concerned about their health. This may well be appreciated in light of the possible side effects which have been noted, including infertility with long term use[101] and possible diabetic symptoms[102]. The drug was no more effective than assertion therapy alone in the long run. Maybe a longer period of drug use would be beneficial. However, long term usage may have unknown adverse effects on the liver and would have to be carefully monitored.

The sex drive reducing properties of antiandrogens may also be suspect. Bancroft, Tennent and Kypros[8] reported in a laboratory study that cyproterone acetate did not influence penile erection but research participants only *said* they were less sexually aroused than control participants. My colleagues and I found in two laboratory studies that cognitive and physiological components of sexual arousal may be autonomous to some extent[50]. In the first study 100 mg. of provera was administered to exhibitionists for 7 weeks in a double blind study. Half received a placebo. Verbal report of sexual arousal and penile tumescence to graded erotic[26] and neutral slides were compared. Sexual arousal was reduced by provera according to verbal reports but penile tumescence was unaffected. In the second similar study on normal controls, there were no differences in research participants' verbal report or in penile arousal to the erotic slides for drugs versus a control placebo condition after 3 weeks on provera. Either much stronger dosages are required, which will often result in erectile difficulties, or perhaps in a greater number of side effects, or the drug may be ineffective at any dosage. A study by Novak, Hendrix and Seckman on prisoners did not show any appreciable effect on self reported sexual arousal after 5 weeks[74]. One pedophilic patient known to the author was a passive man well over 200 lbs. in weight. He was treated with 300 mg. daily by his psychiatrist and yet he reported masturbating. The quality of masturbation was not as exciting as it was without provera and it took longer to climax but he did masturbate nonetheless. Collectively, this information casts doubt on the effectiveness of antiandrogens generally.

Miscellaneous treatments.   A self regulation method has been devised by Freund[27]. He argued that partner novelty is an important facet of the exhibitionists' behaviors as with other courtship disorders. They almost never act out with females who bear a social relationship to them. In addition, there may be an anomalously fast build up of erotic arousal early in the courtship sequence. Thus treatment aims at providing the patient with a less offensive means of effecting this build up of erotic arousal. The patient is taught normal courtship behavior in vivo with cooperative females. In addition, he employs it with as many females as possible to satisfy his need for object novelty.

Married patients are taught a variety of intensive pretactile or foreplay stimulation by viewing erotic films and participating in these activities with their spouses. If these methods do not work, provera is used. No evaluation of the procedure was reported since the project had only begun in this initial paper. The one experimental study of courtship behavior involving penile measurement conducted since this initial report, suggests that the exhibitionist does not differ from normals in his penile reactions. Thus there is no empirical support that there is a fast build up of erotic energy in exhibitionists during approaches to females. Second, there is no empirical study that partner novelty is more prevalent and/or exciting in exhibitionism than in normal or other sex outlets. It has also been demonstrated more recently, that there is no evidence that exhibitionists are deficient in courtship behavior in terms of dating history or marital history, and so forth. It would therefore be interesting if this treatment approach had any effect on treatment outcome. In a current personal communication, Freund noted that he discontinued this method because he found it ineffective.

A broad spectrum approach to exhibitionism has been proposed both by Bastani[10] and Heath[35] in which almost every method of therapy is suggested. It is recommended that treatment be tailored to the individual case. However, one method from the spectrum not noted to date may be used, namely, *thought stopping*[17][84]. There are no research or clinical reports of its use with exhibitionists, but the method would simply involve the patient recognizing the characteristic sequence of thoughts leading to exposing, or to other undesired behavior for that matter, and interrupting this sequence by saying "Stop" either subvocally or aloud. By breaking the chain of thought, he may be able to gain control over his behavior. The therapist can train him by asking him in the office to think about exposing and then yell "Stop."

We do not know if this is effective but presumably it has an aversive quality that can turn it into classical conditioning. The reader who may be disconcerted by the wide array of untested treatments may provide his own intuitive test of the efficacy of these methods by asking if they could alter his/her own behavior. Would thought stopping be effective in changing normal heterosexual relations? Would the average man or woman be able to stop desiring intercourse and settle for masturbation by thought stopping?

The final treatment suggested in the literature is no treatment at all. Gigeroff and his colleagues[30] and Mohr[70] indicated that recidivism for first offenders is about 10-20% and for repeated offenders the likelihood of a third or further offence is about 1 in 2 or 3. Nevertheless in Canada, 45% of all sex offenders are ordered to receive psychiatric service either as assessment, treatment or both. In the case of exhibitionists, it is 67%. This seems highly illogical. Mohr argued that exhibiting is not a disease entity and there is no personality disorder which mental health workers can treat. Why then in fact are we offering a service to these men? Persistent offenders are a different group. Recidivism is high enough that treatment may have some impact. As far as economy is concerned, rarely is imprisonment necessary for exhibitionists since they are not likely to be violent or to harm the female victim involved[72]. They want to be watched and the victim just has to refuse to watch.

Gigeroff and his colleagues[30] recommend such cases be managed by trained probation officers rather than by being sent to a court clinic. The probation officer can be a sounding board for the client's problems and relating "stress" in the patient to other members of his family when appropriate. This would help to reduce stress. Since there is little we can do for the exhibiting itself and since we do not know its origins, the supportive role of the probation officer appears most appropriate and economical. However, if the patient is voluntary and wants treatment, what are the prospects of changing him? Because he does not act out again, does this mean he is not having urges? Is it possible to relieve the suffering of the individual afflicted with the desire to expose in a society which punishes this behavior? Unlike homosexual behavior between consenting adults, exhibiting of necessity appears usually to involve an unwilling female. The element of cooperation is therefore missing to make this a "socially acceptable, laissez faire" act. Guilt is a necessary accompaniment of acting out for many exhibitionists and therapists must seek to deal with these feelings as well.

Treatment of Choice

The outcome of treatments reviewed are summarized in Table l0.3. As far as the exposing behavior itself is concerned, we are again faced with choosing a treatment from method for which there are practically no controlled studies to offer support for their use. The more one knows of the treatment, the less promising they look. The exhibitionist does not seem generally to be dangerous and incarceration would seem unnecessary.

TABLE 10.3
Summary of Treatment Effectiveness for Exhibitionism

Method	Results
1. Electrical Aversion Therapy	Short term gains but poor follow ups, no control studies
2. Shame Aversion Therapy	Only case studies. Problematic
3. Covert Sensitization	Only case studies. Limited success
4. Reciprocal Inhibition Therapy	Only one case report. Unsuccessful
5. Hypnosis	Positive but too few case reports
6. Psychotherapy	Too few cases. Unsuccessful or uncertain
7. Group Therapy	Most used method. Positive outcomes but usually poor or short evluations
8. Assertion Therapy	One controlled study. Only short term gains. Ineffective
9. Antiandrogens	Problem of acceptance by patients. Do not affect penile reactions in moderate doses. Danger of side effects

Interestingly in this anomaly, many of the treatment methods focused on getting the patient to cooperate in treatment; to overcome his denial, and to prevent him dropping out. This adds an additional burden on evaluating what is an effective treatment.

I do not think a program should be instituted for exhibitionists generally, especially if they are incarcerated. In spite of the glowing reports that unwilling patients can be treated, in most cases it is unnecessary. The chance of further legal implication is low enough that such patients are not a special concern to the therapists. Since many are unwilling, they should not waste the time of psychiatric facilities which are already overcrowded.

Once the clinician selects cooperative and willing patients, he may expect to see a relatively normal looking patient who is not different from the average in assertiveness and anxiety level. The patient may be distressed if he faces a change but basically he appears stable. He may be a narcissist who enjoys being admired by females in sexual contexts but he may also indulge in this behavior in other contexts.

Only a few psychotherapy studies have even attempted indirectly to handle narcissism, which appears to be prominent in exposing. In one case, it was considered "in the way of treatment" but progress was made once it was out of the way. One may wish to experiment on psychotherapeutic means of altering exhibitionism by focusing on narcissism. Analysts might consider oral dependency as a factor: the exhibitionist is a taker and he finds it unenjoyable to be a giver in a sexual relationship. The unwillingness to depend on others and give to them may be construed as fear which can be treated. I encourage the reader and challenge him to try different methods of treatment to see which works.

Group therapy has been advocated by several writers but no controlled studies with satisfactory evaluations have been conducted. It certainly warrants further exploration. At the very least, it is economical. Perhaps it adds a dimension to working out problems not treated by the more simpleminded and ineffective assertive training therapy.

I personally reject the aversive therapies because I find them inhumane. They often do not conform to learning principles and are ineffective anyway. I think the therapies directed to treating anger to women are misdirected. They may be angry; they may not. If they are, it does not seem central to exposing. They are not sadists or generally trying to shock females. They are trying to give her a "kick out of the act of exposing". Perhaps, this is a misguided understanding of other's feelings in erotic contexts.

Chemical therapies such as antiandrogens involve an element of risk and in the long run patients do not seem to accept them. I would like to know more about dangerous side effects before considering drugs. None appear to affect penile arousal unless they are given in large doses. Then they may produce an undesirable reduction in all sex behavior. For married patients, this presents an intolerable situation.

I think a necessity in every case of exhibitionism is to recognize the emotional and motivational state of the patient. Is he there because he wants to be or is he being forced? If he is sincere in his desire to change, are there areas of his life which need assistance and which can be helped with counselling? Often such patients feel despondent because they exposed and were caught. Help in recognizing the act as an isolated part of their character is important. This will raise their self esteem and aid in their functioning in society. At that point I tell them if they are willing, I would be interested to try some experimental methods to control or eliminate their exposing. No guarantees offered.

BIBLIOGRAPHY

1. Abel, C. G., Levis, D. J., & Clancy, J. Aversion therapy applied to taped sequences of deviant behavior in exhibitionism and other sexual deviations: A preliminary report. *Journal of Behavior Therapy and Experimental Psychiatry,* 1970, *1,* 59–66.
2. Alberti, R., & Emmons, M. L. *Your perfect right: A guide to assertion behavior.* San Luis Obispo, Ca.: Impact Press, 1970.
3. Allen, C. *Sexual perversions and abnormalities.* London: Oxford University Press, 1949.
4. Allen, C. *A textbook of psychosexual disorders.* London: Oxford University Press, 1969.
5. Arieff, A. J., & Rotman, D. B. One hundred cases of indecent exposure. *Journal of Nervous and Mental Disease,* 1952, *96,* 523–538.
6. Bakker, C., Bakker-Rabdau, M., & Breit, S. The measurement of assertiveness and aggressiveness. *Journal of Personality Assessment,* 1978, *42,* 277–284.
7. Bancroft, J. *Deviant sexual behavior: Modification and assessment.* London: Oxford University Press, 1974.
8. Bancroft, J., Tennent, G., Kypros, L. The control of deviant sexual behavior by drugs. *British Journal of Psychiatry,* 1974, *125,* 310–315.
9. Barnett, I. The successful treatment of exhibitionist: A case report. *International Journal of Offender Therapy and Comparative Criminology,* 1972, *16,* 125–129.
10. Bastani, J. B. Treatment of male genital exhibitionism. *Comprehensive Psychiatry,* 1976, *17*(6), 769–774.
11. Bejke, R. A contribution to the theory of exhibitionism. *Acta Psychiatrica & Neurologica Scandanavica,* 1952, *80,* 233–243.
12. Bergen, A. A self-regulation technique for impulse control. *Psychotherapy: Theory, Research & Practice,* 1969, *6,* 113–118.
13. Bond, J., & Hutchison, H. Application of reciprocal inhibition therapy to exhibitionism. *Canadian Medical Association Journal,* 1960, *83,* 23–25.
14. Brownell, K. D., & Barlow, D. H. Measurement and treatment of two sexual deviations in one person. *Journal of Behavior Therapy and Experimental Psychiatry,* 1976, *7,* 349–354.
15. Brownell, K. D., Hayes, C. S., & Barlow, D. H. Patterns of appropriate and deviant sexual arousal: The behavioral treatment of multiple sexual deviations. *Journal of Consulting and Clinical Psychology,* 1977, *45*(6), 1144–1155.
16. Caprio, F. Case report on scoptophilia and exhibitionism. *Journal of Clinical Psychopathology,* 1949, *10,* 50–72.
17. Cautela, J. R., & Wisocki, P. A. The thought stopping procedure: description, application, and learning theory interpretations. *Psychological Record,* 1977, *1,* 255–268.

18. Christoffel, H. Exhibitionism and exhibitionists. *International Journal of Psychoanalysis*, 1936, *17*, 321–345.
19. Conn, J. Brief psychotherapy of the sex offender. *Journal of Clinical Psychopathology*, 1949, *10*, 347–372.
20. Davies, T. S. Cyproterone acetate in sexual misbehaviour. *Medicine Science and the Law*, 1970, *10*, 237.
21. East, W. H. Observations on exhibitionism. *Lancet*, 1924, *2*, 370–375.
22. Eisler, R. M., Miller, P. M., & Hersen, M. Components of assertive behavior. *Journal of Clinical Psychology*, 1973, *29*, 295–299.
23. Evans, D. R. Masturbatory fantasy and sexual deviation. *Behavior Research & Therapy*, 1968, *6*, 17–19.
24. Evans, D. R. Subjective variables and treatment effects in aversion therapy. *Behavior Research & Therapy,* 1970, *8*, 147–152.
25. Fookes, B. Some experiences in the use of aversion therapy in male homosexuality, exhibitionism and fetishism-transvestism. *British Journal of Psychiatry*, 1969, *115*, 339–341.
26. Freeman, R. J. *The role of subject, context, and stimulus variables in determining evaluative and behavioural reactions to explicit depictions of human sexual behavior.* Unpublished Masters dissertation, University of Waterloo, Waterloo, Ontario, 1976.
27. Freund, K. Diagnosis and treatment of forensically significant anomalous erotic preferences. *Canadian Journal of Criminology and Corrections*, 1976, *18*(3), 181–189.
28. Freund, K. Analysis of disorders of courtship phases. *Archives of Sexual Behavior*, 1982, in press.
29. Freund, K., McKnight, C. K., Langevin, R., & Cibiri, S. The female child as a surrogate object. *Archives of Sexual Behavior*, 1972, *2*, 119–133.
30. Gigeroff, A. K., Mohr, J. W., & Turner, R. E. Sex offenders on probation: The exhibitionist. *Federal Probation*, 1968, *32*, 18–21.
31. Glover, E. Aggression and sadomasochism. In I. Rosen (Ed.), *The pathology and treatment of sexual deviation*. London: Oxford University Press, 1964, 146–162.
32. Hackett, T. P. The psychotherapy of exhibitionists in a court clinic setting. *Seminars in Psychiatry*, 1971, *3*, 297–306.
33. Harwich, A. *Aberrations of sexual life. After the Psychopathia Sexualis of Dr. R.v. Kraft-Ebbing*. London: Staples Press, 1959.
34. Hayes, S. C., Brownell, K., & Barlow, D. H. The use of self-administered covert sensitization in the treatment of exhibitionism and sadism. *Behavior Therapy*, 1978, *9*(2), 283–289.
35. Heath, D. S. Management of exhibitionism. *Canadian Journal of Criminology*, 1978, *20*(3), 252–258.
36. Herman, K., & Schroeder, G. E. Un cas d'exhibitionisme chez une femme. *Acta Psychiatrica Neurologica*, 1935, *10*, 547–564.
37. Hollender, M. H., Brown, C. W., & Roback, H. B. Genital exhibitionism in women. *American Journal of Psychiatry*, 1977, *134*(4), 436–438.
38. Howarth, E. Were Cattell's 'Personality sphere' factors correctly identified in the first instance? *British Journal of Psychology*, 1976, *67*(2), 213–223.
39. Jacobson, E. *Anxiety and tension control*. Philadelphia: Lippincott Co., 1964.
40. Jaffe, J., & Brodie, H. K. The narcissometer: An apparatus for quantification of "self-preoccupation". *Perceptual and Motor Skills*, 1971, *32*, 9–10.
41. Jones, E. *Sigmund Freud: Life and work*. London: Hogarth Press, 1953.
42. Karpman, B. The psychopathology of exhibitionism. *Journal of Clinical Psychopathology*, 1948, *9*, 179–225.

43. Karpman, B. *The sexual offender and his offences.* Washington, D.C.: Julian Press, 1957.
44. Kimble, G. *Hillgard & Marquis' conditioning and learning.* New York: Appleton Century Crofts, Inc., 1961.
45. Kolarsky, A., Madlafousek, J., & Novotna, V. Stimuli eliciting sexual arousal in males who offend adult women: An experimental study. *Archives of Sexual Behavior,* 1978, *7,* 79–87.
46. Kroger, W., & Fezler, W. *Hypnosis and behavior modification.* Philadelphia: Lippincott Co., 1976, 168–175.
47. Kushner, M., & Sandler, J. Aversion therapy and the concept of punishment. *Behavior Research & Therapy,* 1966, *4,* 179–186.
48. Langevin, R. The modification of human sexual behavior. *Proceedings of the National Symposium on Medical Sciences and the Criminal Law,* University of Toronto, 1973.
49. Langevin, R., Paitich, D., Freeman, R., Mann, K., & Handy, L. Personality characteristics and sexual anomalies in males. *Canadian Journal of Behavioral Science,* 1978, *10,* 222–238.
50. Langevin, R., Paitich, D., Hucker, S., Newman, S., Ramsay, G., Pope, S., Geller, G., & Anderson, C. The effects of assertiveness training, provera and sex of therapist in the treatment of genital exhibitionism. *Journal of Behavior Therapy & Experimental Psychiatry,* 1979, *10,* 275–282.
51. Langevin, R., Paitich, D., Ramsay, G., Anderson, C., Kamrad, J., Pope, S., Geller, G., & Newman, S. Experimental studies in the etiology of genital exhibitionism. *Archives of Sexual Behavior,* 1979, *8*(4), 307–331.
52. Langevin, R., Stanford, A., & Block, R. The effect of relaxation instruction on erotic arousal in homosexual and heterosexual males. *Behavior Therapy,* 1975, *6,* 453–458.
53. Laschet, U. Antiandrogen in the treatment of sex offenders: Mode of action and therapeutic outcome. In J. Zubin, & J. Money (Eds.), *Contemporary sexual behavior: Critical issues in the 1970s.* Baltimore: Johns Hopkins University Press, 1973.
54. Laschet, U., & Laschet,L. Antiandrogentherapie der pathologisch gesteigerten und abartigen sexualitat des mannes. *Klinische Wochenschrift,* 1967, *45,* 324.
55. Laschet, U., & Laschet, L. Three years clinical results with cyproterone acetate in inhibiting regulation of male sexuality. *Acta Endocrinologica,* 1969, *138,* Suppl. 232.
56. Laschet, U., & Laschet, L. Antiandrogen in the treatment of sexual deviations in men. *Journal of Steroid Biochemistry,* 1975, *6,* 821–826.
57. Laschet, U., & Laschet, L. *Pharmacotherapy of sexual disorders (Clinical and social indications for treatment with antiandrogens)* Paper presented at the V World Congress of Psychiatry, 1970.
58. Lazarus, A. A. Behavioral therapy for sexual problems. *Professional Psychology,* 1971, 349–353.
59. Lazarus, A. A. On assertive behavior: A brief note. *Behavior Therapy,* 1973, *4,* 697–699.
60. Lazarus, A. A., & Fay, A. *I can if I want to.* New York: William Morrow & Co., 1975.
61. MacCullough, M. J., Williams, C., & Birtles, C. J. The successful application of aversion therapy to an adolescent exhibitionist. *Journal of Behavior Therapy & Experimental Psychiatry,* 1971, *2,* 61–66.
62. Macdonald, J. *Indecent exposure.* Springfield, Illinois: Thomas Co., 1973.
63. Maletzky, B. M. "Assisted" covert sensitization in the treatment of exhibitionism. *Journal of Consulting and Clinical Psychology,* 1974, *42*(1), 34–40.

64. Mathis, J., & Cullens, M. Progressive phases in group therapy of exhibitionists. *International Journal of Group Therapy,* 1970, *20,* 163–169.

65. Mathis, J., & Cullens, M. Enforced group treatment of exhibitionists. In J. H. Masserman (Ed.), *Current psychiatric therapies* (Vol. 11). New York: Grune & Stratton, 1971.

66. Mauger, P., Adkinson, D., Hernandez, S., Fireston, G., & Hook, J. *Can assertiveness be distinguished from aggressiveness using self report data?* Unpublished manuscript, Dept. of Psychology, Georgia State University, Atlanta, Georgia, 1979.

67. McCawley, A. Exhibitionism and acting out. *Comprehensive Psychiatry,* 1965, *6,* 396–409.

68. McCreary, C. P. Personality profiles of persons convicted of indecent exposure. *Journal of Clinical Psychology,* 1975, *31,* 260–262.

69. McGuire, R. J., Carlisle, J. M., & Young B. G. Sexual deviation as conditioned behavior: a hypothesis. *Behavior Research and Therapy,* 1965, *2,* 185–190.

70. Mohr, J. Evaluation of treatment. In H. Resnick, & M. Wolfgang (Eds.), *Sexual behaviors: Social, clinical and legal aspects.* Boston: Little, Brown & Co., 1972, 412–426.

71. Mohr, J., Turner, R. E., & Ball, R. Exhibitionism and pedophilia. *Corrective Psychiatry and Journal of Social Therapy,* 1962, *8,* 172–186.

72. Mohr, J., Turner, R. E., & Jerry, M. *Pedophilia and exhibitionism.* Toronto: University of Toronto Press, 1964.

73. Money, J. Use of an androgen-depleting hormone in the treatment of male sex offenders. *Journal of Sex Research,* 1970, *6,* 165–172.

74. Novak, E., Hendrix, J., & Seckman, C. Effects of medroxyprogesterone acetate on some endocrine functions of healthy male volunteers. *Current Therapeutic Research,* 1977, *21,* 320–326.

75. Paitich, D. Exhibitionism: A Comparative Study. *Toronto Psychiatric Hospital Journal Club,* 1957.

76. Paitich, D. A comprehensive psychological examination and report (CAPER). *Behavioral Science,* 1973, *18,* 131–136.

77. Paitich, D., & Langevin, R. The Clarke parent-child relations questionnaire: A clinically useful test for adults. *Journal of Consulting and Clinical Psychology,* 1976, *44,* 428–436.

78. Paitich, D., Langevin, R., Freeman, R., Mann, K., & Handy, L. The Clarke SHQ: A clinical sex history questionnaire for males. *Archives of Sexual Behavior,* 1977, *6,* 421–436.

79. Peck, M. W. Exhibitionism: A report of a case. *Psychoanalytic Review,* 1924, *11,* 156–185.

80. Quirk, D. A follow up on the Bond-Hutchinson case of systematic desensitization with an exhibitionist. *Behavior Therapy,* 1974, *5,* 428–431.

81. Reitz, W. E., & Keil, W. E. Behavioral treatment of an exhibitionist. *Journal of Behavior Therapy & Experimental Psychiatry,* 1971, *2,* 67–69.

82. Rickles, N. *Exhibitionism.* Philadelphia: Lippincott Co., 1950.

83. Rickles, N. Exhibitionism. *Journal of Social Therapy,* 1965, *1,* 168–181.

84. Rimm, D., & Mathis, J. *Behavior therapy.* New York: Academic Press, 1974.

85. Rooth, G. Changes in the conviction rate for indecent exposure. *British Journal of Psychiatry,* 1972, *121,* 89–94.

86. Rooth, G. Exhibitionism, sexual violence and pedophilia. *British Journal of Psychiatry,* 1973, *122,* 705–710.

87. Rooth, G. Exhibitionism—outside Europe and America. *Archives of Sexual Behavior,* 1973, *2*(4), 351–362.

88. Rooth, G., & Marks, I. Persistent exhibitionism: Short-term response to aversion,

self-regulation and relaxation treatments. *Archives of Sexual Behavior,* 1974, *3*(3), 227–248.

89. Roper, P. The use of hypnosis in the treatment of exhibitionism. *Canadian Medical Association Journal,* 1966, *94,* 72–77.

90. Rosen, I. Exhibitionism, scoptophilia and voyeurism. In I. Rosen (Ed.), *The pathology and treatment of sexual deviation: A methodological approach.* London: Oxford University Press, 1964.

91. Serber, M. Shame aversion therapy. *Journal of Behavior Therapy & Experimental Psychiatry,* 1970, *1,* 213–215.

92. Smukler, A., & Schiebel, D. Personality characteristics of exhibitionists. *Diseases of the Nervous System,* 1975, *36*(11), 600–603.

93. Solomon, R. Punishment. *American Psychologist,* 1964, *19,* 239–253.

94. Sperling, M. The analysis of an exhibitionist. *International Journal of Psychoanalysis,* 1947, *28,* 32–45.

95. Spodak, M., Falck, Z., & Rappeport, J. The hormonal treatment of sexual aggressives with Depo-Provera. *Treatment for Sexual Aggressives,* 1977, *1,* 2–3.

96. Stevenson, J., & Jones, I. Behavior therapy technique for exhibitionism: A preliminary report. *Archives of General Psychiatry,* 1972, *27,* 839–841.

97. Taylor, F. H. Observations on some cases of exhibitionism. *Journal of Mental Science,* 1947, *93,* 631–638.

98. Thomson, P. Some observations on exhibitionism. *Toronto Psychiatric Hospital Journal Club,* March, 1957.

99. Turner, R. E. The group treatment of sexual deviations. *Canadian Journal of Corrections,* 1961, *3,* 485–491.

100. Turner, R. E. The sexual offender. *Canadian Psychiatric Association Journal,* 1964, *9*(6), 533–540.

101. Van Moffaert, M. Social reintegration of sexual delinquents by a combination of psychotherapy and anti-androgen treatment. *Acta Psychiatrica Scandanavica,* 1976, *53,* 29–34.

102. Walker, P., & Meyer, W. J. *Antiandrogen treatment for the paraphiliac sex offender.* Paper presented at the conference on Violence and the Violent Individual, 1978, Houston, Texas.

103. Wardlaw, G. R., & Miller, P. J. A controlled exposure technique in the elimination of exhibitionism. *Journal of Behavior Therapy & Experimental Psychiatry,* 1978, *9,* 27–32.

104. Wickramasakera, I. A technique for controlling a certain type of sexual exhibitionism. *Psychotherapy: Theory, Research & Practice,* 1972, *9*(3), 207–210.

105. Wickramasakera, I. Aversive behavior rehearsal for sexual exhibitionism. *Behavior Therapy,* 1976, *7,* 167–176.

106. Winton, F., & Bayless, L. *Human physiology.* London: Churchill Ltd., 1962.

107. Witzig, J. S. The group treatment of male exhibitionists. *American Journal of Psychiatry,* 1968, *125,* 179–185.

108. Zechnich, R. Exhibitionism: Genesis, dynamics and treatment. *Psychiatric Quarterly,* 1971, *45*(1), 70–75.

11 Voyeurism

INTRODUCTION

One of the most confusing concepts in the study of sexual anomalies is seemingly the simplest one, voyeurism or peeping. In this act the male usually looks at a nude adult female or at heterosexual intercourse and in so doing masturbates to climax. This seems simple enough but often the climax or orgasm is not considered an essential part of the voyeurism. A more nebulous "erotic gratification" or general "satisfaction" is described and herein lies the confusion.

Most people can be described as voyeurs because looking is a safe uninvolved act that offers information and satisfies curiosity. It is the preferred way of experiencing the world even in childhood. In one study, Day and his associates[3] asked a group of Grade 5 children to indicate all the things they would like to experience very much that could be brought into their classroom. A total of 155 items were described and of these the children selected 63% which were specifically visual, and only 10% auditory, 16% tactile, 4% olfactory and 7% gustatory[3]. Marshall McLuhan and Quentin Fiore[13] have clearly indicated how our sensory experience is predominantly visual. Naturally this includes sexual experience as well. The booming pornographic magazine and movie business caters to the average man and not just to the sexually anomalous[18]. This is a testimonial to the widespread "voyeurism" in contemporary society.

Some authors prefer to distinguish voyeurism from the criminal acts by labeling the latter "peeping"[11]. However, in this chapter the term voyeurism is used and the focus is on an erotic preference for looking over other sexual acts, whether criminal or not.

In examining criminal cases, it is noteworthy that often it is difficult to convict someone for voyeurism or peeping because there is no victim contact and the offender usually is not seen at all. Consequently other charges are laid or are dropped altogether. *Mr. A* described how he justified his acts even when apprehended. He often "prowled by night" but also peeped at women's legs from under the bleachers at football games. When the police caught him he would say "I dropped my wallet or I lost my pillow; I'm sure it is down here". As an apartment superintendent he "helped" the police look for the peeping tom in his building. The pretense fooled the police who never knew it was him. *Mr. A* also engaged in fetishism and masochism but seemingly normal individuals may indulge in criminal voyeurism with impunity. A colleague told me of a foreign university department where he sabbaticaled for a year. Everyone in the all male office had binoculars to view the apartment building across the street. The men worked in 15 minute shifts at "peak" hours and when a woman was undressing he would tell the others. They even worked out a two digit code: the first being the floor level and the second, the window numbered from the left. So 14–3 would be fourteenth floor, third window from the left. Then everyone would watch!

Voyeurism as a diagnostic entity or a sexual anomaly can become so broad that it is clinically useless. If one ascertains whether it is orgasmic and if it is preferred, the number of "voyeurs" is very small. In fact as an exclusive anomaly, it is very rare,[12][16]. Most often it has been reported in combination with other sexual behavior such as fetishism, sadism and masochism. Unfortunately it is also uncritically accepted along with other anomalies and causally linked. The eyes are the major instrument of our experiences and voyeurism is the gateway to many anomalies. Its existence as an erotic preference must therefore be carefully ascertained.

THE THEORIES

Sadism and power in looking.   Psychoanalytic theories have focused on the nature of the act of seeing in voyeurism or scoptophilia (lit. love of looking). The eyes are the seat of the soul and through them one can incorporate the world. The act is not allegorical but an oral incorporation of the voyeur's victims. *Mr. B,* a 20-year-old student, described his feelings about peeping:

> "It's really exciting. I'm so close I can touch them but they don't know I'm there. When it's over I feel like I have a part of them I take with me."

All via the act of seeing. Fenichel[4] and Yalom[19] described the great power of the eye in mythology and history. The hypnotist with his gaze sends the subject into a trance in which he must copy the hypnotist and do what he says. The snake supposedly immobilizes its victim in a similar gaze and eats the powerless animal. On the other hand gazing can be a forbidden act that is punishable by death. Lot's wife in the Bible was turned into a pillar of salt for disobeying God and looking at the destruction of Sodom and Gomorrah. Looking at the mythical Medusa or at a Cockatrice can turn the gazer into stone. Psychoanalysts consider both the active sadistic and passive punitive features of the eye to be component elements in voyeurism.

Fenichel[4] has described the sadistic act as the equation of "looking at" and "to devour." The eye in this context can also symbolize the penis so the voyeur is "taking in" the female victim with his penis. Thus there is mixed opinion on whether voyeurism is attributable to regression/fixation at the oral or phallic stage of development. In either case degrading the female victim may be a crucial element in the act. *Mr. B* noted in support of this theory:

> *Mr. B:* "I was so close I could almost touch them (the couple having intercourse). If they knew I was there, they would just die."

This can be construed as an enormous sense of power over the victims or as delight in their imagined humiliation.

Castration anxiety and forbiddenness.   Peeping has also been described as reliving the primal scene of viewing a nude mother or seeing the parents having intercourse. This evokes fears of castration and he allays anxiety by reliving the scene. Like neurotic fixations, reenactment temporarily assures the individual he has a penis. He may identify with the male as father, having intercourse with the female as mother. This is a common psychoanalytic theme in all sexual anomalies. Smith[16] has noted that there may be a link here in voyeurism and triolism. In the latter, one passively watches his sex partner or wife have intercourse with another man. Afterward the troilist may have intercourse with her too. The rarity of this anomaly makes it difficult to test the theory.

Fenichel[4] noted that a self punitive aspect of voyeurism rests in the fear of castration. The eye equals the penis symbolically and it is no accident the label "Oedipal Complex" is applied to this fear since Oedipus himself was punished after killing his father and possessing his mother by blinding himself. The blinding is symbolic of castration. This sadism of the eyes can be displaced from the looker to the victim. Thus the act of voyeurism can be explained by contradictory postulates which are difficult to test in any case.

Yalom[19], Karpman[9], and Kutchinsky[10] think that the *forbiddenness* of the voyeurism is essential for gratification. Yalom claims that none of his patients were interested in attending burlesque shows or watching paid prostitutes strip. Rather they receive pleasure when they observe without detection and were challenged by the forbidden. He noted the pleasure in burglary was similar. He claimed some voyeurs have an uncanny lack of curiosity, which may have been stifled in childhood and channeled into peeping. The forbiddenness of course can also be linked to the oedipal complex and the forbidden desire for incestuous relations with mother. Kutchinsky[10] noted that forbiddeness and aggression to the victim are essential ingredients to peeping.

Psychosomatic effects of voyeurism.   Fenichel[4] has described attempts of psychoanalysts to relate voyeurism to general physical disorders of the eye. The fixed stare of the eye is symbolically the erect penis and very many situations become erotic. Rubbing the eyes for instance is symbolic masturbation. However he noted that the libidinal look is not distinct from ordinary looking so that no operational definition of libidinal looking is possible. This is a serious shortcoming of psychoanalytic theorizing in this area of research. Moreover Fenichel described attempts to link myopia or shortsightedness to sexual anomalies. Constant use of the eye for libidinal gratification in peeping causes it actively to strain in the direction of objects in order to incorporate them psychically. The medical eye specialist will claim that shortsightedness is caused by elongation of the axis of the eyeball due to changes in the muscles of the eye and vegetative changes in the body with aging. This seems like a parsimonious mechanical explanation of shortsightedness but Fenichel asks whether these vegetative changes are not psychically caused.

Rosen[14] has also suggested a link of skin complaints such as eczema and allergies to scoptophilia. He postulated that the voyeurs' excessive aggressive energy and their "lack of fusion with libidinal elements" require other body systems to be more highly charged. Unrestrained by operational definitions, and displaying a tendency to overgeneralize, such an approach can prove anything. However if psychoanalysis is to remain a credible explanation of behavior it is exactly these theoretical tendencies that must be checked.

Exhibiting and peeping.   As noted in more detail in the chapter on Exhibitionism, exposing and peeping have frequently been linked. Freud stated that libidinal energy is totally invested in looking and not in intercourse. Freund (Chapter 10) noted that the two anomalies are aberrations of the progressive phases of courtship along with rape and toucheurism. Courtship was described in four stages; searching for a partner, pretactile interaction, foreplay and intercourse. These correspond to the anomalies of voyeurism, exhibitionism, toucheurism and rape respectively. One possible reason exhibiting and peeping are linked is that the male projects his own desire to exhibit on the woman he is watching. He tries to find in others what he wants to see and satisy in himself[15]. Thus he indirectly satisfies his needs. Exhibitionists, according to Fenichel, are *always unconsciously* voyeurs as well. The desire to peep is determined by both the impulse to injure the female and secondly by a desire to share empathically in her experiences. The contradictory injuring and empathy for the same person are not described in detail but are related in a complicated way to the mechanism of identification.

Violence and other anomalies associated with peeping.   Yalom[19] has linked voyeurism to rape and exhibiting but also to burglary, arson and murder. These acts can be construed as sadistic since the victim is injured or humiliated, but there is also erotic excitement from the risk of being caught in a forbidden act and it helps the voyeur assert his masculinity (masculine protest). Karpman[9] however claimed that relating voyeurism to the threat of assault is wholly without foundation. Yalom disagreed but also suggested that voyeurism may be a defense against aggression.

Both Smith[16] and Yalom[19] have questioned the inclusion in voyeurism, of an interest in filth, feces and urine (mysophilia, coprophilia and urophilia respectively). Some individuals enjoy watching the act of elimination, some even consume the excrement. In psychoanalytic terms feces equal the penis. Scoptophiles including exhibitionists and voyeurs desire to see the female with a penis ("She has been castrated and I have not"). The penis can symbolically become the breast since it also gives off liquid so it is a substitute and the excessive interest in urine is explained. On the surface coprophilia, and such behaviors seem like masochistic and sadistic acts. However, these anomalies are rare and poorly understood so that it is best at present to reserve classification.

Other explanations of voyeurism are lacking. One can invoke learning and conditioning theory or imprinting as Smith suggested but no one has specifically suggested these explanations of voyeurism. Smith indicated that since many sexually anomalous men lack the skills for normal heterosexual behavior, this may be one reason they peep.

THE EXPERIMENTAL EVIDENCE

Smith has reviewed the existing literature on voyeurism. There was only one systematic study, that of Gebbard and his colleagues[6]. Other than this, there are not even uncontrolled descriptive group data. There is a problem in using the Gebhard data here. The study was mainly designed to compare sex offenders with controls in basically a sociological-criminological study. The sex offenders are grouped by offences rather than by orgasmic behavior or erotic preferences. There is overlap in group behavior and statistical tests are not reported. Most important, they are not asking the questions of interest here. Paitich, Russon and I[12] therefore analyzed our forensic data bank on sexual anomalies, specifically for voyeurism.

We compared three groups; "voyeurs", multiple anomaly controls and normal controls in two studies. In the first study, the multiple anomaly group was selected on the basis of lacking a history of peeping whereas the voyeurs had peeped at least ten times. The normal controls also had peeped but then all incidences were fortuitous and nonorgasmic. Nevertheless, a statistical analysis was performed to arrive at the group selection criterion for voyeurs and a minimum of ten times was necessary for inclusion. In the second study, any frequency of orgasmic peeping was acceptable to define a voyeur but the nonvoyeur multiple anomaly group were matched on major erotic preference.

It was difficult to find cases of "pure" voyeurism in a sample of over 600 sexually anomalous men tested over a 10 year period. In the first sample there were no exclusive voyeurs and only 17% of the 45 cases had peeped as their dominant outlet. Similarly in the second sample, 23% of 31 cases were predominantly voyeurs. One may wish to question whether there were any real voyeurs tested in the studies. There were 22% in the first study who had peeped over 100 times and in the second study, orgasm was associated with peeping. The 22% were examined for any differences in sexual history or personality from the remaining voyeurs and few significant results were found. Thus voyeurism, if it is a discrete orgasmic anomaly, is very rare, seldom exists alone or did not come to the attention of our clinic.

Some of the myths about voyeurism were not testable but those that were usually failed to find any support in these empirical studies. It has been suggested that voyeurs are inexperienced sexually. If anything, the opposite is true. The groups under study had more or comparable heterosexual intercourse than the control groups and had a wider range of anomalous sexual experience as well. Voyeurs more often than both control groups engaged in heterosexual pedophilia, obscene calls, and crossdressing. They were comparable to the multiple anomalies control group in showing higher frequencies of homosexual androphilia and pedophilia than normal controls. The hypothesized voyeur's lack of interest in strip shows or "lack of curiosity" was not found. Voyeurs did not differ from the other groups in attendance at strip shows or in measures of curiosity. Contrary to expectation, the more the voyeur peeped at intercourse, the more heterosexual experience he had.

Several writers have noted that voyeurism tends to occur with exhibiting, touching and rape. The one solid finding from our data supported Freud's theory linking peeping and exhibiting. It was found that voyeurism as an orgasmic outlet is associated with genital exhibitionism as an orgasmic preference. However the link was weak. It seems that voyeurism today is a grab bag of sexual behaviors and its usefulness as a concept may be very limited by its association with a wide range of anomalous erotic preferences. As a preference in itself, it seems rare.

From the descriptions of the dynamics of voyeurism one might expect both anxiety and aggression to be prominent features of the voyeur's personality. In both studies the voyeurs did show more manifest and acting out hostility than either control group supporting the hypothesis. Although anxiety was not the most significant feature of their characters, there was considerable emotional disturbance in the first group of voyeurs but not in the second one. The former were diagnosed predominantly as character disorders and secondarily as psychotics. The first sample of voyeurs showed much more pathology than the second better defined group. It has been the theme of this book to examine orgasm first as a criterion of erotic preference and in the voyeur group so defined in the second study, there was not the emotional disturbance found in the group defined by frequency of voyeurism in the first study. In fact we found that the frequency of all outlets was influencing the outcome of the two studies. When the total number of outlets, that is, exposing, homosexual pedophilia, and so forth, are statistically removed from the analysis of the first study, the voyeurs looked much less emotionally disturbed.

The criminal records of the voyeurs showed that they do engage in other than sexual crimes but they are not necessarily involved in aggressive crimes as suggested in the literature. In the first study, 18% of the voyeurs had assault charges including one wounding charge and one arson. Four percent were charged with carrying a concealed weapon and one person was charged with abduction and indecent assault. Only 2% of the multiple anomaly controls had assault charges and 2% were charged with carrying a concealed weapon. The results were reversed in the second study. Only 3% of the voyeurs had violence related charges while 23% of the nonvoyeur control patients did. Thus violence is either a small or incidental part of the voyeurs make up in spite of higher aggression scores on personality tests.

Overall the authors concluded that not only are most of the hypotheses about voyeurism (Table 11.1) unsubstantiated in an empirical test, but the existence of voyeurism as a discrete clinical entity has yet to be established.

TREATMENT

There is only a handful of case reports on the treatment of voyeurism (reviewed by Smith, [16]) but because of the frequent linking theoretically to exhibitionism, one may expect that the same treatments could be used for both anomalies. Some therapists have in fact included voyeurs in with the more numerous exhibitionists in treatment, (for example, Rosen, [14]).

Behavior Therapy

Aversive and positive conditioning have been used in a few cases of voyeurism. None have measured penile reactions or have reported a detailed

TABLE 11.1
Summary of Evidence for Theories of Voyeurism

Theory	Experimental Evidence
1. Voyeurism and exhitionism are linked	Supported but link is weak
2. Voyeurism, exhibitionism, toucheurism and rape co-occur as courtship disorders	Supported but it is related to most sexual anomalies. Apparently a chance relationship except for connection to exhibiting
3. Voyeurs lack satisfactory courtship skills with females	Negative. If anything they have more experience
4. The more habitual the peeping, the less adequate the voyeur's sex life	Negative
5. Voyeurism is associated with murder, arson and burglary	Inconsistent but weak support
6. Voyeurism is sadistic	Not tested
7. Voyeurs are uninterested in strip shows; it is the forbiddenness of peeping and being undetected which is exciting	Negative
8. Voyeurism is a defense against aggression	They show more manifest hostility
9. Voyeurs have a higher incidence of homosexual acts than nonvoyeurs	Negative
10. Voyeurs also have an interest in filth, feces and urine (mysophilia, coprophilia, and urophilia)	Not tested
11. Voyeurs have an unusual lack of curiosity	Negative. They seem normal.

sex history of the patients. Even more than in cases of exhibitionism, the similarities of normal and voyeuristic activities may make it difficult to discriminate the two in treatment[16]. The aim of treatment is to reduce the frequency of voyeurism but maintain or enhance the frequency of normal heterosexual behavior. A study by Jackson[8] illustrates the problem.

A 20-year-old single male wished treatment for anxiety, irritability and depression. He admitted to orgasmic peeping over a 5 year period. Orgasmic reconditioning therapy involved having him masturbate to pornographic pictures in private whenever he had the urge to peep. After 2 weeks he had no desire to peep although he had done so 5 times a week prior to treatment. Then orgasm was associated with pictures of decreasing similarity to the peeping stimuli. He lost his urge to peep and had "two satisfactory heterosexual relations". He maintained the gains after 9 months. The therapist was surprised at the rapidity of change but suggested that motivation to change was probably optimal. Aside from all the criticisms one can level at case studies, the similarity of peeping and normal stimuli is great, which could explain rapid change. However there may also be rapid recidivism as well. It would be difficult to find pornographic material discriminating voyeurs and controls so it makes treatment difficult. One would have to focus on the external trappings of voyeurism—the setting, peculiarities of the fantasies or other unusual acts associated with it —to reduce its occurrence while maintaining normal behavior. The audiotaped procedures devised by Abel and his associates and described in Chapter 2, (p. 11) would seem appropriate. This has not been done to date.

Gaupp and his associates[5] further illustrate the problem of discriminating normal and voyeuristic activities. Their patient peeped *and* masturbated to Playboy magazine centerfolds. Thus he displayed the anomalous behavior of Jackson's patient but also his "cured" behavior! Aversion therapy was used. Statements of the undesirable behavior were conditioning stimuli followed by electric shock. Normal heterosexual statements followed shock as anxiety relief. The latter theoretically should not work. However after three sessions the undesired behaviors were completely absent and therapy was terminated after 12 sessions. Gains were maintained at 8 months follow up but we do not know about the frequency of his normal sexual outlets.

Assertion therapy has been applied to exhibitionism and it may be appropriate for voyeurism. Stoudenmire[17] treated a 44-year-old married man with a long history of peeping. He manifested incestuous desires for his daughters and peeped at them as well as at neighbors. Over a 15 month period, 9 sessions of assertiveness training was used which involved instruction on his rights with respect to his friends, children and employer. His wife was involved and was given explicit instructions on how she could raise his male self esteem. Behavioral management of children was discussed with both husband and wife. In addition the patient was instructed to keep voyeurism on a fantasy level by engaging in intercourse with his wife and if this was not possible to masturbate, presumably to fantasies of intercourse. Although there were transitory problems of excessive drinking and jealousy of his wife's first but deceased husband, overall results were satisfactory. Peeping decreased from 15 times per month pretreatment to less than once per month. Only neighbors were involved and not the daughters. Marital satisfaction increased and they did more things together and increased intercourse. After 6 months the improvement was maintained.

Our own control study[11] of exhibitionists treated by assertion therapy and provera were scrutinized to determine if those who peep were more or less successful in changing. One additional case of an exclusive voyeur treated only with assertion therapy was included for analysis here. In the long run, it made no difference whether they peeped or not. All patients recidivated. (See Chapter 10).

Overall behavior therapy of voyeurs seems problematic and there are too few case studies to make positive assertions. It is perhaps best to examine exhibitionism if one is interested in treatments for his/her patient voyeurs.

Hypnosis has been successfully used by Alexander[1] in one case of voyeurism. As in behavioral conditioning, voyeurism was associated with undesirable and unpleasant outcomes while normal sexual behavior was associated to positive outcomes. Unfortunately this is the only hypnotherapy case reported to date.

Psychotherapy and Group Therapy

There are three reports of interest. Caprio[2] treated a multiple sexual anomaly that included voyeurism. He used psychoanalysis on a 41-year-old married man unsuccessfully. The report is interesting in its detail, a feature generally lacking in psychotherapeutic treatment of sexual anomalies.

The second report of interest is the group therapy treatment of voyeurs and exhibitionists by Rosen[14] described in Chapter 10. Most group members were exhibitionists and it is not clear how many are mixed exhibitionists-voyeurs. Overall there was improvement in 87% of the cases although it is uncertain exactly what this means. In one case where charges were related to voyeurism rather than exposing, no change was evident. However Rosen described an additional case of voyeurism treated with individual psychotherapy which was quite successful in reducing the frequency of acting out. Hamilton[7] also treated a multiple anomaly voyeur and described the psychodynamics of the case but it is not clear what the outcome was. Treatment lasted over 3 years.

Once again the reader is forced to turn to exhibitionism in order to evaluate the treatment of voyeurism. Of course the same problems and criticisms apply as well, and are presented in Chapter 10.

Treatment of Choice

The similarity of much voyeuristic activity to normal sexual behavior makes it a difficult candidate for behavior therapy. Nevertheless carefully devised experimental studies are possible and should be explored.

The most important consideration in selecting a treatment is the nature of the other anomalies typically associated with voyeurism. In conjunction with rape or sadomasochistic tendencies, the latter is a much more important target of treatment. In conjunction with exhibitionism, a focus on narcissistic elements may be important and can be tested in treatment research.

A treatment progam for voyeurism per se at this point in time is premature, until we know more about it.

BIBLIOGRAPHY

1. Alexander, L. Psychotherapy of sexual deviation with the aid of hypnosis. *American Journal of Clinical Hypnosis*, 1967, *9*, 181–183.
2. Caprio, F. S. Scoptophilia—Exhibitionism: A case report. *Journal of Clinical Psychopathology*, 1949, *10*, 50–72.
3. Day, H. I., Langevin, R., Maynes, F., & Spring, M. Prior knowledge and the desire for information. *Canadian Journal of Behavioral Science*, 1972, *4*(4), 330–337. Science Company, 1972, *4*(4), 330–337.
4. Fenichel, O. The scopophilic instinct and identification. *International Journal of Psychoanalysis*, 1943, *18*, 6–34.
5. Gaupp, L. A., Stern, R. M., & Ratlieff, R. G. The use of aversion-relief procedures in the treatment of a case of voyeurism. *Behavior Therapy*, 1971, *2*, 585–588.
6. Gebhard, P. H., Gagnon, J. H., Pomeroy, W. B., & Christenson, C. V. *Sex Offenders*, New York: Harper & Row, 1965.
7. Hamilton, J. W. Voyeurism: some clinical and theoretical considerations. *American Journal of Psychotherapy*, 1972, *26*, 277–287.
8. Jackson, B. T. A case of voyeurism treated by counterconditioning. *Behavior Research & Therapy*, 1969, *7*, 133–134.
9. Karpman, B. *The Sexual Offender and His Offenses*, N.Y. Julian Press Inc., 1957.
10. Kutchinsky, B. Deviance and criminality: the case of voyeur in a peeper's paradise. *Disease of the Nervous System*, 1976, *37*(3), 145–151.
11. Langevin, R., Paitich, D., Hucker, S., Newman, S., Ramsay, G., Pope, S., Geller, G., & Anderson, C. The effect of assertiveness training, provera and sex of therapist in the treatment of genital exhibitionism. *Journal of Behavior Therapy and Experimental Psychiatry*, 1979, *10*, 275–282.
12. Langevin, R., Paitich, D., & Russon, A. Is Voyeurism a distinct sexual anomaly? In R. Langevin (Ed.), *Erotic Preference, Gender Identity & Aggression*. Hillsdale, N.J., Erlbaum Associates, in preparation.
13. McLuhan, M., & Fiore, Q. *The Medium is the Massage*. New York: Bantam Books Inc., 1967.
14. Rosen, I. (ed.) *The Pathology and Treatment of Sexual Deviation*. London: Oxford University Press, 1964.
15. Saul, L. J. A note on exhibitionism and scoptophilia. *Psychoanalytic Quarterly*, 1952, *21*, 224–226.
16. Smith, S. R. Voyeurism: A review of literature. *Archives of Sexual Behavior*, 1976, *5*(6), 585–608.
17. Stoudenmire, J. Behavioral treatment of voyeurism and possible symptom substitution. *Psychotherapy: Theory, Research and Practice*, 1973, *10*(4), 328–330.
18. The report of the Commission on Pornography and Obscenity. Washington, D.C. U.S. Gov't Printing Office, 1970.
19. Yalom, I. Aggression and forbiddenness in voyeurism. *Archives of General Psychiatry*, 1960, *3*(2), 305–319.

12 Sexual Aggression and Rape

INTRODUCTION

According to the law in many countries, rape occurs when the male penetrates the female in intercourse against her will. However, if he forces her to fellate him or perform anal intercourse, he only faces a lesser charge of indecent assault. In Denver in 1975, about half of the sexual aggression cases forced anal intercourse and fellatio[89] which illustrates the misdirection of the law at this point. In fact, many rape charges are reduced to indecent assault because it is so difficult to prove by the legal definition that rape has occurred[14]. The important fact of rape is not that the individual has had intercourse or fellatio but that he has *forced* this body contact on an unwilling victim.

Sexual aggression is defined here as the forceful attainment of erotic gratification from an unwilling female, 16 years of age or older by a physically mature male. The term includes in addition to rape, frotteurism and toucheurism which often appear to be precursors of rape. Frottage refers to rubbing against a female for sexual gratification whereas toucheurism involves active use of the hands in touching her. In general, strangers are involved and crowded transit facilities in large cities are convenient sites for the acts to occur. However, the toucheur who acts out in lonely or deserted places may be more likely to progress to acts of rape. The etiology of various forms of sexual aggression is likely similar but if future work shows they are not, subcategories can be derived at that time. Like other kinds of sexual anomalies, writings on rape are overloaded with theory and are short on facts. One may also suspect some communality between the rapist and

392

individuals who force children or males to sexual intimacy. These are also important social problems but because we may be dealing with differences in erotic preferences, we exclude this category here. Forcing children to have sexual contact was discussed in Chapter 8 on Pedophilia.

Rape is different from all the other sexual anomalies in at least two important respects. Alcohol is a prominent factor in the commission of rapes and other violent offenses[77] and second, rapists tend to have a diverse and extensive criminal history. About half of the men charged with rape are drinking at the time of the offence and a third are chronic alcoholics[73]. As noted in Chapter Two, popular lore and a few experimental studies suggest that erectile ability declines with increased consumption of alcohol. Chronic alcoholism also affects testosterone levels in the blood and may produce chronic impotence and erectile difficulties. How then can such men rape? We return to this question later.

The typical rapist has a history of theft, common assault, indecent assault as well as rape. Theorists are divided on whether rape is simply one more thing that he wants and takes[32] or whether there is something special about rape in the form of erotic preferences. About 6-in-10 rapists are married at the time of the offence and some writers assume that sexual deprivation is not a factor in the commission of the act. The problem is how violence or force is important in the act of rape.

THE THEORIES

The role of force in rape.   Rape has been viewed on a continuum from a desire for intercourse with little or no force to an extreme use of force with or without intercourse. For some men force or threat of force is only a means to an end, namely having the woman yield to their desires for sexual contact. For others, force is essential. Contrast *Mr. A* and *Mr. B*. The former is 23-years-old and living common law with a 19-year-old factory worker. He admitted to committing a series of rapes to his therapist, one typical instance of which was:

> *Mr. A:*   I was feeling horny and had just come out of the bar around 1:00 am. As I turned off Main St., I noticed a young woman heading down toward the park. It was fairly dark and she couldn't see me. I speeded up a little and she sensed I was behind her. When we got to the park, I ran and caught up to her. I said, "Just do what I say and you won't get hurt." I held her forcefully by the arm but not hurting her and led her into the park behind the bushes. I told her to take off all her clothes and she wouldn't get hurt. I said, "We were going to have a nice time." I could feel her shaking and I knew she was afraid and would do what I said. I

took out my privates and told her to kiss it. Then I put it in her. I think she started to enjoy it. When I came I got up and told her not to move until she counted to 50. I got out of there quickly.

On another occasion, *Mr. A* wasn't so lucky because the woman involved screamed when he said, "Do what I tell you and you won't get hurt". He ran into the arms of two male passersby who subdued him and this led to his charges. Clearly, the use of force or threat was instrumental to having intercourse.

Mr. B, on the other hand, seemed to have minimal interest in intercourse and force was prominent in his acts. He was 31, married with two children and worked as a casual laborer at odd jobs. He would be described clinically as a schizoid personality or even as an early process schizophrenic disorder. He had raped and murdered 6 young girls before he was caught. The incident here is perhaps atypical but illustrates the importance of force in his acts. When it was dark, he operated near an open field which many young people used as a shortcut in the suburbs of the city. He used to lie in wait for single females or even pairs of them travelling across the field late at night. He would grab them and beat them to submission. In this one instance, there was no evidence of semen in the cadaver, and when he was questioned, he said he did not have intercourse but may have masturbated afterwards, he wasn't sure. Under sodium amytal interview, he was asked why he did it. He described torturing the girls and simply said at the end, "I liked the look of fear on their faces as they died." Most of his victims were strangled. *Mr. B* would probably be labeled as a sadist by many clinicians and the killings were clearly an important aspect of his crimes.

Often, cases seem to fall between the two extremes of sadism and the use of force for compliance. For example, *Mr. C* was a 42-year-old married man who was a chronic alcoholic and worked as a truck driver. He kept a series of tools on prominent display in his truck and a crowbar was visible to the passenger beside him. He liked to pick up young girls hitchhiking and rape them. The incident for which he was charged was one in which he used a knife. He would not admit to the offence and this is the victim's version of the incident.

Victim: I was thumbing a ride on the main highway and this truck pulled up. He said, "Where are you going?" I told him and he said, "Hop in." He was pretty greasy and dirty and the cabin smelled of liquor. I had to squeeze my feet close to the seat because there were tools on the floor. He started to ask me questions and talk about sex. I said I think I wanted to get out. He said, "You're not going anywhere." He reached over and showed me the crowbar. "See this? If you don't want it between your eyes, you had better do what I say." I was really scared. I thought he was going to kill me. He turned off the road and stopped the truck in a dark sideroad. He reached over to the pile of tools and took out a knife. He said, "Get out." I did so and tried to make a run for it. He tackled me and hit me in the face several times. I cried and he said, "Don't you try that again or I will kill you." He shoved me into the bush and said to get my clothes off. I took everything off and he did too. He kept showing me the knife all the time. He made me do everything. He stuck his thing in my mouth. It was disgusting. Then he said to lie on the grass and he jumped on top of me. He was so rough. He put the knife to my throat and I cried. He started to nick me. He cut my arms all over with the knife. I just wished he would kill me and get it over with. Then he stopped and just walked away. He dressed and left in his truck without saying a word. I dressed and went to the highway where a couple took me to the police.

Even after the victim submitted, he continued to use the knife and sadism may have been fused with the normal desire for intercourse in this case.

One theory of rape and of sexual aggression generally is that force is an essential aspect of the erotic preference. Examining the stimulus response matrix, it seems the rapist prefers the physically mature female as victim but intercourse alone is not sufficient to satisfy him. Freund[31] describes the "pathological rape pattern" in which the victim is followed and stalked, attacked and raped. Although this pattern may not be typical of rapists, it involves force as an essential element in the act. This would explain why sexual intercourse with a consenting partner is not sufficient for his satisfaction. How many wives or lovers are willing to submit to such brutality in day to day activity? On the other hand, Barbaree, Marshall and Lanthier[9] argued that force is not the critical element in rape. The male may be sexually aroused *in spite of* the force used. Since many rapists are used to plundering their world, sexual intercourse with a woman may be just one more thing they take with little or no pangs of conscience. Women's groups have suggested that one way to prevent rape is to do something horrible, like vomiting. *Mr. D* indicated that one of his victims had done this and he described his indifference as follows:

Mr. D: I told her I was going to fuck her and she had better cooperate. She said she was going to throw up. I opened the car door, held her by the neck and stuck her out to vomit. Then I yanked her in and started to feel her up.

He raped in spite of the distress of his victim and one senses he might feel the same way about someone whose car he has stolen.

Madonna Prostitute Complex.   There are many theories that further ask why the act of rape is necessary. One explanation is that rapists dichotomize the female world into pure untouchable women and dirty bad ones. He is not good enough to relate to the decent ones who don't get involved in sex in any case, since they are too pure. The dirty ones are cheap, no good and you can do what you like with them. This has been referred to as the Madonna Prostitute Complex[76].

Mr. E illustrates this theory. He was a 40-year-old married man with many frustrations including a domineering wife. He was milktoast and never seemed to display any anger. At the time of the rape charge, his behavior was quite bizarre and seemed pointless. He drove around in his car up and down streets without any clear goal in mind. He had gone out to buy a loaf of bread about noon time but didn't return. About 9:00 p.m., he picked up two hitchhikers who were in their early teens. In the interim, he had also acquired a gun which he kept in the glove compartment. He didn't know what he was going to do with it. The girls were going out of town about 50 miles to see an aunt. He said he would drive them there. He had been drinking and talked on about his problems. They listened sympathetically and at one point, he started getting sexually aroused. He turned back toward town and led them to a suburban street, not without its passersby. He took out the gun and told them they better do what he said. He noted:

> *Mr. E:* They looked like experienced girls. They looked like they had been around. I told the one nearest me to suck my penis. She did it right away. She sure knew how to do it. I'll bet she had lots of experience. The other one did it too but not as good. But I think she was a slut too!"

Inferiority feelings, sex role rigidity and the Don Juan complex.   Another theory suggests that the rapist suffers from an inferiority complex centered on insecurity about his masculinity[76]. This complex originates in his inappropriate upbringing and hindrances to his childhood development. His poor socialization influences his later sexual relations so that he suffers irrational anxieties about his sexual performance and he develops unrealistic attitudes to women. Women are either pure and untouchable or in control. They call the shots. The men ask for the dates but the women choose to say yes or no. Men are at their mercy. The rapist is at a disadvantage with the female's power over him socially but his physical strength gives him an advantage over them. He further doubts his attractiveness as a mate and that he is proficient sexually. This would certainly make him hesitate to seek voluntary partners but one might expect him to suffer the same impotence in rape. The rape is therefore a desperate attempt to reverse his position and to prove himself not only capable but dominant. The inferiority complex may manifest itself as a rigidity about the male role. He may be very anxious to maintain the male place.

In terms of the stimulus response matrix, he may require rigid adherence to the male gender behavior on his part and to the female role on the part of his mate, without any deviation. One might expect them to show ultra masculine identification. Some men manifest this as a refusal to do any woman's work no matter how slight it may seem, for example, getting his wife a cup of coffee rather than her doing it herself even if she were ill. Thus some writers describe the rapist as persistently possessive and dominating in his relations with women generally.

Dominance–submissiveness has been parallelled to male–female roles and to active–passive. This is an oversimplification and one has to wonder if force and dominance are the same in the rapist. As with many complex terms, the empirical referents to "dominance" are not clear and we are at a loss to know what it means. Sadism seeemingly implies extreme dominance but it is also a rather flexible term as used by social scientists. It includes behaviors involving violent force, even inflicting death, through humiliation and embarrassment of another as a pleasurable outlet. This is certainly a wide range of behaviors and there is considerable room for speculation and labeling any behavior that is negative as "dominant" or "sadistic". At least we can ask one question which has some standardized psychometric instruments to assess it: Does the rapist show high masculine gender identity?

The rapist may be ultramasculine in another way, beside role rigidity and use of force. He may seem to have an exaggerated need to prove his masculinity in the form of having as many sex partners as possible. This has been labeled the "Don Juan" complex[76]. It is not uncommon for men to brag about their exploits and sexual "conquests." Some men are inadequate unless they have an admiring female and can tell their male companions of the number of sex partners they have had. Numbers prove their masculinity and rape can add to the numbers. Such individuals also may accept the double standard. Sex outside of marriage is acceptable for men but not for women. Some writers think that rape is possible only because the double standard exists[76]. This may also be an aspect of the Madonna Prostitute complex mentioned earlier. On the other hand, it has been postulated that rapists lack the skills for establishing normal courtship behavior. For example, they can't talk to women or flirt, and this is significant in their make up. It is interesting how this theorized behavior supposedly recurs throughout the sexual anomalies but fails to find empirical support.

General hostility to women. The rapist seems predisposed to taking things from women in one form or another. Perhaps there is something in his character that creates this condition. Summaries of the research literature indicate that about 2 rapists in 5 are sociopathic personalities[76]. At least half are from homes in which they were abused children. Violence in their home background was a way of life. *Mr. H* noted:

Mr. H: When my old man came home, if he did, he was usually stinking drunk and he would want to hit me right away for no reason. Even if I sat there doing nothing, he would find something, some excuse to whack me. After a while, it didn't hurt anymore. I remember when I was 8-years-old making a promise to myself. He had just smashed me in the mouth and I was wiping away the blood and I wasn't afraid any more. I was mad. I promised myself when I was big enough I would give that old bastard a shit kicking that he would never forget. I waited that day out until I was big enough. It came when I was 13. He came in drunk and took a swing at me and missed; he was so pissed. I kicked him in the stomach and he fell down. I kicked him and kicked him and punched him until I thought he was dead. Then I threw him down the stairs. He just laid there not moving. He was covered in blood. I thought I had killed him. I said good, it's what you deserve you son of a bitch. Unfortunately, he only had a few stitches over his eye and he got better. He was soon up to his old tricks but he never hit me again.

The mothers of rapists have been described as rejective, excessively over-controlling, dominant, and punitive but also as overprotective and seductive. The fathers are distant, uninvolved and absent or passive[76]. Some writers think there is excessive handling of the genitals and incest with a sister, cousin, aunt, or other relative is not infrequent. Parents also engage in flagrant sexual indiscretions.

The force used in rape may reflect a general hostility to women as well as being a specific sexual arousal pattern. Mothers of rapists may be inconsistent in meeting the needs of their sons whose resulting hostility may be displaced to other women and acted out in the rape. His mother may create in him a fear of dependency on women so that he becomes hypermasculine and seemingly independent.

An alternative interpretation of his background is that he grows up in a climate of violence and continues to use it as an adult. It does not seem strange that a child socialized to violence would use it as an adult. The Rotter sentence completion test of *Mr. F* emanates hostility. He was an abused child and came into testing angry at everyone, even when they did nothing to him. His responses were:

My mother . . . . was a stupid bitch.
My father should . . . drop dead.
I always wanted . . . to be big enough to beat up my old man.
Women are . . . just good for screwing.
The people over me . . . are bastards.
I can't understand . . . why no one likes me.

It isn't surprising such a person would rape. It would be surprising if he found someone to have voluntary sex with him!

Some theorists claim that rapists have been seduced as children[76] and some empirical data supports this point of view. According to psycho-analysts, the child desires to have incestuous relations with his mother but usually does not. However, in the case of the rapist, this happens and creates even greater conflicts than in the average family. Especially since the family is often so violent, his castration anxiety must be even greater than average.

Miscellaneous theories.   Rape has been viewed as a sadistic streak in the individual and as an inadequacy. A final way it has been considered is as a defence, against homosexuality, against incest and against flagging sexual interest in women. Since the majority of victims of rape are females, it may seem strange that it is a defence against homosexuality. One can construe the rapist as desperately attempting to prove his adequacy as a heterosexual by forcing a woman to submit to his wishes. In so doing, he proves to himself that he is not homosexual. Once again the homosexuality may be latent and difficult to verify empirically. It is more fruitful to ask whether the rapists' homosexual experience differs from the average nonrapist heterosexual's and whether he shows an erotic preference for men. If the rapist shows a flagging interest in women this may be due to excessive con-sumption of alcohol. Since chronic excessive use of alcohol can result in im-potence, it may be difficult to know if the lack of interest in sex with volun-tary partners is coincidental to the rape.

Typologies of rapists.   A number of attempts have been made to classify types of rape and they have been summarized in a book by R. Rada, *Clinical Aspects of the Rapists*[76] (see also [22] [32] [34] [40] [41]). Most are variants in the use of force or of inadequacy. Some mix in other characteristic prob-lems of rapists as etiologically significant. For example: The drunken ex-plosive type[32] is the male who rapes in a fit of anger which is released when he is drinking. This may be important for treatment but tells little of the etiology of rape. Most of the classification systems were used once and have no further support in empirical studies. Most of the theories and classifica-tions can be reduced to the three questions: To what extent is force necessary for sexual gratification? Is the rapist inadequate as a male? Is he defending against homosexuality, incest, or flagging sexual interest? We can then ask how alcohol and his violent history contribute to the antisocial acts.

Toucheurism and frottage.   Little has been said of other acts of sexual aggression such as toucheurism and frottage. These acts are often precur-sors of rape and are also the forceful taking of some sexual gratification if not the full act of intercourse.

Mr. G was a 19-year-old student, a loner who used to make obscene remarks to girls in the street. He also engaged in touching unknown females on the subway. This started as a passive act. He would ride the trains at rush hour when it was crowded and stand beside some unsuspecting female and take "accidental" feels. Eventually, he became more daring and would try to have physical contact with solitary females travelling the trains at late hours. When he was caught, the victim reported:

> *Victim:*   I was just sitting on the train with my girlfriend talking when this guy (the accused) came on the train and sat down beside us. We ignored him but he started to talk about sex. I told him to shut up but he kept on talking. He reached over and touched my breast. I hit him in the face with my fist and he just sat there then. We got off the train at the next stop and he followed us. He came up beside me and touched my breast again. I grabbed him by the hair and kicked him and took him to the ticket taker at the station who called the police.

One has to wonder how far *Mr. G* would go if it had been a different female, or if she had been alone. Although it has not been documented by systematic research, there appears to be an association of rape, toucheurism and frottage and it may well be that these latter behaviors are precursors of rape or foiled attempts at rape.

THE EXPERIMENTAL EVIDENCE

The importance of force in rape.   It is assumed that the rapist is aroused by force (or in spite of it) but the normal male will not be. So a suitable experiment to test this question would be to compare rapists and nonrapists on the following stimuli: consenting intercourse versus rape versus neutral stimuli. When penile tumescence is measured, rapists should react most to rape but also to consenting intercourse and not to neutral stimuli. Normals or nonrapists should react only to intercourse. These expectations are depicted in Fig. 12.1. Another stimulus which would be informative is the inflicting of force alone on a female with no intercourse or other evident sexual contact. If force were as important or more important than intercourse, rapists may react to it as well. This would provide some perspective on the relationship of force and intercourse in rape.

Kercher and Walker[47] first tested the question by showing rapists and convicted inmate controls pictures of heterosexual interactions, sadomasochism and neutral scenes. Although the study had a number of serious methodological problems, the two groups did not react differently to the sexual materials in terms of penile circumference changes. However, it is not clear whether all stimuli were arousing or not.

Gene Abel and his colleagues[1,2] developed an ingenious way of studying sexual behavior generally by use of audio tapes. Research participants

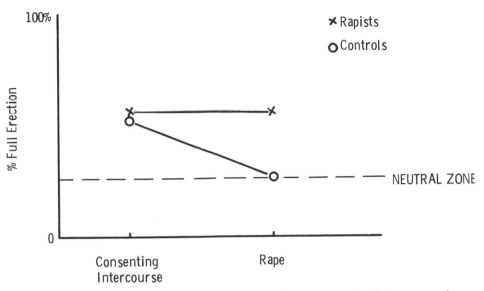

FIG. 12.1   Rapists' versus controls' penile reactions to consenting intercourse and rape.

would be interviewed while attached to a penile circumference strain gauge. Conversational content which was sexually arousing was noted and then statements were presented to the patient to determine which part of his sexual behavior was more arousing. Abel used 10 second intervals between critical segments of the description. In this way, rape cues could be evaluated and later presented in a more orderly and controlled fashion to a number of rapists and control participants in the experimental paradigm described above. However, Abel argued that rape "cues" are highly idiosyncratic and stimuli should therefore be developed for each individual[1].

In his study, subjects were compared on penile circumference changes to consenting and mutually enjoyable intercourse versus rape. An example of intercourse is:

It's in the afternoon, afternoon and you're in a room, on a bed, with Nancy. She really likes you. She's met you and talked with you and she really likes you. She's slipping her clothes off there; slipping her bra off. You can see her tits. She's big, really big, and you're going to have intercourse. She's slipping her clothes off. She's lying there, back, lying on the bed. You can see her. She's got big thighs and a nice ass, a fairly big ass. You're getting on top of her there. You can feel yourself with a nice stiff erection. You're just coming right into her. You can feel your dick right there in her vagina. She really likes it. She's putting her arms around you. You can feel her arms around you. You feel her arms around you. She's really holding you close and you're starting to move up and down on her. She really likes it. She really likes you and really likes you to make love to her. She's holding you real tight and real close. She's starting to move her ass around now. She's really getting excited and she's breathing fast. She's really breathing fast. She's really excited. She's really turned on. You're really turning her on. She really likes it. She's just telling you to go on, really, really to screw her. She really likes it. She can feel your penis in her. She really likes and enjoys the feeling. She can feel your dick . . . really got a nice stiff erection in her. She really likes it. She's holding onto you and moving her ass. She's starting to come now and so are you. She's starting to come and so are you. She starting to climax. She's just letting go. She's just moaning and you're ejaculating into her. Nancy really likes it. She really enjoys it. She really feels good about it.

A companion description of rape involved the same female in the same setting. However, force is evident and the resistance of the female is depicted:

It's in the afternoon and you're in a room. You're in a room with Nancy and you have a knife. You're going to screw her. You tell her you're going to screw her and she might as well give in. She's saying she doesn't want to, that she wants to leave. And you're just taking out the knife. You tell her to take her clothes off. You see her blond hair. She's big. You're telling her to take her clothes off, go on ahead and take her clothes off. She's slipping off her panties. You're going to rape her right there on the bed. She's slipping off her panties and now she's slipping off her bra. You can see her tits there. You tell her to lie back and she's reluctant to, and you just slap her a little, slap her a little and she's lying down now. You feel yourself . . . you've got a nice stiff erection. You're getting right on top of her. She's big. She's got big thighs and you just stick your dick right into her there. All the way, deep into her, really sticking your dick deep into her. And she's fighting you. You slap her a little. You tell her to quiet down, to remain still. She's starting to scream now and cry. You slap her and you tell her to be quiet and you take your hand and you muffle her voice there. You're holding her down; you've got her pinned down there, just forcing yourself on her. You're holding her down, forcing yourself on her. She's telling you to stop, to please stop. She's pleading with you and it's no use. You just hold her down, just hold her down. You're screwing her. You're holding her down, screwing her and fucking her. You've got yourself right on her there, pinned her down. You're just holding her down. You're just too powerful for her, too strong for her. She can't get loose. You're holding her down, screwing her there. Just holding her down and you're starting to come; you're starting to ejaculate into her. It really feels good. You're just ejaculating right into her, holding her down, fucking her there.

Results showed that rapists were equally aroused by intercourse and by rape but the nonrapist controls were more aroused by consenting intercourse than by rape as expected. A further interesting statistic was developed: the rape index. This is the ratio of arousal to rape stimuli divided by arousal to consenting intercourse stimuli. If greater than 1, this suggests rape is the more potent stimulus. It turns out that an index of 0.5 is needed to distinguish the two groups in fact. 75% can be identified correctly with this cut off whereas chance will only identify 65%. An interesting finding was that the higher the rape index, the more frequent was the history of the rapes and the greater was the extent of injury to the victims. The clinical value of the rape index in assessing "dangerousness" seems to be substantial. Obviously, the index needs refinement but it seems to be a very useful tool for the clinician. Unfortunately, we do not know what reaction would be given by subjects to neutral stimuli. Moreover, the study has been criticized on other grounds[9]. Participants in the control group were sexually anomalous, namely bisexuals, exhibitionists, pedophiles and voyeurs who may not have responded to rape because of their own peculiar erotic preferences. A pedophile for example might not react to rape but only to more passive interaction with a female child and perhaps more to a female adult initiating sexual intercourse as in Abel's stimuli. Second, the study used idiosyncratic stimuli. Each person had his own stimuli. Each also had the two largest of his four responses selected as well. The analysis was possibly biased and a more appropriate multivariate statistical analysis could have been performed.

In a second study, Barbaree and his colleagues[9] compared rapists to university students who were not criminals. One might wish to question the use of this control group as well, but all were presumably sexually normal. The same descriptions were presented to all research participants. The questions posed here were whether force alone would be effective in eliciting sexual arousal in rapists, and in addition, the extent to which consent was important. If the female was unwilling to cooperate but offered no resistance, would this be as exciting for the rapists as using force? Seven audiotaped categories of stimulus fantasies were presented. In three, mutually consenting intercourse between the individual being tested and a female adult was described. In the first, she was enthusiastic and initiated sex play. In the second, she was passive, neither rejecting nor accepting. Finally, she was reluctant but was eventually seduced by the subject. This could be interpreted as a degree of consent and/or pleasure in the act. The next three stimuli described rape with varying degrees of consent/force. In the first rape, the female refused sex and is threatened into compliance. In the second rape, he physically restrains her while they have intercourse. In the final rape, he assaults her, punching and slapping her while having sex. In the nonsexual assault stimulus, he physically attacks her but there is no sexual interaction.

The rapists did not react differentially to any stimulus including the nonsexual assault. Controls on the other hand reacted most to consenting intercourse with no differences in the degree of consent/pleasure. They reacted more to rape than to assault alone but less than they did to consenting intercourse. They were less aroused by the violent rape than the ones in which verbal threat and some restraint was used. The authors noted that consent was not the critical variable since the controls were turned on by rape as well as by consenting intercourse and they did not react differently to varying degrees of consent. However, extreme force may have inhibited the sexual arousal of the controls. The authors concluded that rapists may fail to inhibit their arousal when force is used rather than being aroused by force itself. One has to wonder then why the rapists were aroused by the description of nonsexual assault. If neutral stimuli had been used a clearer answer to the question would have been forthcoming. A third study attempted just this.

Quinsey and his colleagues[72] used eighteen audiotaped stimuli: three neutral ones in which a man and a woman interact (opening a bank account, arrange travel plan) and five each of consenting intercourse, with a wife or girlfriend; rape involving significant force, and finally assault on a female with no sexual interaction. This study also varied expectation of the participants in the control group. The rapists were compared to nonsex offenders, to community volunteers with no special instructions and to community volunteers who were told that sexual arousal to rape was normal and expected.

One possible interpretation of the Abel and Barbaree studies was that control participants did not react to rape stimuli because it was expected that they should not. Experimental demands may have biased the results and Quinsey's study tests whether this is the case.

As expected, rapists responded more to rape than uninstructed controls did. The four groups did not differ in their response to intercourse but their overall rape index was different. Using a rape index of 0.80 as cut off, 76% of the men could be classified as rapist or nonrapist. The best one could do by chance and by saying everyone was a rapist, would be 60% correct. While it is not reported in the paper, the present writer did a statistical analysis on the data to show that the assault stimuli did not differ from neutral stimuli in the reactions produced in the four groups. Overall, the results support Barbaree's conclusions that rapists fail to inhibit their arousal in the presence of force rather than being actively aroused by it. They do not seem to be aroused by force alone. This does not rule out the possibility that some special interaction effect is produced by force plus sexual cues. Quinsey's control group with special instructions were interesting. When control participants were told that it is normal and expected to be aroused by rape, they did not differ from rapists in their responses to rape descriptions. On the average rapists reacted more to rape than to intercourse whereas instructed controls did the opposite, although none of the differences were significant. The rape index appears to amplify those weak effects so the index was statistically significant.

One may wonder at this point about the demand on the rapists to respond to the rape cues in the experiments described. In each of the three studies, not only are the rape situations described, that is, the female, hitting her, and so forth, but the participants are also told that they are reacting to the situation. In the example given earlier, the rape stimulus is mixed with the subject's response to it. In fact, he is told how to respond: "You feel yourself . . . you've got a nice stiff erection" and " . . . you're starting to come; you're starting to ejaculate into her. It really feels good." This could create differential demand on the rapist and the controls. The same suggestions about reacting appear in the consenting intercourse stimulus and the rapist may react to both in the same way. Control participants on the other hand may feel that they should not react unless they are given permission as in Quinsey's study. This is not uncommon in laboratory research. A normal control may react, for example, to a nude picture of a pubescent girl or even to a female child on the standard phallometric test (Chapter Two). He may feel uncomfortable and guilty until assured that it is normal to do so.

Each of the three studies suffers the same problem so that conclusions must be treated with caution until more research is done. However, it seems that the force is incidental to the rape in many cases. The foregoing studies did not examine sexual history of the rapists. It is possible that they manifest some sexual anomaly which would be evident from the history.

Presence of other sexual anomalies.   Gebhard[32] and his colleagues from the Kinsey Institute for Sex Research found that sexual aggressors were exceptional in their reported erotic reactions to sadomasochistic activity as well as to animal contacts. Although they also tended to have considerable homosexual experience, Gebhard and his colleagues attribute this to their prison situation.

Earlier results of Sex History Questionnaire data from the Forensic Clinic in my hospital suggested that the rapist displayed multiple sexual anomalies[65]. When one examines the number of sex stimuli men respond to; that is, men, women, children, pubescents; and the range of responses they emit; rape, exhibiting, peeping, intercourse, and so forth, the rapists tend to engage in more outlets than the usual sexually anomalous male. Of all the sexually anomalous cases presenting at our clinic about half displayed multiple anomalies while 80% of rapists did. Rape tends to be associated with exhibiting, voyeurism, and frottage, the so called courtship disorder cluster[65]. It also tends to be associated with acting out with pubescent females. When only multiple anomalies are considered, the category to which rapists seem to belong more appropriately, a similar cluster emerges. Indecent phone calls tend to cluster with courtship disorders but not with rape especially. Of course one is limited by the actual sample which appears at any clinic and another hospital might derive different clusters.

Our concern with the earlier studies was the small number of rapists examined and the wording of some of the questions. Since then we improved our questionnaire to be clearer on the occurrence of orgasm on some items. This is particularly the case for voyeurism, frottage, and obscene calls. Additional items were added to sample sadism and other important anomalies in rape. In a more recent study, Paitich, Macdonald, Russon and I[49] [54] examined forty rapists in a more comprehensive study. We compared two dimensions of sexual behavior: sexual anomaly present or absent versus aggressive history present or absent. The rapists presumably belong in the condition which is positive for both factors. Common assaultives who had no history of sexual anomalies served as another comparison group. A group of multiple sexual anomalies selected from our data bank for charges related to females over 16 and with no history of violence served as the other comparison group. A nonviolent non sexually anomalous normal group completed the design of the study. When sexual history is compared in the groups, the rapists look like the assaultives and not like the other groups. They are normal in most respects but tend to start sexual experience earlier and to have more of it. They do not differ from the other assaultive group in this respect.

Using the new sex history information, we found 42% of the rapists engaged in no other sexually anomalous behavior outside the rape and therefore their erotic preferences may be considered normal. A small group of the rapists exhibited a wide range of sexual behaviors including crossdressing with orgasm. They exhibited, peeped, raped, made obscene calls, touched adult female strangers, and also were more often involved with immature females. However they were not aroused by physically hurting, humiliating, or embarrassing someone, threatening or frightening someone, seeing them unconsious or unable to move, or in pain. They were not aroused by these acts done to them. Seventeen percent had been aroused but did not climax while beating someone. They were not excited by being beaten.

Rapists as homosexuals and toucheurs.   Rapists are less likely to be involved with male children but their experience with adult males is average. This argues against the theory of rape as a defence against homosexuality. Their heterosexual experience appears to be above average and they seem to be active, arguing against a flagging interest in women. Since their dating and experience with women is greater than the control subjects[49][54], can the argument that they are inadequate as males be substantiated? They were only slightly more likely to be involved in touching and rubbing strange females than controls suggesting that frottage and toucheurism may be incidentally related to several sexual anomalies. Less than 30% of any group was involved in touching or frottage. Many instances were apparently chance occurrences.

Problems of impotence.   Karacan[46], Groth[40], and their colleagues have provided some perspective on the question of impotence in rapists. By examining nocturnal penile tumescence, one can determine if there is an organic cause of impotence. Since normal men have several erection periods during sleep, one can diagnose organic impotence which prevents erection altogether. Karacan and his associates compared rapists, other prisoners and controls. There was no evidence of reduced nocturnal tumescence in the rapists, ruling out at least, organic impotence. However, the sample was small and theories relating impotence and rape suggest it is psychological in nature. Groth and Birnbaum in an uncontrolled study of a large number of convicted rapists found only 16% were impotent during the rape and 5% had retarded ejaculation. Although a subjective report was used in this evaluation, it appears that sexual inadequacy is only a sometime companion of rape. Unfortunately, the association of alcoholism and impotence with rape has not been studied adequately to date.

Parent child relations.   The family background of the sexual aggressor has been described as an important determinant of his later antisocial behavior. Violence and sexual abuse are seen as typical. About a third of the parents of rapists are alcoholics and/or are heavy drinkers. Mothers tend to be similar. About a quarter of the parents often and severely beat their sons who are destined to be rapists[76]. However, the story of inappropriate parenting is not peculiar to the rapist but is common in criminal populations. In addition, the lack of studies, especially controlled studies, or rapists versus other relevant clinical groups is noteworthy. One has to wonder why more attention has not been given to this important social problem.

The only controlled study of parent child relations of rapists using a standardized psychometric test was conducted in our clinic[49]. The Clarke Parent Child Relations Questionnaire (PCR) was administered along with a series of questions related to childhood experiences. Our study compared rapists to three contrasting groups: multiple sexual anomalies with no history of violence, common assaultives with normal sex history and nonpatient controls. The study addressed the question whether the rapists were more like assaultive or more like sexually anomalous males. The PCR questionnaire examines the respondant's recollection of familial aggression and his estimation of his parents' competence, affection, indulgence of him and the extent to which he identified with each parent.

The results showed that rapists were more similar to assaultives than to sexually anomalous controls. Both mothers and fathers seemed to provide poor parenting. The most significant factors were that the rapists and assaultives did not identify with either parent. Fathers especially were aggressive and the sons reciprocated. Both parents were seen as low in affection and high in strictness. Mothers were not aggressive like fathers, but were low in affection. The results of the controlled study do suggest that the family background of the rapist is disturbed but it fails to clearly differentiate him from the assaultive individual who is not sexually anomalous. The rapist's profile is more like the assaultive than the sexually anomalous male in that he more often ran away from home as a child and had more fights both before and after 16 years of age. Both parents were often drunk and fathers were in trouble with the police. In spite of this, the rapists also thought they drank too much and were more often drunk in the three months prior to testing than controls were. They were more likely to be jealous over a sib who was father's favorite. Overall the rapists and assaultive individuals appear as abused children growing up in an inhospitable environment. There was no evidence of incest.

All the data taken together suggests that many rapists have normal erotic preferences but they are assaultive individuals. The question of rape then generally becomes one of dealing with violence rather than with a sexual anomaly. The problem is compounded by their extensive history of crime and violence as well as by three other potentially important clinical factors. General and extreme aggression has been associated with alcohol abuse, brain pathology and excessive male sex hormone levels, namely testosterone.

Testosterone, rape and aggression.   Aggression in extreme degrees has been related to elevated testosterone in the blood[25] [26] [27] [48] [59] [60] [62] [68] [83] [88]. Whenever relatively well defined groups of violent individuals have been used, they showed some elevation in testosterone levels. Other studies using questionnaires have not been successful, mainly because they used only normal individuals.

The only study on testosterone levels in rapists carried out by Rada and his colleagues[78] suggest a complex interaction of alcohol use, baseline serum testosterone and rape. Rapists' testosterone levels were within normal limits but there was a positive association of testosterone level and aggressiveness of the rape. This is understandable, but it was found, contrary to expectation, that rapists who were alcoholics had higher testosterone levels than those who were not alcoholics. Alcohol is supposed to lower testosterone level[42] [58] [67] [80] [99] and in its extreme can produce feminization of the male. One possible explanation is that the alcoholic rapists may be peculiar and have higher testosterone levels to begin with for whatever reason. Possibly, their endocrine system adapts to alcohol in the same way. Chronic consumption of alcohol can produce less problems of coordination, etc. than in the casual drinker as noted in Chapter Two. So their bodies are less affected by alcohol than social drinkers.

Mr. I illustrates such a defiance of our expectations. A weekend alcoholic, he consumed in a typical 60 hour drinking bout, 72 pints of beer and 120 oz. of rye whiskey. At blood alcohol levels which would render the average man comatose, he drove about the city in his car, picked up a young lady whom he successfully raped and drove home.

This extreme tolerance to alcohol may be quickly lost under sober conditions so that even by the time of assessment, two to three weeks after the offense, he may lose the tolerance he had. The problem of tolerance to alcohol is complex but it may explain the paradoxical results of Rada et al's study. When the rapists were in prison and had no alcohol, their body may have been showing a compensatory reaction of temporarily higher levels of testosterone. This, of course, is speculation. Rada's study also has important limitations and needs replication. In particular, repeated samples of blood are needed to provide a more accurate assessment of characteristic levels of testosterone. The rapist may show other abnormalities in sex hormones. The level of leutinizing hormone and follicle stimulating hormone may be important in aggression but the question is unresearched.

Brain pathology. Aggressiveness has also been associated with brain pathology. Rapists have been studied as parts of other groups, that is, as parts of aggressive prisoners or as part of sex offenders, but no one to date has specifically studied rapists alone. When there is damage to the limbic system of the brain, this is often reflected as damage to the frontal and temporal lobes which can more readily be measured. Deep damage to the base of the brain is not easily assessed yet[63]. The frontal and the temporal lobes at least reflect possible damage in those areas which results in excessive aggressiveness. Williams[102], in a large scale study, found suport for the hypothesis in a prison sample of aggressive and nonaggressive criminals. Studying the electroencephalogram (EEG), he found 57% of the aggressives' versus 12% of the nonaggressives' tracings were abnormal in the expected anterior part of the brain. However, the research on an exclusively rapist group remains to be done. From the existing literature, we do not know where the damage is or the extent of it. Moreover, we do not know how many rapists are involved in the samples.

One index of brain pathology is low intelligence or a very large discrepancy between verbal and performance intelligence tasks[101]. Samples of verbal tasks are vocabulary, general knowledge and arithmetic while performance tasks are block designs or picture arrangements. The two sets of tasks tend to be associated with activation of different parts of the brain. While most individuals score about the same on verbal and performance tasks, the brain damaged person shows a significant difference on the two. Of course some individuals are retarded and have a general neural deficit. Some authors suggest that rapists compared to other groups of prisoners are retarded or are borderline retarded[86]. Vera and his colleagues[100] in the best controlled study to date compared rapists with nonviolent sex offenders, nonsexual violent offenders, and nonsexual nonviolent offenders. There were no differences in the distribution of scores among the four groups and about 9-in-10 men were average or borderline average intelligence for each group. Our own data confirms this latter finding in four similar groups. To date, no one has reported verbal versus performance IQ differences, which would be a better index of brain pathology.

It is not surprising that aggressive people would suffer some form of brain damage. They lead violent lives and their hostility is often reciprocated so their heads are bashed in from time to time. The demonstrated brain pathology would only be etiologically significant if it occurred in the frontal and temporal lobes or, if it could be measured, in the limbic system. Assuming they do have some sort of brain pathology, how is it influenced by alcohol? By their life style? Is it possible that they can function under normal sober conditions but once they ingest excessive amounts of alcohol, aggressive tendencies manifest themselves? The research remains to be done.

Alcohol abuse in rapists. The final important factor in rape and in violence generally is alcohol abuse. A significant one third of rapists are chronic alcoholics who can unlease their inhibitions chemically[76]. While the average person tends to become happier under the influence of alcohol, the assaultive person may become more aggressive. With possible brain pathology and hormone chemistry predisposing him to violence, the effect of alcohol can be complex and create great difficulties in devising treatment programs or in simply doing forensic assessments[11][21].

There are very few studies relating the effect of alcohol on penile erection and potency[10][16][17][29][85][104]. Collectively, they suggest that with increased consumption and blood alcohol levels, arousability and testosterone levels decline. This indicates that intoxication and rape are unlikely mates. However, with increased tolerance due to habitual consumption of alcohol, sexual arousal may not be influenced. The results of the few laboratory studies offer findings that support a common preconception about alcohol: it may increase the desire for sex but reduce one's ability to perform. This may not be true for the rapist who is often an abuser of alcohol. Moreover, the research studies available have serious methodological problems which need to be corrected in further studies before a firm conclusion can be reached. A design employing different individuals for varying alcohol doses rather than repeated tests on the same people with the same erotic stimuli would be an asset. Phallometric measurement is, of course, essential. The role of participants' expectations about alcohol also seems important but research has provided contradictory findings. Finally, appropriate statistical analyses need to be employed. An interesting addition would be to examine the effect of alcohol and erotica on moderate to heavy drinkers to more closely approximate the drinking habits of rapists.

Personality of the rapist. What contribution does personality make to the picture of the rapist? Certainly, aggression is an important facet but the research studies on aggression in rapists are methodlogically poor and much more work needs to be done. Rapists tend to be sociopathic but there is little evidence for inadequacy. The clinician appears to be facing in the rapist a complex interaction of alcoholism, aggression and sociopathic personality features[28] [50] [75] [81].

Rada[76] who has reviewed personality studies of rapists points out two problems. First, there are very few controlled studies and second, rapists are often grouped together with other sex offenders providing a heterogeneous and uncertain group which may even include docile pedophiles. Karacan and his coworkers[46] compared rapists, other convicted inmates and normal controls on the MMPI. Unfortunately, the validity scales were significantly deviant for the two convict groups which makes other results suspect. However, psychopathic deviate, (Pd), hypomania, (Ma), and depression (D) scales were significant, collectively producing a prototype sociopathic personality profile characterized by immaturity, rebelliousness, low frustration tolerance, superficial friendliness, moodiness, irritability and lack of respect for authority. Rada contrasted alcoholic and nonalcoholic rapists but found only the psychopathic deviate (Pd) scale was significant. This Pd scale is commonly elevated in criminals and may reflect no more than anti-social tendencies, nonconformity and/or family background problems. Quinsey and his associates[71] compared various groups of violent offenders, rapists, pedophiles and property offenders. Rapists did not differ from the other groups in the number of significantly elevated profiles. Again, Pd was most prominent but also schizophrenia and depression scales were. These results suggest the criminal feature of rapists' personalities is more prominent than sexual features.

A few scattered studies have been attempted to ascertain whether the MMPI profile of the rapist is more characteristic of assaultive sexually normal men or nonassaultive sexually anomalous men. Thus Panton[66] and Armentrout and Hauer[6] compared rapists of adults, of children and non-violent pedophiles while Rader[79] examined rapists, exhibitionists and unspecified assaultive men. Individual results are slightly varied but psychopathic deviate scales (MMPI scale #4) and schizophrenia (MMPI scale #8) have been prominent and the so called 4-8 profile appears to describe assaultiveness generally. The clearest result applies to psychopathic deviate scores and other scales seem more influenced by the composition of the group studied and perhaps by their ages[45] [52] [55] [95] [96].

Prison samples may also be different from men awaiting trial and admittors of the crime may differ from nonadmittors. Our own clinical data compared MMPI and 16 PF profiles of rapists, nonsexual assaultives, non-assaultive multiple sex anomalies and controls. Validity scales were within normal limits likely because all clinical participants were cooperative and admitted to their offences. On the MMPI, assaultives and rapists were generally not distinct from each other but were different from controls and nonassaultive sexual anomalies. The most discriminating single scale was psychopathic deviate, similar to the previous studies. However, when clinically deviant profiles are examined, depression, paranoia, psychasthenia, schizophrenia, mania and social introversion were prominent as well. The results suggest considerable emotional disturbance in rapists but once again they are not distinct from sexually normal assaultive men. Another fact emerges about rapists from all the foregoing studies; they do not seem to be ultramasculine as measured by the MMPI. This tends to undermine a number of theories which have this assertion as an integral element in them.

The 16 PF results tend to support the MMPI findings but they were not as clear cut. In consideration of recent research casting doubt on the validity or reliability of the 16 PF test, these results will not be elaborated.

Projective test results have also been reviewed by Rada[76] and results for these tests are more vague, general and uncertain. Because of compounded problems of tester, scorer and test reliability and validity, projective tests have been largely ignored in this book.

Some attention has been directed to other Hostility scales to assess if in fact general hostility is an important component of the rapists' make up. These scales, unfortunately, have been poorly validated and need to be considered with caution as well. Rada and his colleagues[78] found rapists scored higher than normals and pedophiles on the Buss Durkee Hostility Inventory but not on the Megaree Overcontrolled Hostility Rating Scale[57]. Quinsey, Arnold and Pruesse[71] and my colleagues and I[49] also found the latter did not discriminate the rapists from other violent offenders. However, Rada presented pilot data[78] to suggest degree of violence in the rape was positively related to degree of hostility measured by the Buss Durkee test. Fisher and Rivlin[30] compared rapists with other nonsex offenders in prison on the Edwards Personal Preference Schedule (EPPS). Contrary to other reports, rapists were less aggressive than controls but also lower on heterosexuality, change, autonomy and achievement but higher than controls on succorance, abasement, nurturance and endurance. The controls were taken from another study which may have produced the unusual outcome.

Personality data, if anything, generally align the rapist with violent criminals, once again indicating that hostility rather than a sexual anomaly may be a prime factor in his make up.

Conclusion—The Rapists' Stimulus Response Matrix

A summary of theories of rape appear in Table 12.1. The typical rapist presents the most complex picture of any sexual anomaly. He appears to respond to the adult female most and to be normal in his stimulus preference profile. However, he is unusual in his response profile. He seeks out intercourse most, but will do so in the form of rape. He may engage in

TABLE 12.1
Summary of Evidence for Theories of Sexual Aggression and Rape

Theory	Experimental Evidence
1. Force is instrument in rape	Limited evidence suggests this is so
2. Force is essential	Likely in some cases, especially sadism
3. Rapists dichotomize women into pure untouchables or dirty and bad	Untested
4. Rapists suffer feelings of inferiority	They tend to be aggressive and suffer considerable emotional disturbance
5. Rapists are rigid in sex role behavior	Untested
6. Rapists like to "collect female conquests"	Positive. They are "rounders" and have much sexual experience
7. Rapists are hostile to women in general	Untested. They are hostile in general however
8. Mothers of rapists are rejecting, overcontrolling, and punitive but also seductive and overprotective	Only 1 controlled study. Mother is strict and unaffectionate
9. Fathers of rapists are distant, uninvolved, and absent or passive	Similar to mother. Both parents often drunk
10. Rapists had excessive handling of genitals as a child, and incest with sister, parents, etc.	Negative
11. Rape is a defence against homosexuality	Negative

other forms of sexual aggression, in particular, toucheurism and frottage. He is not likely to exhibit or to be involved with men. The complicating factors in his make up is a prominent criminal history which involves a wide range of offenses including assault. This suggests that he is primarily aggressive and rape is incidental. Rape is more likely to be associated with alcoholism than most other sexual anomalies which are not associated with aggression. He may have elevated blood testosterone levels and he may have brain pathology which is associated with aggression. Each of the pieces of his make up indicates that aggression is what should be studied in the rapist while his sexual preferences may be relatively normal. There was little evidence of a fixed preference for violence in intercourse in the rapists studied. Their basic antisocial makeup is one that predisposes them to taking what they want. Alcoholism also reflects this tendency to self indulgence without concern for others. However a smaller percentage of rapists may be sadistic and fuse sexual and aggressive urges.

Rape is one of those acts in which the offender does not care for the needs of others. Their home environment is one that generates a lack of care; they are abused children, their parents are violent, they start a life of crime early, taking what they want perhaps since they are unlikely to get it at home. Brain pathology and unusual serum testosterone levels may interact with their home conditions to generate such a violent individual but more evidence is needed to understand the relative contribution of these factors to their make up. Sadistic rapists seem rarer and they have not been examined to date in any systematic studies.

TREATMENT

There are few treatment programs for rapists and those in existence have not been properly evaluated (See Abel [3]). One may easily have the impression that there is no workable program[40] but in point of fact, little has been tried. Rape is an abhorrent crime and the courts want the assailants off the streets. "Dangerous offender" legislation is an attempt among other things, to remove rapists permanently from society. The focus of interest has been on assessment of dangerousness rather than on treatment and rehabilitation. It is for the rapist that castration seems like the best answer, or perhaps long term imprisonment. One would suspect that assessment of dangerousness will have a bearing not only on treatment effectiveness but also on whether society will permit any treatment to be tested in these cases. Since assessment is so important and complex in the rape cases, we will first discuss it and then possible treatment programs.

Assessment of Dangerousness

The literature on dangerousness is marred by two vague concepts, "sex offender" and "dangerous". Different sexual anomalies are lumped together under the term "sex offender", including homosexuals, pedophiles, exhibitionists, rapists and sadists. Social climates vary over time and the goal of incarceration may seem disparate to the objective viewer. Exhibitionism is currently considered a nuisance and a minor fine is imposed. Homosexuality in Canada, between consenting adults in private is not an offence but prior to 1969, gay men may have spent 5 years in jail for the same acts. The current focus on the "dangerous sex offender" rests generally on rape and pedophilia.

The second vague concept we must deal with is "danger"[97]. The concept is so general that it may even be a threat to our civil liberties[36] [37] [38]. The author recently heard a government representative discuss the problem of "disposition" of dangerous mentally ill offenders. He thought rapists and murderers should be locked away but also mentioned a retarded lady who accidentally but not fatally poisoned her family by leaving meat about in hot weather. He suggested that she should also be detained. The viewpoint would provide enormous and perhaps arbitrary powers to decision makers who may in large numbers be psychiatrists who subscribe to the untested theories noted in this book and who have no established scientifically sound method for making such assessments[84]. Greenland[38] also found such assessments ethically objectionable since the psychiatrist may serve as a double agent securing the conviction of his trusting patient.

Quinsey[70] noted that the study of sexual behavior such as rape has an advantage over other less clearly defined "dangerous" acts. We can ask two questions: "Will the rapists seek forced sexual gratification from a woman in the forseeable future given the opportunity?" and "How much force is he likely to use[84]?". While this does not weigh the psychological damage done to the victim, it assesses the probability of inflicting *some* psychological damage and physical harm. It provides quantifiable and clear measures of danger unavailable in other crimes. There are at least four factors which are implicated in the two questions but the research evidence is unsatisfactory so their relative importance is unknown; history of violence; of alcohol and drug abuse; organic factors like frontal-temporal brain pathology or elevated testosterone levels; and an erotic preference for force (sadism)[7] [18] [19] [20] [24] [61] [103].

The single best predictor of future violence is past violence[56]. Although this may be a useful index, it is easy to overpredict violence and detain harmless individuals who would not act out again[37]. Nevertheless, the fact remains: past violence predicts more violence.

A predisposition to violence can interact with alcohol abuse in individuals who are self indulgent and prone to act out their impulses. Alcoholism is a complicating treatment factor because the addiction itself must be treated in individuals who are not anxious to be helped. Further complications involve possible brain pathology and hormone chemistry. Finally, a small minority of rapists may be truly sadistic and erotically prefer violence over consenting intercourse. The latter group requires special treatment considerations as well. All of these factors could be weighted in an equation to predict violence and future rapes as follows:

A_1. History of Violence + A_2. Alcohol Abuse + A_3. Organic Factors (Brain pathology/testosterone) + A_4. Sadism = Future rape with Violence

where A_1, A_2, A_3, A_4 are mathematical constants that determine the relative importance of each factor. The more important the factor, the larger the mathematical constant. It would be gratifying if we could fill in the values in the equation now but there is so little research, we cannot do it. For the present, the clinician must rely on his intuitions and experience.

No mention has been made of the vague terms "mental illness" or "not guilty by reason of insanity", which have a bearing on the presentation of the psychiatric assessment before the courts. Generally, the sexually anomalous male is not mentally ill by anyone's definition[37]. However, in the case of rapists, this assessment is more complex and mental illness may be invoked as a defense for the patient. While the most frequent diagnosis is sociopathy or psychopathy, the complicating alcoholism, drug abuse and/or brain pathology may make it difficult in practice to distinguish the rapists from psychotic individuals (See Grinspoon and Bakalar[39]). It is therefore important that a thorough assessment be done which includes phallometric testing of erotic preferences, a complete Sex History Questionnaire and interview, extent of alcohol abuse (MAST scale is useful, See Skinner,[93] [94]) and drugs, serum testosterone as determined by a three blood samples and radioimmunoassay, prior crimes from the police record with special reference to violence both sexual and nonsexual assaults, other violence, brain pathology assessed by Reitan battery and CT-Scan if possible and a thorough neurological exam. Other psychological tests like the MMPI and PCR[49] [64] are also helpful. In this way, "mental illness" may be better defined and predicting future acting out may be clearer.

One thing is clear. Any treatment program for rape is complex. First and foremost, it generally needs to be directed to aggression management.

Behavior Therapy

Abel and his colleagues[3] have described a five point treatment program for rape: establishing an emphatic relationship with the rapist; confronting him with his responsibility for the rape; courtship skills training, enhance arousal to mature females; and reducing sexual arousal to rape. There are individual differences in the extent of deficits in the problem areas of rapists so that individual assessments are first carried out. They then apply a variety of behavior therapy methods: electrical aversion therapy, covert sensitization, heterosocial skills training, masturbatory conditioning, and assertive training. They tailored each treatment to the individual.

The aversion therapies have been described throughout the book and in the case of the rapist the conditioning stimulus would be rape cues followed by eletric shock or by an imagined unpleasant stimulus. Abel, Blanchard and Becker[3] do not spell out the exact stimuli they used in their study. Heterosocial skills training also involves increasing appropriate reactions to females. The skills developed can be tested "dating" prison staff within the institution. The remaining procedures are described in Chapter 3 but Abel and his colleagues offer no details on exactly what they are doing. Moreover they present no outcome data so an evaluation of their program must await further reports.

In reviewing the treatment literature on rape, only a couple of rapists or frotteurs treated with aversive conditioning can be found[90]. The long term effectiveness of the behavior therapy methods for rape therefore remains largely untried and uncertain.

Psychotherapy, Group Therapy and Prison Programs

At a 1977 conference in Memphis, Tennessee[4], most major programs for rapists in the United States and Canada were described. It would be evident to the uninitiated listener that there was considerable conviction and enthusiasm on the part of the speakers but that evaluations of the programs were either very poor or nonexistent. Moreover, we are uncertain in many cases whom they are treating under the rubrics "sexual offender" or "sexual aggressive."

Brancale and his co workers[15] at Rahway prison in New Jersey treated sex offenders and 23% were rapists but the majority appeared to be pedophilic. They believed group therapy is more effective than individual therapy because it is more successful and long lasting. Because the offenders are sexually ignorant, passive and inadequate, they also require a more directive approach including sex education. The authors believed that homogeneous groups are undesirable and may even be detrimental to treatment. The sex offense is understood only as symptomatic of an underlying problem. Emotional release is an essential part of treatment which involved marathon sessions. Continued contact and treatment for parolees were maintained. Over half the treated inmates were recommended for probation and an unspecified number were "highly successful".

Macdonald and Di Furia[53] also described a group treatment program with an 87% success rate. However, only those believed to be sufficiently motivated for treatment were selected. Each participant spent a minimum of 25 hours a week in the group. The basic precepts of the program are that sex behavior is learned and changeable, that, as in Alcoholics Anonymous, offenders can do much to help each other; that the treatment milieu must reflect and confront the realities of the community, and that a major goal of treatment is to give participants a sense of dignity which is progressively enhanced. Staff relate in a free, open, friendly, and honest way and expect the same in return from participants. As the program progresses, the men are given more responsibilities and liberties until they meet daily without staff.

Volunteers, male and female, meet weekly with group members. Men serve as role models and women participate in psychodrama. The latter is important in improving the social skills of the men. The program lasts at least a year and the men are gradually released to half way houses in the community. Wives and children are invited to become involved in the program.

Other programs or case studies[4][23][87] could be described but they would leave the same uncertainty about who is being treated and for what. The programs lack control measures and assessments are not reported at all. Clearly, sex history and phallometric measures are absent. The connection between the behavior of the sex offenders and the treatment is at best nonspecific. Recidivism rates for sex offences are low without any treatment and even violent offenders tend to outgrow their antisocial behavior by their late thirties[69]. Evaluation of the programs must consider differences in first and repeated offenders and indicate age at discharge as well as improving and reporting both assessment, treatment and group breakdowns in specific categories. As it now stands, nothing which is clear and replicable can be said about the psychotherapeutic treatment of rape.

Castration

An apparently easy solution to the problem of rape is castration which removes the testicles that produce the main source of testosterone in the male body. It would not matter that the rapist remained alcoholic or continued to display brain pathology. Castration should render him docile and presumably impotent so that his violent tendencies would be reduced and he would not rape again.

The uncontrolled studies of castration for "sex offenders" described in Chapter 3 have indicated a successful outcome. Unfortunately, the heterogeneity of the castrates is so great, it is difficult to draw conclusions about rape per se. There are no controlled studies of castration of rapists which leaves the question of recidivism open. Such a treatment certainly does not attempt to alter erotic preferences but rather attempts to remove erotic behavior altogether.

Unfortunately, there is a worrisome 1-in-5 cases of recidivism even several years after castration[5]. Moreover, in the one study examining penile erections to erotic stimuli after castration, half the sample of castrates could still have full erections. Heim[43] also reported that in a sample of 31 sex offenders including 12 rapists (39%) who were castrated and released into the community, 31% were still able to engage in sexual intercourse. The rapists were relatively more sexually active than homosexuals and pedophiles. Heim concluded that castration does not have an immediate effect on sexual behavior and appears to be most effective for men 46-to-59-years-old.

The physical health problems of castration have been noted in Chapter 3 with obesity and osteoporosis being problems of concern. The effectiveness of castration remains to be demonstrated. Heim and Hursch[44] concluded from a review of European literature that "there is no scientific or ethical basis for castration in the treatment of sex offenders.''

Chemotherapy

The use of antiandrogens such as provera has a distinct advantage over castration. Degenerative changes are reversible and perhaps more important, all testosterone production may be counteracted. When the testicles are removed, significant amounts of androgens can still be produced and sexual arousal is possible. With antiandrogen drugs, this is presumably not the case[35]. Unfortunately, cooperation by the patient is necessary but not always readily obtainable. Many therapists are unwilling to try this method on rapists.

Bancroft and his associates[8] examined the effectiveness of cyproterone acetate and ethinyl oestradiol on sexual arousal of 12 sex offenders. Six cases involved rape or sadism. Generally, the results suggested a reduction in a sexual interest and arousal with both drugs. Nevertheless, treatment was only for experimental purposes and no patient was released into the community.

Bierer and Van Someren[12] described a bizarre case of a 33-year-old schizoid patient who had obsessive thoughts of raping women. He was shy and retiring, usually locking himself in his room and having food delivered to him in a basket through the window. He had not worked for 15 years at the time of assessment. He was treated with stilboestrol. Although he never actually raped anyone, his desire to do so left him after treatment. A year later, he was mixing socially and interacting normally at home.

One may speculate on the effectiveness of these drugs generally as they influence ''sex offenders'' but there is no clear evaluation of rapists. Since the existing controlled studies on cyproterone acetate and provera question their effectiveness in reducing penile arousal, (see Chapter 10) caution is advised in trying them especially with aggressive sex offenders.

The rapist may also be considered a sexually normal male who is aggressive and a treatment program could be devised solely for his violent tendencies. Blumer and Migeon[13] found provera not only could reduce sexual drive but aggressiveness in temporal lobe epileptics and other behavior disorders.

Lithium carbonate used in the treatment of mania has also been found effective in reducing aggressiveness[91][92][98]. Sheard found that lithium increased serum leutinizing hormone while it did not change the level of testosterone. Aggression progressively diminished over a 3 month course of treatment. There was less fighting, threatening and fewer infractions of rules in the lithium group than in a placebo group. Sheard[91] has reviewed the promising work in this area but the reader should be cautioned that rape specifically was not studied and research participants remained incarcerated. One must also be concerned with side effects in all these drugs. Lion[51] has reviewed the literature on the variety of drugs used in treating aggression and has described the problems with each. He concluded that drug treatment should not obscure the need for verbal therapies.

Psychosurgery

Writers have long considered sexual behaviors to have a genital and a psychological component. Castration attempts to destroy the genital source of excitation whereas psychosurgery removes the brain matter presumably related to sexual arousal. Lobotomies and leucotomies have been used for a variety of problems, and they have been viewed as one approach to problems of aggression and presumably to rape as well[76]. Current techniques are refined so that only small areas of the brain are destroyed. The patient can be conscious during surgery and electrodes placed at various sites in the brain. The patient can report what has happened when a site is electrically stimulated. Presumably those sites associated with erotic fantasies control sexual behavior and these can be destroyed. The former rapist, in theory, should think little about sex.

For such a serious intervention into the human body, the research reports are so poor that they are ethically unsound[82]. It is immoral to subject human beings to risky procedures in a study which is so badly designed that its outcome is uncertain. We do not know for sure who had psychosurgery but it included some pedophiles, exhibitionists and homosexuals in treatments mostly carried out in Europe. Assessments, outcomes, methods and side effects are uncertain in many cases. Its effectiveness remains to be established but many communities are ethically opposed to this treatment so it is not likely to be widely used. We can say nothing about rape in this regard.

Treatment of Choice

I find it alarming and disturbing that so little effort, even misguided effort, has been directed to treating rapists (Table 12.2). Hundreds of studies exist on homosexuality now legal in many places while few studies exist on rapists. The former acts with the consent of his partner, the latter does not. The difference is striking and understandable in some ways. Rapists are difficult to deal with. They are dangerous and there are many problem of both informed consent[74] and releasing them into the community to test effectively the outcome of therapy. Their problems are multiple and difficult to deal with. Long term incarceration therefore seems like the most sensible goal to protect the community.

Nonetheless, there are several desirable goals in understanding and treating rapists. First, more controlled studies on alcohol and drug abuse, on brain pathology, sex hormones, erotic preferences and history of violence in sexually aggressive men need to be done to better understand

TABLE 12.2
Summary of Treatment Effectiveness for Rape and Sexual Aggression

Method	Results
1. Behavior Therapy	Untested
2. Psychotherapy and group therapy	Untested, sexually aggressive patients mixed with other offenders
3. Castration	Limited use. Unknown if more effective than untreated cases with only a prison term
4. Chemotherapy	Provera reduces sex drive but method depends on offender's cooperation in taking medication
5. Psychosurgery	No sound therapy available

what we are dealing with. A second step is prevention of rape by intervening early in the patient's behavior. It is clear that many rapists are abused children who may be socialized into an aggressive life style. Some attempts to prevent abuse are being made by changing the law but education in parenting and rethinking the value of the foster home may be helpful. Possibly, foster grandparents who are proven effective parents and who are near retirement or retired could find purpose in parenting and, at the same time, provide stable warm environments for the young abused child. Third, funds could be directed to develop adequate assessments of existing prison programs. Finally, rape can be prevented by the public at large. For example, hitchhiking is one factor in rape. Geller[33] in an interesting study examined the number of sexual offenses against hitchhikers prior to and during a transit strike in a large city. There was a dramatic increase in the number of sexual assaults during the strike when many women were forced to thumb a ride to and from work. He recommended several ways to prevent rape. Individuals should be warned not to hitchhike. This can be done by advertising or police visits to schools. Other methods are less practical or have been inadequately tested for their effectiveness, for example: recognize typical characteristics of rapists or make loud noises. Many Women's Centres and Rape Crisis Centres are up to date on the effectiveness of various methods of preventing rape and the interested readers may wish to consult one in their area.

Two features of the rapists are noteworthy in considering preventive measures: their tendency to violence and to abuse alcohol or drugs. Half of rapists are drinking at the time of their offense and so are a quarter of the victims. Some measures to avoid rape may come to the reader knowing this fact but excessive drinkers should clearly be avoided and not be permitted to be alone with a potential victim. Hostile men who may seem masculine and attractive to the inexperienced female should be avoided. A man who fights a lot or is a known fighter should also be avoided. Rape is just one aspect of his violence.

BIBLIOGRAPHY

1. Abel, G. G., Barlow, D. H., Blanchard, E. B., & Guild, D. The components of rapists' sexual arousal. *Archives of General Psychiatry,* 1977, *34,* 895–903.
2. Abel, G. G., Blanchard, E. B., Barlow, D. H., & Mavissakalian, M. Identifying specific erotic cues in sexual deviations by audio-taped descriptions. *Journal of Applied Behavior Analysis,* 1975, *8,* 244–260.
3. Abel, G., Blanchard, E., Becker, J. Psychological treatment of rapists in Walker, M. & Brodsky, S. (Eds.) *Sexual Assault,* Lexington, Mass.: Heath & Co., 1976.
4. Abel, G. Conference on Sexual Aggressives, Memphis, Tennessee, 1977. *TSA Newsletter,* 1977, *1.*
5. Anonymous. Castration of sex offenders. *British Medical Journal,* 1955, *1,* 897–898.
6. Armentrout, J. A., & Hauer, A. I. MMPIs of rapists of adults, rapists of children, and non-rapist sex offenders. *Journal of Clinical Psychology,* 1978, *34*(2), 330–332.
7. Bach-y-Rita, G., & Veno, G. Habitual violence: A profile of 62 men. *American Journal of Psychiatry,* 1974, *131*(9), 1015–1017.
8. Bancroft, J., Tennent, G., Loucas, K., & Cass, J. The control of deviant sexual behaviour by drugs: I. Behavioural changes following oestrogen and anti-androgens. *British Journal of Psychiatry,* 1974, *125,* 310–315.
9. Barbaree, H. E., Marshall, W. L., & Lanthier, R. D. Deviant sexual arousal in rapists. *Behavior Research & Therapy,* 1979, *17*(3), 215–222.
10. Barbaree, H. E., Marshall, W. L., Lightfoot-Barbaree, L. O., & Yates, E. *Alcohol intoxication and anti-social behavior: Two laboratory studies.* Paper presented at the Annual Meeting of the Ontario Psychological Association, 1979.
11. Bennett, R. M. A. H., & Carpenter, J. A. Alcohol and human physical aggression. *Quarterly Journal of Studies in Alcohol,* 1969, *30,* 870–876.
12. Bierer, J., & Van Someren, G. A. Stilboestrol in out-patient treatment of sexual offenders. *British Medical Journal,* 1950, *1,* 935–936.
13. Blumer, D., & Migeon, C. Hormone and hormonal agents in the treatment of aggression. *Journal of Nervous & Mental Disease,* 1975, *160*(2), 127–137.
14. Bowden, P. Rape. *British Journal of Hospital Medicine,* 1978, *20*(3), 286–290.
15. Brancale, R., Vuocolo, A., & Prendergast, W. E. The New Jersey program for sex offenders. In H. L. Resnik, & M. E. Wolfgang (Eds.), *Sexual behaviors: Social, clinical, and legal aspects.* Boston: Little, Brown & Co., 1972, 331–350.
16. Briddell, D. W., Rimm, D. C., Caddy, G. R., Krawitz, G., Sholis, D., & Wunderlin, R. J. Effects of alcohol and cognitive set on sexual arousal to deviant stimuli. *Journal of Abnormal Psychology,* 1978, *87*(4), 418–430.
17. Briddell, D. W., & Wilson, G. T. Effects of alcohol and expectancy set on male sexual arousal. *Journal of Abnormal Psychology,* 1976, *85*(2), 225–234.
18. Chase, M. M., & Krames, L. Situational determinants of violence and aggression. Ottawa Canada, Solititor General of Canada, 1977.
19. Climent, C. E., & Ervin, F. R. Historical data in the evaluation of violent subjects. *Archives of General Psychiatry,* 1972, *27,* 621–624.

20. Cocozza, J. J., & Steadman, H. J. Some refinements in the measurement and prediction of dangerous behavior. *American Journal of Psychiatry*, 1974, *131*(9), 1012–1014.

21. Coger, R. W., Dymond, M., Serafetinides, E. A., Lowensteam, I., & Pearson, D. EEG signs of brain impairment in alcoholism. *Biological Psychiatry*, 1978, *13*(6), 729–739.

22. Cohen, M. L., Garofalo, R., Boucher, R., & Seghorn, T. The psychology of rapists. *Seminars in Psychiatry*, 1971, *3*(3), 307–326.

23. Cook, G. H. Problem of the criminal sexual psychopath. *Diseases of the Nervous System*, 1949, *10*, 137–142.

24. Dix, G. E. Determining the continued dangerousness of psychologically abnormal sex offenders. *Journal of Psychiatry & Law*, 1975, *3*, 327–344.

25. Doering, C. H., Brodie, H. K. H., Kraemer, H., Becker, H., & Hamburg, D. A. Plasma testosterone levels and psychologic measures in men over a 2-month period. In R. C. Friedman, R. M. Richart, V. L. Vandoriete, & L. O. Stern (Eds.), *Sex differences in behavior*. New York: Wiley & Sons, 1974, 413–431.

26. Doering, C. H., Brodie, K. H., Kraemer, H. C., Moos, R. H., Becker, H. B., & Hamburg, D. A. Negative affect and plasma testosterone: A longitudinal human study. *Psychosomatic Medicine*, 1975, *37*(6), 484–491.

27. Ehrenkranz, J., Bliss, E., & Sheard, M. H. Plasma testosterone: Correlation with aggressive behavior and social dominance in man. *Psychosomatic Medicine*, 1974, *36*(6), 469–475.

28. Elliott, F. A. Neurological aspects of antisocial behavior. In W. H. Reid (Ed.), *The psychopath: A comprehensive study of antisocial disorders and behaviors*. New York: Brenner/Mazel, 1978, 146–158.

29. Farkas, G. M., & Rosen, R. C. Effect of alcohol on elicited male sexual response. *Journal of Studies on Alcohol*, 1976, *37*(3), 265–272.

30. Fisher, G., Rivlin, E. Psychological needs of rapists. *British Journal of Criminology*, 1971, *11*, 182–185.

31. Freund, K. Diagnosis and treatment of forensically significant anomalous erotic preferences. *Canadian Journal of Criminology & Corrections*, 1976, *18*(3), 181–189.

32. Gebhard, P. H., Gagnon, J. H., Pomeroy, W. B., & Christenson, C. V. *Sex offenders: An analysis of types*. London: Heinemann, 1965.

33. Geller, S. H. The sexually assaulted female: Innocent victim or temptress? *Canada's Mental Health*, 1977, *25*(1), 26–29.

34. Gibbens, T. C. N., Way, C., & Soothill, K. L. Behavioural types of rape. *British Journal of Psychiatry*, 1977, *130*, 32–42.

35. Golla, F. L., & Hodge, R. S. Hormone treatment of the sexual offender. *Lancet*, 1949, *1*, 1006–1007.

36. Greenland, C. *Dangerous sexual offenders in Canada*. Paper presented at the interdisciplinary meeting of Law, Psychiatry and Corrections, Royal Society of Medicine, London, 1971.

37. Greenland, C. Evaluation of violence and dangerous behavior associated with mental illness. *Seminars in Psychiatry*, 1971, *3*(3), 345–356.

38. Greenland, C. Psychiatry and the dangerous sexual offender. *Canadian Psychiatric Association Journal*, 1977, *22*, 155–159.

39. Grinspoon, L., & Bakalar, J. B. Drug abuse, crime, and the antisocial personality: Some conceptual issues. In W. H. Reid (Ed.), *The psychopath: A comprehensive study of antisocial disorders and behavior*. New York: Brunner/Mazel, 1978, 234–243.

40. Groth, A., & Birnbaum, H. *Men who rape: The psychology of the offender*. New York: Plenum Press, 1979.

41. Groth, A., Burgess, A. W., & Holmstrom, L. Rape: power, anger, and sexuality. *American Journal of Psychiatry,* 1977, *134*(11), 1239–1243.

42. Hartocollis, P. Drunkenness and suggestion: An experiment with intraveneous alcohol. *Quarterly Journal of Studies in Alcohol,* 1962, *23,* 376–389.

43. Heim, N. Sexual behavior of castrated sex offenders. *Archives of Sexual Behavior,* 1981, *10*(1), 11–19.

44. Heim, N., & Hursch, C. Castration for sex offenders: treatment or punishment? A review and critique of recent European literature. *Archives of Sexual Behavior,* 1979, *8*(3), 281–304.

45. Huesmann, L. R., Lefkowitz, M. M., & Eron, L. D. Sum of MMPI scales F, 4, and 9 as a measure of aggression. *Journal of Consulting and Clinical Psychology,* 1978, *46*(5), 1071–1078.

46. Karacan, I., Williams, R. L., Guerrero, M. W., Salis, P. J., Thornby, J. I., & Hursch, C. J. Nocturnal penile tumescence and sleep of convicted rapists and other prisoners. *Archives of Sexual Behavior,* 1974, *3*(1), 19–26.

47. Kercher, G. A., & Walker, C. E. Reactions of convicted rapists to sexually explicit stimuli. *Journal of Abnormal Psychology,* 1973, *81*(1), 46–50.

48. Kreuz, L. E., & Rose, R. M. Assessment of aggressive behavior and plasma testosterone in a young criminal population. *Psychosomatic Medicine,* 1972, *34*(4), 321–332.

49. Langevin, R., Paitich, D., & Russon, A. Are rapists sexually anomalous, aggressive, or both? *Archives of Sexual Behavior,* 1982 (In press).

50. Leaff, L. A. The antisocial personality: Psychodynamic implications. In W. H. Reid (Ed.), *The psychopath: A comprehensive study of antisocial disorders and behavior.* New York: Brunner/Mazel, 1978, 69–116.

51. Lion, J. R. Conceptual issues in the use of drugs for the treatment of aggression in man. *Journal of Nervous and Mental Disease,* 1975, *160*(2), 76–82.

52. Lothstein, L. M., & Jones, P. Discriminating violent individuals by means of various psychological tests. *Journal of Personality Assessment,* 1978, *42*(3), 237–243.

53. Macdonald, G. J., & Di Furia, G. A guided self-help approach to the treatment of the habitual sex offender. *Hospital and Community Psychiatry,* 1971, *22,* 34–37.

54. McDonald, A., Paitich, D. Rape: an examination of psychological test findings. Unpublished manuscript. *Clarke Institute of Psychiatry,* Toronto, 1978.

55. McCreary, C. P. Trait and type differences among male and female assaultive and nonassaultive offenders. *Journal of Personality Assessment,* 1976, *40*(6), 617–621.

56. Megargee, E. I. The prediction of dangerous behavior. *Criminal Justice and Behavior,* 1976, *3*(1), 3–22.

57. Megargee, E. I., Cook, P. E., & Mendelsohn, G. A. Development and validation of an MMPI scale of assaultiveness in over-controlled individuals. *Journal of Abnormal Psychology,* 1967, *72*(6), 519–528.

58. Mello, N. K., & Mendelson, J. H. Alcohol and human behavior. In *Handbook of Psychopharmacology,* Iversen, L. L., Iversen, S. D., & Snyder, S. H. (Eds.). New York: Plenum Press, 1978.

59. Mendelson, J. H. Endocrines and aggression. *Psychopharmacology Bulletin,* 1977, *13*(1), 22–23.

60. Meyer-Bahlburg, H. F., Boon, D. A., Sharma, M., & Edwards, J. A. Aggressiveness and testosterone measures in man. *Psychosomatic Medicine,* 1974, *36*(3), 269–274.

61. Mesnikoff, A. M., & Lauterbach, C. G. The association of violent dangerous behavior with psychiatric disorders: A review of the research literature. *Journal of Psychiatry & Law,* 1975, *3,* 415–445.

62. Monti, P. M., Brown, W. A., & Corriveau, D. P. Testosterone and components of aggressive and sexual behavior in man. *American Journal of Psychiatry,* 1977, *134*(6), 692–694.

63. Munroe, R. R. *Brain Dysfunction in Aggressive Criminals,* Lexington, Massachusetts, Lexington Books, 1978.

64. Paitich, D., & Langevin, R. The Clarke Parent Child Relations Questionnaire: a clinically useful test for adults. *Journal of Consulting and Clinical Psychology,* 1976, *44,* 428–436.

65. Paitich, D., Langevin, R., Freeman, R., Mann, K., & Handy, L. The Clarke SHQ: a clinical sex history questionnaire for males. *Archives of Sexual Behavior,* 1977, *6,* 421–436.

66. Panton, J. H. Personality differences appearing between rapists of adults, rapists of children and non-violent sexual molesters of female children. *Research Communications in Psychology, Psychiatry, and Behaviour,* 1978, *3*(4), 385–393.

67. Persky, H., O'Brien, C. P., Fine, E., Howard, W. J., Khan, M., & Beck, R. W. The effect of alcohol and smoking on testosterone function and aggression in chronic alcoholics. *American Journal of Psychiatry,* 1977, *134*(6), 621–625.

68. Persky, H., Smith, K. D., & Basu, G. K. Relation of psychologic measures of aggression and hostility to testosterone production in man. *Psychosomatic Medicine,* 1971, *33*(3), 265–277.

69. Pincus, J. H., & Tucker, G. J. Violence in children and adults: A neurologic view. *American Academy of Child Psychiatry,* 1978, *17*(2), 277–288.

70. Quinsey, V. L. Assessments of the dangerousness of mental patients held in maximum security. *International Journal of Law and Psychiatry,* 1979, *2,* 389–406.

71. Quinsey, V. L., Arnold, L. S., & Pruesse, M. G. MMPI profiles of men referred for a pre-trial psychiatric assessment as a function of offense type. *Journal of Clinical Psychology,* 1980, *36,* 410–417.

72. Quinsey, V. L., Chaplin, T., & Varney, G. A comparison of rapists' and non-sex offenders' sexual preferences for mutually consenting sex, rape, and sadistic acts. *Behavioral Assessment,* 1981, *3,* 127–135.

73. Rada, R. T. Alcoholism and forcible rape. *American Journal of Psychiatry,* 1975, *132*(4), 444–446.

74. Rada, R. T. Legal aspects in treating rapists. *Criminal Justice and Behavior,* 1978, *5*(4), 369–378.

75. Rada, R. T. Sociopathy and alcohol abuse. In W. H. Reid (Ed.), *The psychopath: A comprehensive study of antisocial disorders and behaviours.* New York: Brunner/Mazel, 1978, 223–233.

76. Rada, R. T. *Clinical Aspects of the Rapist.* New York: Grune and Stratton, 1978.

77. Rada, R. T., Kellner, R., Laws, D. R., & Winslow, W. W. Drinking, alcoholism, and the mentally disordered sex offender. *Bulletin of the American Academy of Psychiatry and the Law,* 1978, *6*(3), 296–300.

78. Rada, R. T., Laws, D. R., & Kellner, R. Plasma testosterone levels in the rapist. *Psychosomatic Medicine,* 1976, *38,* 257–268.

79. Rader, C. M. MMPI profile types of exposers, rapists, and assaulters in a court services population. *Journal of Consulting and Clinical Psychology,* 1977, *45*(1), 61–69.

80. Rankin, J. G., Orrego-Matte, H., Deschenes, J., Medline, A., Findlay, J. E., & Armstrong, A. I. Alcoholic liver disease: The problem of diagnosis. *Alcoholism: Clinical and Experimental Research,* 1978, *2*(4), 327–338.

81. Reid, W. H. Diagnosis of antisocial syndromes. In W. H. Reid (Ed.), *The psychopath: A comprehensive study of antisocial disorders and behaviors.* New York: Brunner/Mazel, 1978.

82. Rieber, I., & Sigusch, V. Psychosurgery on sex offenders and sexual "deviants" in West Germany. *Archives of Sexual Behavior,* 1979, *8*(6), 523–528.

83. Rose, R. Testosterone, aggression and homosexuality: a review of the literature and implications for future research. In *Topics on Psychoendocrinology,* Sachar, E. J.

(Ed.). New York: Grune and Stratton, 1975.

84. Rubin, B. Prediction of dangerousness in mentally ill criminals. *Archives of General Psychiatry*, 1972, *27*, 397–407.

85. Rubin, H. B., & Henson, D. E. Effects of alcohol on male sexual responding. *Psychopharmacology*, 1976, *47*, 123–134.

86. Ruff, C. F., Templer, D. I., Ayers, J. L. The intelligence of rapists. *Archives of Sexual Behavior*, 1976, *5*(4), 327–329.

87. Sadoff, R. L. Treatment of violent sex offenders. *International Journal of Offender Therapy and Comparative Criminology*, 1975, *19*, 75–80.

88. Scaramella, T. J., Brown, W. A. Serum testosterone and aggressiveness in hockey players. *Psychosomatic Medicine*, 1978, *40*(3), 262–265.

89. Selkin, J. Rape. *Psychology Today*, 1975, *8*(8), 71–76.

90. Serber, M., & Wolpe, J. Behavior therapy techniques. In H. L. Resnik, & M. E. Wolfgang (Eds.), *Sexual behaviors: Social, clinical, and legal aspects*. Boston: Little, Brown & Co., 1972, 239–254.

91. Sheard, M. H. Lithium in the treatment of aggression. *Journal of Nervous and Mental Disease*, 1975, *160*(2), 108–118.

92. Sheard, M. H., Marini, J. L., & Giddings, S. S. The effect of lithium on luteinizing hormone and testosterone in man. *Diseases of the Nervous System*, 1977, *38*(10), 765–769.

93. Skinner, H. A. A multivariate evaluation of the Michigan alcoholism screening test. *Journal of Studies in Alcohol*, 1979, *40*(9), 319–325.

94. Skinner, H. A. *"What if you ask a simple qustion?"*: *An evaluation of alcohol use scales*. Addiction Research Foundation Substudy No. 1012, Toronto, Canada, 1978.

95. Spellacy, F. Neuropsychological differences between violent and nonviolent adolescents. *Journal of Clinical Psychoogy*, 1977, *33*(4), 966–969.

96. Spellacy, F. Neuropsychological discrimination between violent and nonviolent men. *Journal of Clinical Psychology*, 1978, *34*(1), 49–52.

97. Tennent, T. G. The dangerous offender. *British Journal of Hospital Medicine*, 1971, *6*, 269–274.

98. Tupin, J. P., Smith, D. B., Clanon, T. L., Kim, L. I., Nugent, A., & Groupe. A. The long-term use of lithium in aggressive prisoners. *Comprehensive Psychiatry*, 1973, *14*(4), 311–317.

99. Van Thiel, D. H., & Lester, R. Sex and alcohol. *New England Journal of Medicine*, 1974, *291*(5), 251–253.

100. Vera, H., Barnard, G. W., & Holzer, C. The intelligence of rapists: New data. *Archives of Sexual Behavior*, 1979, *8*(4), 375–378.

101. Wechsler, D. *Manual of the Wechsler Adult Intelligence Scale*. New York: The Psychological Corporation, 1955.

102. Williams, D. Neural factors related to habitual aggression. *Brain*, 1969, *92*, 503–520.

103. Williams, W., & Miller, K. S. The role of personal characteristics in perceptions of dangerousness. *Criminal Justice and Behavior*, 1977, *4*(3), 241–252.

104. Wilson, G. T. Alcohol and human sexual behavior. *Behavior Research and Therapy*, 1977, *15*, 239–252.

13 Sadism and Masochism

INTRODUCTION

Sadism and masochism are paradoxical conditions in which erotic gratification is obtained in association with humiliation, enslavement, domination and even with physical pain. The sadist is the donor and the masochist is the recipient of the degrading or cruel acts. The two anomalies are often thought to be fused in one person so that the term sadomasochism is used. Gebhard[17] claimed that partners are so difficult to find, that sadists must take turns being the masochist. This presupposes a preference for the sadism and explains both behaviors in the same person. Sack and Miller[42] on the other hand indicated that the interchangeability of the two behaviors has not been demonstrated satisfactorily in case material.

Sadism and masochism are rather loosely applied terms which entail not only sexual pleasure in pain but a wide range of nonsexual and cruel acts (cf. Panken[37]). Siomopoulos and Goldsmith[45] have reviewed and classified the various forms of nonsexual sadism. They note that it may be associated with sexual and aggressive drives and neuroses but also in nonsexual ways with psychosis, seizures, and, as a characterological trait. In some cases, it is not clear if the sadistic act is erotic. Lust-murder falls between the two extremes of sexual and nonsexual sadism. Usually the victim is mutilated and parts of the body may even be eaten. In rape-murder sexual assault is clearly involved but in lust-murder it is not. Lust-murder may involve generalized excitement or perhaps masturbation, but not always, so this rare act may be nonerotic. It is uncertain if all sadistic and masochistic acts have a common etiology but in any case, the material of this chapter is restricted to sexual sadism and masochism. More attention has been directed in the professional literature to masochism in which aggression is directed inwards. Perhaps sadism has received less attention because hurting another seems more logical than hurting oneself. The two anomalies are considered in turn.

THE THEORIES

Masochism

The obvious question about masochism is how pain can be pleasurable. The major theories are psychoanalytic and have been reviewed by Lowenstein[26], Brenner[5] and Sach and Miller[42]. Freud noted that pain itself is not pleasurable but that it is a *condition* allowing sexual release to follow. The masochist experiences considerable guilt about his sexual desires and must protect himself against that guilt. The sexual partner therefore has control of him either by tying him up or abusing and ordering him around, forcing him to comply with socially unacceptable demands. This relieves the masochist of the responsibility for whatever happens and he is free to enjoy the sex. *Mr. A* who was a masochist described one of his favourite fantasies which illustrate this theory:

> *Mr. A:* "I would like to be abducted by three young women, around eighteen or nineteen years old, who would grab me off the street and throw me in the back of a car. They might even tie me up so I wouldn't be able to get away. They would drive me out to a country house or some place no one was around so I couldn't get away even if I wanted to. Then they take me into the house and throw me on the floor. They are in high leather boots which they force me to lick. They make me perform all sorts of sexual things like licking their privates. They tell me I had better do it or I'll be sorry. One takes out a whip and threatens me, telling me to kiss the others' asses or she will beat me mercilessly. Then the one with the whip jumps on my private and pumps away until she is satisfied. Then they untie me and let me go."

Mr. A described his abduction with such relish that one does not appreciate any pain on his part.

Psychoanalysts explain the protective nature of masochism in that control is exercised over the sadist partner, a symbol of the parent, and this offers him a sense of omnipotence. Passive aggression, such as sulking, can be quite controlling for the helpless child and it may be the genesis of masochism. The basic aggressiveness of such behavior shows how sadism and masochism have a common root. Masochism is simply the weapon of the weak[26].

The fear of the masochist is the fear of incest and/or castration. The passivity and helplessness he enacts may reflect an implicit appeal to the mercy of the threatening and protective parental figure[5][26]. The threats and punishment used are more or less veiled threats of castration according to Lowenstein[26]. They reenact childhood situations in which sexual fantasies, erotic games or attempts to sexually approach the forbidden, especially mother, were met with real or imagined disapproval, threat and/or punishment. By reliving the scene, the castration threat is annulled and the threat rebuffed. One can also conceptualize this as identifying with the aggressor. By taking on their characteristics, in one way he controls them. It is a way of aiming to actively master a passively experienced danger[26].

A second psychoanalytic hypothesis is that masochism is a feminine-passive genital wish toward the father, regressively experienced as being beaten. Such wishes have been considered determining factors in transvestism and transsexualism. Possibly masochists do not like the culturally stereotyped sex roles and desire to switch. The pain and humiliation may be a precondition to allow him to play the female role which he can surreptitiously enjoy. *Mr. B* expressed a desire for passivity in his sex role which psychoanalysts equate with femininity. In describing sex with his wife, he noted:

> *Mr. B:* "I don't necessarily want her to be boss but to take the initiative—seduce me. But she doesn't. I always start sex. It would be nice if she would come up and kiss me or touch me sexually. I would like her to get on top sometimes when we make love but she doesn't like it".

Another way to describe masochism in psychoanalytic theory is in terms of the three parts of the human psyche; id, ego and superego. The id is the storehouse of instinctive impulses, our needs for food, sex, and so forth, and it is present at birth. The ego is the executive of the personality, our cognitions and perceptual apparatus which mediates between the id and the real world. These two functions appear first, and later the superego develops, which is the internal representative of society. Our conscience punishes us with guilt for wrong doing and our ego ideal praising us for doing good. These constitute the two aspects of the superego. The three divisions of the psyche develop differently and we may experience pleasure in one part and pain in another concurrently. Thus masochism may be pleasurable genital gratification for the id but a painful experience in the superego[26]. Freud later modified this theory to note that masochism was a manifestation of the death instinct[5]. We all have an impulse to self-destruction which may be manifested in suicide attempts or masochism.

A learning theory of masochism. Lowenstein[26] had described what might be labelled a social learning theory of masochism. Parents engage their children in games which involve threat or mild pain but which are followed by loving attention. The child is chased, grabbed and hugged or scared by a hiding parent, tickled, poked, hit in banter, teased or thrown, all followed by laughter, attention and love. Lowenstein noted that the threat is followed by its pleasurable removal and it is well known how eagerly children wish to repeat these games. The parental attention and loving can stamp in or reinforce these mildly masochistic acts. In fact, Brenner[5] argued we are all masochistic in varying degrees and it is a fine line between normal and pathological acts.

Even the extremely sadistic parent may not be rejected by the child. Children's Aid Workers are familiar with cases in which children want to be with their parents in spite of beatings and hospitalizations. The sadism is a form of loving which the child perceives in spite of the punishment.

Laboratory studies[11] [19] have suggested that punishment may be instrumental to reward. In fact research animals and humans will work harder under punishing conditions for escape or reward. Aronfreed[2] noted that if punishment is very aversive and inconsistent, it may actually cause the child to pursue the punishment to "get it over with" since the tension of waiting is so great. The behavior to be eliminated may be increased in frequency by punishment. For example, punishing running away may increase its frequency because it is a response that naturally occurs from the punishment.

Distinguishing pleasure and pain. Few psychoanalysts have explicitly questioned the nature of pain itself but Freud suggested that any sensation including pain may give rise to pleasure when they reach a certain intensity; beyond this limit they are only painful. If we examine any sensation such as sound, there is a lower limit of intensity which we do not perceive (subliminal). At some narrow range of intensity (threshold or limen) we start to perceive the sound. As it increases in intensity it can be more or less pleasurable until it gets so intense it is painful. At that extreme intensity our brain, especially the reticular activation system, has difficulty modulating the input and it can be painful even causing tissue damage. There are wide individual differences in the threshold of awareness and of pain. It is perhaps that pain for the normal individual is not perceived in this way by masochists. By way of analogy, a discotheque may be very unpleasantly loud and visually annoying for one person but a pleasant experience for another. So with apparent pain and sex. A number of activities are painful, pain relieving and pleasurable, such as scratching, teeth grinding and biting[26]. These easily fit Freud's formulation. However, pain and pleasure may be fused together at high intensity, as in the experience of childbirth. For some mothers only the pain is manifest but for others it is the greatest experience of their lives. One could argue this is masochism because of the ultimate link of childbirth with sexual intercourse but the fusion of pain and pleasure appear to be physical experiences in themselves akin to masochism but nonsexual in nature and not necessarily related to guilt. Freud believed that in infancy any increase in psychic tension, even as painful stimulation produced sexual responses. An unusual constitutional predisposition in this respect may result in later masochism[5].

Pain and imprinting.   One may wish to invoke an imprinting process to explain masochism. In childhood the connection of pain and sexual arousal are likely and they may become inextricably intertwined. However, later in life they are resistant to change because a critical period of association has passed. This phenomenon has been observed in birds and may occur in humans. Punishment of behavior during imprinting has the paradoxical effect of increasing approaches to the mother. Thus if one tried to prevent following the mother by shocking baby chicks, the behavior would occur all the more, an apparently masochistic behavior[21][42]. Moreover when one interferes with early postnatal sensory experiences, bizarre masochistic-like behaviors emerge. Melzach and Scott[34] found that early sensory deprivation of puppies was correlated with lack of escape or avoidance of noxious stimuli. The dogs were deprived of light and tactile stimulation while in sensory isolation. Upon release from the experience, the experimenter could pat them with one hand and shock them with the other and they would not run away like other dogs. However, blindness in some cases may have been a factor in results of the sensory deprivation studies.

Arousal theory.   Activation or arousal theory[12] may explain masochism. There are three postulates of interest here. Humans strive to maintain an optimal level of stimulation to their bodies. The Reticular Activation System[36] controls the inputs. If too much stimulation is coming in, it reduces the flow of nerve impulses from the sense organs to the cortex, reducing its overall impact. The second postulate is that many behaviors are a curvilinear function of the arousal level. If one is not alert, as when awakened from a sleep, behavior is poorly organized and coordinated; performance is poor. As alertness increases up to a point, performance improves. However, if one is hyperalert as in anxiety states, performance again becomes disorganized and poor. The third postulate was basically similar to Freud's theory, that is, different sources of stimulation could add together to affect overall arousal. Presumably having sexual intercourse with lights on and the radio playing can be more stimulating than the same behavior in darkness and silence. Similarly pain and sexual stimulation should summate to produce better sexual performance, up to a point, and then interfere with it. For arousal-activation theory, the nature of the additional stimulation is irrelevant. Pain or anything else may enhance the sexual experience. No further etiological explanation is necessary. Chance or accidental association of the two may be sufficient explanation.

Defining pain. Freud also hinted at another factor influencing masochism; constitutional predispositions or individual differences. Melzack[32] [33] who has conducted the most extensive empirical work to date on pain noted that it is not a fixed response to a hurting stimulus. Its perception is influenced by our experiences, our expectations, and our culture. Most important he noted that pain is usually not defined by researchers and that it is a private experience. Since pain is such a subjective experience, is what we label pain experienced by the masochist as painful? Being bound by ropes has been labeled "helpless" which is an undesirable state for many. Being told you are going to have sex or be whipped may be seen as threatening. However, "helpless" may be equated rather with "being held" or "being contained" and the threat of whipping may be perceived as "desirability". *Mr. C* who had fantasies of a woman in leather boots with a whip forcing him to have sex with her described it this way:

> *Mr. C:* The whip is not so much to hurt me as to show me she means what she says. She is in charge. She really wants me to have sex with her and she will go to any extent to get it. I guess she is so turned on by me, she can't help herself and she will have me at any price.

Mr. C's sexual history revealed a longstanding inferiority with respect to women which may be considered reflected in his fantasy. One can perceive guilt in his desires but it is almost as if he had a different social convention for relating with women.

The variable nature of pain is illustrated (1) by major surgery carried out under hypnosis, (2) by soldiers who are happy in spite of wounds, because they will now be taken to safety and, (3) by the relief of a wrist slasher who experienced unbearable tension before cutting himself[42]. In the latter case tension is reduced rather than induced as we expect. Social convention is also a factor in what is labeled painful or insulting. This is illustrated by the Eskimo husband who is expected to offer his wife to guests[15]. Adultery does not arouse jealousy or anger. Rather, the husband would be insulted if a male guest refused to take his wife. Such behavior in our culture as seen in triolism, or folie a trois, is considered pathological. The Eskimo thinks of his wife as his property which he can give or share, nothing more. We consider the masochist to experience jealousy and degradation by letting another man copulate with his wife in his presence, typical of Western man's feeling but some other social convention may be operative.

Sadism

Pain as instrumental.   The sadist might receive pleasure from indignant anger at the sexually provocative behaviour of his partner or of a masochist. The exhibitionist, *Mr. F* (page 327) displayed such an attitude. He would expose to sleezily dressed attractive young women who "could not handle their sexuality". By exposing to them, he "taught them a lesson. They got what they deserved". One can find examples of such righteous indignation in the popular *Boccaccio* or *The Grapes of Wrath*. One senses through the righteousness that the sexual wish is satisfied at the same time. The sadist like the masochist can also be construed as relieving his own guilt through projecting the sexual wish to the other person. The masochist says "He/she is forcing me to have sex and is hurting me, I will comply", whereas the sadist says "I'll punish this evil person for their sexual impulse by making sex unpleasant for them." However, some theorists do not conceive of the pain, humiliation, and so forth, as instrumental but as sexually pleasurable in themselves.

Pain as a goal in itself. Karpman[22][23] described excessive acts of sadism, including necrophilia, in which sexual gratification is obtained with corpses. The dead body may be violated or the victim may first be killed and then violated by rape, mutilation, or eating (necrophagy). It is the total passivity and helplessness of the corpse which arouses the necrophile and in this way parallels other acts of sadism. Such acts are not necessarily associated with masochism but, according to Karpman, almost always are associated with psychosis or epilepsy which was not previously recognized.

The agonistic behavior of animals appears to bear a relationship to sadism. They may express aggression and sexual arousal concomitantly. In the mating of the stickleback fish, the male becomes increasingly hostile to females as courtship progresses. Since the male will court several females, the last one he mates may be treated with considerablae aggression as his mating urge subsides (cf. Tinbergen, [48]).

Organic factors in sadism. In humans, the sex hormone, testosterone, has been associated with both sexual arousal and aggression. If it is injected into the human body, heightened sexual arousal results. On the other hand, violent individuals may have excessive amounts of testosterone in the bloodstream although other factors are also primary in aggressivity (See Chapter 12). In the sadistic rapist, the fusion of sexual and aggressive drives may be prominent. Thus constitutional predispositions, the nature of the human brain and/or other organic factors may be significant in sadism as well as in other sexual anomalies. Temporal lobe dysfunction in the brain has also been linked to aggressive outbursts and sexual arousal. Possibly a disorder of this sort underlies both sadism and masochism.

Sadomasochism

Karpman[23] noted that sadism and masochism have been considered manifestations of the same instinct. In sadism, the object of the inflicted pain is someone else whereas in masochism the object is oneself. The painful infliction is an end in itself and it relieves inner tension or anxiety. The sadist does to others what he fears will be done to him. The masochist needs punishment and suffering as sexual experiences. In its extreme this could result in suicide. The logic seems reasonable in the sadist: "I'll get you before you get me" but not for the masochist or sadomasochist who lets the partner punish him. Yet the self-castrating behavior of the masochist is specifically invoked to annul castration threats. By the very act of sexual gratification in conjunction with the threat behavior, he triumphs by showing he still has orgasm.

The sadist and masochist may grow up in a culturally deviant family which models the sexual behavior involving cruelty, seductiveness and restriction simultaneously[5]. The behavior may be especially prominent in the mothers.

A modelling theory offers an easy explanation of why sadism and masochism occur in the same person. Their behavior is unconventional but it is still a reciprocation. Normal sexual interaction may be described as: "You stimulate me in ways I like and I'll do the same to you." Partners may take turns stimulating and receiving stimulation. The reciprocity may also be true of sadists and masochists who after all do have a relationship.

The importance of make believe. The behaviors enacted in sadomasochism are very much prescribed, make believe and agreed upon by the partners. Exceeding those limits may mean the end of the relationship[13 17 26]. *Mr. B* was basically a masochist who attempted to induce his wife to step on him and abuse him as preludes to sexual intercourse. However, he only "wanted her to be boss" in a sexual context and in other respects wanted to be boss himself. When asked what would happen if she really hurt him or tried to do so while having sex, he said: "I wouldn't like it. I wouldn't let it happen. Sometimes my fantasies run away but I end them before I can really be harmed. Even in my imagination."

Aggression underlying sadomasochism. Glover[18] has argued that aggressive and libidinal impulses are antagonistic and one inhibits the other. Aggressive reactions on the part of male or female will inhibit sexual drive during intercourse. The reverse may be true as well. One function of sexual arousal is to cancel unconscious guilt and sadism. In the sadomasochist this apparently fails. The clinical evidence for these postulates are lacking, Glover noted, but he suggested directions for research.

Stoller[47] has suggested that aggression underlies all sexual "perversions" and calls them erotic forms of hatred. Thus sadism need not be centered out.

Menninger[35] has suggested that the erotic object in sadomasochism is unimportant and the responses themselves are primary. Thus man, woman, boy, girl is immaterial, the humiliation, and so forth, are ends in themselves.

The majority of theories of sadism and masochism are psychoanalytic in origin. Collectively they suffer from two major problems. First, the notion of instinct is difficult to operationalize, that is, to test empirically. Particularly the death instinct has been criticized and generally has been ignored more recently by psychoanalysts themselves[26]. However all the instincts in Freudian theory have the same problem: they are names for classes of behavior which have been given motivational significance. Empirical referents get lost in discussions which tend to be overgeneralizations from the concepts. Second, sadism and masochism lack clear empirical referents. The two anomalies have been considered etiologically the same. All masochistic acts are basically sadistic, only the object is different. One aggresses against himself instead of others. However, one can find both behaviors in the same person. If one asks how to empirically separate masochism and sadism according to these definitions, it is not possible. However, it would seem that aggressive acts against the self, if that is in fact what masochism entails, are different from such acts against others but psychoanalytic theory allows no clear way to separate the two behaviors.

THE EXPERIMENTAL EVIDENCE

In spite of extensive interest in sadism and masochism, the facts are very few indeed. There are no systematic or controlled studies examining sex history or phallometric reactions. This is in part due to the rarity of the anomalies. Nevertheless some facts are suggestive.

Co-occurrence of sadism and masochism. Sadism and masochism are presumably interchangeable. Sach and Miller indicate this fact is not often demonstrated in case reports. Shore and his associates[44] developed a 100 item questionnaire to sample theoretically postulated behaviors in masochism. The validation data was collected on 146 general psychiatric patients and then examined on 26 masochists. The term masochism was used in a general sense and only 7 were clearly sexual masochists. It is not certain how many were males. However in none of the 26 cases was sadism described supporting the hypothesis that the two are distinct.

The largest sample to date, 243 respondants, was reported by Spengler[46] in West Germany. He collected data from sadomasochism clubs and sent questionnaires out in response to newspapers contact ads seeking partners for sadomasochism. The question used to classify respondants was "Do you prefer the active role (lord, master, teacher) or the passive role (servant, slave, pupil) in sadomasochistic sex?"

About a third each of the group was heterosexual, homosexual and bisexual. In the total sample, 13% were exclusive sadists and 16% exclusive masochists but an additional 19% were versatile although mainly sadistic and 22% were versatile but mainly masochistic. Only 29% were fully versatile or sadomasochistic. One can interpret the versatile groups as mainly favoring the hypothesis that sadism and masochism tend to co-occur since 70% are versatile. On the other hand if one accepts Gebhard's statement that partners are hard to come by and one must play both roles, one can group "sadist", and "mainly sadist" for 32% and "masochist", and "mainly masochist" for 38%, suggesting that the majority are one or the other. In any case, about a third are exclusively active or passive and one can expect the behaviors to be independent in some patients.

Pain and humiliation as sexually arousing.   A second question which has been indirectly studied is whether inflicting pain is sexually arousing. Although no clearly defined sadists have been studied, rapists have been compared to nonrapist controls on penile reactions to rape, consenting intercourse, non sexual violence and neutral stimuli. The various detailed results have been described in Chapter 12. It can be concluded from those studies that violence itself is not sexually arousing. Rather, rape is sexually arousing in spite of the force which may be used. Normal men can be sexually aroused by rape descriptions as well.

It has also been postulated that exhibitionists are engaging in sadistic behavior, the aim of this anomaly being to shock, humiliate or embarrass the female victim. Detailed results are described in Chapter 10. The exhibitionists studied did react to exposing with such outcomes but not differently from normal controls. They also reacted more to positive responses from women, that is, to the sexually aroused female or to a female exposing. Reactions to violence without sex did not differ from those to neutral stimuli. It seems that the use of physical pain is not sexually arousing to rapists, exhibitionists or normals but the use of psychical pain aroused both exhibitionists and controls alike. In a sex history questionnaire, exposing frequency and orgasm was not related to sadistic or masochistic acts, namely, physically hurting, humiliating, or embarrassing someone; having this done to you; threatening or frightening someone; having this done to you; beating someone; being beaten; seeing someone unconscious or unable to move. The foregoing results can only be considered suggestive since there is little evidence that either rapists or exhibitionists in general are sexual sadists. Aggression or sadism as a general theme underlying all sexual anomalies does not appear to be the case.

Kotzwarraism.   Resnik[40], Dietz[10] and Knight[24] have summarized case reports of masochism which suggest a link of sexual arousal to true pain and danger. These cases of eroticized repetitive hangings currently called Kotzwarraism after a Czech musician Katzwarra who practiced the behavior, resulted in accidental death. The erotic nature of the acts was inferred from evidence of masturbation or orgasm by the presence of semen, partial or complete nudity, pornographic literature, and at times the presence of female attire. The accidental nature of the deaths was inferred because there was no apparent motive to die. Ropes, belts and other binding materials were arranged to produce compression on the neck but they could be controlled voluntarily. The behavior was repetitive and done so it left no visible marks. The adolescents or young men who performed these acts alone bound their bodies, feet and hands or genitals with ropes, chains or leather.

Resnik noted that in criminal hangings erection and spontaneous emission occur. The lumbar cord reflex center of the nervous system controls erection and ejaculation. Both excitation and inhibition are involved and after hanging, the inhibitory impulses are ineffective. In eroticized hangings, the constriction of the neck reduces blood flow to the brain resulting in giddiness, lightheadedness and exhilaration which reinforce masturbation sensations. Although no dynamics can be derived from verbal interaction in these cases, Resnik postulated that they are eroticizing dying which comes about in an attempt to escape overwhelming anxiety and depression. Of course psychoanalytic themes are possible explanations as well.

Shankel and Carr[43] and Edmondson[14] have described living cases of eroticized hanging. Shankel and Carr's patient was psychopathic and hanged himself and dressed simultaneously in female attire for erotic pleasure. Although psychoanalytic interpretations are possible, the patient stressed his curiosity about a variety of sexual matters, discovering the erotic pleasure of hanging by chance and subsequently repeated it.

Edmondson's patient was almost uneducable and his Stanford Binet IQ was between 75 and 85. Guilt appeared to play a role in his erotic hangings because he used the rope to hamper his state of consciousness in order to prevent awareness of his masturbation activities. His feelings of guilt may have led to a need to punish himself.

In general the "pain" is sadism and masochism may be considered non-painful to the experiencing individual. Self injurious behavior generally may serve to increase sensory input[3] or to establish "body reality"[8]. Melzack[32][33] has described anecdotal and experimental evidence to show that people attach variable meanings to pain producing situations and these meanings greatly influence the degree and quality of pain they feel. One common assumption is obviously not true; that is, the biological value of pain is to signal tissue damage and the greater the pain the more damage there is. The topic of general pain cannot be discussed in detail here and the interested reader may wish to read Melzack's pioneering writings. This literature does suggest that the masochist may not experience pain even from stimuli ordinarily perceived as painful. No direct studies of pain thresholds in masochists have been done.

Masochism and feminine gender identity.   Psychoanalytic theory suggests that masochism is associated with a wish to be female. One might then expect it to occur more often in transsexuals or transvestites. Only one study addresses this question and it is noted in Chapter 6. Basically transsexuals say they do not have masochistic desires in wanting sex reassignment surgery. Rather they show extreme feminine gender identity.

Biological and miscellaneous factors.   There are no existing personality or biological studies in sadism or masochism. Evidence reviewed in Chapter 12 on rape indicates that there is a positive association of serum testosterone levels and aggression in criminals but not necessarily in sexual sadists. Studies of brain pathology in sadomasochism have yet to be done.

Menninger's interesting suggestion that the stimulus person is not important in sadomasochism has been partially refuted by Spengler's sample of 245 men. They tended to classify themselves as heterosexual, bisexual or homosexual. However we do not know if they would interact with children or what their actual sex histories were. They showed a predominant preference for cane, whip, bonds and for leather and boots. Only 15% climaxed exclusively via sadomasochistic practices while 45% could do so without them. Their data indicated that 78% think their sexual orientation is different from the ordinary but acceptable and less than 5% think it is morbid or immoral. Most feel positively about it and want to do it again. Only 10% have seen a mental health professional about their anomaly, and 9% have attempted suicide. This may explain why there is so little psychological data on them.

The Stimulus Response Matrix of Sadists and Masochists

The two anomalies have been so inadequately researched, it is almost impossible to draw conclusions. Sadism and masochism may or may not co-occur. They may be heterosexual, homosexual or "bisexual". They apparently can be satisfied by normal heterosexual or homosexual contact. Dominance-submission appears to be important but has not been defined by any authors. The acts in sadomasochism may or may not be painful in the usual sense of the term. The existing data suggest that the behaviors are unusual but not painful. There is no evidence that masochism is associated with high feminine gender identity. There are no studies of biological correlates of sadomasochism. (see Table 13.1)

Directions for Research

It would be useful to study sadists and masochists with the phallometer and sex history questionnaire to establish their erotic preferences and history. Administration of a standard phallometric test (Chapter 2) to determine if

TABLE 13.1
Summary of Theories of Sadism and Masochism*

Theory	Theory
1. Pain is a precondition of sexual release for the masochist but is not pleasurable in itself	10. Masochists suffer from feelings of guilt and inferiority
2. The masochist fears incest and/or castration	11. Pain may be perceived as indignant anger when inflicted by the sadist
3. Masochism is a feminine-passive genital wish toward the father	12. Inflicting pain on others is an end in itself and is a means to make the recipient helpless, passive or degraded
4. Masochism is a manifestation of the death instinct	
5. Games of chasing and scaring the child followed by loving attention may be the genesis of masochism	13. Hormones, constitutional predispositions or heredity may fuse sex and aggression
6. Pain is subjective and may be pleasurable under certain circumstances and/or be pleasurable to certain individuals	14. Sadomasochism exists because partners are difficult to find so each partner takes a turn playing the sadist
7. Pain may be associated with sexual release through imprinting	15. Sadomasochism is an unconditional behavior but a reciprocation nonetheless; a make-believe
8. Pain itself may add to sexual drive to enhance the sexual pleasure experienced	
9. Pain may be culturally or idiosyncratically defined as helplessness or being desired	16. Aggression underlies all sexual anomalies including sadism and masochism
	17. The erotic object is not important in sadomasochism but responses themselves are primary

*Note: There is no empirical systematic controlled study to test any of the theories in this Table.

they generally react more to men, women or children has yet to be done.

A study of pain thresholds would be useful. Melzack[33] has developed a pain meter consisting of a pressure cuff used in measuring blood pressure. Inside are teeth which stick into the arm and one can read the amount of pressure sustained by the research participant. My guess is that sadists and masochists have normal pain thresholds compared to controls but this fact should be demonstrated. The "pain" is more psychical than physical.

The nature of the sadomasochistic acts need to be more fully described. If pain is instrumental to sexual arousal but is not sexually arousing in itself, this should easily be demonstrated by phallometric study. Penile responses to pain alone (humiliation, etc.) should not be different from reactions to neutral stimuli while reactions to intercourse would be. One might find *both* pain and intercourse necessary for arousal. One might ascertain at the same time if sadism and masochism are equally arousing to the same individual.

Biological studies also need to be done, brain scans, EEG, hormone assays, and constitutional differences in pain perception. Since masochism has been associated with suicide, personality pathology in this group needs systematic study as well.

TREATMENT

Behavior Therapy

Aversion therapy. The majority of case reports in the professional literature involves aversion therapy. A full range of treatment variations have been used from classical faradic conditioning to aversive imagery. The conditioning stimulus would be the whips, canes, boots, and so forth, or their imagined use by the patient. This would be followed by unconditioned shock or imagined aversive events like eating feces or throwing up. One might expect that punishment would increase the frequency, at least of masochistic acts, since the shock or nausea could be perceived as rewarding rather than as aversive. This procedure would appear inadvisable and, in fact, Bancroft[4] warns against using aversive procedures contingent upon erectile responses. However there are two reasons for believing that sadomasochistic acts can be treated like any other sexual anomaly. If one accepts Freud's theory that pain is a precondition for sexual arousal and gratification, the usual stimulus for the masochist is pain then pleasure—a stimulus followed by a positive reinforcer. However in aversive conditioning the sequence would be opposite: pain—pleasure (sexual arousal) and pain (electric shock). The whole sequence should become aversive. In fact, if Freud is correct, the masochists' fantasies should become unpleasant simply by reversing the usual sequence. Positive reinforcers such as sexual release increase the frequency of behaviors which immediately follow it while negative reinforcers like electric shock decrease the frequency. The sequence of pain followed by sexual release should make the pain more pleasant whereas the reverse sequence, sexual release followed by pain, should make sexual release less pleasant.

The second reason sadomasochism may be like any other sexual anomaly is that the "pain" is not experienced as such by the patient. It is pain to us but not to him. In this case being humiliated or excited by a boot or leather is analogous to kissing or being excited by a man or woman.

The results of aversion therapy have been positive but only case studies have been reported and the same problems and cautions about this method noted earlier must also be taken into consideration here. (Chapter 3).

Marks, Rachman and Gelder[28] treated a 34-year-old married man who was sexually excited by fantasies of men or women wearing rubber boots or high heeled shoes while kicking him. His wife had initially cooperated in these acts but later refused.

First, an operant conditioning task was used to determine if shock was an effective reinforcer. The patient pressed a lever initially at 70 times per minute and then did so while holding a sexually arousing rubber boot. The rate increased to 85 times per minute. Finally he was shocked for pressing the lever in excess of 70 times per minute. He reported the shocks were very unpleasant. He was treated twice daily for two weeks with approximately 25-to-30 trials per session. He was asked to imagine his favorite objects and was shocked following his signal that he had imagined them. Thus classical conditioning was used with 100% reinforcement by shock. After 3 months, the anomalous behavior was neutral rather than aversive. Intercourse with his wife occurred without the masochistic fantasies. However the therapists were not optimistic about outcome. In each session the patient still had fantasies of masochistic activity but they took longer to image once shock was administered. If they had been extinguished, they would occur less with subsequent sessions even before shocks. The anomalous behavior was only suppressed, that is, in a matter of time the unshocked behavior would recur. The "mild hostility" of the patient expressed during treatment may be a reflection of his unwillingness to give up his sexual behavior.

Marks, Michael and Bancroft[29], later treated five patients; three sadomasochists, one sadist and one masochist, with similar electrical aversion therapy. Three showed a 50% reduction in deviant behavior and two a 25% reduction up to two years after therapy.

Bancroft[4] was not so enthusiastic about aversion procedures for masochists. He reported two cases in which shock facilitated erection, as he feared. It is noteworthy that his homosexual patient was examined in a single case experimental design while penile circumference was measured. Homosexual and masochistic fantasies were each compared under aversive and nonaversive trials. There was little reaction to homosexual fantasies under either condition but penile erection increased over nonaversive trials for masochistic fantasies when shock was *anticipated*. Shock was delivered on an intermittent reinforcement schedule. It is perhaps the combination of anticipated rather than real shock plus intermittent application of actual shock that enhanced the erections. Masochists enjoy anticipated punishment or threat but not actual pain so that threat of shock may have appeared as their preferred erotic stimulus. If the reinforcement schedule and shock intensity were inadequate for these patients, learning would not occur. This study points out the importance of measuring penile erection and carefully monitoring therapy progress. It also suggests that aversion therapy be used with caution if at all with sadomasochists.

McGuire and Vallence[27] and Pinard and Lamontagne[38] each successfully treated a masochist and Mees[31], a sadistic with similar aversive procedures. The latter study is noteworthy in that 6,000 trials were used with unpleasant shock over 14 weeks and progress was slow. The patient still had a few fantasies but no associated orgasm. Follow-ups were all short.

Laws, Meyer and Holmen[25] used olfactory aversion therapy on a 29-year-old sadist who had acted out his fantasies to injure women and was incarcerated as criminally insane. Although he enjoyed mutually consenting intercourse, he also enjoyed a range of torturing activities and had attacked a woman with an axe. Slides of various sadistic acts were shown while he inhaled valeric acid which has a foul odor. He was to imagine his anomalous fantasies during the two minutes the slides were presented. Penile circumference was monitored. Sessions were three to five times per week for eight weeks. Penile reactivity to deviant stimuli rapidly dropped to near zero level while reactions to nondeviant stimuli stayed high. After eight months the patient had 3% erection to deviant stimuli and 93% to nondeviant ones.

Overall, aversive methods have been used in sadomasochism with some success. Such procedures do not appear generally to enhance the anomalous behavior. Follow ups have been exceptionally short and longer term outcome is uncertain.

Other Methods

Marquis[30] used orgasmic reconditioning on a 30-year-old married executive he described as sadomasochistic. The patient switched from his anomalous fantasies to one of his wife's face during masturbation, once orgasm was inevitable. After 9 sessions he could have intercourse with his wife without fantasies. No follow up was reported.

Davison[9] applied both orgasmic reconditioning and covert sensitization to a sadistic 21-year-old single student. He was uninterested in dating females and masturbated to fantasies of torturing women. The patient was upset because he had read about the poor prognosis for his problem as interpreted by psychoanalysts. The behavior therapist spent the first session refuting this interpretation. Then the patient masturbated using Playboy pictures and both normal and sadistic fantasies. The latter were only used to maintain erection and so this was not standard orgasmic reconditioning. He was encouraged to date. Then he was administered covert sensitization. The sadistic fantasy of torturing a female served as the conditioning stimulus. The unconditioned aversive stimulus was having his eyes burned with a branding iron and drinking a bowl of feces in urine. A total of six sessions were used and in telephone follow-up a month later he said he had no sadistic fantasies but was still not dating. After sixteen months he had a temporary relapse but stopped and was dating.

Brownell, Hayes and Barlow[6] also treated five patients with orgasmic reconditioning and covert sensitization. Among the cases were a masochist, sadist and sadomasochist. After six months each had no anomalous behavior but was engaging in normal sexual relationships. They reported[20] an additional successful case of sadism treated only with covert sensitization who was well after an eight week follow-up.

Abel and his colleagues[1] used a variant of orgasmic reconditioning to treat an 18-year-old sadist who had acted out some of his fantasies to injure women. He stole women's clothes and had jabbed girls in the backs with pins. He had fantasies of torturing and killing girls so that he was worried about his behavior and stopped masturbating to such fantasies and sought help. His sexual knowledge was poor and he did not date. The aim of treatment was to increase sexual arousal to normal heterosexual themes and reduce it to sadistic ones.

The procedure started with masturbation to sadistic fantasies and then to sandwich normal fantasies in between, gradually increasing their duration until the total fantasy was normal. This offers more opportunities to reinforce normal fantasies than the usual reconditioning method in which reinforcement occurs only once. However there is still the theoretical problem that everything should become uninteresting. Abel's patient lost his reactivity to pure sadistic fantasies but responded to a mixture of normal and sadistic ones. Outside the clinic he reported a reduced interest in sadistic fantasy after seven weeks but maintained his interest in stealing women's clothes.

In an unreported case study, I treated a 33-year-old married masochist by positive operant conditioning after Quinn[39]. The patient who had an inordinate interest in boots and shoes had previously been treated unsuccessfully by psychoanalysis. His favorite masturbation fantasy was to be kicked by a woman who might stand on his face and then have sex with him. His wife would not cooperate in this activity and was urging him to have treatment. He reluctantly came to see me. He showed average intelligence and significantly high femininity and feminine gender identity on both the MMPI MF scale and Freund's FGI scale. No other psychopathology was evident and he appeared to enjoy his masochistic sexual outlet.

Initial phallometric testing to the body parts of male and female[16] showed he reacted most to the feet, next to the face, vagina and breasts of the female and not to men at all. He fasted from liquids for twenty-four hours prior to treatment. The goal of treatment was first to rearrange the order of his response hierarchy to body parts, so that the largest reactions would be to the vagina and breasts and then second, to decrease his masochistic fantasies. Any reaction over baseline to the vagina or fantasies of touching it or of initiating intercourse were reinforced with an ounce of liquid. In four sessions he showed a positive response to treatment and a reversal of the arousal to feet versus vagina. However, the effect was treatment specific because a retest on body parts showed the legs were still producing the greatest reaction and, if anything, the reaction to them was larger than the baseline measure. Through a series of missed appointments and the therapist's vacation, treatment was not resumed.

Carr[7] described a case of a 25-year-old divorced man which might be labeled masochistic. He climaxed via self-administered enemas while dressing in female clothes. His wife left him because of the behaviors. The treatment was unique in that the patient was completely in control of it. Therapy aimed to decrease the number of enemas and the extent of crossdressing while increasing social contacts with women. This was accomplished by decreasing his opportunities for enemas and crossdressing by scheduling competing rewarding activities, for example, movies, out to dinner, and so forth. He had to do one new and unusual activity each week to extend his social contacts, such as opera, sports, and the like. The latency between enema and orgasm was increased so the association of the two was weakened. Success in heterosexual relations was shaped by having him dating only women with an obvious sexual interest in him. This was likely because he was good looking and intelligent. He engaged in sex only when highly motivated. He thought of the enema only when it was unlikely he could have one, for example, in the office and at specified times when no reinforcement was possible. Treatment was successful and gains were maintained after five months.

There are too few cases to offer a sound evaluation of behavior therapy methods. Obviously better studies are needed.

Psychotherapy

There are only a few reports of psychotherapy with sadomasochists. Freud was pessimistic about treatment outcome because of transference resistance. His followers seem to have taken his advice, although Brenner[5] was optimistic. In theory, the patient enacts a sadomasochistic relationship with the therapist and gets worse or does not improve with psychoanalytic interpretations, as expected. In fact the patient may receive gratification by depriving the therapist of an obvious important possession; his therapeutic potency[5].

Berliner (in Brenner[5]) stressed, to be successful, the analyst must be warm and friendly to avoid seeming like the patient's real parents and he must take the patient's side against those whom the patient feels are hostile to him. The analyst must also show that the patient's hostility is not his own but is derived from his parents' real hostility to him during childhood.

Brenner thought masochism should be treated like any other character disorder. The transference resistance should be treated as an object of analysis for the patient, and viewed objectively to reveal its role in the patient's present life as much as possible. His two masochistic patients who liked to be beaten were treated by psychoanalysis and had different outcomes. The more "severe" case had relatively rapid symptom relief whereas the less "severe" one "dragged on for years." The expected transference resistance developed only in the case treated longer. Brenner suggested than analysts are more likely to be successful in understanding a masochist's transference reaction if they are not unconsciously tempted to participate with the patient in some sort of sadomasochistic behavior, for example, to become angry at him or to demonstrate either affection or aversion in whatever way. Analysts must be aware of the various meanings and purposes that the masochist's behavior serves in his mental life. A model for dealing with them is the reasonable handling of a sulky, stubborn, and provocative child. One should not be emotionally involved or upset but be calm and understanding during attempts to provoke the therapist into sadomasochistic episodes.

Romm[41] described the dynamics in a case of fetishism but sadomasochism was most evident. The patient could only achieve orgasm with his wife by cutting her hair during foreplay and, at times, after intercourse had started. He had fantasies occasionally of gouging out pieces of her scalp. His reaction to having his own hair cut relieved general tension but it was not orgasmic. He experienced a thrill in having his hair cut but he had it cut so close to his scalp he was ashamed of his appearance. This would seem masochistic because he invariably left his hat somewhere. Romm considered this exhibitionistic but the element of shame is not typical of exhibitionists. The patient shaved all his hair away from his body and masturbated with a sense of feeling clean. This also seems masochistic.

The patient made permanent gains in psychoanalysis after he released much hostility toward his father who was symbolized in his dreams as a vicious dog, a dangerous lion or a cruel person. In one dream he delighted to see his father humiliated since his penis was exposed during his speech to an audience. The patient was seen for "several years" and developed a "genital relationship with his wife" as well as "improved self esteem and interpersonal relationships." However "on rare occasions" when under stress he had his anomalous fantasies but with no impulse to act out. He retained a great interest in his wife's hair. Typical of psychotherapy cases, the outcome and methodology is poorly reported so replicating the procedures is almost impossible.

As Freud suggested, psychoanalysis has met with mixed success in treating sadomasochism. Writers have been concerned about transference resistance and clearly more work needs to be done on this problem.

Treatment of Choice

Treatments used for sadism and masochism are summarized in Table 13.2. Both behavior therapists and psychoanalysts have been cautious and concerned about treating sadomasochism. Ironically behavior therapists were worried about aversive conditioning increasing the habit strength of the sadistic or masochistic behavior, but that is the treatment they used most.

TABLE 13.2
Summary of Treatment Effectiveness for Sadism and Masochism

Method	Results
1. Aversion Therapy	Some success. Results comparable to other anomalies
2. Orgasmic Reconditioning	Case studies. Positive outcome
3. Operant Conditioning	Limited succession in a case study
4. Environmental manipulations and scheduling	Positive case study
5. Psychotherapy	Freud pessimistic but a few cases treated with some success

One has to wonder why they did not try some other method first. Psychoanalysts were worried about negative transference resistance but have presented only a very few cases to empirically test their concern. It would appear that more work is necessary and should be encouraged to determine if in fact psychoanalysis works. Some writers are optimistic that it can. I am hesitant to suggest that researchers focus on feelings of inferiority in treating such patients because it has been so often considered important in sexual anomalies but has failed to be significant in controlled research studies. However in the case of masochism and sadism, domination and submissiveness are part of the sexual acts themselves and in the few cases I have had the opportunity to see, pronounced feelings of inferiority were involved in the sexual act. If this is etiologically significant, therapeutic efforts at increasing self esteem may be useful in changing these anomalies.

As far as behavior therapy is concerned, considerable analysis is necessary before a treatment program can be undertaken. Sadistic and masochistic behavior involve a complex fantasy life with much elaboration of detail. In clinical cases perhaps the best treatment approach would be to focus on the fantasy in whatever method is employed. However the sequencing of guilt, submission, and so forth, is important and must be carefully examined before treatment. Punishment as a precondition of sexual release may produce very different results from pain intertwined with sexual arousal. Assertion training would most likely interfere with sadism and masochism. However every reasonable method should be tried in what are generally unexplored anomalies.

BIBLIOGRAPHY

1. Abel, G. G., Barlow, D. H., & Blanchard, E. B. Developing heterosexual arousal by altering masturbatory fantasies: A controlled study. *Paper presented to 7th Annual Convention of Association for Advancement of Behavior Therapy,* December 8, 1973, Miami, Florida.
2. Aronfreed, J. Aversive control of socialization. *Nebraska Symposium on Motivation,* 1968, *16,* University of Nebraska Press.
3. Bachman, J. A. Self-injurious behavior: A behavioral analysis. *Journal of Abnormal Psychology,* 1972, *80*(3), 211–224.
4. Bancroft, J. *Deviant Sexual Behavior.* London: Oxford University Press, 1974.
5. Brenner, C. The masochistic character: Genesis and treatment. *Journal of American Psychoanalytic Association,* 1959, *7,* 197–226.
6. Brownell, K. D., Hayes, S. C., & Barlow, D. H. Patterns of appropriate and deviant sexual arousal: The behavioral treatment of multiple sexual deviations. *Journal of Consulting and Clinical Psychology,* 1977, *45*(6), 1144–1155.
7. Carr, E. G. Behavior therapy in a case of multiple sexual disorders. *Journal of Behavior Therapy and Experimential Psychiatry,* 1974, *5,* 171–174.
8. Carr, E. G. The motivation of self-injurious behavior: A review of some hypotheses. *Psychological Bulletin,* 1977, *84*(4), 800–816.
9. Davison, G. C. Elimination of a sadistic fantasy by a client-controlled counter-conditioning technique: A case study. *Journal of Abnormal Psychology,* 1968, *73*(1), 84–90.
10. Dietz, P. Kotzwarraism: Sexual induction of cerebral hypoxia. Medical Criminology Research Centre, McLean Hospital, 1978.
11. Dreyer, P., & Renner, K. E. Self-punitive behavior—masochism or confusion. *Psychological Review,* 1971, *78*(4), 333–337.
12. Duffy, E. *Activation and Behavior.* New York: J. Wiley and Sons, 1962.
13. Eidelberg, L. Humiliation in masochism. *Journal of the American Psychoanalytic Association,* 1959, *7,* 274–283.
14. Edmondson, J. A case of sexual asphyxia without fatal termination. *British Journal of Psychiatry,* 1972, *121,* 437–438.
15. Flynn, C. P. Sexuality and insult behavior. *The Journal of Sex Research,* 1976, *12*(1), 1–13.
16. Freund, K., McKnight, C., Langevin, R., & Ciberi, S. The female child as a surrogate object. *Archives of Sexual Behavior,* 1972, *2*(2), 119–133.

17. Gebhard, P. H. Fetishism and sadomasochism. In J. Masserman (Ed.), *Dynamics of Deviant Sexuality,* New York: Grune & Stratton, 1969, 71–80.
18. Glover, E. Aggression and sado-masochism. In Rosen, I. (Ed.), *The Pathology and Treatment of Sexual Deviation.* London: Oxford University Press, 1964, 146–162.
19. Green, P. C. Masochism in the laboratory rat: An experimental demonstration. *Psychonomic Science,* 1972, *27*(1), 41–44.
20. Hayes, S. C., Brownell, K., & Barlow, D. H. The use of self administered covert sensitization in the treatment of exhibitionism and sadism. *Behavior Theraphy,* 1978, *9*(2), 283–289.
21. Hess, E. Imprinting. *Science,* 1959, *130,* 133–141.
22. Karpman, B. The obsessive paraphilias (perversions): a critical review of Stekel's works on sadism, masochism and fetishism. *Archives of Neurology and Psychiatry,* 1934, *32,* 577–626.
23. Karpman, B. *The Sexual Offender and His Offenses.* New York: Julian Press, 1957.
24. Knight, B. Fatal masochism—accident or suicide. *Medical Science,* 1979, *19*(2), 118–120.
25. Laws, D. R., Meyer, J., & Holmen, M. L. Reduction of sadistic sexual arousal by olfactory aversion: a case study. *Behavior Research and Therapy,* 1978, *16,* 281–285.
26. Loewenstein, R. M. A contribution to the psychoanalytic theory of masochism. *Journal of American Psychoanalytic Association,* 1957, *5,* 197–234.
27. McGuire, R. J., & Vallance, M. Aversion therapy by electric shock: A simple technique. *British Medical Journal,* 1964, *1,* 151–153.
28. Marks, I. M., Rachman, S., & Gelder, M. G. Methods for assessment of aversion treatment in fetishism and masochism. *Behavior Research & Therapy,* 1965, *3,* 253–258.
29. Marks, I., Michael, G., & Bancroft, J. Sexual deviatns two years after electric aversion. *British Journal of Psychiatry,* 1970, *117,* 173–185.
30. Marquis, J. Orgasmic reconditioning: changing sexual object choice through controlling masturbation fantasies. *Journal of Behavior Therapy and Experimental Psychiatry,* 1970, *1,* 263–271.
31. Mees, H. L. Sadistic fantasies modified by aversive conditioning and substitution: a case study. *Behavior Research Therapy,* 1966, *4,* 317–320.
32. Melzack, R. The perception of pain. *Scientific American,* 1961.
33. Melzack, R. *The Puzzle of Pain.* New York: Basic Books Inc., 1973.
34. Melzack, R., & Scott, T. The effects of early experience on the response to pain. *Journal of Comparative and Physiological Psychology,* 1957, *50,* 155–161.
35. Menninger, K. *Man Against Himself.* New York: Harcourt Brace & World, 1938.
36. Moruzzi, G., & Magoun, H. Brain stem reticular formation and activation of the EEG. *Electroencephalography and Clinical Neurophysiology,* 1949, *1,* 455–473.
37. Panken, S. *The Joy of Suffering.* New York: Jason Aronson Inc., 1973.
38. Pinard, G., Lamontagne, Y. Electrical aversion, aversion relief and sexual retraining in treatment of fetishism with masochism. *Journal of Behavior Therapy and Experimental Psychiatry,* 1976, *7,* 71–74.
39. Quinn, J. T., Harbison, J. J. M., & McAllister, H. An attempt to shape human penile responses. *Behavior Research and Therapy,* 1970, *8,* 213–216.
40. Resnik, H. L. P. Erotized repetitive hangings: A form of self-destructive behavior. *American Journal of Psychotherapy,* 1972, *26*(1), 4–21.
41. Romm, M. E. Some dynamics in fetishism. *Psychoanalytic Quarterly,* 1949, *18,* 137–153.
42. Sack, R. L., & Miller, W. Masochism: A clinical and theoretic overview. *Psychiatry,* 1975, *38,* 244–257.
43. Shankel, L., & Carr, A. Transvestism and hanging episodes in a male adolescent. *Psychiatric Quarterly,* 1956, *30,* 478–493.

44. Shore, M. F., Clifton, A., Zelin, M., & Myerson, P. G. Patterns of masochism: an empirical study. *Journal of Medical Psychology,* 1971, *44,* 59–65.

45. Siomopoulos, V., & Goldsmith, J. Sadism revisited. *American Journal of Psychotherapy,* 1976, *30*(4), 631–640.

46. Spengler, A. Manifest sadomasochism of males: results of an empirical study. *Archives of Sexual Behavior,* 1977, *6*(6), 441–456.

47. Stoller, R. *Perversion: The Erotic Form of Hatred.* New York: Random House, 1975.

48. Tinbergen, N. The curious behavior of the stickelback. *Scientific American,* 1952.

IV PHYSICAL DISORDERS

14

The Intersexes: Physical and Genetic Abnormalities

INTRODUCTION

Normal sex organ development and functioning is mainly dependent on the programming of the genes and on an adequate endocrine system in a healthy body. Sometimes nature (and man) errs so that sex organs are incomplete or aspects of both the male and female bodies are present. These resulting intersexes are usually problems to be dealt with by physicians but interesting questions arise that have a bearing on the study of sexual anomalies. For example, if a genetic woman is raised as a male, what is her object choice and/or gender identity? Will sexually anomalous behavior be present? This chapter examines these questions but for more complete medical information other sources should be consulted[25] [29] [33] [47] [49].

Physical sexual abnormalities stem from two main sources: from unusual hereditary in the genes and from an unusual endocrine system which produces sex hormones. The two are not independent. Usually anatomical sex is programmed in the X and Y chromosomes of the genes. These so called sex chromosomes are usually paired as XX or XY, one chromosome coming from each parent. an XX combination usually produces a normal female and the XY a normal male. One of at least 3 mistakes can occur: to many X's, too many Y's or only 1 X and no second X or Y chromosome. The major resulting genetic abnormalities are presented in Table 14.1.

In the case of the Triple X syndrome, no abnormalities of the external genitalia are necessarily evident but the female may be mentally retarded, have infantile genitalia, and she carries an unusual heredity. Similarly in the XYY syndrome, a physically normal and perhaps tall male results but he

TABLE 14.1
Genetic Abnormalities

Medical Name	Description	Chromosomal Sex	External Genitalia	Treatment
XXX Syndrome	Extra female chromosome. Looks normal and may be mentally retarded.	Female +	Normal female	None required
XYY Syndrome	Extra male chromosome. May be very tall or delinquent.	Male +	Normal male	None required
Klinefelter's or XXY Syndrome	Mixed female and male chromosomes. May be mentally or socially impaired. Inadequate personality, low sex drive, wide range of sexual anomalies present.	Mixed	Male but penis and testes small, may develop female breasts at puberty; sterile.	Sterility problem-counselling/sperm donor.
Turner's or XO Syndrome	Missing or "broken" X chromosome. Short stature, infantile appearance. May have webbed neck, fingers and toes, small receding chin, pigmented moles, "oriental eyes", heart or kidney and urethra defects.	Female –	Female but no ovaries	Female sex hormones produce adult sex characteristics and menstruation. Counselling for sterility.

451

may be delinquent or antisocial and may be found in a penitentiary.

Sexual anomalies paradoxically paired with low sex drive have been noted in the XXY or Klinefelter's Syndrome. The range of sexually anomalous behavior in Klinefelter's Syndrome is wide including homosexuality, pedophilia, firesetting with erotic fantasy, sadomasochism, "polymorphous perversion" with interest in breaking and entering, self burning, hitting women, and exhibitionism. In addition there may be antisocial acts including larceny and arson. The genitals are male but small. Female breasts may develop at puberty. A host of problems may accompany this genetic anomaly including sterility, mental retardation and/or psychiatric disorders.

Turner's Syndrome is the name given to the condition in which only one X chromosome is present or if a second X is present, it is "broken" in some way. Accompanying physical abnormalities which may be present range from short stature and webbed neck to heart or kidney defects. The afflicted person is female but has no ovaries and is sterile. Administration of female sex hormones or oestrogens produces adult sex characteristics and menstruation.

Hormonal imbalances can produce a number of physical anomalies as well and some are described in Table 14.2. The XX chromosomes require female oestrogen hormones for development and differentiation of female genitals. Similarly the XY chromosomes need male androgen hormones. Initially the fetus has the rudiments of both male and female genitalia and under the influence of sex hormones they differentiate as male or female; one at the expense of the other. If the XY chromosomes lack androgens or male sex hormones, the external body looks female. In this Androgen Insensitivity Syndrome (Table 14.2), adaptation to the female sex role seems more appropriate. The vagina is blind or closed and too short for satisfactory intercourse but it can be surgically lengthened so that intercourse can be satisfactory. Inside are testes instead of ovaries.

For the female XX chromosomes, an excess of androgens masculinizes the fetus in the Adrenogenital Syndrome or Female Hermaphroditism. The adrenal glands are supposed to produce cortisone but make androgens instead. This syndrome may also develop from an excess of androgens passed from the mother to her fetus. This can be caused by a tumor or administration of diethyl stilbestrol to prevent abortion. In both male and female hermaphroditism, the genitals are unfinished and ambiguous. Hormone replacement therapy or surgery may be used to help correct the problems.

THE THEORIES

The physical appearance of an individual can be an important determinant of gender identity and gender role. If one looks like a male, he tends to be treated like a male, so there is considerable momentum to behave like one. In the transsexual males (Chapter 6) I described men who were anatomically and genetically normal but nevertheless felt like they were women. A persistent feeling of being a woman, or gender identity, does not necessarily correspond to gender behavior. Children particularly may show cross sex behavior but nevertheless feel like normal individuals of their anatomical sex. In this section we are presented with clashes of genetic and hormonal sex and sex of rearing. The resulting gender behavior may therefore offer another perspective on the relationship of gender behavior and physical sex. As noted in Chapter 4, preferred sex object and gender behavior may not be related. Homosexual men, for instance, may be masculine or feminine identified. Given an abnormal sexual development, what will the resulting gender identity and object choice be? Some of the patients afflicted with genetic abnormalities may have little or no sex drive which makes their evaluation of relationships, erotic object choice, and gender identity difficult but for some the need to resolve their sexual identity is still a powerful force in their lives.

Two main theoretical positions have been developed to explain the gender behavior of individuals with the variety of physical anomalies just described. Money and the Hampsons[32] claimed that hormones and genes are secondary to sex of rearing as a determinant of gender *role*. If a child is raised as a male, that is the overriding factor in gender behavior. Up to 2 years of age, gender preference is flexible and changing sex role assignment is possible but after that it is not. Money & the Hampsons[32] have likened this to *imprinting* in birds. In avian species soon after birth a period of "following" the mother occurs and her absence produces great distress. If this behavior is prevented or disrupted, it has far reaching consequences on adult sexual behavior. However, important to Money and the Hampsons' theory is that the bond to mother and its species becomes irreversible. There is a flexible period of 24-to-72 hours after birth and when it is over, imprinting for the birds is no longer possible. A similar phenomenon may occur in humans. Gender behavior may be flexible up to 2 years of age but after that it is fixed.

Other writers stress that gender behavior is determined by an interaction of neurochemical factors. Dorner[6] argued that there is both a male and a female center in the brain. Androgens favor development of the male center, oestrogens the female center. These hormonal factors override the social environmental influences on gender noted by Money.

Reinisch[45] argued that the presence or absence of androgens during a critical period of brain organization and differentiation is the operative agent in human sex differences in behavior. However psychosexual differentiation is the end result of a complex of environmental and hormonal factors.

TABLE 14.2
Hormonal and External Genital Abnormalities

Medical Name	Description	Chromosomal Sex	Genitalia	Treatment
1. Cryptorchidism	Undescended or missing testes, lower testosterone in blood, lower sexual activity level	Male	Male	Hormones or corrective surgery. May need sterility counselling
2. Androgen insensitivity or testicular feminizing syndrome	Seems normal female but chromosomes are male	Male	Female but blind or closed vagina unsatisfactory for intercourse but internal testes. Sterile and no menstruation	Surgical lengthening of vagina. Sterility counselling
3. Female hermaphroditism or adrenogenital syndrome (AGS)	Adrenal glands produce male androgens instead of cortisone due to recessive genetic trait or due to excess androgen from mother to fetus. Affects development of sex organs	Female	Unfinished and ambiguous. Female with enlarged clitoris. Unusual urethral opening. May be labial fusion	Cortisone replacement therapy
4. Male adrenogenital syndrome	Like female AGS	Male	Male but early puberty even premature	Cortisone replacement therapy delays puberty to normal time

TABLE 14.2 (continued)
Hormonal and External Genital Abnormalities

Medical Name	Description	Chromosomal Sex	Genitalia	Treatment
5. Male hermaphroditism	Mixed genitalia. Psychosexual females. Youthful appearance	Male	Varying degrees of feminizing of genitals. Develops breasts. No ejaculate.	If infant responds to androgens, raise as a male; if not raise as female. Adult – Plastic surgery to remove breasts
6. Stein Leventhal Syndrome	Ovaries enlarged by cysts; miss periods and grow excess hair. Like hyperadrenocortical condition but different source	Female	Female	Cortisone therapy

THE EXPERIMENTAL EVIDENCE

The intersexes offer us an opportunity to examine which components of human sexuality are most important in gender identity and erotic object choice. If the genes or the malfunctioning hormone system of the individual override sex assigned by the physician and parents, this would indicate that they are most important. However, if the sex of rearing and gender identity contradicts the genetic sex or the hormone system of the individual, this would suggest that social factors can override the biological determinants or are themselves the important sources of gender identity and erotic object choice. First the major genetic abnormalities are discussed and then hormonal ones.

Genetic Abnormalities

Klinefelter's syndrome. Baker and Stoller[2] [3] have argued that a biological force can contribute to gender identity. They reviewed the existing literature up to 1968 of all case studies and reports. The majority of cases they describe are Klinefelter's Syndrome or the XXY Syndrome. Of the 28 cases of their own, 7 genetic males wanted to change to the female sex at puberty. This of course means that 75% did not and Baker and Stoller argue that a biological force can contribute *sometimes* to gender identity but it is not the final answer.

The cases are ambiguously reported, making definitive statements impossible. Often the genetic sex was not determined. The use of the Barr body[36] was only available in the early fifties and it has been superceded by analysis of chromosomes themselves[41]. The Barr body in the cell nucleus is insensitive to the missing or abnormal Y chromosome but detects the presence of X chromosomes. Thus some abnormalities may be missed. Baker and Stoller themselves complained that the existing literature is poor because many workers are not psychiatrists and do not search for pertinent information on gender and erotic object choice. They described the articles as both appealing and dreadful, noting that one cannot systematize the existing literature because the data both reported and unreported make comparison impossible. However it seems that in approximately a quarter of Klinefelter cases there is crossdressing, opposite sex play and a desire for sex reassignment surgery. While some authors report the prominent finding of homosexuality accompanied by feminine gender identification[15] [21], it should be noted that there is no evidence that the converse is true. That is, homosexual men are not necessarily afflicted with Klinefelter's Syndrome and in fact there is no sound evidence that homosexual men have any genetic or endocrine abnormalities. (See Chapter 4). The same applies to pedophilia and any other sexual anomaly which may cooccur with intersexes. The studies do suggest that intersex genetic abnormalities may relate to cross gender identity and to a sexually anomalous object choice.

Baker and Stoller made one further point which needs detailed investigation. Hermaphrodites may develop *ambiguous* gender identity or no identity. Parents may accept that their child is neither male or female, or both male and female, and treat the child accordingly. We do not know the details of these individuals' lives other than that some felt ambivalence about their gender identity. It is conceivable that parents' uncertainty would permit adoption in the child of bits and pieces of the sexual and gender behavior of both males and females. In the six of the 27 cases Baker and Stoller studied, the genitals were unambiguously male and yet the desire to be female emerged in spite of parental acceptance of the maleness of their child.

Money and Polett[35] made an interesting comparison between transvestites and Klinefelter's Syndrome and found the former genetically normal. Many Klinefelter Syndrome cases were homosexual and/or transsexual suggesting a link of the genetic abnormality to sexually confused behavior. Pasqualini, Vidal and Bur[40] presented a low incidence of sexual abnormality among 31 Klinefelter cases. Sampling methods in the foregoing studies may have played an important role in the results.

The low sex drive in the XXY syndrome has more recently been associated with reduced testosterone by Raboch, Mellan and Starka[43]. Unfortunately the psychological information on these individuals is impressionistic without even a report of interviewer reliability. There are no phallometric or standardized psychological tests or sexual histories. All of the issues and problems with uncontrolled case reports noted earlier are present here. Is there true cross gender identity or only feminine behavior in males? Are the sexual anomalies reported coincidental? Are they fixed patterns of behavior? In particular, is homosexual behavior any different than that in the general population? Since over a third of normal males engage in homosexual behavior at some time in their lives without having a homosexual object preference, these results are to be considered with extreme caution.

Hoaken, Clarke and Breslin[15] reviewed findings in Klinefelter's Syndrome and two main results recur: mental retardation and psychopathology may accompany the problem. They made the interesting suggestion that the greater the number of X chromosomes in the variants of the XXY syndrome, that is, XXXY and XXXXY cases, the more severe the retardation. This offers interesting prospects for research investigation, however rare the cases. They also noted a general low libido in the syndrome and "sexuality" is poorly differentiated. The personality pathology in their patients included schizophrenia, psychopathic personality, brain pathology, passive aggressive personality and paranoia. A later study by Baker and his colleagues[1] and a review of the literature by Hook[16] of XYY and XXY Syndromes among the mentally retarded confirmed their findings.

Turner's syndrome. Three case studies of Hypopituitary Dwarfism and of Turner's Syndrome are illustrative of the possible problems which may be encountered by patients afflicted with intersex abnormalities. Raft, Spencer, & Toomey[44] did not describe the cases for the examination of gender and object choice hypotheses but illustrate that parental pressure can be conducive to psychiatric pathology. Turner's syndrome may be accompanied not only by genital defects, that is, no ovaries, but general appearance can be markedly infantile. Short stature is common to all cases (less than 5 feet tall).

In the three cases Raft and his associates described, the patients were force fed and dragged from clinic to clinic to improve their condition, mainly to grow in stature. Parents were alarmed by lack of age appropriate growth. The problem of emotional growth not matching physical growth may also be important in the mother-daughter or father daughter conflicts noted. One patient who wanted to drive a car was told by her parents: "you are too little and not fast enough". Social pressures in school were also noted and alarmed the parents. Sexual and gender feelings were not clearly reported although the MMPI administered to one patient was described as unremarkable. Presumably if there was a gender disturbance it would be reflected to some degree at least in the masculinity–femininity scale of the MMPI. All three cases were assigned to the female sex. It was noted that short stature and its accompanying psychological abnormalities need not be a barrier to treatment.

Kusalic and her colleagues[20] studied 11 cases of Turner's Syndrome and found from clinical assessments that they were passive and showed a strong inhibition of aggression. They suffered from feelings of low self esteem which developed into strong depression during hormone treatment to increase stature. However we do not know what effect the hormones themselves were having on this abnormal condition.

Money and his colleagues have made the first efforts to systematically study Turner's Syndrome[13][14] although they incorrectly describe their cases as having male chromosomes which indicates the state of knowledge at the time. The cases were Turner's syndrome as indicated by the external features, especially short stature in all cases. All seemed normal in respect to marriage and romantic fantasies and there was little evidence of homosexual interest. Intelligence appeared to be normally distributed but Money noted in another study[26] that a cluster of results suggestive of parietal lobe dysfunctions appeared on psychological testing. In particular, there was a space form and directional sense deficit and there was a numerical disability. Others have confirmed the findings[37].

The greatest problem for the girls was their short stature and infantile appearance. Later Ehrhardt, Greenberg and Money[8] compared Turner's Syndrome cases to normal girls and found little difference in development. If anything, they were more feminine in interests. From their data, Turner's Syndrome seems to be associated with feminine gender identity. The authors concluded that neither a second X chromosome or a fetal ovary is necessary for differentiation of feminine gender identity. We do not know however about erotic object choice and we do not know how the single X chromosome is functioning. As Zuger[51] noted, the role of the chromosomes is uncertain and not normal in many cases of intersexes making conclusions about its importance in normal functioning uncertain. Later studies by Money and his colleagues suffer many of the same problems.

The XYY-syndrome.   The interesting suggestion of early workers on the XYY Syndrome was that the afflicted male may show particular tendencies to be aggressive. One might construe such men to be supermasculine and so link genes and masculine gender behavior. Researchers however have not been particularly concerned about gender identity in any of the intersex problems and in the case of XYY males, they were concerned with aggressiveness. Owen[39] and others[16][19] have provided thorough reviews of the XYY Syndrome for the interested reader so only a brief summary is given here. A number of physical abnormalities have been noted: tallness, genital abnormalities including small and/or undescended testicles, low sperm counts or infertility, bone and/or joint disorders like osteoarthropathy, dental irregularities like enamel hypoplasia, or teeth in irregular order, cardiac disorders, skin problems like excessive acne, neurological disorders, and unusual thumb print patterns among others. Noteworthy was the fact that XYY males did not differ from matched controls in testosterone. In case reports they were generally normal on pituitary gonadotropins, follicle stimulating hormone, leutinizing hormone and growth hormone. Very few studies have been done and controls were poor, as Owen noted, so reported conclusions were often unwarranted. For example, the conclusion about tallness may be biased because it has often been a starting point of studies to examine only prisoners or mentally retarded men 6 feet or taller. This may distort the results in the direction of support for the hypothesis. When *all* cases have been examined, the results were not so impressive. Unfortunately this applies to the studies of aggression in XYY men as well.

Owen noted that XXY men have been described with a range of characteristics from schizophrenic to hard working to aggressive, passive aggressive, and plain passive. However these terms are clinical impressions from case studies. There is little in the way of psychometric data and what there is, fails to support the hypothesis that XYY men are aggressive. Sex anomalies have been inconsistently reported but rape and indecent exposure have been noted. Criminal records also generally fail to show them as more aggressive or having more charges. Finally Owen noted that karyotyping in XYY cases is often reported only for peripheral leukocytes and other tissue should be examined. Researchers could more often note mosaics of chromosomes as well.

Conclusion.   As a group the genetic studies are methodologically so poor that conclusions should be treated with extreme caution. It seems that sex of assignment even if it is incongruent with genetic sex is maintained in about three quarters of the cases but that in one quarter, genetic sex overrides sex of rearing and reassignment surgery may be sought out. However a sound study using karyotyping of genes from several tissues, hormone assay, a detailed sexual history, phallometry where possible, psychiatric evaluation with standardized instruments and the use of a suitable control group has yet to be done. The reader needs to be particularly cautious because there may be no incongruity between genetic sex and sex of rearing in many of the reports. Authors include such congruous cases as markers of success that environment overrides biology when this hypothesis has not really been tested.

Hormone Abnormalities

Adrenogenital syndrome.   The effect of hormone abnormalities (Table 14.2) have been better studied than genetic abnormalities but by no means *adequately* examined to date. There are few controlled studies. In the better conducted studies, the clinicians are members of large established clinics which do fine work so that mistakes in sex assignment at birth are few in number and treatments to correct hormone deficiencies are started early in life. Thus clinical setting totally confounds the effect of biological and environmental factors and makes evaluation of the relative contribution of these two dimensions impossible.

Lev-Ran[22] from the Soviet Union has illustrated the poor state of knowledge in this area. He reported the first case of congenital adrenal hyperplasia in 1963 and before that it was never reported correctly. In his 1974 article he noted that in the majority of cases neither the patients nor the doctors knew the methods of diagnosing and treating these diseases. However, he noted that his cases provide a natural experiment in which there was no ambiguity on the part of the parents about the child's sex in spite of the physical anomaly. This of course is conjecture but Lev-Ran made this assumption. The secretiveness and ignorance about sexual matters would also help mitigate against accurate reporting of information and record keeping.

Lev-Ran studied 24 cases. One was a true hermaphrodite with genitals of both sexes, three had mixed gonadal dysgenesis, nine were male hermaphrodites with tests in various stages of descent and 11 were females with congenital adrenal hyperplasia. In all but two cases, according to the author, the patients accepted the sex of assignment regardless of the genetic sex. He concluded that the cases demonstrate that gender identity is not determined by biological influences prenatally but that it is postnatally learned and determined by sex assignment in infancy and by resulting socializing experiences. However a careful examination of the results show that such an interpretation is not so clear cut.

On the basis of chance alone, the infants with ambiguous external genitals would be correctly assigned to their genetic sex half of the time. Since about 50% of the population are male one can expect that agreement between social assigned and biological sex is about 50%. In Lev-Ran's sample that is the case. Since he determined the chromatin of each case, it turns out that 12 of the 24 cases are congruent in genetic and socially assigned sex. These cases are therefore lost to a test of the theory that socially assigned sex is more important than genetic sex. Incidentally, one patient was reassigned at 7 years of age satisfactorily suggesting that 2 years of age is not a critical cut off point for gender change. Of his 12 test cases, one genetic male was not sure of his gender assignment and 2 additional cases were later correctly assigned from male to female. This is approximately a quarter of the cases which were dissatisfied with their assigned gender. This is a similar proportion to the number reported by Baker and Stoller. It seems that both social and biological environment play a part in the gender feelings of the patients. One has to wonder about the part played by the individuals' own assessment of their gender identity and erotic preference. We have almost no information on the sex drive level of the patients in any of these studies. If they are aroused, to whom do they respond?

Perhaps there is an ambiguity for them, an uncertainty that allows them to be more flexible than the anatomically normal individual. One of Lev Ran's patients who was quite bright described her feelings: "I agree (not) to go on living as a man or as a woman but as somebody definite in order to get rid of this unbearable uncertainty, even if only in the eyes of others." In reference to being male or female she said, "A lot would depend on my appearance." For her the worst thing was not knowing if the sex of assignment was correct. She thought of herself as having only a social and not a sexual life. Unfortunately we have no detailed and systematic data on this question in general.

The Hampsons and Money presented a series of papers[13] [14] [30] [31] which describe the adrenogenital syndrome and prescribe the treatment of the problem of hermaphroditism. It is one of the most frequently quoted series of articles offered as support for the theory than environment overrides genetic sex in determining gender identity. They recommend that external genital appearance be a primary consideration unless gender identity is well established in which case it should be given precedence. They also presented data which suggests that sex of rearing is an overriding influence compared to genetic sex. They note that gender role and orientation were congruous with sex of rearing in 72 of 76 cases despite contradictions in chromosomal sex, gonadal sex, hormonal sex and internal reproductive organs. However their data is confusing. The selection of cases is not clearly defined making evaluation difficult. They use subsets of the group of 76 cases to evaluate the importance of chromosomal sex, hormonal sex, and so forth; and different cases or perhaps overlapping ones are used to illustrate their points. However if one used their different tables, contradictory results emerge. They maintain in one table that gender role is congruent with sex of rearing but 100% discordant with genetic sex. If one uses their other tables, this is true for 85% of the cases in one instance and as low as 63% in another. All cases should have been used in the evaluation for a proper assessment. The same problem of course emerges in comparing sex of rearing and hormonal sex. The criteria they use for gender role and "orientation", which are not well spelled out, seem like soft clinical impressions. Zuger[51] criticized the Money and Hampson studies. He noted that changes in one of the sex determinants, that is, genetic, gonadal, and so forth, affects the others and it is not an either/or condition.

Money and Ogunro[34] reported on 10 patients who were genetically male but who were partially androgen insensitive and were born with hermaphroditic incompletely differentiated genitals, looking more female than male. Eight were raised as boys, one changed from girl to boy at 2 years of age and the last case reared as a girl. It appears that clinical intervention started early in the lives of these individuals. Surgery and hormone treatments were involved to correct the androgen deficiency. Erotic behavior was heterosexual and the authors incorrectly noted that the results fail to support a hormonal hypothesis of homosexuality when this hypothesis was never testable in this population. Only one case is pertinent, the one raised as a female past the age of two. Interestingly she was the only one who was ambivalent about her assigned sex and apparently she was also "bisexual" indicating the conflict in genetic and assigned sex. However the whole study is uncontrolled and in the final analysis there is only one case which tests the hypothesis contrasting genetic and social sex assignment.

An *expected* feature of Money and Ogunro's study was *the relative insensitivity* of the patients to orgasm. Since it is believed that androgens control orgasmic behavior, their hormone deficiency would interfere with such experience. In fact when patients did report it, it was described as a gradual or a spasmic peak of feeling and some had no discharge of fluid.

In another uncontrolled group report, Money and Dalery[28] studied seven genetic females; four reared as girls and three as boys. The latter are of interest and support the hypothesis that sex of rearing is all important. The patients reared as girls were discovered early in life and treatment begun before 1 year of age. All were prepubertal at the time of the study. The three raised as males were seen at 6, 13 and 19 years of age respectively and were followed up into adulthood. Each considered himself to be a male and sexually interacted satisfactorily with females. All found sexual intercourse pleasurable and none had difficulty in obtaining and maintaining an erection. None had erotic fantasies to men and only one was "slightly dissatisfied" with his sex life. Money and Dalery argued that the postnatal social factors are important in determining gender identity.

Masica, Money and Ehrhardt[23] compared 10 chromosomal males who were androgen insensitive with 23 chromosomal females who were treated adrenogenital syndrome cases. All cases were female in physical appearance. The male group had a lower sex drive level and were less keenly aware of it although both groups were within the limits of feminine as defined in our culture. Although the 23 cases of adrenogenital syndrome were not suitable test cases to compare the genetic versus social sex hypotheses, the 10 androgen insensitivity cases were. These ten cases appear to support the hypothesis that sex of rearing overrides biological factors. There were no cases of lesbianism, transsexualism or transvestism. All patients were within the limits of feminine on the Guilford Zimmerman Temperament Survey Masculinity-Femininity Scale. Once again the results must be weighted by the fact that the 10 androgren insensitive patients were administered oestrogens to increase their feminine features. This suggests that hormones as well as social sex of rearing can influence gender behavior but that genetic sex may only be a secondary factor.

Ehrhardt[7][10] has summarized her work with Money and their colleagues by noting that androgen excess (adrenogenital syndrome) in girls who are reared as females and have corrective hormone surgery do not seem different in gender identity and erotic object preference from normal girls. They tend to display a higher level of physical energy expenditure in rough outdoor play but so do males with the same condition. The girls were considered long term tomboys and preferred boys' company over girls' and were less interested in dolls and female toys but were within normal limits on these factors nonetheless. None had a conflict about their gender role in spite of one item "satisfaction with gender role" being scored lower by experimental girls than by sib controls. This suggests the questions used in this series of studies should be carefully scrutinized for meaning. No homosexual behavior was evident.

A study by Imperato-McGinley[17] and her colleagues on 24 male pseudohermaphrodites in the Dominican Republic shows how social and biological influences can interact. It is one of the few existing study of intersexes which reported a thorough hormone analysis. All patients were genetic (XY) males who had marked ambiguity of external genitalia at birth and were raised as girls before the disorder became evident to the community. The disorder was genetically traced back to a single woman in this closed society. The interesting and paradoxical feature of this study was that at puberty the patients had a marked virilization and developed a typical male phenotype with increased muscle mass and an enlarged and functional penis. There was no breast enlargement. The testes descended and the scrotum became rugated and there was ejaculation. There was fertility although the prostate gland remained small and beard growth was scanty. In general the birth defect was corrected and masculinization of internal structures was normal. The authors noted that psychosexual orientation was unequivocally male and while 18 of the 24 men were reared as females, they were able to change their gender identity at puberty, contrary to what Money and his associates predicted, once again. They considered themselves as males with libido directed toward women. A chemical study of these 24 cases suggested that there was a marked decrease in plasma dihydrotestosterone secondary to a decrease activity in the steroid enzyme, alpha reductase. It seems that chemistry was important in determining final gender identity and erotic preference but the attitude of the community in readily adjusting to the change was equally important in gender adjustment. These cases are unusual in that the change in genitals was complete and new "males" were totally functional, different from the typical intersex case where genital ambiguity, uncorrected, remains permanently. Perhaps the environment has a negative effect on the emergence of a new gender identity once one has been established, in spite of the feelings of the individual. If such pressures exist, suppression of any gender or erotic preference may result.

Money[27] criticized the Imperato-McGinley study because of insufficient information on parent child relationships with respect to sex of rearing and gender identity and because the researchers disregarded early socialization experience as if they did not exist (See [18] for a reply).

Progestins administered to pregnant mothers.   A number of studies have been reported in which progestins have been administered to pregnant mothers to prevent threatening miscarriages. As a result, genetically female babies were born with partially masculinized genitals[7 9 11 46 50]. At puberty normal feminization occurred and no treatment was necessary. If masculinization is extreme, corrective surgery may be necessary, the sooner the better according to Ehrhardt and Money[11] and the babies should always be assigned as female. A karyotyping would be a useful confirmation as well.

Since these girls have been reared as female and are genetically and hormonally female, there is little expectation that they will differ from the norm. There was no clearly defined difference in gender development or object choice reported.

One finding has captured the fancy of workers in the area. There was a noticeable trend for the hormone treated children to be above average intelligence. However the two studies in which the IQ scores on standardized tests, namely the Wechsler Intelligence Scales, were used to compare the hormone affected children with sibs who were unaffected, showed there were no significant differences in the groups and both were above average. This suggests that brighter families submit to research studies or attend clinics with the problems earlier or that some other extraneous factor is involved. Although the two studies are not conclusive, they suggest that the IQ results are not attributable to the administration of hormones. An incidental finding in the Ehrhardt and Money[11] report is that two patients showed a WAIS verbal IQ and performance IQ difference large enough to suggest brain damage. Few authors have reported to date on the neurological status of intersexes and it is an open question if brain abnormalities may play a part in emotional and gender disturbances in general.

Cryptorchidism.   Raboch et al[42] have presented the most extensive study of adult cryptorchids' undescended testicles sexual development and history. They found that plasma testosterone was reduced after 13 years of age in contrast to controls and that sexual outlet was developed somewhat later and was lower in general. There was also the earlier appearance of prolonged periods of sexual abstinence. There was no explicit discussion of gender identity or erotic preference but it seems that *all cases* were normal in this respect.

CONCLUSION

There has yet to appear in the literature a satisfactory study to test the hypothesis that sex of rearing is an overriding factor in gender identity or object choice. Although this claim is made, there are so few studies with a suitable control group that the conclusion is not yet a sound one but remains a theory. Moreover, in the majority of better documented studies, the genetic and/or hormonal sex is congruent with the sex of rearing making a test of this hypothesis impossible. There has yet to appear a study that uses a standardized sexual history questionnaire or gender identity scale along with a psychometric evaluation of psychological health. Few psychological studies to date have reported on the hormonal status of the intersex patients and often it is difficult to know exactly who has had karyotyping to determine genetic sex. The measures of energy level are not satisfactory discriminators of males and females but appear to be a factor in both males and females with excessive androgen levels. The concept of tomboyism is ambiguous and is not identical with gender identity. The studies reviewed in Chapter 6 on Transsexualism have illustrated that cross sex behavior in children is not clearly related to later gender identity or to homosexuality. There is an important distinction between femininity and feminine gender identity which has not been made to date in the studies on intersexes. The rarity of such cases makes it unlikely that many studies will be generated which are definitive. The area of intersexes therefore remains an obscure interesting problem (cf. Green[12]).

The assertion has been made that it is important to establish the sex of the child as male or female by approximately two years of age. Money has paralleled the phenomenon to imprinting in birds and indicated that gender reversal is very difficult if not impossible after that age because core gender identity is established and fixed like the species attachment of the birds[29]. I disagree with that assertion on two counts. First there is no satisfactory empirical evidence that this is the case. Patients have been described who have changed later in life and have made a satisfactory adjustment. The most striking example is the community in the Dominican Republic in which hermaphrodites changed at puberty from female to male without apparent psychopathology and stress. The role and acceptance of the community in this transformation was noteworthy. Perhaps the *uncertainty* of gender identity in such patients is more important than a *change* of gender identity. Little has been said about the feelings of these patients or of ambiguous gender identity. With such an evident physical reminder of their sexual ambiguity; this uncertainty may be the norm.

The second reason for disagreement with Money is that the analogy of imprinting to gender identity formation is not a satisfactory one. Money and Ehrhardt[29] argued that imprinting is a type of learning which satisfies the following criteria: A responding nervous system and a special set of stimulus signals meet at a sensitive developmental period. Bonding of signals in the brain at this sensitive period is rapid, tenacious and long lasting. They argued further that it may not be correct to apply the term imprinting to human beings but the concept is important. They distinguish the acquisition of language and core gender identity from more transient learning. Errors of core gender identity are very resistant to change, they argued, and they implied that these early experiences are important in later gender attachments and object choice. The transsexual syndrome would appear to contradict this assertion, because early gender role assignment is clearly in line with anatomical sex and yet these individuals are insistent that there has been an error and they are members of the opposite sex. Whereas the parents may not discourage later feminine behavior it is not clear that they necessarily support it before 2 years of age. Moreover, crossdressing appears to start later and it seems that the programs described in Chapter 6 on Transsexualism indicate that effeminate male children are quite amenable to change, even though the child is 6-to-10 years of age. The hermaphrodite on the other hand may not desire to change his/her gender identity but only to be certain what it is. Since societies around the world and throughout history all appear to divide along age and sex lines, the pressure to be one or the other, male or female, is important. Ambiguity may be the greatest problem they face.

Language acquisition and imprinting are not the fixed all or none phenomena it is claimed they are. Shapiro[48] referred to imprinting as a Cheshire cat, which in Alice in Wonderland was forever appearing and disappearing. Shapiro asks if it is possible that imprinting has disappeared like the cat and all we have left, like the cat's grin, is the "following" response of the birds? Imprinting has been prematurely labeled as the measure of attachment, the feature of imprinting which has most concerned theorists in sexology. Shapiro made several pertinent points. First, the following response can be elicited by many different stimuli, not all of which have anything to do with attachment formation in the precocial bird. Second, following is only one way of measuring attachment. There may be many different mechanisms mediating the formation of attachment in precocial birds and these mechanisms may occur at different ages. Third, imprinting is used to explain a variety of phenomena and a common underlying mechanism is thereby implied. However the literature on imprinting is a "compendium of contradictory evidence" indicating that it is not as established as we may like to believe. Fourth, and perhaps most important for the problem of intersexes, attachments formed early in life do not necessarily automatically control the nature of attachments to be formed later in life. Fifth, color, smell or other stimuli may mediate attachment and following may only be the result of the formed attachment. In fact it may be the mother bird who follows her brood rather than the other way around. The same assertions may be made about gender identity and language acquisition. Language acquisition is a continuing process in which the child first uses single words at approximately 18 months, increasing vocabulary throughout adolescent years. Short sentences start to appear at 2 1/2 years and complex sentences about 3 1/2 years[5]. The average child is over 4-years-old before the rudiments of language acquisition are well formed but it is a continuing process which suggests that there is no definitive point in time when language is fixed in the brain of the child.

Similarly, measures of gender identity for preschool children as young as 4 years of age have been developed but lower age norms do not exist at present. Preferred toys is one index of masculinity-femininity and perhaps gender identity but even the 4-to-5-year-olds may be flexible in their choice of toys.

The attitude of the family and of the individual afflicted with an intersex problem may be all important in establishing negative feelings evidenced at adulthood or in changing an incorrectly assigned child. However Money and his colleagues make the point that treatment and diagnosis should be made early in life and this certainly is important since many of the problems described in the foregoing cases can be avoided.

TREATMENT

There are no systematic psychological studies of treatment effects in the intersexes. Understandably there are so few cases that this is extremely difficult and impractical. Most of the treatments used have been medical ones to correct a hormonal imbalance or surgical intervention to correct the malformed sex organs. Some of the treatments are outlined in Tables 14.1 and 14.2. More detail of medical treatment and of illustrations of the various disorders may be found in Money[25], Money and Ehrhardt[29], Smith[48] and Rosenthal[47]. Counselling for sterility may be important in some cases and Money[25] offers suggestions on approaches to take. He has indicated how misdiagnosis and mismanagement of the problems have added to the distress of the individuals afflicted. He suggests that early intervention and a thorough work up are important.

Treatment of Choice

Medical intervention is the most important facet of treatment for intersex problems. As Money suggested this should be done as soon after birth as possible and, if necessary, corrective changes made. Since the intersex problems are so poorly understood generally, specialists should be consulted who have long experience in this area. Karyotyping to determine genetic sex would seem an essential part of treatment but it is not clear that it is always done. Some confusion in cases described in the literature may not have happened if the determination of genetic sex has been made earlier. An important consideration in seeking early medical attention is that ambiguous sex organs may be associated with cancer[38] and early surgery can be performed to remove the carcinogenic tissue.

Little has been said of psychiatric intervention in the intersexes. If there is distress in these cases, it is poorly documented. Ehrhardt indicated that girls with adrenogenital sydrome appear to have made a satisfactory psychological adjustment but usually we do not know what psychological problems intersex individuals may face. No psychological treatment therefore can be recommended.

The whole question of changing sex or gender role in intersex patients should be reconsidered. There is little impelling evidence that a satisfactory adjustment cannot be made at any age. The claim that 2-to-3 years of age is critical has not been supported by empirical fact. Gender identity may be an overriding factor in a satisfactory sex change in intersex patients but it remains to be shown that any change that will bring certainty of sex role with an acceptable physical appearance is not the most important feature in treatment of these patients.

BIBLIOGRAPHY

1. Baker, D., Telfer, M., Richardson, C., & Clark, G. Chromosome errors in men with antisocial behavior: comparison of selected men with Klinefelter's Syndrome and XYY chromosome pattern. *Journal of the American Medical Association*, 1970, *214*(5), 869–878.
2. Baker, H. J.,& Stoller, R. J. Can a biological force contribute to gender identity. *American Journal of Psychiatry*, 1968, *124*(12), 1653–1658.
3. Baker, H. J., & Stoller, R. J. Sexual psychopathology in the hypogonadal male. *Archives of General Psychiatry*, 1968, *18*, 631–633.
4. Bartlett, D. J. Chromosomes of male patients in a security prison. *Nature*, 1968, *219*, 351–353.
5. Beasley, J. Language origins and development. *The Child: A Book of Readings*. Seidman, J. M. (Ed.), New York: Holt Rhinehart & Winston, 1964.
6. Dorner, G. Hormones and sexual differentiation of the brain. In *Sex, Hormones and Behavior*. New York: Ciba Foundation Symposium, 1979.
7. Ehrhardt, A. A. Prenatal hormonal exposure and psychosexual differentiation. In E. J. Sachar (Ed.), *Topics in Psychoendocrinology*, New York: Grune & Stratton, 1975, 67–82.
8. Ehrhardt, A. A., Greenberg, N., & Money, J. Female gender identity and absence of fetal gonadal hormones: Turner's syndrome. *The Johns Hopkins Medical Journal*, 1970, *126*(5), 237–248.
9. Ehrhardt, A. A., Grisanti, G. C., & Meyer-Bahlburg, H. F. L. Prenatal exposure to Medroxyprogesterone Acetate (MPA) in girls. *Psychoneuroendocrinology*, 1977, *2*, 391–398.
10. Ehrhardt, A. A., & Meyer-Bahlburg, H. F. L. Psychosexual development: an examination of the role of prenatal hormones. *Sex, Hormones and Behavior*. New York: Ciba Foundation Symposium, 1979, 41–57.
11. Ehrhardt, A. A., & Money, J. Progestin-induced hermaphroditism: IQ and psychosexual identity in a study of ten girls. *The Journal of Sex Research*, 1967, *3*(1), 83–100.
12. Green, R. Sexual identity: Research strategies. *Archives of Sexual Behavior*, 1975,
13. Hampson, J. G. Hermaphroditic genital appearance, rearing and eroticism in hyperadrenocorticism. *Bulletin of the Johns Hopkins Hospital*, 1955, *96*, 265–273.
14. Hampson, J. L., Hampson, J. G., & Money, J. The syndrome of gonadal agenesis (ovarian agenesis) and male chromosomal pattern in girls and women: psychologic studies. *Bulletin of the Johns Hopkins Hospital*, 1955, *97*, 207–226.
15. Hoaken, P. C. S, Clarke, M., & Breslin, M. Psychopathology in Klinefelter's Syndrome. *Psychosomatic Medicine*, 1964, *26*, 207–223.
Psychosomatic Medicine, 1964, *26*, 207–223.
16. Hook, E. B. Behavioral implications of the human XYY genotype. *Science*, 1973, *179*, 139–150.
17. Imperato-McGinley, J., Guerrero, L, Gauther, T., & Peterson, R. E. Steroid 5 alpha Reductase deficiency in man: an inherited form of male pseudohermaphroditism. *Science*, 1974, *186*, 1213–1215.

18. Imperato-McGinley, J., Peterson, R. E., & Gauther, T. Gender identity and hermaphroditism. *Science,* 1976, *191,* 872.

19. Kessler, S., & Moos, R. The XYY karyotype and criminality: a review. *Journal of Psychiatric Research,* 1970, *7,* 153-170.

20. Kusalic, M., Fortin, C., & Gauthier, Y. Psychodynamic aspects of dwarfism. *Canadian Psychiatric Association Journal,* 1972, *17,* 29-34.

21. Kvale, J., & Fishman, J. The psychosocial aspects of Klinefelter's Syndrome. *Journal of the American Medical Association,* 1965, *193*(7), 567-572.

22. Lev-Ran, A. Gender role differentiation in hermaphrodites. *Archives of Sexual Behavior,* 1974, *3*(5), 391-424.

23. Masica, D. N., Money, J., Ehrhardt, A. Fetal feminization and female gender identity in the testicular feminizing syndrome of Androgen insensitivity. *Archives of Sexual Behavior,* 1971, *1*(2), 132-142.

24. Money, J. Hermaphroditism, gender and precocity in hyperadrenocorticism: psychologic findings. *Bulletin of Johns Hopkins Hospital,* 1955, *96,* 253-264.

25. Money, J. *Sex Errors of the Body: Dilemmas, Education, Counseling.* Baltimore: Johns Hopkins Press, 1968.

26. Money, J. Turner's Syndrome and parietal lobe functions. *Cortex,* 1973, *9,* 387-393.

27. Money, J. Gender identity and hermaphroditism. *Science,* 1976, *191,* 871-872.

28. Money, J., & Dalery, J. Iatrogenic homosexuality. *Journal of Homosexuality,* 1976, *1*(4), 357-370.

29. Money, J., & Ehrhardt, A. A. *Man and Woman, Boy and Girl.* Baltimore: Johns Hopkins Press, 1972.

30. Money, J., Hampson, J. G., & Hampson, J. L. Hermaphroditism: Recommendations concerning assignment of sex, change of sex, and psychologic management. *Bulletin of Johns Hopkins Hospital,* 1955, *97,* 214-300.

31. Money, J., Hampson, J. G., & Hampson, J. L. An examination of some basic sexual concepts: The evidence of human hermaphroditism. *Bulletin of Johns Hopkins Hospital,* 1955, *97,* 301-319.

32. Money, J., Hampson, J. G., & Hampson, J. L. Imprinting and the establishment of gender role. *Archives of Neurology and Psychiatry,* 1957, *77,* 333-336.

33. Money, J., & Musaph, H. (Eds.). *Handbook of Sexology,* Amsterdam: Excerpta Medica, 1977.

34. Money, J., & Ogunro, C. Behavioral sexology: Ten cases of genetic male intersexuality with impaired prenatal and pubertal androgenization. *Archives of Sexual Behavior,* 1974, *3*(3), 183-205.

35. Money, J., & Pollitt, E. Cytogenic and psychosexual ambiguity. *Archives of General Psychiatry,* 1964, *11,* 589-595.

36. Moore, K. L., Graham, M. A., Barr, M. The detection of chromosomal sex in hermaphrodites from a skin biopsy. *Surgery, Gynecology, and Obstetrics,* 1953, *96,* 641-648.

37. Nyborg, H., & Nielsen, J. Sex chromosome abnormalities and cognitive performance: field dependence, frame dependence, and failing development of perceptual stability in girls with Turner's Syndrome. *The Journal of Psychology,* 1977, *96,* 205-211.

38. Overzier, C. (Ed.). *Intersexuality,* London, Academic Press, 1963.

39. Owen, D. R. The 47, XYY male: a review. *Psychological Bulletin,* 1972, *78*(3), 209-233.

40. Pasqualini, R. Q., Vidal, G, & Bur, G. E. Psychopathology of Klinefelter's Syndrome. *Lancet,* 1957, *2,* 164-167.

41. Pritchard, M. Homosexuality and genetic sex. *Journal of Mental Science,* 1962, *108,* 616-623.

42. Raboch, J., Mellan, J., & Starka, L. Adult cryptorchids: sexual development and activity. *Archives of Sexual Behavior,* 1977, *6*(5), 413–419.

43. Raboch, J., Mellan, J., & Starka, L. Klinefelter's Syndrome: sexual development and activity. *Archives of Sexual Behavior,* 1979, *8*(4), 333–339.

44. Raft, D., Spencer, R. F., & Toomey, T. C. Ambiguity of gender identity fantasies and aspects of normality and pathology in hypopituitary dwarfism and Turner's Syndrome: Three cases. *The Journal of Sex Research,* 1976, *12*(3), 161–172.

45. Reinisch, J. M. Fetal hormones, the brain, and human sex differences: A heuristic, integrative review of the recent literature. *Archives of Sexual Behavior,* 1974, *3*(1), 51–90.

46. Reinisch, J. M., & Karow, W. G. Prenatal exposure to synthetic progestins and estrogens: Effects on human development. *Archives of Sexual Behavior,* 1977, *6*(4), 257–288.

47. Rosenthal, D. *Genetic Theory and Abnormal Behavior.* New York: McGraw Hill Company, 1970.

48. Shapiro, J. L. Imprinting: Another look at the Cheshire Cat. *Paper presented at the Sixty-Fourth Annual Meeting of the Southern Society for Philosophy,* St. Louis, Missouri, March 30, 1972.

49. Smith, D. W. *Recognizable Patterns of Human Malformation.* Philadelphia: Saunders and Company, 1976.

50. Yalom, I. D., Green, R., & Fish, N. Prenatal exposure to female hormones. *Archives of General Psychiatry,* 1973, *28,* 554–561.

51. Zuger, B. A critical review of the evidence from hermaphroditism. *Psychosomatic Medicine,* 1970, *32*(5), 449–467.

15 Sexual Dysfunction

INTRODUCTION

Men with normal erotic preferences may experience difficulties during sexual intercourse. Some are *impotent* since they either cannot obtain an erection or are unable to maintain it once they do have it. This is one of the most common sexual dysfunctions seen clinically. Another problem is premature ejaculation in which the male climaxes too soon to allow his female partner to attain orgasm as well. The concept of premature ejaculation can be particularly difficult to define. Kilmann and Auerbach[33] who reviewed the literature on this topic noted that time to orgasm was often important in defining the problem. Obler[56] used "ejaculation in less than 2 minutes" as significant while Masters and Johnson[50], noting the variability in each couple's performance, suggested that a male who could not delay ejaculation long enough on 50% of sexual occasions for the female to climax was impotent. The female's contribution is ignored for, as Kilmann and Auerbach noted, a male who could only delay ejaculation 30 minutes for his female partner who took 45 minutes would be considered a premature ejaculator. All men might be premature ejaculators in some instances with a partner or may not be dysfunctional for one partner but would be for another (cf. [77]).

Mr. A was an exhibitionist who had intercourse with over 100 women. He was charming and when he first came to my office, several female staff commented on his good looks after he left. He illustrates how different women as partners can define the sexual dysfunction.

Mr. A: You know women fall into two groups. Some are eager and enjoy sex as a participant. But others are like boards. They lie back and expect you to do all the work. When it's all over I still don't know where I'm at. I get the feeling they are giving me a gift and they are reluctant to do so. I think they see me as someone who has to entertain them. It's a pain. I find good-looking broads like that. It's the plain ones who are more eager. Then there are the dogs. I guess I shouldn't say that, they can't help being ugly. But I've gone to bed with homely women because they had nice personalities and they seemed turned on. Sometimes I found it even hard to get an erection.

Doctor: Which women do you like best for sex?

Mr. A: The plain ones who are nice and look ok. Sex should be fun and not work. Some women think they are God's gift to men and I don't like them at all. At first I thought it was me and I wasn't a man unless I satisfied the woman. But now I see both the man and woman have an active part to play.

If *Mr. A* has less experience he might be judged sexually dysfunctional, either as a premature ejaculator or impotent and even with his experience, he might be judged to suffer both sexual dysfunctions.

Who exactly is sexually dysfunctional is open to a wide range of interpretations so that a booming business has been created for a sometimes gullible but normal population. Sex therapists who have little or no qualifications and even well meaning untrained professionals have come into the business of treating sexual dysfunctions. The charlatans have also capitalized on the market with untested procedures, with sex surrogates and a wide range of sexual aids and gadgets to serve as stimulants. The line between trained professional and untrained entrepreneur has been a difficult one to draw. Many ethical issues arise which have not been worked out clearly to date. The boundary between sensation seeking and science has been abused making the whole problem difficult for laymen to evaluate. Phallometry has an important role to play in assessing sexual dysfunction and it provides the patient and therapist with a guide to diagnosis and treatment. We will return to this later.

It has been claimed often but inappropriately that men with sexual anomalies are sexually dysfunctional[22][33][43][73]. The impotent male usually wants to have sex with a mature female and cannot whereas the sexually anomalous male may not desire her at all. For example, a homosexual may not desire the mature female and cannot be aroused by her. He may come to the attention of a clinician because he is married and there is discord over sexual relations. The true object of his erotic desire is not his wife whom he has married for social rather than sexual reasons. However, he mistakenly may be treated for impotence.

Mr. B had lived a secret homosexual life for over 20 years unknown to his wife or business associates. Because his therapist had been recommended by a gay community organization, he revealed for the first time the extent of his homosexual commitment.

> *Mr. B:* I have a thing about men. I can't stay away from them. I like sex with a man and I wonder if I shouldn't go all the way and be gay and leave my wife.
>
> *Doctor:* How do you feel about your wife?
>
> *Mr. B:* Not so good. Sex is less than it is with a man and half the time I can't get it up or I don't come. I guess our relationship is in the pits. We fight a lot and we don't even have sex that much any more.

He made it quite clear he would not discuss with another therapist that he was homosexual and the remaining facts of his case present as a picture of an impotent heterosexual in an unhappy marriage. By making the sexual anomaly into a sexual dysfunction, the arousal and directional components of sexual motivation are confused.

In sexual dysfunction the arousal component or sex drive may be excessively high or too low but the preferred object, the female, is appropriate. In contrast, there may be no evident problem with arousal itself in sexual anomalies but the direction or object choice for orgasm is unusual or socially unacceptable. In fact, not infrequently one hears that the homosexual or exhibitionist "has a compulsion to engage in his socially deviant behavior." This attests to the strength of the sex drive although "compulsion" seems an inappropriate term. The average man is not described as a "compulsive heterosexual." In sexual anomalies, the arousal component of sexual behavior seems normal but the direction is different. Confusion arises because sometimes sexually anomalous men may also be impotent or premature ejaculators for their preferred object. Masters and Johnson[51] in fact, conducted a long term study on sexual dysfunction in homosexual men and treated them in analogous fashion to heterosexual dysfunctional men by restoring their full homosexual functioning.

The main questions in this section are: what causes sexual dysfunctions and how often are they associated with sexual anomalies.

THE THEORIES

There are several review articles or books available and only an overview is presented here[2] [25] [29] [33].

Anxiety as a causal factor.   The most frequent cause of sexual dysfunction is assumed to be anxiety. Several authors have suggested that the new wave of women's sexual liberation has produced problems in their male partners. The women think that they are entitled to orgasm like their male partners and a competition may be developed to see how well one man performs compared to another[27][39]. This takes the problem of sexual dysfunction out of the psychological realm and into the social. Many theorists postulate that anxiety is the basis of both sexual anomalies and dysfunctions. The homosexual, the exhibitionist, the rapist, and so forth, are afraid of intercourse with a woman. As we have seen throughout the book, most of these theories are seriously wanting. Moreover it is important to distinguish object choice from arousability. If we assume that the homosexual, for example, is impotent with females, is it also not fair to say that the heterosexual male who cannot perform in homosexual relations is impotent? Clearly the problem must be defined within the limits of arousability to preferred sex objects. There are impotent homosexuals who, during their relationships with other men, experience arousal difficulties and this can readily be defined as sexual dysfunction in a homosexual male. However it is not the case that he is impotent because he cannot be aroused by women. The literature does not always make this clear and treatment goals become confused. Erotic object choice seems very resistant to change but arousability level does appear to be readily modifiable in many cases.

Depression, anger and loss of libido.   Tamburello and Seppecher[71], Proctor[61], and Goldberg[28] suggested that depression is an important cause of impotence. Severe depression is not only a mood characterized by sadness, hopelessness and poor self esteem, but there are also the so called physiological signs of sleep disturbance, loss of appetite and loss of libido. The depressed male may appear impotent and, according to Tamburello and Seppecher, this may further add to his feelings of incompetence and deepen the depression. Thus, an impotent male may become depressed because of his poor sexual performance or vice versa.

Anger may be another causal emotion in impotence[26]. It may stem from marital problems, infidelity or domination by the wife, needs not being met, and so forth. Psychoanalysts also view its source as unconscious rage to women as well as fear of castration.

Physical abnormalities, disease and chemicals versus psychological factors.   Many physical abnormalities are associated with sexual dysfunction. a dichotomy has been made between primary and secondary impotence and between organic and psychogenic impotence. The male with primary impotence has never had satisfactory sexual intercourse with ejaculation whereas the one with secondary impotence has done so at least once[33]. Either form of impotence may be psychogenic, that is, have causal factors which are psychological rather than physical. For the male who has never experienced satisfactory intromission, an organic or physical cause may be suspected.

Austino[5], Ellenberg[19], Lundberg[47], Simpson[69], Tordjman[73], and Vas[75], have outlined the wide range of conditions that can result in impotence. In some instances, such as certain cases of diabetes, it may be the only presenting symptom suggesting that great care is required in assessing this disorder. Known factors associated with it are: diabetes, prostatitis (inflammation of the prostate gland), lumbar disc disease, Le Riche's Syndrome which is a circulatory disturbance in the lower aorta, sympathectomy involving the lumbar ganglia, brain or spinal cord tumors or injuries, especially temporal lobe tumors including epilepsy, (See Chapter 7 and Lundberg[47]), trauma or injury to perineal nerves, multiple sclerosis, endocrine disorders which involve sex hormones, severe systemic disease of any nature, priapism (sustained painful erection of the penis) which may result from obstruction of vessels that drain the organ, in turn, caused by nerve damage, bladder stones, prostatitis, and also sickle cell anemia and leukemia. Venous stasis or slowing of normal flow of blood into the penis can have several causes. Often there is valvular incontinence of the deep dorsal vein of the penis so the blood is drained off from it. Thus a male may be able to have an erection for a short time and then lose it because of the weakness in the dorsal vein. Tordjman and his co-workers[74] have studied the venous vascular process involved in erection and indicated that erectile impotence of venous origin may be suspected by the ability of a male to maintain erection more easily when standing. Coronary heart disease is also associated with both impotence and premature ejaculation but not consistently. A study of patients[76] with acute myocardial infarction showed two thirds were impotent, 28% had a significant decrease in sexual outlet, and 8% were premature ejaculators.

Chemicals have also been connected with impotence: heroin addiction, excessive alcohol results in temporary impotence, chronic barbiturate intoxication, Banthene-like drugs or anti-cholinergic agents, Phenothiazine, tranquilizers such as Thorazine, Compazine, Mellaril, Phenergan, Sparine and Trilafon, monoamine oxidase inhibitors such as Nardil, Marplan or Parnate; drugs used to treat high blood pressure such as Guanethedine, Ismulen and Esimil. The antiandrogens and estrogens will also produce impotence in men: cyproterone acetate and medroxyprogesterone acetate (Provera, Depo Provera).

Urological surgery such as prostate gland operations may produce impotence. Amelar[1] noted that potency is *retained in* operations for *benign enlargements* of the prostate gland but when the perineal nerves are involved even in *benign* disease or in radical prostatectomy for cancer, potency is lost. Retrograde ejaculation usually occurs after these operations when potency is restored. Loss of the penis itself accidentally or surgically can be seriously depressing to the patient and his wife. However, erotic satisfaction may still be possible by stimulating other parts of the body[71].

Amelar pointed out an important diagnostic feature distinguishing organic and psychogenic impotence. Psychological impotence is characteristically *selective* such that the male is arousable under certain conditions but not others. For instance, a man may be aroused by his mistress or by magazine pictures but not by his wife or he may show morning erection or nocturnal tumescence or erection during sleep. Erections under any circumstance suggest psychogenic impotence.

Premature ejaculation and impotence may be considered similar in etiology, especially if psychogenic origins are prominent in the theory, for example, in psychoanalysis. However the range of organic factors which produce impotence do not apply to premature ejaculation. The latter seems mainly psychogenic[42]. Kaplan noted that the premature ejaculator is unaware of sensations warning of impending orgasm. This may be due to unconscious conflict or early sexual experiences with women whose sexual satisfaction was not valued so a lasting conditioned low physiological threshold for ejaculation was set up. Levine[42] noted that premature ejaculation may be masking a female sexual dysfunction which manifests itself as short vaginal containment of the penis or attempts to "get it over with" in one way or another.

THE EXPERIMENTAL EVIDENCE

This cursory review of sexual dysfunction shows that the phenomenon is quite complex conceptually and diagnostically. Unfortunately there is a dearth of pertinent controlled studies.

Sexual anomaly versus dysfunction. The association of sexual dysfunctions with anomalies has not been adequately investigated to date. Gebhard and his associates[24] found that a range of sex offenders reported from 31% to 61% incidence of impotence, the highest being incest offenders, the lowest voyeurs. However they apparently contradict these figures in stating that 25% of exhibitionists reported erectile impotence. The results are ambiguous since they are based on self reports of prisoners and it is not clear if the sexually anomalous outlet as distinguished from heterosexual coitus is the object of orgasms. The authors warned that they are not sure in homosexual offenders if the dysfunction refers to male or female partners. Karacan and his associates[31] found that nocturnal penile tumescence in rapists was normal suggesting that the erectile apparatus was functioning and organic impotence was not important in this condition. However psychogenic impotence could not be ruled out.

In our own data banks of sexual anomalies, impotence has not been a frequently reported problem. In one report on exhibitionists my colleagues and I[37] found that in reference to sexual intercourse with a mature female, 82%

reported no problem, 12% were not applicable because of inexperience and 6% reported a problem of impotence. Considering that these men have an erotic preference for exhibiting and not for intercourse per se, this incidence seems rather low to be of etiological significance. A higher incidence would be expected in homosexual men since they show very little or no sexual arousal to women. In exhibitionists who at least prefer the *body* characteristics of women, sexual dysfunction would seem to be a poor explanation of their sexual behavior. No other data are currently available on sexual anomalies and further studies need to be done. The arousal and direction components of erotic interest would have to be clearly separated and defined.

It is noteworthy that a sexual anomaly is not frequently explored as a reason for dysfunction so that psychogenic anxiety is often assumed. Annon[2] indicated that 90% to 95% of dysfunctional cases are psychogenic in origin. Yet Kilmann and Auerbach[33] complained of poor evaluations in treatment studies. Obviously much greater care is needed in diagnosis. It seems the importance of organic factors are not considered as often as they should be. Since a wide range of physical problems and disease processes can be associated with impotence, even as the only presenting symptom, both researcher and therapist need to be more cautious.

Organic versus psychogenic impotence.   Karacan and his colleagues[30] used nocturnal penile tumescence as a diagnostic aid in identifying organic versus psychogenic impotence. Psychogenic cases show erections during sleep about every 45 minutes in conjunction with REM (Rapid Eye Movement) sleep. REM has been associated also with dreaming[20]. If psychogenic impotence is present, erections will occur when the patient's anxiety or guard is down during sleep.

Karacan and his coworkers[32] found that in 20-to-26 year old men there were 4-to-5 episodes of penile tumescence nightly each lasting about 33 minutes. Over 9-in-10 of the episodes occurred during REM sleep. One may wish to make an association of dreams and tumescence but this phenomenon seems to serve some other perhaps organic function since it is found in newborn babies. Karacan et al., noted that there is not a one to one relationship of REM sleep and erection. They did point out the diagnostic significance of the phenomenon for impotence.

Marshall and his associates[49] have studied nocturnal erection in impotent men. Using a careful diagnostic procedure to sort out organic and psychogenic cases, they tested the value of nocturnal erection in diagnosis. They found that almost 100% of cases could be classified. Their results suggest that the method could be a primary diagnosis in itself without the necessity of more complex examination. At least it serves as a primary criterion of organic impotence. It is uncertain whether the nocturnal penile erections are erotic in nature but at least their presence rules out organic impotence. Their absence however may not. Usually nocturnal penile tumescence has been studied in laboratories and changes in sleep setting can influence sleep pattern during the first couple of nights[9]. This is a possible but unlikely factor influencing nocturnal erections which should be controlled. More important, anxiety states which influence erections as well as sleep have not been thoroughly studied, nor have the interfering influence of drugs used to treat these conditions. Drugs need to be ruled out as significant factors in sexual dysfunction. The importance of a physician in assessment is apparent.

Age and impotence. Age has been studied as a possible confounding factor in interpreting sexual dysfunction. The incidence of impotence (sexual disinterest?) is believed to increase with age. Karacan and his colleagues[32] examined males 3-to-79 years of age for nocturnal penile tumescence. Total full erection time during sleep decreased from 40 minutes per night to 30 minutes per night between ages 12 and 70. This result was also influenced by the total amount of sleep time. However it is clear that the phenomenon occurred consistently throughout the life span. Its importance as a diagnostic aid remains regardless of age.

Kinsey and his associates[35] found impotence common in men over 50 years of age and Edwards and Husted[18] noted in an experimental study using penile tumescence measures to erotica that decreased sensitivity of the penis occurred with age. It is noteworthy in their study that no direct measure of the two was reported without statistical manipulation of confounding variables. A replication of the study is warranted. Pfeiffer, Verwoerdt and Davis[57] noted that while there is a decline in sexual interest in men with age and more so with women, sex continues to play an important role. The decline is not so dramatic that it would produce frequent impotence however.

Solnick and Birren[70] conducted the most interesting study to date relating age and sexual potency. They compared two groups of normal men ages 19-to-30 and 48-to-65 on temperature change and rate of erection in the penis to an erotic film. Penile circumference was monitored and they found that the younger group erected almost 6 times faster than the older group. The younger group was also more sexually active and reported 2.95 ejaculations in the previous week compared to 1.75 in the older group. The lowered responsiveness of the older group may be due to physiological changes but it may also be due to the reduced effectiveness of the stimuli to elicit arousal. Older organisms are generally less curious than younger ones and experience in general reduces arousability to repeated stimuli. It would be interesting while controlling for age, to determine if less experienced men are more reactive to erotic films than those more experienced.

Endocrine disorders.   The question of androgen deficiencies have been suggested as factors in impotence and the results are confusing at first glance. There are numerous problems in assessing endocrine hormones in sexual behavior which have been discussed in Chapter Two. It is important to take several blood samples and to use an established radio immunoassay method to measure the serum levels of hormones. In addition, it is important to establish that the impotence is organic, psychogenic or uncertain in origin. One might expect in some cases of organic impotence that testosterone levels would be influenced by endocrine disorders but there is less reason to suspect such a change in psychogenic disorders. The reports which fail to satisfy these minimum criteria are the ones reporting significant results[14] [40] [62] [67]. In a more detailed study, Pirke and his associates[59] attempted to classify psychogenic impotence and compared this group of men to controls. There were no significant differences in leutinizing hormone or in plasma testosterone. Data on normals suggest that sex hormones and erectile function are related weakly and in a complex way. Schiavi and his coworkers[65] found that testosterone and leutinizing hormone (LH) were unrelated to erection cycles and REM sleep in healthy males. In a better controlled study on a larger sample, Pirke and his colleagues[58] found that there was an average increase of 35% in testosterone level in relation to an explicit erotic movie. They measured plasma testosterone every fifteen minutes and the maximum concentration was observed 60 to 90 minutes after the film. Control volunteers did not show such changes to a neutral movie.

The studies collectively suggest that psychological causes of impotence are not clearly related to hormones in the blood but that some cases of organic impotence will show a relationship and a careful assessment is necessary.

Mood and impotence.   There are almost no systematic psychological studies on personality traits or states in sexually dysfunctional men in spite of claims that anxiety, anger and depression are prominent. Depression is presumably related to reduced sexual outlet but it is not uncommon for severely depressed patients to say they are incompetent or declining in various aspects of their lives and to say sex is not what it was. Depressed patients also tend to be older. In the few studies which control for age and examine the relationship of depression and actual performance, there is little difference between depressed and control volunteers[6]. It seems that the depressed person suffers more from an attitude toward himself than an actual performance impairment. In a widely used depression measure, the Beck Depression Inventory, Stancer and I found that the so called physiological signs of depression, loss of appetite, loss of libido and sleep disturbance were not correlated with the state of depression and in fact were unrelated to each other[38]. Moreover the whole measure of depression reflected a socially undesirable response set. That is, the depressed person prefers to report himself in a negative way. Depression however does not seem to influence sexual performance to an appreciable extent, even in severe cases of depression. In a paper poorly translated from Italian, Tamburello and Seppecher[71] appear to indicate that frequency of coitus in severely depressed patients is substantial although reduced. However, their numerical tabulations appear to indicate that coital frequency increased slightly with depression. In examining my own unpublished data on sexually anomalous men, I found that there was no connection between depression scores on the MMPI and the frequency of sexual relations in the past week prior to testing. Lidberg[44] reported on the clinical evaluation of 201 Swedish men complaining of premature ejaculation and impotence. Psychiatrically they were unremarkable and only 11% were classified as having anxiety neurosis; the type of diagnosis one would expect more frequently based on the anxiety theory of sexual dysfunction. The author noted that the incidence of emotional disturbance was low and so was the use of alcohol and barbiturates. It is not clear from their report which cases were organic or psychogenic.

Cooper[12] [14] found that premature ejaculators scored higher on a neuroticism scale than controls who were suffering from primary impotence. However all scores were within normal limits although the premature ejaculators were clinically rated more often as neurotic. There were no apparent differences in femininity, submissiveness or depression. Among impotent groups, psychogenic types appeared more neurotic than constitutional (organic) types and were more hostile. While no analysis is presented, the claim is made that the two groups did not differ on these personality measures.

Derogatis and Meyer[17] compared sexually dysfunctional men to normal heterosexual controls on the Brief Symptom Inventory which measures symptoms and affect, and on the Derogatis Sexual Functioning Inventory (DSFI) which measures sexual information, experience, drive, liberal versus conservative attitudes, gender role definition and number of sex fantasy themes. 81% of the male patients suffered from unspecified impotence and the rest from premature ejaculation. The dysfunctional group scored as significantly less adjusted than controls on all scores except attitudes and gender role. In particular, the dysfunctional group scored lower on joy, contentment, vigor and affection but higher on anxiety, depression, guilt and hostility. While the results support the stereotyped personality of sexually dysfunctional men, the groups were not well defined and the range of variables which can relate to both the sexual dysfunction and the DSFI is considerable. Perhaps subgroups would reveal differences of clinical interest.

It seems that the relationship of depression as well as anxiety and anger is yet to be evaluated fully in well controlled studies and their etiological significance remains an assumption of treatment. Derogatis and Meyer's study suggests that anxiety, hostility and depression may be important in sexual dysfunction and should be further examined. In consideration of the poor assessment of sexual dysfunction and the variable meanings assigned to the terms premature ejaculation and impotence, studies examining personality traits must be especially careful to specify the criteria classifying the patient groups.

Social changes.   It has been suggested that there is a new impotence in our society due to the increased sexual freedom. Women are demanding and searching for their right to sexual experience and presumably this is generating a new wave of impotence in their men. However these are only speculations and the one study which offers empirical facts suggests that just the opposite is the case. Welch and Kartub[78] studied sexual attitudes and the incidence of impotence in 30 societies. Although this anthropological approach has its limitations, they found that the best predictor of impotence was the restrictiveness of attitudes toward premarital sex in females. Greater restriction related to reduced frequency of premarital intercourse and, to a much lesser extent, to negative attitudes towards rape, to degree of danger imputed to sexual intercourse, and to restrictiveness of attitudes towards sexual intercourse in marriage and towards extramarital affairs.

Sexual Dysfunction and the Stimulus Response Matrix

A summary of theories of sexual dysfunction appears in Table 15.1. The arousal and object choice components of sexual behavior have not been clearly separated in sexual dysfunction. Whereas the presence of a sexual anomaly may be the real reason for "impotence", rarely has an attempt been even made to establish that fact. In most cases no detailed sexual history has been provided. The very few existing studies suggest that men with sexual anomalies need not be impotent or premature ejaculators. Therefore the stimulus response matrix for sexually dysfunctional men is presumably as broad as the spectrum of sexual behavior itself.

It is important to separate out organic and psychological or psychogenic impotence. When this is done in the research literature, it is usually poorly described. A wide range of factors can cause impotence and careful medical examination is essential for anyone suspected of having a sexual dysfunction. A urologist is the likely specialist to investigate the problem but endocrinologists and neurologists may also be involved. The prevalence of

TABLE 15.1
Summary of Evidence for Theories of Sexual Dysfunction

Theory	Experimental Results
1. Anxiety plays a major role	Some positive support but systematic studies on well defined groups are few in number
2. Depression and anger can be important	Not clearly established to date
3. Sexual anomalies are due to sexual dysfunction	Limited evidence suggests they are not
4. Most impotence is psychogenic in origin	Very limited evidence to support this assertion. Many organic factors are associated with sexual dysfunction and careful medical investigation by specialists should be undertaken before conclusions are drawn

psychogenic and organic impotence is unknown at present and difficult to assess from the existing literature.

Psychological factors have been poorly evaluated so the connection of anxiety and other traits to impotence and premature ejaculation remains unclear. Sexual intercourse is a pleasure in which one must be relaxed to perform and enjoy. "Anxiety" that causes sexual dysfunction may not be pathological but reflect no more than a preoccupation with other matters, such as job, marital problems, and so forth. Anxiety about sexual performance per se has been implicit in the theory of impotence and premature ejaculation but we do not know the extent to which it is important. Any anxiety may block sexual performance and careful assessment of this factor needs to be reported in research studies. Therapy often has been based on the assumption that anxiety is prominent in sexual dysfunction and techniques have focused on reducing it.

TREATMENT

The treatment reports in the literature are not always clear on the type of sexual dysfunction treated[33] and this hampers our evaluation. It is important to keep organic factors distinct from psychogenic ones.

Medical Intervention

In many cases of organic impotence there is a medical technique available to correct the problem and no psychological procedures are necessary. Loss of libido associated with temporal lobe tumors may be restored with corrective surgery (See Chapter 7). In these cases there is a sudden loss of libido where it existed before. This might be interpreted as psychogenic without an adequate medical assessment. Marshall and his colleagues[48] found the drug Afrodex (nux vomica, methyl testosterone and yohimbene) to be effective in restoring potency in about one third of clearly defined cases of organic impotence. It operates by increasing blood flow to the penis. Karacan and his colleagues[32] reported that a prosthetic implant to the penis which makes it permanently hard, resulted in satisfactory physical and psychological postsurgery adjustments of 55 impotent men although they presented no systematic data (See also Austino et al.,[5]). Cole[10] had discussed a program in human sexuality for paraplegics and other physically disabled individuals available at the University of Minnesota Medical School. Although men with this affliction are insensitive from the chest down, they are capable of reflexive erection and intercourse but not ejaculation and orgasm. However there is a mental equivalent of orgasm experienced which seems fully satisfying. Possibly mental and physical sexual arousal are separate entities as discussed in Chapter 10 in reference to provera studies. In any case, Cole noted the importance of sex counselling for the paraplegic in a program that stresses his remaining abilities rather than his losses. The range of medical problems involved and the result of impotence are beyond the scope of this book and cannot be reviewed here (cf Cooper[13]). However I do want to point out that organic impotence does not necessarily mean permanent loss of sexual functioning and medical specialists should be consulted for any form of sexual dysfunction to determine accurately its organic or psychogenic nature.

Behavior Therapy

Case reports are not presented here because they are reviewed by Kilmann and Auerbach and others and because case reports are suspect due to publishing practices of journals. Unsuccessful cases are not reported and only controlled studies offer us anywhere near the complete picture of the true effectiveness of treatment approaches.

Desensitization. It seems that the psychiatric and psychological literature on sexual dysfunction has assumed impotence and premature ejaculation usually are psychogenic. The most frequent and logical method used with sexual dysfunction has been anxiety reducing systematic desensitization described in Chapter 3[16] [39] [45] [63]. In some cases of premature ejaculation, the desensitization treatment has been supplemented with Brevital (methohexitone sodium), a short acting barbiturate which aids in relaxation[23] [36].

The patient is first trained in deep muscle relaxation and then desensitized to a hierarchy of sexual stimuli. Weaker stimuli focused on sexual intercourse are introduced first and fantasized while the patient is in a state of deep relaxation. The anxiety to the stimulus should extinguish because it is not possible to be relaxed and tense at the same time. When the weak stimulus is extinguished, the previously strong stimuli become weaker. For example, a patient may find walking into his bedroom produces weak anxiety reactions whereas lying nude in bed with his wife generates much anxiety. The order of presenting stimuli would be in this case, walking into the room and then lying down. Usually 20-to-25 stimuli are used although more and less are noted by various therapists. Very few sessions are required in some cases raising the question of how ingrained the problem is. In some cases, all that may be necessary is to relax the patient. Deep muscle relaxation itself may be effective in bringing about sexual arousal.

Prohibition of anxiety provoking sexual behavior during desensitization is usually requested by the therapist so that the patient's daily sex life is not counter therapeutic. In some cases it may be a relief for the patient not to engage in the anxiety provoking sexual behavior. The command from the authority figure, the therapist, may be sufficient to relax him to the extent that he finds himself involuntarily sexually aroused. These confounding influences on treatment and the problem of diagnostic classification make it difficult to know exactly what the effective ingredients are in desensitization therapy of sexual dysfunctions. The concurrent use of other treatments like psychotherapy and simple sex education instruction have also been confounding influences in interpreting studies. The treatment forms such a good fit to the problem that one hesitates to criticize its effectiveness but Kilmann and Auerbach reviewed the literature up to 1970 and noted that there existed mainly case studies and only a few systematic controlled studies. They complained that this offers very little on which to base the claims of treatment effectiveness. Their claim remains true today. Controlled studies are to be trusted first although they are by no means the final answer and should not be accepted uncritically. It is important not to form premature closure on treatment. Many more controlled studies are needed.

Obler[56] conducted a controlled study on the effectiveness of desensitization, group therapy and no treatment on a group of unspecified sexually dysfunctional university students. Females were also studied but are not discussed here. There were nine males in each group and they had to be free of other psychological problems. They were selected according to scores on the Taylor Manifest Anxiety Scale but it is unclear how. A variety of *psychological* measures were taken as well as heart rate and Galvanic skin responses (GSR). The group therapy was "traditional" but involved discussion of social and sexual problems as well. The desensitization was superior to the group therapy or no treatment. The latter two were not different. The change due to treatment was reflected in most measures although the meaning of some of them is unclear from the report. Even the GSR was unusual in the amount of change reported. There were large individual differences in GSR results which may have distorted the outcome. A confounding factor in the evaluation of the treatment is that the desensitization group also received assertiveness training at the same time.

Auerbach and Killman[4] compared two facets of desensitization: The use of relaxation with a hierarchy versus the use of relaxation alone in the treatment of secondary impotence. The group receiving a hierarchy improved in 40% of cases based on an examination of self reported sexual experience whereas the group that had only relaxation showed a 3% improvement. This suggests that the hierarchy is important. It is noteworthy that in this well defined study, the success rate was quite low, namely 40%, suggesting that although it offers some positive results, other features of the problems are likely being missed. The Masters and Johnson methods are more powerful as noted later.

Asirdas and Beech[3] compared desensitization to positive conditioning and no treatment control groups using two cases of ejaculatory incompetence, seven of secondary impotence, and two of primary impotence. Women were also treated and reported together because their results were comparable in the three treatment conditions. Positive conditioning was used because the authors felt anxiety was not always present in dysfunctional cases and that boredom or indifference may have been important factors. In this method a stimulus representing the currently nonarousing wife or mate was paired with something that was sexually stimulating so as to increase her attractiveness. Fantasies of the coital partner were used as conditioning stimuli while slides of erotic scenes were used as unconditioned stimuli since they were capable of arousing the male patients. There was a significant increase in coital frequency from pre-to-post treatment in the two treatment conditions while the controls did not change. Satisfaction with intercourse also improved in both groups significantly but not as much in the desensitization group as in the positive conditioning group. It was unchanged in the untreated controls. The interesting finding was that the positive conditioning group showed significantly more improvement than the desensitization group. If the coital partner was anxiety provoking or all women were anxiety provoking then the positive conditioning should not have worked at all. If the partner alone was anxiety provoking then following her by nonanxiety provoking stimuli would be the equivalent of anxiety relief conditioning or backward conditioning which supposedly does not work. On the other hand if all heterosexual stimuli were anxiety provoking, then two aversive scenes would be used in this procedure so the patient would be shunted from one negative stimulus (his mate) to another (erotic scenes). Thus the anxiety theory of sexual dysfunction should not predict positive outcome in this method but the results were significant. Therefore the hypothesis that boredom may be important in sexual dysfunction may be entertained.

Biofeedback.   Reynolds[64] presented one of the very few studies using penile measurement in evaluation and treatment. He compared the effectiveness of biofeedback in changing erectile difficulties. All cases were considered to be psychogenic dysfunctions although five men never completed coitus because of insufficient erections and were labeled primary erectile dysfunction. There were three groups. In two groups penile circumference was monitored while participants were given continuous sound feedback on increases in the level of erection to an erotic film. The first group had erection contingent feedback while the second group had noncontingent feedback to demonstrate that timing was an important factor in the outcome. A third group saw the film and had no feedback. Follow up after one month showed that the three groups did not differ in self reported satisfaction. It seems treatment did little to them. However immediately after treatment, the group that had contingent feedback was more aroused than the other groups. The latter did not differ from each other. The author argued that the feedback in the form of a tone interfered with the effects of the erotic film. However the great variability in responsiveness of participants, the influence of their age on penile erection and the variability in duration of the problem (from 2-to-31 years) casts doubt on the effectiveness of this method.

Csillag[15] in a feedback study of six psychogenic cases of impotence found that the method was quite effective. The cases were compared to a group of controls all ranging in age from 18-to-35. Both pictures and fantasies were used first without feedback and then with visual and auditory feedback to enhance penile diameter. The patients showed a steady improvement over treatment sessions while the controls' reactions declined with repetition as expected with any stimulus as it becomes boring. Possibly the simple repetition of the stimuli for the impotent patients helped to reduce anxiety and allowed them to respond as well. Self reports of patients showed that 5% improved their sex lives although one man with primary erectile impotence did not. The improvement of a bisexual patient is noteworthy since he had erections in homosexual situations, but he did not have the opportunity to test out his therapy gains in heterosexual situations. He was also described as having primary impotence. As noted in Chapter 5, bisexual men who marry usually erotically prefer men and the impotence they experience may simply reflect their lack of interest in the female. They do not experience a problem of impotence with men. Csillag's study does serve to show that the use of biofeedback can be effective although more studies which are better defined need to be done.

Evaluation of behavior therapy.   Lobitz and his colleagues[46] have indicated that behavior therapy is simplistic in the treatment of sexual dysfunction and that marital problems and marital discord may be an overriding influence on treatment outcome. The therapist may have to alter his approach continuously. Changing the attitude of the male and/or his partner may be the essence of therapy. To date only a simplistic approach has been taken to a complex problem.

McCarthy[53] has outlined the range of procedures which have been used as anxiety reducing methods for sexual problems generally. Some clearly may have educative effects on the individual rather than changing personality pathology. There are 14 methods: bibliotherapy (reading), use of audiovisual materials, in vivo desensitization via written programmed exercises, self exploratory masturbation training, orgasmic reconditioning, stimulated orgasm experiences, implosion techniques, sex word desensitization, sexual assertion training, therapist modelling, self disclosure, systematic desensitization and cue controlled relaxation. While all are used, most of the procedures do not have demonstrated effectiveness in the treatment of sexual dysfunction. Rather they reflect the heterogeneous range of problems which are cast under the label sex dysfunction and which may be minor, transitory, or, life long problems.

Hypnosis

There is a striking parallel in hypnotherapy and conditioning therapy practiced by behavior therapists. Beigel[7] indicated that impotence is related to a lack of self confidence, general inadequacy and body overconcern. Hypnosis serves to identify and confirm causative factors in the problem, eliminate mental blocks, bring back repressed memories and allows imaging and planting ideas essential to a change in attitude of the patient towards himself and others. Posthypnotic suggestion allows execution of tasks supporting the goal of therapy and allows a check on progress.

Only a few case studies have been reported with success[33] indicating it is an alternative method which can be used to treat sexual dysfunction. However contemporary hypnotherapists see the role of their treatment as more limited than Beigel does. One is faced with the unwillingness of individuals to undergo hypnosis while they will accept behavior therapy which is similar in outcome.

Psychotherapy

Psychotherapy has been infrequently used in sexual dysfunction cases and and has generally been found too time consuming and expensive as well as relatively ineffective for the problem[13]. Moisso[54] has provided an outline for transactional analysis therapy of sexual dysfunction but no outcome details are reported. In the only study using more than a case report, O'Connor and Stern[55] treated premature ejaculators and impotent men via psychotherapy. Three quarters of the premature ejaculators and 2/3 of the impotent men improved but they did not say what was meant by this. All of the foregoing programs would appear to be superceded by the demonstrated effectiveness of Masters and Johnson's method.

The Masters and Johnson Techniques

By far the best tested procedure to date in the area of sexual dysfunction is the Masters and Johnson method[50]. It has been widely copied and modifed in minor ways with great success. Premature ejaculation is treated with almost 100% success by most therapists using it while impotence is cured in 60% to 90% of cases[8 11 33 41 52 60 72].

The therapists carry out a careful assessment of both marital or sexual partners. This step allows an examination of the marital relationship and the extent to which confounding factors may be present over and above the dysfunction itself. Obviously a couple with overt hostility will not be eager to give each other sensual pleasure which is the next step in the sequence. In sensate focus training each partner finds what is pleasurable to the other in sensuous ways. No sexual pleasure is included at this phase, just general sensual pleasure. Later this is extended to incorporate the genital sensations.

The crux of treating premature ejaculation in the Masters and Johnson method is the squeeze method employed earlier by Semans[68]. The method is simple: during intercourse or masturbation ejaculation is delayed by the male or his partner squeezing the penis at the glans or corona to prevent ejaculation. Erection is maintained and after a few moments, intercourse or masturbation can be resumed. There may be some loss of erection (10% to 30%) and about half a minute is needed for the reduction of the urge to ejaculate before resumption of sex. This can be repeated up to 10 times[8]. Usually the procedure starts with masturbation, the female may masturbate the male but he could do it to himself as well. Then intercourse is introduced and delayed in the same fashion. The method is remarkably effective and Masters and Johnson report over 90% success rate with heterosexuals and over 85% success with homosexuals. The unique feature of their study is the evaluation period which lasted 5 years during which there was almost no reduction in success rate. The total program is two weeks long and involves a team of male and female therapists. However some authors have reduced the time and used a single therapist with successful results. It is still not clear which part of the procedure is most important[34] but the method is among the best techniques available to the therapist working on sexual dysfunction.

Kinder and Blakeney[34] have criticized the Masters and Johnson method and other researchers using it. The selection of patients for treatment is important and Masters and Johnson do considerable screening of couples before allowing them into their program. Extreme marital problems of other pathology, which they do not specify in detail, will disqualify the couple for treatment and they will be referred elsewhere for traditional methods of intervention. It is unclear how or who to select. Their method suggests that if premature ejaculation is the only symptom in an otherwise intact and healthy couple then the Masters & Johnson program will work.

Negative effects of treatment have been reported by others but not by Masters and Johnson. Marital relationship may deteriorate and even end in divorce. However this may have been imminent before treatment. In a summary evaluation of the method, Kinder and Blakeney call for more accurate pretreatment assessment and reporting, clearer diagnoses, data on the treatment process, better post therapy evaluations, more information on changes in other areas than the sexual, data on unsuccessful cases, more objective and quantifiable measures in all data collection, and, on success rate in reference to specific diagnoses.

Treatment Evaluation

Kilmann and Auerbach have reviewed treatment studies to date and offer the following general criticisms. The most glaring problem has been the lack of attention to critical subject variables. There is often little information on the type of sexual dysfunction or the extent of the disorder. The treatment is not spelled out in detail with the exception of behavior therapy studies. More than one treatment often is used and they have not been evaluated for their relative effectiveness. Few studies control for expectation effects. Follow ups are almost nonexistant with the exception of Masters and Johnson's excellent efforts. It would be interesting to see in other studies how lasting the effects are. The critera of successful treatment are usually not spelled out so "improved" can mean a wide range of changes. More data should be provided on the sexual functioning of the partner since she may be a causal factor in the disorder and may be dysfunctional herself creating the illusion her husband is. An anorgasmic woman will not climax so her husband has to be a "premature ejaculator". Fordney-Settlage[21] reported in a selected sample that 27% of male dysfunctions were accompanied by female problems. A careful assessment of both husband and wife is essential and treatment outcome should be crossvalidated by partner consensus of success or failure[33].

I am surprised at the infrequent use of penile measures in both assessment and treatment since they can be used effectively in at least three ways. First, diagnosis of organic versus psychogenic impotence may be made via nocturnal penile tumescence. Absence of any tumescence indicates that organic factors are likely while the clear presence of erection of usual durations during sleep (30 minutes) suggests psychogenic factors are important. Unusual conditions like venous stasis in which the penis engorges but the valve is incontinent and the erection is gone, may be reflected in very short tumescence cycles. The second way penile measures can be useful in diagnosis is via a standard test of erotic preference to verify arousability and to rule out a sexual anomaly as a significant factor in the seemingly sexual dysfunction. If a married man can show erections to pictures but not to his wife, then the notion of impotence is suspect. He may be bored or angry or simply satiated with his wife. The discrepancy in self report about marital problems and in reaction to pictures is evident. Extremely arousing movies may also be used to assess the state of erection that is obtained and to determine if it is maintained. The standard test of erotic preference described in Chapter 2 indicates in cooperative individuals whether homosexuality or pedophilia are ready explanations of the problem. However the presence of a sexual anomaly suggests that simple treatment of the inability to be aroused by a female partner will not be easily effective. Sexual anomalies are different from sexual disorders. The former involve a difference in object choice and the latter problems of arousability. Finally, phallometry is useful in assessment of treatment. Desensitization or biofeedback may be evaluated in an ongoing way by the presence of a penile strain gauge or volumetric device during treatment sessions. The "anxiety" is evident by loss of erection, which is, after all, the primary target of change.

Treatment of Choice

Of all the treatments in Table 15.2, the Masters and Johnson method is by far the most impressive for sexual dysfunction in spite of shortcomings which have been noted and it can be recommended. However the problem arises in exactly what to recommend it for. Impotence and premature ejaculation can be due to organic factors, an anomalous preference, psychological factors such as anxiety, depression and anger, although none of these have been adequately documented; to sheer ignorance, to poor partner affinity, to marital discord, to drugs, alcohol, lack of interest, extramarital interest and even trivial factors the sex partners are not aware of. Schimel[66] noted the following "trivial" interfering factors: too much diaphragm gel as a contraceptive, shouting a climax by the wife, pain to the penis from the female pubic bone, athletic movement on the part of the wife involving extreme force, fear of laughing at silliness of partner's behavior, and excessive foreplay. We lack information on the importance of each of these factors and their contribution to treatment success and/or failure. It seems appropriate that organic impotence is best treated primarily by chemical or or medical means. Sexual anomalies do not appear to be amendable to these procedures, although they might be effective once object choice was changed. The problem is that we have no satisfactory technique to change object choice fully at present so that homosexual men who are dysfunctional should be best adapted to becoming functional homosexuals rather than attempting to make them heterosexuals. The technique might be useful in adapting pedophilic men to the adults of their preferred sex but not to the nonpreferred sex. Homosexual pedophiles would seem to be poor

TABLE 15.2
Summary of Treatment Effectiveness for Sexual Dysfunctions

Method	Results
1. Medical intervention and drugs	Depending on the problem, outcome is positive in organic impotence
2. Systematic densensitization	Positive but mainly case studies. Effective ingredients in therapy have yet to be studied systematically
3. Biofeedback	Only a few cases, mixed results
4. Hypnosis	Only case studies, positive outcome
5. Psychotherapy	Little evaluation of this method. Appears too expensive
6. Masters & Johnson method	Apparently the best method to date. 90% success. Problem of patient selection bias. No control group for comparison. Widely copied procedures

training candidates for heterosexual adult relations at present with our existing technology. In general there has been confusion of sexual anomalies and dysfunctions and Masters & Johnson's data suggest that it is easier to make someone functional to his anomaly than to change him.

Marital discord has been poorly assessed and the seeming impotence may only reflect that fact. If some other problem such as money, shared time, consideration, etc. were tackled, then the dysfuction might vanish itself. It would seem senseless to encourage sexual relations in a couple when the only expression of discontent and hostility is denial of sex relations to a partner. Working out the hostility or other problem by marital counselling or trying to counsel for divorce would seem more appropriate. Increased communication could be one of the most important therapeutic changes improving sex.

Ignorance and poor partner affinity should not be overlooked or underestimated. The inexperienced male who was a virgin at marriage may have no idea of what to expect from a woman or vice versa. A premature ejaculator may reflect a slow responding insensitive woman who could learn to enhance her own responsiveness or see her sexual role as a more active one. It would seem that the Masters and Johnson method is clearly indicated for psychogenic problems in which extraneous factors are minimal. In selecting patients for this method, it is critical that a medical examination be undertaken. This has been ignored or at least glossed over in reports to date and organic factors can be critical in determining outcome in treatment. Not only is it time consuming and wasteful but a serious problem can be left unattended by assuming that psychogenic factors are primary in dysfunctions. This area of research offers clear goals of treatment and progress should be straightforward in the near future.

BIBLIOGRAPHY

1. Amelar, R. D. Therapeutic approaches to impotence in the male. *The Journal of Sex Research,* 1971, *7*(3), 163–167.
2. Annon, J. S. *The Behavioral Treatment of Sexual Problems, Volume 1: Brief Therapy.* Honolulu: Enabling Systems Inc., 1975.
3. Asirdas, S., & Beech, H. The behavioral treatment of sexual inadequacy. *Journal of Psychosomatic Research,* 1975, *19*, 345–353.
4. Auerbach, R., & Kilman, P. The effects of group systematic desensitization on secondary erectile failure. *Behavior Therapy,* 1977, *8*, 330–339.
5. Austino, E., & Mantovani, F. Prosthetic implants in the treatment of impotence. In *Medical Sexology: The Third International Congress.* Forleo, R., & Pasini, W. (Eds.). Littleton, Mass., PSG Publishing Company, 1978.
6. Beck, A. T. *Depression: Causes and Treatment.* Philadelphia: University of Philadelphia Press, 1967.
7. Beigel, H. G. The hypnotherapeutic approach to male impotence. *The Journal of Sex Research,* 1971, *7*(3), 168–176.
8. Clarke, M., & Parry, L. Premature ejaculation treated by the dual sex team method of Masters and Johnson. *Australian and New Zealand Journal of Psychiatry,* 1973, *7*, 1–6.
9. Coble, P., McPartland, R., Silva, W., & Kupfer, D. Is there a first night effect? *Biological Psychiatry,* 1974, *9*, 215–219.
10. Cole, T. Sexuality and physical disability. In *New Directions in Sex Research.* Rubinstein, E., Green, R., & Brecher, E. (Eds.). New York: Plenum Press, 1976.
11. Cooper, A. J. A factual study of male potency disorders. *British Journal of Psychiatry,* 1968, *114*, 719–731.
12. Cooper, A. J. 'Neurosis' and disorders of sexual potency in the male. *Journal of Psychosomatic Research,* 1968, *12*, 141–144.
13. Cooper, A. J. Treatments of male potency disorders: the present studies. *Psychosomatics,* 1971, *12*, 235–244.
14. Cooper, A. J., Ismail, A. A. A., Smith, C. G., & Loraine, J. A. Androgen function in "Psychogenic" and "Constitutional" types of impotence. *British Medical Journal,* 1970, *3*, 17–20.
15. Csillag, E. R. Modification of penile erectile response. *Journal of Behavior Therapy & Experimental Psychiatry,* 1976, *7*, 27–29.
16. Dengrove, E. Behavior therapy of impotence. *The Journal of Sex Research,* 1971, *7*(3), 177–183.
17. Derogatis, L., & Meyer, J. A psychological profile of the sexual dysfunctions. *Archives of Sexual Behavior,* 1979, *8*(3), 201–223.

18. Edwards, A. E., & Husted, J. R. Penile sensitivity, age, and sexual behavior. *Journal of Clinical Psychology,* 1976, *32*(5), 697–700.

19. Ellenberg, M. Impotence in diabetics: A neurologic rather than an endocrinologic problem. *Medical Aspects of Human Sexuality,* 1973, *7*(4), 12–28.

20. Fisher, C., Gross, J., & Zuck, J. Cycle of penile erection synchronous with dreaming (REM) sleep: preliminary report. *Archives of General Psychiatry,* 1965, *12,* 29–45.

21. Fordney-Settlage, D. Heterosexual dysfunction: evaluation of treatment procedures. In *New Directions in Sex Research.* Rubinstein, E. A., Green, R., Brecher, E. (Eds.). New York: Plenum Press, 1976.

22. Freund, K. Assessment of anomalous erotic preferences in situational impotence. *Journal of Sex & Marital Therapy,* 1976, *2*(8), 173–183.

23. Friedman, D. The treatment of impotence by brietal relaxation therapy. *Behavior Research & Therapy,* 1968, *6,* 257–261.

24. Gebhard, P., Gagnon, J., Pomeroy, W., & Christenson, C. *Sex Offenders: An Analysis of Types.* London: Heineman Co., 1965.

25. Gemme, R., & Wheeler, C. *Progress in Sexology,* New York: Plenum Press, 1976.

26. Gill, H., Temperley, J. Time-limited marital treatment in a foursome. *British Journal of Medical Psychology,* 1974, *47,* 153–161.

27. Ginsberg, G. L. The new impotence. *Archives of General Psychiatry,* 1972, *26,* 218–220.

28. Goldberg, M. Selective impotence. *Medical Aspects of Human Sexuality,* 1973, *7,* 13–32.

29. Jehu, D. *Sexual Dysfunction: A Behavioral Approach to Causation, Assessment, and Treatment.* Toronto: J. Wiley & Sons, 1979.

30. Karacan, I., Scott, F., Salis, P., Attia, S., Ware, J., Attinel, A., & Williams, R. Nocturnal erections, differential diagnoses of impotence and diabetes. *Biological Psychiatry,* 1977, *12,* 373–380.

31. Karacan, I., Williams, R., Guerrero, M., Salis, P., Thornby, J., & Hursch, C. Nocturnal penile tumescence and sleep of convicted rapists and other prisoners. *Archives of Sexual Behavior,* 1974, *3*(1), 19–26.

32. Karacan, I., Williams, R. L., Thornby, J. I., & Salis, P. J. Sleep-related penile tumescence as a function of age. *American Journal of Psychiatry,* 1975, *132*(9), 932–937.

33. Kilman, P., & Auerbach, R. Treatments of premature ejaculation and psychogenic impotence: a critical review of the literature. *Archives of Sexual Behavior,* 1979, *8*(1), 81–100.

34. Kinder, B. N., & Blakeney, P. Treatment of sexual dysfunction: A review of outcome studies. *Journal of Clinical Psychology,* 1977, *33*(2), 523–530.

35. Kinsey, A., Pomeroy, W., & Martin, C. *Sexual Behavior in the Human Male.* Philadelphia: Saunders Co., 1948.

36. Kraft, T., & Al-Issa, I. The use of Methohexitone Sodium in the systematic desensitization of premature ejaculation. *British Journal of Psychiatry,* 1968, *114,* 351–352.

37. Langevin, R., Paitich, D., Ramsay, G., Anderson, C., Kamrad, J., Pope, S., Geller, G., Pearl, L., & Newman, S. Experimental studies of the etiology of genital exhibitionism. *Archives of Sexual Behavior,* 1979, *8,* 307–331.

38. Langevin, R., & Stancer, H. Evidence that depression rating scales primarily measure a social undesirability response set. *Acta Psychiatrica Scandanavica,* 1979, *59,* 70–79.

39. Lazarus, A. A. The treatment of a sexually inadequate man. In *Case Studies of Behavior Modification,* Ulmann, L., & Krasner, L. (Eds.). New York: Holt Rinehart & Winston Inc., 1965.

40. Legros, J., Franchemont, P., Palemvlier, M., & Servais, J. FSH, LH and testosterone blood level in patients with psychogenic impotence. *Endocrinologia Experimentalis,* 1973, *7,* 59–63.

41. Levay, A., Weisberg, J., & Blaustein, A. Concurrent sex therapy and psychoanalytic psychotherapy by separate therapists: effectiveness and implications. *Psychiatry,* 1976, *39,* 355–363.

42. Levine, S. B. Premature ejaculation: Some thoughts about its pathogenesis. *Journal of Sex & Marital Therapy,* 1975, *1*(4), 326–334.

43. Levine, E. M., & Ross, N. Sexual dysfunction and psychoanalysis. *American Journal of Psychiatry,* 1977, *134*(6), 646–651.

44. Lidberg, L. Social and psychiatric aspects of impotence and premature ejaculation. *Archives of Sexual Behavior,* 1972, *2*(2), 135–146.

45. Lobitz, W. C., & LoPiccolo, J. New methods in the behavioral treatment of sexual dysfunction. *Journal of Behavior Therapy and Experimental Psychiatry,* 1972, *3,* 265–271.

46. Lobitz, W. C., LoPiccolo, J., Lobitz, G. K., & Brockway, J. A closer look at "Simplisitc" behavior therapy for sexual dysfunction: Two case studies. In *Case Studies in Behavior Therapy,* H. J. Eysenck (Ed.), London: Routledge & Kegan Paul, 1976.

47. Lundberg, P. Sexual dysfunction in patients with neurological disorders. In *Progress in Sexology,* Gemme, R., & Wheeler, C. (Eds.). New York: Plenum Press, 1976.

48. Marshall, P., Surridge, D., & Delva, N. *Nocturnal penile tumescence recording in the assessment of impotence: results of a pilot study.* Paper presented at the annual Ontario Psychiatric Association Meeting, January, 1979.

49. Marshall, P., Surridge, D., & Delva, N. The role of nocturnal penile tumescence in differentiating between organic and psychogenic impotence: the first stage of validation. *Archives of Sexual Behavior,* 1981, *10*(1), 1–10.

50. Masters, W., & Johnson, V. *Human Sexual Inadequacy.* Boston: Little, Brown & Co., 1970.

51. Masters, W. H., & Johnson, V. *Homosexuality in Prospective.* Boston: Little Brown & Co., 1979.

52. McCarthy, B. W. A modification of Masters and Johnson sex therapy model in a clinical setting. *Psychotherapy: Theory, research & practice.* 1973, *10*(4), 290–293.

53. McCarthy, B. W. Strategies and techniques for the reduction of sexual anxiety. *Journal of Sex and Marital Therapy,* 1977, *3,* 243–248.

54. Moiso, C. Transactional analysis integrated approach to sexual dysfunctions. In *Medical Sexology: The Third International Congress.* Forleo, R., & Pasini, W. (Eds.). Littleton, Mass., PSG Publishing Company, 1975.

55. O'Connor, J., & Stern, L. Results of treatment in functional disorders. *New York State Journal of Medicine,* 1972, *72,* 1927–1934.

56. Obler, M. Systematic desensitization in sexual disorders. *Journal of Behavior Therapy & Experimental Psychiatry,* 1973, *4,* 93–101.

57. Pfeiffer, E., Verwoerdt, A., & Davis, G. C. Sexual behavior in middle life. *American Journal of Psychiatry,* 1972, *128*(10), 1262–1267.

58. Pirke, K. M., Kockott, G., & Dittmar, F. Psychosexual stimulation and plasma testosterone in man. *Archives of Sexual Behavior,* 1974, *3*(6), 577–584.

59. Pirke, K., Kockott, G., Aldenhoff, J., Besinger, U., & Feil, W. Pituitary gonadal system function in patients with erectile impotence and premature ejaculation. *Archives of Sexual Behavior,* 1979, *8*(1), 41–48.

60. Prochaska, J. O., & Marzilli, R. Modification of the Masters and Johnson approach to sexual problems. *Psychotherapy: Theory, Research and Practice,* 1973, *10*(4), 294–296.

61. Proctor, R. Impotence as a symptom of depression. *North Carolina Medical Journal,* 1973, *34,* 876–878.

62. Raboch, J., Mellan, J., & Starka, L. Plasma testosterone in male patients with sexual dysfunction. *Archives of Sexual Behavior,* 1975, *4*(5), 541–545.

63. Razani, J. Ejaculatory incompetence treated by deconditioning anxiety. *Journal of Behavior Therapy & Experimental Psychiatry,* 1972, *3,* 65–67.

64. Reynolds, B. S. Biofeedback and facilitation of erection in men with erectile dysfunction. Paper presented at the Meeting of the American Psychological Association, Toronto, Ontario, 1978.

65. Schiavi, R., Davis, D., Fogel, M., White, D., Edwards, A., Igel, G., Szechter, R., & Fisher, C. Luteinizing hormone and testosterone during nocturnal sleep: relation to penile tumescent cycles. *Archives of Sexual Behavior,* 1977, *6*(2), 97–104.

66. Schimel, J. L. Some practical considerations in treating male sexual inadequacy. *Medical Aspects of Human Sexuality,* 1971, *3,* 24–31.

67. Schwartz, M., Kolodny, R., & Masters, W. Plasma testosterone levels of sexually functional and dysfunctional men. *Archives of Sexual Behavior,* 1980, *9*(5), 355–366.

68. Semans, J. H. Premature ejaculation: a new approach. *Southern Medical Journal,* 1956, *49,* 353–358.

69. Simpson, S. L. Impotence. *British Medical Journal,* 1950, *1,* 692–697.

70. Solnick, R., & Birren, J. Age and male erectile responsiveness. *Archives of Sexual Behavior,* 1977, *6*(1), 1–9.

71. Tamburello, A., & Seppecher, M. The effects of depression on sexual behavior: preliminary results of research. In *Progress in Sexology,* Gemme, R., & Wheeler, C. (Eds.). New York: Plenum Press, 1976.

72. Tanner, B. A. Two case reports on the modification of the ejaculatory response with the squeeze technique. *Psychotherapy: Theory, Research and Practice,* 1973, *10*(4), 297–300.

73. Tordjman, G. Male erectile impotence. In *Progress in Sexology,* Gemme, R., & Wheeler, C. (Eds.). New York: Plenum Press, 1976.

74. Tordjman, G., Tkierree, R., & Michel, J. Advances in the vascular pathology of male erectile dysfunction. *Archives of Sexual Behavior,* 1980, *9*(5), 391–398.

75. Vas, C. J. Sexual impotence and some autonomic disturbances in men with multiple sclerosis. *Acta Neurologica Scandinavica,* 1969, *45,* 166–182.

76. Wabrek, A., & Burchell, R. Male sexual dysfunction associated with coronary heart disease. *Archives of Sexual Behavior,* 1980, *9*(1), 69–75.

77. Weiner, M. F. Wives who refuse their husbands. *Psychosomatics,* 1973, *14,* 277–282.

78. Welch, M. R., & Kartub, P. Socio-cultural correlates of incidence of impotence: A cross-cultural study. *The Journal of Sex Research,* 1978, *14*(4), 218–230.

V CONCLUDING REMARKS

16 Concluding Remarks

Writing this book has forced me to review all the pertinent literature on sexual anomalies including the work my colleagues and I have done over the past ten years. I have experienced many emotions doing so, among them delight, anger and hope.

It has been a pleasure seeing all the pieces in one place and integrated. It offers a new starting point for research. I am amazed how much I had forgotten or tucked away deep in my memory and which now appears in the foregoing pages.

At times I have felt great anger about the wide range of theoretical folly which has been used in diagnosis and treatment of trusting and unsuspecting patients. There is no room for such confidence. We need many more facts before we can make even rudimentary conclusions. This theme has run through the book and for some it may mean disappointment. For me it has helped dissipate my anger which has been replaced by hope.

Although the evidence has been an indictment for some theories and treatments, at the same time many paths have been suggested for new directions in understanding and treating sexual anomalies. It is my hope that some readers will examine the hypotheses with empirical studies.

In comparing case studies and controlled experiments in groups, I am constantly amazed at how divergent conclusions can be. Some of my clinical colleagues refuse to accept research findings which do not agree with their own experience. To me, this represents an uncontrolled case or group study. How often does a theory hold for clinicians because they have one patient who displayed certain features fitting their theory? It is not perceived as an accidental association but etiologically significant. My viewpoint for these colleagues is "Test your hypothesis". My advice to patients is to select a therapist who does not act out of faith but keeps up on the state of knowledge. I think the best therapist is one actively involved in research. In fact a treatment program which is under investigation is beneficial to everyone including the patient. He will get the best of assessments and careful treatment. The therapists will know what does and does not work.

Dramatic differences appear between studies using some assessment of erotic preferences, especially phallometry, and those which do not. In the treatment of homosexuality, the greatest successes came from uncontrolled and single case studies, the least success from controlled experiments. The more frequent the success, the less likely the study used penile measures. My experience has taught me to be more trusting of the controlled group study and I hope that the reader will understand why, having read this far.

One other factor has aroused my anger and perplexed me. It is the selection of aversion therapy as a first and most frequent choice in treating sexual anomalies. I was trained to use these methods and used them initially but quickly saw they were incomplete and ineffective both in individual cases and in literature articles. The people who trained me and whom I know use the methods, were not ogres and did not see themselves as inhumane. Now the evidence is in. Aversion methods have no greater effect in changing behavior than the less noxious positive behavior therapies or psychotherapies. Can we continue to permit patients to suffer unnecessarily? The success rate is relatively low. Can we continue to hold out false hope of cure? A range of behavioral and psychotherapy methods is available and should be tried out. Any growth experience or change can be painful but if the patient feels he is the master of his destiny, it is a mutual concern of therapist and client to change and the patient has dignity and control. It is my hope that these methods will be studied experimentally and replace aversion therapy as top choice.

It would be ideal if we could understand the sexual anomalies before we treated them but we cannot. Experimental methods should be tried out to determine if any treatment has a lasting impact on the behavior of the patient and on reducing their personal suffering. We can improve on the searching process by collecting as much etiological information as possible while we see patients. With computer facilities and the technology available to set up data banks in efficient and useful ways, we can collect sufficient information to do the necessary research without a significant increase in processing time for patients or in increased personnel. This will allow us to further our knowledge while treating the problems as best we can.

Some anomalies have not been discussed in the foregoing chapters mainly because there is extremely little information on them. Karpman[3] offers the interested reader a tree of unusual sexual behaviors which he theoretically ties into each other. Most clinicians I know have never seen any of the cases he described, for example, vampirism or necrophilia. I have nothing to say about them. Obscene telephone calls would seem to be a prominent nuisance which should have been researched but it has not. It is very difficult to catch these men and I know of no study in which they are assessed. The one case study reported in the literature was treated by shame aversion therapy[1]. I have yet to see a case in which the act of calling is a primary orgasmic outlet in itself. Usually it is imbedded in other behaviors which are more interesting to the patient, for example exposing or rape. Of the half dozen to a dozen cases in our data bank, all had multiple sexual anomalies.

The problem of classifying the multiple anomalies has not been tacked to any great extent in the book because our information is so uncertain. One fact is pertinent for assessment; the more orgasmic outlets a patient acknowledges, the more emotionally disturbed he seems to be. This must be qualified since some behaviours seem to go together such as exhibiting and peeping. Currently my colleagues and I are working on the mathematics involved in properly assessing the problem. It would seem to be an important question to answer because half of the presenting cases are multiple anomalies. However many can be reduced to single anomalies if erotic preference is used as a criterion.

The use of the stimulus response matrix and the concept of orgasmic preference have been of great service to me. They serve as clear thumbnail sketches of each anomaly and have allowed me to talk to my clinic patients with an understanding they can accept readily. The whole gamut of sexual anomalies are clearly laid out so gaps in our knowledge are evident to me. My colleagues and I are already investigating some of the interesting problems at this time. I hope the stimulus response matrix and the idea of orgasmic preference will be as useful to the reader.

It is characteristic at this juncture to offer an integrating theory to encompass all the facts. This had been tried many times in the past and it would be the antithesis of this book to attempt it here. Theories have been based on too much speculation and too little fact. That is still true today. We need many more specific hypotheses and no new grand theories at this time. Some specific questions to research have been raised throughout the book.

Having written so far, I have looked over the whole area of research and asked what is the most promising avenue to follow at this point in time. Two themes appear to me. First, sexually anomalous men in general seem to direct their sexual energy inwards. The psychoanalyst recognizes this as narcissism[2,5]. However the function of narcissism is to allay anxiety and/or feelings of inferiority. Many groups of anomalies discussed in the foregoing chapters were supposed to manifest a feeling of inferiority which could not be found when systematic studies were employed. Perhaps the directing of interest inwards is due to some other factor. Narcissism may also be described as egocentrism in the sense Piaget uses the term to describe early learning and functioning of the child. It is difficult to take the perspective of another person at this stage of development and this may be true as well for the sexually anomalous adult male. This may be the way he experiences the world. This hypothesis is testable using Piagetian tasks which are now more or less standardized at least for children. This problem in turn may relate to a second avenue of investigation, brain pathology. Not gross damage, but subtle differences which have been found in temporal lobe disorders may be important. With the recent changes in computer technology, especially computer tomography brain scans (CT Scan), there has been a quantitative change in our ability to understand the brain. Possibly some subtle factor in temporal lobe functioning in sexually anomalous men will be evident in the near future. It is my hypothesis that either altered brain states or egocentrism (narcissism) will link some sexual anomalies together. Homosexualities may be different from the remaining anomalies because there is a different sex object preference. However in cases in which object choice is appropriate but behavior or responses are not, faulty learning may relate to temporal lobe damage.

The explanations of "sexual learning" have been very limited. Classical and operant conditioning have been the main learning paradigms employed to explain sexual anomalies and to develop treatment methods for them. While classical conditioning is too limited to explain the phenomena, more basic research on the efficiency and on the parameters of operant conditioning could be explored in clinical analog studies. We know very little about brain activity during sexual behavior and learning. Systematic controlled EEG studies of sexual behavior may open new avenues of understanding. I am optimistic that we will have answers to many of the questions raised in the book during the next twenty years.

BIBLIOGRAPHY

1. Anonymous. A modified shame aversion therapy for compulsive obscene telephone calling. *Behavior Therapy,* 1975, *6,* 704–706.
2. Goldberg, A. Narcissism and the readiness for psychotherapy termination. *Archives of General Psychiatry,* 1975, *32*(6), 695–699.
3. Karpman, B. *The Sexual Offender and His Offenses.* New York: Julian Press, 1957.
4. McKnight, C., & Goldstein, C. *Indecent Phone Calls.* Law Reform Commission and The Clarke Institute of Psychiatry, July 1975.
5. Stolorow, R. Narcissus revisited. *American Journal of Psychoanalysis,* 1975, *35*(3), 286.

APPENDIX ONE

SEXUAL HISTORY QUESTIONNAIRE - MALE

1. About how many girls or women have you gone out with on dates?
    a) none   b) 1 only   c) 2-3   d) 4-5   c) 6-10
    f) 11-20   g) 21-40   h) 41-70   i) 71-100   j) over 100

2. How many girls or women have you kissed on the lips since the age of 16?
    a) none   b) 1 only   c) 2-3   d) 4-5   e) 6-10
    f) 11-20   g) 21-40   h) 41-70   i) 71-100   j) over 100

3. Have you ever wanted to do this?
    a) Yes   b) No

4. Would this be disgusting to you?
    a) Yes   b) No

5. How many girls or women have you touched on the breasts since the age of 16?
    a) none   b) 1 only   c) 2-3   d) 4-5   e) 6-10
    f) 11-20   g) 21-40   h) 41-70   i) 71-100   j) over 100

6. Have you ever wanted to do this?
    a) Yes   b) No

7. Would this be disgusting to you?
    a) Yes   b) No

8.   How many girls or women have you touched on the naked breasts since the age of 16?
    a) none   b) 1 only   c) 2-3   d) 4-5   e) 6-10
    f) 11-20   g) 21-40   h) 41-70   i) 71-100   j) over 100

9. Have you ever wanted to do this?
    a) Yes   b) No

10. Would this be disgusting to you?
    a) Yes   b) No

11. How many girls or women have you kissed or put your mouth on their breasts since you were 16 years of age?
    a) none   b) 1 only   c) 2-3   d) 4-5   e) 6-10
    f) 11-20   g) 21-40   h) 41-70   i) 71-100   j) over 100

12. Have you ever wanted to do this?
    a) Yes   b) No

13. Would this be disgusting to you?
    a) Yes   b) No

14. Since the age of 16, how many females 16 and older have you
    touched between the legs with your hands
    a) none   b) 1 only   c) 2–3   d) 4–5   e) 6–10
    f) 11–20   g) 21–40   h) 41–70   i) 71–100   j) over 100

15. Have you ever wanted to do this?
    a) Yes   b) No

16. Would this be disgusting to you?
    a) Yes   b) No

17. Since the age of 16, how many females 16 and older have done this to
    you?
    a) none   b) 1 only   c) 2–3   d) 4–5   e) 6–10
    f) 11–20   g) 21–40   h) 41–70   i) 71–100   j) over 100

18. Have you ever wanted a girl or woman to do this to you?
    a) Yes   b) No

19. Would this be disgusting to you?
    a) Yes   b) No

20. What is the total number of girls or women that you have had inter-
    course with from age of 16 up to now?
    a) none   b) 1 only   c) 2–3   d) 4–5   e) 6–10
    f) 11–20   g) 21–40   h) 41–70   i) 71–100   j) over 100

21. How old were you when you first had intercourse with a girl or
    woman?
    a) 12 or younger b) 13–14   c) 15–16   d) 17–18   e) 19–20
    f) 21–22   g) 23–24   h) 25–26   i) 27–28   j) 29 & older

22. How old was the girl or woman?
    a) 12 or younger b) 13–14   c) 15–16   d) 17–18   e) 19–20
    f) 21–22   g) 23–24   h) 25–26   i) 27–28   j) 29 & older

23. Do you wish now that you had had intercourse with more women?
    a) Yes   b) No

24. Would you like to have intercourse with other women in the future?
    a) Yes   b) No

25. Is the act of intercourse with a girl or woman unpleasant for you or
    disgusting?
    a) Yes   b) No

26. How many girls or women have you had intercourse with once and no more?
    a) none   b) 1 only   c) 2–3   d) 4–5   e) 6–10
    f) 11–20   g) 21–40   h) 41–70   i) 71–100   j) over 100

27. What is the most often that you have had intercourse with the same girl or woman while you were single?
    a) none   b) once only   c) 2–3 times   d) 4–5 times   e) 6–10 times
    f) 11–20   g) 21–40   h) 41–70   i) 71–100   j) over 100
    times   times   times   times   times

For Single Men Only:

28. Over the past month, how often have you had intercourse with a girl or woman?
    a) none   b) once only   c) 2–3 times   d) 4–5 times   e) 6–10 times
    f) 11–20   g) 21–40   h) 41–70   i) 71–100   j) over 100
    times   times   times   times   times

For Married Men Only: (Others skip to 35)

29. Over the past month how often have you had intercourse with your wife?
    a) 7 or more times a week b) 5–6 times a week c) 3–4 times a week
    d) twice a week   e) once a week   f) 2–3 times a month
    g) once a month   h) less than once a month

30. Did you have intercourse with your wife before you were married?
    a) Yes   b) No

31. How many girls or women have you had intercourse with since you were married (not including your wife)?
    a) none   b) 1 only   c) 2–3   d) 4–5   e) 6–10
    f) 11–20   g) 21–40   h) 41–70   i) 71–100   j) over 100

32. Have you ever wanted this?
    a) Yes   b) No

33. What is the most often that you had intercourse with the same girl or woman since you were married (not including your wife)?
    a) none   b) once only   c) 2–3 times   d) 4–5 times   e) 6–10 times
    f) 11–20   g) 21–40   h) 41–70   i) 71–100   j) over 100
    times   times   times   times   times

34. Have you ever enjoyed sexual relations with any other woman at any time in your life, more than with your wife?
    a) Yes   b) No

For Single And Married Men

35. How many times have you paid money to a girl or woman so that you could have intercourse with her?
    a) none   b) once only   c) 2–3 times   d) 4–5 times   e) 6–10 times
    f) 11–20   g) 21–40   h) 41–70   i) 71–100   j) over 100
    times   times   times   times   times

36. How many girls or women that were married and living with their husbands have you had intercourse with?
    a) none   b) 1 only   c) 2–3   d) 4–5   e) 6–10
    f) 11–20   g) 21–40   h) 41–70   i) 71–100   j) over 100

37. If you had exactly the right sexual partner, how often do you think that you would have intercourse?
    a) 7 or more times a week b) 5–6 times a week c) 3–4 times a week
    d) twice a week   e) once a week   f) 2–3 times a month
    g) once a month   h) less than once a month

38. How many *times* have you kissed or put your mouth between the legs of a girl or woman, since the age of 16?
    a) none   b) once only   c) 2–3 times   d) 4–5 times   e) 6–10 times
    f) 11–20   g) 21–40   h) 41–70   i) 71–100   j) over 100
    times   times   times   times   times

39. Have you ever wanted to do this?
    a) Yes   b) No

40. Would this be disgusting to you?
    a) Yes   b) No

41. With how many different girls 16 and older have you done this?
    a) none   b) 1 only   c) 2–3   d) 4–5   e) 6–10
    f) 11–20   g) 21–40   h) 41–70   i) 71–100   j) over 100

42. How many *times* have girls or women done this to you, since the age of 16?
    a) none   b) once only   c) 2–3 times   d) 4–5 times   e) 6–10 times
    f) 11–20   g) 21–40   h) 41–70   i) 71–100   j) over 100
    times   times   times   times   times

43. Have you ever wanted a girl or woman to do this to you?

    a) Yes   b) No

44. Would this be disgusting to you?
    a) Yes   b) No

45. How many different girls or women have done this to you?
    a) none   b) once only   c) 2–3 times   d) 4–5 times   e) 6–10 times
    f) 11–20   g) 21–40   h) 41–70   i) 71–100   j) over 100
       times   times   times   times   times

46. How many times have you put your finger into the rear end (rectum)
    of a girl or woman since the age of 16?
    a) none   b) once only   c) 2–3 times   d) 4–5 times   e) 6–10 times
    f) 11–20   g) 21–40   h) 41–70   i) 71–100   j) over 100
       times   times   times   times   times

47. Have you ever wanted to do this?

    a) Yes   b) No

48. Would this be disgusting to you?
    a) Yes   b) No

49. How many times have girls or women done this to you?
    a) none   b) once only   c) 2–3 times   d) 4–5 times   e) 6–10 times
    f) 11–20   g) 21–40   h) 41–70   i) 71–100   j) over 100
       times   times   times   times   times

50. Have you ever wanted a girl or women to do this to you?
    a) Yes   b) No

51. Would this be disgusting to you?
    a) Yes   b) No

52. How many times have you put your penis into the rear end (rectum)
    of a girl or woman since the age of 16?
    a) none   b) once only   c) 2–3 times   d) 4–5 times   e) 6–10 times
    f) 11–20   g) 21–40   h) 41–70   i) 71–100   j) over 100
       times   times   times   times   times

53. Have you ever wanted to do this?
    a) Yes   b) No

54. Would this be disgusting to you?
    a) Yes   b) No

55. Since the age of 16, have you ever felt that you would like to have
    sexual contact with a girl 12-years-old or younger?
    a) Yes   b) No

56. How many times have you felt this way?
    a) none   b) once only   c) 2–3 times   d) 4–5 times   e) 6–10 times
    f) 11–20   g) 21–40   h) 41–70   i) 71–100   j) over 100
       times   times   times   times   times

57. Would this be disgusting to you?
     a) Yes   b) No

If there has been NO sexual contact between you and girls 12 and younger since you were 16, and no desires of this kind on your part, leave out the items up to #71 and begin answering again at #72.

58. What is the total number of times that you have touched girls 12 and younger in a sexual way since the age of 16?
     a) none   b) once only   c) 2–3 times   d) 4–5 times   e) 6–10 times
     f) 11–20   g) 21–40   h) 41–70   i) 71–100   j) over 100
        times   times   times   times   times

59. Since the age of 16 how many girls 12 and younger have you touched between the legs with your hands?
     a) none   b) 1 only   c) 2–3   d) 4–5   e) 6–10
     f) 11–20   g) 21–40   h) 41–70   i) 71–100   j) over 100

60. Have you ever wanted to do this?
     a) Yes   b) No

61. Would this be disgusting to you?
     a) Yes   b) No

62. Since the age of 16, how many girls 12 and younger have done this to you?
     a) none   b) once only   c) 2–3 times   d) 4–5 times   e) 6–10 times
     f) 11–20   g) 21–40   h) 41–70   i) 71–100   j) over 100
        times   times   times   times   times

63. Have you ever wanted a girl of this age to do this to you?
     a) Yes   b) No

64. Would this be disgusting to you?
     a) Yes   b) No

65. How many girls 12 and younger have you rubbed against with your penis since the age of 16?
     a) none   b) 1 only   c) 2–3   d) 4–5   e) 6–10
     f) 11–20   g) 21–40   h) 41–70   i) 71–100   j) over 100

66. Have you ever wanted to do this?
     a) Yes   b) No

67. Would this be disgusting to you?
     a) Yes   b) No

68. Since the age of 16 how many girls 12 and younger have you tried to have intercourse with?

a) none   b) 1 only   c) 2–3   d) 4–5   e) 6–10
f) 11–20   g) 21–40   h) 41–70   i) 71–100   j) over 100

69. Have you ever wanted to do this?
a) Yes   b) No

70. Would this be disgusting to you?
a) Yes   b) No

71. What is the most often that you have had sexual contact with the same girl 12 and younger, since you were 16?

a) none   b) once only   c) 2–3 times   d) 4–5 times   e) 6–10 times
f) 11–20   g) 21–40   h) 41–70   i) 71–100   j) over 100
   times   times   times   times   times

72. Since the age of 21, have you ever felt that you would like to have sexual contact with a girl 13 to 15 years of age?
a) Yes   b) No

73. How many times have you felt this way?

a) none   b) once only   c) 2–3 times   d) 4–5 times   e) 6–10 times
f) 11–20   g) 21–40   h) 41–70   i) 71–100   j) over 100
   times   times   times   times   times

74. Would this be disgusting to you?
a) Yes   b) No

75. What is the total number of times that you have touched girls 13 to 15 years old in a sexual way since the age of 21?

a) none   b) once only   c) 2–3 times   d) 4–5 times   e) 6–10 times
f) 11–20   g) 21–40   h) 41–70   i) 71–100   j) over 100
   times   times   times   times   times

76. Since the age of 21 how many girls 13 to 15 have you touched between the legs with your hands?

a) none   b) 1 only   c) 2–3   d) 4–5   e) 6–10
f) 11–20   g) 21–40   h) 41–70   i) 71–100   j) over 100

77. Have you ever wanted to do this?
a) Yes   b) No

78. Would this be disgusting to you?
a) Yes   b) No

79. Since the age of 21 how many girls 13 to 15 have done this to you?
    a) none   b) 1 only   c) 2–3   d) 4–5   e) 6–10
    f) 11–20   g) 21–40   h) 41–70   i) 71–100   j) over 100

80. Have you ever wanted to do this?
    a) Yes   b) No

81. Would this be disgusting to you?
    a) Yes   b) No

82. Since the age of 21 how many girls 13 to 15 have you rubbed against with your penis?
    a) none   b) 1 only   c) 2–3   d) 4–5   e) 6–10
    f) 11–20   g) 21–40   h) 41–70   i) 71–100   j) over 100

83. Have you ever wanted to do this?
    a) Yes   b) No

84. Would this be disgusting to you?
    a) Yes   b) No

85. Since the age of 21 how many girls 13 to 15 have you tried to have intercourse with?
    a) none   b) 1 only   c) 2–3   d) 4–5   e) 6–10
    f) 11–20   g) 21–40   h) 41–70   i) 71–100   j) over 100

86. Have you ever wanted to do this?
    a) Yes   b) No

87. Would this be disgusting to you?
    a) Yes   b) No

88. What is the most often that you have had sexual contact with the same girl 13 to 15 years, since you were 21?
    a) none   b) once only   c) 2–3 times   d) 4–5 times   e) 6–10 times
    f) 11–20   g) 21–40   h) 41–70   i) 71–100   j) over 100
       times   times   times   times   times

89. Do you think that masturbating (playing with yourself) is harmful or wrong?
    a) Yes   b) No

90. Over the past 3 months how often have you masturbated?
    a) 7 or more times a week b) 5–6 times a week c) 3–4 times a week
    d) twice a week   e) once a week   f) 2–3 times a month
    g) once a month   h) less than once a month   i) none

91. What is the most often that it has ever been?
    a) 7 or more times a week b) 5-6 times a week c) 3-4 times a week
    d) twice a week   e) once a week   f) 2-3 times a month
    g) once a month   h) less than once a month   i) none

92. Do you think that you should masturbate less than you do?
    a) Yes   b) No

93. Do you think that you should not masturbate at all?
    a) Yes   b) No

Whom do you think of when you masturbate *or* when you are thinking sexually?

94.	girls 12 and younger	a) Yes	b) No
95.	girls 13-15 years	a) Yes	b) No
96.	girls 16-20 years	a) Yes	b) No
97.	women 21-30 years	a) Yes	b) No
98.	women 31 and older	a) Yes	b) No

Whom do you think of when you masturbate *or* when you are thinking sexually?

99.	boys 12 and younger	a) Yes	b) No
100.	boys 13-15 years	a) Yes	b) No
101.	boys 16-20 years	a) Yes	b) No
102.	males 21-30 years	a) Yes	b) No
103.	males 31 and older	a) Yes	b) No

104. Since the age of 16, have you ever felt that you would like to have
     sexual contact with a man or boy?
     a) Yes   b) No

105. How many times have you felt this way?
     a) none   b) once only   c) 2-3 times   d) 4-5 times   e) 6-10 times
     f) 11-20   g) 21-40   h) 41-70   i) 71-100   j) over 100
        times   times   times   times   times

106. Would this be disgusting to you?
     a) Yes   b) No

Since the age of 16 has a man or boy ever handled your private parts? (answer only the numbered questions)

107. How many boys 12 or younger?
     a) none   b) 1 only   c) 2-3   d) 4-5   e) 6-10
     f) 11-20   g) 21-40   h) 41-70   i) 71-100   j) over 100

108.   How many boys 13-15 years old?
 a) none   b) 1 only   c) 2–3   d) 4–5   e) 6–10
 f) 11–20   g) 21–40   h) 41–70   i) 71–100   j) over 100

109.   How many boys 16-20 years old?
 a) none   b) 1 only   c) 2–3   d) 4–5   e) 6–10
 f) 11–20   g) 21–40   h) 41–70   i) 71–100   j) over 100

110.   How many males 21 years and older?
 a) none   b) 1 only   c) 2–3   d) 4–5   e) 6–10
 f) 11–20   g) 21–40   h) 41–70   i) 71–100   j) over 100

Have you ever wanted a man or boy to do this to you?

111.   A boy 12 years and younger?   a) Yes   b) No
112.   A boy 13-15 years?   a) Yes   b) No
113.   A boy 16-20 years old?   a) Yes   b) No
114.   A male 21 years and older?   a) Yes   b) No

Would this be disgusting to you?

115.   With a boy 12 and younger?   a) Yes   b) No
116.   With a boy 13-15 years old?   a) Yes   b) No
117.   With a boy 16-20 years old?   a) Yes   b) No
118.   With a male 21 years and older? a) Yes   b) No

Have you ever handled the private parts of a man or boy with your hands since the age of 16?

119.   How many boys 12 and younger?
 a) none   b) 1 only   c) 2–3   d) 4–5   e) 6–10
 f) 11–20   g) 21–40   h) 41–70   i) 71–100   j) over 100

120.   How many boys 13-15 years old?
 a) none   b) 1 only   c) 2–3   d) 4–5   e) 6–10
 f) 11–20   g) 21–40   h) 41–70   i) 71–100   j) over 100

121.   How many boys 16-20 years old?
 a) none   b) 1 only   c) 2–3   d) 4–5   e) 6–10
 f) 11–20   g) 21–40   h) 41–70   i) 71–100   j) over 100

122.   How many males 21 years and older?
 a) none   b) 1 only   c) 2–3   d) 4–5   e) 6–10
 f) 11–20   g) 21–40   h) 41–70   i) 71–100   j) over 100

Have you ever wanted to do this?

123.   With boys 12 years and younger? a) Yes   b) No
124.   With boys 13-15 years old?   a) Yes   b) No
125.   With boys 16-20 years old?   a) Yes   b) No
126.   With males 21 years and older   a) Yes   b) No

Would this be disgusting to you?

127.	With boys 12 and younger?	a) Yes	b) No
128.	With boys 13-15 years old?	a) Yes	b) No
129.	With boys 16-20 years old?	a) Yes	b) No
130.	With males 21 and older?	a) Yes	b) No

If there has been *NO* sexual contact of any kind between you and other men or boys since you were 16, and no desires of this kind on your part, leave out the items up to #187 and begin answering again at #188.

Have you ever kissed a man or boy on the lips since the age of 16?

131. How many boys 12 years and younger?
    a) none   b) 1 only   c) 2-3   d) 4-5   e) 6-10
    f) 11-20   g) 21-40   h) 41-70   i) 71-100   j) over 100

132. How many boys 13-15 years old?
    a) none   b) 1 only   c) 2-3   d) 4-5   e) 6-10
    f) 11-20   g) 21-40   h) 41-70   i) 71-100   j) over 100

133. How many boys 16 to 20 years old?
    a) none   b) 1 only   c) 2-3   d) 4-5   e) 6-10
    f) 11-20   g) 21-40   h) 41-70   i) 71-100   j) over 100

134. How many males 21 years and older?
    a) none   b) 1 only   c) 2-3   d) 4-5   e) 6-10
    f) 11-20   g) 21-40   h) 41-70   i) 71-100   j) over 100

135. Have you ever wanted to do this?
    a) Yes   b) No

136. Would this be disgusting to you?
    a) Yes   b) No

Have you ever kissed or put your mouth on the private parts of a man or boy since you were 16?

137. How many boys 12 and younger?
    a) none   b) 1 only   c) 2-3   d) 4-5   e) 6-10
    f) 11-20   g) 21-40   h) 41-70   i) 71-100   j) over 100

138. How many boys 13-15 years old?
    a) none   b) 1 only   c) 2-3   d) 4-5   e) 6-10
    f) 11-20   g) 21-40   h) 41-70   i) 71-100   j) over 100

139. How many boys 16-20 years old?
    a) none   b) 1 only   c) 2-3   d) 4-5   e) 6-10
    f) 11-20   g) 21-40   h) 41-70   i) 71-100   j) over 100

140. How many males 21 and older?
    a) none   b) 1 only   c) 2–3   d) 4–5   e) 6–10
    f) 11–20   g) 21–40   h) 41–70   i) 71–100   j) over 100

141. Have you ever wanted to do this?
    a) Yes   b) No

142. Would this be disgusting to you?
    a) Yes   b) No

Has a man or boy ever done this to you since you were 16?

143. How many boys 12 and younger?
    a) none   b) 1 only   c) 2–3   d) 4–5   e) 6–10
    f) 11–20   g) 21–40   h) 41–70   i) 71–100   j) over 100

144. How many boys 13-15 years old?
    a) none   b) 1 only   c) 2–3   d) 4–5   e) 6–10
    f) 11–20   g) 21–40   h) 41–70   i) 71–100   j) over 100

145. How many boys 16-20 years old?
    a) none   b) 1 only   c) 2–3   d) 4–5   e) 6–10
    f) 11–20   g) 21–40   h) 41–70   i) 71–100   j) over 100

146. Have you ever wanted a man or boy to do this to you?
    a) none   b) 1 only   c) 2–3   d) 4–5   e) 6–10
    f) 11–20   g) 21–40   h) 41–70   i) 71–100   j) over 100

147. Have you ever wanted a man or boy to do this to you?
    a) Yes   b) No

148. Would this be disgusting to you?
    a) Yes   b) No

Have you ever put your finger into the rear end of a man or boy since the age of 16?

149. How many boys 12 and younger?
    a) none   b) 1 only   c) 2–3   d) 4–5   e) 6–10
    f) 11–20   g) 21–40   h) 41–70   i) 71–100   j) over 100

150. How many boys 13-15 years old?
    a) none   b) 1 only   c) 2–3   d) 4–5   e) 6–10
    f) 11–20   g) 21–40   h) 41–70   i) 71–100   j) over 100

151. How many boys 16-20 years old?
    a) none   b) 1 only   c) 2–3   d) 4–5   e) 6–10
    f) 11–20   g) 21–40   h) 41–70   i) 71–100   j) over 100

152. How many men 21 and older?
     a) none   b) 1 only   c) 2–3   d) 4–5   e) 6–10
     f) 11–20   g) 21–40   h) 41–70 i) 71–100 j) over 100

153. Have you ever wanted to do this?
     a) Yes   b) No

154. Would this be disgusting to you?
     a) Yes   b) No

Has a man or boy ever done this to you, since you were 16?

155. How many boys 12 and younger?
     a) none   b) 1 only   c) 2–3   d) 4–5   e) 6–10
     f) 11–20   g) 21–40   h) 41–70 i) 71–100 j) over 100

156. How many boys 13-15 years old?
     a) none   b) 1 only   c) 2–3   d) 4–5   e) 6–10
     f) 11–20   g) 21–40   h) 41–70 i) 71–100 j) over 100

157. How many boys 16-20 years old?
     a) none   b) 1 only   c) 2–3   d) 4–5   e) 6–10
     f) 11–20   g) 21–40   h) 41–70 i) 71–100 j) over 100

158. How many men 21 years and older?
     a) none   b) 1 only   c) 2–3   d) 4–5   e) 6–10
     f) 11–20   g) 21–40   h) 41–70 i) 71–100 j) over 100

159. Have you ever wanted a man or boy to do this to you?
     a) Yes   b) No

160. Would this be disgusting to you?
     a) Yes   b) No

Have you ever put your penis into the rear end of a man or boy since the age of 16?

161. How many boys 12 and younger?
     a) none   b) 1 only   c) 2–3   d) 4–5   e) 6–10
     f) 11–20   g) 21–40   h) 41–70 i) 71–100 j) over 100

162. How many boys 13-15 years old?
     a) none   b) 1 only   c) 2–3   d) 4–5   e) 6–10
     f) 11–20   g) 21–40   h) 41–70 i) 71–100 j) over 100

163. How many boys 16-20 years old?
     a) none   b) 1 only   c) 2–3   d) 4–5   e) 6–10
     f) 11–20   g) 21–40   h) 41–70 i) 71–100 j) over 100

164. How many men 21 and older?
a) none   b) 1 only   c) 2–3   d) 4–5   e) 6–10
f) 11–20   g) 21–40   h) 41–70   i) 71–100   j) over 100

165. Have you ever wanted to do this?
a) Yes   b) No

166. Would this be disgusting to you?
a) Yes   b) No

Has a man or boy ever done this to you?

167. How many boys 12 and younger?
a) none   b) 1 only   c) 2–3   d) 4–5   e) 6–10
f) 11–20   g) 21–40   h) 41–70   i) 71–100   j) over 100

168. How many boys 13-15 years old?
a) none   b) 1 only   c) 2–3   d) 4–5   e) 6–10
f) 11–20   g) 21–40   h) 41–70   i) 71–100   j) over 100

169. How many boys 16 to 20 years old?
a) none   b) 1 only   c) 2–3   d) 4–5   e) 6–10
f) 11–20   g) 21–40   h) 41–70   i) 71–100   j) over 100

170. How many men 21 years and older?
a) none   b) 1 only   c) 2–3   d) 4–5   e) 6–10
f) 11–20   g) 21–40   h) 41–70   i) 71–100   j) over 100

171. Have you ever wanted to do this?
a) Yes   b) No

172. Would this be disgusting to you?
a) Yes   b) No

With how many boys or men have you had sexual contact once and no more since you were 16? (Answer only the numbered questions).

173. With how many boys 12 and younger once only?
a) none   b) 1 only   c) 2–3   d) 4–5   e) 6–10
f) 11–20   g) 21–40   h) 41–70   i) 71–100   j) over 100

174. With how many boys 13-15 once only?
a) none   b) 1 only   c) 2–3   d) 4–5   e) 6–10
f) 11–20   g) 21–40   h) 41–70   i) 71–100   j) over 100

175. With how many boys 16-20 once only?
a) none   b) 1 only   c) 2–3   d) 4–5   e) 6–10
f) 11–20   g) 21–40   h) 41–70   i) 71–100   j) over 100

176. With how many men 21 and over once only?
   a) none   b) 1 only   c) 2–3   d) 4–5   e) 6–10
   f) 11–20   g) 21–40   h) 41–70   i) 71–100   j) over 100

177. What is the most often that sexual contact has taken place between you and the same man or boy since you were 16?
   a) none   b) once only   c) 2–3 times   d) 4–5 times   e) 6–10 times
   f) 11–20   g) 21–40   h) 41–70   i) 71–100   j) over 100
   times   times   times   times   times

178. How old was he at the time?
   a) 12 or younger   b) 13–15   c) 16–20   d) 21 & older

179. How old were you?
   a) 12 or younger   b) 13–15   c) 16–20   d) 21 & older

180. How many boys 12 and younger have you had sexual contact with 5 times or more?
   a) none   b) 1 only   c) 2–3   d) 4–5   e) 6–10
   f) 11–20   g) 21–40   h) 41–70   i) 71–100   j) over 100

181. How many boys 13-15 years old have you had sexual contact with 5 times or more?
   a) none   b) 1 only   c) 2–3   d) 4–5   e) 6–10
   f) 11–20   g) 21–40   h) 41–70   i) 71–100   j) over 100

182. How many boys 16-20 years old have you had sexual contact with 5 times or more?
   a) none   b) 1 only   c) 2–3   d) 4–5   e) 6–10
   f) 11–20   g) 21–40   h) 41–70   i) 71–100   j) over 100

183. How many men 21 and over have you had sexual contact with 5 times or more?
   a) none   b) 1 only   c) 2–3   d) 4–5   e) 6–10
   f) 11–20   g) 21–40   h) 41–70   i) 71–100   j) over 100

184. Over the past month (4 weeks) how many *TIMES* have you had sexual contact with boys 12 and younger?
   a) none   b) once only   c) 2–3 times   d) 4–5 times   e) 6–10 times
   f) 11–20   g) 21–40   h) 41–70   i) 71–100   j) over 100
   times   times   times   times   times

185. Over the past month (4 weeks) how many *TIMES* have you had sexual contact with boys 13-15 years?
   a) none   b) once only   c) 2–3 times   d) 4–5 times   e) 6–10 times
   f) 11–20   g) 21–40   h) 41–70   i) 71–100   j) over 100
   times   times   times   times   times

186. Over the past month (4 weeks) how many *TIMES* have you had
     sexual contact with boys 16-20 years?
     a) none   b) once only   c) 2–3 times   d) 4–5 times   e) 6–10 times
     f) 11–20   g) 21–40   h) 41–70   i) 71–100   j) over 100
        times   times   times   times   times

187. Over the past month (4 weeks) how many *TIMES* have you had
     sexual contact with men 21 and over?
     a) none   b) once only   c) 2–3 times   d) 4–5 times   e) 6–10 times
     f) 11–20   g) 21–40   h) 41–70   i) 71–100   j) over 100
        times   times   times   times   times

**Have you ever worn articles of women's clothing or tried them on,
since the age of 16?**

188. Skirt or dress? How many times?
     a) none   b) once only   c) 2–3 times   d) 4–5 times   e) 6–10 times
     f) 11–20   g) 21–40   h) 41–70   i) 71–100   j) over 100
        times   times   times   times   times

189. Undergarments? How many times?
     a) none   b) once only   c) 2–3 times   d) 4–5 times   e) 6–10 times
     f) 11–20   g) 21–40   h) 41–70   i) 71–100   j) over 100
        times   times   times   times   times

190. Stockings? How many times?
     a) none   b) once only   c) 2–3 times   d) 4–5 times   e) 6–10 times
     f) 11–20   g) 21–40   h) 41–70   i) 71–100   j) over 100
        times   times   times   times   times

191. Shoes? How many times?
     a) none   b) once only   c) 2–3 times   d) 4–5 times   e) 6–10 times
     f) 11–20   g) 21–40   h) 41–70   i) 71–100   j) over 100
        times   times   times   times   times

192. Jewelry? How many times?
     a) none   b) once only   c) 2–3 times   d) 4–5 times   e) 6–10 times
     f) 11–20   g) 21–40   h) 41–70   i) 71–100   j) over 100
        times   times   times   times   times

193. Wig? How many times?
     a) none   b) once only   c) 2–3 times   d) 4–5 times   e) 6–10 times
     f) 11–20   g) 21–40   h) 41–70   i) 71–100   j) over 100
        times   times   times   times   times

**Have you ever watched a man or woman having sexual relations,
since you were 16?**

194. How many times?
    a) none   b) once only   c) 2–3 times   d) 4–5 times   e) 6–10 times
    f) 11–20   g) 21–40   h) 41–70   i) 71–100   j) over 100
    times   times   times   times   times

195. Have you ever wanted to watch this?
    a) Yes   b) No

Since you were 16 have you ever secretly tried to see this or women undressing by looking in windows or by other means?

196. How many times?
    a) none   b) once only   c) 2–3 times   d) 4–5 times   e) 6–10 times
    f) 11–20   g) 21–40   h) 41–70   i) 71–100   j) over 100
    times   times   times   times   times

197. How many strip-tease shows have you seen?
    a) none   b) 1 only   c) 2–3   d) 4–5   e) 6–10
    f) 11–20   g) 21–40   h) 41–70   i) 71–100   j) over 100

198. Were they enjoyable?
    a) Yes   b) No

199. Were they disgusting?
    a) Yes   b) No

Have you ever telephoned a girl or woman who did not know you in order to have a sexual conversation or talk dirty to her?

200. How many times?
    a) none   b) once only   c) 2–3 times   d) 4–5 times   e) 6–10 times
    f) 11–20   g) 21–40   h) 41–70   i) 71–100   j) over 100
    times   times   times   times   times

Since you were 16 have you ever rubbed up against women who did not know you in a sexual way in a crowd?

201. How many times?
    a) none   b) once only   c) 2–3 times   d) 4–5 times   e) 6–10 times
    f) 11–20   g) 21–40   h) 41–70   i) 71–100   j) over 100
    times   times   times   times   times

Since you were 16, have you ever touched a women who did not know you in a sexual way, in a crowd, with your hands?

202. How many times?
    a) none   b) once only   c) 2–3 times   d) 4–5 times   e) 6–10 times
    f) 11–20   g) 21–40   h) 41–70   i) 71–100   j) over 100
    times   times   times   times   times

Since you were 16, have you ever touched women who did not know you in a sexual way, against their will, in a lonely place?

203.   How many times?
   a) none   b) once only   c) 2–3 times   d) 4–5 times   e) 6–10 times
   f) 11–20   g) 21–40   h) 41–70   i) 71–100   j) over 100
      times   times   times   times   times

Have you ever tried to have sexual intercourse with a female against her will?

204.   How many times?
   a) none   b) once only   c) 2–3 times   d) 4–5 times   e) 6–10 times
   f) 11–20   g) 21–40   h) 41–70   i) 71–100   j) over 100
      times   times   times   times   times

Have you ever succeeded in this?

205.   How many times?
   a) none   b) once only   c) 2–3 times   d) 4–5 times   e) 6–10 times
   f) 11–20   g) 21–40   h) 41–70   i) 71–100   j) over 100
      times   times   times   times   times

Have you ever masturbated, with your penis out of your pants, in some place such as a car, alleyway or park, thinking that nobody could see you?

206.   How many times?
   a) none   b) once only   c) 2–3 times   d) 4–5 times   e) 6–10 times
   f) 11–20   g) 21–40   h) 41–70   i) 71–100   j) over 100
      times   times   times   times   times

Have you ever exposed your penis on purpose to a girl who did not know you, in a more or less public place such as a street, a park, or a field, an alleyway, a car, in a show, or through a window?

207.   How many times altogether?
   a) none   b) once only   c) 2–3 times   d) 4–5 times   e) 6–10 times
   f) 11–20   g) 21–40   h) 41–70   i) 71–100   j) over 100
      times   times   times   times   times

208.   How many times to girls 12 or younger?
   a) none   b) once only   c) 2–3 times   d) 4–5 times   e) 6–10 times
   f) 11–20   g) 21–40   h) 41–70   i) 71–100   j) over 100
      times   times   times   times   times

209. How many times to girls 13–15 years?
a) none b) once only c) 2–3 times d) 4–5 times e) 6–10 times
f) 11–20 g) 21–40 h) 41–70 i) 71–100 j) over 100
times times times times times

210. How many times to girls 16–20 years?
a) none b) once only c) 2–3 times d) 4 5 times e) 6–10 times
f) 11–20 g) 21–40 h) 41–70 i) 71–100 j) over 100
times times times times times

211. How many times to women 21 – 30 years?
a) none b) once only c) 2–3 times d) 4–5 times e) 6–10 times
f) 11–20 g) 21–40 h) 41–70 i) 71–100 j) over 100
times times times times times

212. How many times to women 31 – 40 years?
a) none b) once only c) 2–3 times d) 4–5 times e) 6–10 times
f) 11–20 g) 21–40 h) 41–70 i) 71–100 j) over 100
times times times times times

213. How many times to women 40 and over?
a) none b) once only c) 2–3 times d) 4–5 times e) 6–10 times
f) 11–20 g) 21–40 h) 41–70 i) 71–100 j) over 100
times times times times times

214. Have you ever felt that you would like to expose your penis to a girl or woman in the ways mentioned?
a) Yes b) No

Answer The Following Questions Only If Your Answer To 207 Is 1, Or More

215. How often have you had an erection (enlarged penis) when you exposed yourself?
a) never b) sometimes c) often d) almost always e) always

216. How often have you masturbated while exposing yourself?
a) never b) sometimes c) often d) almost always e) always

217. How often has the indecent exposure happened suddenly?
a) never b) sometimes c) often d) almost always e) always

218. Do you feel that you are in a fog mentally or that things are unreal when you expose yourself?
a) never b) sometimes c) often d) almost always e) always

219. When you expose yourself to females do you hope that they will get enjoyment out of seeing your penis?
   a) never   b) sometimes   c) often   d) almost always e) always

220. Do you hope that they will be impressed by the size of your penis?
   a) never   b) sometimes   c) often   d) almost always e) always

221. Have you ever tried to have sexual relations with the person that saw you?
   a) Yes   b) No

222. Have you ever felt an urge to do this?
   a) Yes   b) No

223. When is the last time you exposed your penis in public?
   a) 1 or 2 days ago   b) 3–7 days ago   c) 2–3 weeks ago
   d) 1 or 2 months ago   e) 3–6 months ago   f) 7–12 months ago
   g) 1–2 years ago   h) 2–3 years ago   i) 4–5 years ago
   j) over 5 years ago

224. If the girl or woman who saw you wanted to go some place to have sexual relations with you, what would you do?
   a) run away   b) walk away   c) go with her

225. Have you ever used vulgar language on the person who saw you? How many times altogether?
   a) none   b) once only   c) 2–3 times   d) 4–5 times   e) 6–10 times
   f) 11–20   g) 21–40   h) 41–70   i) 71–100   j) over 100
     times   times   times   times   times

APPENDIX TWO

A SAMPLE SHQ PROFILE

NAME   - Mr. A   NUMBER   - 123456

BORN   - July 1, 1948 AGE   - 32

MARITAL STATUS   - Single   TEST DATE   - May 4, 1980

EDUCATION   - Grade 10   OCCUPATION - Laborer

PRESENTING PROBLEM - Genital Exhibitionism

Sex History Questionnaire

Has endorsed 13 of 14 items indicative of a convention heterosexual orientation toward females 16 and over:

Has dated about 15 girls or women

Has kissed about 15 girls or women on the lips

Has had intercourse with 4 or 5 women

Has endorsed 6 of 7 items dealing with genital exhibitionism:

Has exposed to girls 13–15 on 100 or more occasions

Has exposed to girls 16 to 20 on 100 or more occasions

Has exposed to women 21 or older on 100 or more occasions

Has not tried to have sexual contact with the females seeing him

Genital exhibitionism last occurred 1 or 2 days ago

Acknowledges homosexual urges:

Has had contact a few times with men 21 and older

Over the past month the frequency of sexual contact with men 21 and older has been nil

Has worn female underclothing:

Female undergarments 7 or 8 times

Stockings 2 or 3 times.

Has peeped in windows on 15 or more occasions

Has made indecent phone calls 2 or 3 times

Has molested women who did not know him in a lonely place on 2 or 3 occasions

Has carried out forcible intercourse once

PROFILE

Conventional heterosexual outlet	-	85 centile
Exhibitionism	-	95 centile
Homosexual	-	10 centile
Crossdressing	-	20 centile
Voyeurism	-	65 centile
Indecent calls	-	30 centile
Rape	-	30 centile

Subject Index

X,Y,Z